Minimali

Linguistics: The Essential Readings

This series consists of comprehensive collections of classic and contemporary reprinted articles in a wide range of fields within linguistics. The primary works presented in each book are complemented by outstanding editorial material written by key figures in the field. Each volume stands as an excellent resource on its own, as well as an ideal companion to an introductory text.

Minimalist Syntax

The Essential Readings

Edited by

Željko Bošković
and
Howard Lasnik

Blackwell Publishing

Editorial material and organization © 2007 by Blackwell Publishing Ltd

BLACKWELL PUBLISHING
350 Main Street, Malden, MA 02148-5020, USA
9600 Garsington Road, Oxford OX4 2DQ, UK
550 Swanston Street, Carlton, Victoria 3053, Australia

The right of Željko Bošković and Howard Lasnik to be identified as the Authors of
the Editorial Material in this Work has been asserted in accordance with the UK Copyright,
Designs, and Patents Act 1988.

First published 2007 by Blackwell Publishing Ltd

1   2007

Library of Congress Cataloging-in-Publication Data

Minimalist syntax : the essential readings / edited by Željko Bošković and Howard Lasnik.
p. cm. — (Linguistics ; 6)
Includes bibliographical references and index.
ISBN-13: 978-0-631-23303-9 (alk. paper)
ISBN-10: 0-631-23303-2 (alk. paper)
ISBN-13: 978-0-631-23304-6 (pbk. : alk. paper)
ISBN-10: 0-631-23304-0
1. Grammar, Comparative and general—Syntax.   2. Minimalist theory (Linguistics)   I.
Bošković, Željko.   II. Lasnik, Howard.

P295.M56 2006
415—dc22
2006044679

A catalogue record for this title is available from the British Library.

Set in 10.5/12.5pt Ehrhardt
by Graphicraft Limited, Hong Kong

The publisher's policy is to use permanent paper from mills that operate a sustainable
forestry policy, and which has been manufactured from pulp processed using acid-free and
elementary chlorine-free practices. Furthermore, the publisher ensures that the text paper
and cover board used have met acceptable environmental accreditation standards.

For further information on
Blackwell Publishing, visit our website:
www.blackwellpublishing.com

Contents

Acknowledgments

First, we must thank Noam Chomsky for creating and often (as in the case of Minimalism) reinventing the field of generative transformational grammar, and for constantly stimulating its practitioners to find better data, arguments, and analyses. Several of the works collected here are his, and all were inspired by him. Next, we are grateful to Blackwell Publishing for their encouragement in this project (and their patience). We should particularly mention Sarah Coleman, who always displays good sense and good cheer. Valery Rose and Pandora Kerr Frost have been careful and conscientious copy-editors, raising just the right questions and offering us good answers. Finally, this project would not have been possible at all without the extensive assistance of our students Tomohiro Fujii (who did almost all of the initial physical preparation of the manuscript, and also prepared the index) and Duk-Ho An.

Z.B.
H.L.

Text Credits

The editors and publisher gratefully acknowledge the permission granted to reproduce the copyright material in this book. This is ordered below by appearance in this book.

Chapter 1
Noam Chomsky, "Minimalist Inquiries: The Framework," p. 94, from Roger Martin, David Michaels, and Juan Uriagereka (eds.), *Step by Step: Essays on Minimalist Syntax in Honor of Howard Lasnik* (Cambridge, MA: MIT Press, 2000). © 2000 by Massachusetts Institute of Technology. Reprinted by permission of The MIT Press.

Noam Chomsky, "Derivation by Phase," p. 1, from Michael Kenstowicz (ed.), *Ken Hale: A Life in Language* (Cambridge, MA: MIT Press, 2001). © 2001 by Massachusetts Institute of Technology. Reprinted by permission of The MIT Press.

Noam Chomsky, "Minimalist Inquiries: The Framework," pp. 95, 112–13, 114, 117–19, from Roger Martin, David Michaels, and Juan Uriagereka (eds.), *Step by Step: Essays on Minimalist Syntax in Honor of Howard Lasnik* (Cambridge, MA: MIT Press, 2000). © 2000 by Massachusetts Institute of Technology. Reprinted by permission of The MIT Press.

Željko Bošković, "D-Structure, Theta-Criterion, and Movement into Theta-positions," pp. 247–73, from *Linguistic Analysis* 24 (1994). © 1994 by Linguistic Analysis. Reprinted by permission of the author.

Noam Chomsky, "A Minimalist Program for Linguistic Theory," pp. 191–9, 202–12, 215–17, from his *The Minimalist Program* (Cambridge, MA: MIT Press, 1995). © 1995 by Massachusetts Institute of Technology. Reprinted by permission of The MIT Press.

Samuel D. Epstein, Erich M. Groat, Ruriko Kawashima, and Hisatsugu Kitahara, pp. 11–13, from *A Derivational Approach to Syntactic Relations* (New York: Oxford University Press, 1998). © 1998 by Samuel David Epstein, Erich M. Groat, Ruriko Kawashima, and Hisatsugu Kitahara. Reprinted by permission of Oxford University Press, Inc.

Noam Chomsky, "Minimalist Inquiries: The Framework," pp. 131–2, 150, from Roger Martin, David Michaels, and Juan Uriagereka (eds.), *Step by Step: Essays on Minimalist Syntax in Honor of Howard Lasnik* (Cambridge, MA: MIT Press, 2000). © 2000 by Massachusetts Institute of Technology. Reprinted by permission of The MIT Press.

Noam Chomsky, "Beyond Explanatory Adequacy," pp. 107–8, 111, 124–6 (notes), from Adriana Belletti (ed.), *Structures and Beyond: The Cartography of Syntactic Structure*, vol. 3 (New York: Oxford University Press, 2004). © 2004 by Noam Chomsky. Reprinted by permission of the author.

Chapter 2
Howard Lasnik and Mamoru Saito, "On the Subject of Infinitives," pp. 8–15, 17–19, 23–4, from L. Dobrin, L. Nichols, and R. Rodriguez (eds.), *Papers from the 27th Regional Meeting of the Chicago Linguistic Society* (Chicago Linguistic Society, 1991). © 1991 by The Chicago Linguistic Society. Reprinted with permission of The Chicago Linguistic Society.

Noam Chomsky, "A Minimalist Program for Linguistic Theory," pp. 173–6, 213, from his *The Minimalist Program* (Cambridge, MA: MIT Press, 1995). © 1995 by Massachusetts Institute of Technology. Reprinted by permission of The MIT Press.

Noam Chomsky, "Minimalist Inquiries: The Framework," pp. 122–5, 127–8, 128–9, 130–1, 147–8, 149, 150, from Roger Martin, David Michaels, and Juan Uriagereka (eds.), *Step by Step: Essays on Minimalist Syntax in Honor of Howard Lasnik* (Cambridge, MA: MIT Press, 2000). © 2000 by Massachusetts Institute of Technology. Reprinted by permission of The MIT Press.

Željko Bošković, pp. 7–25, 63–5, 177, 184, 195–6, from *The Syntax of Nonfinite Complementation: An Economy Approach* (Cambridge, MA: MIT Press, 1997). © 1997 by Massachusetts Institute of Technology. Reprinted by permission of The MIT Press.

Norbert Hornstein, "Movement and Control," pp. 69–74, 77–90, from *Linguistic Inquiry* 30 (1999). © 1999 by Massachusetts Institute of Technology. Reprinted by permission of MIT Press Journals.

Noam Chomsky and Howard Lasnik, "The Theory of Principles and Parameters," pp. 90–1, from J. Jacobs, A. von Stechow, W. Sternefeld, and T. Vennemann (eds.), *Syntax: An International Handbook of Contemporary Research* (Berlin: Walter de Gruyter, 1993). © 1993 by Walter de Gruyter. Reprinted by permission of Mouton de Gruyter, a division of Walter de Gruyter & Co. KG Publishers.

Noam Chomsky, "A Minimalist Program for Linguistic Theory," pp. 181–2, from his *The Minimalist Program* (Cambridge, MA: MIT Press, 1995). © 1995 by Massachusetts Institute of Technology. Reprinted by permission of The MIT Press.

Chris Collins, "Economy of Derivation and the Generalized Proper Binding Condition," pp. 45–57, from *Linguistic Inquiry* 25 (1994). © 1994 by Massachusetts Institute of Technology. Reprinted by permission of MIT Press Journals.

Hisatsugu Kitahara, pp. 68–76, 120–1, from his *Elementary Operations and Optimal Derivations* (Cambridge, MA: MIT Press, 1997). © 1997 by Massachusetts Institute of Technology. Reprinted by permission of The MIT Press.

Noam Chomsky, "Categories and Transformations," pp. 262–5, 271, 277–9, 281, 294–7, 304–6, 309–10, 355–8, 383, 385, 387–9, 393, from his *The Minimalist Program* (Cambridge, MA: MIT Press, 1995). © 1995 by Massachusetts Institute of Technology. Reprinted by permission of The MIT Press.

Chris Collins, pp. 4–5, 9–10, 25–6, 131–2, 134, from *Local Economy* (Cambridge, MA: MIT Press, 1995). © 1997 by Massachusetts Institute of Technology. Reprinted by permission of The MIT Press.

Masao Ochi, "Move or Attract?" pp. 319–32, from E. Curtis, J. Lyle, and G. Webster (eds.), *WCCFL16: Proceedings of the Sixteenth West Coast Conference on Formal Linguistics* (Stanford, CA: CSLI Publications, 1997). © 1998 by CSLI Publications, Stanford University, Stanford, CA 94305-4115, USA. Reprinted by permission of CSLI Publications.

Željko Bošković, "A-movement and the EPP," pp. 167–72, 178–98, 203–4, from *Syntax* 5: 3 (2002). © 2002 by Syntax. Reprinted by permission of Blackwell Publishing Ltd.

Noam Chomsky, "Minimalist Inquiries: The Framework," pp. 102, 106–7, 107–8, 109, 110, 144, 145, from Roger Martin, David Michaels, Juan Uriagereka (eds.), *Step by Step: Essays on Minimalist Syntax in Honor of Howard Lasnik* (Cambridge, MA: MIT Press,

2000). © 2000 by Massachusetts Institute of Technology. Reprinted by permission of The MIT Press.

Noam Chomsky, "Derivation by Phase," pp. 12–14, 44–5, from Michael Kenstowicz (ed.), *Ken Hale: A Life in Language* (Cambridge, MA: MIT Press, 2001). © 2001 by Massachusetts Institute of Technology. Reprinted by permission of The MIT Press.

Klaus Abels, pp. 9–13, from "Successive Cyclicity, Anti-locality and Adposition Stranding" (University of Connecticut, PhD dissertation, 2003). © 2003 by Klaus Abels. Reprinted by permission of the author.

Chapter 3

Noam Chomsky, "Categories and Transformations," pp. 241–9, 382–3, from his *The Minimalist Program* (Cambridge, MA: MIT Press, 1995). © 1995 by Massachusetts Institute of Technology. Reprinted by permission of The MIT Press.

Noam Chomsky, "Beyond Explanatory Adequacy," p. 109, from Adriana Belletti (ed.), *Structures and Beyond: The Cartography of Syntactic Structure*, vol. 3 (New York: Oxford University Press, 2004). © 2004 by Noam Chomsky. Reprinted by permission of the author.

Noam Chomsky, "Minimalist Inquiries: The Framework," pp. 100–2, 104, 106, 142, 143, from Roger Martin, David Michaels, and Juan Uriagereka (eds.), *Step by Step: Essays on Minimalist Syntax in Honor of Howard Lasnik* (Cambridge, MA: MIT Press, 2000). © 2000 by Massachusetts Institute of Technology. Reprinted by permission of The MIT Press.

Norvin Richards, pp. 38–46, from his *Movement in Language: Interactions and Architectures* (New York: Oxford University Press, 2001). © 2001 by Norvin Richards. Reprinted by permission of Oxford University Press and Iris Mulders.

Noam Chomsky, "Minimalist Inquiries: The Framework," pp. 132, 136–7, 150, from Roger Martin, David Michaels, and Juan Uriagereka (eds.), *Step by Step: Essays on Minimalist Syntax in Honor of Howard Lasnik* (Cambridge, MA: MIT Press, 2000). © 2000 by Massachusetts Institute of Technology. Reprinted by permission of The MIT Press.

Željko Bošković, "LF Movement and the Minimalist Program," pp. 43–55, from P. N. Tamanji and K. Kusumoto (eds.), *Proceedings of the North Eastern Linguistics Society* (Amherst, MA: GLSA, 1998). © 1998 by Željko Bošković. Reprinted by permission of the author.

Noam Chomsky, "Categories and Transformations," pp. 349–53, 354–5, 368, 392–3, from his *The Minimalist Program* (Cambridge, MA: MIT Press, 1995). © 1995 by Massachusetts Institute of Technology. Reprinted by permission of The MIT Press.

Chapter 4

Howard Lasnik, "Verbal Morphology: *Syntactic Structures* meets *The Minimalist Program*," pp. 251–75, from H. Campos and P. Kempchinsky (eds.), *Evolution and*

Revolution in Linguistic Theory: Essays in Honor of Carlos Otero (Washington, DC: Georgetown University Press, 1995). © 1995 by Georgetown University Press. Reprinted by permission of Georgetown University Press.

Noam Chomsky, "Derivation by Phase," pp. 37–8, 48–9, from Michael Kenstowicz (ed.), *Ken Hale: A Life in Language* (Cambridge, MA: MIT Press, 2001). © 2001 by Massachusetts Institute of Technology. Reprinted by permission of The MIT Press.

Cedric Boeckx and Sandra Stjepanović, "Head-ing toward PF," pp. 346–53, from *Linguistic Inquiry* 32 (2001). © 2001 by Massachusetts Institute of Technology. Reprinted by permission of MIT Press Journals.

Chapter 5

Richard S. Kayne, pp. 3–11, 15–24, 30–6, 47–9, 133–5, 137, 139, from *The Antisymmetry of Syntax* (Cambridge, MA: MIT Press, 1994). © 1994 by Massachusetts Institute of Technology. Reprinted by permission of The MIT Press.

Noam Chomsky, "Categories and Transformations," pp. 334–40, 390–1, from his *The Minimalist Program* (Cambridge, MA: MIT Press, 1995). © 1995 by Massachusetts Institute of Technology. Reprinted by permission of The MIT Press.

Samuel D. Epstein, "Un-principled Syntax: The Derivation of Syntactic Relations," pp. 323–38, from Samuel D. Epstein and N. Hornstein (eds.), *Working Minimalism* (Cambridge, MA: MIT Press, 1999). © 1999 by Massachusetts Institute of Technology. Reprinted by permission of The MIT Press.

Juan Uriagereka, "Multiple Spell-Out," pp. 251–60, 277, from Samuel D. Epstein and N. Hornstein (eds.), *Working Minimalism* (Cambridge, MA: MIT Press, 1999). © 1999 by Massachusetts Institute of Technology. Reprinted by permission of The MIT Press.

Jairo Nunes and Juan Uriagereka, "Cyclicity and Extraction Domains," pp. 20–1, 22–6, 28, from *Syntax* 3: 1 (2000). © 2000 by Syntax. Reprinted by permission of Blackwell Publishing Ltd.

Chapter 6

Jairo Nunes, pp. 13, 15–18, 22–3, 23–7, 27–8, 30–4, 35–6, 37–43, 62–3, 163, 164–9, from his *Linearization of Chains and Sideward Movement* (Cambridge, MA: MIT Press, 2004). © 2004 by Massachusetts Institute of Technology. Reprinted by permission of The MIT Press.

Jonathan Bobaljik, pp. 348–9, from "Morphosyntax: The Syntax of Verbal Inflection" (Cambridge, MA: MIT, PhD dissertation). © 2005 by Jonathan David Bobaljik.

Jonathan Bobaljik, "A-chains at the PF-interface: Copies and 'Covert' Movement," p. 199, from *Natural Language and Linguistic Theory* 20: 2 (2002). © 2002 by Natural Language and Linguistic Theory.

Chapter 7

Noam Chomsky, "A Minimalist Program for Linguistic Theory," pp. 200–1, from his *The Minimalist Program* (Cambridge, MA: MIT Press, 1995). © 1995 by Massachusetts Institute of Technology. Reprinted by permission of The MIT Press.

Noam Chomsky, "Categories and Transformations," pp. 272–6, 286–8, 364, 384, 386, from his *The Minimalist Program* (Cambridge, MA: MIT Press, 1995). © 1995 by Massachusetts Institute of Technology. Reprinted by permission of The MIT Press.

Howard Lasnik, "Last Resort," pp. 125–42, 145–8, from his *Minimalist Analysis* (Cambridge, MA: MIT Press, 1999). © 1999 by The Massachusetts Institute of Technology. Reprinted by the permission of The MIT Press.

Noam Chomsky, "Derivation by Phase," pp. 16 and 45, from Michael Kenstowicz (ed.), *Ken Hale: A Life in Language* (Cambridge, MA: MIT Press, 2001). © 2001 by Massachusetts Institute of Technology. Reprinted by permission of The MIT Press.

Noam Chomsky, "Minimalist Inquiries: The Framework," p. 126, from Roger Martin, David Michaels, and Juan Uriagereka (eds.), *Step by Step: Essays on Minimalist Syntax in Honor of Howard Lasnik* (Cambridge, MA: MIT Press, 2000). © 2000 by Massachusetts Institute of Technology. Reprinted by permission of The MIT Press.

Noam Chomsky, "Beyond Explanatory Adequacy," pp. 113–14, 126 (notes), from Adriana Belletti (ed.), *Structures and Beyond: The Cartography of Syntactic Structure*, vol. 3 (New York: Oxford University Press, 2004). © 2004 by Noam Chomsky. Reprinted by permission of the author.

Chapter 8

Danny Fox, "Economy and Scope," pp. 283–300, 302–4, from *Natural Language Semantics* 3: 3 (1995). © 1995 by Natural Language Semantics. Reprinted by permission of Springer Science and Business Media.

Danny Fox, "Reconstruction, Binding Theory, and the Interpretation of Chains," pp. 180–7, 188, from *Linguistic Inquiry* 30 (1999). © 1999 by Massachusetts Institute of Technology. Reprinted by permission of MIT Press Journals.

Norbert Hornstein, "Minimalism and Quantifier Raising," pp. 45–60, 69–71, from Samuel D. Epstein and N. Hornstein (eds.), *Working Minimalism* (Cambridge, MA: MIT Press, 1999). © 1999 by Massachusetts Institute of Technology. Reprinted by permission of The MIT Press.

Every effort has been made to trace copyright holders and to obtain their permission for the use of copyright material. The publisher apologizes for any errors or omissions in the above list and would be grateful if notified of any corrections that should be incorporated in future reprints or editions of this book.

Introduction

The goal of this collection is to introduce the reader to the Minimalist Program. The collection undeniably does not contain all one needs to read from the burgeoning literature on Minimalism. Due to space limitations, we have been forced to omit a number of topics that have proved to be important in the development of the program. This in turn forced us to omit a number of influential works. However, we believe that the collection does give a pretty good picture, if not a completely comprehensive one, of the major theoretical and empirical issues in the Minimalist Program, including its current state of affairs and its development, and thus represents a good illustration of what the Minimalist Program is about.

1 The Leading Ideas of the Minimalist Program

A Background

Minimalism is the most recent instantiation of transformational generative grammar. As in the previous instantiations, a sentence is regarded as the result of a computation producing a derivation, beginning with an abstract structural representation sequentially altered by structure-dependent transformations. The Minimalist Program maintains that these derivations and representations conform to an economy criterion demanding that they be minimal in a sense determined by the language faculty (perhaps ultimately by general properties of organic systems): no extra steps in derivations and no extra symbols in representations, and no representations beyond those that are necessary for the system to function at all in connecting sound (or, in the case of signed languages, gesture) and meaning.

Minimalism can best be understood against the background of its immediate predecessor, the so called "Government-Binding" (GB), or Principles and Parameters, model. In that model, there are four significant *levels of representation*, related by derivation as in diagram (1):

(1)   D(eep)-structure
                                          |
                                 S(urface)-structure
                              ╱   ╲
                        PF   LF
                 (Phonetic form)   (Logical form)

Under the traditional view that a human language is a way of relating sound and meaning, the interface levels PF and LF were assumed to be ineliminable. Minimalism begins
with the position that these levels of representation are the only levels, which has led to
exploration of the possibility of movement into θ-positions (see Bošković 1994) for the
initial attempt) and reanalyses of S-structure conditions as either PF/LF or derivational
conditions (see e.g. Chomsky 1993). Eventually, as will be discussed below, even the PF
and LF levels are eliminated. Minimalism differs in several technical ways from its predecessor, but also in perspective. Early work in transformational grammar concentrated
heavily on *descriptive adequacy*, that is, on the task of formulating grammars that correctly describe the intrinsic competence of the idealized native speaker. Beginning with
Chomsky (1965), the focus began to shift towards *explanatory adequacy*, the formulation
of models of linguistic theory that show how the child can succeed in selecting a descriptively adequate grammar on the basis of primary linguistic data. This was the central
concern of the GB program, instantiated in terms of *principles*, universal properties argued
to be innately given by the human language faculty, and *parameters*, limited options set
by the language learner based on simple, readily available data. Minimalism, too, is a
principles and parameters approach, but one that aims to move even beyond explanatory adequacy, by raising the question of why the language faculty has just the properties it has, given that alternative organizations of the computational system can easily be
imagined that also provide good solutions to the puzzle of how children acquire their
language so quickly and easily.

B   Syntactic Interfaces and Levels of Representation

The connection between the syntactic derivation and semantic and phonological interfaces has been a central research question throughout the history of generative grammar. In the earliest generative model, the interface is the T-marker, which includes all
of the syntactic structures created in the course of the derivation. Subsequent models
had the following interfaces with semantics:

(2) a. The "standard theory"   D-structure
     b. Government-Binding (GB)   LF (via S-structure)
     c. Early Minimalism   LF (via an uninterrupted transformational
                                     derivation beginning with the numeration, which
                                     contains lexical items to be used in the derivation)

As will be discussed below, the current Minimalist approach to structure building is much
more similar to that of the 1950s than to any of the intervening models, suggesting that
interpretation in the Minimalist model also could be more like that in the early model,

distributed over many structures. Chomsky (2000, 2001a, 2001b) argues for a general instantiation of this distributed approach to phonological and semantic interpretation, based on ideas of Epstein (1999), and Uriagereka (1999), who called the approach "Multiple Spell-Out." Simplifying somewhat, at the end of each cycle (or "phase" in Chomsky 2001b) the syntactic structure thus far created is encapsulated and sent off to the interface components for phonological and semantic interpretation. Thus, while there are still what might be called PF and LF *components*, there are no *levels* of PF and LF. Epstein argues that such a move represents a conceptual simplification (in the same way that elimination of D-structure and S-structure does), and several authors, e.g. Uriagereka (1999), Chomsky (2000), Franks and Bošković (2001), Simpson (2002), and Fox and Pesetsky (2005), among others, provide empirical justification. The role of syntactic derivation, always very important in Chomskian theorizing, becomes even more central on this view, as there are no levels of representation at all. Epstein argues that the centrality of c-command (as opposed to one of a whole range of other conceivable geometric relations) in syntax is also predicted on this strongly derivational view, but not in a more "representational" theory.

Returning to Multiple Spell-Out, the mechanism effectively deals with a range of "reconstruction" phenomena, situations where a moved item behaves for certain interpretive processes as if it had not moved. For example, a reflexive such as *himself* normally requires an antecedent that c-commands it:

(3)   John criticized himself
(4)   *Himself criticized John

But in many cases where the reflexive is fronted from a position c-commanded by an antecedent to a position not in that structural relation, the anaphoric connection is nonetheless still available:

(5)   Himself, John criticized

This possibility follows straightforwardly if anaphoric connection can be interpreted prior to movement.

C   The "Last Resort" Nature of Syntactic Movement

One major Minimalist concern involves the driving force for movement. From its inception in the early 1990s, Minimalism has insisted on the "last resort" nature of movement: in line with the leading idea of economy, movement must happen for a reason, and in particular, a formal reason. The Case Filter, which was a central component of the GB system, was thought to provide one such driving force. A standard example involves subject raising, an instance of movement proposed in one form or another from the earliest days of transformational generative grammar. This operation captures the thematic relatedness in pairs of examples like the following:

(6)   Mary is certain to win the race
(7)   It is certain that Mary will win the race

In (6), as in (7), *Mary* is the understood subject of *win the race*. This fact is captured by deriving (6) from an underlying structure like that of (7), except with an infinitival embedded sentence instead of a finite one:

(8) __ is certain [Mary to win the race]

Crucially, *Mary* in (8) is not in a position appropriate to any Case. By raising to the higher subject position, the thematic subject of the lower clause can rectify its Case theoretic inadequacy, since, in this instance, the raised position is one licensing nominative Case. But notice that if the Case requirement of *Mary* provides the driving force for movement, the requirement will not be satisfied immediately upon the introduction of that nominal expression into the structure. Rather, satisfaction must wait until the next cycle, or, in fact, until an unlimited number of cycles later, as raising configurations can iterate, and it is only the ultimate landing site that licenses nominative Case:

(9)   Mary seems to be likely to win the race
(10) Mary is believed to seem to be likely to win the race

A Minimalist critique favors an alternative where the driving force for movement can be satisfied immediately, rather than indefinitely later in the derivation. In the present instance, suppose the crucial inadequacy lies not in the nominal expression but rather in the item that licenses its Case, say the Tense/Inflection head of the clause. That is, Tense has a feature that must be checked against the NP. Then as soon as that head has been introduced into the structure, it can *attract* the NP that will check (and consequently delete) its feature. Movement is then seen from the point of view of the target rather than the moving item itself. The Case of the NP apparently does get checked as a result of the movement, but that is simply a beneficial side effect of the satisfaction of the requirement of the attractor. In an elegant metaphor, Uriagereka (1998) likens the attractor to a virus. Immediately upon its introduction into the body, it is dealt with (by the production of antibodies in the case of physical viruses, by movement to check the "viral" feature in the syntactic instance). The earlier Minimalist approach to the driving force of movement was called "Greed" by Chomsky. This later one developed out of what Lasnik (1995a) called "Enlightened Self Interest." There is still one residue of Greed, though. As discussed by Lasnik (1995b) and Chomsky (2001b), once the Case feature of a nominal expression has been checked, that expression is no longer available for A-movement, either to another Case position, or even to a non-Case position:

(11) *John is certain [t will fail the exam]
(12) *The belief [John to be likely [t will fail the exam]]

2 The Role of Government in Syntactic Analysis

A Case

One early Minimalist objective was to examine all posited relations, with the goal of eliminating any that were arbitrary. Attention immediately focused on the structural relation *government*, which played a central role in virtually every module of the GB theory. This was a virtue, in that it provided substantial unification. But it was a defect in that it was an arbitrary notion. Consider first the Case module. On GB assumptions, structural Case involves three distinct structural configurations. Structural nominative is licensed in the SPEC-head relation with the functional head finite INFL. Structural accusative Case is licensed in the head-complement relation with V. Exceptional Case marking didn't seem to fall under any true X-bar relation, being head-SPEC of complement. These three distinct relations were incorporated under a general notion of government, but at the expense of positing a rather arbitrary notion, with a very arbitrary exception:

(13)   Head H governs XP if no YP boundary [other than IP] intervenes between H and XP.

As a more principled alternative, Chomsky (1991) and Lasnik and Saito (1991) proposed that structural Case licensing is invariably a SPEC-head relation with a functional head. Just as nominative subject raises (to SPEC of AGR_S), accusative object and accusative ECM subject raise to SPEC of AGR_O. Chomsky assumed that the latter movement is covert, but by the logic of the situation, it could just as well be overt (as long as V raises overtly to a still higher position, at least in VO languages).

B   PRO

One of the great early descriptive achievements of GB theorizing was the "PRO theorem" account of the distribution of PRO, the null thematic subject of certain non-finite clauses. Chomsky (1981) proposed that PRO is a pronominal anaphor, therefore subject to both Condition A and Condition B of the binding theory:

(14)   Condition A: An anaphor must be bound in its governing category.
(15)   Condition B: A pronominal must be free in its governing category.

Since "free" means not bound, these requirements are contradictory. PRO can thus exist only where it has no governing category. By Chomsky's definitions, this will only be true when PRO is ungoverned. Though this provided a far more accurate account than any of the competitors at the time, it was not without troubling aspects. First, the government approach to the distribution of PRO requires positing a number of stipulations as to which elements do or do not count as governors. Furthermore, it is actually not clear that government in the definition of governing category is needed to account for anaphors and pronouns other than PRO. Next, it is fairly widely assumed that Case is necessary for θ-role assignment (the "visibility hypothesis"). Under the GB view that Case demands government, PRO, which is always an argument, stood as an exception to visibility. Given this, Chomsky and Lasnik (1993), followed by Martin (1996) and Bošković (1996), propose that PRO actually is Case-marked (with a special "null" Case). An alternative non-government approach to the distribution of PRO relying on the possibility of movement into θ-positions was proposed by Hornstein (1999b). These works reduce further (likely eliminate) the need for government in binding theory (see also Hornstein 2001 and Kayne 2003 regarding Conditions A and B. The reader is also referred to Bošković and Lasnik (2003) for elimination of government in the domain of the distribution of null complementizers, where government was previously assumed to play a crucial role (see Stowell 1981).

C Locality

GB conditions on the locality of movement often were formulated in terms of government. The ECP of Chomsky (1981) was crucially based on government. Subjacency was not, in that work; however, to solve certain problems of the classical formulation of Subjacency, Chomsky (1986a) presented a new formulation making essential use of government. More recent proposals have attempted to deduce locality from Relativized Minimality (RM) (for example, in the form of Shortest Move, see Chomsky and Lasnik 1993 and Takahashi 1994). Some of the Subjacency effects not falling under RM have been argued to follow from the theory of phases (Chomsky 2001b), in particular the Phase Impenetrability Condition. Chomsky suggested that when a phase is sent off for semantic and phonological interpretation, its "edge" (typically a specifier position) remains until the next phase, thus is available as an "escape hatch." Assuming that CP is a phase, the moving Wh-phrase will have to move to the Spec of each CP on the way to its ultimate destination. Accommodating other "island" constraints on movement in a Minimalist way has been a lively research area (for recent discussion, see Bošković 2002, Boeckx 2003, Nunes and Uriagereka 2000, Starke 2001, and Stepanov 2001, among others).

3 Structure Building

As noted above, Minimalism, in a partial return to the technical apparatus of pre-1965 transformational theory, has no level of D-structure. Rather, lexical items are inserted "on-line" in the course of the syntactic derivation. The derivation proceeds cyclically with the most deeply embedded structural unit created first, then combined with the head of which it is the complement to create a larger unit, and so on, all in accord with X′-theory. The processes merging independent units into new combined structures (generalized transformations) are intermingled with those manipulating existing structures (singular transformations). There is thus no one representation following all lexical insertion and preceding all (singular) transformations. That is, there is no D-structure. The constraint that derivations proceed strictly monotonically, bottom–up, had been introduced, along with D-structure, in the "standard theory" of Chomsky (1965). Chomsky argued that this requirement of cyclicity explains the absence of certain kinds of derivations in language. This was presented at the time as an argument against generalized transformations and for D-structure. But it was cyclicity, rather than D-structure, that was crucial in the account. Minimalism rejects D-structure, reinstates generalized transformations, and preserves cyclicity, still ruling out the kind of anti-cyclic derivations that were the original concern. One Minimalist version of the cyclic principle, the Extension Condition, demands that both movement of material already in the structure (singular transformation) and merger of a lexical item not yet in the structure (generalized transformation) target the top of the existing tree. An important question is whether covert operations also obey the Extension Condition (see e.g. Bures

1993, Branigan and Collins 1993, and Jonas and Bobaljik 1993), and if so, how. Chomsky (1995b) suggests an additional way of deducing cyclicity, based on a particular theory of the "strong features" forcing overt movement in which strong features must be checked immediately upon insertion; Bošković and Lasnik (1999) pursue this possibility, proposing that it should completely replace the Extension Condition. Another question related to theories of cyclicity and structure building is whether covert lexical insertion exists, an issue addressed in Bošković (1998). For items with phonological content, the answer is straightforwardly negative, but for those lacking phonological content, the issue is more subtle and more interesting.

Another interesting issue centers on the fact that the model in question allows essentially free interaction between generalized and singular transformations. However, Chomsky (2000), developing a suggestion of Chomsky (1995b), argues that whenever a specific derivational point allows either kind of operation, the former (Merge) is preferred over the latter (Move). This is intended to rule out examples like (16).

(16)   *There seems [someone to be in the room]

The relevant derivational point is shown in (17).

(17)   [to be someone in the room]

Since *there* is available for Merge, Move of *someone* is blocked. Chomsky suggests that this preference follows from considerations of (local) economy, since Move is a compound operation including Merge as one of its sub-parts. The Merge-over-Move analysis, however, has been challenged in several recent works (see e.g. Bošković 2002, Epstein and Seely 1999, and Grohmann et al. 2000).

4 Verbal Morphology and Parametric Properties

One recurrent theme in GB and Minimalist theorizing is that human languages are syntactically much more similar than they appear to be. The standard GB and early Minimalist approach was the proposal that apparent differences result from derivational "timing" differences among languages. In a language where the effects of a transformation are phonetically observable, that operation has happened in overt syntax (i.e. before "Spell-Out," the branch point towards PF). If the effects are not phonetically observable, the operation has happened in covert syntax. Under both circumstances, LF would reflect the results of the transformation. For example, the "Wh-movement" operative in English interrogative sentences is overt. In many other languages, including Chinese and Japanese, the interrogative expressions seem to remain in situ. Huang (1981/2) presented a very influential argument that even in such languages, there is movement but that it is covert. Huang's argument was based on his discovery that certain well-established locality constraints on Wh-movement also constrain the distribution and interpretation of certain seemingly unmoved Wh-expressions in Chinese. This argument laid the groundwork for much GB and Minimalist research. Along similar lines, Chomsky (1993) discussed V-raising, overt in virtually all the Romance languages, among many others, and argued by Chomsky to be covert in English. Consider the following examples from English and French:

(18) a.   John often kisses Mary
     b.   *John kisses often Mary
(19) a.   *Jean souvent embrasse Marie
     b.   Jean embrasse souvent Marie

Recall that under the "last resort" concept, movement is driven by a feature needing to be checked. For V-raising, the feature is assumed to be one that resides in Tense/Infl. Now what of the difference between French and English? As indicated above, Chomsky proposed that features driving movement come in two flavors, "strong" and "weak." While all such features must be checked eventually (i.e. by the end of all LF operations), strong features must be checked specifically before Spell-Out. (See Lasnik 1999b for comparison of three theories of strong features.) Considerations of computational complexity suggest that a strong feature must be checked immediately upon its introduction into a structure. Thus, in French there is a strong feature in Tense forcing overt raising. The corresponding feature in English is weak. This accounts for (19) and (18a), leaving just (18b) mysterious. In that example, overt movement took place even though only covert movement should have been required. Chomsky argued that this state of affairs should be excluded in general and formulated the principle Procrastinate disallowing overt movement except when it is necessary (i.e. for the satisfaction of a strong feature).

Procrastinate was often called an economy principle, but it was not obvious that it was. Why is delaying an operation until LF more economical than performing it earlier? In part to answer this question and in part to account for the fact that most of the hypothesized instances of covert movement did not have the expected semantic effects (with respect to quantifier scope, anaphora, etc.) that corresponding overt movements have, Chomsky (1995b), followed by Lasnik (1995b), proposed a modified theory of covert movement. The leading idea of this modified theory is that if movement is driven by the need for formal features to be checked, all that should really move is formal features, in particular Case and agreement features. When movement is overt, this will generally not suffice, since phonology will not be able to deal with the resulting "scattered object." Thus the entire word or phrase hosting the features moves along with them, an extension of a phenomenon dubbed "pied-piping" by Ross (1967). Since covert movement does not feed into PF, feature movement in the LF component will not necessitate pied-piping. Now if only formal features of an element raise, plausibly the semantic features relevant for such phenomena as scope and anaphora are left behind. For such semantic purposes, then, it is as if no movement took place. Further, Procrastinate now would follow from reasonable notions of economy. Delaying a movement until LF means that pied-piping will not be necessary; only formal features will have to move. And moving less is more economical than moving more.

Chomsky (2000, 2001b) takes this line of reasoning even further, proposing that there is no feature movement. Rather, a process of agreement (potentially at a substantial distance) relates the two items that need to be checked against each other. Many of the phenomena that had been analyzed as involving covert movement are reanalyzed as involving no movement at all, just the operation Agree. (However, see Lasnik 2002 for some evidence that feature movement cannot be entirely dispensed with.) This, of course, again creates the question of why movement takes place at all. Chomsky conjectures that phrasal movement is largely to convey discourse-oriented notions such as topic-comment information (though this is not what formally drives it). V-movement, on the other hand, has PF motivation (guaranteeing that the Infl affix will ultimately be attached to a proper host, V), and may even be a PF process, as Chomsky, followed by Boeckx and Stjepanović (2001), suggests for all head movement.

5   C-command and the Linear Correspondence Axiom

Asymmetric c-command is of central importance in Minimalist syntax (as it was in the GB framework). A very influential research line, initiated by Kayne (1994), extends the importance of c-command to PF as well. Generative syntax has always been concerned with the hierarchical organization of representations, and the overwhelming majority of syntactically and semantically significant structural relations are hierarchical: domination, immediate domination, c-command, sisterhood. None of these relations involves linear order, though linear order is obviously manifest in phonological representation. Kayne's hypothesis is that linear order is established via his Linear Correspondence Axiom (LCA), which states that asymmetric c-command is mapped on to linear order. In a natural extension of this line of research, Chomsky (1995a) proposes that linear order, established via the LCA, is manifested *only* in PF. The LCA has the far-reaching consequence that structures must always be right-branching, a consequence that is, on the face of it, flagrantly violated in the vast majority of languages. For example, SVO languages like English are broadly consistent with the requirement, but SOV languages like Japanese are not. Further, given that movement is always to a c-commanding position, leftwards movement is fine but rightwards movement is prohibited, contrary to the apparent existence of "extraposition" type operations. The "antisymmetry" approach reanalyzes SOV languages as underlyingly SVO (as all languages must be by this hypothesis) with the SOV order derived by (leftwards) movement. Similarly, apparent rightwards movement is typically reanalyzed as a series of leftwards movements, many of them "remnant movements" in which X moves out of Y, then the residual Y moves to a position higher than X. Many phenomena have been productively analyzed in these terms, but one crucial unanswered question at this point is the source of the "driving force" for all of the required leftwards movements.

6   The Copy Theory of Movement

Chomsky (1993, 1995b) proposed an approach to movement based on a condition that he calls "Inclusiveness." This condition demands that a syntactic derivation merely combines elements of the numeration, without creating any new entities. Traces, traditionally conceived as new objects created by movement, violate this condition. Chomsky therefore proposed that a "trace" of movement is actually a *copy* of the item that moved, rather than a new sort of entity. Interestingly, this is yet another return to much earlier generative approaches (wherein movement was seen as a compound of copying and deletion, as in Ross 1967). The copy left behind is normally deleted in the phonological component (though, as shown by Bobaljik 2002, Bošković 2001, and Franks 1998, among others, under certain circumstances lower copies are pronounced, in order to "rescue" what would otherwise be PF violations) but could well persist for semantic purposes, such as the licensing of anaphoric connection. The copy theory of movement has incited a great deal of research in both the syntax/phonology and the syntax/semantics interface. For the former, the reader is referred to Nunes (2004). Regarding the latter, Fox (2000) presents an extensive analysis of scope and anaphora reconstruction effects in terms of the copy theory (see also Hornstein 1999a regarding scope). Lasnik (1999a, 2001) examines the presence and, especially, the absence of certain reconstruction effects with A-movement. For dealing with reconstruction effects, the proper division of labor between Multiple Spell-Out and the copy theory of movement is an important ongoing research topic.

7 Existential Constructions

The existential construction, illustrated by (20), has been one of the most hotly debated topics within the Minimalist Program, due to a number of questions that the construction raises with respect to Case (whether or not *there* has Case and the source of Case for the indefinite NP); agreement (regarding the agreement relation between the verb and the postverbal NP); the nature of covert movement and Full Interpretation, issues that are related to the proposal of Chomsky (1986b) that the indefinite replaces the associate in LF; and the EPP and the driving force of movement, issues that are tied to the resolution of the Case issue and the expletive replacement hypothesis.

(20)   There have been two soldiers in the garden today.

8 Syntax/Semantics Interface

The Minimalist Program has raised a number of important issues regarding the nature of the syntax–semantics interface. As noted above, some of them are tied to the question of how exactly syntax feeds into semantics (see the discussion in section 1.B, above) and the copy theory of movement (see the discussion in section 6). Regarding the latter, reconstruction effects and the syntactic treatment of quantifiers have attracted a great deal of attention. Another important question, addressed by Fox (1995) and Fox (2000), is what role economy principles play in the syntax/semantics interface.

9 Conclusion

Minimalism, Chomsky emphasizes, is as yet still just an approach, a conjecture about how human language works ("perfectly"), and a general program for exploring and developing the conjecture. The explanatory success attained thus far gives reason for optimism that the approach can be developed into an articulated theory of language.

Final Comment for the Reader

In our effort to include as many works as possible, we have included excerpts of the selected papers, [. . .] being used to indicate places where material has been left out. As noted in section 1.A, we believe that the best way to understand the Minimalist Program is through a comparison with its immediate predecessor, the GB model. This is reflected in the organization of the collection, which starts with the Minimalist departures from the GB tradition regarding the basic design of language and the interaction with interfaces, the notion of government, and phrase structure building. While organizing the collection, we had in mind that the collection may be used in a graduate seminar on the Minimalist Program. The order of chapters thus represents what seems to us to be a natural order in which major issues in the Minimalist Program can be presented in such a class.[1] The best way of using the collection in the class may be to omit the Recent Developments sections in the initial discussion, returning to them after the rest of the material has been presented. The selections that crucially rely on the material presented in the Recent Development sections (e.g. some of the material from sections 1.1 and 2.3, below) can be discussed together with the latter.

Note

1 In fact, the organization loosely follows the second semester of graduate syntax at the University of Connecticut, which is devoted to the Minimalist Program.

References

Bobaljik, J. 2002. A-chains at the PF interface: Copies and "covert" movement. *Natural Language and Linguistic Theory* 20: 197–267.

Boeckx, C. 2003. *Islands and chains: Resumption as stranding*. Amsterdam: John Benjamins.

Boeckx, C. and S. Stjepanović. 2001. Head-ing toward PF. *Linguistic Inquiry* 32: 345–55.

Bošković, Ž. 1994. D-structure, Theta-Criterion, and movement into theta-positions. *Linguistic Analysis* 24: 247–86.

Bošković, Ž. 1996. Selection and the categorial status of infinitival complements. *Natural Language and Linguistic Theory* 14: 269–304.

Bošković, Ž. 1998. LF movement and the Minimalist Program. In *Proceedings of the North East Linguistic Society*, 28, 43–57. GLSA, University of Massachusetts.

Bošković, Ž. 2001. *On the nature of the syntax – phonology interface: Cliticization and related phenomena*. Amsterdam: Elsevier Science.

Bošković, Ž. 2002. A-movement and the EPP. *Syntax* 5: 167–218.

Bošković, Ž. and H. Lasnik. 1999. How strict is the cycle? *Linguistic Inquiry* 30: 691–703.

Bošković, Ž. and H. Lasnik. 2003. On the distribution of null complementizers. *Linguistic Inquiry* 34: 527–46.

Branigan, P. and C. Collins. 1993. Verb movement and the quotative construction in English. In *MIT working papers in linguistics* 18: 1–13.

Bures, A. 1993. There is an argument for a cycle at LF here. In *CLS 28* vol. 2, 14–35. Chicago Linguistic Society.

Chomsky, N. 1965. *Aspects of the theory of syntax*. Cambridge, MA: MIT Press.

Chomsky, N. 1981. *Lectures on government and binding*. Dordrecht: Foris.

Chomsky, N. 1986a. *Barriers*. Cambridge, MA: MIT Press.

Chomsky, N. 1986b. *Knowledge of language*. New York: Praeger.

Chomsky, N. 1991. Some notes on economy of derivation and representation. In *Principles and parameters in comparative grammar*, ed. R. Freidin, pp. 417–54, Cambridge, MA: MIT Press. [Reprinted in Chomsky (1995), *The Minimalist Program*, Cambridge, MA: MIT Press.]

Chomsky, N. 1993. A minimalist program for linguistic theory. In *The view from Building 20: Essays in linguistics in honor of Sylvain Bromberger*, ed. K. Hale and S. J. Keyser, pp. 1–52. Cambridge, MA: MIT Press. [Reprinted in Chomsky (1995), *The Minimalist Program*, Cambridge, MA: MIT Press.]

Chomsky, N. 1995a. Bare phrase structure. In *Government and binding theory and the minimalist program*, ed. G. Webelhuth, Oxford: Basil Blackwell pp. 383–439. [Also in *Evolution and revolution in linguistic theory: Essays in honor of Carlos Otero*, ed. H. Campos and P. Kempchinsky, Washington, DC: Georgetown University Press (1995).]

Chomsky, N. 1995b. Categories and transformations. In *The Minimalist Program*, Cambridge, MA: MIT Press, pp. 219–394.

Chomsky, N. 2000. Minimalist inquiries: The framework. In *Step by step: Essays on minimalist syntax in honor of Howard Lasnik*, ed. R. Martin, D. Michaels. and J. Uriagereka, Cambridge, MA: MIT Press, pp. 89–155.

Chomsky, N. 2001a. Beyond explanatory adequacy. In *MIT Occasional Papers in Linguistics* 20: 1–28.

Chomsky, N. 2001b. Derivation by phase. In *Ken Hale: A life in language*, ed. M. Kenstowicz, Cambridge, MA: MIT Press, pp. 1–52.

Chomsky, N. and H. Lasnik. 1993. The theory of principles and parameters. In *Syntax: An international handbook of contemporary research*, vol. 1, ed. J. Jacobs, A. von Stechow, W. Sternefeld, and T. Vennemann, Berlin: Walter de Gruyter, pp. 506–69. [Reprinted in Chomsky (1995), *The Minimalist Program*, Cambridge, MA: MIT Press.]

Epstein, S. D. 1999. Un-principled syntax: The derivation of syntactic relations. In *Working minimalism*, ed. S. D. Epstein and N. Hornstein, Cambridge, MA: MIT Press, pp. 317–45.

Epstein, S. D. and T. D. Seely. 1999. SPEC-ifying the GF "subject"; eliminating A-chains and the EPP within a derivational model. Ms; University of Michigan and Eastern Michigan State University.

Fox, D. 1995. Economy and scope. *Natural Language Semantics* 3: 283–341.

Fox, D. 2000. *Economy and semantic interpretation*. Cambridge, MA: MIT Press.

Fox, D. and Pesetsky, D. 2005. Cyclic linearization of syntactic structure. *Theoretical Linguistics* 31: 1–45.

Franks, S. 1998. Clitics in Slavic. Paper presented at the Comparative Slavic Morphosyntax Workshop. Bloomington, Indiana.

Franks, S. and Ž. Bošković. 2001. An argument for multiple spell-out. *Linguistic Inquiry* 32: 174–83.

Grohmann, K. J. Drury, and J. C. Castillo. 2000. No more EPP. In *Proceedings of the Nineteenth West Coast Conference on Formal Linguistics*, Somerville, MA: Cascadilla Press, pp. 139–52.

Hornstein, N. 1999a. Minimalism and quantifier raising. In *Working minimalism*, ed. S. D. Epstein and N. Hornstein, Cambridge, MA: MIT Press.

Hornstein, N. 1999b. Movement and control. *Linguistic Inquiry* 30: 69–96.

Hornstein, N. 2001. *Move! A minimalist theory of construal*. Malden, MA: Blackwell.

Huang, C.-T. J. 1981/2. Move *wh* in a language without *wh*-movement. *The Linguistic Review* 1: 369–416.

Jonas, D. and J. Bobaljik. 1993. SPECs for subjects: The role of TP in Icelandic. In *MIT Working Papers in linguistics* 18, 59–98.

Kayne, R. S. 1994. *The antisymmetry of syntax*. Cambridge, MA: MIT Press.

Kayne, R. 2002. Pronouns and their antecedents. In *Derivation and explanation in the Minimalist Program*, ed. S. D. Epstein and T. D. Seely, Oxford: Blackwell, pp. 133–66.

Lasnik, H. 1995a. Case and expletives revisited: On Greed and other human failings. *Linguistic Inquiry* 26: 615–33. [Reprinted in Lasnik (1999), *Minimalist analysis*, Oxford: Blackwell.]

Lasnik, H. 1995b. Last resort. In *Minimalism and linguistic theory*, ed. S. Haraguchi and M. Funaki, Tokyo: Hituzi Syobo pp. 1–32. [Reprinted in Lasnik (1999), *Minimalist analysis*, Oxford: Blackwell.]

Lasnik, H. 1999a. Chains of arguments. In *Working minimalism*, ed. S. D. Epstein and N. Hornstein, Cambridge, MA: MIT Press pp. 189–215. [Reprinted in Lasnik (2003), *Minimalist investigations in linguistic theory*, London: Routledge.]

Lasnik, H. 1999b. On feature strength: Three minimalist approaches to overt movement. *Linguistic Inquiry* 30: 197–217. [Reprinted in Lasnik (2003), *Minimalist investigations in linguistic theory*, London: Routledge.]

Lasnik, H. 2001. Subjects, objects, and the EPP. In *Objects and other subjects: Grammatical functions, functional categories, and configurationality*, ed. W. D. Davies and S. Dubinsky, Dordrecht: Kluwer Academic, pp. 103–21.

Lasnik, H. 2002. Feature movement or agreement at a distance? In *Dimensions of movement*, ed. A. Alexiadou, E. Anagnostopoulou, S. Barbiers, and H.-M. Gärtner, Amsterdam: John Benjamins, pp. 189–208.

Lasnik, H. and M. Saito. 1991. On the subject of infinitives. In *Papers from the 27th Regional Meeting of the Chicago Linguistic Society, Part I: The general session*, ed. L. M. Dobrin, L. Nichols, and R. M. Rodriguez, Chicago Linguistic Society, University of Chicago, pp. 324–43. [Reprinted in Lasnik (1999), *Minimalist analysis*, Oxford: Blackwell.]

Martin, R. 1996. *A minimalist theory of PRO and control*. Doctoral dissertation, University of Connecticut, Storrs.

Nunes, J. 2004. *Linearization of chains and sideward movement*. Cambridge, MA: MIT Press.

Nunes, J. and J. Uriagereka. 2000. Cyclicity and extraction domains. *Syntax* 3: 20–43.

Ross. J. R. 1967. *Constraints on variables in syntax*. Doctoral dissertation, MIT. Published as *Infinite syntax!* Norwood, NJ: Ablex (1986).

Simpson, A. 2002. IP-raising, tone sandhi and the creation of S-final particles: Evidence for cyclic spell-out. *Journal of East Asian Linguistics* 11: 67–99.

Starke, M. 2001. *Move dissolves into Merge: A theory of locality*. Doctoral dissertation, University of Geneva.

Stepanov, A. 2001. *Cyclic domains in syntactic theory*. Doctoral dissertation, University of Connecticut, Storrs.

Stowell, T. 1981. *Origins of phrase structure*. Doctoral dissertation, MIT.

Takahashi, D. 1994. *Minimality of movement*. Doctoral dissertation, University of Connecticut, Storrs.

Uriagereka, J. 1998. *Rhyme and reason: An introduction to minimalist syntax*. Cambridge, MA: MIT Press.

Uriagereka, J. 1999. Multiple Spell-Out. In *Working minimalism*, ed. S. D. Epstein and N. Hornstein, Cambridge, MA: MIT Press, pp. 251–82.

1

The Basic Design of Language: Levels of Representation and Interaction with Interfaces

1.1 General Background

From "MINIMALIST INQUIRIES: THE FRAMEWORK"
Noam Chomsky

We have assumed two external systems: sensorimotor systems and systems of thought, each with its own characteristics independent of FL [the faculty of language]. The former can only use information presented in a specific form: with temporal order, prosodic and syllable structure, certain phonetic properties and relations. The systems of thought require information about units they can interpret and the relations among them: certain arrays of semantic features, event and quantificational structure, and so on. Insofar as we can discover the properties of these external systems (an empirical problem, however difficult), we can ask how well the language organ satisfies the design specifications they impose, providing legible representations at the interface levels. That is the minimal condition FL must satisfy to be usable at all.

From "DERIVATION BY PHASE"
Noam Chomsky

The shared goal is to formulate in a clear and useful way – and to the extent possible to answer – a fundamental question of the study of language, which until recently could hardly be considered seriously and may still be premature: to what extent is the human faculty of language FL an optimal solution to minimal design specifications, conditions that must be satisfied for language to be usable at all? We may think of these specifications as "legibility conditions": for each language L (a state of FL), the expressions generated by L must be "legible" to systems that access these objects at the interface between FL and external systems – external to FL, internal to the person.

The strongest minimalist thesis SMT would hold that language is an optimal solution to such conditions.

From "MINIMALIST INQUIRIES: THE FRAMEWORK"
Noam Chomsky

To introduce some terminology of *MP* [the Minimalist Program], we say that a computation of an expression Exp *converges at an interface level IL* if Exp is legible at IL, consisting solely of elements that provide instructions to the external systems at IL and arranged so that these systems can make use of them; otherwise, it *crashes* at IL. The computation *converges* if it converges at all interfaces. Call the expression Exp so formed *convergent* as well. As in *MP*, we keep here to a restricted version of the concept of convergence, setting aside the matter of legible arrangement (which raises all sorts of complex issues), and tentatively assuming it to be irrelevant – no slight simplification. Certain features of lexical items are *interpretable*, that is, legible to the external systems at the interface; others are *uninterpretable*. We assume, then, that if an expression contains only features interpretable at IL, it converges at IL.

[. . .]

Assume that FL provides no machinery beyond what is needed to satisfy minimal requirements of legibility and that it functions in as simple a way as possible. We would like to establish such conclusions as these [. . .]:

(1) a. The only linguistically significant levels are the interface levels.
     b. The *Interpretability Condition*: LIs [lexical items] have no features other than those interpreted at the interface, properties of sound and meaning.
     c. The *Inclusiveness Condition*: No new features are introduced by C_{HL} [computational system of human language].
     d. Relations that enter into C_{HL} either (i) are imposed by legibility conditions or (ii) fall out in some natural way from the computational process.

Condition (1a) requires that there is no Deep or Surface Structure, or other levels that have been proposed. It holds that everything accounted for in these terms has been misdescribed and is better understood in terms of legibility conditions at the interface: that includes the Projection Principle, binding theory, Case theory, the Chain Condition, and so on.

Condition (1b) is transparently false.

Condition (1c) permits rearrangement of LIs and of elements constructed in the course of derivation, and deletion of features of LI – but optimally, nothing more.

Condition (1d) has to be spelled out. Properties induced by legibility conditions might include adjacency, argument structure, scope, and the like. Those of category (ii) should include at least (perhaps at most) the relations provided directly by the indispensable computational operation Merge. But there should be no government, no stipulated properties of chains, no binding relations internal to language, no interactions of other kinds. It is hardly necessary to observe that all of this is highly unlikely. There is substantial empirical evidence supporting the opposite conclusion at every point. Furthermore, a basic assumption of the work in the P&P [Principles and Parameters] framework, with its impressive achievements, is that everything just suggested is false: that language is highly "imperfect" in these respects. It would be no small task, then, to show that this apparatus is a kind of descriptive technology, and that if we abandon it, we can maintain or even extend descriptive and explanatory force. Nevertheless, recent work suggests that such conclusions, which seemed out of the question a few years ago, are at least plausible, possibly correct in nontrivial respects.

[. . .]

Consider condition (1c). It requires that there be no phrasal categories or bar levels, hence no X-bar theory or other theory of phrase structure, apart from bare phrase structure, which will be simplified further below. It also rules out introduction of traces, indices, λ-operators, and other new elements in the course of operation of C_{HL}. Recourse to such devices could be innocuous (e.g. if used for convenience to annotate properties that can be determined by inspection at LF), but questions arise if they enter into interpretation and function significantly within the computation – for example, percolation of indices, or operations that apply specifically to trace.

[. . .]

If α in the syntactic object SO is merged somewhere else (by the operation Move) to form SO′, then the two occurrences of α constitute a chain, the original occurrence called the *trace* or *copy* of the new one. The terminology is misleading, for several reasons. First, each of the elements is a "copy" of the other. Second, copy theory is the simplest version of transformational grammar, making use only of Merge, not Merge followed by an operation that deletes the original – and, under trace theory, a further operation that creates a new kind of element, trace, a serious violation of the Inclusiveness Condition. These are "imperfections," to be avoided unless shown to be necessary.

[. . .]

There are some respects in which the strong thesis seems untenable, and we find what appear to be "design flaws" that are not necessary for language-like systems. The most obvious involve the phonological component, which takes syntactic objects constructed by the computational operations C_{HL} and converts them to representations at the PF interface. Here there are radical violations of the Interpretability and Inclusiveness Conditions (1b,c). The Inclusiveness Condition is violated by operations that introduce such new elements as prosodic structure and narrow phonetics. The Interpretability Condition is violated by the discrepancy between the phonological properties of LIs ("morphophonemes," "phonological units," etc., within various frameworks and terminologies) and the narrow phonetic instantiations of combinations of such elements.

[. . .]

The strongest sustainable inclusiveness/interpretability requirement, then, is (2).

(2)   Inclusiveness holds of narrow syntax, and each feature is interpreted at the level LF or associated with phonetic features by the phonological component.

The phonological component is generally assumed to be isolated in even stronger respects: there are *true* phonological features that are visible only to the phonological component and form a separate subsystem of FL, with its own special properties. Assume this to be true. Then in the course of construction of LF, an operation Spell-Out delivers the structure already formed to the phonological component, which converts it to PF [phonetic form]. If LIs express Saussurean arbitrariness in the conventional way, then Spell-Out "strips away" the true phonological features, so that the derivation can converge at LF; it will crash if later operations introduce LIs with phonological features.

1.2   Levels of Representation

From "D-STRUCTURE, THETA-CRITERION, AND MOVEMENT INTO THETA-POSITIONS"
Željko Bošković

1   The minimalist program and D-structure

The starting assumptions of the minimalist program (Chomsky 1993) fall within the domain of virtual conceptual necessity. Language is embedded in two performance systems: articulatory–perceptual and conceptual–intentional. Two linguistic levels, the phonological component (PF) and logical form (LF), are postulated as interfaces with the performance systems, providing the instructions for the two systems. Each linguistic expression is a pair (P, L) satisfying interface conditions and generated in the most economical way. The interface levels PF and LF are the only conceptually necessary linguistic levels. Any additional level represents a departure from the conceptual necessity and must be empirically justified. D-structure (DS), with its all-at-once-application of the operation SATISFY, which selects an array of lexical items and presents them in a way that satisfies X-bar theory, is one such additional level of representation. In contrast to PF and LF, external interface levels with the performance systems, DS is an internal interface level with the lexicon, which is conceptually not necessary. As a result, Chomsky concludes, elimination of DS would represent a move toward the minimalist program of language design.

Chomsky notes that the existence of DS raises several problems. Consider the status of DS as a pure representation of thematic structure, a consequence of the Projection Principle, which requires that lexical properties be satisfied at all levels of representation, and the Theta-Criterion (1).[1]

(1)   The Theta-Criterion (Chomsky 1981)
      Each argument bears one and only one theta-role and each theta-role is assigned to one and only one argument.

As Chomsky notes, the extension of the Theta-Criterion and the Projection Principle from LF, where they hold by virtue of interpretation, to DS is conceptually rather problematic. At LF, the Theta-Criterion and the Projection Principle are trivial; if they are not satisfied, the expression in question receives a deviant interpretation. At DS, on the other hand, the Theta-Criterion and the Projection Principle have a primary role. In fact, their role is to ensure that DS has the basic properties of LF.

Another well-known and more obvious problem with the extension of the Theta-Criterion to DS is that, given the extension, we have to assume that different elements function as arguments at different levels of representation. Consider (2a), with its DS given in (2b).

(2)   a.   Who did John kiss t
      b.   John kissed who

In (2b), *who* is the argument bearing the object theta-role. At LF, the variable bound by *who* rather than *who* itself functions as the argument. Due to the extension of the Theta-Criterion to DS, enforced by the Projection Principle, we thus need to have two different concepts of argument: argument at DS and argument at LF.

It is well-known that the concept of DS as a pure representation of thematic properties also has empirical difficulties. Consider (3).

(3)   John is tough [Op PRO to please t]

Example (3) contains an argument, namely *John*, located in a DS position to which no theta-role is assigned. To account for this, Chomsky (1981) suggested that *John* is inserted later in the derivation, as a result of which (3) does not violate the Theta-Criterion. However, as noted in Chomsky (1993), the matrix subject in (3) can involve a complex structure that itself involves theta-relations.

(4)   That John would do that is tough [Op PRO to believe t]

To save (3) from violating the Theta-Criterion at DS we are forced to assume that the subject of such constructions is inserted after DS. However, the assumption causes the Theta-Criterion to be violated in (4), because the arguments contained in the clause located in subject position are not present at DS.

Tough constructions aside, in recent years several works have appeared which challenge the existence of DS as a level at which all thematic relations are established. Thus, Larson (1988) argues that in double object constructions, thematic relations are established during derivation in the overt syntax. Given Larson's analysis of double object constructions, the thematic relation between *John* and *give* in (5) can be established only after *give* undergoes head-movement.

(5)   John$_i$ [$_{VP}$ t$_i$ gave$_j$ [$_{VP}$ Mary t$_j$ a book]]

In her analysis of *except* ellipsis, Reinhart (1991) argues that the subject NP in (6) adjoins to NP1 at LF. A lambda-predicate is then formed in IP, which takes NP1 as its argument. The thematic relation between IP and NP1 is not established before LF.

(6) a. [$_{IP}$[$_{IP}$ everyone smiled] [$_{NP1}$ except [$_{NP1}$ John]]] SS
    b. [$_{IP}$[$_{IP}$ t$_i$ smiled] [$_{NP1}$ everyone$_i$ [$_{NP1}$ except [$_{NP1}$ John]]]] LF

In work in progress, Hoshi and Saito provide evidence that in Japanese light verb constructions such as (7), thematic relations are also established at LF. They argue that the noun *aiseki* incorporates into the light verb *shita* at LF, after which it theta-marks its arguments *John-wa* and *Bill-to*. They show that, given their analysis, a number of properties of light verb constructions can be accounted for in a principled way.

(7) John-wa Bill-to [$_V$. aiseki-o   shita]
    top   with table-sharing-acc did
    'John shared a table with Bill'

The relevance of ellipsis for determining the status of DS, the Theta-Criterion, and the Projection Principle is often overlooked. Consider, for example, the following instance of antecedent contained deletion (ACD).

(8) I met everyone who John did [$_{VP}$ e]

A number of linguists have argued that the missing VP of the relative clause in (8) is intepreted by copying the matrix VP into the gapped VP position (Williams 1977; Baltin 1987; May 1985; Hornstein 1994; Takahashi 1995, among others). Since the matrix VP itself contains the empty VP that must be filled, doing this at SS would lead to an interpretative regress. May, Hornstein, and Takahashi solve the regress problem by having the object NP undergo LF movement outside the matrix VP. For May the movement is QR [quantifier raising], for Hornstein and Takahashi it is A-movement to SpecAgroP motivated by Case-checking. The matrix VP can then be copied into the gapped VP without causing regress. Under the May/Hornstein/Takahashi analysis, the VP of the relative clause is thus filled only at LF. As a result, *John* in the subject position of the relative clause cannot receive a theta-role before LF. At DS and SS, (8) thus contains an argument that bears no theta-role. One could, however, argue that (8) involves PF deletion of the relative clause VP under identity with the matrix VP rather than LF copying.[2] A PF deletion account would be, however, highly implausible for the Norwegian surface anaphor *det*, unless we go back to the pronominalization transformation and assume that it applies at PF, a position that has been conclusively shown to be untenable (cf. for example, Hankamer and Sag 1976 for convincing arguments that pronouns are present underlyingly and not derived transformationally from full NPs). Hankamer and Sag (1976) establish a difference between deep and surface anaphors. They show that only surface anaphors must be replaced by their antecedent at some level of representation. Lødrup (1993) shows that the Norwegian proform *det* is a surface anaphor when it functions as a complement of epistemic modals. For one thing, when it is a complement of epistemic modals, *det* cannot be deictic, i.e. it must have an antecedent in the linguistic context. Thus, the modal in (9b), where *det* is deictic, can only have a root interpretation. As shown by Hankamer and Sag, the obligatory presence of a linguistic antecedent is a property of surface anaphors ((9a–b) are taken from Lødrup 1993).[3]

(9) a. (Kan bussen ha kommet nå?) Nei, den kan ikke det
         Can the bus have come now? No, it can not it
     b. [I see a man juggling and say]
         Det vil jeg også.
         That I will too

Being a surface anaphor, at some level of representation *det* in (9a) must be replaced by its antecedent. Translating from Lødrup's Lexical Functional Grammar analysis, the replacement of *det* in (9a) takes place at LF. Note now that, as is well-known, epistemic modals do not assign subject theta-roles, therefore the subject of the relevant clause in (9a) cannot receive a theta-role before replacement takes place. Like several other constructions discussed above, (9a) thus seems to contain an argument that bears no theta-role at either DS or SS.

In conclusion, we seem to have both empirical and conceptual evidence against the existence of DS, a result of an all-at-once application of the operation SATISFY with thematic structure fully represented, and the conditions applying to it.[4] In the place of D-structure, Chomsky argues that elements taken from the lexicon project separate X′-subtrees which are combined to form a phrase marker by generalized transformations.[5] The empirical consequences of DS, however, still remain to be accounted for. Chomsky notes that the most important consequence of DS and the conditions applying to it is the ban on substitution into theta-positions. In a system assuming DS, the ban is readily derivable. Given the Theta-Criterion and the Projection Principle, there can be no empty theta-positions at DS; therefore substitution into a theta-position deletes the argument that occupied the position at DS, which violates Recoverability. In this paper we examine whether the ban on substitution into theta-positions can be derived if DS is eliminated.

Two questions should be considered here:

(10) a. Can the ban on substitution into theta-positions be derived by keeping the Theta-Criterion as it is and applying it to LF?
      b. Can the ban on substitution into theta-positions be derived without reference to the LF Theta-Criterion?

Obviously, the latter is the preferred option. Since, like the Projection Principle, the Theta-Criterion loses its primary role by the elimination of DS, it would be desirable to eliminate it along with DS. It should be pointed out here that although the Theta-Criterion does not seem to have independent *syntactic* significance at LF, something like (11), however, must hold by virtue of interpretation.

(11) a. Every theta-role must be assigned to some argument.
      b. Every argument must be assigned some theta-role.

However, as noted by Brody (1993), (11) follows from general considerations of interpretation. There is nothing syntactic about it. What is syntactic about the Theta-Criterion is the biuniqueness requirement. As noted above, semantically, there is nothing wrong with one argument bearing two theta-roles. Problems arise when the association of one argument with more than one theta-role arises as a result of movement. It is highly unlikely that such a constraint on association of arguments and theta-roles can be of a semantic nature. Rather, syntax seems to be responsible for it. The Theta-Criterion in (10) then should be taken to mean the syntactic Theta-Criterion. In the next two sections we address the questions in (10). We show that the answer to (10a) is negative. The answer to (10b), on the other hand, turns out to be positive. We argue that not only can we derive the ban on substitution into theta-positions in a framework in which DS is eliminated, but that this can be done without reference to the LF Theta-Criterion. Furthermore, no new assumptions have to be made to achieve this. All the mechanisms that are needed are already available and independently motivated.[6]

2   Eliminating the Theta-Criterion

2.1   The LF Theta-Criterion

The first potential problem for the minimalist framework, with DS dispensed with, is raised by constructions such as (12).[7]

(12)   *John [$_{VP}$ t believes [$_{IP}$ t to [$_{VP}$ t like Mary]]]

John in (12) is associated with two theta-positions thus ending up with subject theta-roles of both *believe* and *like*. Notice, however, that we do not need to invoke the LF Theta-Criterion to rule out (12). If ECM [exceptional case marking] subjects are assigned Accusative Case in the embedded SpecIP, (12) is ruled out by the Last Resort Condition because it involves movement from a Case-checking position (embedded SpecIP) into a Case-checking position (matrix SpecIP). On the other hand, if Accusative Case is checked under Spec-head agreement with Agro (Chomsky (1991, 1993), Chomsky and Lasnik (1993), among others) it does not seem to be possible to rule out (12) by the Last Resort Condition without ruling out constructions such as *John kissed Mary*. To avoid violation of the Last Resort Condition in simple transitive constructions it is often assumed that SpecAgroP is generated at LF in English. Given that assumption, SpecAgroP is not present at the level at which subject moves to SpecIP and it does not interfere with subject movement via the Last Resort Condition. Assuming that the matrix SpecAgroP is generated at LF in (12), as in simple transitive constructions, it does not interfere with overt subject movement to SpecIP. However, since *John* is Case-checked in the matrix SpecIP, and assuming that *believe* has Accusative Case features, (12) can still be ruled out because Case features of *believe* remain unchecked.[8] In order to get around the problem, suppose that, as suggested by Brody (1993), we replace *believe* by BELIEVE, which would have the same thematic structure as *believe* but would not check Accusative Case.

(13)   John [$_{VP}$ t BELIEVES [$_{IP}$ t to [$_{VP}$ t like Mary]]]

In fact, *remark* might be a verb of the BELIEVE class. Given Pesetsky's (1982) claim that verbs that cannot take NP complements cannot assign Accusative Case, the ungrammaticality of constructions such as **John remarked Mary's arrival* provides evidence that *remark* has no Accusative Case features.[9] The question is now why there are no verbs that allow the configuration in (13), or, if *remark* is indeed a verb of the BELIEVE class, why (14) is ungrammatical.

(14)   *John [$_{VP}$ t remarked [$_{IP}$ t to t like Mary]]

It is easy to verify that (13–14) cannot be ruled out by appealing to the Case Theory. However, since *John* ends up with two theta-roles, examples (13–14) still violate the syntactic Theta-Criterion at LF. Consider, however, (15).

(15)   a.   John [$_{VP}$ t' BELIEVES [$_{IP}$ t to [$_{VP}$ seem that Peter likes Mary]]]
       b.   *John [$_{VP}$ t' remarked [$_{IP}$ t to [$_{VP}$ seem that Peter likes Mary]]]

John in (15a–b) moves to a theta-position from a nontheta-position. As a result, the constructions satisfy the LF Theta-Criterion. Yet, there are no verbs that allow the configuration in (15a), and (15b) is ungrammatical.

The relevant point can be made even clearer with respect to (16).[10]

(16)   a.   SS   *It believes [$_{IP}$ John to seem that Peter likes Mary]
       b.   LF   *It believes$_i$ [$_{AgroP}$ John$_j$ t$_i$ [$_{VP}$ t$_j$ t$_i$ [$_{IP}$ t$_j$ to seem that Peter likes Mary]]]
       c.   SS   *It$_i$ is likely [$_{IP}$ t$_i$ to believe [$_{IP}$ John to seem that he likes Mary]]
       d.   LF   *It$_i$ is likely [$_{IP}$ t$_i$ to [$_{AgroP}$ John$_j$ believe$_k$ [$_{VP}$ t$_i$ t$_k$ [$_{IP}$ t$_j$ to seem that he likes Mary]]]]

In the LF of (16a,c) *John*, which is inserted into SpecIP at SS, moves to SpecAgroP via the Spec of the VP headed by *believe*, where it picks up the subject theta-role of *believe*. The movement is motivated by Case-checking. The Last Resort Condition is thus satisfied in (16). Since *John* moves to SpecVP from a nontheta-position we cannot rule out (16a,c) by appealing to the LF syntactic Theta-Criterion. We conclude, therefore, that the answer to the question in (10a) is negative. Once DS is eliminated, the ban on movement into theta-positions cannot be derived by simply maintaining the syntactic Theta-Criterion at LF.[11] In the next section, however, we will show that the ban on movement into theta-positions is derivable from principles independent of the Theta-Criterion. Since our analysis of (13–16) is crucially based on broadening the typology of syntactic positions, in the next section we will make a short digression to discuss the issue in question.

2.2   Deriving the effects of the Theta-Criterion

Chomsky (1981) defines A-positions as potential theta-positions. However, given the VP Internal Subject Hypothesis and the DP Hypothesis, the traditional A/A' distinction in terms of theta (T)/nontheta (T')-positions can no longer be maintained. Chomsky and Lasnik (1993) and Chomsky (1993) propose to divide T'-positions into A and A'-positions. According to them, in addition to T-positions, certain T'-positions such as SpecAgrP and SpecTP should be considered A-positions. Given this proposal, the intuitive appeal and simplicity of the traditional A/A' distinction is lost. Furthermore, in recent work it has become clear that the A/A' distinction does not sufficiently account for the full range of facts relevant to the typology of syntactic positions. Thus, to account for mixed properties of Scrambling with respect to the A/A' distinction, Webelhuth (1989) proposes that Scrambling involves movement into a third kind of position, namely a nonA nonoperator position. Müller and Sternefeld (1993) show that a number of different properties of *wh*-movement, Scrambling, and Topicalization can be accounted for by fine-graining the typology of syntactic positions. According to Müller and Sternefeld, all the operations in question involve movement into different types of positions. Fukui (1993) argues that positions adjoined to phonological lexical heads and positions adjoined to projections of functional heads are fundamentally different kinds of syntactic positions. For several languages it has been proposed that SpecIP can function as an A'-position when Nominative Case is assigned into SpecVP (Bonet 1989; Diesing 1990; Rögnvaldsson and Thráinsson 1990, among others). Masullo (1992) shows, however, that even when it functions as an A'-position, SpecIP differs from typical A'-positions such as SpecCP in several respects.[12] Li (1990) argues that we still need a distinction between theta and nontheta-positions. He shows convincingly that the T/T' distinction is crucially needed to account for locality effects on head-movement. He extends the notion of T-positions to cover heads as well as maximal projections by defining T-positions as positions to which or from which a theta-role in principle can be assigned. Given this, since INFL and C do not assign theta-roles they are fundamentally different kinds of syntactic positions from V, a theta-role assigner. Certain facts concerning V-incorporation (VI) provide evidence that this is indeed the case. It is well-known that complementizers are absent from XPs from which VI takes place. Furthermore, verbs undergoing VI generally lack INFL features. Li argues that the absence of complementizers and the lack of INFL features on the verbs undergoing VI indicate that VI can take place only from VPs. This is only expected given that nontheta-role assigners INFL and C are fundamentally different kinds of syntactic positions from V. Since both the initial and the landing site of VI is a T-position, VI from within either IP or CP inevitably results in an Improper Movement, namely T–T'–T movement.[13] Li's proposals also account for the nonexistence of VI compounds containing NEG that negates only the lower verb, which would involve V-adjunction to Neg, a T'-position, prior to VI. Since such constructions involve T–T'–T movement they are ruled out as instances of Improper Movement. The data considered by Li thus indicate that Chomsky's (1981) division of syntactic positions in terms of T and T'-positions represents a fundamental insight into the typology of syntactic positions. What we need now is a more fine-grained typology of T'-positions.[14]

Bearing in mind that theta and nontheta-positions are fundamentally different kinds of syntactic positions let us reconsider (15).

(15) a.   John [$_{VP}$ t' BELIEVES [$_{IP}$ t to seem that Peter likes Mary]]
      b.   *John [$_{VP}$ t' remarked [$_{IP}$ t to seem that Peter likes Mary]]

John in (15a–b) is inserted into the embedded SpecIP to satisfy the Extended
Projection Principle (EPP), or, in Chomsky's (1993) terms, to check the N feature
of the embedded INFL. It moves to the matrix SpecIP, where it is Case-checked,
via matrix SpecVP, where it picks up a theta-role. The derivation involves movement from T' to T and back to a T'-position. Given this, regardless of which of the
current approaches to Improper Movement is adopted, the derivation in question
is straightfowardly ruled out as an instance of Improper Movement. For concreteness let us adopt Saito's (1994) and Takahashi's (1992) Economy account of
Improper Movement. Consider (17).[15]

(16) α   t'   t

X   Y   X (where X and Y are different types of syntactic positions)

Saito (1994) and Takahashi (1992) note that to form a single X–chain (α, t) the
derivation in (17) in fact creates two chains, namely a Y–chain (t', t) and a X–chain
(α, t'). As a result, it is ruled out by the Principles of Economy of Derivation, in
particular, Make the Fewest Steps Condition (Chomsky 1991, MIT lectures 1991),
which chooses the more economical derivation in which α moves directly to X
creating a single X chain.[16] Returning now to (15), notice that the derivation on
which *John* passes through the matrix SpecVP on its way to SpecIP creates two
chains, a T-chain (t', t) and a T'-chain (*John*, t'), to form a single T' chain (*John*, t).
As a result, it is excluded by the Principles of Economy of Derivation, which force
the more economical derivation resulting in the formation of a single chain, namely
direct movement of *John* to SpecIP.[17] Let us now reconsider (16), another problem
for the LF Theta-Criterion.

(17) a.   SS   *It believes [$_{IP}$ John to seem that Peter likes Mary]
      b.   LF   *It believes$_i$ [$_{AgroP}$ John$_j$ t$_i$ [$_{VP}$ t$_j$ t$_i$ [$_{IP}$ t$_j$ to seem that Peter likes Mary]]]
      c.   SS   *It$_i$ is likely [t$_i$ to believe [$_{IP}$ John to seem that he likes Mary]]
      d.   LF   *It$_i$ is likely [$_{IP}$ t$_i$ to [$_{AgroP}$ John$_j$ believe$_k$ [$_{VP}$ t$_j$ t$_k$ [$_{IP}$ t$_j$ to seem that
              he likes Mary]]]]

As in (15), *John* in (16a,c) is inserted into a T'-position and at LF moves to a T
and back to a T'-position. Since the derivations create two chains to form a single
T'-chain they are ruled out by the Principles of Economy of Derivation. It is easy
to verify that the constructions in (18) are also readily ruled out as instances of
Improper Movement (for ease of exposition we will continue to use the term
Improper Movement).

(18) a.   *John$_i$ [$_{VP}$ t$_i$ BELIEVES/remarked [$_{IP}$ t$_i$ to [$_{VP}$ t$_i$ like Mary]]]
      b.   SS   *It believes [$_{IP}$ John$_j$ to [$_{VP}$ t$_j$ like Mary]]
      c.   LF   *It believes$_i$ [$_{AgroP}$ John$_j$ t$_i$ [$_{VP}$ t$_j$ t$_i$ [$_{IP}$ t$_j$ to [$_{VP}$ t$_j$ like Mary]]]]

     d.   SS   *It$_i$ is likely [$_{IP}$ t$_i$ to believe [$_{IP}$ John$_j$ to [$_{VP}$ t$_j$ like Mary]]]

     e.   LF   *It$_i$ is likely [$_{IP}$ t$_i$ to [$_{AgroP}$ John$_j$ believe$_k$ [$_{VP}$ t$_j$ t$_k$ [$_{IP}$ t$_j$ to [$_{VP}$ t$_j$ like Mary]]]]]

If *John* skips the embedded SpecIP no problems with respect to Improper Movement arise in (18). However, the constructions are then ruled out by the EPP because they contain a SpecIP that remains empty. In other words, the N-feature of the relevant INFL remains unchecked. Recall now that the derivations in question are also ruled out by the syntactic LF Theta-Criterion. However, in addition to the conceptual reasons discussed above, the very fact that the Improper Movement analysis can account for (15) and (16), which cannot be accounted for by the LF Theta-Criterion, provides evidence that the Improper Movement analysis is to be preferred to the LF Theta-Criterion analysis.[18]

   Given that (15–16) and (18) are accounted for as shown above, we can go a long way towards eliminating the Theta-Criterion as a syntactic condition. In fact, constructions such as (19) are the only potential problem for the Improper Movement account of the effects of the Theta-Criterion.

(19)   *[$_{IP}$ John [$_{VP}$ t [$_{V'}$ hit t]]]

John in (19) is generated in object position and then moves to SpecVP, where it picks up the subject theta-role of *hit*. The derivation in (19) clearly does not involve Improper Movement. However, given that *hit* has Accusative Case features, if *John* is Case-checked in SpecIP, (19) is ruled out because the Case features of *hit* remain unchecked. If, on the other hand, *John* is Case-checked in SpecAgroP the construction violates the Last Resort Condition, which rules out movement from Case-checking into Case-checking positions, and the Principle Procrastinate, which delays Accusative Case-checking in English until LF. Furthermore, Nominative Case-features of Tense remain unchecked. Like other relevant constructions discussed above, (19) is thus straightforwardly ruled out independently of the Theta-Criterion. Suppose, however, that we replace *hit* by HIT, which would differ from *hit* only in that it would not be specified with the feature [+Accusative]. The question is why such verbs do not exist.

(20)   [$_{IP}$ John [$_{VP}$ t [$_{V'}$ HIT t]]]

Because HIT has no Case-features, if *John* is Case-checked in SpecIP the construction cannot be ruled out on a par with (19). However, since HIT has no Accusative Case features but assigns subject theta-role, (20) can be accounted for by invoking Burzio's generalization, which prohibits the existence of verbs such as HIT. We could thus simply assume that whatever accounts for Burzio's generalization should also account for (20). However, since Burzio's generalization is not a primitive of the theory (cf., for example, the discussion concerning (15a,b) above), let us see if we can account for (20) independently of Burzio's generalization. In fact, the configuration in question is ruled out independently by the following condition, proposed by Saito and Murasugi (1999), which Saito and

Murasugi argue is derivable from the Principles of Economy, in particular, Chomsky's ban on superfluous steps.[19]

(21)   a.   Each chain link must be at least of length 1.
         b.   A chain link from α to β is of length n if there are n XPs that cover β but not α.[20]

Example (21) requires that each chain link have some length, which, according to Saito and Murasugi, is necessary to avoid violating the ban on superfluous steps. The condition has considerable motivation. Thus, given the Minimize Chain Links Principle (Chomsky and Lasnik 1993), which requires that every chain link be as short as possible, it is clear that we need a constraint like (21). Without (21), the Minimize Chain Links Principle would force a phrase in an adjoined position to keep adjoining the same node. As (22) shows, the Minimize Chain Links Principle aside, even in the *Barriers* framework, without a constraint like (21) we could get around island effects by adjoining a phrase to the same node twice, as a result of which the relevant traces would be antecedent governed by each other. (The observation is generally attributed to D. Bouchard.)

(22)   *How did John wonder whether Peter [$_{VP}$ t [$_{VP}$ [$_{VP}$ fixed the car] t]]

Saito and Murasugi (1999) argue that (21) is also responsible for the ungrammaticality of (23), which, if allowed, could void the Comp-trace effect.

(23)   *Who do you think [$_{CP}$ t that [$_{IP}$ t [$_{IP}$ loves Mary]]]

Chomsky (1986a) accounts for (23) by banning *wh*-adjunction to IP. Given recent theoretical developments, there is no compelling reason for banning *wh*-adjunction to IP. If the ban is lifted, a question arises as to why (23) has the status of an ECP violation.[21] According to Saito and Murasugi, the derivation in (23) is ruled out because the chain-link from SpecIP to the IP adjoined position has the length 0, thus violating the ban on superfluous steps. Example (21) also rules out short subject Topicalization (24a), which is a desirable result (cf. Lasnik and Saito 1992). Given the arguments presented in Bošković (1996) and Law (1991) that zero null operator relatives are IPs with the null operator adjoined to IP, the facts in (24b–d) also follow from (21).[22]

(24)   a.   *I think that [$_{IP}$ Mary, [$_{IP}$ t likes John]]
         b.   *the man [$_{IP}$ Op [$_{IP}$ t likes Mary]]
         c.   the man [$_{IP}$ Op [$_{IP}$ Mary likes t]]
         d.   the man [$_{IP}$ Op [$_{IP}$ you think t likes Mary]]

Let us return now to the non-existence of HIT which, if accounted for only by Burzio's generalization – not a primitive of the theory – raises a potential problem for our claim that the effects of the Theta-Criterion follow from independently needed principles. Notice now that the chain link from object position to SpecVP in (20) has the length 0 and therefore violates (21). Example (20) is thus ruled out independently of Burzio's generalization on a par with (22), (23), and (24a–b).[23] Given this, the Theta-Criterion as stated in (1) redundantly rules out the configuration in (20). As noted above, other effects of the Theta-Criterion follow from the Improper Movement Constraint or, to be more precise, Make the Fewest Steps Condition. Given this, the syntactic part of the Theta-Criterion, i.e. the biuniqueness requirement, does not seem to be needed any more. The Theta-Criterion is thus reduced to (11), which holds by virtue of interpetation.[24]

To sum up the discussion so far, we have argued that the ban on movement into theta-positions is derivable independently of DS, the Projection Principle, and the Theta-Criterion. Since DS and the conditions in question do not seem to be either conceptually or empirically necessary they can be eliminated in accordance with the minimalist program. Given that all the constructions that are ruled out by the application of the Theta-Criterion at DS, or that are forced by the Projection Principle, are independently excluded, by eliminating DS and the conditions in question we also eliminate a redundancy in the system.[25]

3   Empirical problems with the Theta-Criterion and DS

In all the examples we have examined so far the NP moving from a theta-position of one predicate into a theta-position of another predicate was forced to move through a nontheta-position by independent principles of grammar. A question arises as to whether there are any instances of movement from a theta-position into a theta-position that are not mediated by nontheta-positions. If there are no other interfering factors such as chain length, this would be exactly the case where the Improper Movement and the DS/Theta-Criterion analysis would make different predictions. In the next section we will argue that there are indeed grammatical constructions that involve movement into a theta-position. In fact, we will argue that movement into theta-positions is possible exactly in those cases in which it is allowed by the analysis presented in section 2, above. In this respect we will argue against Chomsky (1994), who suggests that movement into theta-positions such as SpecVP is always ruled out by the Principle Greed (cf. Chomsky 1993), which requires that every movement be motivated by feature checking of the moved element.[26] Interestingly, Lasnik (1995) shows that Chomsky's (1993) version of Greed is too strong. He shows convincingly that it fails to account for the syntactic properties of *there* constructions, which were its original motivation. Lasnik argues for relaxing Greed by allowing movement to take place iff it contributes to convergence regardless of whether or not the movement results in feature checking of the moved element. As shown by Lasnik, this version of Greed is empirically superior to Chomsky's (1993) version.[27] Now, Chomsky (1994) argues that violations of the Theta-Criterion lead to non-convergence and not merely defective interpretation.[28] Given that violations of the Theta-Criterion lead to non-convergence and given Lasnik's version of Greed, which allows movement driven by convergence and has strong empirical motivation, movement into theta-positions is no longer ruled out by Greed. We thus lose the Greed account of the ban on movement into theta-positions.[29] We will argue that this is desirable. As shown above, all the ungrammatical instances of movement into theta-positions are ruled out independently of Greed. Furthermore, the analysis presented above does not in principle rule out movement into theta-positions. As noted above, movement into theta-positions is still allowed in certain restricted contexts. It is argued in the next section that exactly in these contexts movement into theta-positions actually takes place. We will first examine Romance restructuring constructions.

3.1 Restructuring verbs

Over the years there have been a number of different analyses of restructuring constructions. Most of them, including Rizzi's (1982) reanalysis account, which violates Recoverability, and parallel structure analyses (Manzini 1983; Zubizarreta 1985; Goodall 1987, which posit two structures for every restructuring construction with arbitrary statements concerning which principles apply to which structure, are clearly excluded under current theoretical assumptions even if we disregard the empirical problems they raise (cf. Moore 1989 for discussion of theoretical anomalies and note 39 for some empirical problems that arise on these analyses).

Several linguists (Zubizarreta 1982; Picallo (1990)) have argued that restructuring verbs are essentially adverbials. The adverbial analysis, however, lacks both theoretical and empirical foundations. Consider, for example, Zubizarreta's (1982) analysis. Zubizarreta introduces the notion of *adjunct theta-roles* and proposes that, in contrast to the main verb *querer* 'to want', the restructuring verb *querer* assigns an adjunct theta-role to its subject. However, as Zubizarreta herself notes, there is no semantic difference between the subject theta-role assigned by the main verb *querer* and the restructuring verb *querer*. Furthermore, under Zubizarreta's analysis both the restructuring and main verb *querer* assign a theta-role to their subject in the same structural configuration. We believe that all this makes Zubizarreta's analysis untenable.[30]

Picallo's (1990) adverbial analysis of restructuring verbs is somewhat more plausible, given that she locates the restructuring and main verb *querer* in different structural positions. She argues that when they have a root intepretation, restructuring verbs are base-generated adjoined to VP, where they are interpreted as subject-oriented secondary predicates.

(25)   Juan lo [$_{VP}$ quiere [$_{VP}$ ver]]
         Juan it   wants   to see

Syntactically, the structure in (25) is rather problematic. First, it seems to require head movement out of an adjunct (*quiere*-to-INFL), which should be ruled out by the ECP. Second, given that main verbs freely move across VP-adjuncts in Romance, a question arises as to why (26) is bad on Picallo's analysis.

(26)   *Juan$_i$ toma$_j$ [$_{VP}$ querer [$_{VP}$ t$_i$ t$_j$ café]]
         Juan drank   to want   coffee

Picallo provides evidence that, in contrast to *querer*, root modals do not have main verb counterparts. As a result, she claims that they always function as subject-oriented secondary predicates. There is, however, strong evidence that root modals assign a primary rather than secondary theta-role to their subject. Recall Hankamer and Sag's (1976) distinction between deep and surface anaphors. As shown by Hankamer and Sag, in contrast to surface anaphors, deep anaphors do not undergo replacement by their antecedent. Hankamer and Sag also show that deep and surface anaphors differ in that only the former can be deictic, i.e. allow for the possibility of a nonlinguistic antecedent. Given this, the grammaticality of (27) provides evidence that root modals can take a deep anaphor complement.

(27) [Juan watches Javier jump into the icy cold sea and says]
      Yo puedo también
      'I can too!'

Given that the complement of the modal in (27) is a deep anaphor, which does not undergo replacement by its antecedent, the only source of theta-role assignment for the subject is the modal verb. Since, as shown by the ungrammaticality of constructions such as **John seems that Peter loves Mary angry* with *angry* assigning a secondary theta-role to *John*, bearing a secondary theta-role cannot license an argument with respect to the Theta-Criterion, it must be the case that the modal assigns a primary theta-role to its subject. The grammaticality of constructions such as (27) provides strong evidence against the secondary predicate analysis of root restructuring verbs.[31] Given the discussion above, we reject the secondary predicate analysis of restructuring verbs.

Most often restructuring verbs have been analyzed as either control or raising verbs (cf. for example, Burzio 1986). Recently, Rosen (1990a, 1990b) has proposed that restructuring verbs are light verbs with an unspecified argument structure. Below we will give several arguments against the control and light verb analysis. Before that, notice that if, as argued by a number of researchers (Manzini 1983; Moore 1989; Rosen 1990a, 1990b; Strozer 1981, among others), the complement of restructuring verbs is a bare VP, the following derivation is available in the minimalist system.[32]

(28) Juan$_i$ lo$_k$ quiere$_j$[$_{VP}$ t$_i$ t$_j$[$_{VP}$ t$_i$ ver t$_k$]]
      Juan it wants   to see
      'Juan wants to see it'

Since there are no intervening functional projections between VPs in (28), under the proposals made here we would expect (28) to be grammatical in spite of the fact that it involves movement into a theta-position.[33] It is beyond the scope of this paper to present a comprehensive analysis of the full range of facts associated with restructuring verbs. We will argue, however, that there is evidence which suggests that constructions in question indeed involve movement into a theta-position.[34] Consider the following constructions from González (1988, 1990), with the psych verb *gustar*, which following Belletti and Rizzi (1988) we assume has no external argument, embedded under a restructuring verb.

(29) a. Marta le quiere gustar a Juan
          Marta cl. wants to please to Juan
          'Marta wants for Juan to like her'
      b. A Juan le quiere gustar Marta
          'Juan wants to like Marta'

González points out that (29a) and (29b) differ in meaning.[35] According to
González, in (29b) it is *Juan* who does wanting, in (29a) it is *Marta*. On the other
hand, as González notes, when the psych verb *gustar* is embedded under a raising
verb the construction has the same meaning, regardless of which NP is raised to
the matrix SpecIP.

(30) a. Las estudiantes le empezaron a gustar al profesor
      b. Al profesor le empezaron a gustar las estudiantes
          'The profesor began to like the students'
          *'The students began for the profesor to like them'

Given that *empezar* assigns no subject theta-role, no matter which NP raises to the
matrix subject position only internal theta-roles are relevant for the interpretation
of (30a,b). The fact that, in contrast to (30a) and (30b), (29a) and (29b) do not have
the same meaning provides strong evidence against analyzing restructuring constructions with *querer* as traditional raising constructions (see below for more evidence).
It also militates against Rosen's (1990a, 1990b) analysis of restructuring verbs as
light verbs. According to Rosen, restructuring verbs have no argument specification.
They obtain argument specification by merging with the embedded verb's argument
structure. The argument structure of the embedded verb then becomes the argument
structure of both verbs.[36] Rosen's analysis makes an interesting prediction with respect
to operations that are sensitive to the external vs. internal theta-role distinction.
In fact, Rosen herself claims that when the embedded verb has no external theta-role
the restructuring verb should also behave as if it had no external theta-role. Returning
now to (29a,b) notice that, given Rosen's proposal, since the embedded verb assigns
no external theta-role, we would expect *querer* in (29a,b) to exhibit the same behavior
as traditional raising verbs such as *empezar*. In other words, given that the only theta-
positions in (29) are those internal to the lowest VP it is difficult to explain the
difference in meaning between (29a) and (29b). Let us see now how (29a,b) could
be analyzed under Rosen's proposals. Rosen (1990a) assumes that (31a) is the Lexical
Conceptual Structure (LCS) of *querer* (we are disregarding here the possibility of
querer taking "Thing" as its complement). Under Rosen's proposals (31b) is the
argument structure of *querer* prior to merger with *gustar* (e refers to the event argument). Example (31c), on the other hand, is the argument structure of *gustar*, which
has two internal arguments.[37] After merger takes place, (31d) becomes the argument
structure of the complex verb *querer-gustar*. The complex verb projects into syntax
as shown in (31e). (Example (31e) contains the relevant part of (29a,b).)

(31) a. *querer*: [x] desires [Event y] to occur
      b. *querer* ( ) [e]

  c. *gustar* (experiencer (theme)) [e]
  d. *querer gustar* (experiencer (theme)) [e]
  e. [$_{VP}$ querer [$_{VP}$ gustar Marta a Juan]]

Let us now concentrate on the operations leading to (3le). On the mapping from LCS to argument structure the variable x in the LCS of *querer* is linked to one of the internal arguments of the complex verb. It seems plausible to assume that x is linked to the higher argument, namely the experiencer. However, given that x is linked to the experiencer (32a), we have no way of accounting for the interpretation of (29a), where the theme is interpreted as x. If, on the other hand, x is linked to the theme (32b), we cannot account for the interpretation of (29b), where the experiencer is the wanter.

(32) a. [$_{VP}$ querer [$_{VP}$ [$_{V}$ · gustar Marta] a Juan]]

    argument structure: ((exp) (theme))

    LCS of *querer*: x desires [Event y] to occur

  b. [$_{VP}$ querer [$_{VP}$ [$_{V}$ · gustar Marta] a Juan]]

    argument structure: ((exp) (theme))

    LCS of *querer*: x desires [Event y] to occur

Finally, if we allow x to freely link to either the theme or the experiencer we incorrectly predict both (29a) and (29b) to be ambiguous with respect to who does wanting. The problem that arises on the argument structure merger analysis is that to get the right interpretation, the mapping from LCS to argument structure *must* depend on which element moves to the subject position of the complex verb. However, it is simply not possible to ensure this kind of dependency between syntactic movement and the mapping from LCS to argument structure.

 Let us now turn to the widely accepted control analysis of *querer* constructions. The fact that both the matrix and the embedded verb impose selectional restrictions in (33) is fully in line with the control analysis (it also provides further evidence against the raising analysis).

(33) a. *Juan quiere llover
    'Juan wants to rain'
  b. *El agua quiere correr
    'The water wants to flow'

However, the facts in (29) raise an unsurmountable problem for the control analysis. Let us focus on (29b). Under the control analysis (29b) has the following structure.

(34)   A Juan le quiere [PRO₍ᵢ₎ gustar Marta t₍ᵢ₎]

Notice now the presence of *a* on the NP functioning as the matrix clause subject. In their analysis of corresponding constructions in Italian, Belletti and Rizzi (1988) argue convincingly that *a* is an overt instantiation of the inherent Case that *gustar* assigns to the NP bearing its experiencer theta-role. As argued by Belletti and Rizzi, the inherent Case moves together with the NP to the subject position (35a).[38] Note also that, in contrast to *gustar*, *querer* does not assign *a* to any of its arguments (35b–c).

(35)   a.   [A Juan]₍ᵢ₎ le gusta la musica t₍ᵢ₎
             'Juan likes music'
       b.   *A Juan le quiere la fama
             'Juan wants fame'
       c.   *A Juan le quiere comer la torta
             'Juan wants to eat the cake'

Given this, the presence of *a* with *Juan* provides strong evidence that at some point of the derivation *Juan* was located within the embedded VP and assigned the experiencer theta-role by *gustar*. Under the control analysis we have no way of accounting for this (see below for more evidence against the control analysis). This is also a problem for Rizzi's reanalysis approach and parallel structure approaches, which at the same time assign two structures – a monoclausal one and a biclausal one – to the constructions in question.[39] On the other hand, the presence of *a* with *Juan* is exactly what is predicted given the proposal that association of one argument with two theta-roles and movement into theta-positions are allowed as long as they do not violate Economy Principles. In fact, given the discussion of the alternative analyses of (29b) above, we seem to have no choice but to accept the movement into a theta-position analysis of (29b).

(36)   A Juan₍ᵢ₎ le quiere₍ⱼ₎ [$_{VP}$ t₍ᵢ₎ t₍ⱼ₎ [$_{VP}$ gustar Marta t₍ᵢ₎]]

Juan in (36) is inserted into a position that is assigned the experiencer theta-role of *gustar*, as a result of which it acquires *a*, and then moves to SpecIP via the matrix SpecVP, where it picks up the subject theta-role of *querer*. Although (36) involves movement into a theta-position it does not violate the relevant Principles of Economy. Furthermore, as shown above, by admitting (36) under the proposals made here we do not rule in constructions such as (15–16) and (18–20). As noted above, (36) also straightforwardly accounts for the presence of *a* with *Juan*. The fact that both the matrix verb and the embedded verb impose selectional restrictions on the matrix subject in (33) is also expected under the movement into a theta-position analysis.

Before we conclude the discussion of restructuring+psych verb constructions, it should be pointed out that the ambiguity of (37), taken from González (1990), in Chilean Spanish provides an interesting piece of evidence for the VP Internal Subject Hypothesis and the XP + X⁰ movement analysis of cliticization.

(37)   pro te   quiero   gustar
               you-dat want-1SG to like
   a.   'I want you to like me'
   b.   'You want to like me'

The readings in (37a) and (37b) have the structures given in (38a) and (38b) respectively.

(38)   a. pro_i $[_{I'}$ te_j $quiero_k$ $[_{VP}$ t_i t_k $[_{VP}$ gustar t_i $t_j]]]$
         b. pro_i $[_{I'}$ te_j $quiero_k$ $[_{VP}$ t_i t_k $[_{VP}$ gustar t_i $t_j]]]$

In (38a), pro picks up the subject theta-role of the matrix verb on its way to the matrix SpecIP. In (38b), on the other hand, *te* picks up the subject theta-role of *querer* while undergoing clitic climbing (note that, being located in a T-position, t_j does not block movement of pro to SpecIP, a T'-position, via Relativized Minimality). Given that only XPs can serve as arguments, (38b) provides evidence for Chomsky's claim that cliticization involves XP + X^0 movement rather than only X^0 movement. In other words, cliticization starts as XP movement; only in a later stage of the derivation does the head move out of its XP and adjoin to another head. Notice also that subject–verb agreement and external theta-role assignment are divorced in (38b). Whereas pro, located in SpecIP, undergoes agreement with *querer*, the clitic *te* bears the external theta-role of *querer*. The split between subject–verb agreement and external theta-role assignment provides evidence for the VP Internal Subject Hypothesis, according to which the two processes are triggered in different positions; external theta-roles are assigned in SpecVP and agreement with the verb takes place in SpecIP. It is difficult to see how the facts under consideration can be accounted for if both subject–verb agreement and external theta-role assignment take place in SpecIP.

Notes

1   Chomsky (1981, 1986b) in fact notes that an argument can bear more than one theta-role as long as it does not acquire them through movement. Thus in *John left angry*, *John* is assigned a theta-role by both *left* and *angry*. The construction, however, does not involve movement into a theta-position. Chomsky (1986b) explicitly allows for the possibility of one argument being assigned two theta-roles in its base-generated position. He incorporates the Theta-Criterion into the Chain Condition, which merely requires that all theta-roles be assigned to the foot of the chain.

   (i)   The Chain Condition

   If $C = (\alpha_1, \ldots, \alpha_n)$ is a maximal CHAIN, then α_n occupies its unique theta-position and α_1 its unique Case-marked position.

   The way of deriving Theta-Criterion effects proposed in the text derives both (1) and the theta-theoretic part of the Chain Condition. Given this, since the Theta-Criterion in (1) is defined without interference from Case Theory, for ease of exposition where it is not crucial, we will assume (1) rather than (i).

2   Sag (1976) offered a PF deletion account of ACD. However, to account for the interpreta-
    tion of ellipted VPs Sag had to assume that the phonological rule of deletion is crucially
    subject to semantic constraints, which are generally assumed to operate at LF. This renders
    Sag's analysis untenable under the current conception of grammar.

3   Cf. Lødrup (1993) for more evidence for the surface anaphor status of *det* with epistemic
    modals. Note that the acceptability of the deictic *det* in (9b) shows that the complement of
    root modals can be a deep anaphor. Since deep anaphors are not replaced by their antecedent,
    (9b) provides evidence that root modals are primary theta-role assigners (as is well-known,
    secondary theta-roles cannot license arguments with respect to the Theta-Criterion (cf. **John
    seems that Peter likes Mary angry*)). The deep anaphora option for *det* with epistemic modals is
    ruled out because it would leave the subject of the epistemic modal without a theta-role. [...]

4   For arguments against the existence of DS as a level that serves as an input for all trans-
    formational rules, the reader is also referred to the generative semantics literature of the
    late 1960s and early 1970s. To give a few references: Lakoff (1971), Lakoff and Ross (1976),
    McCawley (1968), Morgan (1969), and Postal (1970). That there is no independent level
    of D-structure was in fact one of the central assumptions of generative semantics.

5   Here we have a residue of the Projection Principle. As Chomsky himself notes, an element
    X, taken from the lexicon, still has to be projected to one of the following X-bar struc-
    tures, with $X = X^0 = [_X X]$.

(i)   a. $[_X X]$
      b. $[_{X'} X]$
      c. $[_{X''} X]$

6   Actually, in section 3 we will argue that there are instances of movement into theta-
    positions that are not ungrammatical. What we will show in the next section is that instances
    of movement into theta-positions that result in ungrammatical structures are ruled out
    independently of the Theta-Criterion.

    It should be noted here that after this paper was written, Chomsky (1994) appeared, where
    it is argued that movement into theta-positions is ruled out by the Principle Greed because
    it has no morphological motivation of its own. The Greed account is intended to rule out
    altogether movement into theta-positions. However, it is argued in section 3 that movement
    into theta-positions is allowed in certain cases. The intended empirical coverage aside, in
    section 3 we note that ruling out ungrammatical instances of movement into theta-positions
    by appealing to Greed is also problematic. Given this, in the next section we will explore
    alternative ways of ruling out ungrammatical instances of movement into theta-positions.

7   Throughout this paper we will be assuming the VP Internal Subject Hypothesis. In fact,
    to the extent that it is successful, the analysis presented here will provide support for the
    VP Internal Subject Hypothesis.

8   Cf. Authier (1991) and Martin (1992) for relevant discussion. Notice that under this ana-
    lysis, we have to assume that clauses can check Accusative Case to account for *John believes
    that Peter will leave*. Bošković (1995) argues that clauses can indeed have Case features.

9   The question is, however, whether *remark* can take (l-select in terms of Pesetsky 1992) an
    infinitival complement. Unfortunately, it does not seem to be possible to determine this con-
    clusively. The problem is that even if an infinitival complement could match l-selectional
    restrictions of *remark*, constructions involving *remark* taking an infinitival complement would
    still be ruled out by independent principles. It is well-known that propositional-attitude verbs
    in English can take ECM but not control infinitival complements (*claim* is the only exception
    we are aware of). Bošković (1996) argues that this is a result of s-selectional properties of
    the verbs in question. More precisely, Bošković argues that control infinitivals cannot be inter-
    preted as Propositions. Given this, since *remark* is a propositional verb, it cannot take a control
    infinitival complement (ia). The possibility of *remark* taking an ECM infinitival comple-

ment, which is allowed with most propositional verbs, is ruled out via Case Theory. Since *remark* has no Accusative Case features, the embedded subject in (ib) cannot be Case-checked.

    (i) a.   *John remarked [PRO to like Mary]
         b.   *John remarked [Mary to be crazy]

10   As shown by McCloskey (1991), in contrast to *there* constructions, in constructions containing the expletive *it*, the verb agrees with the expletive rather than with the clause that is assumed to be 'associated' with it. Given this, we assume that *it* is not replaced by a clausal argument at LF, which in the case of (16a) would result in a Proper Binding Condition (PBC) violation. Cf. also Collins (1994), where it is argued that the PBC should be eliminated.

11   The same conclusion is reached by Brody (1993), who discusses (15a). Cf. below for discussion of Brody's analysis of constructions under consideration.

12   Thus, in contrast to SpecCP, even when it counts as an A'-position, SpecIP does not block *wh*-extraction (for more evidence cf. Masullo 1992). To account for this Masullo argues that SpecCP is specified as [+Op], whereas SpecIP is specified as [−Op] even when it is a nonCase-position. Masullo then makes the next logical step by proposing that A and A' are derivative notions that should be decomposed into more primitive features such as [+/− theta], [+/− Case] and (+/− Operator].

    (i)

	Operator	Case	Theta
SpecCP	+	−	−
SpecIP	−	+	−
SpecVP	−	−	+

13   Cf. below for discussion of the mechanism of Improper Movement. Notice also that to avoid violating the Empty Category Principle (ECP), the verb undergoing incorporation cannot skip the intervening INFL and C.

14   A question arises as to how the fact that both elements located in Case and theta-positions count as binders for the Binding Theory should be handled if Case and theta-positions are different kinds of syntactic positions. Notice, however, that given the decomposition of the A/A' distinction into features such as Op, Theta, and Case (cf. note 12), it is only natural that the A/A' binding should be decomposed into more primitive notions as well. In fact, there is empirical evidence that this is the correct approach. Take, for example, Condition A. It is well known that Scrambled elements located in [−Case, −theta] positions can count as binders for anaphors. The following Japanese example is from Saito (1992).

    (i) ?[karera-o$_i$ [[otagai$_i$ -no sensei]-ga [t$_i$ hihansita]]] (koto)
        them   each other gen teacher nom criticized   fact
        'Them$_i$ each other's$_i$ teacher criticized t$_i$'

Saito (1992) shows convincingly that Scrambling is a semantically vacuous operation that does not establish an Operator-variable relation. Given this, the landing site of Scrambling in (i) should be specified as [−Op], in addition to [−Case] and [−theta]. The grammaticality of constructions such as (i) then provides evidence that what is relevant for Condition A is the feature [Op]. As noted by Saito (1992), Condition A could be stated as follows: an anaphor must be non-operator bound in its governing category. The traditional A/A' approach to Binding Theory, on the other hand, is hard pressed to account for the grammaticality of (i). Notice that, even under Chomsky and Lasnik's (1993) and Chomsky's (1993) proposal concerning the A/A' distinction, being a nonCase position, the landing site of Scrambling would still count as an A'-position (cf., however, Abe 1993 for arguments that the A/A' distinction is not relevant for Binding Conditions).

15   For alternative approaches to improper movement, see Abe (1993), Fukui (1993), and Müller and Sternefeld (1993). Fukui and Takahashi show that May's (1981) Condition C account of Improper Movement is untenable for two reasons. First, it cannot account for the full range of relevant facts. Second, given that Binding Conditions apply at LF and that traces belonging to non-uniform chains undergo deletion (Chomsky 1991), it no longer accounts even for the cases it was originally intended for, namely those involving A–A′–A movement. Being a member of a non-uniform chain, the intermediate trace in an A–A′–A chain (which makes the initial trace a variable thus causing a Condition C violation on May's analysis), is deleted before the level of LF (where Binding Conditions apply), is reached (cf. the works cited for detailed discussion). Fukui (1993), Saito (1994), and Takahashi (1992) argue that constructions involving Improper Movement should be ruled out by a derivational rather than a representational constraint. Thus, Fukui rules out such constructions by proposing a uniformity condition on chain formation which prevents formation of a chain that, with the exception of the initial trace, contains elements located in different types of syntactic positions.

16   Note that chain formation counts as one step (cf. Chomsky 1991; Collins 1994). Given this, the two step derivation in (17) is blocked by the possibility of a single step derivation involving direct movement to α. Note that in (i), where the intermediate position is also an X-type position, movement can proceed successive cyclically since it results in the creation of a single X chain. As a result, the whole movement counts as one step.

(i)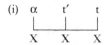

It should be pointed out that a derivation D can block another derivation via Economy of Derivation only if D converges at LF, i.e. if it forms a representation that consists only of legitimate LF objects with all their features checked (cf. Chomsky 1993).

17   Note that this derivation converges at LF. According to Chomsky 1993, a derivation that involves only a violation of the Theta-Criterion converges at LF. However, it receives a defective interpretation.

18   Constructions in (15–16) and (18) in fact may be ruled out independently of the Improper Movement Constraint. Each of the constructions in question contains a mixed chain consisting of theta and potential Case positions. Chomsky (1991) argues that with the exception of operator-variable chains, mixed chains are not legitimate LF objects. Even if we add Case-theta chains to the list of legitimate LF objects, in order to derive legitimate LF chains in each of the constructions under consideration we would have to delete either a trace in a theta-position (SpecVP) or a Case-position (SpecIP), which could lead to a violation of either the Theta-Criterion or the EPP.

19   We have slightly revised Saito and Murasugi's definition of (21b). In fact, for reasons that will become clear shortly we have adopted the definition of chain length that was considered by Saito (University of Connecticut lectures 1993) but not ultimately adopted in Saito and Murasugi (1999).

20   α covers β iff a segment of α dominates β.

21   Note that we assume that the head-government requirement, which is superfluous empirically and highly problematic conceptually (cf. Frampton 1991), should be eliminated.

22   An alternative way of ruling out the relevant constructions is to posit a condition such as (i) (this condition also rules out (20)).

(i)   X can bear only one local relation to Y

where local relations are defined as specifier of, complement of, and adjunct of.

23 Consider also ergative constructions such as (i).

(i)   John [$_{VP}$ arrived t]

Note that the shortest first link for the chain originating in object position in (i) is created by movement to SpecVP. Given this, the Minimize Chain Links Principle (MCLP) of Chomsky and Lasnik (1993), which requires that each chain link be as short as possible, might force the object argument of ergative verbs to move through SpecVP. (Under a strictly derivational approach to the MCLP, argued for in Bošković 1995, this would be the case.) This could have serious consequences. For example, it could trigger selection of *avere* rather than *essere* in Italian ergative constructions, an undesirable result. However, given (21), the problem does not arise. [. . .] Movement from *t* to SpecVP would create a chain link of length 0 and is, therefore, ruled out by (21) on a par with the derivation in (20).

24 Recall that Chomsky (1986b) incorporates the Theta-Criterion into the Chain Condition. It is easy to verify that the theta-theoretic part of the Chain Condition is also deducible as shown above.

25 Brody (1993) also offers an account of the ban on movement into theta-positions that makes no reference to DS and the Theta-Criterion. As a result, Brody argues that his analysis is compatible with the minimalist program. However, he crucially needs the Projection Principle and has to introduce the notion of *D-sets*, which are defined as sets of all chain-root positions. D-sets are defined on chain structure, which is formed presyntactically in Brody's analysis. He argues that the Projection Principle requires all theta-positions to be present in D-sets. In (15a), for example, there is a theta-position that is not a root of the chain and, therefore, is not a member of the D-set of the sentence. As a result, Brody argues, the construction is ruled out by the Projection Principle. There are several problems with Brody's analysis. First, although Brody claims to have dispensed with DS, he has to maintain the Projection Principle as a *syntactic* non-interface condition, holding of D-sets. He also makes an additional assumption concerning the existence of D-sets. It is clear that neither the syntactic non-interface view of the Projection Principle nor the notion of D-sets is conceptually necessary. Moreover, their postulation is not empirically justified since, as shown above, the relevant constructions can be ruled out by the mechanisms that are needed independently. Given this, the very postulation of D-sets as well as Brody's view of the Projection Principle goes against the spirit of the minimalist program. Furthermore, the notion of D-sets in fact seems to correspond to a level of representation. If this is not the case, it is difficult to see how the Projection Principle could force D-set to contain all thematic positions (recall that if a theta-position is not a member of a D-set, the Projection Principle is violated). The notion of D-sets thus seems to be a D-structure in disguise. The only difference is that, in Brody's view, DS is a representation of chain rather than thematic structure, with chains being formed presyntactically. Since chain roots are present at LF one might be able to get around the problem by restating the Projection Principle as an LF interface condition on chain roots. Notice, however, that, under this view, even at LF the Projection Principle could not hold by virtue of interpretation. Such an extension of the Projection Principle seems unwarranted. Even if we disregard the conceptual problems, given the data presented below, like the Theta-Criterion itself, Brody's analysis is simply empirically inadequate since it rules out certain grammatical constructions. In fact, since Brody's analysis is designed to have the same empirical effects as the Theta Criterion, all the empirical arguments against the Theta-Criterion given below can be taken as arguments against Brody's analysis.

26 It is actually not clear that Greed can by itself rule out all instances of movement into SpecVP. It is a standard assumption that *wh*-phrases undergoing long *wh*-movement can land in intermediate SpecCPs although such movement has no morphological motivation (cf. Collins

1994 and references therein for empirical evidence for successive cyclic *wh*-movement). If SpecCP can serve as an intermediate landing site for movement even when no feature checking takes place we would expect the same to hold for SpecVP. Cf. also Lasnik (1995) for criticism of Chomsky's Greed account of movement into theta-positions.

27 Actually, in his discussion of the EPP, Chomsky (1994) appears to accept Lasnik's (1995) version of the Greed Principle since he seems to allow for the possibility of movement to SpecIP being driven by checking the N feature of INFL.

28 Chomsky (1994) proposes that theta-roles are formal features of predicates that must be discharged. On this view, (11a) follows from lexical properties of theta-assigning heads.

29 Note that the assumption that violations of the Theta-Criterion lead to non-convergence might require a different approach to Improper Movement from the one proposed by Saito (1994) and Takahashi (1992) and adopted above. However, the generalization to be captured there and hopefully reduced to independently motivated principles is clear: X–Y–X movement, where X and Y are different types of syntactic positions, is not allowed.

30 Cf. also below for arguments that Romance root modals assign primary theta-roles to their subjects (in note 3, above it is shown that Norwegian and English root modals are primary theta-role assigners). Cf. also Rochette (1988) for arguments that verbal elements never assign adjunct theta-roles. Under the analysis presented below it is not necessary to stipulate that Romance root restructuring verbs assign an adjunct theta-role to their subject.

31 There are also several differences between subject-oriented adverbs and root restructuring verbs that further undermine Picallo's adverbial analysis. Thus, restructuring verbs can cooccur with subject-oriented adverbs and precede speaker-oriented adverbs, which is not possible with subject-oriented adverbs. For a detailed discussion of the phenomena in question the reader is referred to Jackendoff (1972), who considers and rejects the subject-oriented secondary predicate analysis for English root modals on the grounds that, among other things, the analysis cannot account for the occurrence of root modals with subject-oriented and speaker-oriented adverbs.

32 It is well-known that restructuring verbs can never take a +*wh* or a negated complement, which is expected under the VP analysis.

33 Given the strictly derivational approach to the Minimize Chain Link Principle (MCLP) argued for in Bošković (1995), *Juan* in (28) would in fact be forced by the MCLP to pass through the higher SpecVP.

It should be pointed out here that the movement into a theta-position analysis of (28) would be possible even if there is a functional projection above the embedded VP (this would make V-movement across VP-adjuncts possible) as long as the embedded subject is not forced to move through the Spec of the functional projection in question by independent principles of grammar. Note that there may have to be an AgroP in the complement of *querer*, which contains a transitive verb. However, [. . .] the presence of Agro does not affect the possibility of a movement into a theta-position analysis. The complement of *querer*, however, cannot be an AgrsP, otherwise (28) would be ruled out either by the Improper Movement Constraint or the EPP (cf. the references cited above for arguments against the AgrsP analysis).

34 The reader should bear in mind that, as argued above, root restructuring verbs are primary and not secondary theta-role assigners.

35 This may not be true in all dialects of Spanish. We will examine here *only* the dialects in which (29a) and (29b) are not synonymous. González, whose judgement we follow here, is a native speaker of Chilean Spanish. Other Chilean Spanish speakers González consulted also share her judgement. Moore (1989) reports that his informants also share González' judgement. The same holds for one Chilean Spanish speaker we were able to consult. A *Linguistic Analysis* reviewer, however, claims that there are Chilean Spanish speakers that do not share González' judgement. It thus seems that we are dealing here with a more fine-grained dialectal difference. It should be pointed out that J. Ormazabal, one of the

European Spanish speakers we consulted, also finds the difference in meaning between (29a) and (29b) noted above.

36   Rosen's analysis crucially depends on the existence of argument structure serving as a mediator between Lexical Conceptual Structure (LCS), which contains grammatically relevant syntactic information about particular lexical items (cf. Hale and Keyser 1986, 1987, among others) and syntax (including LF). However, given the spirit of the minimalist program, the status of argument structure, which is certainly not conceptually necessary, should be reconsidered. Jackendoff (1990) in fact shows that there is no need to posit argument structure as an independent level of representation. Dispensing with argument structure would render Rosen's analysis untenable.

37   Theta-role labels, which do not seem to have any theoretical significance (cf. for example, Jackendoff 1987 and Levin and Rappaport 1986), are given only for ease of exposition.

38   We will not be concerned here with the issue of what drives movement of quirky subjects to SpecIP.

39   Notice that it will not do to assume that, under the reanalysis account, *Juan* acquires *a* after *querer* and *gustar* are restructured under a single V node, since, crosslinguistically, inherent Case is never assigned to clausal subjects (cf. Burzio 1986; Rosen 1990b, among others, for discussion of other problems that arise on the reanalysis account). Under parallel structure approaches the presence of *a* could be accounted for if we assume that (29b) involves movement into a theta-position. However, as shown below, given this assumption we no longer need parallel structures, which are theoretically rather problematic.

References

Abe, J. 1993. *Binding conditions and scrambling without A/A′ distinction.* Doctoral dissertation, University of Connecticut, Storrs.

Authier, J.-M. 1991. V-governed expletives, case theory, and the projection principle. *Linguistic Inquiry* 22: 721–40.

Baker, M., K. Johnson and I. Roberts. 1989. Passive arguments raised. *Linguistic Inquiry* 20: 219–52.

Baltin, M. 1987. Do antecedent contained deletions exist? *Linguistic Inquiry* 18: 579–95.

Belletti, A. and L. Rizzi. 1988. Psych-verbs and theta-theory. *Linguistic Inquiry* 6: 291–352.

Bonet, E. 1989. Subjects in Catalan. Ms., MIT.

Bošković, Ž. 1995. Case properties of clauses and the Greed Principle. *Studia Linguistica* 49: 32–53.

Bošković, Ž. 1996. Selection and the categorial status of infinitival complements. *Natural Language and Linguistic Theory* 14: 269–304.

Brody, M. 1993. Theta-theory and arguments. *Linguistic Inquiry* 24: 1–23.

Burzio, L. 1986. *Italian syntax: A government and binding approach.* Dordrecht: Reidel.

Chomsky, N. 1981. *Lectures on government and binding.* Dordrecht: Foris.

Chomsky, N. 1986a. *Barriers.* Cambridge, MA: MIT Press.

Chomsky, N. 1986b. *Knowledge of language: Its nature, origin, and use.* New York: Praeger.

Chomsky, N. 1991. Some notes on economy of derivation and representation. In R. Freidin (ed.), *Principles and parameters in comparative grammar*, Cambridge, MA: MIT Press, pp. 417–54. [Reprinted in Chomsky (1995), *The Minimalist Program*, Cambridge, MA: MIT Press, pp. 128–66.]

Chomsky, N. 1993. A minimalist program for linguistic theory. In K. Hale and S. J. Keyser (eds.), *The view from Building 20: Essays in linguistics in honor of Sylvain Bromberger*, Cambridge, MA: MIT Press, pp. 1–52. [Reprinted in Chomsky (1995), *The Minimalist Program*, Cambridge, MA: MIT Press, pp. 167–217.]

Chomsky, N. 1994. *Bare phrase structure. MIT Occasional Papers in Linguistics 5.* Cambridge, MA: MITWPL. [Published in P. Kempchinsky (ed.) (1994), *Evolution and revolution in linguistic theory: Essays in honor of Carlos Otero*, Washington, DC: Georgetown University Press, pp. 51–109. Also published in G. Webelhuth (ed.) (1994), *Government and binding theory and the minimalist program*, Cambridge, MA: MIT Press, pp. 383–439.]

Chomsky, N. and H. Lasnik. 1993. The theory of principles and parameters. In J. Jacobs, A. von Stechow, W. Sternefeld, and T. Vennemann (eds.), *An international handbook of contemporary research*, Berlin/New York: Walter de Gruyter, pp. 506–69. [Reprinted in Chomsky (1995), *The Minimalist Program*, Cambridge, MA: MIT Press, pp. 13–127.]

Collins, C. 1994. Economy of derivation and the generalized proper binding condition. *Linguistic Inquiry* 25: 45–61.

Diesing, M. 1990. Verb movement and the subject position in Yiddish. *Linguistic Inquiry* 8: 41–79.

Frampton, J. 1991. Relativized minimality, a review. *The Linguistic Review* 8: 1–46.

Fukui, N. 1993. A note on improper movement. *The Linguistic Review* 10: 111–26.

González, N. 1988. *Object raising in Spanish.* New York: Garland.

González, N. 1990. Unusual inversion in Chilean Spanish. In P. M. Postal and B. Joseph (eds.), *Studies in relational grammar*, vol. 3, Chicago: University of Chicago Press.

Goodall, G. 1987. *Parallel structures in syntax: Coordination, causatives, and restructuring.* Cambridge: Cambridge University Press.

Hale, K. and S. J. Keyser. 1986. Some transitivity alternations in English. *Lexicon Project Working Papers 7.* Cambridge, MA: MIT Center for Cognitive Science.

Hale, K. and S. J. Keyser. 1987. A view from the Middle. *Lexicon Project Working Papers 10.* Cambridge, MA: MIT Center for Cognitive Science.

Hankamer, J. and I. Sag. 1976. Deep and surface anaphora. *Linguistic Inquiry* 7: 391–428.

Hornstein, N. 1994. An argument for minimalism: the case of antecedent-constrained deletion. *Linguistic Inquiry* 25: 455–80.

Jackendoff, R. 1972. *Semantic interpretation in generative grammar.* Cambridge, MA: MIT Press.

Jackendoff, R. 1987. The status of thematic relations in linguistic theory. *Linguistic Inquiry* 18: 369–412.

Jackendoff, R. 1990. *Semantic structures.* Cambridge, MA: MIT Press.

Lakoff, G. 1971. On generative semantics. In D. Steinberg and L. Jakobovits (eds.), *Semantics: An interdisciplinary reader in philosophy, linguistics and psychology*, Cambridge: Cambridge University Press, pp. 232–96.

Lakoff, G. and J. R. Ross. 1976. Is deep structure necessary? In J. McCawley (ed.), *Syntax and semantics 7*, New York: Academic Press, pp. 159–64.

Larson, R. 1988. On the double object construction. *Linguistic Inquiry* 19: 335–91.

Lasnik, H. 1995. Case and expletives revisited: On Greed and other human failings. *Linguistic Inquiry* 26: 615–33.

Lasnik, H. and M. Saito. 1992. *Move α.* Cambridge, MA: MIT Press.

Law, P. 1991. *Effects of head movement on theories of subjacency and proper government.* Doctoral dissertation, MIT.

Levin, B. and M. Rappaport. 1986. What to do with theta-roles. *Lexicon Project Working Papers 11.* Cambridge, MA: MIT Center for Cognitive Science.

Li, Y. 1990. *Conditions on X^0-movement.* Doctoral dissertation, MIT.

Lødrup, H. 1993. "Surface proforms" in Norwegian and the definiteness effect. In M. González, *Proceedings of the 24th Annual Meeting of the Annual Meeting of the North East Linguistic Society*, Amherst, MA: GLSA, pp. 303–15.

McCawley, J. 1968. Concerning the base component of a transformational grammar. *Foundations of Language* 4: 243–69.

McCloskey, J. 1991. There, it, and agreement. *Linguistic Inquiry* 22: 563–67.

Manzini, M. R. 1983. *Restructuring and reanalysis*. Doctoral dissertation, MIT.

Martin, R. 1992. Case theory, A-chains, and expletive replacement. Ms., University of Connecticut, Storrs.

Masullo, P. J. 1992. Quirky subjects in Spanish and the non-nominative subject parameter. In A. Kathol and J. Beckman (eds.), *MIT Working Papers in Linguistics 16*, Cambridge, MA: MITWPL, pp. 82–103.

May, R. 1881. Binding and movement. *Linguistic Inquiry* 12: 215–43.

May, R. 1985. *Logical form*. Cambridge, MA: MIT Press.

Moore, J. 1989. Spanish restructuring and psych verbs: A case for VP complementation. In J. Fee and K. Hunt (eds.), *Proceedings of the 8th West Coast Conference on Formal Linguistics*, Stanford: CSLI, pp. 262–75.

Morgan, J. 1969. On arguing about semantics. *Papers in Linguistics* 1: 49–70.

Müller, G. and W. Sternefeld. 1993. Improper movement and unambiguous binding. *Linguistic Inquiry* 24: 461–507.

Pesetsky, D. 1982. *Paths and categories*. Doctoral dissertation, MIT.

Pesetsky, D. 1992. Zero syntax, vol. 2. Ms., MIT.

Picallo, M. C. 1990. Modal verbs in Catalan. *Linguistic Inquiry* 8: 285–312.

Postal, P. 1970. On the surface verb *remind*. *Linguistic Inquiry* 1: 37–120.

Reinhart, T. 1991. Elliptic conjunctions – Non-quantificational LF. In A. Kasher (ed.), *The Chomskyan turn*, Oxford: Blackwell, pp. 360–84.

Ritter, E. and S. T. Rosen. 1991. Causative have. In T. Sherer (ed.), *Proceedings of the 21st Annual Meeting of the North East Linguistic Society*, Amherst, MA: GSLA, pp. 323–36.

Rizzi, L. 1982. *Issues in Italian syntax*. Dordrecht: Reidel.

Rochette, A. 1988. *Semantic and syntactic aspects of Romance sentential complementation*. Doctoral dissertation, MIT.

Rögnvaldsson, E. and H. Thráinsson. 1990. On Icelandic word order once more. In J. Maling and A. Zaenen (eds.), *Syntax and semantics 24*, New York: Academic Press, pp. 3–40.

Rosen, S. T. 1990a. *Argument structure and complex predicates*. New York: Garland.

Rosen, S. T. 1990b. Restructuring verbs are light verbs. In A. Halpern (ed.), *Proceedings of the 9th West Coast Conference on Formal Linguistics*, Stanford: CSLI, pp. 477–91.

Sag, I. 1976. *Deletion and logical form*. Doctoral dissertation, MIT.

Saito, M. 1985. *Some asymmetries in Japanese and their theoretical implications*. Doctoral dissertation, MIT.

Saito, M. 1992. Long distance scrambling in Japanese, *Journal of East Asian Linguistics* 1: 68–118.

Saito, M. 1994. Additional-WH effects and the adjunction site theory. *Journal of East Asian Linguistics* 3: 195–240.

Saito, M. and K. Murasugi. 1999. Subject predication within IP and DP. In K. Johnson and I. Roberts (eds.), *Beyond principles and parameters*, Dordrecht: Kluwer, pp. 167–88.

Strozer, J. R. 1981. An alternative to restructuring in Romance syntax. In *Papers in Romance* 3, Seattle: University of Washington, pp. 177–84.

Takahashi, D. 1992. Improper movements and chain formation. Ms., University of Connecticut, Storrs.

Takahashi, D. 1995. On antecedent-contained deletion. In E. Laurencot, R. Lee, and M.-K. Park (eds.), *University of Connecticut Working Papers in Linguistics 5*, Cambridge, MA: MITWPL, pp. 65–80.

Webelhuth, G. 1989. *Syntactic saturation phenomenon and the modern Germanic languages*. Doctoral dissertation, University of Massachusetts, Amherst.

Williams, E. 1977. Discourse and logical form. *Linguistic Inquiry* 8: 101–39.

Zubizarreta, M. L. 1982. *On the relationship of the lexicon to syntax*. Doctoral dissertation, MIT.

Zubizarreta, M. L. 1985. The relation between morphophonology and morphosyntax: The case of Romance causatives. *Linguistic Inquiry* 16: 247–89.

From "A MINIMALIST PROGRAM FOR LINGUISTIC THEORY"
Noam Chomsky

3.4 Beyond the interface levels: S-Structure

Suppose that D-Structure is eliminable along these lines. What about S-Structure, another level that has only theory-internal motivation? The basic issue is whether there are S-Structure conditions. If not, we can dispense with the concept of S-Structure, allowing Spell-Out to apply freely in the manner indicated earlier. Plainly this would be the optimal conclusion.

There are two kinds of evidence for S-Structure conditions.

(1) a. Languages differ with respect to where Spell-Out applies in the course of the derivation to LF. (Are *wh*-phrases moved or in situ? Is the language French-style with overt V-raising or English-style with LF V-raising?)

   b. In just about every module of grammar, there is extensive evidence that the conditions apply at S-Structure.

To show that S-Structure is nevertheless superfluous, we must show that the evidence of both kinds, though substantial, is not compelling.

In the case of evidence of type (1a), we must show that the position of Spell-Out in the derivation is determined by either PF or LF properties, these being the only levels, on minimalist assumptions. Furthermore, parametric differences must be reduced to morphological properties if the Minimalist Program is framed in the terms so far assumed. There are strong reasons to suspect that LF conditions are not relevant. We expect languages to be very similar at the LF level, differing only as a reflex of properties detectable at PF; the reasons basically reduce to considerations of learnability. Thus, we expect that at the LF level there will be no relevant difference between languages with phrases overtly raised or in situ (e.g. *wh*-phrases or verbs). Hence, we are led to seek morphological properties that are reflected at PF. Let us keep the conclusion in mind, returning to it later.

With regard to evidence of type (1b), an argument against S-Structure conditions could be of varying strength, as shown in (2).

(2) a. The condition in question *can* apply at LF alone.
   b. Furthermore, the condition sometimes *must* apply at LF.
   c. Furthermore, the condition must *not* apply at S-Structure.

Even (2a), the weakest of the three, suffices: LF has independent motivation, but S-Structure does not. Argument (2b) is stronger on the assumption that, optimally, conditions are unitary: they apply at a single level, hence at LF if possible. Argument (2c) would be decisive.

To sample the problems that arise, consider binding theory. There are familiar arguments showing that the binding theory conditions must apply at S-Structure, not LF. Thus, consider (3).

(3)   a.   you said he liked [the pictures that John took]
       b.   [how many pictures that John took] did you say he liked *t*
       c.   who [*t* said he liked [$_\alpha$ how many pictures that John took]]

In (3a) *he* c-commands *John* and cannot take *John* as antecedent; in (3b) there is no c-command relation and *John* can be the antecedent of *he*. In (3c) *John* again cannot be the antecedent of *he*. Since the binding properties of (3c) are those of (3a), not (3b), we conclude that *he* c-commands *John* at the level of representation at which Condition C applies. But if LF movement adjoins α to *who* in (3c), Condition C must apply at S-Structure.

The argument is not conclusive, however. [. . .] we might reject the last assumption: that LF movement adjoins α of (3c) to *who*, forming (4), *t'* the trace of the LF-moved phrase.

(4)   [[how many pictures that John took] who] [*t* said he liked *t'*]

We might assume that the only permissible option is extraction of *how many* from the full NP α, yielding an LF form along the lines of (5), *t'* the trace of *how many*.[1]

(5)   [[how many] who] [*t* said he liked [[*t'* pictures] that John took]]

The answer, then, could be the pair (*Bill, 7*), meaning that Bill said he liked 7 pictures that John took. But in (5) *he* c-commands *John*, so that Condition C applies as in (3a). We are therefore not compelled to assume that Condition C applies at S-Structure; we can keep to the preferable option that conditions involving interpretation apply only at the interface levels. This is an argument of the type (2a), weak but sufficient. We will return to the possibility of stronger arguments of the types (2b) and (2c).

The overt analogue of (5) requires "pied-piping" of the entire NP [*how many pictures that John took*], but it is not clear that the same is true in the LF component. We might, in fact, proceed further. The LF rule that associates the in-situ *wh*-phrase with the *wh*-phrase in [Spec, CP] need not be construed as an instance of Move α. We might think of it as the syntactic basis for absorption in the sense of Higginbotham and May (1981), an operation that associates two *wh*-phrases to form a generalized quantifier.[2] If so, then the LF rule need satisfy none of the conditions on movement.

There has long been evidence that conditions on movement do not hold for multiple questions. Nevertheless, the approach just proposed appeared to be blocked by the properties of Chinese- and Japanese-type languages, with *wh*- in situ throughout but observing at least some of the conditions on movement (Huang 1982). Watanabe (1991) has argued, however, that even in these languages there is overt *wh*-movement – in this case movement of an empty operator, yielding the effects of the movement constraints. If Watanabe is correct, we could assume that a *wh*-operator always raises overtly, that Move α is subject to the same conditions everywhere in the derivation to PF and LF, and that the LF operation that applies in multiple questions in English and direct questions in Japanese is free of these conditions. What remains is the question why overt movement of the operator is always required, a question of the category (1a). We will return to that.

Let us recall again the minimalist assumptions that I am conjecturing can be upheld: all conditions are interface conditions; and a linguistic expression is the optimal realization of such interface conditions. Let us consider these notions more closely.

Consider a representation π at PF. PF is a representation in universal phonetics, with no indication of syntactic elements or relations among them (X-bar structure, binding, government, etc.). To be interpreted by the performance systems A-P, π must be constituted entirely of *legitimate PF objects*, that is, elements that have a uniform, language-independent interpretation at the interface. In that case we will say that π satisfies the condition of *Full Interpretation* (FI). If π fails FI, it does not provide appropriate instructions to the performance systems. We take FI to be the convergence condition: if π satisfies FI, the derivation D that formed it converges at PF; otherwise, it crashes at PF. For example, if π contains a stressed consonant or a [+ high, + low] vowel, then D crashes; similarly, if π contains some morphological element that "survives" to PF, lacking any interpretation at the interface. If D converges at PF, its output π receives an articulatory-perceptual interpretation, perhaps as gibberish.

All of this is straightforward – indeed, hardly more than an expression of what is tacitly assumed. We expect exactly the same to be true at LF.

To make ideas concrete, we must spell out explicitly what are the legitimate objects at PF and LF. At PF, this is the standard problem of universal phonetics. At LF, we assume each legitimate object to be a chain $CH = (\alpha_1, \ldots, \alpha_n)$: at least (perhaps at most) with CH a head, an argument, a modifier, or an operator-variable construction. We now say that the representation λ satisfies FI at LF if it consists entirely of legitimate objects; a derivation forming λ converges at LF if λ satisfies FI, and otherwise crashes. A convergent derivation may produce utter gibberish, exactly as at PF. Linguistic expressions may be "deviant" along all sorts of incommensurable dimensions, and we have no notion of "well-formed sentence". Expressions have the interpretations assigned to them by the performance systems in which the language is embedded: period.

To develop these ideas properly, we must proceed to characterize notions with the basic properties of A- and Ā-position. These notions were well defined in the [*Lectures on government and binding*] framework [Chomsky 1981], but in terms of assumptions that are no longer held, in particular, the assumption that θ-marking is restricted to sisterhood, with multiple-branching constructions. With these assumptions abandoned, the notions are used only in an intuitive sense. To replace them, let us consider more closely the morphological properties of lexical items, which play a major role in the minimalist program we are sketching.

Consider the verbal system of (6).

(6)

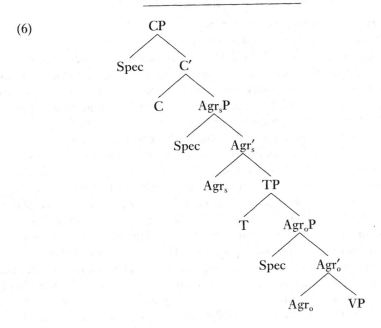

The main verb typically "picks up" the features of T and Agr (in fact, both Agr_s and Agr_o in the general case), adjoining to an inflectional element I to form [V I]. There are two ways to interpret the process, for a lexical element α. One is to take α to be a bare, uninflected form; PF rules are then designed to interpret the abstract complex [α I] as a single inflected phonological word. The other approach is to take α to have inflectional features in the lexicon as an intrinsic property (in the spirit of lexicalist phonology); these features are then checked against the inflectional element I in the complex [α I].[3] If the features of α and I match, I disappears and α enters the PF component under Spell-Out; if they conflict, I remains and the derivation crashes at PF. The PF rules, then, are simple rewriting rules of the usual type, not more elaborate rules applying to complexes [α I].

I have been tacitly assuming the second option. Let us now make that choice explicit. Note that we need no longer adopt the Emonds-Pollock assumption that in English-type languages I lowers to V. V will have the inflectional features before Spell-Out in any event, and the checking procedure may take place anywhere, in particular, after LF movement. French-type and English-type languages now look alike at LF, whereas lowering of I in the latter would have produced adjunction structures quite unlike those of the raising languages.

There are various ways to make a checking theory precise, and to capture generalizations that hold across morphology and syntax. Suppose, for example, that Baker's Mirror Principle is strictly accurate. Then we may take a lexical element – say, the verb V – to be a sequence V = (α, $Infl_1$, . . . , $Infl_n$), where α is the morphological complex [R-$Infl_1$- . . . -$Infl_n$], R a root and $Infl_i$ an inflectional feature.[4] The PF rules only "see" α. When V is adjoined to a functional category F (say, Agr_o), the feature $Infl_1$ is removed from V if it matches F; and so on. If any $Infl_i$ remains at LF, the derivation crashes at LF. The PF form α always satisfies the

Mirror Principle in a derivation that converges at LF. Other technologies can readily be devised. In this case, however, it is not clear that such mechanisms are in order; the most persuasive evidence for the Mirror Principle lies outside the domain of inflectional morphology, which may be subject to different principles. Suppose, say, that richer morphology tends to be more "visible," that is, closer to the word boundary; if so, [. . .] we would expect nominative or absolutive agreement (depending on language type) to be more peripheral in the verbal morphology.

The functional elements T and Agr therefore incorporate features of the verb. Let us call these features *V-features*: the function of the V-features of an inflectional element I is to check the morphological properties of the verb selected from the lexicon. More generally, let us call such features of a lexical item L *L-features*. Keeping to the X-bar-theoretic notions, we say that a position is *L-related* if it is in a local relation to an L-feature, that is, in the internal domain or checking domain of a head with an L-feature. Furthermore, the checking domain can be subdivided into two categories: nonadjoined (Spec) and adjoined. Let us call these positions *narrowly* and *broadly* L-related, respectively. A structural position that is narrowly L-related has the basic properties of A-positions; one that is not L-related has the basic properties of Ā-positions, in particular, [Spec, C], not L-related if C does not contain a V-feature. The status of broadly L-related (adjoined) positions has been debated, particularly in the theory of scrambling.[5] For our limited purposes, we may leave the matter open.

Note that we crucially assume, as is plausible, that V-raising to C is actually I-raising, with V incorporated within I, and is motivated by properties of the (C, I) system, not morphological checking of V. C has other properties that distinguish it from the V-features.

The same considerations extend to nouns (assuming the D head of DP to have N-features) and adjectives. Putting this aside, we can continue to speak informally of A- and Ā-positions, understood in terms of L-relatedness as a first approximation only, with further refinement still necessary. We can proceed, then, to define the legitimate LF objects $CH = (\alpha_1, \ldots, \alpha_n)$ in something like the familiar way: heads, with α_i an X^0; arguments, with α_i in an A-position; adjuncts, with α_i in an Ā-position; and operator-variable constructions, to which we will briefly return.[6] This approach seems relatively unproblematic. Let us assume so, and proceed.

The morphological features of Tense and Agr have two functions: they check properties of the verb that raises to them, and they check properties of the NP (DP) that raises to their Spec position; thus, they ensure that DP and V are properly paired. Generalizing the checking theory, let us assume that, like verbs, nouns are drawn from the lexicon with all of their morphological features, including Case and ϕ-features, and that these too must be checked in the appropriate position:[7] in this case, [Spec, Agr] (which may include T or V). This checking too can take place at any stage of a derivation to LF.

A standard argument for S-Structure conditions in the Case module is that Case features appear at PF but must be 'visible' at LF; hence, Case must be present by the time the derivation reaches S-Structure. But that argument collapses under a checking theory. We may proceed, then, with the assumption that the Case Filter is an interface condition – in fact, the condition that all morphological features must be checked somewhere, for convergence. There are many interesting and subtle problems to be addressed; reluctantly, I will put them aside here, merely asserting without argument that a proper understanding of economy of derivation goes a long way (maybe all the way) toward resolving them.

Next consider subject–verb agreement, as in *John hits Bill*. The φ-features appear in three positions in the course of the derivation: internal to *John*, internal to *hits*, and in Agr_S. The verb *hits* raises ultimately to Agr_S and the NP *John* to [Spec, Agr_S], each checking its morphological features. If the lexical items were properly chosen, the derivation converges. But at PF and LF the φ-features appear only twice, not three times: in the NP and verb that agree. Agr plays only a mediating role: when it has performed its function, it disappears. Since this function is dual, V-related and NP-related, Agr must in fact have two kinds of features: V-features that check V adjoined to Agr, and NP-features that check NP in [Spec, Agr]. The same is true of T, which checks the tense of the verb and the Case of the subject. The V-features of an inflectional element disappear when they check V, the NP-features when they check NP (or N, or DP; see note 7). All this is automatic, and within the Minimalist Program.

Let us now return to the first type of S-Structure condition (1a), the position of Spell-Out: after V-raising in French-type languages, before V-raising in English-type languages (we have now dispensed with lowering). As we have seen, the Minimalist Program permits only one solution to the problem: PF conditions reflecting morphological properties must force V-raising in French but not in English. What can these conditions be?

Recall the underlying intuition of Pollock's approach, which we are basically assuming: French-type languages have "strong" Agr, which forces overt raising, and English-type languages have "weak" Agr, which blocks it. Let us adopt that idea, rephrasing it in our terms: the V-features of Agr are strong in French, weak in English. Recall that when the V-features have done their work, checking adjoined V, they disappear. If V does not raise to Agr overtly, the V-features survive to PF. Let us now make the natural assumption that "strong" features are visible at PF and "weak" features invisible at PF. These features are not legitimate objects at PF; they are not proper components of phonetic matrices. Therefore, if a strong feature remains after Spell-Out, the derivation crashes.[8] In French overt raising is a prerequisite for convergence; in English it is not.

Two major questions remain: Why is overt raising barred in English? Why do the English auxiliaries *have* and *be* raise overtly, as do verbs in French?

The first question is answered by a natural economy condition: LF movement is "cheaper" than overt movement (call the principle *Procrastinate*). [. . .] The intuitive idea is that LF operations are a kind of "wired-in" reflex, operating mechanically beyond any directly observable effects. They are less costly than overt operations. The system tries to reach PF "as fast as possible," minimizing overt syntax. In English-type languages, overt raising is not forced for convergence; therefore, it is barred by economy principles.

To deal with the second question, consider again the intuition that underlies Pollock's account: raising of the auxiliaries reflects their semantic vacuity; they are placeholders for certain constructions, at most "very light" verbs. Adopting the intuition (but not the accompanying technology), let us assume that such elements, lacking semantically relevant features, are not visible to LF rules. If they have not raised overtly, they will not be able to raise by LF rules and the derivation will crash.[9]

Now consider the difference between SVO (or SOV) languages like English (Japanese) and VSO languages like Irish. On our assumptions, V has raised overtly to I (Agr_S) in Irish, while S and O raise in the LF component to [Spec, Agr_S] and [Spec, Agr_O], respectively.[10] We have only one way to express these differences: in terms of the strength of the inflectional features. One possibility is that the NP-feature of T is strong in English and weak in Irish. Hence, NP must raise to [Spec, [Agr T]] in English prior to Spell-Out or the derivation will not converge. The principle Procrastinate bars such raising in Irish. The Extended Projection Principle, which requires that [Spec, IP] be realized (perhaps by an empty category), reduces to a morphological property of T: strong or weak NP-features. Note that the NP-feature of Agr is weak in English; if it were strong, English would exhibit overt object shift. We are still keeping to the minimal assumption that Agr_S and Agr_O are collections of features, with no relevant subject-object distinction, hence no difference in strength of features: Note also that a language might allow both weak and strong inflection, hence weak and strong NP-features: Arabic is a suggestive case, with SVO versus VSO correlating with the richness of visible verb inflection.

Along these lines, we can eliminate S-Structure conditions on raising and lowering in favor of morphological properties of lexical items, in accord with the Minimalist Program. Note that a certain typology of languages is predicted; whether correctly or not remains to be determined.

If Watanabe's (1991) theory of *wh*-movement is correct, there is no parametric variation with regard to *wh-* in situ: language differences (say, English–Japanese) reduce to morphology, in this case, the internal morphology of the *wh*-phrases. Still, the question arises why raising of the *wh*-operator is ever overt, contrary to Procrastinate. The basic economy-of-derivation assumption is that operations are driven by necessity: they are "last resort," applied if they must be, not otherwise (Chomsky 1986). Our assumption is that operations are driven by morphological necessity: certain features must be checked in the checking domain of a head, or the derivation will crash. Therefore, raising of an operator to [Spec, CP] must be driven by such a requirement. The natural assumption is that C may have an operator feature (which we can take to be the Q- or *wh*-feature standardly assumed in C in such cases), and that this feature is a morphological property of such operators as *wh-*. For appropriate C, the operators raise for feature checking to the checking domain of C: [Spec, CP], or adjunction to Spec (absorption), thereby satisfying their scopal properties.[11] Topicalization and focus could be treated the same way. If the operator feature of C is strong, the movement must be overt. Raising of I to C may automatically make the relevant feature of C strong (the V-second phenomenon). If Watanabe is correct, the *wh*-operator feature is universally strong.

[. . .]

Recall that for a derivation to converge, its LF output must be constituted of legitimate objects: tentatively, heads, arguments, modifiers, and operator-variable constructions. A problem arises in the case of pied-piped constructions such as (7).

(7)   (guess) [[$_{wh}$ in which house] John lived t]

The chain (wh, t) is not an operator-variable construction. The appropriate LF form for interpretation requires "reconstruction," as in (8).

(8)   a.   [which x, x a house] John lived [in x]
      b.   [which x] John lived [in [x house]]

Assume that (8a) and (8b) are alternative options. There are various ways in which these options can be interpreted. For concreteness, let us select a particularly simple one.[12]

Suppose that in (8a) x is understood as a DP variable: regarded substitutionally, it can be replaced by a DP (the answer can be *The old one*); regarded objectually, it ranges over houses, as determined by the restricted operator. In (8b) x is a D variable: regarded substitutionally, it can be replaced by a D (the answer can be *that* (*house*)); regarded objectually, it ranges over entities.

Reconstruction is a curious operation, particularly when it is held to follow LF movement, thus restoring what has been covertly moved, as often proposed (e.g. for (3c)). If possible, the process should be eliminated. An approach that has occasionally been suggested is the "copy theory" of movement: the trace left behind is a copy of the moved element, deleted by a principle of the PF component in the case of overt movement. But at LF the copy remains, providing the materials for "reconstruction." Let us consider this possibility, surely to be preferred if it is tenable.

The PF deletion operation is, very likely, a subcase of a broader principle that applies in ellipsis and other constructions. Consider such expressions as (9a–b).

(9)   a.   John said that he was looking for a cat, and so did Bill
      b.   John said that he was looking for a cat, and so did Bill [$_E$ say that he was looking for a cat]

The first conjunct is several-ways ambiguous. Suppose we resolve the ambiguities in one of the possible ways, say, by taking the pronoun to refer to Tom and interpreting *a cat* nonspecifically, so that John said that Tom's quest would be satisfied by any cat. In the elliptical case (9a), a parallelism requirement of some kind (call it *PR*) requires that the second conjunct must be interpreted the same way – in this case, with *he* referring to Tom and *a cat* understood nonspecifically (Lakoff 1970; Lasnik 1972; Sag 1976; Ristad 1993). The same is true in the full sentence (9b), a nondeviant linguistic expression with a distinctive low-falling intonation for E; it too must be assigned its properties by the theory of grammar. PR surely applies at LF. Since it must apply to (9b), the simplest assumption would be that only (9b) reaches LF, (9a) being derived from (9b) by an operation of the PF component deleting copies. There would be no need, then, for special mechanisms to account for the parallelism properties of (9a). Interesting questions arise when this path is followed, but it seems promising. If so, the trace deletion operation may well be an obligatory variant of a more general operation applying in the PF component.

Assuming this approach, (7) is a notational abbreviation for (10).

(10) [$_{wh}$ in which house] John lived [$_{wh}$ in which house]

The LF component converts the phrase *wh* to either (11a) or (11b) by an operation akin to QR.

(11) a. [which house] [$_{wh}$ in *t*]
      b. [which] [$_{wh}$ in [*t* house]]

We may give these the intuitive interpretations of (12a–b).

(12) a. [which *x*, *x* a house] [in *x*]
      b. [which *x*] [in [*x* house]]

For convergence at LF, we must have an operator-variable structure. Accordingly, in the operator position [Spec, CP], everything but the operator phrase must delete; therefore, the phrase *wh* of (11) deletes. In the trace position, the copy of what remains in the operator position deletes, leaving just the phrase *wh* (an LF analogue to the PF rule just described). In the present case (perhaps generally), these choices need not be specified; other options will crash. We thus derive LF forms interpreted as (8a) or (8b), depending on which option we have selected. The LF forms now consist of legitimate objects, and the derivations converge.

Along the same lines, we will interpret *which book did John read* either as '[which *x*, *x* a book] [John read *x*]' (answer: *War and Peace*) or as '[which *x*] [John read [*x* book]]' (answer: *that* (*book*)).

The assumptions are straightforward and minimalist in spirit. They carry us only partway toward an analysis of reconstruction and interpretation; there are complex and obscure phenomena, many scarcely understood. Insofar as these assumptions are tenable and properly generalizable, we can eliminate reconstruction as a separate process, keeping the term only as part of informal descriptive apparatus for a certain range of phenomena.

Extending observations of Riemsdijk and Williams (1981), Freidin (1986) points out that such constructions as (13a–b) behave quite differently under reconstruction.[13]

(13) a.   which claim [that John was asleep] was he willing to discuss
      b.   which claim [that John made] was he willing to discuss

In (13a) reconstruction takes place: the pronoun does not take *John* as antecedent. In contrast, in (13b) reconstruction is not obligatory and the anaphoric connection is an option. While there are many complications, to a first approximation the contrast seems to reduce to a difference between complement and adjunct, the bracketed clause of (13a) and (13b), respectively. Lebeaux (1988) proposed an analysis of this distinction in terms of generalized transformations. In case (13a) the complement must appear at the level of D-Structure; in case (13b) the adjunct could be adjoined by a generalized transformation in the course of derivation, in fact, after whatever processes are responsible for the reconstruction effect.[14]

The approach is appealing, if problematic. For one thing, there is the question of the propriety of resorting to generalized transformations. For another, the same reasoning forces reconstruction in the case of A-movement. Thus, (13) is analogous to (13a); the complement is present before raising and should therefore force a Condition C violation.

(14)   The claim that John was asleep seems to him [$_{IP}$ t to be correct]

Under the present interpretation, the trace t is spelled out as identical to the matrix subject. While it deletes at PF, it remains at LF, yielding the unwanted reconstruction effect. Condition C of the binding theory requires that the pronoun *him* cannot take its antecedent within the embedded IP (compare **I seem to him [to like John]*, with *him* anaphoric to *John*). But *him* can take *John* as antecedent in (14), contrary to the prediction.

The proposal now under investigation overcomes these objections. We have moved to a full-blown theory of generalized transformations, so there is no problem here. The extension property for substitution entails that complements can only be introduced cyclically, hence before *wh*-extraction, while adjuncts can be introduced noncyclically, hence adjoined to the *wh*-phrase after raising to [Spec, CP]. Lebeaux's analysis of (13) therefore could be carried over. As for (14), if "reconstruction" is essentially a reflex of the formation of operator-variable constructions, it will hold only for Ā-chains, not for A-chains. That conclusion seems plausible over a considerable range, and yields the right results in this case.

Let us return now to the problem of binding-theoretic conditions at S-Structure. We found a weak but sufficient argument (of type (2a)) to reject the conclusion that Condition C applies at S-Structure. What about Condition A?

Consider constructions such as those in (15).[15]

(15)   a.   i.   John wondered [which picture of himself] [Bill saw t]
            ii.   the students asked [what attitudes about each other] [the teachers
                  had noticed t]
       b.   i.   John wondered [who [t saw [which picture of himself]]]
            ii.   the students asked [who [t had noticed [what attitudes about each
                  other]]]

The sentences of (15a) are ambiguous, with the anaphor taking either the matrix or embedded subject as antecedent; but those of (15b) are unambiguous, with the trace of *who* as the only antecedent for *himself, each other*. If (15b) were formed by LF raising of the in-situ *wh*-phrase, we would have to conclude that Condition A applies at S-Structure, prior to this operation. But we have already seen that the assumption is unwarranted; we have, again, a weak but sufficient argument against allowing binding theory to apply at S-Structure. A closer look shows that we can do still better.

Under the copying theory, the actual forms of (15a) are (16a–b).

(16) a. John wondered [$_{wh}$ which picture of himself] [Bill saw [$_{wh}$ which picture of himself]]

　　　b. the students asked [$_{wh}$ what attitudes about each other]
　　　　　[the teachers had noticed [$_{wh}$ what attitudes about each other]]

The LF principles map (16a) to either (17a) or (17b), depending on which option is selected for analysis of the phrase *wh*.

(17) a. John wondered [[which picture of himself] [$_{wh}$ *t*]] [Bill saw [[which picture of himself] [$_{wh}$ *t*]]]

　　　b. John wondered [which [$_{wh}$ *t* picture of himself]] [Bill saw [which [$_{wh}$ *t* picture of himself]]]

We then interpret (17a) as (18a) and (17b) as (18b), as before.

(18) a. John wondered [which *x*, *x* a picture of himself] [Bill saw *x*]
　　　b. John wondered [which *x*] [Bill saw [*x* picture of himself]]

Depending on which option we have selected, *himself* will be anaphoric to *John* or to *Bill*.[16]

The same analysis applies to (16b), yielding the two options of (19) corresponding to (18).

(19) a. the students asked [what *x*, *x* attitudes about each other] [the teachers had noticed *x*]

　　　b. the students asked [what *x*] [the teachers had noticed [*x* attitudes about each other]]

In (19a) the antecedent of *each other* is *the students*; in (19b) it is *the teachers*.

Suppose that we change the examples of (15a) to (20a–b), replacing *saw* by *took* and *had noticed* by *had*.

(20) a. John wondered [which picture of himself] [Bill took *t*]
　　　b. the students asked [what attitudes about each other]
　　　　　[the teachers had]

Consider (20a). As before, *himself* can take either *John* or *Bill* as antecedent. There is a further ambiguity: the phrase *take . . . picture* can be interpreted either idiomatically (in the sense of 'photograph') or literally ('pick up and walk away with'). But the interpretive options appear to correlate with the choice of antecedent for *himself*: if the antecedent is *John*, the idiomatic interpretation is barred; if the

antecedent is *Bill*, it is permitted. If *Bill* is replaced by *Mary*, the idiomatic interpretation is excluded.

The pattern is similar for (20b), except that there is no literal–idiomatic ambiguity. The only interpretation is that the students asked what attitudes each of the
teachers had about the other teacher(s). If *the teachers* is replaced by *Jones*, there
is no interpretation.

Why should the interpretations distribute in this manner?

First consider (20a). The principles already discussed yield the two LF options
in (21a–b).

(21)　a.　John wondered [which x, x a picture of himself] [Bill took x]
　　　b.　John wondered [which x] [Bill took [x picture of himself]]

If we select the option (21a), then *himself* takes *John* as antecedent by Condition
A at LF; if we select the option (21b), then *himself* takes *Bill* as antecedent by the
same principle. If we replace *Bill* with *Mary*, then (21a) is forced. Having abandoned D-Structure, we must assume that idiom interpretation takes place at LF,
as is natural in any event. But we have no operations of LF reconstruction. Thus,
take . . . picture can be interpreted as 'photograph' only if the phrase is present as
a unit at LF – that is, in (21b), not (21a). It follows that in (21a) we have only the
nonidiomatic interpretation of *take*; in (21b) we have either. In short, only the option
(21b) permits the idiomatic interpretation, also blocking *John* as antecedent of the
reflexive and barring replacement of *Bill* by *Mary*.

The same analysis holds for (20b). The two LF options are (22a–b).

(22)　a.　the students asked [what x, x attitudes about each other]
　　　　　[the teachers had x]
　　　b.　the students asked [what x] [the teachers had [x attitudes about each
　　　　　other]]

Only (22b) yields an interpretation, with *have . . . attitudes* given its unitary sense.

The conclusions follow on the crucial assumption that Condition A *not* apply
at S-Structure, prior to the LF rules that form (21).[17] If Condition A were to apply
at S-Structure, *John* could be taken as antecedent of *himself* in (20a) and the later
LF processes would be free to choose either the idiomatic or the literal interpretation, however the reconstruction phenomena are handled; and *the students*
could be taken as antecedent of *each other* in (20b), with reconstruction providing the interpretation of *have . . . attitudes*. Thus, we have the strongest kind of
argument against an S-Structure condition (type (2c)): Condition A *cannot* apply
at S-Structure.

Note also that we derive a strong argument for LF representation. The facts
are straightforwardly explained in terms of a level of representation with two properties: (1) phrases with a unitary interpretation such as the idiom *take . . . picture*
or *have . . . attitudes* appear as units; (2) binding theory applies. In standard EST
approaches, LF is the only candidate. The argument is still clearer in this minimalist theory, lacking D-Structure and (we are now arguing) S-Structure.

Combining these observations with the Freidin-Lebeaux examples, we seem to face a problem, in fact a near-contradiction. In (23a) either option is allowed: *himself* may take either *John* or *Bill* as antecedent. In contrast, in (23b) reconstruction appears to be forced, barring *Tom* as antecedent of *he* (by Condition C) and *Bill* as antecedent of *him* (by Condition B).

(23)　a.　John wondered [which picture of himself] [Bill saw *t*]
　　　　b.　i.　　John wondered [which picture of Tom] [he liked *t*]
　　　　　　ii.　　John wondered [which picture of him] [Bill took *t*]
　　　　　　iii.　John wondered [what attitude about him] [Bill had *t*]

The Freidin-Lebeaux theory requires reconstruction in all these cases, the *of*-phrase being a complement of *picture*. But the facts seem to point to a conception that distinguishes Condition A of the binding theory, which does not force reconstruction, from Conditions B and C, which do. Why should this be?

In our terms, the trace *t* in (23) is a copy of the *wh*-phrase at the point where the derivation branches to the PF and LF components. Suppose we now adopt an LF movement approach to anaphora, assuming that the anaphor or part of it raises by an operation similar to cliticization – call it *cliticization$_{LF}$*. This approach at least has the property we want: it distinguishes Condition A from Conditions B and C. Note that cliticization$_{LF}$ is a case of Move α; though applying in the LF component, it necessarily precedes the "reconstruction" operations that provide the interpretations for the LF output. Applying cliticization$_{LF}$ to (23a), we derive either (24a) or (24b), depending on whether the rule applies to the operator phrase or its trace TR.[18]

(24)　a.　John self-wondered [which picture of *t*$_{self}$] [NP saw [$_{TR}$ which picture of himself]]
　　　　b.　John wondered [which picture of himself] [NP self-saw [$_{TR}$ which picture of *t*$_{self}$]]

We then turn to the LF rules interpreting the *wh*-phrase, which yield the two options (25a–b) (α = either *t*$_{self}$ or *himself*).

(25)　a.　[[which picture of α] *t*]
　　　　b.　[which] [*t* picture of α]

Suppose that we have selected the option (24a). Then we cannot select the interpretive option (25b) (with α = *t*$_{self}$); that option requires deletion of [*t* picture of *t*$_{self}$] in the operator position, which would break the chain (*self*, *t*$_{self}$), leaving the reflexive element without a θ-role at LF. We must therefore select the interpretive option (25a), yielding a convergent derivation without reconstruction:

(26)　John self-wondered [which *x*, *x* a picture of *t*$_{self}$] NP saw *x*

In short, if we take the antecedent of the reflexive to be *John*, then only the non-reconstructing option converges.

If we had *Tom* or *him* in place of *himself*, as in (23b), then these issues would not arise and either interpretive option would converge. We thus have a relevant difference between the two categories of (23). To account for the judgments, it is only necessary to add a preference principle for reconstruction: Do it when you can (i.e. try to minimize the restriction in the operator position). In (23b) the preference principle yields reconstruction, hence a binding theory violation (Conditions C and B). In (23a) we begin with two options with respect to application of cliticization$_{LF}$: either to the operator or to the trace position. If we choose the first option, selecting the matrix subject as antecedent, then the preference principle is inapplicable because only the nonpreferred case converges, and we derive the non-reconstruction option. If we choose the second option, selecting the embedded subject as antecedent, the issue of preference again does not arise. Hence, we have genuine options in the case of (23a), but a preference for reconstruction (hence the judgment that binding theory conditions are violated) in the case of (23b).[19]

Other constructions reinforce these conclusions, for example, (27).[20]

(27) a. i.   John wondered what stories about us we had heard
        ii'.   *John wondered what stories about us we had told
        ii".   John wondered what stories about us we expected Mary to tell
      b. i'.   John wondered what opinions about himself Mary had heard
        i".   *John wondered what opinions about himself Mary had
        ii'.   they wondered what opinions about each other Mary had heard
        ii". *they wondered what opinions about each other Mary had
      c. i.   John wondered how many pictures of us we expected Mary to take
        ii.   *John wondered how many pictures of us we expected to take
            (idiomatic sense)

Note that we have further strengthened the argument for an LF level at which all conditions apply: the LF rules, including now anaphor raising, provide a crucial distinction with consequences for reconstruction.

The reconstruction process outlined applies only to operator-variable constructions. What about A-chains, which we may assume to be of the form CH = (α, t) at LF (α the phrase raised from its original position t, intermediate traces deleted or ignored)? Here t is a full copy of its antecedent, deleted in the PF component. The descriptive account must capture the fact that the head of the A-chain is assigned an interpretation in the position t. Thus, in *John was killed t, John* is assigned its θ-role in the position t, as complement of *kill*. The same should be true for such idioms as (28).

(28) several pictures were taken t

Here *pictures* is interpreted in the position of t, optionally as part of the idiom *take . . . pictures*. Interesting questions arise in the case of such constructions as (29a–b).

(29) a.   the students asked [which pictures of each other] [Mary took t]
      b.   the students asked [which pictures of each other] [t' were taken t by Mary]

In both cases the idiomatic interpretation requires that t be [x *pictures of each other*] after the operator-variable analysis ("reconstruction"). In (29a) that choice is blocked, while in (29b) it remains open. The examples reinforce the suggested analysis of Ā-reconstruction, but it is now necessary to interpret the chain (t', t) in (29b) just as the chain (*several pictures*, t) is interpreted in (28). One possibility is that the trace t of the A-chain enters into the idiom interpretation (and, generally, into θ-marking), while the head of the chain functions in the usual way with regard to scope and other matters.

Suppose that instead of (23a) we have (30).

(30)   the students wondered [$_{wh}$ how angry at each other (themselves)] [John was t]

As in the case of (23a), anaphor raising in (30) should give the interpretation roughly as 'the students each wondered [how angry at the other John was]' (similarly with reflexive). But these interpretations are impossible in the case of (30), which requires the reconstruction option, yielding gibberish. Huang (1990) observes that the result follows on the assumption that subjects are predicate-internal (VP-, AP-internal), so that the trace of *John* remains in the subject position of the raised operator phrase *wh-*, blocking association of the anaphor with the matrix subject (anaphor raising, in the present account).

Though numerous problems remain unresolved, there seem to be good reasons to suppose that the binding theory conditions hold only at the LF interface. If so, we can move toward a very simple interpretive version of binding theory as in (31) that unites disjoint and distinct reference (D the relevant local domain), overcoming problems discussed particularly by Howard Lasnik.[21]

(31)   a.   If α is an anaphor, interpret it as coreferential with a c-commanding phrase in D.
         b.   If α is a pronominal, interpret it as disjoint from every c-commanding phrase in D.
         c.   If α is an r-expression, interpret it as disjoint from every c-commanding phrase.

Condition A may be dispensable if the approach based upon cliticization$_{LF}$ is correct and the effects of Condition A follow from the theory of movement (which is not obvious); and further discussion is necessary at many points. All indexing could then be abandoned, another welcome result.[22]

Here too we have, in effect, returned to some earlier ideas about binding theory, in this case those of Chomsky (1980), an approach superseded largely on grounds of complexity (now overcome), but with empirical advantages over what appeared to be simpler alternatives (see note 21).

I stress again that what precedes is only the sketch of a minimalist program, identifying some of the problems and a few possible solutions, and omitting a wide range of topics, some of which have been explored, many not. The program has been pursued with some success. Several related and desirable conclusions seem within reach.

(32) a. A linguistic expression (SD) is a pair (π, λ) generated by an optimal derivation satisfying interface conditions.

  b. The interface levels are the only levels of linguistic representation.

  c. All conditions express properties of the interface levels, reflecting interpretive requirements.

  d. UG provides a unique computational system, with derivations driven by morphological properties to which syntactic variation of languages is restricted.

  e. Economy can be given a fairly narrow interpretation in terms of FI, length of derivation, length of links, Procrastinate, and Greed.

Notes

1 See Hornstein and Weinberg (1990) for development of this proposal on somewhat different assumptions and grounds.

2 The technical implementation could be developed in many ways. For now, let us think of it as a rule of interpretation for the paired *wh*-phrases.

3 Technically, α raises to the lowest I to form [$_I$ α I]; then the complex raises to the next higher inflectional element; and so on. Recall that after multiple adjunction, α will still be in the checking domain of the "highest" I.

4 More fully, Infl$_i$ is a collection of inflectional features checked by the relevant functional element.

5 The issue was raised by Webelhuth (1989) and has become a lively research topic. See Mahajan (1990) and much ongoing work. Note that if I adjoins to C, forming [$_c$ I C], [Spec, C] is in the checking domain of the chain (I, t). Hence, [Spec, C] is L-related (to I), and non-L-related (to C). A sharpening of notions is therefore required to determine the status of C after I-to-C raising. If C has L-features, [Spec, C] is L-related and would thus have the properties of an A-position, not an Ā-position. Questions arise here related to proposals of Rizzi (1990) on agreement features in C, and his more recent work extending these notions; these would take us too far afield here.

6 Heads are not narrowly L-related, hence not in A-positions, a fact that bears on ECP issues.

7 I continue to put aside the question whether Case should be regarded as a property of N or D, and the DP–NP distinction generally.

8 Alternatively, weak features are deleted in the PF component so that PF rules can apply to the phonological matrix that remains; strong features are not deleted so that PF rules do not apply, causing the derivation to crash at PF.

9 Note that this is a reformulation of proposals by Emmon Bach and others in the framework of the Standard Theory and Generative Semantics: that these auxiliaries are inserted in the course of derivation, not appearing in the semantically relevant underlying structures. See Tremblay (1991) for an exploration of similar intuitions.

10 This leaves open the possibility that in VSO languages subject raises overtly to [Spec, TP] while T (including the adjoined verb) raises to Agr$_S$; for evidence that that is correct, see Bures (1992), Bobaljik and Carnie (1992), and Jonas (1992).

11 Raising would take place only to [Spec, CP], if absorption does not involve adjunction to a *wh*-phrase in [Spec, CP]. See note 2. I assume here that CP is not an adjunction target.

12 There are a number of descriptive inadequacies in this overly simplified version. Perhaps the most important is that some of the notions used here (e.g. objectual quantification) have no clear interpretation in the case of natural language, contrary to common practice.

Furthermore, we have no real framework within which to evaluate "theories of interpretation"; in particular, considerations of explanatory adequacy and restrictiveness are hard to introduce, on the standard (and plausible) assumption that the LF component allows no options. The primary task, then, is to derive an adequate descriptive account, no simple matter; comparison of alternatives lacks any clear basis. Another problem is that linking to performance theory is far more obscure than in the case of the PF component. Much of what is taken for granted in the literature on these topics seems to me highly problematic, if tenable at all. See *LGB* for some comment.

13 The topicalization analogues are perhaps more natural: *the claim that John is asleep* (*that John made*), . . . The point is the same, assuming an operator-variable analysis of topicalization.

14 In Lebeaux's theory, the effect is determined at D-Structure, prior to raising: I will abstract away from various modes of implementing the general ideas reviewed here. For discussion bearing on these issues, see Speas (1990), Epstein (1991). Freidin (1994) proposes that the difference has to do with the difference between LF representation of a predicate (the relative clause) and a complement; as he notes, that approach provides an argument for limiting binding theory to LF (see (2)).

15 In all but the simplest examples of anaphora, it is unclear whether distinctions are to be understood as tendencies (varying in strength for different speakers) or sharp distinctions obscured by performance factors. For exposition, I assume the latter here. Judgments are therefore idealized, as always; whether correctly or not, only further understanding will tell.

16 Recall that LF *wh*-raising has been eliminated in favor of the absorption operation, so that in (15b) the anaphor cannot take the matrix subject as antecedent after LF raising.

17 I ignore the possibility that Condition A applies irrelevantly at S-Structure, the result being acceptable only if there is no clash with the LF application.

18 I put aside here interesting questions that have been investigated by Pierre Pica and others about how the morphology and the raising interact.

19 Another relevant case is (i),

(i) (guess) which picture of which man he saw *t*

a Condition C violation if *he* is taken to be bound by *which man* (Higginbotham 1980). As Higginbotham notes, the conclusion is much sharper than in (23b). One possibility is that independently of the present considerations, absorption is blocked from within [Spec, CP], forcing reconstruction to (iia), hence (iib),

(ii) a. which *x*, he saw [*x* picture of which man]
      b. which *x*, *y*, he saw *x* picture of [$_{NP}$ *y* man]

a Condition C violation if *he* is taken to be anaphoric to NP (i.e. within the scope of *which man*). The same reasoning would imply a contrast between (iiia) and (iiib),

(iii) a. who would have guessed that proud of John, Bill never was
       b. *who would have guessed that proud of which man, Bill never was

(with absorption blocked, and no binding theory issue). That seems correct; other cases raise various questions.

20 Cases (27ai), (27aii) correspond to the familiar pairs *John* (*heard, told*) *stories about him*, with antecedence possible only in the case of *heard*, presumably reflecting the fact that one tells one's own stories but can hear the stories told by others; something similar holds of the cases in (27b).

21 See the essays collected in Lasnik 1989.
22 A theoretical apparatus that takes indices seriously as entities, allowing them to figure in operations (percolation, matching, etc.), is questionable on more general grounds. Indices are basically the expression of a relationship, not entities in their own right. They should be replaceable without loss by a structural account of the relation they annotate.

References

Bobaljik, J. and A. Carnie. 1992. A minimalist approach to some problems of Irish word order. Ms., MIT. [Published as Bobaljik, J. and A. Carnie. 1996. A minimalist approach to some problems of Irish word order. In I. Roberts and R. Borsley (eds.), *The syntax of the Celtic languages*. Cambridge: Cambridge University Press, pp. 223–40.]

Branigan, P. 1992. *Subjects and complementizers*. Doctoral dissertation, MIT.

Bures, T. 1992. Re-cycling expletive (and other) sentences. Ms., MIT.

Chomsky, N. 1980. On binding. *Linguistic Inquiry* 11: 1–46.

Chomsky, N. 1981. *Lectures on government and binding*. Dordrecht: Foris.

Chomsky, N. 1986. *Knowledge of language: Its nature, origin, and use*. New York: Praeger.

Epstein, S. D. 1991. *Traces and their antecedents*. Oxford: Oxford University Press.

Freidin, R. 1986. Fundamental issues in the theory of binding. In B. Lust (ed.), *Studies in the acquisition of anaphora*, vol. 1. Dordrecht: Reidel, pp. 151–88.

Freidin, R. 1994. The principles and parameters framework of generative grammar, In R. E. Asher and J. M. Y. Simpson (eds.), *The encyclopedia of language and linguistics*, Oxford: Pergamon Press.

Higginbotham, J. 1980. Pronouns and bound variables. *Linguistic Inquiry* 11: 679–708.

Higginbotham, J. and R. May. 1981. Questions, quantifiers and crossing. *The Linguistic Review* 1: 41–79.

Hornstein, N. and A. Weinberg. 1990. The necessity of LF. *The Linguistic Review* 7: 129–67.

Huang, C.-T. J. 1982. *Logical relations in Chinese and the theory of grammar*. Doctoral dissertation, MIT.

Huang, C.-T. J. 1990. A note on reconstruction and VP movement. Ms., Cornell University.

Jonas, D. 1992. Transitive expletive constructions in Icelandic and Middle English. Ms., Harvard University.

Lakoff, G. 1970. *Irregularity in syntax*. New York: Holt, Rinehart, and Winston.

Lasnik, H. 1972. *Analyses of negation in English*. Doctoral dissertation, MIT.

Lasnik, H. 1989. *Essays on anaphora*. Dordrecht: Kluwer.

Lebeaux, D. 1988. *Language acquisition and the form of the grammar*. Doctoral dissertation, University of Massachusetts, Amherst.

Mahajan, A. 1990. *The A/A-bar distinction and movement theory*. Doctoral dissertation, MIT.

Riemsdijk, H. C. van and E. Williams. 1981. NP structure. *The Linguistic Review* 1: 171–217.

Ristad, E. 1993. *The language complexity game*. Cambridge, MA: MIT Press.

Rizzi, L. 1990. *Relativized minimality*. Cambridge, MA: MIT Press.

Sag, I. 1976. *Deletion and logical form*. Doctoral dissertation, MIT.

Speas, M. 1990. Generalized transformations and the D-Structure position of adjuncts. Ms., University of Massachusetts, Amherst.

Tremblay, M. 1991. *Possession and datives*. Doctoral dissertation, McGill University.

Watanabe, A. 1991. *Wh-in-situ, subjacency and chain formation. MIT Occasional Papers in Linguistics 2*. Cambridge, MA: MITWPL.

Webelhuth, G. 1989. *Syntactic saturation phenomenon and the modern Germanic languages*. Doctoral dissertation, University of Massachusetts, Amherst.

1.3   Recent Developments: Multiple Spell-Out

From *A DERIVATIONAL APPROACH TO SYNTACTIC RELATIONS*
Samuel D. Epstein, Erich M. Groat, Ruriko Kawashima, and Hisatsugu Kitahara

Recall that the minimalist approach eliminates the mechanism of syntactic filters applying to syntactic levels, replacing them by appeal to what are currently largely undetermined interpretive requirements imposed by post-syntactic computation, the "Bare Output Conditions" (Chomsky 1994, 1995), which determine allowable interface representations on the basis of the interpretive requirements of semantic and phonological computation external to the syntactic component. In the formalization of this approach, Chomsky distinguishes between objects (syntactic categories and features) that are *legitimate* and those that are *illegitimate* at the interfaces (Chomsky 1991). As an example, unchecked formal features are hypothesized to be uninterpretable to semantic – *non-syntactic* – computation. Thus such features must be checked before the phrase-marker can be interpreted; unchecked features are *illegitimate*. At the same time, the *syntactic* operation Move is hypothesized to be constrained by Greed, which states that Move applies only in order to check features that would otherwise be uninterpretable – that is, only in order to create legitimate objects. In fact, any syntactic operation other than binary Merge (such as Move) is generally constrained by the requirement that legitimate, interpretable objects result from the application of that operation (Last Resort; see also Epstein 1992; Lasnik 1995). Notice that the notion of "legitimacy" is defined only with respect to *non-syntactic* interpretation. But if post-syntactic interpretation applies only to a single output phrase-marker, generated by syntactic structure-building rules (such as Move), how can there be a well-defined notion of legitimacy characterizing "licit rule-application" at some *intermediate* point in the derivation, to which post-syntactic computation has no access? By requiring that, internal to the syntax, each rule-application be constrained by the ultimate requirements of the interfaces (the Bare Output Conditions), we arrive at a paradox: the requirements of the interfaces, by hypothesis, apply exclusively at the interfaces, and not internal to a derivation – yet Last Resort, requiring that rules apply only to yield "legitimacy," entails that legitimacy must be defined with respect to rule-application within a derivation.

In our model, no such paradox arises. Given that syntactic relations in our theory are properties of rule-application, and hence of derivations, the post-syntactic computational systems must examine not "output representations" to determine such relations but, rather, the derivation, which consists of the partially ordered application of syntactic rules. Hence, at each point in the derivation at which a rule (such as Move) is applied, interface conditions hold, and the notion of "legitimacy" remains well-defined internal to the derivation. In the case of feature checking, for example, Move will be allowed only if it has the property that a Checking Relation is established that renders legitimate some otherwise uninterpretable feature. Effectively, this result is the same as the current minimalist Last Resort requirement "Greed" – but differs crucially in that the "legitimacy" of a category remains a purely *extrasyntactic* notion: the computational systems beyond the interfaces "see" the operation Move, and thus "see" the Checking Relation that results in the legitimacy of the feature being checked.

Semantic and phonological interpretation is thus "invasive" to the syntax, being isomorphic to the syntactic derivation and interpreting it as it proceeds, rather than interpreting an output phrase-marker representation generated by the derivation. There is no phrase-marker that serves as the sole object of semantic interpretation (the minimalist carry-over of an LF "level" of representation); nor is there a phrase-marker that is "Spelled-Out" to the phonological component (the minimalist analog of an S-Structure "level" of representation). The "Y-model" of syntax is thus eliminated. For every syntactic operation there is a corresponding interpretive operation in the semantic and/or PF components.

This theory of syntax might comport well with a compositional approach to semantic interpretation. Instead of cyclic, syntactic construction of an entire phrase-marker *followed by* cyclic, semantic composition which retraces the steps of the syntax, the syntax instead serves as a set of instructions to the semantic component to build cyclically composed structures, in the manner of Montagovian categorial grammar.

This simplification resembles the resolution (attained by the minimalist return to Generalized Transformations) of a long-standing problem with respect to purely syntactic strict cyclicity in preminimalist theories. Why should phrase-structure rules create a complete (deep) structure representation, only to have transformational rules apply cyclically to subtrees of that representation? Cyclic transformational rule-application applies exactly as if higher structure didn't yet exist. Why? These questions disappear when deep structure is eliminated and structure-building subsumes both base generation and transformations on the structure built so far – that is, derivationally. Similarly, why should the syntax build a structure cyclically, only to have compositional semantic computation apply cyclically to the already constructed subtrees of the completed interface structure? In our model, this question also disappears, since semantic interpretation is "invasive," proceeding concurrently with structure-building, i.e. derivationally.

References

Chomsky, N. 1991. Some notes on economy of derivation and representation. In R. Freidin (ed.), *Principles and parameters in comparative grammar*, Cambridge, MA: MIT Press, pp. 417–54. [Reprinted in Chomsky (1995), *The Minimalist Program*, Cambridge, MA: MIT Press, pp. 128–66.]

Chomsky, N. 1994. *Bare phrase structure. MIT Occasional Papers in Linguistics 5.* Cambridge, MA: MITWPL. [Published in P. Kempchinsky (ed.) (1994), *Evolution and revolution in linguistic theory: Essays in honor of Carlos Otero*, Washington, DC: Georgetown University Press, pp. 51–109. Also published in G. Webelhuth (ed.) (1994), *Government and binding theory and the minimalist program*, Cambridge, MA: MIT Press, pp. 383–439.]

Chomsky, N. 1995. Categories and transformations. In Chomsky (1995), *The Minimalist Program*, Cambridge, MA: MIT Press, pp. 219–394.

Epstein, S. D. 1992. Derivational constraints on A'-chain formation. *Linguistic Inquiry* 23: 235–60.

Lasnik, H. 1995. Last resort. In S. Haraguchi and M. Funaki (eds.), *Minimalism and linguistic theory*, Tokyo: Hituzi Syobo, pp. 1–32. [Reprinted in Lasnik (1999), *Minimalist Analysis*, Malden, MA/Oxford: Blackwell, pp. 120–50.]

From "MINIMALIST INQUIRIES: THE FRAMEWORK"
Noam Chomsky

A crucial property of deletion is that a deleted feature is invisible at LF and inaccessible to C_{HL} (the [±active] property), but accessible to the phonological component. This property poses a problem on the assumption made in [Chomsky 1995] that Spell-Out applies at a single point in a derivation: pre-Spell-Out, the probe must delete when checked yet remain until Spell-Out.[1] The natural conclusion is that Spell-Out is associated with agreement. Deleted features are literally erased, but only after they are sent to the phonological component along with the rest of the structure Σ – possibly at the phase level. Spell-Out therefore applies cyclically in the course of the (narrow syntactic) derivation. I will assume that this approach, apparently the simplest and most principled one, is correct.[2]

The single Spell-Out thesis of *MP* retains the flavor of the Extended Standard Theory model, distinguishing overt from covert operations – pre- and post-Spell-Out, respectively. If both overt and covert operations are cyclic, then there are two independent cycles – and if operations of the phonological component are cyclic, a third cycle as well. With cyclic Spell-Out, contingent on feature-checking operations, these distinctions collapse. There is a single cycle; all operations are cyclic. Within narrow syntax, operations that have or lack phonetic effects are interspersed. There is no distinct LF component within narrow syntax, and we can dispense with troublesome questions about its apparently cyclic character. Agree alone, not combined with Merge in the operation Move, can precede overt operations, contrary to the assumptions made in *MP* and related work. Crucial cases are long-distance agreement, *wh*-in-situ, and others. Many questions arise, but they do not seem obviously unanswerable.

Notes

1 The problem is noted in [Chomsky (1995): 385, n. 50] but left unresolved.
2 The conception is similar to the strict derivational interpretation of Spell-Out proposed by Epstein et al. (1998); for similar suggestions, on different grounds, see Uriagereka (1996, 1999). The basic architecture resembles that of Bresnan (1971); her results on the interaction of phonological and transformational rules fall into place more directly than in the Extended Standard Theory model. See several papers in Abraham et al. (1996) and Yang (1997) for related discussion.

References

Abraham, W., S. D. Epstein and H. Thráinsson (eds.). 1996. *Minimal ideas: Syntactic studies in the Minimalist framework*. Amsterdam/Philadelphia: John Benjamins.
Bresnan, J. 1971. Sentence stress and syntactic transformations. *Language* 47: 257–81.
Chomsky, N. 1995. *The Minimalist Program*. Cambridge, MA: MIT Press.
Epstein, S. D., E. Groat, R. Kawashima and H. Kitahara. 1998. *A derivational approach to syntactic relations*. New York: Oxford University Press.

Uriagereka, J. 1996. Formal and substantive elegance in the Minimalist Program. In C. Wilder, Hans-Martin Gartner, and Manfred Bierwisch (eds.), *The Role of Economy Principles in Linguistic Theory*, Berlin: Akademie Verlag, pp. 170–204.

Uriagereka, J. 1999. Multiple spell-out. In S. D. Epstein and N. Hornstein (eds.), *Working minimalism*, Cambridge, MA: MIT Press, pp. 251–82.

Yang, C. 1997. *Minimal computation: Derivation of syntactic structures*. Master's thesis, Artificial Intelligence Laboratory, MIT.

From "BEYOND EXPLANATORY ADEQUACY"
Noam Chomsky

Assume further that L has three components: *narrow syntax* (NS) maps LA to a derivation D-NS; the *phonological component* Φ maps D-NS to PHON; the *semantic component* Σ maps D-NS to SEM. Σ is assumed to be uniform for all L; NS is as well, if parameters can be restricted to LEX (as I will assume). Φ, in contrast, is highly variable among Ls. Optimally, mappings will satisfy the *inclusiveness condition*, introducing no new elements but only rearranging those of the domain. Assume this strong condition to be true of NS. It is surely not true of Φ nor (on usual assumptions) of Σ.[1]

Assume that all three components are cyclic, a very natural optimality requirement and fairly conventional. In the worst case, the three cycles are independent;[2] the best case is that there is a single cycle only. Assume that to be true. Then Φ and Σ apply to units constructed by NS, and the three components of the derivation of <PHON, SEM> proceed cyclically in parallel. L contains operations that transfer each unit to Φ and to Σ. In the best case, these apply at the same stage of the cycle. Assume so. Then there is an operation TRANSFER, applying to the narrow-syntactic derivation D-NS:

(1)   TRANSFER hands D-NS over to Φ and to Σ.

We focus here primarily on the mapping to Φ, returning to its integration later: call it *Spell-Out* (S-O).[3]

In this conception there is no LF: rather, the computation maps LA to <PHON, SEM> piece by piece, cyclically. There are, therefore, no LF properties and no interpretation of LF, strictly speaking, though Σ and Φ interpret units that are part of something like LF in a noncyclic conception.

Call the relevant units "phases."[4] It remains to determine what the phases are, and exactly how the operations work. I will assume, following [Chomsky 2001], that the phases are CP and vP, but crucially not TP, returning later to some reasons for this.[5] When a phase is transferred to Φ, it is converted to PHON. Φ proceeds in parallel with the NS derivation. Φ is greatly simplified if it can "forget about" what has been transferred to it at earlier phases; otherwise, the advantages of cyclic computation are lost. Although the assumption may be somewhat too strong, let us assume it to be basically true, so that global properties of phonology (e.g. intonation contour) are superimposed on the outcome of the cyclic operation of Φ.

Applied to a phase PH, S-O must be able to spell out PH in full, or root clauses would never be spelled out.[6] But we know that S-O cannot be *required* to spell out PH in full, or displacement would never be possible. Consider a typical phase (2), with H as its head:

(2) PH = [α [H β]]

Call α-H the *edge* of PH. It is a fact that elements of the edge may (or sometimes must) raise. A natural condition, which permits spell-out of root phrases and allows for meaningful cyclic computation, is that β must be spelled out at PH, but not the edge: that allows for head-raising, raising of Predicate-internal subject to Spec-T, and an "escape hatch" for successive-cyclic movement through the edge. Call this condition the Phase Impenetrability Condition (PIC). However PIC is formulated exactly, it should have as a consequence that, at the phase ZP containing phase HP,

(3) The domain of H is not accessible to operations, but only the edge of HP.

[. . .]

By definition, the operation TRANSFER [see (1)] applies at the phase level. At this level, internal Merge can apply either before or after TRANSFER, hence before or after Spell-Out S-O. The former case yields overt movement, the latter case covert movement, with the displaced element spelled out in situ.[7]

Covert and overt movements yield pairs <α, β>, α an edge element c-commanding β, where either α or β loses its phonological features under S-O: α under covert Move, β under overt Move.

Notes

1 These asymmetries allow for investigation of the internal structure of NS and Φ in ways that are not possible for Σ, which is invariant and does not satisfy economy conditions [. . .] in any obvious way. It is somewhat paradoxical, perhaps, that logically equivalent versions of Σ, decomposing it in different ways, have important consequences. A further asymmetry is that Φ introduces only elements that are in [F] (though typically not in LEX), whereas the new elements introduced by Σ never enter NS and are accordingly not in [F]; and if inclusiveness holds for NS, it introduces no features, even of [F].

2 A still worse case is the EST-model, with two cycles in NS, overt and covert.

3 For a very strong version of the thesis, see Epstein (1999). On cyclic Spell-Out see [Chomsky 2000, 2001]; and for related ideas, see Uriagereka (1999). S-O removes from NS all features that do not reach SEM. For expository simplicity, I refer to all these as "phonological."

4 For an intriguing generalization of the notion to incorporate binding theory properties, see Freidin and Vergnaud (2001).

5 Possibly DP as well, but this raises many questions. I will put the topic aside here, keeping to the basic clausal architecture and the phases CP, *v*P.

6 This requirement could reduce to Spell-Out of sister of the head if we adopt some variant of Ross's phonologically empty performative analysis; Nissenbaum, personal communication.

7 See Nissenbaum (2000). See also Pesetsky (2000). I will assume this to be correct, contrary to Chomsky (2000) and Chomsky (2001), which interpreted covert movement as long-distance agreement.

References

Chomsky, N. 2000. Minimalist inquiries: The framework. In R. Martin, D. Michaels and J. Uriagereka (eds.), *Step by step: Essays on minimalism in honor of Howard Lasnik*, Cambridge, MA: MIT Press, pp. 89–155.

Chomsky, N. 2001. Derivation by phase. In M. Kenstowicz (ed.), *Ken Hale: A Life in Linguistics*, Cambridge, MA: MIT Press, pp. 1–52.

Epstein, S. D. 1999. Un-principled syntax: The derivation of syntactic relations. In S. D. Epstein and N. Hornstein (eds.), *Working minimalism*, Cambridge, MA: MIT Press, pp. 317–45.

Freidin, R. and J.-R. Vergnaud. 2001. Exquisite connections: Some remarks on the evolution of linguistic theory. *Lingua* 111: 639–66.

Nissenbaum, J. W. 2000. *Investigations of covert phrase movement*. Doctoral dissertation, MIT.

Pesetsky, D. 2000. *Phrasal movement and its kin*. Cambridge, MA: MIT Press.

Uriagereka, J. 1999. Multiple spell-out. In S. D. Epstein and N. Hornstein (eds.), *Working minimalism*, Cambridge, MA: MIT Press, pp. 251–82.

2

Eliminating Government

2.1 Case

From "ON THE SUBJECT OF INFINITIVES"
Howard Lasnik and Mamoru Saito

2 Evidence for raising

Since the earliest detailed investigations of sentential complementation within a transformational framework, the dual nature of the immediately postverbal (italicized) NP in examples like (1) has been noted. In some respects, that NP behaves like the subject of the lower predicate, while in other respects, it behaves like the object of the matrix verb.

(1) I believe *John* to have convinced Bill

Rosenbaum (1967), for example, argues persuasively that at least in underlying structure, *John* in (1) must be a subject. He observes the synonymy between infinitival embedding and finite embedding, as in (2).

(2) I believe that John convinced Bill

As Rosenbaum notes, this will be expected if *John* is the subject of the lower clause in (1) as well as in (2). He also points out the contrast between *believe*-type constructions, on the one hand, and clear instances of NP + S complementation, on the other hand, with respect to semantic import of active vs. passive in the complement. (3) is synonymous with (1), but (5) is not synonymous with (4).

(3) I believe Bill to have been convinced by John
(4) I compelled the doctor to examine John
(5) I compelled John to be examined by the doctor

As noted in Rosenbaum (1967) and Bach (1974), the underlying subject status of the NP in question is confirmed by the fact that the existential *there* and idiom chunks associated with the embedded clause can appear in this position. Thus, (6)–(7) contrast with (8)–(9), which are instances of NP + S complementation.

(6)   I believe there to be a man in the garden
(7)   I believe advantage to have been taken of John
(8)   *I forced there to be a man in the garden
(9)   *I forced advantage to have been taken of John

Alongside these arguments for lower subject status, Postal (1974) lists three "traditional arguments" for higher object status, based on passivization, reflexivization, and reciprocal marking. All three of these processes typically establish a relation between an object position and a subject position in the same clause. But they can also establish a relation between the underlying subject of the complement clause and the subject of the matrix under certain limited circumstances including, in particular, the infinitival constructions under discussion. The following examples are from Postal (1974: 40–2):

(10)   a.   Jack believed Joan to be famous
        b.   Joan was believed to be famous by Jack
(11)   a.   *Jack$_i$ believed him$_i$ to be immoral
        b.   Jack$_i$ believed himself$_i$ to be immoral
(12)   They believed each other to be honest

This class of arguments centrally involves the nature of the boundary separating the two linked NP positions. For Postal, any clause boundary would suffice to block the relevant relations, hence the second NP position must have become a clause-mate of the first (via "raising to object"). Chomsky (1973) offered a somewhat different perspective on these phenomena. For Chomsky, the relevant structural property is not **whether** there is a clause boundary separating the two NPs, but rather **what sort** of clause boundary there is. Metaphorically, an infinitival clause boundary is weaker than a finite clause boundary. While the latter is strong enough to block the relations in question, the former is not. Chomsky formulated this relative inaccessibility of material in finite clauses (and of non-subjects of infinitives) in terms of his Tensed Sentence Condition (TSC) and Specified Subject Condition (SSC).

In addition to the much discussed phenomena alluded to above, where boundary strength at least potentially provides the needed distinctions, Postal sketches certain other arguments for raising in which the actual surface structure height of the deep structure subject is implicated. One argument is based on a scope difference between (13) and (14):

(13)   The FBI proved that few students were spies
(14)   The FBI proved few students to be spies

Postal indicates that *few students* can have wide or narrow scope in (13) while it can have only wide scope in (14), and that this distinction is best described in terms of the hierarchical notion "command." The precise semantic difference between (13) and (14) is not crystal clear, but there does seem to be some difference, and it is reasonable to assume that it has something to do with scope. Given this, it is plausible to reason, with Postal, that some sort of transformational reorganization is implicated. As Postal notes, notions of hierarchical clause membership, such as command, are independently known to play a role in describing quantifier scope.

Postal bases another similar argument on "a fundamental pronominalization constraint" due to Langacker (1969), which states that a pronoun cannot both precede and command its antecedent. There are a number of recent formulations of this constraint, including the noncoreference rule of Lasnik (1976) and Binding Condition C of Chomsky (1981). Any of these formulations can distinguish (15) from (16), but only if the embedded subject in (16) has raised into the higher clause.

(15)   Joan believes he$_i$ is a genius even more fervently than Bob$_i$ does
(16)   *Joan believes him$_i$ to be a genius even more fervently than Bob$_i$ does

Once again, hierarchical notions are known to play a role in determining such constraints on pronominal coreference, but if *him* in (16) remains in the lower clause, there cannot be a difference between (15) and (16) with respect to command, c-command, etc. The structural relation between *he* and *Bob* in (15) would be the same as that between *him* and *Bob* in (16) in relevant respects.[1]

The logic of the argument based on (15)–(16) is compelling, but there is a potentially confounding factor in the specific examples Postal presents, namely, the VP ellipsis in the adverbial clause. If the elided VP is restored in (16), arguably we have (17).

(17)   *Joan believes him$_i$ to be a genius even more fervently than Bob$_i$ believes him$_i$ to be a genius

But now notice that in (17), the illicit relation could be that between *Bob* and the second, rather than the first, *him*. And this relation falls into the category of those in (10)–(12) above, where boundary strength rather than height could be the determining factor. In fact, there is reason to believe that this potential complication does not seriously interfere. The noncoreference effects that would be expected if the constraints on pronominal anaphora applied to reconstructed VPs do not materialize in any strong way. For example, (18) is far better than (19), the latter displaying a clear Condition B effect.

(18)   ?Mary believes him$_i$ to be a genius, and Bob$_i$ does too
(19)   *Bob$_i$ believes him$_i$ to be a genius

Similarly, (20) displays little of the Condition C effect of (21).

(20)   ?Mary believes Bob$_i$ to be a genius, and he$_i$ does too
(21)   *He$_i$ believes Bob$_i$ to be a genius

But to control even for the slight residual effect displayed in (18), (15)–(16) can be modified as follows:

(22)   Joan believes he$_i$ is a genius even more fervently than Bob's$_i$ mother does

(23)   ?*Joan believes him$_i$ to be a genius even more fervently than Bob's$_i$ mother does

Postal's contrast still obtains, though in slightly weakened form. (23) does not seem quite as bad as (16). The important comparison is with (24), however, and (24) and (23) are quite close in acceptability.

(24)   ?*Joan believes him$_i$ even more fervently than Bob's$_i$ mother does

Thus, as Postal indicates, the subject of the infinitival complement is patterning with objects in this regard: it seems to be approximately as high in the structure as an object.

    Before exploring possible accounts of this property, we want to present several other paradigms displaying similar behavior. The first of these involves the distribution of reciprocal expressions. One aspect of this distribution constituted one of Postal's traditional arguments, as in (12) above, and was essentially neutral between a raising analysis and one in terms of boundary strength. The relative height of reciprocal and antecedent was not necessarily at issue in such constructions. But there is another aspect of the distribution where relative height is significant. Note that (25) is not significantly worse than (26).

(25)   ?The DA proved [the defendants to be guilty] during each other's trials

(26)   ?The DA accused the defendants during each other's trials

They both are considerably better than (27), the finite counterpart of (25).

(27)   ?*The DA proved [that the defendants were guilty] during each other's trials

Given usual assumptions, the antecedent of a reciprocal must bear a command relation to the reciprocal, c-command, for example. But an embedded subject does not c-command an adverbial in the matrix clause. This indicates that at the point in the derivation relevant to the licensing of reciprocals, or anaphors in general, the structure of (25) has changed in such a way that the position of *the defendants* is comparable to what it is in (26).

    Negative polarity item licensing is also known to display asymmetries characteristic of c-command determined relations. Thus, a negative subject of a simple sentence can license *any* in the object, but not vice versa:

(28)   No one saw anything

(29)   *Anyone saw nothing

Further, a negative object can, to a reasonably acceptable extent, license *any* in an adverbial:

(30)   The DA accused none of the defendants during any of the trials

Now notice that to roughly the same extent, a negative subject of an infinitival can license *any* in an adverbial attached to the higher VP.

(31)   ?The DA proved [none of the defendants to be guilty] during any of the trials

This is in rather sharp contrast to a corresponding finite complement:

(32)   ?*The DA proved [that none of the defendants were guilty] during any of
        the trials

Once again, there is reason to believe that at the relevant level of representation, the subject of the infinitival complement is approximately as high in the structure as an NP complement would be.

"Binominal *each*," a construction presented in Postal (1974) and explored in detail by Safir and Stowell (1988), also involves c-command relations (at least for many speakers). The "antecedent" of *each* must c-command it.

(33)   The students solved three problems each
(34)   *Three students each solved the problems (i.e., on the reading "The prob-
        lems were solved by three students each")

Postal shows that there is what we have been calling a boundary strength effect with this *each*, presenting the following contrast, among others.

(35)   *The students proved that three formulas each were theorems (i.e., on the
        reading "Each of the students proved that three formulas were theorems")
(36)   ?The students proved three formulas each to be theorems

But there is an additional finite/non-finite asymmetry displayed by binominal *each*. Safir and Stowell present the "small clause" in (37); the full infinitival in (38) seems equally good.

(37)   Jones proved the defendants guilty with one accusation each
(38)   Jones proved the defendants to be guilty with one accusation each

(37) and (38) are comparable to (39).

(39)   Jones prosecuted the defendants with one accusation each

However, the finite counterpart of (37) and (38) is degraded:[2]

(40)   ??Jones proved that the defendants were guilty with one accusation each

In this paradigm, it is apparently not (just) boundary strength that is at issue, but, once again, structural height.

3   When does raising take place?

The examples discussed so far indicate that the subject of the embedded infinit-ival has roughly the height of the matrix object at some level of representation. And

the level of representation in question must be where the possibility of pronominal coreference is explained and where anaphors, negative polarity items, and binominal *each* are licensed. According to Postal's (1974) "raising to object" analysis, the
relevant level is S(urface)-structure, since the subject becomes a structural object
by the operation of a syntactic transformation. But there is an alternative possibility that we might consider.

Chomsky (1991) notes that structural Case assignment (or checking) appears to take
place in two distinct basic configurations. Assuming that Agreement (or some related
functional category) is responsible for nominative Case assignment/checking, such Case
assignment can be regarded as an instantiation of Spec–head agreement. Accusative
Case assignment, on the other hand, is standardly viewed as arising from a government relation between a verb and the accusative NP. Chomsky speculates that the
second type of Case assignment might be reducible to the first if, inside of the subject
agreement (Agr_s) projection, there is an object agreement (Agr_o) projection. Then the
structural relation necessary for accusative Case could once again be a Spec–head
relation, this time holding between the Spec and head of Agr_o (with the contribution
of V to the Case assignment process presumably following from the amalgamation
of V with Agr_o). As Chomsky indicates, in a language like English, movement to [Spec,
Agr_o] does not take place between D(eep)-structure and S(urface)-structure. Specs
in English are phrase initial, but the accusative direct object of a verb follows the
verb, hence follows the Agr head that takes the VP as its complement. But this leaves
open the possibility that the movement takes place "later," between S-structure
and LF. Chomsky thus suggests the following phrase structure for sentences:

(41)

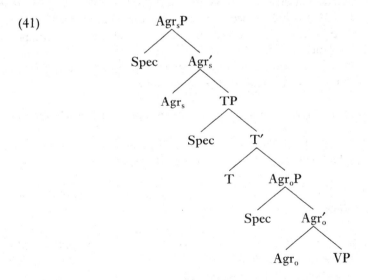

Assuming that in English, NPs with accusative Case must move to [Spec, Agr_o]
in the LF Component for the purpose of Case assignment/checking, this hypothesis,
then, implies that the subject of the embedded infinitival and the matrix object
are in the same position at the level of LF. Thus, a possibility arises that the subject is raised to the matrix not by S-structure but by LF.

In this section, we will explore the question of whether the raising that we have already seen evidence for takes place prior to S-structure, as Postal (1974) proposes, or after S-structure, along the lines of Chomsky's conjecture. We will find some reason to believe that the raising operation argued for in the preceding section is not LF movement to [Spec, Agr_o], but rather is an independent S-structure operation.

[. . .]

Uriagereka (1988) suggests one further test to determine the level at which anaphors must be licensed, based on Chomsky's (1986) proposal that at LF, expletives are replaced by the arguments with which they are associated. For example, S-structure (42) becomes LF (43).

(42)   There arrived a man
(43)   A man arrived t

Based on the acceptability of (44), Uriagereka proposes that anaphors need not be licensed at S-structure, reasoning that the required c-command relation between *two knights* and *each other* holds at LF (45) but not at S-structure (44).[3]

(44)   There arrived two knights on each other's horses
(45)   Two knights arrived t on each other's horses

However, this interesting argument is not entirely conclusive, since we have seen repeatedly that direct objects do, in fact, seem to c-command certain adjuncts. We defer to a later section discussion of how this could be possible, but given that it is, the anaphor in (44) could be licensed at S-structure. However, Uriagereka's test can be applied in less equivocal fashion to our central concern – the properties of raising constructions. As seen earlier, the subject of an infinitival can serve as the antecedent of a reciprocal within an adjunct in the higher clause. (46) is an example, similar to those above, of this phenomenon.

(46)   The DA proved [two men to have been at the scene] during each other's trials

However, (47), which should be identical to (46) at LF in relevant respects, under the expletive replacement hypothesis, is severely degraded.

(47)   *The DA proved [there to have been two men at the scene] during each other's trials

S-structure, rather than LF, is the level at which (46) can be appropriately distinguished from (47) with respect to anaphor licensing. Thus, this contrast implies that anaphors must be licensed at S-structure.

There is also some (slight) evidence that the licensing of negative polarity items is based on S-structure, rather than LF, configurations. May (1977) discusses the ambiguity of sentences involving subject raising to subject position, such as (48).

(48)   Some politician is likely to address John's constituency

He points out that the quantifier in subject position can have either wide or narrow scope with respect to the predicate *likely*. On the narrow reading, (48) is roughly synonymous with (49).

(49)   It is likely that some politician will address John's constituency

May proposes that this reading of (48) is derived via the LF lowering of the quantifier to the embedded clause. Next, notice that while a negative raising predicate in a configuration like that in (49) can license *any*, as in (50), *any* is nonetheless impossible as the surface subject of the negative predicate, as shown in (51).

(50)   It is unlikely that anyone will address the rally
(51)   *Anyone is unlikely to address the rally

(50) is unsurprising: the negative predicate c-commands *anyone*. (51) is also unsurprising based on its S-structure configuration: *unlikely* does not c-command *anyone*. However, if quantifier lowering is possible, the LF of (51) should be like (50) in relevant respects. Thus, this is potentially a strong argument that such licensing must take place at S-structure, and consequently, that the licensing negative in examples like (31) above must have already raised by S-structure.

The one weakness in the argument above is that, for reasons that are unclear, quantifier lowering across a negative predicate is degraded. Thus, (52) does not readily permit the narrow scope interpretation.

(52)   Someone is unlikely to address the rally

But if such lowering is barred, then even at LF *anyone* in (51) will not be in a licit configuration. The relevant factual question, then, is whether (51) is even worse than the narrow scope reading of (52). While the judgment is not as clear as one might hope, (51) does, in fact, seem to be worse. And just to the extent that it is worse, we have evidence that negative polarity items must be licensed at S-structure, and, hence, that raising must take place by S-structure.

4   Postal's B-verbs versus W-verbs

[. . .]
There are two further theoretical questions that must be addressed. The first specifically involves the Condition C effect in (17) and (23) above. Since in this instance, the relevant phenomenon is a filtering effect, rather than a licensing effect as with polarity *any*, binominal *each*, reciprocals, it is crucial that the raising process be obligatory. If it were optional, it could simply refrain from applying, and there then should be no detectable noncoreference phenomenon. This is significant since we assume, following Chomsky and Lasnik (1977), that obligatoriness is not simply a stipulated property of transformational operations, but rather, must follow from deeper principles. Note that under Chomsky's approach, while

the level of application was argued to be wrong, obligatoriness is straightforward. The Case of an accusative NP would not be appropriately licensed if it did not raise to [Spec, Agr$_o$]. It is less clear under the classic transformational account. Interestingly, Postal and Pullum (1988) suggest an answer that is Case-based, much like the one we just sketched, conjecturing that raising is necessary in order for the accusative NP to be close enough to the verb that assigns Case to it:

> the transclausal boundary Case-marking alternatives to Raising-to–Object analyses violate what would otherwise be a possible restrictive constraint on Case marking. (1988: 666)

The final theoretical question was alluded to earlier. We noted that with respect to all of the paradigms considered, the subject of the infinitive was behaving like an object of the higher verb. We further observed that it was unclear why even true objects were behaving the way they were, since all of the paradigms involved c-command phenomena, and objects do not obviously c-command adjuncts. Here, again, an approach in terms of [Spec, Agr$_o$] could (apart from the question of level of applicability) give exactly the right structural relations. The [Spec, Agr$_o$] c-commands everything in, or adjoined to, VP.

Notes

1   Aoun and Sportiche (1982/3) actually propose a boundary strength account of a phenomenon like (16). Taking c-command to be defined in terms of maximal projections, and S to be non-maximal, they indicate that the ECM subject would c-command out of the embedded clause. However, if S is a maximal projection (IP, or AgrP), that line of reasoning fails.

2   We are, frankly, puzzled by the fact that these finite complements are as good as they are. As far as we know, under no analysis do subjects of finite clauses undergo raising, so one would expect all such examples to be completely impossible.

3   Actually, according to the specific analysis of expletive–argument pairs in Chomsky (1986), (44) would straightforwardly satisfy the binding requirement of the anaphor at S-structure, since Chomsky claimed that throughout the derivation expletives are coindexed with their associated arguments. But see Lasnik (1992) for arguments against this position.

References

Aoun, J. and D. Sportiche. 1982/3. On the formal theory of government. *The Linguistic Review* 2: 211–36.

Bach, E. W. 1974. *Syntactic theory.* New York: Holt, Rinehart, and Winston.

Chomsky, N. 1973. Conditions on transformations. In S. Anderson and P. Kiparsky (eds.), *A Festschrift for Morris Halle,* New York: Holt, Rinehart, and Winston, pp. 232–86.

Chomsky, N. 1981. *Lectures on government and binding.* Dordrecht: Foris.

Chomsky, N. 1986. *Knowledge of language: Its nature, origin, and use.* New York: Praeger.

Chomsky, N. 1991. Some notes on economy of derivation and representation. In R. Freidin (ed.), *Principles and parameters in comparative grammar,* Cambridge, MA: MIT Press, pp. 417–54. [Reprinted in Chomsky (1995), *The Minimalist Program,* Cambridge, MA: MIT Press, pp. 128–66.]

Chomsky, N. and H. Lasnik. 1977. Filters and control. *Linguistic Inquiry* 8: 425–504.

Langacker, R. W. 1969. On pronominalization and the chain of command. In D. A. Reibel and S. A. Shane (eds.), *Modern studies in English, Englewood Cliffs,* N. J. Prentice-Hall, pp. 160–86.

Lasnik, H. 1976. Remarks on coreference. *Linguistic Analysis* 2: 1–22.

Lasnik, H. 1992. Two notes on control and binding. In K. R. Larson, S. Iatridou, U. Lahiri and J. Higginbotham (eds.), *Control and grammar*, Dordrecht: Kluwer, pp. 235–52.

May, R. 1977. *The grammar of quantification*. Doctoral dissertation, MIT.

Postal, P. M. 1974. *On raising*. Cambridge, MA: MIT Press.

Postal, P. M. and G. K. Pullum. 1988. Expletive noun phrases in subcategorized positions. *Linguistic Inquiry* 19: 635–70.

Rosenbaum, P. S. 1967. *The grammar of English predicate complement constructions*. Cambridge, MA: MIT Press.

Safir, K. and T. Stowell. 1988. Binominal *each*. In J. Blevins and J. Carter (eds.), *Proceedings of the 18th Annual Meeting of the North East Linguistic Society*, Amherst, MA: GLSA, pp. 426–50.

Uriagereka, J. 1988. *On government*. Doctoral dissertation, University of Connecticut, Storrs.

From "A MINIMALIST PROGRAM FOR LINGUISTIC THEORY"
Noam Chomsky

Take Case theory. It is standardly assumed that the Spec–head relation enters into structural Case for the subject position, while the object position is assigned Case under government by V, including constructions in which the object Case-marked by a verb is not its complement (exceptional Case marking).[1] The narrower approach we are considering requires that all these modes of structural Case assignment be recast in unified X-bar-theoretic terms, presumably under the Spec–head relation. [. . .] [A]n elaboration of Pollock's (1989) theory of inflection provides a natural mechanism, where we take the basic structure of the clause to be (1).

(1)

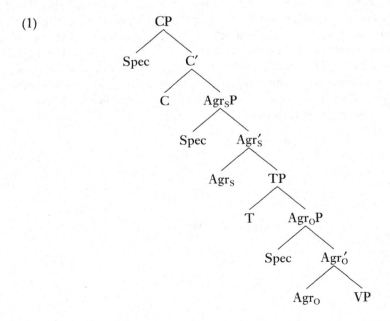

Omitted here are a possible specifier of TP ([Spec, TP]) and a phrase headed by the functional element *Neg(ation)*, or perhaps more broadly, a category that includes an affirmation marker and others as well (Pollock 1989; Laka 1990). *Agr$_S$*

and *Agr$_O$* are informal mnemonics to distinguish the two functional roles of Agr. Agr is a collection of φ-features (gender, number, person); these are common to the systems of subject and object agreement, though Agr$_S$ and Agr$_O$ may of course be different selections, just as two verbs or NPs in (1) may differ.[2]

We now regard both agreement and structural Case as manifestations of the Spec–head relation (NP, Agr). But Case properties depend on characteristics of T and the V head of VP. We therefore assume that T raises to Agr$_S$, forming (2a), and V raises to Agr$_O$, forming (2b); the complex includes the φ-features of Agr and the Case feature provided by T, V.[3]

(2)   a.   [$_{Agr}$ T Agr]
      b.   [$_{Agr}$ V Agr]

The basic assumption is that there is a symmetry between the subject and the object inflectional systems. In both positions the relation of NP to V is mediated by Agr, a collection of φ-features; in both positions agreement is determined by the φ-features of the Agr head of the Agr complex, and Case by an element that adjoins to Agr (T or V). An NP in the Spec–head relation to this Agr complex bears the associated Case and agreement features. The Spec–head and head–head relations are therefore the core configurations for inflectional morphology.

Exceptional Case marking by V is now interpreted as raising of NP to the Spec of the AgrP dominating V. It is raising to [Spec, Agr$_O$], the analogue of familiar raising to [Spec, Agr$_S$]. If the VP-internal subject hypothesis is correct (as I henceforth assume), the question arises why the object (direct, or in the complement) raises to [Spec, Agr$_O$] and the subject to [Spec, Agr$_S$], yielding unexpected crossing rather than the usual nested paths. We will return to this phenomenon below, finding that it follows on plausible assumptions of some generality, and in this sense appears to be a fairly "deep" property of language. If parameters are morphologically restricted in the manner sketched earlier, there should be no language variation in this regard.

The same hypothesis extends naturally to predicate adjectives, with the underlying structure shown in (3) (*Agr$_A$* again a mnemonic for a collection of φ-features, in this case associated with an adjective).

(3)

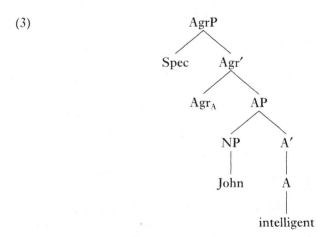

Raising of NP to Spec and A to Agr_A creates the structure for NP–adjective agreement internal to the predicate phrase. The resulting structure is a plausible candidate for the small clause complement of *consider*, *be*, and so on. In the former construction (complement of *consider*), NP raises further to [Spec, Agr_O] at LF to receive accusative Case; in the latter (complement of *be*), NP raises overtly to receive nominative Case and verb agreement, yielding the overt form *John is intelligent* with *John* entering into three relations: (1) a Case relation with [T Agr_S] (hence ultimately the verbal complex [[T Agr_S] V]), (2) an agreement relation with Agr_S (hence the verbal complex), and (3) an agreement relation with Agr of structure (3) (hence the adjectival complex). In both constructions, the NP subject is outside of a full AP in the small clause construction, as required, and the structure is of a type that appears regularly.[4]

An NP, then, may enter into two kinds of structural relations with a predicate (verb, adjective): agreement, involving features shared by NP and predicate; or Case, manifested on the NP alone. Subject of verb or adjective, and object of verb, enter into these relations (but not object of adjective if that is an instance of inherent, not structural, Case). Both relations involve Agr: Agr alone, for agreement relations; the element T or V alone (raising to Agr), for Case relations.

The structure of CP in (1) is largely forced by other properties of UG, assuming the minimalist approach with Agr abstracted as a common property of adjectival agreement and the subject–object inflectional systems, a reasonable assumption, given that agreement appears without Case (as in NP–AP agreement) and Case appears without agreement (as in transitive expletives, with the expletive presumably in the [Spec, Agr_S] position and the subject in [Spec, T], receiving Case; see note 3). Any appropriate version of the Case Filter will require two occurrences of Agr if two NPs in VP require structural Case; conditions on Move α require the arrangement given in (1) if structural Case is construed as outlined. Suppose that VP contains only one NP. Then one of the two Agr elements will be "active" (the other being inert or perhaps missing). Which one? Two options are possible: Agr_S or Agr_O. If the choice is Agr_S, then the single NP will have the properties of the subject of a transitive clause; if the choice is Agr_O, then it will have the properties of the object of a transitive clause (nominative-accusative and ergative-absolutive languages, respectively). These are the only two possibilities, mixtures apart. The distinction between the two language types reduces to a trivial question of morphology, as we expect.

Note that from this point of view, the terms *nominative*, *absolutive*, and so on, have no substantive meaning apart from what is determined by the choice of "active" versus "inert" Agr; there is no real question as to how these terms correspond across language types.

The "active" element (Agr_S in nominative-accusative languages and Agr_O in ergative-absolutive languages) typically assigns a less-marked Case to its Spec, which is also higher on the extractability hierarchy, among other properties. It is natural to expect less-marked Case to be compensated (again, as a tendency) by more-marked agreement (richer overt agreement with nominative and absolutive than with accusative and ergative). The C-Command Condition on anaphora leads us to expect nominative and ergative binding in transitive constructions.[5]

Similar considerations apply to licensing of *pro*. Assuming Rizzi's theory (1982, 1986), *pro* is licensed in a Spec–head relation to "strong" Agr_S, or when governed by certain verbs V^*. To recast these proposals in a unitary X-bar-theoretic form: *pro* is licensed only in the Spec–head relation to $[_{Agr} \alpha \, Agr]$, where α is [+tense] or V, Agr strong or $V = V^*$. Licensing of *pro* thus falls under Case theory in a broad sense. Similar considerations extend rather naturally to PRO.[6]

Suppose that other properties of head government also have a natural expression in terms of the more fundamental notions of X-bar theory. Suppose further that antecedent government is a property of chains, expressible in terms of c-command and barriers. Then the concept of government would be dispensable, with principles of language restricted to something closer to conceptual necessity: local X-bar-theoretic relations to the head of a projection and the chain link relation.

Notes

1 In Chomsky (1981) and other work, structural Case is unified under government, understood as m-command to include the Spec–head relation (a move that was not without problems); in the framework considered here, m-command plays no role.

2 I will use *NP* informally to refer to either NP or DP, where the distinction is playing no role. *IP* and *I* will be used for the complement of C and its head where details are irrelevant.

3 I overlook here the possibility of NP-raising to [Spec, T] for Case assignment, then to [Spec, Agr_S] for agreement. This may well be a real option. For development of this possibility, see Bures (1992), Bobaljik and Carnie (1992), Jonas (1992), and Chomsky (1995: sections 4.9 and 4.10).

4 Raising of A to Agr_A may be overt or in the LF component. If the latter, it may be the trace of the raised NP that is marked for agreement, with further raising driven by the morphological requirement of Case marking (the Case Filter); I put aside specifics of implementation. The same considerations extend to an analysis of participial agreement along the lines of Kayne (1989); see Chomsky (1995: ch. 2), Branigan (1992).

5 For development of an approach along such lines, see Bobaljik (1992a, 1992b). For a different analysis sharing some assumptions about the Spec–head role, see Murasugi (1991, 1992). This approach to the two language types adapts the earliest proposal about these matters within generative grammar (De Rijk 1972) to a system with inflection separated from verb. See Levin and Massam (1985) for a similar conception.

6 See Chomsky (1995: ch. 1).

References

Bobaljik, J. 1992a. Ergativity, economy, and the Extended Projection Principle, Ms., MIT.

Bobaljik, J. 1992b. Nominally absolutive is not absolutely nominal. In J. Mead (ed.), Proceedings of the 11th West Coast Conference on Formal Linguistics, Stanford: CSLI, pp. 44–60.

Bobaljik, J. D. and A. Carnie. 1992. A Minimalist approach to some problems of Irish word order. In B. Borsley and I. Roberts (eds.), *The syntax of the Celtic languages*, Cambridge: Cambridge University Press, pp. 223–40.

Branigan, P. 1992. *Subjects and complementizers*. Doctoral dissertation, MIT.

Bures, T. 1992. Re-cycling expletive (and other) sentences. Ms., MIT.

Chomsky, N. 1981. *Lectures on government and binding*. Dordrecht: Foris.

Chomsky, N. 1995. *The Minimalist Program*. Cambridge, MA: MIT Press.

De Rijk, R. 1972. *Studies in Basque syntax*. Doctoral dissertation, MIT.

Jonas, D. 1992. Transitive expletive constructions in Icelandic and Middle English. Ms., Harvard University.

Kayne, R. S. 1989. Facets of past participle agreement. In P. Benincà (ed.), *Dialect variation and the theory of grammar*, Dordrecht: Foris, pp. 85–103.

Levin, J. and D. Massam. 1985. Surface ergativity: Case/theta relations reexamined. In S. Berman, J.-W. Choe and J. McDonough (eds.), *Proceedings of the 15th Annual Meeting of the North East Linguistic Society*, Amherst, MA: GLSA, pp. 286–301.

Murasugi, K. G. 1991. The role of transitivity in ergative and accusative languages: The case of Inuktitut and Japanese. Paper presented at the Association of Canadian Universities for Northern Studies.

Murasugi, K. G. 1992. *Crossing and nested paths: NP movement in accusative and ergative languages*. Doctoral dissertation, MIT.

Pollock, J.-Y. 1989. Verb movement, universal grammar, and the structure of IP. *Linguistic Inquiry* 20: 365–424.

Rizzi, L. 1982. *Issues in Italian syntax*. Dordrecht: Reidel.

Rizzi, L. 1986. Null objects in Italian and the theory of *pro*. *Linguistic Inquiry* 17: 501–57.

2.1.1   Recent Developments

From "MINIMALIST INQUIRIES: THE FRAMEWORK"
Noam Chomsky

Suppose that the derivation has constructed the SO [syntactic object] (1), having merged T with the copula-headed phrase.

(1)   T be elected an unpopular candidate

The new element T has uninterpretable features of two types: its ϕ-set and its selectional feature, the Extended Projection Principle (EPP). Like other selectional features, EPP seeks an XP to merge with the category it heads. The ϕ-set we can think of as a *probe* that seeks a *goal*, namely, "matching" features that establish agreement, The relation of the probe of T to its goal is the *T-associate* relation.

For the ϕ-set of T in (1), there is only one choice of matching features: the ϕ-set of *candidate*. Locating this goal, the probe erases under matching. Taking structural Case to be a reflex of an uninterpretable ϕ-set,[1] it too erases under matching with the probe. The erasure of uninterpretable features of probe and goal is the operation we called *Agree*. But the EPP-feature of T must also be satisfied – in this case by "pied-piping" of a phrase P(G) determined by the goal of T's probe, which merges with (1), becoming [Spec, T]. The combination of selection of P(G), Merge of P(G), and feature deletion under matching (Agree) is the composite operation Move, which dislocates *an unpopular candidate*, eliminating all uninterpretable features.

Matching is a relation that holds of a probe P and a goal G. Not every matching pair induces Agree. To do so, G must (at least) be in the *domain* D(P) of P and satisfy locality conditions. The simplest assumptions for the probe-goal system are shown in (2).

(2)   a.   Matching is feature identity.
      b.   D(P) is the sister of P.
      c.   Locality reduces to "closest c-command."

Thus, D(P) is the c-command domain of P, and a matching feature G is *closest to* P if there is no G′ in D(P) matching P such that G is in D(G′).

In the absence of evidence to the contrary, we adopt (2), with a qualification taken over from earlier work.[2]

(3)   Terms of the same minimal domain are "equidistant" to probes.

The minimal domain of a head H is the set of terms immediately contained in projections of H.

With matching restricted to identity, Case and lexical category cannot enter into Agree or Move, since the probes do not manifest these features. And OS [Object Shift] must be an implementation of (here invisible) object agreement, with ancillary Case checking.

If uninterpretable features serve to implement operations, we expect that it is structural Case that enables the closest goal G to select P(G) to satisfy the EPP by Merge. Thus, if structural Case has already been checked (deleted), the phrase P(G) is "frozen in place," unable to move further to satisfy the EPP in a higher position. More generally, uninterpretable features render the goal *active*, able to implement an operation: to select a phrase for Merge (pied-piping) or to delete the probe. The operations Agree and Move require a goal that is both local and active.[3]

We therefore have the possibility of *defective intervention constraints* in a structure (4), where > is c-command, β and γ match the probe α, but β is inactive so that the effects of matching are blocked.

(4)   α > β > γ

We will return to some illustrations.[4]

In [Chomsky 1995b] Agree is analyzed in terms of feature movement (Attract) and a concept of matching that is left unclear. Here we take matching to be identity and dispense with Attract, with complications it induces about extended MLIs [modified lexical items], feature chains, and other matters. Checking reduces to deletion under matching with an active local goal and ancillary deletion of the uninterpretable feature that rendered the goal active. I will use the terms *checking* and *attract* only for convenience.

Suppose that the EPP-feature of T could be satisfied more simply than by the full operation Move. That is the case in (5).

(5)   there [$_\alpha$ T-was elected an unpopular candidate]

Here the lexical array includes the expletive *there*. At stage α of the derivation (= (1)), the independent operations Agree and pure Merge suffice: Agree deletes the φ-set of T and the structural Case of *candidate*, and Merge (of *there*) satisfies the EPP-feature of T. The more complex operation Move is preempted; dislocation does not take place, though we have long-distance agreement of T and its goal (its associate).[5]

Manifestation of structural Case depends on interpretable features of the probe: finite T (nominative), v (accusative), control T (null), on our earlier assumptions. We may therefore regard structural Case as a single undifferentiated feature. The same would be expected for the uninterpretable φ-set of the probe. Its manifestation depends on interpretable features (namely, φ-features) of the goal, so that it too can be taken to be undifferentiated with respect to the value of the individual features of the φ-set ([+/−plural], etc.). For both probe and goal, the form of the uninterpretable features is determined by Agree. To rephrase in traditional terms, verbs agree with nouns, not conversely, and Case is assigned.

We therefore understand "feature identity" in (2a) to be identity of the choice of feature, not of value. More important, defective intervention effects are induced whether or not β and γ of (4) are identical in φ-feature value (singular blocks plural agreement, etc.). This lends theory-internal support to the earlier observation that φ-features are interpretable only for N; their value is specified only in this case. Notice also that only the most underspecified element, PRO, can have null Case, so raising of α ≠ PRO to [Spec, T] causes the derivation to crash when T is a control infinitival.

We take deletion to be a "one fell swoop" operation, dealing with the φ-set as a unit. Its features cannot selectively delete: either all delete, or none. The φ-features of T do not agree with different NPs, for example. In the same spirit, we assume that only a probe with a full complement of φ-features is capable of deleting the feature that activates the matched goal. Suppose that the probe for participial (like adjectival) α is a φ-set lacking the feature [person] and that G is the closest matching goal in its search space: P(G) = DP may be attracted to [Spec, α], deleting the probe of α (participial agreement), but the operation will not delete structural Case in DP, which can move on to [Spec, T], deleting the probe of T and the Case of DP (subject agreement). v and nondefective T, with a full complement of φ-features, delete the uninterpretable feature that activates the matched goal (raised or not).[6]

How would noncontrol infinitivals (T_{def}) and weak expletives Expl of the *there-type* fit into this picture? The former category falls into place if T always has at least a minimal feature complement, perhaps only [person] for T_{def}. If so, Move of α to [Spec, T_{def}] will delete the φ-set of T (= uninterpretable [person]) but not the structural Case feature of α, so that α can undergo further movement and agreement. The phase head v/C have no counterpart to T_{def} with a reduced φ-set and therefore do not provide an "escape hatch" for successive-cyclic A-movement.

Weak Expl shares the basic movement/attraction properties of nominals. That is expected if Expl has an uninterpretable feature F that activates it until erased and a φ-set G that matches a probe in T. But G is uninterpretable for Expl, so a distinct F is unnecessary, obviating the need for structural Case in Expl. The composition of G is determined by two conditions: (a) Expl can raise to [Spec, T_{def}]; (b) Expl cannot delete the probe of nondefective T. Condition (a) requires that G contain a feature to match the probe of T_{def} ([person], if what precedes is correct).

From (b) it follows that G must be less than a full φ-set, hence optimally just [person]. That (b) holds is shown by long-distance agreement structures such as (6b–d), (6b) surfacing commonly as (6c), or in English more naturally as (6d), as noted.

(6) a. they declared [three men guilty]
     b. there were declared [three men guilty]
     c. there were declared guilty three men
     d. there were three men declared guilty

If the matching feature of the probe were deleted by the operation, it would not be available for associate matching and the nominative Case of the associate would remain unchecked because of the lack of a full complement of features in T (compare participial agreement). The problem does not arise if (b) holds and uninterpretable features delete in an "all or none" fashion, not selectively. In (6b–d) the full complement of φ-features of T deletes the uninterpretable feature G of *there*, barring further raising. When Expl raises to [Spec, T_{def}], the probe (a single feature) deletes under matching as before, but G does not, because deletion requires matching with a full complement of φ-features of the probe. Therefore, successive-cyclic raising through [Spec, T_{def}] is possible.[7]

Reinterpretation of Attract in terms of Agree eliminates the need to introduce "checking domains." That is a step forward. The notion is complex, and furthermore unnatural in minimalist terms; feature checking should involve features, nothing more, and there is no simpler relation than identity. More important, the notion is irrelevant for the core cases: elements merge in checking domains for reasons independent of feature checking; and feature checking takes place without dislocation to a checking domain.

[. . .]

With this shift of perspective, structural Case is demoted in significance. The Case Filter still functions indirectly in the manner of Vergnaud's original proposal, to determine the distribution of noun phrases. But what matters primarily are the probes, including φ-features of T, v. That reverses much of the recent history of inquiry into these topics and also brings out more clearly the question of why Case exists at all. The question arises still more sharply if matching is just identity, so that Case can never be attracted; operations are not induced by Case-checking requirements. Recall that lexical category also cannot be attracted and does not induce operations, raising the same questions.[8] For Case, a plausible answer is the one already suggested: uninterpretable features activate the goal of a probe, allowing it to implement some operation (Agree or Move).[9] It follows that after structural Case of DP is deleted, the phrase cannot move further to an A position and its φ-set cannot induce deletion (though it is still "visible" to a probe, allowing defective intervention effects as in (4)). Suppose quirky Case is (θ-related) inherent Case with an additional structural Case feature, as often suggested in one or another form. Then it too is immobile once it reaches a Case-checking position.[10] If the φ-features of T that check the structural Case of raised quirky Case themselves delete, we have default T; if they remain, we have remote agreement with some lower accessible nominative.

[. . .]

The head of an A-chain can undergo Ā-movement, of course, with different features accessed. Take *wh*-movement. This would be point by point analogous to A-movement if the *wh*-phrase has an uninterpretable feature [wh] and an interpretable feature [Q], which matches the uninterpretable probe [Q] of a complementizer in the final stage; successive cyclicity could then function in the manner discussed.[11] The *wh*-phrase is active until [wh] is checked and deleted. The *Wh*-Island Constraint is then a defective intervention effect of the type (4): [Q] of the already checked *wh*-phrase (β in (4)) bars attraction of lower [Q], but cannot move or check the uninterpretable feature of the probe. A possible analysis of *wh*-in-situ constructions is that [wh] pied-pipes only the head (overtly or covertly).[12]

The reasoning extends to such constructions as (7a–d) ((7b) based on OS).

(7)   a.   *[John to seem [t^I is intelligent]] (would be surprising)

      b.   *(we hoped) [PRO to be decided [t^I to be killed at dawn]]

      c.   *[$_{DO}$ this book] seem [t_{DO} to read [$t_{DO}{}^I$ [never [[$_{Subj}$ any students] t_{read}]]]]

      d.   *there seem [$_\alpha$[$_{Subj}$ several people]^I are [$_{Pred}$ friends of yours]]

The EPP is satisfied throughout, and if local matching sufficed for agreement, the expressions should converge with uninterpretable features deleted. Appeal to such principles as "maximal checking" would not make the proper distinctions locally (e.g., barring (7c) in favor of subject raising). But in all cases the position superscripted *I* is inactive, hence unable to raise (7a–c) or to delete the features of a matched probe (7d). Case (7d) illustrates a defective intervention effect of type (4): Subj is visible (barring Pred as goal) but inactive, unable to establish agreement with matrix T.[13] The same property holds in (8).

(8)   a.   *there were decided [$_\alpha$ PRO to stay with friends]

      b.   *XP T-seem that [$_\alpha$ it was told friends CP]

PRO and *it* are inactive, their structural Case feature having been checked and deleted in α. But their φ-features remain visible and block association of matrix T to *friends*, both of which therefore retain uninterpretable features. Case (8b) is therefore barred with pure Merge of Expl, or raising of *it* or *friends* ("superraising").[14]

[. . .]

Further insight into these matters should derive from raising constructions with quirky Case moving to matrix subject, as in (9).[15]

(9)   a.   me(dat) thought(pl) [t_{me} [they(pl,nom) be industrious]]

      b.   *me(dat) seem(pl) [t_{me} [John(dat) to like horses(pl,nom)]]

      c.   *John seems(sg) me(dat) [t_{John} to like horses]

The matrix verb agrees with the embedded nominative in (9a), but not in (9b), which requires default inflection because of the defective intervention effect: the φ-features of *John* block the T-associate relation between T-*seem* and nominative *horses.* In (9a) as well a phrase with φ-features intervenes between matrix T and nominative, namely, the trace of the quirky dative *me*. But the latter is not the head of an A-chain, unlike in (9b) (also (7d) and (8)). Case (9c) is blocked by locality; quirky dative, with structural Case, is accessible. The conclusions are as before, but sharpened: it is only the head of the A-chain that blocks matching under the locality condition (2c). A-movement traces are "invisible" to the probe–associate relation; or from another perspective, the A-chain itself (regarded as a set of occurrences of α) constitutes the barrier.

Notes

1   If a reflex of an interpretable φ-set, it would be erased in situ by the φ-set of *candidate* itself.

2   See [Chomsky 1995b], Ura (1996). The condition stated there refers only to Specs of the same head. Whether the generalization (3) is appropriate depends on answers to questions about the structure of more complex constructions (double object verbs, etc.). These and other questions, including parameterization, are put aside here. See Bošković (1997) and McGinnis (1998), among others. The notion "feature occurrence" used implicitly here for expository convenience can be eliminated by restatement in terms of the heads to which features belong.

3   Among the problems that arise is the status of scrambling. The logic would suggest that for at least some cases, a scrambling feature induces pied-piping even after Case assignment, the pied-piped element being "attracted" by a higher probe, whereas other cases fall into a category distinct from feature-driven movement. For exploration of alternatives in a comparative study, see Sauerland (1998).

4   For a similar configuration in phonology, with > = linear order, see the discussion in Halle (1995) of coronal assimilation in Sanskrit, barred by an intervening (nonassimilating) coronal.

5   On the assumptions made in [Chomsky 1995b] sec. 4.10, multiple-subject (including transitive expletive) options are parameterized in terms of deletion of EPP-features. See particularly Ura (1996), and for skepticism about the option, Zwart (1997). Agreement in the sense discussed here is to be distinguished from concord, with different properties.

6   The analysis of structural Case is along the lines proposed by George and Kornfilt (1981). As they observe, structural Case linked to φ-features may be dissociated from finiteness. Matters become more complex when we consider ergative/absolutive and mixed systems, and languages in which φ-features without finiteness do not suffice for nominative Case assignment (see Iatridou 1993).

7   For a different approach, on the assumption that *there* has structural Case, see Lasnik (1995). For a different perspective on a wide range of related issues, see Moro (1997).

8   Perhaps substantive lexical categories do not exist, only bare roots. Configurational and morphological properties, along with interpretable noncategorial features of the root, would then determine relevant structural properties, as in Semitic. The possibility is suggested by work since the 1960s on derivational versus transformationally induced morphology. See Marantz (1997) for pertinent discussion.

9   A different motivation, based on the need to overcome ambiguity in the composite verbal element at LF, is developed by Uriagereka (1996). One can also think of various functional arguments: the familiar trade-off between order rigidity and richness of inflection, facilitation of search for attracted elements, and so on.

10   Pure inherent Case I take to be a distinct phenomenon, "invisible" to matching, as if inherent Case inactivates the φ-set. [. . .] For more on the topic, [see] McGinnis (1998) and sources cited there.

11   To complete the analogy, C (and v with its ϕ-set deleted) may have a nonspecific P-feature analogous to [person] for T_{def}, perhaps contingent on assignment of the EPP-feature to a phase.

12   Following ideas of Watanabe (1992) and Hagstrom(1998). This is not to be confused with the distinction between pied-piping of a full XP and pied-piping of a minimal operator (e.g., interrogatives/raising relatives vs. comparatives/complex adjectivals/nonraising relatives), a choice fixed by context (with various questions about relatives; see Sauerland 1998). The *wh*-island analysis extends to other constructions if the feature that drives movement shares properties with [wh] (assuming here a hierarchy of features); see Hagstrom (1998) for supporting evidence. Multiple overt *wh*-movement as in some Slavic languages might be analogous to multiple head options for A-movement along with a principle to overcome the Subjacency effect. See Richards (1997), adapting ideas in Brody (1995), and for a general critical review, Bošković (1998). As is well known, pied-piping in Ā-movement differs from the A-chain analogue, with variation among languages and constructions that is poorly understood.

13   The perennial troublemaker (i) falls into place if the (undeleted) [person] feature of embedded *there* bars association of matrix T to *three men*.

(i)   *there seem there to be three men in the room

Groat (1997) points out further complications. Thus, whatever its status, (ii) is more acceptable.

(ii)   there look as though there are three men (vs. *[a man]) in the room

That suggests that the [person] barrier may be overridden in some manner.

14   The [Chomsky 1995b] analysis of superraising assumed that *it* raises to matrix T by locality and the derivation crashes because *friends* cannot be Case-checked. But covert attraction of the ϕ-features of *friends* by matrix T should still be possible, with convergence (Eduardo Raposo, personal communication). See Raposo and Uriagereka (1996) for a different approach.

15   Translations of Icelandic examples: (9a), with a default variant, from Sigurðsson (1996); (9b,c) from Boeckx (2000); these and other examples, and discussion, in Schütze (1997).

References

Boeckx, C. 2000. Quirky agreement. *Studia Linguistica* 54: 354–80,

Bošković, Ž. 1997. *The syntax of nonfinite complementation: An economy approach.* Cambridge, MA: MIT Press.

Bošković, Ž. 1998. Wh-phrases and wh-movement in Slavic. Ms., Presented at the Comparative Slavic Morphosyntax Workshop, Bloomington, Indiana.

Brody, M. 1995. *Lexico-logical form: A radically minimalist theory.* Cambridge, MA: MIT Press.

Chomsky, N. 1995a. Categories and transformations. In Chomsky (1995b), pp. 219–394.

Chomsky, N. 1995b. The Minimalist Program. Cambridge, MA: MIT Press.

Frampton, J. and S. Gutmann. 1999. Cyclic computation: A computationally efficient minimalist syntax. *Syntax* 2: 1–27.

George, L. and J. Kornfilt. 1981. Finiteness and boundedness in Turkish. In F. Heny (ed.), *Binding and filtering*, Cambridge, MA: MIT Press, pp. 105–27.

Groat, E. 1997. *A derivational program for linguistic theory.* Doctoral dissertation, Harvard University.

Hagstrom, P. 1998. *Decomposing questions*. Doctoral dissertation, MIT.

Halle, M. 1995. Feature geometry and feature spreading. *Linguistic Inquiry* 26: 1–46.

Iatridou, S. 1993. On nominative case assignment and few related things. In C. Phillips (ed.), *Papers on Case and agreement II. MIT Working Papers in Linguistics 19*, Cambridge, MA: MITWPL, pp. 175–96.

Lasnik, H. 1995. Case and expletives revisited: On Greed and other human failings. *Linguistic Inquiry* 26: 615–33.

McGinnis, M. 1998. *Locality in A-movement*. Doctoral dissertation, MIT.

Marantz, A. 1997. No escape from syntax: Don't try morphological analysis in the privacy of your own lexicon. In A. Dimitriadis, L. Siegel, C. Surek-Clark and A. Williams (eds.), *University of Pennsylvania Working Papers in Linguistics 4.2*, Philadelphia: Penn Linguistics Club, University of Pennsylvania, pp. 201–25.

Moro, A. 1997. *The raising of predicates*. Cambridge: Cambridge University Press.

Raposo, E. and J. Uriagereka. 1996. Indefinite *se*. *Natural Language and Linguistic Theory* 14: 749–810.

Richards, N. 1997. *What moves where when in which language?* Doctoral dissertation, MIT.

Sauerland, U. 1998. *The meaning of chains*. Doctoral dissertation, MIT.

Sauerland, U. 1999. Erasability and interpretation. *Syntax* 2: 161–88.

Schütze, C. 1997. *INFL in child and adult languages: Agreement, Case and licensing*. Doctoral dissertation, MIT.

Sigurðsson, H. A. 1996. Icelandic finite verb agreement. *Working Papers in Scandinavian Syntax* 57: 1–47.

Ura, H. 1996. *Multiple feature-checking: A theory of grammatical function splitting*. Doctoral dissertation, MIT.

Uriagereka, J. 1996. Formal and substantive elegance in the Minimalist Program. In C. Wilder. H.-M. Gartner, and M. Bierwisch (eds.), *The role of economy principles in linguistic theory*. Berlin: Akademie Verlag, pp. 170–204.

Watanabe, A. 1992. Subjacency and S-structure movement of wh-in-situ. *Journal of East Asian Linguistics* 1: 255–91.

Zwart, J.-W. 1997. Transitive expletive constructions and the evidence supporting the multiple specifier hypothesis. In W. Abraham and E. van Gelderen (eds.), *German: Syntactic problems problematic syntax*, Tübingen: Niemeyer, pp. 105–34.

2.2 PRO

2.2.1 Null Case

From *THE SYNTAX OF NONFINITE COMPLEMENTATION: AN ECONOMY APPROACH*
Željko Bošković

2.1 Introduction

The development of the Minimalist Program has led to the abandonment of a number of conditions and mechanisms, either because their effects overlap with those of other conditions or because they are arbitrary in nature. The goal of this chapter is to explore the possibility of a minimalist reduction in the phenomena of infinitival complementation and the distribution of PRO.[1]

The standard account of the phenomena is crucially based on two mechanisms that no longer seem to play any role in the grammar: government and c-selection.

In the preminimalist framework, government played a central role in the theory. The minimalist framework has witnessed a dramatic decline in the importance of government. A number of phenomena that had previously been defined in terms of government are now characterized independently of it. Thus, [...] structural Case assignment, which was previously assumed to take place under government, is now reduced to a single X-bar-theoretic configuration, namely, the Spec-head relation. Locality conditions on movement are also formulated in terms of notions independent of government; more precisely, they seem to follow from general considerations of economy of derivation (see Chomsky and Lasnik 1993 and Takahashi 1994, among others). With the advent of the theory of LF anaphor movement (see Chomsky 1986), government no longer seems to play a role in binding theory either. In fact, under the standard account of the distribution of PRO and infinitival complementation, which rests on the assumption that PRO cannot be governed, government is still crucially needed only to account for the phenomena in question. Given this and the fact that government is a rather heterogeneous and arbitrary notion, it would be desirable to account for the phenomena in question without making recourse to government. This would open up the possibility that government could be completely eliminated from the grammar.

Another mechanism whose role seems to be limited to infinitival complementation is c-selection. Grimshaw (1979) argues that lexical entries of predicates contain information concerning selection for both syntactic categories (c-selection) and the semantic type of the complement (s-selection). She argues for the autonomy of c-selection and s-selection by noting that there is no one-to-one correspondence between semantic types of complements and their syntactic categories. Crucial examples are provided by the fact that verbs that take the same semantic type may or may not take an NP object. Thus, although both *wonder* and *ask* s-select Question (Q), only the latter allows Q to be realized as an NP.

(1) a.   John wondered [$_{CP}$ what the time was]
     b.   *John wondered [$_{NP}$ the time]
     c.   John asked [$_{CP}$ what the time was]
     d.   John asked [$_{NP}$ the time]

Pesetsky (1982, 1992), on the other hand, argues that c-selection should be eliminated as an independent syntactic mechanism. Whether or not a predicate can take an NP object is determined by whether or not it can assign Case. Thus, if *ask* but not *wonder* is marked [+accusative], c-selection need not be invoked to rule out (1b). The construction is ruled out independently by the Case Filter.

A potential argument against Pesetsky's claim that c-selection can be eliminated comes from certain facts concerning infinitival complementation. Consider (2a–d).

(2) a.   *John$_i$ is illegal [$_{CP}$ t$_i$ to park here]
     b.   It is illegal [$_{CP}$ PRO to park here]
     c.   John$_i$ appears [$_{IP}$ t$_i$ to like Mary]
     d.   *It appears to Bill [$_{IP}$ PRO to like Mary]

(2a–d) are generally accounted for by invoking c-selection: whereas *illegal* c-selects CP, *appear* c-selects IP. (2a) is then ruled out because it involves NP movement crossing a CP boundary. (2d), on the other hand, is excluded because PRO is governed by *appear*.[2] To the extent that this analysis of (2a–d) is correct, it provides evidence for the existence of c-selection as an autonomous syntactic mechanism. However, if it can be shown that (2a) and (2d) can be excluded by independently needed syntactic mechanisms that do not make reference to c-selection, the data in (2) would not be in-consistent with Pesetsky's position. This would be desirable, given that the facts in (1), which have previously been argued to provide strong evidence for the existence of c-selection, can in fact be accounted for independently of c-selection. Accounting for (2a,d) independently of c-selection would then open up the possibility that c-selection could be altogether eliminated from the theory of grammar.

In this chapter I show that neither c-selection nor the notion of government need be invoked to account for (2a–d). I provide evidence that the standard c-selection/binding-theoretic account, which crucially depends on the notion of government, is empirically inadequate, and I give an account of infinitival complementation based on the Case-theoretic approach to the distribution of PRO and the s-selectional properties of the relevant predicates. [. . .]

2.2 Infinitival complementation and c-selection

The discussion in this section centers around the well-known paradigm given in (3). I first briefly sum up the standard c-selection/binding-theoretic account of (3) and then develop an account of infinitival complementation based on the Case-theoretic approach to the distribution of PRO that dispenses with c-selection for different types of infinitival clauses. I then provide evidence that the Case-theoretic account of infinitival complementation and the distribution of PRO is superior to the binding-theoretic account.

(3) a.   John believed$_i$ [$_{Agr_oP}$ him$_j$ t$_i$ [$_{IP}$ t$_j$ to be crazy]]
     b.   *John believed [$_{IP}$ PRO to be crazy]
     c.   John tried [$_{CP}$ PRO to win]
     d.   *John tried$_i$ [$_{Agr_oP}$ him$_j$ t$_i$ [$_{CP}$[$_{IP}$ t$_j$ to win]]]

Under the standard analysis (3a–d) are accounted for by recourse to c-selection. Whereas *try* c-selects CP, *believe* c-selects IP.[3] Given that accusative Case is checked in SpecAgr$_o$P, *him* in (3a) and (3d) must undergo LF A-movement to the matrix SpecAgr$_o$P in order to be Case-checked. [. . .] In (3d) the movement is blocked by the intervening CP. In (3c) the CP protects PRO from being governed by *try*. In (3b), on the other hand, PRO is governed by *believe* and the construction is ruled out by either Condition A or Condition B of the binding theory.

It is well known that the standard account of (3) faces a number of conceptual problems. First, it is based on the assumption that, in contrast to all other NPs,

PRO is not Case-marked. This raises an obvious conceptual question, especially if Case marking is a prerequisite for θ-marking, as argued by Chomsky (1981, 1986).

Second, the account is based on a number of stipulations concerning which elements count as governors. Thus, to maintain the standard account of the ditribution of PRO, it is necessary to stipulate that, in contrast to finite I, nonfinite I is not a governor. The same stipulation has to be made for I of Balkan subjunctives, which allow PRO although they exhibit the same verbal morphology as indicatives, including person/number agreement.[4] It is also necessary to stipulate that the null complementizer heading the infinitival complement of *try* in (3c), as well as overt complementizers that head control infinitival complements in the Romance languages (see Rochette 1988 and references therein), does not count as a governor.[5]

Third, the standard binding-theoretic account of (3) is crucially based on the assumption that the infinitival complement of *believe* is an IP, and that of *try* a CP, which is another stipulation. Furthermore, both the mechanism that is responsible for the difference in the categorial status of the infinitival complements in (3) (namely, c-selection) and the notion of government (which plays the central role in the standard account) are theoretically very problematic. In fact, as noted above, in the current theoretical framework they seem to be needed merely to account for the facts in (3a–d).

Chomsky and Lasnik's (1993) proposal that PRO is always Case-marked opens up a new way of analyzing (3a–d) that makes no reference to either c-selection or government. Chomsky and Lasnik note that, as illustrated by (4), PRO must undergo NP-movement from non-Case positions and is not allowed to undergo NP-movement from Case positions even to escape government.

(4) a.   John tried PRO$_i$ to be arrested t$_i$
     b.   *John tried PRO$_i$ to seem to t$_i$ that the problem is unsolvable

To account for (4a–b), Chomsky and Lasnik reject the binding-theoretic account of the distribution of PRO and argue that, like all other argument NPs, PRO is always Case-marked. They propose that PRO is marked for null Case, which is restricted to PRO and checked via Spec-head agreement with nonfinite I. They show that, given this proposal, (4b) is ruled out by the Last Resort Condition, which forbids NP-movement from Case-checking to Case-checking positions.[6] NP-movement in (4a), on the other hand, is in accordance with the Last Resort Condition; PRO moves from a non-Case position to a position in which Case can be checked. Given the data in (4a–b), I will adopt Chomsky and Lasnik's Case-theoretic account of the distribution of PRO, with a modification proposed by Martin (1992b).[7]

Martin modifies Chomsky and Lasnik's (1993) account by arguing that not every nonfinite I has the ability to check null Case. Restricting attention to infinitival complements, only [+tense] nonfinite I can check null Case. Martin adopts Stowell's (1982) proposal that, in contrast to ECM infinitives, control infinitives are specified for Tense. More precisely, they denote a possible future; this is, they specify a time frame that is unrealized with respect to the Tense of the matrix clause (note, for example, the interpretation of *John remembered to bring the wine*). To account for this, Stowell proposes that infinitival complements of control verbs have an independent Tense value; that is, they are specified as [+tense]. In contrast to control infinitives, ECM infinitives have no independent Tense value; that is, they are specified as [−tense]. Their time frame is determined by the time frame of the higher clause. They have no internally organized Tense.[8]

Martin notes that certain facts concerning the occurrence of eventive predicates in infinitival complements confirm the correctness of Stowell's proposal. Enç (1991) argues that eventive predicates contain a temporal argument that needs to be bound. Tense, the aspectual *have* and *be*, and adverbs of quantification serve as binders for the temporal argument. It is well known that under the nonhabitual reading eventive predicates can be embedded under control predicates, but not under ECM predicates.

(5)   a.   John tried to bring the beer
      b.   *John believed Peter to bring the beer

Martin (1992b) observes that, given Stowell's proposal concerning the presence versus absence of Tense in infinitival complements and Enç's claim that eventive predicates contain a temporal argument that must be bound, the contrast in (5) can readily be accounted for. The Tense of the control infinitival can serve as a binder for the temporal argument of *bring* in (5a). On the other hand, (5b) is ruled out because, ECM [exceptional case marking] infinitivals being Tenseless, the temporal argument of *bring* remains unbound.[9] Stowell's proposal concerning temporal properties of control and ECM infinitivals thus seems to be well motivated. Building on Stowell's proposal, Martin (1992b) modifies Chomsky and Lasnik's Case-theoretic approach to the distribution of PRO by proposing that the [+tense] feature of nonfinite I ([+tense, −finite] I) rather than nonfinite I in general checks null Case via Spec–head agreement.

Independent evidence for Martin's proposal is provided by certain facts concerning VP-ellipsis. Lobeck (1990) and Saito and Murasugi (1990) note that functional heads can license ellipsis of their complement only when they undergo Spec–head agreement. Thus, (6a–f) show that tensed I, *'s*, and [+wh]-C, which according to Fukui and Speas (1986) undergo Spec–head agreement, license ellipsis, whereas the nonagreeing functional categories *to*, *the*, and *that* do not.[10]

(6)   a.   John liked Mary and Peter [$_{I'}$ did e] too
      b.   *John believed Mary to know French but Peter believed Jane [$_{I'}$ to e]
      c.   John's talk about the economy was interesting but Bill [$_{D'}$'s e] was boring
      d.   *A single student came to the class because [$_{D'}$ the e] thought that it was important
      e.   John met someone but I don't know who [$_{C'}$ [+wh]-C e]
      f.   *John thinks that Peter met someone but I don't believe [$_{C'}$ that e]

Note now that, in contrast to what happens in ECM infinitives, VP-ellipsis is not blocked in control infinitives.

(7)   John was not sure he could leave, but he tried PRO [$_{\mathrm{I'}}$ to e]

Martin notes that this contrast between ECM and control infinitives is exactly what is expected if, in contrast to what happens in ECM infinitives, Tense in control infinitives checks null Case via Spec-head agreement with PRO in SpecIP. Since *to* in (7) undergoes Spec-head agreement, its complement can be deleted. The contrast between (6b) and (7) thus provides evidence for the Case-theoretic approach to the distribution of PRO.[11] Given the ellipsis data discussed above, I will adopt Martin's proposal that PRO is Case-checked under Spec-head agreement with [+tense, −finite] I.

I believe that the difference between *believe* and *try* with respect to the Tense specification of their complement, which is responsible for the contrast between (6b) and (7), can best be stated in terms of s-selection. Suppose that, in contrast to *believe*, which s-selects Proposition (here I am ignoring constructions in which *believe* and *try* take NP complements), *try* s-selects a nonpropositional complement, which I will refer to as "Irrealis." This seems plausible given that there are several semantic differences between the infinitival complements of *believe* and *try*. For example, it is well known that truth and falsity can be predicated of the infinitival complement of *believe* but not *try* (e.g. *John believed Peter to have played football, which was false* vs. **John tried to play football, which was false*). Let us assume that the defining property of irrealis complements is that the truth of the complement is left unspecified at the time of the utterance, which straightforwardly explains the impossibility of predicating truth or falsity of the complement of *try*. Given this defining property, the presence of Stowell's unrealized Tense in the complement of *try* may well be a consequence of the s-selectional properties of *try*. If *try* takes a finite or [−tense] infinitival complement, its complement will not be interpreted as irrealis and its s-selectional properties will not be satisfied. As for *believe*, the possibility of its taking an infinitival complement specified for unrealized Tense can also be excluded via s-selection; if *believe* takes such a complement, which I assume can have only irrealis interpretation, its s-selectional requirements will not be satisfied.

Note that verbs taking factive infinitival complements (8a), which presuppose the truth of their complement, and verbs taking implicative infinitival complements (8b), which assert the truth or falsity of their complement, can be treated in the same way as verbs taking irrealis infinitival complements.

(8)   a.   John hated to win the championship last year
       b.   John managed to bring the beer yesterday

Pesetsky (1992) argues that factive and implicative *to* are modalized Tense morphemes whose presence is necessary to yield factive and implicative interpretations; that is, their presence is forced by the s-selectional properties of the higher predicates. Given that, in the absence of adverbs of quantification and the aspectual *have* and *be*, eventive predicates are allowed only in clauses that are specified as [+tense], the grammaticality of (8a–b) on the nonhabitual reading indicates that, like irrealis infinitivals and unlike propositional infinitivals, factive and implicative infinitivals are specified as [+tense]. As noted above with respect to irrealis infinitivals and as discussed at length below, given that factive and implicative infinitivals are specified as [+tense, –finite], the possibility of PRO in these infinitivals is predicted under the Case-theoretic account of the distribution of PRO. Note also that, as expected under this account, VP-ellipsis is allowed with implicative and factive infinitivals, just as it is with irrealis infinitivals.

(9)   a.   Peter liked to play football and John hated to
       b.   I didn't think Sam could finish the job but he managed to

Since implicative and factive infinitivals pattern with *try* in all relevant respects, from here on I will use the term *"try*-class verbs" to refer not only to irrealis but also to implicative and factive infinitivals.

In summary, under the Case-theoretic approach to the distribution of PRO, like other NP arguments, PRO is always Case-marked. Its Case is checked via Spec-head agreement with [+tense, –finite] I. As a result of the s-selectional properties of the relevant predicates, this element is present in the infinitival complement of *try*-class verbs but not *believe*-class verbs.[12]

2.2.1   Case checking with ECM verbs

Now that the Case-theoretic account of the distribution of PRO has been introduced, we are ready to return to the paradigm in (3). Let us first reconsider the infinitival complement of *believe* in (3a–b), repeated here as (10a–b).

(10)   a.   John believed$_i$ [$_{Agr_OP}$ him$_j$ t$_i$ [$_{IP}$ t$_j$ to be crazy]]
      b.   *John believed [$_{IP}$ PRO to be crazy]

Under the Case-theoretic approach to the distribution of PRO, (10b) is excluded by Case theory: since the embedded Tense does not check null Case, PRO in (10b) cannot be Case-checked. Notice that (10b) is now ruled out regardless of whether the embedded clause is a CP or an IP. Even if the embedded clause is a CP, (10b) is still excluded via Case theory. Given this, we do not need to stipulate that *believe* c-selects IP. We can let *believe* take either a CP or an IP complement and rule out ungrammatical constructions by independently needed mechanisms. Thus, if *believe* takes a CP complement in (10a), the construction is ruled out because it involves A-movement – namely, movement of *him* to the matrix SpecAgr$_O$P – across a CP boundary. More specifically, under the standard analysis it is ruled out either by the Empty Category Principle (ECP) (if *him* moves directly to the matrix SpecAgr$_O$P, crossing the CP/IP pair) or by the Improper Movement Constraint (if *him* moves via the embedded SpecCP).[13] The derivation in which the complement of *believe* is an IP, however, proceeds without problems. Given this, I conclude that under the Case-theoretic approach to the distribution of PRO there is no need to appeal to c-selection to account for (10a–b). *Believe* can be allowed to take either a CP or an IP infinitival complement. As for raising predicates such as *appear*, the reader can verify that (2c–d), repeated here as (11a–b), can also be accounted for without invoking c-selection.

(11) a.   John$_i$ appears [t$_i$ to like Mary]
      b.   *It appears to Bill [PRO to like Mary]

2.2.2 Try-class verbs and Case checking

Let us now turn to control verbs, which under the binding-theoretic account of
the distribution of PRO c-select CP. I will show that under the Case-theoretic
account control verbs can be allowed to take either a CP or an IP complement.
This will enable us to account for the possibility of PRO and the impossibility of
NP-trace in control infinitivals without recourse to c-selection. Notice first that
since the Case-theoretic account permits PRO to be governed, there is nothing
wrong with the complement of *try* being an IP. What is important is that the [+tense]
feature of the complement can check null Case, which PRO is marked for. The
question remains, however, whether (12a–c) can be ruled out if *try* is allowed to
take an IP complement.

(12) a.   *John$_i$ was tried [t$_i$ to leave]
      b.   *John tried [him to leave]
      c.   *Who$_i$ did John try [t$_i$ to leave]

If the embedded clauses in (12a–c) are IPs, we cannot appeal to the impossibility
of A-movement out of CPs to rule them out. (12b–c), as well as (12a) under the
standard assumption that only [+accusative] verbs can be passivized [. . .] could
be ruled out via Case theory if *try* is not a Case assigner. However, the grammaticality of *John tried something* provides evidence that *try* is a Case assigner. Some
other control verbs (e.g. *demand*, which behaves like *try* in all relevant respects)
also uncontroversially assign Case, as *John demanded Mary's resignation* illustrates.
    Given that, as argued by Hornstein and Lightfoot (1987), Larson (1991), Koster
(1984), and Sportiche (1983), among others, (13) is ruled out because PRO lacks
an appropriate controller, the ungrammaticality of (12a) cannot be related to the
ungrammaticality of (13).[14]

(13) *It was tried [PRO to leave]

This is so because, unlike (13), (12a) does not contain PRO. Recall, however, that
under the Case-theoretic approach to the distribution of PRO the possibility of
having PRO in a particular position provides evidence that null Case can be checked
in that position. As discussed above and as illustrated by (3c), PRO can appear in
the subject position of the infinitival complement of *try*. Given this, *John* in (12a)
is located in a Case-checking position prior to movement to the matrix SpecIP.
What we have in (12a), then, is NP-raising originating from a Case-checking position, a possibility that is ruled out by the Last Resort Condition.[15] Assuming that
him in (12b) and *who* in (12c) must move to the matrix SpecAgr$_o$P for Case checking,
(12b–c) also involve NP-movement from a Case-checking position and therefore
are ruled out by the Last Resort Condition. (12a–c) can then be ruled out in the
same way as (4b), discussed above. Given that (12a–c) are ruled out by the Last

Resort Condition, I conclude that it need not be specified in the lexicon that control verbs such as *try* take a CP infinitival complement in order to account for the impossibility of ECM and passive raising with such verbs. Under the Case-theoretic approach to the distribution of PRO, control verbs can take either a CP or an IP complement. ECM and passive raising with control verbs are ruled out by the Last Resort Condition.

Control adjectives such as *illegal* are amenable to the same analysis as control verbs. Under the Case-theoretic approach, the infinitival clause in (2b) can be either a CP or an IP. Like (3d), (2a) is ruled out by the Last Resort Condition regardless of the categorial status of the embedded clause.

In summary, in the preceding two sections I have considered the behavior of *try*-class and *believe*-class verbs with respect to ECM, passive raising, and the licensing of PRO. I have shown that under the Case-theoretic approach to the distribution of PRO the relevant facts can be accounted for without appealing to c-selection. Stowell's (1982) difference in the temporal properties of *try*-class and *believe*-class infinitivals, which determine the status of infinitival SpecIP with respect to Case checking, plays a crucial role in the phenomena under consideration. Since the difference in the temporal properties is a result of the s-selectional requirements of *try*-class and *believe*-class verbs, the systematic difference with respect to the licensing of PRO and NP-trace in the subject position of the infinitival complement of the verbs ultimately follows from their s-selectional requirements.

2.2.3 Case checking with *want*-class verbs

So far I have considered infinitival complements in which PRO and lexical subjects are in complementary distribution. The complementary distribution breaks down with *want*-class verbs.

(14) a. I want him to leave
      b. I want PRO to leave

The grammaticality of (14a) is potentially problematic for the analysis developed here. Under this analysis *him* cannot be Case-checked in the matrix SpecAgr$_O$P. Given that the infinitival clause receives irrealis interpretation and that its subject position can be filled by PRO and is therefore a Case-checking position, NP-raising into the matrix clause is ruled out by the Last Resort Condition. The ungrammaticality of (15), where passivization has occurred, confirms this.

(15) *John was wanted to leave

Following Bach (1977), Lasnik and Saito (1991) provide evidence that, in contrast to *him* in (3a), *him* in (14a) does not move into the matrix clause. Consider (16), taken from Lasnik and Saito 1991.

(16) a. ?Joan wants him$_i$ to be successful even more fervently than Bob's$_i$ mother does

b.   ?*Joan believes him$_i$ to be a genius even more fervently than Bob's$_i$ mother does

Given that the embedded subject in (16b) raises to SpecAgr$_O$P in LF for Case checking, it c-commands the matrix adverbial at LF, thus causing a Condition C violation. The grammaticality of (16a) indicates that Condition C is not violated in this construction, which in turn provides evidence that the embedded subject does not undergo A-movement into the matrix clause. It follows that it must be Case-checked within the infinitival complement. The constructions in (14a) and (16a) thus do not raise a problem for the Last Resort account given above.

The following constructions from Lasnik and Saito (1991) involving anaphor binding (17) and negative polarity item (NPI) licensing (18) provide further evidence that the subject of the infinitival complement of *believe*, but not *want*, undergoes A-movement into the matrix clause. In (17a) and (18a) the embedded-clause subject can license an anaphor and an NPI located within a matrix adverbial; such licensing is not possible in (17b) and (18b).

(17)   a.   ?I believed [those men$_i$ to be unreliable] because of each other's$_i$ statements
       b.   ??*I wanted [those men$_i$ to be fired] because of each other's$_i$ statements

(18)   a.   ??I believed [none of the applicants to be qualified] after reading any of the reports
       b.   ??*I wanted [none of the applicants to be hired] after reading any of the reports

A question now arises about how the embedded subject is Case-checked in constructions such as (14a). In Bresnan (1972), Chomsky (1981), Snyder and Rothstein (1992), and Bošković (1994), among others, it is argued that the infinitival complement in (14a) is headed by a null complementizer, a phonologically null counterpart of the complementizer *for*, which heads the infinitival complement of *want* in (19). The embedded-clause subject in (14a) can then be Case-checked in essentially the same way as in (19).[16]

(19)   I want (very much) for him to leave

An important clue to how exactly the embedded-clause subject is Case-checked in (14a) and (19) is provided by the possibility of VP-ellipsis in (20a–b).

(20)   a.   ?You wanted for Mary to cook but Peter wanted for John [$_{I'}$ to e]
       b.   Mary didn't ask Peter to leave but she really wanted C him [$_{I'}$ to e]

Recall Lobeck's (1990) and Saito and Murasugi's (1990) generalization that only complements of agreeing functional heads can undergo ellipsis. As discussed above, Martin (1992b) argues that, given this generalization, the possibility of VP-ellipsis with control infinitivals (as in (7)) and its impossibility with ECM infinitivals (as in (6b)) indicate that the subject of control infinitivals but not the subject of ECM infinitivals is Case-checked under Spec-head agreement with the infinitival I. Returning now to (20a–b), note that the grammaticality of these constructions indicates that, like PRO in (7) and unlike *Jane* in (6b), the embedded subject in (20a–b) is Case-checked under Spec-head agreement with the embedded-clause I. What we need to do now is capture the standard assumption that C and *for* are responsible for Case-checking the infinitival subject in (20a–b) and still have the embedded subject undergo Case checking under Spec-head agreement in the embedded SpecIP. Watanabe's (1993) analysis of *for-to* constructions achieves this result. Following a suggestion by Noam Chomsky, Watanabe proposes that the *for-to* complex is generated under I, with *for* undergoing movement to C^0. (Roger Martin (personal communication) has suggested a similar analysis.) Under this proposal, *John* in (20a) is Case-checked in SpecIP under Spec-head agreement with the *for-to* complex, prior to the raising of *for*.[17] I assume that the null counterpart of *for* in (20b) behaves like *for* in all relevant respects. Note incidentally that the contrast between (20b) and (6b) provides more evidence that, in contrast to the subject of the infinitival clause embedded under *believe*, the embedded subject in constructions such as (20b) and (14a) is Case-checked within the embedded clause, and not by undergoing object shift to the matrix $SpecAgr_0P$. If the latter were the case, we would expect VP-ellipsis to be disallowed in (20b), just as it is in (6b).

One question concerning the infinitival complement of *want* that still has to be addressed is why *for* and its null counterpart are allowed with *want*. The answer may lie in Pesetsky's (1992) l-selection. Pesetsky argues that regardless of whether or not c-selection is eliminated, in addition to s-selection, which may simply be a coherence condition on semantic interpretation, we need selection for terminal elements, which he refers to as "l-selection." L-selection is limited in scope and involves arbitrary selection for lexical items and features associated with them that cannot be reduced to either s-selection or c-selection. L-selection does not refer to syntactic categories, but instead refers to individual lexical items and specific features such as [+/–finite]. For example, it involves selection for individual prepositions. The fact that the noun *love* allows either *for* or *of*, whereas *desire* requires *for*, is a matter of l-selection. According to Pesetsky, l-selection can see a particular lexical item such as *for*, but it cannot see the node P^0 that dominates it. L-selection thus has nothing to do with syntactic selection. Note that c-selection itself cannot make the necessary distinction between *love* and *desire*, since c-selection could only provide information that both the noun *love* and the noun *desire* take a PP complement.

Concerning *want*, it seems plausible that the presence of *for* and its null counterpart with *want* is a result of the l-selectional properties of *want*, given that we are dealing here with selection for particular terminal elements and not merely selection for CP. (In fact, even under the standard c-selection account of infinitival complementation we still need a way of saying that some verbs taking a CP infinitival allow *for* and some do not.) Given the facts concerning the mobility of infinitival complements to be discussed in section 2.2.4.1, I assume that l-selection for a prepositional complementizer with *want*-class verbs is optional [. . .]. However, I should note here that Kiparsky and Kiparsky (1970) observe that the complementizer *for* (and I assume that the same holds for its null counterpart) occurs only with a

particular class of predicates, namely, emotive predicates. Building on their observation, Bresnan (1972) argues that the complementizer *for* is semantically active.
It expresses subjective reason or cause, purpose, use, or goal. Given Bresnan's proposal, we could perhaps let *for* freely appear in any infinitival complement as long
as its meaning is compatible with the semantics of the higher predicate. (Pesetsky
(1992) also argues that whether or not an infinitival complement can be introduced
by *for* is determined by the semantics of the higher predicate, in fact, the whole
higher clause.)[18]

To sum up, I have shown in this section that the lack of complementary distribution of lexical subjects and PRO in the infinitival complement of *want*-class
verbs does not pose a problem for the Case-theoretic account of the distribution
of PRO and the Last Resort account of the impossibility of ECM and passive raising out of control infinitival complements. The relevant facts are accounted for
without invoking c-selection.

2.2.4 The categorial status of control infinitives

We have seen that we no longer need to specify that control verbs c-select CP infinitival complements. In this section I show in fact that were we to specify this,
certain grammatical constructions would be ruled out. In other words, I show
that under certain circumstances complements of control verbs must be IPs, a possibility that is not available under the c-selection/binding-theoretic account of
infinitival complementation, but is consistent with the s-selection/Case-theoretic
account.

2.2.4.1 *Empty complementizers and the ECP*
Stowell (1981) argues that the distribution of empty complementizers can be
accounted for if they are subject to the ECP. In (21a) the empty complementizer
is properly governed by the verb; in (21b–c) it is not.[19]

(21) a. It is believed [$_{CP}$ C [$_{IP}$ he is crazy]]
      b. *[$_{CP}$ C [$_{IP}$ He would buy a car]] was believed at that time
      c. *It was believed at that time [$_{CP}$ C [$_{IP}$ you would fail her]]

Infinitival clauses behave quite differently from finite clauses in the relevant respect.

(22) a. I tried at that time [$_{CP}$ C [$_{IP}$ PRO to fail her]]
      b. [$_{CP}$ C [$_{IP}$ PRO to buy a car]] was desirable at that time

The grammaticality of (22a–b) is unexpected. Since the empty C in (22) is not
properly governed, we would expect (22a–b) to be ruled out by the ECP on a par
with (21b–c). The grammaticality of the constructions suggests that the infinitives
in (22a–b) are not CPs and therefore do not contain a null complementizer. Under
the analysis developed here (22a–b) can be accounted for. Given that under the
Case-theoretic approach to the distribution of PRO control infinitivals can be
IPs, the CP projection does not have to be present in (22a–b). Since the null

complementizer is not present, no problems with respect to the ECP arise in (22a–b) under this analysis. The contrast between (22a–b) and (21b–c) is thus straightforwardly accounted for.[20]

(23) also shows that control infinitivals can be IPs.

(23) a.   What the terrorists tried was [$_\alpha$ PRO to hijack an airplane]
       b.   They demanded and we tried [$_\alpha$ PRO to visit the hospital]
       c.   *What the terrorists believe is [$_\alpha$ they will hijack an airplane]
       d.   *They suspected and we believed [$_\alpha$ Peter would visit the hospital]

Assuming that (23c–d) are ruled out by the ECP because the null head of α is not properly governed, the question arises why (23a–b) are grammatical. It seems plausible that α in (23a–b) must match the selectional restrictions of the relevant predicates. Since under the c-selection account of infinitival complementation both *demand* and *try* are assumed to take a CP complement, (23a–b) are ruled out by the ECP on a par with (23c–d). On the other hand, given my assumption that *demand* and *try* can freely take an IP complement, the grammaticality of (23a–b) can readily be accounted for.

Consider also (24a–b), which provide more evidence that control infinitivals can be IPs.

(24) a.   *Mary believed Peter finished school and Bill [$_\alpha$ Peter got a job]
       b.   Mary tried to finish school and Peter [$_\alpha$ PRO to get a job]

Aoun et al. (1987) argue that governing heads cannot be gapped. Given this, (24a) is ruled out by the ECP because the null C heading α cannot be properly governed. The grammaticality of (24b), then, provides evidence that control infinitivals can be IPs; if they had to be CPs, (24b) would be ruled out by the ECP on a par with (24a).

Factive infinitivals (25a–c) and implicative infinitivals (25d–f) pattern with irrealis infinitivals in all relevant respects; this behavior suggests that they can also be IPs.

(25) a.   John hated at that time to play football early in the morning
       b.   What John hated was to play football early in the morning
       c.   John loved and Sam hated to play football early in the morning
       d.   John managed at that time to leave
       e.   What John managed was to leave as soon as they arrived
       f.   John disdained and Sam declined to work for a living

The line of reasoning employed here leads me to conclude that adjunct infinitivals, such as the one in (26), are also IPs.

(26)   John went there [PRO to meet Mary]

If the infinitival in (26) were a CP, the construction would be ruled out by the ECP because the null complementizer is not properly governed, the adjunct CP being a barrier to government.

Note that the CP-deletion approach to infinitival complementation fares no better than the c-selection approach with respect to (22)–(25). Given the assumption that *try*, *demand*, *desirable*, and the verbs taking factive and implicative infinitivals in (25) do not trigger CP-deletion, the infinitival clauses in (22)–(25) would have to be CPs, and, as a consequence, the relevant constructions would be ruled out by the ECP. To maintain the CP-deletion hypothesis in light of these data, we would have to assume that, in contrast to ECM predicates, which always trigger CP-deletion, control predicates trigger CP-deletion only in the contexts given in (22)–(25). Since triggering CP deletion is a lexical property, this cannot be done in a principled way.

To sum up, I have argued in this section that in certain contexts control infinitives must be IPs. Given that the infinitives in (22)–(25) are IPs, I see no principled way of ruling out the IP option for the infinitives in (12a–c) and (3c–d). Since the standard binding-theoretic account of the distribution of PRO is crucially based on the CP status of control infinitival complements, this leads me to reject this account in favor of the Case-theoretic account.[21]

2.2.4.2 Scrambling out of control infinitives

Certain facts concerning scrambling out of control infinitives provide more evidence for the IP status of such infinitives and for the Last Resort Condition analysis of A-movement out of infinitival complements. As noted by Mahajan (1990) and Nemoto (1991), in contrast to scrambling out of finite CPs, scrambling out of control infinitives exemplifies A-movement. The following examples from Serbo-Croatian, involving the scrambled quantifier *nekoga* 'someone', illustrate this.

(27) a. Nekoga$_i$ njegov$_{j/?*i}$ otac veruje da oni mrze t$_i$
    someone his father believes that they hate
    'Someone, his father believes that they hate'
 b. Nekoga$_i$ njegov$_i$ otac planira PRO kazniti t$_i$
    someone his father is-planning to-punish
    'Someone, his father is planning to punish'

It is well known that, as illustrated by (28), Ā-movement, but not A-movement, induces weak crossover effects. In other words, quantifiers moved to A-positions, but not Ā-positions, can locally bind pronouns.

(28) a. Everyone$_i$ seems to his$_i$ father t$_i$ to be crazy
 b. Everyone$_i$, his$_{j/?*i}$ father kissed t$_i$

The fact that the preposed quantifier in (27a) cannot be coindexed with the pronoun it c-commands indicates that, like *everyone* in (28b), it is located in an Ā-position. It is generally assumed in the literature on scrambling that the lack of weak crossover effects in constructions such as (27b) indicates that, like *everyone* in (28a), the scrambled quantifier in (27b) is located in an A-position. Bearing this in mind, consider (29a), where passive raising out of an infinitival complement has occurred.

(29) a.   *Jovan$_i$ je planiran [t$_i$ poljubiti Mariju]
           Jovan is planned   to-kiss   Maria
           'Jovan was planned to kiss Maria'
      b.   cf. Jovan je planirao [PRO poljubiti Mariju]
           'Jovan planned to kiss Maria'

Given that A-movement out of the control infinitival in (27b) is possible, the question is why (29a) is bad. Under the standard approach to the distribution of PRO, it is not clear how the contrast between (27b) and (29a) can be accounted for. Assuming that control complements are CPs, we would expect *both* (29a) and (27b) to be ruled out because they involve A-movement crossing a CP boundary, which, as is well known, is not allowed (see note 13). If, as suggested above, infinitival passives such as (13) are ruled out because they lack an appropriate controller for PRO, (29a) cannot be ruled out in the same way, because PRO is not present in (29a). However, the contrast between (29a) and (27b) receives a straightforward account under the Case-theoretic approach. Given that a position in which PRO can appear is a Case-checking position, (29a) is ruled out by the Last Resort Condition because it involves movement from a Case-checking position into a Case-checking position. The grammatical (27b), on the other hand, does not involve movement into a Case-checking position.[22]

As for the contrast between (27b) and (27a), the fact that long-distance scrambling in (27a) does not exhibit properties of A-movement is not surprising, since it is well known that A-movement cannot take place across a CP boundary. As noted above, A-movement out of CPs is ruled out either by the ECP or by the Improper Movement Constraint, both of which are reducible to economy principles (see note 13). Since, as shown by the lack of weak crossover effects in (27b), scrambling out of control infinitivals has properties of A-movement, it must be the case that the movement in question does not cross a CP boundary. It follows that the control infinitival in (27b) cannot be a CP, a conclusion that is consistent with the proposals made here, but not with the traditional accounts of infinitival complementation.[23]

To summarize the discussion in this section, I have argued that the traditional c-selection and CP-deletion accounts of infinitival complementation and the binding-theoretic account of the distribution of PRO should be rejected in favor of the Case-theoretic account of the distribution of PRO and infinitival complementation. I have provided evidence that in certain contexts control infinitival complements must be of category IP, contrary to what is predicted by the c-selection/binding-theoretic account, but in accordance with the Case-theoretic account. (For more evidence for the Case-theoretic account based on French pro-positional infinitivals and English *wager*-class verbs, see Bošković (1997: ch. 3).) In addition to accounting for the phenomena discussed in this section, the Case-theoretic account of the distribution of PRO enables us to dispense with c-selection for different types of infinitival clauses and a number of stipulations concerning which elements count as governors. I have shown that infinitival complements can be allowed to vary freely between IP and CP within the limits set by the l-/s-selectional properties of the higher predicate, the Case requirements of the infinitival subject, and economy conditions responsible for the impossibility of A-movement out of CPs.

[. . .]

3.4 Infinitival complementation in French

Kayne (1984) notes a systematic difference in Case marking and the occurrence of PRO between English and French infinitivals, which appears to raise a serious problem for the Case-theoretic account of the distribution of PRO. As (30) shows, in contrast to their English counterparts, French *believe*-class infinitivals allow PRO to appear in their subject position.

(30) a. Pierre croit   [PRO avoir   convaincu son auditoire]
          Pierre believes   to-have convinced his audience
      b. Pierre a   constaté [PRO avoir   convaincu son auditoire]
          Pierre has noticed   to-have convinced his audience

If, as argued by Martin (1992b), only [+tense, −finite] I can check null Case, which PRO is marked for, and if, like their counterparts in English, propositional infinitivals in French are specified as [−tense], (30a–b) should be ruled out under the Case-theoretic account because PRO cannot be Case-checked. In Bošković (1996) I suggest that the grammaticality of (30a–b) indicates that regardless of its Tense specification, nonfinite I can check null Case in French. In other words, what is needed for null Case checking in French is simply the presence of [−finite] I. (A similar proposal is made independently by Watanabe (1993).) The grammaticality of (30a–b) can then readily be accounted for.[24] This account is conceptually problematic, however, since it would be preferable to keep the source of null Case checking constant in English and French.

However, in contrast to English propositional infinitivals, the infinitival complement of French *croire*-class verbs can receive a nonhabitual interpretation even in the absence of an auxiliary or adverbs of quantification. Thus, in contrast to the corresponding constructions in English, (31a–e) are grammatical on the nonhabitual reading.[25]

(31) a. Je crois   rêver
          I believe to-dream
          'I believe that I am dreaming'
      b. Anna croyait arriver   en retard hier   alors qu'en fait
          Anna believed to-arrive late   yesterday although in fact
          elle était à l'heure
          she was   at the time
          'Anna believed that she arrived late yesterday although in fact she was
          on time'
      c. Je crois   réussir   l'examen demain
          I believe to-succeed the exam tomorrow
          'I believe that I will pass the exam tomorrow'

   d. [There is no light in the room. Pierre is hitting somebody but is not
      sure who it is]
      Pierre croit   frapper un voleur
      Pierre believes to-hit   a   burglar
      'Pierre believes he is hitting a burglar'
   e. Pierre croyait   embrasser Marie
      Pierre believed to-kiss   Marie
      'Pierre believed he was kissing Marie'

Recall that, as discussed in section 2.2, in the absence of aspectual elements such as *have* and adverbs of quantification, on the nonhabitual reading eventive predicates are allowed only in clauses that are specified as [+tense]. The Tense is needed to bind the temporal argument of eventive predicates. Following Martin (1992b), the ungrammaticality of **John believed Peter to arrive late yesterday* was in fact interpreted in section 2.2 as evidence that the infinitival complement of *believe* is specified as [–tense]. **John believed Peter to arrive late yesterday* is, then, ruled out because the temporal argument of the embedded eventive predicate remains unbound. Given this, the grammaticality of (31a–e) on the nonhabitual reading should be taken as indicating that, in contrast to English propositional infinitivals, French propositional infinitivals are specified as [+tense]. The presence of PRO in (30)–(31) can then be straightforwardly accounted for without positing a parametric difference between English and French with respect to which elements function as null Case checkers, which was done in Bošković (1996). In fact, the possibility of PRO in (30)–(31) confirms the Case-theoretic approach to the distribution of PRO. As shown above, French *believe*-class infinitivals differ from English *believe*-class infinitivals in that they are specified as [+tense]. As expected under the Case-theoretic approach to the distribution of PRO, on which the presence of [+tense] in an infinitival complement is necessary for licensing of PRO, French *believe*-class infinitivals also differ from their English counterparts in that they allow PRO in their subject position. I conclude, therefore, that the correlation between the possibility of PRO and temporal properties of infinitival complements, the pillar of the Case-theoretic account, holds not only in English but also in French, a language that at first sight appeared to be problematic for the Case-theoretic approach but upon closer scrutiny turns out to provide surprising evidence in its favor.[26]

Notes

1   This chapter is a revised and considerably expanded version of Bošković (1996). The earliest version of the chapter is Bošković (1992).

2   Chomsky (1981) achieves the same result by assuming that *appear* but not *illegal* is lexically specified as triggering CP-deletion. See section 2.2.4.1 for arguments against this account.

3   Since Tense is assumed to be adjoined to Agr$_S$ at SS in English, when the distinction between Agr$_S$ and Tense is not crucial I will refer to the Agr$_S$+Tense complex as I and its maximal projection as IP. (It is actually not quite clear whether Agr$_S$P is present in infinitives.)

4   Terzi (1992) shows convincingly that the subject position of the embedded clause in the following Greek example can be filled by PRO. For relevant discussion, see also Watanabe (1993).

(i) O Yiannis theli   PRO na   fai
     Yiannis wants   SUBJ.PART eats
     'Yiannis wants to eat'

5 (i) is an example of an infinitival complement headed by a lexical complementizer from Italian (however, see Kayne 1991 for an alternative analysis and Watanabe 1993 for criticism of the analysis).

(i) Gianni decise di   PRO vincere
     Gianni decided COMPL   to-win
     'Gianni decided to win'

6 The Last Resort Condition "requires that movement is permitted only to satisfy some condition" (Chomsky and Lasnik 1993: 523). The tacit assumption here is that NP raising is driven by the need to check the Case features of the NP undergoing movement, in accordance with Chomsky's (1993) Greed, which requires that α move only to satisfy a requirement on α.

Note that prior to NP-movement PRO in (4b) is located in a Case-checking position that does not match the Case PRO is marked for. Still, PRO is not allowed to move to a position in which null Case can be checked. The same point can be made with respect to *he* in (i), due to Howard Lasnik (personal communication).

(i) *He$_i$ seems to t$_i$ that Mary is ill

Apparently, an NP located in a Case-checking position is not allowed to undergo movement to another Case-checking position even if its Case feature does not match the Case feature of the position the NP is already located in. To maintain the Last Resort Condition account of (4b) and (i), we need to assume that regardless of whether the Case features of the Case checker and Case checkee match, when an NP is found in a Case-checking position a Case-checking relation is established, thus preventing the NP from moving into another Case-checking position. This view is apparently adopted by Chomsky and Lasnik (1993). There is, however, an alternative way of ruling out movement from Case-checking to Case-checking position that readily extends to (i) and (4b). Suppose that such movement is in principle allowed. As Martin (1992a) shows, constructions involving such movement can still be ruled out if Case features of traditional Case assigners must be "discharged" or, in minimalist terms, checked. On this view, if *he* undergoes Case checking in the matrix SpecIP in (i), the construction is ruled out because the Case feature of *to* remains unchecked. In this chapter, following Chomsky and Lasnik (1993), I will refer to all instances of movement from Case-checking to Case-checking position as "Last Resort Condition violations" without committing myself to one of the two possible analyses of the ungrammaticality of such movement (Greed or the requirement that Case features of traditional Case assigners be discharged). [. . .]

7 Attempts were made before Chomsky and Lasnik (1993) to account for the distribution of PRO via Case theory. It has often been suggested that the distribution of PRO can be captured if it is assumed that PRO does not tolerate Case. The proposal is empirically seriously flawed, however, as Chomsky and Lasnik demonstrate.

8 As noted in chapter 1, I do not discuss gerunds in this book. For some relevant discussion of gerunds, see Martin (1992b), where it is argued, contra Stowell (1982), that gerunds are specified as [+tense].

9 As noted by Pesetsky (1992), who essentially follows Enç (1991), when either an overt (ia) or an implicit (ib) adverb of quantification is present, eventive predicates can be embedded under *believe*.

(i)   a.   John believed Mary to always sing the anthem
      b.   John believed Mary to sing the anthem

In such constructions, the adverb of quantification binds the temporal argument of the eventive predicate – hence the obligatoriness of the habitual reading in (i). (The grammaticality of (5a) on the nonhabitual reading shows that an implicit adverb of quantification does not have to be present when an eventive predicate is embedded under a control predicate.)

As for constructions such as *John believed Peter to have brought the beer* and *John believes Peter to be bringing the beer right now*, Martin (1992b) argues that *have* and *be*, which can be taken to be specified as [+tense], serve as binders of the temporal argument of the embedded-clause main verb.

It is worth noting in this context that, on the basis of the obligatoriness of the habitual reading in constructions such as *Mary sings the anthem*, which contrasts in the relevant respect with *Mary sang the anthem*, Enç (1991) argues that English has no "present tense." As a result, the temporal argument of *sing* can be bound only by an implicit adverb of quantification (or some kind of habitual/generic operator) – hence the obligatoriness of the habitual reading. (This implies that finite I can check nominative Case regardless of its Tense specification.) Some other languages apparently differ from English in the relevant respect. Thus, in French *Marie chante l'hymne* can either have the habitual reading or mean that Marie is singing the anthem right now, which indicates that French has "present tense"; that is, the I of the construction is specified as [+tense] and therefore can bind the temporal argument of *chanter*.

10   Notice also the ungrammaticality of (i).

(i)   *John met someone but I don't know who$_i$ Peter said [$_{CP}$ t$_i$ [$_{C'}$ C e]]

If the null C in (i) can undergo agreement with the trace in its Spec, we would expect that, in contrast to what we find in (6f), IP-ellipsis can be licensed in (i). The fact that (i) is ungrammatical provides evidence against the accounts of the C-trace effect that are crucially based on the assumption that, in contrast to *that*, the null complementizer undergoes Spec-head agreement with the trace in its Spec (see Lasnik and Saito 1992 and Rizzi 1990, among others).

11   As illustrated by *I don't believe they will win the World Cup, but John believes they are likely to*, VP-ellipsis is possible with some traditional raising predicates such as *likely*, a possibility that seems unexpected given the standard assumption that their complement contains no PRO. However, Lasnik and Saito (1992) and Martin (1992b), provide convincing evidence that *likely* is ambiguous between a control and a raising predicate, which accounts for the fact that it allows VP-ellipsis. Martin notes that, as expected, when we rule out the control option by using expletive *there*, which cannot control PRO, VP-ellipsis becomes unacceptable (e.g. *John doesn't believe there is likely to be any Asian team in the final game, but I believe there is likely to*). Martin shows that some other traditional raising predicates, such as *seem*, which allow VP-ellipsis, also allow the control option (see section 3.4). According to Martin, the infinitival complement of the predicates in question can be specified either as [+tense], which results in a control structure, or [–tense], which results in a raising structure.

12   Note that the clean semantic division between the verbs that allow PRO in the subject position of their infinitival complement and those that do not is unexpected under the standard CP-deletion/binding-theoretic account of the phenomena under consideration, on which whether or not a verb allows PRO in its infinitival complement depends on arbitrary lexical properties (i.e. whether or not the verb is lexically specified as a CP deleter). As shown in the text, the relevant facts can be accommodated in a more principled way under the Case-theoretic account of the distribution of PRO.

13 As shown by Motapanyane (1994), an example of the impossibility of A-movement out of CPs is provided by Romanian subjunctive complements, which can be introduced by the complementizer *ca* (ia). However, when A-movement takes place out of a subjunctive complement, the complementizer cannot be present (ib–c). ((ia–c) are from Rivero 1989.)

(i)   a.   Trebuia   ca   studenţii   să   plece
           must-3SG that students-the SUBJ.PART leave
           'It must have been that the students left'
      b.   Studenţii   trebuiau   să   plece
           students-the must-3PL SUBJ.PART leave
           'The students must have left'
      c.   *Studenţii   trebuiau   ca · să   plece
           students-the must-3PL that SUBJ.PART leave

This can be accounted for if A-movement is not allowed to take place out of CPs. [. . .] Note that there is no *that*-trace effect in Romanian, so that (ic) cannot be ruled out on a par with *Who do you think that left*. (Watanabe 1993 proposes an alternative account of (ib–c) crucially based on his two-layered theory of Case checking. However, I show in note 21 that this theory of Case checking cannot be maintained.)

For more examples of the impossibility of A-movement out of CPs, see (for Serbo–Croatian and French) sections 2.2.4.2 and 3.4 and (for Japanese) Murasugi and Saito (1994) and Saito (1994).

The impossibility of A-movement out of CPs may actually be a consequence of the economy principles. Manzini's (1994) Locality, an economy constraint that requires every movement to be as short as possible, in fact forces *studenţii* in (ic) to pass through the embedded SpecCP. (In Manzini's system, movement must proceed through the domain of each head.) The Improper Movement Constraint then prevents *studenţii* from undergoing A-movement. Saito (1994) proposes a similar analysis of the ban on A-movement out of CPs that is also based on the interaction of the Minimize Chain Links Principle and the Improper Movement Constraint. Notice also that if, as argued by Saito (1992) and Takahashi (1994), the Improper Movement Constraint can be deduced from the economy principles, the impossibility of A-movement out of CPs actually follows from those principles.

14 As *John was persuaded to leave* illustrates, object control passives, where a controller is present, are acceptable. This suggests that the failure of control is indeed responsible for the ungrammaticality of (13).

15 That (12a) can be ruled out by the Last Resort Condition was also noticed independently by Howard Lasnik (personal communication).

16 Evidence for the presence of the null C is provided by the ungrammaticality of (i).

(i)   *I wanted very much [$_{CP}$ C [$_{IP}$ him to leave]]

Given that a null complementizer must be present in (i), under standard assumptions the construction is ruled out by the ECP because the null complementizer is not properly governed (see section 2.2.4.1 for relevant discussion and possible treatments of this phenomenon within the minimalist system).

It is possible that the null C receives Case features from the higher verb, given the ungrammaticality of the passive (ii).

(ii)   *It was wanted [$_{CP}$ C [$_{IP}$ him to leave]]

This can be implemented as follows: In Bošković (1995) I suggest that Agr has N and V Case features, which are matched against the Case features of V or Tense adjoined to Agr and the NP in SpecAgrP. (On this view Case features are treated like φ features.) Suppose that, like Agr, the null C in constructions such as (14a) and (ii) also has N and V Case features. Its N Case feature could be checked against the NP in the infinitival subject position (see the discussion directly below in the text). In (14a) its V Case feature would be checked by adjunction to the higher verb, which is specified as [+accusative]. Since the higher verb is passivized and therefore not specified as [+accusative] in (ii), the V Case feature of the null C remains unchecked in (ii).

17 Under this analysis we need to assume that the *for-to* I checks accusative rather than null Case.

18 Two *Natural Language & Linguistic Theory* reviewers argue that *expect* raises a problem for the analysis developed here. Like *want*, *expect* allows PRO (e.g. *I expected to leave*), lexical subjects (e.g. *I expected (for) John to leave*), and VP-ellipsis (e.g. *They didn't expect John to win, but they expected Mary to*). However, unlike *want* and like *believe*, *expect* allows passive raising (e.g. *John is expected to leave*). Bresnan (1972) provides convincing evidence that *expect* is three-ways ambiguous. On its intentional reading, which describes the subject's desire, it belongs to the *want*-class. *I expect for John to go there* illustrates this reading. On its predictive reading, which describes beliefs, *expect* belongs to the *believe*-class. *There are expected to be soldiers in the town* illustrates this reading. As expected, ellipsis is not allowed on this reading (e.g. **John doesn't believe there are any soldiers in the town, but there are expected to*). Finally, on its compulsive reading, *expect* belongs to the *persuade*-class and takes an animate NP complement in addition to the infinitival complement. This reading is illustrated by *You are expected to remove the tables after the dinner*. It is easy to verify that, given the three-way ambiguity of *expect*, the potentially problematic behavior noted above can readily be accounted for.

19 Stowell does not discuss (21c). Note that I use here the traditional terms "ECP" and "government" for ease of exposition. As noted above, the status of government is dubious. In the current framework Stowell's proper government requirement on null heads can readily be reformulated as a condition on identification of null heads. (It is well known that null elements do not occur freely in the structure.) C-command would probably have to be involved in the proper statement of the condition. Thus, a null C would have to be c-commanded by the higher verb.

An alternative, proposed by Pesetsky (1992), is to treat the null complementizer as an affix that must undergo affixation to a verbal head, which could be a result of a more general requirement that all null morphemes be affixes. The requirement could provide a single uniform way of licensing null heads. On Pesetsky's analysis (see also Ormazabal 1995), affixation takes place through head movement of C to V, which may be blocked in (21b–c) because the affixed C does not c-command its trace after the embedded clause undergoes movement. An alternative is to assume that C-V affixation takes place through the process of merger (see Halle and Marantz 1993; Bobaljik 1994; Lasnik 1995) under PF adjacency. In (21b–c) merger would be blocked because the null C and the matrix V are not adjacent at PF, and the constructions would be ruled out because of the presence of a stranded affix. The affixation analysis is appealing. Unfortunately, it cannot account for the full range of relevant facts. Thus, it is well known that null complementizers that enter into a Spec-head relation with an operator (or its trace) are for some reason exempt from the traditional head government requirement. (Here I consider binding of a variable to be a prerequisite for operator status.)

(i)   a.   [$_{CP}$ What$_i$ C [$_{IP}$ John likes t$_i$]] is apples
      b.   Who$_i$ do you believe sincerely [$_{CP}$ t$_i$ C [$_{IP}$ t$_i$ is crazy]]

I see no principled way of accounting for the contrast between (i) and (21b–c) under the affixation analysis. ((24a) is also potentially problematic for the C-to-V movement analysis.) [. . .] The contrast seems to be more amenable to an analysis whereby the head government requirement on null heads is reformulated as a condition on identification of null elements. Here, for ease of exposition, I will continue to use the traditional term "ECP". (For an ECP analysis of (ib), see Snyder and Rothstein 1992.)

20 Stowell (1982) suggests that the embedded clause in (22b) is specified as [−tense]. If this were the case, since C is not required in [−tense] clauses under Stowell's analysis, the ECP would not be violated in (22b). I believe, however, that the infinitival I in (22b) is specified as [+tense], though it is somewhat difficult to see this owing to the stativity of the matrix predicate. It is clear, however, that whether the act of buying a car has happened or will yet happen is left unspecified in (22b); this fact can be accounted for if we assume that the infinitival complement of *desirable* contains [+tense, −finite] I, associated with irrealis interpretation. Certain facts concerning the interpretation of the infinitival in question provide evidence for this assumption. It is well known that, as *John tried to have won* illustrates, perfective *have* is incompatible with irrealis infinitivals, specified as [+tense, −finite], plausibly because of a Tense clash between perfective *have* and irrealis Tense. Given this, the ungrammaticality of *To have bought a car was desirable at that time* indicates that the infinitival complement of *desirable* also contains irrealis Tense or, more precisely, [+tense, −finite] I. Note also that eventive predicates are allowed in the infinitival complement of *desirable* (e.g. *To win was desirable at that time*). Recall now that eventive predicates are allowed only in clauses that are specified as [+tense] (see (5)). Given this, the possibility of eventive predicates in the infinitival complement of *desirable* also indicates that, like the infinitival complement of *try* and unlike the infinitival complement of *believe*, the infinitival embedded under *desirable* is specified as [+tense].

21 The data under consideration also provide evidence against Watanabe's (1993) two-layered theory of Case checking. Watanabe argues that Case checking under Spec–head agreement with Agr creates a feature that forces Agr to raise to a functional head above it. Under this proposal, Case-checking SpecIPs must be dominated by a CP. However, the data considered in this section [. . .] provide evidence that the SpecIP position in which null Case and nominative Case are checked does not have to be dominated by a CP. [. . .]

22 Given Chomsky's (1993) claim that all movement is driven by morphological considerations, scrambling would have to involve some kind of feature checking. The precise nature of the feature in question, however, is not clear. Saito (1989) suggests that it is some kind of focus feature. For a discussion of scrambling and economy, see Fukui (1993), where it is argued that scrambling operations are costless in languages that allow them; that is, they are exempt from the Last Resort Condition.

23 It is tempting to interpret the data in (i) as providing more evidence against the binding-theoretic account of the distribution of PRO.

(i)   a.   *What the terrorists believe is [CP they will hijack an airplane]
      b.   *They believed and we claimed [CP Peter would visit the hospital]
      c.   *It was believed at that time [CP John would fail Mary]
(ii) a.   *What the terrorists believed was [PRO to have hijacked an airplane]
      b.   *They suspected and we believed [PRO to have visited the hospital]
      c.   *They believed at that time [PRO to have failed Mary]

As noted above, under the standard analysis (ia–c) are ruled out by the ECP because the null C heading the embedded clauses is not properly governed. The ungrammaticality of the constructions thus provides evidence that the embedded clauses in (i) are barriers to government, and the same should then hold for the embedded clauses in (ii). Given that the embedded clauses in (ii) are barriers to government, PRO is ungoverned in (iia–c), as required under the binding-theoretic account. Notice also that, as (22) and (23a–b) show, PRO can in principle appear in the relevant configurations so that nothing seems to go wrong with respect to control in (ii). The data considered in this note can be taken to indicate that regardless of whether or not PRO is governed, it cannot appear in the subject position of the infinitival complement of *believe*. This is expected under the Case-theoretic account of the distribution of PRO, which rests on the requirement that PRO be Case-checked by [+tense, –finite] I, but not under the binding-theoretic account, on which PRO can in principle appear in the subject position of the infinitival complement of *believe* as long as PRO is ungoverned. However, it may still be possible to account for (ii) under the binding-theoretic account by assuming that the relevant clauses in (ii) undergo LF reconstruction to a position governed by *believe* [. . .] and that the binding conditions, which determine the distribution of PRO, are checked at LF after reconstruction, whereas the head government requirement on null heads holds at a level prior to reconstruction.

24 A question arises about what happens with the Case feature of *croire* and *constater*. One possibility is that *croire* and *constater* only optionally bear Case features; that is, they can be taken from the lexicon without Case features. Alternatively, the Case features of the matrix verbs in (30a–b) could be checked by the infinitival complements. Under this analysis French infinitivals would at least have the option of bearing Case features, an option that has been proposed in the literature (see Rochette 1988 and references therein).

25 Thanks are due to Michèle Bacholle and Viviane Déprez for discussion of possible interpretations of some of the French examples in (31). ((31a) is taken from Déprez 1989.) Note that since the nonhabitual reading is usually not very salient, some contextualization is generally necessary. (We seem to be dealing here with some poorly understood contextual conditions.) Note also that when the matrix verb is in the past tense, a sort of a counterfactual implication is present (see, for example, (31b)). The implication is not enforced. Thus, *Anna croyait arriver en retard hier* can also be continued as follows: *et elle est arrivée en retard* 'and she did arrive late'. No counterfactual implication is present when the matrix verb is in the present tense (31a,c,d). English *believe* behaves in a similar way. Thus, in *John believed Mary to be intelligent* there seems to be an implication that Mary was not intelligent. The implication is not enforced since the sentence can be continued with *and she was intelligent*. As in French, such an implication is not present when the matrix verb is in the present tense. Even the English finite counterpart of (31b), *Anne$_i$ believed that she$_i$ arrived late yesterday* (the same holds for French), seems to have an implication that Anne did not arrive late, which can be canceled by continuing the sentence with *and she did arrive late*. Given that the facts concerning counterfactuality mentioned in this note are present in both French and English and in both finite and nonfinite clauses, they clearly do not interfere with the point made here.

26 Portuguese, Spanish, and Italian behave like French in the relevant respects. They allow PRO in propositional infinitivals. As expected, they also allow eventive predicates.

(i) a. A Ana julgou chegar atrasada ontem   ma afinal   chegou
         the Ana believed to-arrive late   yesterday but actually she-arrived
         a horas (Portuguese)
         on time

     b. Anna creía   llegar   tarde ayer   aunque en verdad estaba
         Anna believed to-arrive late   yesterday though in fact   she-was
         bien de tiempo (Spanish)
         right on time

     c. Anna credeva di arrivare in ritardo ieri   mentre era   in realtà
         Anna believed to arrive late   yesterday though she-was actually
         in orario (Italian)
         on time

Note in this context that, as discussed by Pesetsky (1992), English also has one verb, *claim*, that allows PRO in its infinitival complement although its infinitival complement is purely propositional (e.g. *John claimed to know French*). This can be accounted for if the infinitival complement of *claim* is specified as [+tense]. Constructions such as ?*John claimed to arrive late yesterday*, however, do not seem to be much better than *John believed Peter to arrive late yesterday*. *Claim* thus remains problematic.

References

Bach, E. W. 1977. Review article *On Raising: One rule of English grammar and its implications*. *Language* 53: 621–54.

Bobaljik, J. D. 1994. What does adjacency do? In H. Harley and C. Phillips (eds.), *The morphology-syntax connection. MIT Working Papers in Linguistics 22*, Cambridge, MA: MITWPL.

Bošković, Ž. 1992. Clausal selection, subjacency, and minimality. Ms., University of Connecticut, Storrs.

Bošković, Ž. 1994. Categorial status of null operator relatives and finite declarative complements. *Language Research* 30.

Bošković, Ž. 1995. Case properties of clauses and the Greed principle. *Studia Linguistica* 49: 32–53.

Bošković, Ž. 1996. Selection and the categorial status of infinitival complements. *Natural Language and Linguistic Theory* 14: 269–304.

Bošković, Ž. 1997. *The syntax of nonfinite complementation: An economy approach*. Cambridge, MA: MIT Press.

Bresnan, J. 1972. *Theory of complementation in English syntax*. Doctoral dissertation, MIT.

Chomsky, N. 1981. *Lectures on government and binding*. Dordrecht: Foris.

Chomsky, N. 1986. *Knowledge of language: Its nature, origin, and use*. New York: Praeger.

Chomsky, N. 1993. A minimalist program for linguistic theory. In K. Hale and S. J. Keyser (eds.), *The view from Building 20: Essays in linguistics in honor of Sylvain Bromberger*, Cambridge, Mass.: MIT Press, pp. 1–52. [Reprinted in Chomsky (1995), *The Minimalist Program*, Cambridge, Mass.: MIT Press, pp. 167–217.]

Chomsky, N. and H. Lasnik. 1993. The theory of principles and parameters. In J. Jacobs, A. von Stechow, W. Sternefeld and T. Vennemann (eds.), *An international handbook of contemporary research*, Berlin/New York: Walter de Gruyter, pp. 506–69. [Reprinted in Chomsky (1995), *The Minimalist Program*, Cambridge, Mass.: MIT Press, pp. 13–127.]

Déprez, V. 1989. *On the typology of syntactic positions and the nature of chains: Move α to the specifier of functional projections*. Doctoral dissertation, MIT.

Enç, M. 1991. On the absence of the present tense morpheme in English. Ms., University of Wisconsin, Madison.

Fukui, N. 1993. Parameters and optionality. *Linguistic Inquiry* 24: 399–420.

Fukui, N. and M. Speas. 1986. Specifiers and projection. In N. Fukui, T. R. Rapoport and E. Sagey (eds.), *Papers in Theoretical Linguistics. MIT Working Papers in Linguistics 8*, Cambridge, MA: MITWPL, pp. 128–72.

Grimshaw, J. 1979. Complement selection and the lexicon. *Linguistic Inquiry* 10: 279–326.

Halle, M. and A. Marantz. 1993. Distributed Morphology and the pieces of inflection. In K. Hale and S. J. Keyser (eds.), *The view from Building 20: Essays in linguistics in honor of Sylvain Bromberger*, Cambridge, MA: MIT Press, pp. 111–76.

Hornstein, N. and D. Lightfoot. 1987. Predication and PRO. *Language* 63: 23–52.

Kayne, R. S. 1984. *Connectedness and binary branching*. Dordrecht: Foris.

Kayne, R. S. 1991. Romance clitics, verb movement, and PRO. *Linguistic Inquiry* 22: 647–86.

Kiparsky, P. and C. Kiparsky. 1970. Fact. In M. Bierwisch and K. Heidolph (eds.), *Progress in linguistics*, The Hague: Mouton, pp. 143–73.

Koster, J. 1984. On binding and control. *Linguistic Inquiry* 15: 417–59.

Larson, R. 1991. *Promise* and the theory of control. *Linguistic Inquiry* 22: 103–39.

Lasnik, H. 1995. Verbal morphology: *Syntactic structures* meets the Minimalist Program. Ms., University of Connecticut, Storrs. [Published in H. Campos and P. Kempchinsky (eds.) (1995), *Evolution and revolution in linguistic theory*, Washington, DC: Georgetown University Press, pp. 251–75, and reprinted in Lasnik (1999), *Minimalist analysis*, Malden, MA: Blackwell, pp. 97–119.]

Lasnik, H. and M. Saito. 1991. On the subject of infinitives. In L. Dobrin, L. Nichols, and R. Rodriguez (eds.), *Papers from the 27th Regional Meeting of the Chicago Linguistics Society*, Chicago: Chicago Linguistics Society, pp. 324–43. [Reprinted in Lasnik (1999), *Minimalist analysis*, Malden, MA/Oxford: Blackwell, pp. 7–24.]

Lasnik, H. and M. Saito. 1992. *Move α*. Cambridge, MA: MIT Press.

Lasnik, H. and T. Stowell. 1991. Weakest crossover. *Linguistic Inquiry* 22: 687–720.

Lobeck, A. 1990. Functional heads as proper governors. In J. Carter, R.-M. Dechaine, B. Philip and T. Sherer (eds.), *Proceedings of the 20th Annual Meeting of the North East Linguistic Society*, Amherst, MA: GLSA, pp. 348–62.

Mahajan, A. 1990. *The A/A-bar distinction and movement theory*. Doctoral dissertation, MIT.

Manzini, M. R. 1994. Locality, minimalism, and parasitic gaps. *Linguistic Inquiry* 25: 481–508.

Martin, R. 1992a. Case theory, A-chains, and expletive replacement. Ms., University of Connecticut, Storrs.

Martin, R. 1992b. On the distribution and Case features of PRO. Ms., University of Connecticut, Storrs.

Motapanyane, V. 1994. An A-position for Romanian subjects. *Linguistic Inquiry* 25: 722–34.

Murasugi, K. and M. Saito. 1994. Adjunction and cyclicity. In R. Aranovic, W. Byrne, S. Preuss and M. Senturia (eds.), *Proceedings of the 13th West Coast Conference on Formal Linguistics*, Stanford: CSLI, pp. 302–17.

Nemoto, N. 1991. Scrambling and conditions on A-movement. In D. Bates (ed.), *Proceedings of the 10th West Coast Conference on Formal Linguistics*, Stanford: CSLI, pp. 349–58.

Ormazabal, J. 1995. *The syntax of complementation: On the connection between syntactic structures and selection*. Doctoral dissertation, University of Connecticut, Storrs.

Pesetsky, D. 1982. *Paths and Categories*. Doctoral dissertation, MIT.

Pesetsky, D. 1992. Zero syntax, vol. 2. Ms., MIT.

Rivero, M.-L. 1989. Barriers in Rumanian. In D. Wanner and D. A. Kibbee (eds.), *New analyses in Romance linguistics*, Amsterdam: John Benjamins, pp. 289–312.

Rizzi, L. 1990. *Relativized minimality*. Cambridge, MA: MIT Press.

Rochette, A. 1988. *Semantic and syntactic aspects of Romance sentential complementation*. Doctoral dissertation, MIT.

Saito, M. 1989. Scrambling as semantically vacuous A'-movement. In M. Baltin and A. Kroch (eds.), *Alternative conceptions of phrase structure*, Chicago: University of Chicago Press, pp. 182–200.

Saito, M. 1992. Long distance scrambling in Japanese. *Journal of East Asian Linguistics* 1: 69–118.

Saito, M. 1994. Improper adjunction. In H. Ura and M. Koizumi (eds.), *Formal approach to Japanese linguistics I. MIT Working Papers in Linguistics 24*, Cambridge, MA: MITWPL, pp. 263–93.

Saito, M. and K. Murasugi. 1990. N' deletion in Japanese. In J. Ormazabal and C. Tenny (eds.), *University of Connecticut Working Papers in Linguistics 3*, pp. 86–107. University of Connecticut, Storrs.

Snyder, W. and S. Rothstein. 1992. A note on contraction, Case, and complementizers. *The Linguistic Review* 9: 251–66.

Sportiche, D. 1983. *Structural invariance and symmetry in syntax*. Doctoral dissertation, MIT.

Stowell, T. 1981. *Origins of phrase structure*. Doctoral dissertation, MIT.

Stowell, T. 1982. The tense of infinitives. *Linguistic Inquiry* 13: 561–70.

Takahashi, D. 1994. *Minimality of movement*. Doctoral dissertation, University of Connecticut, Storrs.

Terzi, A. 1992. *PRO in finite clauses: A study of the inflectional heads in the Balkan languages.* Doctoral dissertation, CUNY Graduate Center.

Watanabe, A. 1993. Agr-based Case theory and its interaction with the A-bar system. Doctoral dissertation, MIT.

2.2.2   Eliminating PRO: Movement into θ-positions

From "MOVEMENT AND CONTROL"
Norbert Hornstein

1   Introduction

This article is an exercise in grammatical downsizing. Since the earliest days of generative grammar (Rosenbaum 1967), control and raising constructions have been treated differently, with different rules and/or formatives involved in the two structures. In the beginning there was Equi-NP Deletion. Equi, a deletion process, contrasted with Subject-to-Subject Raising, a movement process. Subsequently, in most versions of the Extended Standard Theory, control was relegated to binding theory – the binding of an abstract expression PRO – whereas raising remained an instance of movement. This dual-track approach persisted into the Government-Binding (GB) era.

In GB, control sentences like (1a) have structures like (1b). These contrast with raising sentences, (2a), and their phrase markers, (2b). In particular, the relation between *John* and the embedded subject position in (1a) is mediated through the binding of a grammatically distinctive lexical formative in control configurations, namely, PRO. In raising structures like (2a) the relation between the matrix and embedded subjects is a by-product of movement and results in an A-chain in which the head, the antecedent, binds the tail, its trace.

(1)   a.   John expects to win.
      b.   John$_i$ expects [PRO$_i$ to win]
(2)   a.   John seemed to win.
      b.   John$_i$ seemed [t$_i$ to win]

The differences do not stop here. The distribution of PROs in GB is attributed to binding theory – the PRO Theorem, to be precise. The distribution of NP-traces, in contrast, is the province of the Empty Category Principle (ECP). Traces must be properly governed. PROs, on the other hand, cannot be governed at all. PROs head their own chains; traces, by definition, cannot. PROs are base-generated; traces are produced through movement. Thus, in most every respect, GB fundamentally distinguishes NP-traces from PROs. Their one commonality within GB is that both are Caseless and phonetically null.

To date, standard work in the Minimalist Program has left matters pretty much in this GB state.[1] There are good reasons for this. Empirically, the distinction reflects the fact that the antecedent of PRO in cases like (1a) bears two θ-roles whereas the subject in (2a) has but one. This semantic difference is theoretically ensconced in the different *kinds* of binding assumed to hold in control versus raising. The theoretical basis for the distinction in GB technically rests on distinguishing a level of D-Structure. D-Structure is the sole locus of lexical insertion, an operation that precedes all other transformations. Lexical insertion is subject to θ-requirements. In particular, D-Structure is defined as the phrase marker that purely represents GF-θ, the level at which all and only thematic positions of the sentence are occupied by lexical material. Subsequent transformations move the lexical expressions located in θ-positions to non-θ-positions. These movements are further restricted by the θ-Criterion so that going from one θ-position to another is strictly forbidden.

This GB package of assumptions (the combination of D-Structure and the θ-Criterion) forces a distinction between PRO and trace, and thereby between binding and control. Two suppositions are central, and both are retained in the Minimalist Program: first, the θ-Criterion (the assumption that (A-)chains are constrained to possess but a single θ-position; i.e. movement from one θ-position to another is strictly forbidden); second, the priority of θ-marking over movement (i.e. the requirement that θ-positions coincide with the foot of a chain).

The first requirement prevents movement to θ-positions in the course of a derivation, just as it did in GB theories. The second retains a central feature of D-Structure. Chomsky (1995) operationalizes the thematic restriction on lexical insertion by restricting θ-assignment to the merger of trivial chains. This recapitulates within the Minimalist Program the assumption that D-Structure is the locus of pure GF-θ. Thus, in Chomsky's (1995) version of the Minimalist Program, a D/NP can legitimately enter a derivation only through the thematic door; that is, nominal expressions all enter the derivation via Merge. Given the provision that only trivial chains can be θ-marked, an NP so merged must merge to a θ-position on pain of never receiving a θ-role. Chomsky (1995) further assumes that all subsequent movement is restricted to nonthematic targets. This is technically executed by assuming (3).

(3)   a.   θ-roles are not features.
      b.   Movement must be greedy.

As θ-roles are not "checkable" features, movement to θ-positions cannot be greedy and so is prohibited. In short, the Minimalist Program retains the θ-Criterion.

All of this suggests that the minimalist abandonment of D-Structure as a level (Chomsky 1993) is less radical than often perceived. Chomsky's argument does not lead to a general repudiation of the core characteristics of D-Structure. Rather, D-Structure's earlier properties are packed into restrictions on the computational operations. In fact, the only feature of D-Structure that the Minimalist Program forswears is the principle that *all* lexical insertion precedes the application of *all* other transformations; in other words, the rule Satisfy has been dropped (Chomsky 1993). The other features of D-Structure have been retained.

This article submits these other assumptions to minimalist scrutiny. How well motivated are they? Why assume that chains are biuniquely related to θ-roles? What goes wrong if movement takes place from one θ-position to another? Why distinguish trace from PRO? As is generally the case with minimalist meditations, I assume that the burden of proof is on those who wish to promote these assumptions and invoke these distinctions. What is not at issue is that control and raising sentences manifest different properties. The minimalist question is whether these differences require the technical apparatus standardly invoked to distinguish them.

In the particular case of control, methodological skepticism is fully warranted. The distinction between raising and control multiplies the inventory of empty categories. Furthermore, the distinction massively complicates the grammar. PRO brings with it two big theoretical complications: (a) a control module whose job it is to specify how PRO is interpreted and (b) theoretical modifications to account for PRO's distribution. In GB (b) is handled by the binding theory. PRO is analyzed as a pronominal anaphor. The contradictory requirements that standard versions of the binding theory place on pronouns and anaphors within governing domains force such expressions to be ungoverned. Hence, PROs can appear only in ungoverned positions (see Chomsky 1986).

This GB approach to (b) has several conceptual and empirical problems (see Bouchard 1984; Chomsky and Lasnik 1993). Furthermore, the Minimalist Program cannot adopt the PRO Theorem, since it relies on the notion of government, which is not an acceptable minimalist primitive. Consequently, governing categories and domains cannot be defined or theoretically exploited.

Chomsky and Lasnik (1993) propose that the distribution of PRO is regulated by Case theory.[2] Theirs is the standard minimalist account for the distribution of PRO.[3] In particular, they propose that PRO has "null" Case. This is a Case special to PRO in the sense that only PRO bears it and Is that assign/check it license no other sorts of Case. It is fair to say that null Case accounts for the distribution of PRO largely by stipulation.

The theory of the control module does not fare much better. What principles determine the antecedents of PRO, and whether or not all instances of control are actually the same, is quite controversial. It seems safe to say that control theory has not been one of the bright stars in the GB firmament.

In sum, neither part of the control conglomerate has been uncontroversial even within GB. Given a minimalist sensibility, its technical complexities are ripe for reevaluation.

The article is organized as follows. Section 2 reviews why we need a theory of PRO and control. In particular, sections 2 and 3 review the distribution and interpretive requirements of PRO in obligatory control (OC) and nonobligatory control (NOC) configurations. Sections 4 and 5 argue that the general properties of OC structures can be reduced to movement if we abandon the residues of D-Structure still extant within the Minimalist Program and abandon the θ-Criterion-based prohibition against moving into θ-positions. [. . .]

2 The issues

Section 1 has tersely outlined the twin problems that theories of control must deal with: the distribution and interpretation of PRO. The GB solutions to these problems often pull in opposite directions. This tension is resolved in minimalist approaches. Consider the details.

The GB PRO Theorem treats PRO simultaneously as an anaphor subject to Principle A of the binding theory and a pronoun subject to Principle B. In the context of the binding theory, this dual status of PRO implies that it is ungoverned. Were it governed, it would possess a governing category and would have to meet both Principles A and B. As being both bound and free *within a given domain* is impossible, it must be that pronominal anaphors (i.e. PROs) evade this contradiction by not having governing categories. An XP with no governor (i.e. a governing X^0) is without a governing category. Thus, if PROs do not have governors (i.e. exclusively appear in ungoverned positions), they can meet their binding requirements. If one further assumes that the [Spec, IP] position of infinitives and gerunds is ungoverned, the observed distribution of PRO is explained.

This reasoning offers an additional bonus: it explains why PRO is phonetically null. In GB a D/NP is assigned Case by a Case-marking head that governs it. Since PROs cannot be governed, they cannot be Case-marked. If phonetically full D/NPs must be Case-marked, then PRO's lack of a governor precludes its having phonetic content. In sum, the PRO Theorem and Case theory combine to account both for PRO's distribution and for its phonetic status.

This GB account is less successful in dealing with PRO's interpretive characteristics. Williams (1980) argues that there are two types of control; obligatory control (OC) and nonobligatory control (NOC). This distinction, which has generally been accepted,[4] is based on several interpretive phenomena that distinguish OC from NOC constructions. Consider the following OC paradigm:[5]

(4) a.   *It was expected PRO to shave himself.
     b.   *John thinks that it was expected PRO to shave himself.
     c.   *John's campaign expects PRO to shave himself.
     d.   John expects PRO to win and Bill does too. (= Bill win)
     e.   *John$_i$ told Mary$_j$ PRO$_{i+j}$ to wash themselves/each other.
     f.   The unfortunate expects PRO to get a medal.
     g.   Only Churchill remembers PRO giving the BST speech.

(4a) shows that OC PRO must have an antecedent. (4b) indicates that this antecedent must be local, and (4c) that it must c-command the PRO. (4d) indicates that OC PRO only permits a sloppy interpretation under ellipsis. (4e) shows that OC PRO cannot have split antecedents. PRO in (4f) has only the *de se* interpretation, in that the unfortunate believes *of himself or herself* that he or she will be a medal recipient. In theory, (4g) could have two paraphrases, (5a) and (5b). In fact, however, only paraphrase (5a) – on which only Churchill could have this memory, for Churchill was the sole person to give the speech – is available. This contrast follows on the assumption that OC PRO must have a c-commanding antecedent. This requires *only Churchill* to be the binder.

(5) a.   Only Churchill remembers himself giving the BST speech.
     b.   Only Churchill remembers that he gave the BST speech.

These properties of OC PRO are not shared by PRO in NOC environments.[6]

(6) a. It was believed that PRO shaving was important.
     b. John$_i$ thinks that it is believed that PRO$_i$ shaving himself is important.
     c. Clinton's$_i$ campaign believes that PRO$_i$ keeping his sex life under control is necessary for electoral success.
     d. John thinks that PRO getting his resume in order is crucial and Bill does too.
     e. John$_i$ told Mary$_j$ [that [[PRO$_{i+j}$ washing themselves/each other] would be fun]].
     f. The unfortunate believes that PRO getting a medal would be boring.
     g. Only Churchill remembers that PRO giving the BST speech was momentous.

(6a) indicates that NOC PRO does not require an antecedent. (6b) demonstrates that if it does have an antecedent, the antecedent need not be local. (6c) shows that the antecedent need not c-command the NOC PRO. (6d) contrasts with (4d) in permitting a strict reading of the elided VP (i.e. the reading on which it is John's resume that is at issue). (6e) indicates that split antecedents are readily available in NOC contexts. (6f) can have a non-*de se* interpretation. (6g) is consistent with the notion that many people other than Churchill recall that the BST speech was momentous.

The OC cases in (4) and the NOC cases in (6) contrast in one further interesting way; it is possible to paraphrase the former by replacing PRO with reflexives, and the latter by replacing it with pronouns. (7) illustrates this with the counterparts of (4c) and (6c).

(7) a. *John's$_i$ campaign expects himself$_i$ to shave himself.
     b. Clinton's$_i$ campaign believes that his$_i$ keeping his sex life under control is crucial for electoral success.

In short, the differences between OC and NOC structures duplicate, where applicable, the differences between structures with locally bound anaphors and pronouns (see (5a) and (5b) as well). This makes sense if PRO is actually ambiguous – an anaphoric expression in OC configurations and a pronominal in NOC structures – rather than simultaneously a pronoun and an anaphor, as the PRO Theorem requires. This, then, speaks against reducing the distribution of PRO to the binding theory by way of the PRO Theorem.
     [. . .]
     [. . .]
Given minimalist inclinations, the deepest question concerning PRO is whether such a formative even exists. PRO is a theory-internal construct.[7] In GB, PRO is structurally analogous to NP-traces and *wh*-traces. All have the same shape, namely, [$_{NP}$ e]. The main difference between traces and PRO is the source of their indices: the former derive from movement, the latter are assigned via the control module. In the Minimalist Program, however, this machinery is all suspect. There

is little reason to think that traces (qua distinctive grammatical constructs) exist at all. Traces are not grammatical formatives but the residues of the copy-and-deletion operations necessary to yield PF/LF pairs. As such, traces have no common structure in the Minimalist Program as they do in GB. They are simply copies of lexical material and so have no specific shapes whatsoever. Thus, they cannot be structurally analogous to PRO. This leaves the theoretical status of PRO up in the air. What kind of empty category is it? Why do grammars have it?

Section 1 has provided answers to these questions. PRO exists because of θ-theory. If chains could bear more than one θ-role and if θ-roles could be accreted in the course of a derivation, there would be little reason to distinguish PROs in OC configurations from NP-traces. As these restrictions on θ-assignment are not conceptually necessary, the theoretical basis for distinguishing PROs from NP-traces weakens. Put more bluntly, distinguishing trace from PRO requires *additional* assumptions about θ-assignment and chains. The burden of proof, therefore, resides with those who favor such assumptions. In section 4 I argue that forgoing these stipulations permits a more empirically and theoretically adequate account of OC. I propose that PRO, like NP-trace, is the residue of movement. Strictly speaking, then, there is no grammatical formative like PRO. Rather, PRO is simply a residue of movement – simply the product of copy-and-deletion operations that relate two θ-positions.[8]

4   An alternative

I have argued that the null hypothesis is that OC PRO is identical to NP-trace; that is, it is simply the residue of movement. NOC PRO is to be identified with pro, the null pronominal found in various Romance and East Asian languages. This section is concerned with demonstrating the empirical virtues of these assumptions. The main focus is on OC PRO, since handling the OC data requires the most radical departures from standard GB and minimalist technicalia. For what follows, I adopt the following assumptions:

(8)   a.   θ-roles are features on verbs.
      b.   Greed is Enlightened Self-Interest.
      c.   A D/NP "receives" a θ-role by checking a θ-feature of a verbal/predicative phrase that it merges with.
      d.   There is no upper bound on the number of θ-roles a chain can have.
      e.   Sideward movement is permitted.

(8a) treats θ-roles as morphological features.[9] This is required if movement to a θ-position is to conform to the principle of Greed. If OC is to be reduced to movement, then this assumption is conceptually required given other minimalist assumptions. (8b) interprets Greed as requiring at least one of the relata to check a feature (Lasnik 1995). Thus, if A moves to merge with B, then at least one feature of either A or (the head of) B is checked. Treating θ-roles as features on the verb or predicate allows a D/NP to move to a θ-position and respect Greed by checking this feature.[10] Analyzing θ-roles thus permits us to "mechanize" θ-role assignment as in (8c): to receive a θ-role is just to check the relevant thematic feature of the predicate. One might think of this as "transferring" the verbal θ-feature to the nominal expression. In effect, checking conforms to Chomsky's (1995: 226) vision of syntactic operations as the "rearrangements of properties of the lexical items of which they are ultimately constituted" – that is, the features of the elements in the array. (8d) is logically required to analyze OC in terms of movement given that control involves the relation of at least two θ-positions. It is also the null hypothesis, I believe. The requirement that chains be restricted to a single θ-role needs substantial empirical justification. (8e) comes into play in the analysis of adjunct OC. I discuss it further in that context. What is important here is that c-command is not part of the *definition* of movement. Thus, the computational system does not prohibit the copying of an expression to a position that does not c-command the "movement" site.[11]

The assumptions in (8) suffice to accommodate OC in terms of movement given standard minimalist technology. Their empirical virtue is that they permit a radical simplification of the grammar of control and a derivation of the basic properties of OC structures. Consider the details.

First, consider the basic interpretive properties of OC structures. As noted in section 2, these structures require c-commanding local antecedents (see (4a–c)). This is what one expects if OC PROs are NP-traces. For illustration, let us look at (9).

(9) a. John hopes to leave.
    b. [IP John [VP John [hopes [IP John to [VP John leave]]]]]

The derivation begins with *John* merging with *leave*, thereby checking the verb's θ-role. *John* then "raises" to the embedded [Spec, IP] to check the D-feature of the IP. This is *not* a Case-marking position, so the Case of *John* cannot be checked here. *John* raises again to [Spec, VP] of *hope* and checks the external θ-feature of the verb. By (8c), each time *John* checks a θ-feature of a predicate, it assumes that θ-role. Thus, *John* (or the chain it heads) has two θ-roles, the leaver role and the hoper role. *John* raises one last time to [Spec, IP] of the matrix, where it checks the D-feature of the IP and nominative Case. Note that this is the only place where *John* checks Case. On the assumption that it was inserted into the derivation with nominative Case features, the derivation converges. In more conventional notation, the copy *John* in the embedded [Spec, IP] corresponds to PRO, and the copy in the matrix [Spec, IP] is the antecedent. The requirement that OC have a local c-commanding antecedent follows from the fact that PRO is an intermediate link in an A-chain. As such, it must have an antecedent. Furthermore, the antecedent must conform to general A-chain strictures and thus both c-command the traces in the A-chain (i.e. the PRO in [Spec, IP]) and be local to it, given conditions on movement like the MLC. In short, the first three properties of OC PRO follow straightforwardly (see (4a–c)).

Treating OC PRO as the residue of movement also derives the prohibition against split antecedents. Two (nonconjoined) expressions cannot both antecede OC PRO because they cannot have both moved from the same position. In other words, the ban against split antecedents in this case is equivalent to the ban against one and the same trace having two distinct antecedents. In the Minimalist Program this reduces to the fact that two distinct expressions cannot be merged into a single position.[12]

The required sloppy reading of OC PRO follows as well. Note that in raising constructions only a sloppy reading is available.

(10)   Mary seems to be happy and Sally does too.

(10) must be understood to mean that it seems that Sally is happy. For the same reason, OC PRO must carry the sloppy reading since it too is an NP-trace.[13]

The movement analysis also accounts for the required *de se* interpretation of OC PRO. The movement underlying OC PRO ends up assigning two θ-roles to a single expression; for example, in (9a) *John* has two θ-roles. The semantic form of the predication in (9) is equivalent to (11), a predication that ascribes a reflexive property to the subject *John*.

(11)   John λx [x hopes x leave]

Movement, then, semantically forms a compound monadic predicate by having one and the same expression saturate two argument positions. Salmon (1986) discusses these semantic issues at some length. Of importance here is his observation that relating the semantic value of an expression to two θ-positions via the formation of a reflexive predicate is semantically very different from relating two expressions in different θ-positions to each other via coreference. The former operation results in changing the semantic argument structure of the predicate; the latter leaves it intact. The former operation reflexivizes the predicate and thus forces a *de se* reading; the latter does not. Treating OC as the reflex of movement, then, yields the correct interpretation for the structures – the one exemplified in (11).

Finally, the observed reading in (4g) (repeated here) follows as well.

(12)   Only Churchill remembers giving the BST speech.

The reading on which someone other than Churchill could recall this event requires the paraphrase in (13).

(13)   Only Churchill remembers Churchill giving the BST speech.

This cannot underlie the structure of (12). The PRO here is of the OC variety. This means that *only Churchill* has raised from the embedded position and has the reflexive property noted in (14). This is semantically equivalent to the reading on which Churchill alone has the required memory.

(14)   only Churchill λx [x remembers x giving the BST speech]

In sum, the six basic properties of OC reviewed in section 2 follow directly from assuming that OC PRO is identical to NP-trace, the residue of movement. In addition, these properties are derived without the problems reviewed in section 3. Once again, consider the details.

The distribution of OC PRO does not require the services of null Case. This Case, specially designed for PRO by Chomsky and Lasnik (1993), is unnecessary if OC PRO is an NP-trace. In fact, the existence of null Case in [Spec, IP] of control infinitives is *incompatible* with the movement analysis, since it would prevent raising out of the embedded [Spec, IP].

Abandoning null Case in this context does not lead to any empirical difficulties. Recall that null Case has been postulated to replace the assumption that PRO must be ungoverned. Its principal empirical effect is to block the derivation of (15) and license PRO only in [Spec, IP] of nonfinite clauses.

(15) *We never expected [PRO_i to appear to t_i that . . .

The proposed account rules (15) out on the same basis as an account that postulates null Case. On the latter view, PRO cannot move to [Spec, IP] of the embedded clause because it would be moving from one Case-marking position (inside PP) to another ([Spec, IP]). This either violates Greed or causes a feature mismatch. In either case the derivation fails to converge. However, if [Spec, IP] is an *intermediate* NP-trace, as it would be on the proposed account, then the same reasoning prohibits movement through this position. In effect, a PRO in (15) should be no better than an NP-trace in (16).

(16) *We_i were expected [t_i to appear to t_i that . . .

Furthermore, on the proposed account we expect to find OC PRO in positions from which movement is licit. This should roughly coincide with non-Case-marked positions, such as [Spec, IP] of nonfinite clauses. Note that this is compatible with treating inherently reflexive verbs like *wash*, *dress*, and *shave* as simply not Case-marking their objects – in effect, as allowing derivations like (17) to be licit.

(17) a. Mary washed.
      b. [$_{IP}$ Mary [past [$_{VP}$ Mary [wash Mary]]]]

Case is checked in [Spec, IP]. *Mary* receives two θ-roles since it checks both the internal and external θ-role of *wash*.[14]
[. . .]

The movement approach to OC PRO also accommodates the classical data used to distinguish raising from control. It was argued, for example, that idiom chunks and expletives could raise but not control.

(18) a. The shit seems [t to have hit the fan].
      b. There seems [t to be a man in the garden].
(19) a. *The shit expects [PRO to hit the fan].
      b. *There expects [PRO to be a man in the garden].

The distinction between these cases is preserved in the present account even if PRO in (19) is just an NP-trace. The basis for the distinction is that in (18) *the shit* and *there* bear the external θ-role of *expect*. If this θ-role is not checked, then, I assume, the derivation fails to converge since there is an unchecked θ-feature at LF.[15] However, the only nominals that can check the relevant θ-roles, *there* and *the shit*, are not expressions that can bear θ-roles because of their inherent idiomatic or expletive semantics. As a result, we retain a difference between raising and control structures in cases such as these but attribute it not to an inability to control PRO but to an inability to support a θ-role that must be discharged for grammaticality to ensue.

This section has demonstrated that OC structures can be treated in terms of movement and that there is considerable empirical payoff in doing so. In particular, we can dispense with null Case, and we can derive the six basic properties of OC exemplified in (4). The next section turns to perhaps the biggest advantage. It appears that treating OC PRO as the residue of movement comes very close to allowing us to eliminate the PRO module entirely.

5 The Minimal Distance Principle reduced to the Minimal Link Condition

The PRO module has two primary functions. First, it designates the controller in an OC structure. Second, it determines how a controlled PRO is to be interpreted in a given configuration (e.g. Does it permit split antecedents? Is it obligatorily *de se*?). The latter function of the PRO module is no longer required. The various interpretive options of OC and NOC PRO follow from whether the PRO in question is a null pronominal – pro – or a residue of A-movement – an NP-trace.[16] Still to be explained is how the controller in OC cases is determined. Note that this is not an issue for NOC configurations, since in these cases no antecedent is required. This is the topic of this section.

The chief descriptive principle regulating this part of the PRO module is the Minimal Distance Principle (MDP).[17] Its effect is to designate NP_i the controller in the configurations in (20).

(20)   a. NP_i [V [PRO ...]]
        b.   NP [V NP_i [PRO ...]]

Thus, the MDP picks the closest c-commanding potential antecedent as controller; that is, α is the controller of PRO iff α c-commands PRO, and for all β different from α that c-command PRO, β c-commands α. The MDP picks the subject to be the controller in (20a) and the object in (20b). If the MDP is treated as a markedness condition, then verbs like *persuade* become the unmarked case and verbs like *promise* are highly marked. This state of affairs closely coincides with the observed data and I assume its accuracy here.

The MDP makes perfect sense from the perspective of a movement approach to OC. We have already seen the derivation of a structure like (20a) in (9b). Now consider the derivation of an object control sentence.

(21) a. John persuaded Harry to leave.
      b. [$_{IP_2}$ John [$_{I^0}$ past [$_{VP_3}$ John v + persuaded [$_{VP_2}$ Harry persuaded [$_{IP_1}$ Harry [to [$_{VP_1}$ Harry leave]]]]]]]

The array consists of the following set of expressions: {John, Harry, persuaded, to, leave, past, v, other assorted functional categories}. The derivation starts by selecting *leave* and *Harry* and merging them. This allows *Harry* to check the θ-feature of *leave* and assume the internal argument role – (8a,c). *To* then merges with the VP headed by *leave*, and *Harry* moves to [Spec, IP$_1$] to check the D-feature of the embedded clause (the Extended Projection Principle).

Note that this move violates Procrastinate, since *John* could have been inserted here. However, if *John* had been inserted, the derivation would not have been able to converge. I return to the details after limning the rest of the derivation.

IP$_1$ then merges with *persuaded*, checking the propositional θ-role of the verb. *Harry* then raises and merges with VP to form [Spec, VP$_2$]. This too is a θ-position of *persuade*, and this move provides *Harry* with a second θ-role. Once again Procrastinate is violated, since *John* could have been inserted. Had it been, however, the derivation would have failed to converge, so the insertion is blocked (see below). The next step is to raise *persuaded* to merge with *v*. Then *John* is taken from the array and merged with the *v* + *persuaded* projection, forming [Spec, VP$_3$]. This is a θ-position, and *John* checks the external θ-role. Past tense features then merge with VP$_3$. *John* raises and forms [Spec, IP$_2$]. Here the D-features and nominative Case features of T are checked, as are the Case features of *John*. At LF *Harry* raises and forms an outer [Spec, VP] (or alternatively merges with Agr$_O$ and forms [Spec, Agr$_O$]), where it checks its Case features and those of *v* + *persuade*. All features that must be checked ate checked, and the derivation converges.

Observe that [Spec, IP$_1$], the so-called position of PRO, is occupied by an intermediate copy of *Harry*. This expression has been inserted with Case features. Assume that it has accusative Case; otherwise, the derivation does not converge. Each move in the derivation is licit with respect to Greed because some feature is checked at every step. The two violations of Procrastinate must still be accounted for, however. Let's turn to them now.

Harry is inserted into the derivation with some Case features.[18] If these features are accusative, then there is no way to check the features on *John*. There are two possibilities. If *John* has accusative features, then either its features or those on *Harry* cannot be checked, since only one accusative head is available: *v* + *persuaded*. If the features on *Harry* are nominative, then the Minimal Link Condition (MLC) will prevent movement of *Harry* across *John* if *Harry* is inserted into [Spec, IP$_1$] and raised again. The full LF phrase marker given this derivation is (22).

(22) [$_{IP_2}$ Harry [$_{I^0}$ past [John [$_{VP_3}$ John v + persuaded [$_{VP_2}$ John persuaded [$_{IP_1}$ John [to [$_{VP_1}$ Harry leave]]]]]]]]

To check nominative Case requires moving *Harry* to I^0. This traverses several copies of *John*, all of which are closer. This violates the MLC and so is illicit (see below).

Consider the second option. *John* is inserted with nominative Case, *Harry* with accusative. *John* is merged into [Spec, IP_1]. It then raises through the two θ-positions of *persuade* and *v* up to [Spec, IP_2], where it checks its nominative Case and that of T, as well as the D-feature of IP_2. The accusative features on *Harry* need to be checked. This could be done by moving to the outer [Spec, VP_3]. The relevant LF phrase marker is (23).

(23) $[_{IP_2}$ John $[_{I^0}$ past [Harry $[_{VP_3}$ John v + persuaded $[_{VP_2}$ John persuaded $[_{IP_1}$ John [to $[_{VP_1}$ Harry leave]]]]]]]]]

The derivation in (23) must be illicit if the one in (21b) is well formed as required by the present analysis. The derivation in (23) violates the MLC on the assumption that *John* in [Spec, IP_1], [Spec, VP_2], or [Spec, VP_3] prevents the movement of *Harry* in [Spec, VP_1] to the outer [Spec, VP_3] (or to Agr_O to form [Spec, Agr_O]) to check accusative Case at LF. This, in turn, requires that copies formed by movement be relevant for the MLC. *Harry* cannot check its Case because it is farther from the relevant Case-checking position than are *copies* of *John*. If we make the assumption that such copies are visible to the computational system (and thereby block movement across them via the MLC), then the derivation in (23) does not converge. This, in turn, permits Procrastinate to be violated in the derivation of (21b).

Interestingly, the assumption that copies are relevant for the MLC is required independently once the assumption that only trivial chains can be θ-marked – (8d) – is dropped. Given the assumption (8d) that there is no upper bound on the number of θ-roles an expression can have – a conceptually necessary assumption if OC is to be reduced to movement – (24) provides independent motivation for making the MLC sensitive to copies. Chomsky (1995: 345) asks why (24b) does not exclude (24c).

(24)   a.   I expected someone to be in the room.
       b. $[_{IP_1}$ I expected $[_{IP_2}$ I to be [someone in the room]]]
       c. $[_{IP_1}$ I expected $[_{IP_2}$ someone to be [someone in the room]]]

The derivation of (24b) proceeds as follows. The small clause *someone in the room* is constructed via successive mergers. The result is merged with *be* and then with *to*. *I* is merged in the [Spec, IP_2] position, discharging the D-feature on the embedded I. The result is merged with *expected*. Chomsky argues that this structure is illicit because *I* cannot receive a θ-role given either the assumption that only trivial chains can be θ-marked or the assumption that θ-features do not count for Greed so that movement via the [Spec, VP] of *expect* is illicit. If convergence requires nominals to have θ-roles, then (24b) does not converge. This then licenses the derivation in (24c) in which Procrastinate is violated. In other words, instead of merging *I* to [Spec, IP_2], *someone* can be raised, violating Procrastinate. This is how (24a) is licitly derived.

The assumptions in (8) preclude adopting this analysis. Given (8b,d), there is nothing that prohibits moving *I* to [Spec, VP] of *expect* to receive a θ-role. Thus,

(24b)'s failure to converge cannot be due to the requirement that nominals have θ-roles. However, the derivation can be excluded in the same way that (23) is. *Someone* needs to check its Case features. The only available Case position is the outer Spec of *expected* (or the Agr_O above it). Movement to this outer Spec is blocked by I in [Spec, IP_2] if copies count for the MLC.[19] In short, the same reasoning required for (23) extends to cover this case as well.

(24) is of particular interest, for it indicates that treating copies as the computational equals of originals from the array is virtually unavoidable if OC is reduced to movement in the context of the Minimalist Program. (24b) must be prohibited from converging. θ-theory is unavailable once (8b,d) eliminate the last vestiges of D-Structure. In particular, there is nothing amiss with the derivation in (24b) if *someone* can check Case. Thus, it must be that it cannot. This is accomplished if the I in [Spec, IP_2] triggers the MLC.[20]

The above has been in the service of a single conclusion: that object control can be derived via movement given a general minimalist setting amended by (8). There is a further conclusion. Subject control in *persuade* clauses is ungrammatical. To derive a structure of subject control involves violating the MLC. Consider the derivation of a subject control structure like (25a).

(25) a. John$_i$ persuaded Harry [PRO$_i$ to leave].
      b. [$_{IP_2}$ John [$_{I^0}$ past [$_{VP_3}$ John v + persuaded [$_{VP_2}$ Harry persuaded [$_{IP_1}$ John [to [$_{VP_1}$ John leave]]]]]]]

The relevant structure is (25b). If *John* is the controller, it must have been merged with *leave* and raised to [Spec, IP_1], the locus of "PRO." *Harry* has the object-of-*persuade* θ-role, as indicated by its merger in [Spec, VP_2]. Now, the external θ-feature of *v* + *persuaded* must be checked. In (25b) *John* is raised to [Spec, VP_3]. Note that it crosses *Harry* in [Spec, VP_2]. This violates the MLC and is prohibited. As noted earlier, this is consistent with the traditional observation (see Chomsky 1969) that subject control verbs like *promise* are highly marked.

To conclude: I have argued that a derivational approach to OC can account for the prevalence of object control with *persuade* verbs. This is what is expected given minimalist technology supplemented with the assumptions in (8). In effect, OC structures conform to the traditional MDP just in case their derivational histories respect the MLC. The control module and MDP are superfluous in cases like these.

Consider now the absence of object control in structures like (26), illustrated in (27).

(26) NP$_i$ V NP$_j$ [$_{Adjunct}$ PRO$_{i/*j}$ . . .]
(27) John$_i$ heard Mary$_j$ [without/before/after [PRO$_{i/*j}$ entering the room]].

The account for these structures can also be reduced to the MDP if it is assumed that objects do not c-command adjuncts. In minimalist terms, this requires assuming that objects fail to c-command adjuncts *at LF*, the locus of binding requirements in a minimalist theory. This assumption is doubtful, however, given that objects can license bound pronouns within adjuncts.

(28)   John read every book$_i$ without reviewing it$_i$.

If *every book* can bind *it*, then *every book* c-commands *it* at LF. If so, it c-commands PRO as well. Regardless of whether the MDP can be made to operate in these cases, the movement approach to PRO derives the data in (26)–(27). Consider the details.

The numeration for (27) consists of the set of items {John, heard, Mary, without, entering, the, room, assorted functional categories}. We build the adjunct phrase by merging *the* with *room*, *entering* with *the room*, and *John* with *entering the room*. The two θ-roles of *enter* are checked by the merger of the two D/NPs. *-ing* heads its own I projection. This merges with the previously formed VP small clause. The strong feature of this I is checked by raising *John*. (Observe that this violates Procrastinate; I return to this issue after completing the proper derivation.) After the adjunct has merged with the IP, we have a structure like (29).[21]

(29)   [$_{Adjunct}$ without [$_{IP}$ John [$_{I^0}$ ing [$_{VP}$ John [entering the room]]]]]

Next we build the main clause. *Mary* merges with *heard*. The internal θ-role is thereby discharged. (29) then merges with this VP, forming an adjunction structure.[22]

(30)   [$_{VP/VP}$[$_{VP}$ heard Mary] [$_{Adjunct}$ without [$_{IP}$ John [$_{I^0}$ ing [$_{VP}$ John [entering the room]]]]]]

The external θ-feature of *heard* must be checked. If *John* raises, then the derivation proceeds as follows: *John* raises and discharges the external θ-role by merging with the VP of *heard*.[23] It then raises to [Spec, IP] to check its own Case, those of I, and the latter's D-features. At LF *Mary* raises to check accusative Case in either the outer [Spec, VP] or Agr$_O$P. The derivation converges with the overt structure in (31).

(31)   [$_{IP}$ John [$_{I^0}$ past [$_{VP/VP}$[$_{VP}$ John [heard Mary]] [$_{Adjunct}$ without [$_{IP}$ John [$_{I^0}$ ing [$_{VP}$ John [entering the room]]]]]]]]

This derivation requires explanation at two points. First, the movement of *John* to [Spec, ing] within the adjunct violates Procrastinate. *Mary* could have been inserted. Had it been, however, *John* could never have checked its Case features. *Mary* or a copy of *Mary* would have blocked movement out of the adjunct to a Case position in the matrix. In short, once again the MLC would prevent a convergent derivation. Thus, Procrastinate is violable at this point.

Second, *John* moves to check the external θ-feature of *heard*. Doesn't this violate the MLC? In other words, isn't *Mary* closer to this position, and shouldn't *Mary* block this movement? The MLC is not involved in this move. The reason is that *Mary* in the complement position of *heard* and *John* in [Spec, IP] of the adjunct do not c-command one another, nor does the target of movement c-command them both (see note 24). Thus, they are not in a "proximity" relation relevant for the MLC. The combination of movement from an adjunct and move-ment to a non-c-commanding position makes it possible for *Mary* and *John* to be equidistant from the [Spec, VP] of *heard*. Hence, moving *John* to [Spec, VP] does not violate the MLC. Furthermore, if *Mary* moves to [Spec, VP] in place of *John*, then the derivation cannot converge, for the Case features on *John* will not be checked.[24] Thus, the only convergent derivation is the one reviewed in (29)–(31).[25] This is the desired result, for it deduces, correctly, that OC PROs inside adjuncts are necessarily controlled by subjects. [. . .]

Notes

1   This is not quite accurate. Recently control has become a hot area of research. My pro-posal shares with O'Neil's (1995) the intuition that control should be reduced to move-ment. Though the details of the two approaches differ, they are conceptually very similar. There are two other approaches to control set within minimalist assumptions. Martin (1996) develops a theory exploiting the notion of null Case proposed by Chomsky and Lasnik (1993) to account for the distribution of PRO. Manzini and Roussou (1997) develop a theory of control in terms of feature movement of heads at LF. The wealth of approaches is to be welcomed given the awkward position that the control module has in the Minimalist Program. In what follows I lay out a view of control that differs from those noted here. For reasons of space, I keep comparisons to a minimum.

2   This was first suggested by Bouchard (1984). Chomsky and Lasnik adopt Bouchard's basic proposal, though their particular version differs in certain details.

3   This theory has been elaborated and expanded in Martin (1996).

4   See, for example, Bouchard (1984); Koster (1984); Manzini (1983); Lebeaux (1985); Hornstein and Lightfoot (1987).

5   (4a–e) are presented in Lebeaux (1985). (4f) is discussed in Higginbotham (1992). (4g) was first discussed in Fodor (1975).

6   It is even possible to "control" an NOC PRO across a sentence boundary. I believe that this was first noted by Emmon Bach, though I cannot recall where.

(i)   John$_i$ even shaved for the interview. PRO$_i$ making himself presentable is very import-ant to the success of the project.

7   See Nunes (1995) for a discussion of the status of traces as formatives in the Minimalist Program.

8   It is interesting to observe that earlier theories of control that distinguished OC and NOC assume that OC PRO is governed (see, e.g. Manzini 1983; Hornstein and Lightfoot 1987). In many versions of the ECP, government by a head is required for all empty categories resulting from movement (see, e.g. Aoun et al. 1987; Rizzi 1990). The fact that OC PROs are the head-governed ones once again suggests that they, like traces in general, are the residues of movement.

9   This has already been proposed by Lasnik (1995), Bošković (1994), and Bošković and Takahashi (1998).

10   Chomsky (1995) suggests that it is odd to think of θ-roles as features. This is correct if one thinks of them as properties of D/NPs. There is no "paradigm" that groups nominals by their thematic status. However, verbs (and other predicates) are indeed grouped by adicity. In other words, verbs are categorized by their thematic status. This makes it quite natural to treat θ-roles as features of predicates as proposed here.

11 See Nunes (1995) for elaborate discussion. This option does not prohibit making c-command a property of chains, however. Thus, sideward movement might be allowed, but the resulting copies might have to be in a c-command sequence to be interpretable objects. I am not advocating this here, however. The negative thesis suffices for the time being. See section 5 for discussion of sideward movement.

12 This actually follows from the definition of Merge together with the analysis of movement as copy and deletion and of traces as copies. The fact that it does so is interesting, for in a representational theory that treats traces as real base-generated formatives (one version of GB), this prohibition against split antecedents must be stipulated.

13 This does not say how sloppy readings are derived, whether interpretively (Sag 1976; Williams 1977) or via deletion operations at PF under some sort of parallelism requirement (Chomsky 1995). For current purposes, which of these proves to be correct is irrelevant. All that is required is that the ultimately correct approach should treat movement in an interpretively uniform fashion.

14 The question remains, why this operation is not generally valid. If we assume that the difference between *wash* and *see* is that the latter must assign accusative Case whereas the former can suppress it, then we expect (i) to violate Case theory.

(i) John saw PRO.

The underlying structure would leave either the accusative Case of *saw* or the nominative Case of IP unchecked.

    Note that if this is correct, then *expect* is like *wash* in optionally suppressing its accusative Case, and *believe* is like *see*. This permits the contrast in (ii).

(ii) a. John expects PRO to be leaving.
      b. *John believes to be leaving.

15 If one is reluctant to require that θ-features be checked, one might recast the θ-Criterion to require that every θ-role be "expressed" by being attached to a DP. This would then make (19a–b) θ-Criterion violations. Note that the analysis proposed above requires dropping the assumption that a DP can bear only one θ-role. It does not require dropping the assumption that all θ-roles must be assigned.

16 There remains the issue of when pro-headed propositions are permitted (see section 6 of the original paper).

17 This was first formulated in Rosenbaum (1967).

18 The standard assumption, adopted here, is that nominal expressions cannot be doubly Case-marked. This is also the minimal assumption given standard minimalist reasoning: universally, nominals require Case. This is minimally satisfied with one set of Case features. As no more are required, no more are permitted, at least in the unmarked case.

19 Note that, strictly speaking, the *I* in the embedded [Spec, IP] is not a copy but the original element selected from the array. The higher *I*s are the copies if movement is copying plus deletion as Chomsky (1995) assumes. The point in the text is that the grammar does not (and should not) distinguish copies from originals in any relevant sense. This is contrary to Chomsky's proposal that the foot of a chain differs from the head in not being visible to the computational system. Chomsky's proposal amounts to encoding in minimalist terms a distinction between expressions and their traces. In effect, it implicitly postulates the existence of traces as grammatical formatives. As usual, the postulation of abstract entities must be empirically justified. The null position is that NP-traces, qua distinctive grammatical objects, do not exist. This is what the copy theory presupposes and what I assume here. For further critical discussion of this assumption, see Nunes (1995).

    Treating all copies as grammatically equal raises the question of whether chains are "real" objects, that is, have distinctive properties of their own. When introduced in Chomsky (1981), chains were a notational shorthand used for summarizing the properties of local movement. Rizzi (1986) was the first to argue that chains had an independent grammatical existence. In the context of the Minimalist Program, it is not at all clear that chains should be treated as independent entities. For example, their existence appears to contradict "inclusiveness" (Chomsky 1995: 228), which bars the addition of "new objects" in the course of the computation from the numeration to LF. Chains are not lexical objects. Therefore, inclusiveness should bar their presence at LF. This is not to deny that movement exists. The existence of "displacement" operations in the grammar is undeniable. However, this does not imply that chains exist, with well-formedness conditions of their own. For further discussion of these issues, see Hornstein (1998b).

20   The reasoning in (24) is the sole argument given in Chomsky (1995) for assuming that NPs must have θ-roles for a derivation to converge. The reasoning in terms of Case removes this argument.

There is another problem, however, that leads to the same conclusion. Consider (i) (with the structure in (ii)), brought to my attention by Juan Carlos Castillo (see also Martin 1996: 26, (21)).

(i)   *John expects to seem that he is smart.

(ii)   [$_{IP_1}$ John [$_{VP}$ John expects [$_{IP_2}$ John to seem [$_{CP}$ that he . . .]]]]

According to the derivation in (ii), *John* is first merged into [Spec, IP$_1$]. It raises to [Spec, VP], checking the external θ-role of *expect*, and then raises to [Spec, IP$_1$] to check Case and D-features. This derivation is ruled out if movement cannot take place to a θ-position or if only trivial chains can receive θ-roles. However, these assumptions are rejected here, and so another way must be found to prevent the derivation in (ii). Two solutions are possible.

The first option is to deny that *John* can be inserted into [Spec, IP$_2$] since it fails to check some relevant feature. One possibility is that the I^0 of a control predicate differs from the I^0 in a raising construction. This is proposed by Martin (1996: ch. 2), following earlier work by Stowell (1982) on the tense of infinitives. The proposal is that control and raising infinitives have a [T] feature. The two types are distinguished in that control infinitives have [+T] I and raising infinitives have [–T] I. Say that this is correct. We now make a further assumption concerning [+T] infinitives: namely, that the [+T] control infinitive I (in contrast to the [–T] raising infinitive I) has a feature that can only be checked by an NP that has a θ-feature (i.e. is θ-marked). For concreteness, assume that the D-feature associated with [+T] infinitives can only be checked by a DP with a θ-feature. Recall that the account I am proposing treats θ-roles as features that an expression receives by checking the θ-features of a predicate under merger. In effect, the θ-features of the verb are transferred to the DP that merges with it. If they are indeed features, then we would expect them to enter into typical checking relations. The proposal is that this is what happens in control IPs; that is, only DPs having θ-features can check the I of a [+T] OC infinitive. Note that this will prevent the derivation in (ii), for *John* merged into [Spec, IP$_2$] has not yet been θ-marked. It receives a θ-feature only by moving to [Spec, VP]. Thus, it cannot check the postulated θ-sensitive feature of the [+T] infinitive I. Note that this same assumption will suffice to block control by expletive arguments like *it* in sentences like (iii).

(iii)   *It was hoped to be believed that Fran left.

(iii) cannot be interpreted as parallel to (iv).

(iv)   It was hoped that it was believed that Fran left.

The question is, why not? The relevant structure is (v).

(v) $[_{IP_2}$ it was hoped $[_{IP_1}$ it to be believed [that . . .

This is illicit if we assume that *it* – not endowed with a θ-role (or endowed with the "wrong kind" of pseudoargument θ-role in the sense of Chomsky 1986) – cannot check the postulated feature of the embedded [+T] infinitive that *hope* selects. Note that if PRO were a formative, it is not clear how (v) would be ruled out except by stipulating that it cannot be bound by a non-θ-marked antecedent in these sorts of constructions. This, however, runs against the observation that such control is possible in adjunct structures (see Chomsky 1986, where (via) is discussed).

(vi) a. It$_i$ always rains [before PRO$_i$ snowing].
      b. It$_i$ seemed that Clinton won reelection without PRO$_i$ appearing that he had won a majority.

In short, postulating a feature on [+T] infinitives that must be checked by θ-marked DPs suffices to handle (i).

A second option for dealing with (i) is to recognize that when predicates like *seem* take finite complements, they require *it* subjects. If, as Chomsky (1986) suggests, *it* carries a weak kind of θ-role, then one can treat this requirement as a selection fact about predicates with finite complements: they select thematically marked subjects like *it*. If so, then (i) is ruled out because it violates a selection restriction. Note that the intimate relation between *it* and finite complements has long been observed. The proposal here is to exploit that fact to block the derivation in (i). A similar sort of account would block the derivation of (vii), which Chomsky (1995) treats as a selection restriction violation.

(vii) *I expect $[_{IP_1}$ John to seem [that t left]].

This raising should be licensed by the requirement to check the D-feature in IP$_1$. It is blocked if the finite complement requires that *seem* have an *it* subject.

For current purposes, either approach suffices. I assume that one of them can be more fully worked out to accommodate the problematic (i); thus, (i) does not threaten the basic assumptions required for a movement theory of OC.

21 I remain agnostic on the exact status of the adjunct – that is, whether it is a complementizer or head of a PP.

22 I represent adjunction as *VP/VP*, modifying slightly the convention in Chomsky (1995). The adjunct is adjoined at this point in the derivation to conform to the assumption that movement requires a connected tree (see Epstein 1996). It is not obvious that this assumption is required. It does not affect the discussion here in any serious way if movement between unconnected subtrees is sanctioned. See Nunes (1995), Uriagereka (1998), and note 23 for further discussion.

23 Note that moving *John* from the adjunct to the higher VP is not movement to a c-commanding position. Recall that (8) sanctions such movement. This is required if the "D-Structure" position of the subject is not to c-command the adjunct, as appears to be empirically required. For discussion, see Hornstein (1995: ch. 8; 1998a).

Theoretically this sort of movement is important in two ways. First, it suggests that θ-marking must take place in the immediate domain of the relevant verb. In this case the external θ-marking must take place within the VP, not VP/VP. This suggests that the adjunct is adjoined, not to what eventually becomes a V′, but to the VP itself. Second, at least in cases such as these, *v* seems superfluous. If it assigned a θ-role, then we would expect the subject to c-command the adjunct. This seems to be incorrect in general, as the above references argue. A final point is that "extension" in the sense of Chomsky (1993) appears to ignore adjuncts. This is consistent with the position Chomsky takes in that work.

There is another, more interesting way to look at this derivation that exploits proposals made by Nunes (1995) for parasitic gap phenomena. He observes that extension can be applied to adjuncts as well if we assume that sideward movement is possible. In effect, movement is permitted out of the adjunct before the adjunct is adjoined to the VP that it modifies. Movement out of the adjunct to a θ-position inside VP "extends" the VP. Adjunction of the adjunct to the VP then extends the VP. In each case extension is respected. An interesting corollary is that adjuncts are not actually islands. However, extraction from an adjunct via sideward movement is *only* permitted given other natural assumptions (for details see Hornstein 1998a). If this is so, then *there* should not be able to control PRO.

(i)   There arrived several men before there erupted a riot.
(ii)   *There arrived several men before PRO erupting a riot.

For further discussion and details, see Nunes (1995) and Hornstein (1998a).

24 This raises an interesting problem. What blocks *Mary* from bearing nominative Case and *John* from bearing accusative and thereby deriving (i), in which *John* checks its Case at LF?

(i)   *Mary heard before John entering the room.
(ii)   [$_{IP}$ Mary [$_{I^0}$ past * [$_{VP/VP}$[$_{VP}$ Mary [heard Mary]] [$_{Adjunct}$ before [$_{IP}$ John [$_{I^0}$ ing [$_{VP}$ John [entering the room]]]]]]]]]

As (ii) indicates, *Mary* would have two θ-roles and *John* would check its accusative Case at LF.

This derivation is plausibly blocked by the MLC as follows. Assume that the Case-checking position for accusative is at the left edge of VP/VP, as it would be if accusative is checked in [Spec, Agr$_O$] or if it is checked in the outer Spec of the full VP including the adjoined clause, that is, in the outer [Spec, VP/VP] (the position of * in (ii)). This position c-commands both the adjunct and the arguments of *heard*. Consequently, this sort of movement could be blocked by the MLC if we compute distance by relativizing it to the target in cases where the potential fillers do not c-command one another. In this case distance is relevant only if the target c-commands its potential fillers. Thus, movement to a c-commanding position would trigger the MLC and related minimality restrictions, whereas sideward movement would not. (iii) would suffice for current purposes.

(iii)   If a target T c-commands α, β, then α is closer to T than β is if fewer nodes intervene between T and α than between T and β.

Mary and its copies are in different domains from *John* in (ii). If the target of movement is at least as high as VP/VP, and if distance is measured as in (iii), the MLC will prevent movement out of the adjunct since *Mary* is closer to the accusative Case checker than is *John*. In other words, moving out of the adjunct is critical if the accusative Case on *heard* is to be licitly checked.

Note that something like (iii) is required if we are to make the movement analysis of PRO empirically adequate. The text relies on movement out of an adjunct. However, this is clearly not generally available. The current proposal follows Nunes (1995) in assuming that sideward movement can extract a D/NP out of an adjunct. This is how Nunes analyzes parasitic gap constructions. Such constructions also involve sideward movement to a θ-position. What needs to be blocked is extraction from an adjunct "directly" to a c-commanding position (e.g. [Spec, CP]). In other words, being in a c-command relation with the target appears to restrict movement in certain ways. This is what (iii) intends to capture. Another approach to these issues that gets the desired results exploits a proposal by Uriagereka (1998) regarding linearization. Uriagereka suggests that to obey the Linear Correspondence Axiom, elements that are not in a c-command relation must be linearized before they form a single subtree. Assume that this holds for adjuncts. It has the effect that adjuncts are islands, once merged with the VPs they modify. If this is correct, then LF movement *out* of the adjunct is not allowed. This derives the unacceptability of (i), as the Case on *John* remains unchecked. This is a more attractive solution than the one mooted above. However, further details require elaboration before it can be made fully operational. I leave the very complex issues involved here to further research. See Hornstein (1998a) for a possible approach to these issues.

25   This argument requires that we adopt a non-Larsonian approach to adjuncts; that is, it requires claiming that they are not like syntactic arguments. In fact, the difference between where adjuncts are merged and where complements are merged is central to explaining why the latter case (typically) manifests object control and the former, subject control.

References

Aoun, J., N. Hornstein, D. Lightfoot and A. Weinberg. 1987. Two types of locality. *Linguistic Inquiry* 18: 537–77.

Bošković, Ž. 1994. D-Structure, Theta Criterion, and movement into theta positions. *Linguistic Analysis* 24: 247–86.

Bošković, Ž. and D. Takahashi. 1998. Scrambling and last resort. *Linguistic Inquiry* 29: 347–66.

Bouchard, D. 1984. *On the content of empty categories*. Dordrecht: Foris.

Chomsky, C. 1969. *The acquisition of syntax in children from 5 to 10*. Cambridge, MA: MIT Press.

Chomsky, N. 1981. *Lectures on government and binding*. Dordrecht: Foris.

Chomsky, N. 1986. *Knowledge of language: Its nature, origin, and use*. New York: Praeger.

Chomsky, N. 1993. A minimalist program for linguistic theory. In K. Hale and S. J. Keyser (eds.), *The view from Building 20: Essays in linguistics in honor of Sylvain Bromberger*, Cambridge, MA: MIT Press. pp. 1–52. [Reprinted in Chomsky (1995), *The Minimalist Program*, Cambridge, MA: MIT Press, pp. 167–217.]

Chomsky, N. 1995. *The Minimalist Program*. Cambridge. MA: MIT Press.

Chomsky, N. and H. Lasnik. 1993. The theory of principles and parameters. In J. Jacobs, A. von Stechow, W. Sternefeld and T. Vennemann (eds.), *An international handbook of contemporary research*, Berlin/New York: Walter de Gruyter, pp. 506–69. [Reprinted in Chomsky (1995), *The Minimalist Program*, Cambridge, MA: MIT Press, pp. 13–127.]

Epstein, S. D. 1996. Un-principled syntax: The derivation of syntactic relations. Ms., Harvard University. [Published in S. D. Epstein and N. Hornstein (eds.), *Working minimalism*, Cambridge, MA: MIT Press, pp. 317–45.]

Fodor, J. A. 1975. *The language of thought*. New York: Thomas Y. Crowell.

Fukui, N. and M. Speas. 1986. Specifiers and projection. In N. Fukui, T. R. Rapoport and E. Sagey (eds.), *Papers in theoretical linguistics. MIT Working Papers in Linguistics 8*, Cambridge, MA: MITWPL, pp. 128–72.

Higginbotham, J. 1992. Reference and control. In K. R. Larson, S. Iatridou, U. Lahiri and J. Higginbotham (eds.), *Control and grammar*, Dordrecht: Kluwer, pp. 79–108.

Hornstein, N. 1995. *Logical form: From GB to minimalism*. Malden, MA: Blackwell.

Hornstein, N. 1998a. Adjunct control and parasitic gaps. In E. Murguia, A. Pires and L. Quintana (eds.), *University of Maryland Working Papers in Linguistics 6*, College Park, MD: Linguistics Department, University of Maryland, pp. 102–21.

Hornstein, N. 1998b. Movement and chains. *Syntax* 1: 99–127.

Hornstein, N. and D. Lightfoot. 1987. Predication and PRO. *Language* 63: 23–52.

Koster, J. 1984. On binding and control. *Linguistic Inquiry* 15: 417–59.

Lasnik, H. 1995. Last resort and Attract F. In *Papers from the 6th Annual Meeting of the Formal Linguistics Society of Mid-America*, Bloomington: Indiana Linguistics Club, pp. 62–81.

Lebeaux, D. 1985. Locality and anaphoric binding. *The Linguistic Review* 4: 343–63.

Manzini, M. R. 1983. Control and control theory. *Linguistic Inquiry* 14: 421–46.

Manzini, M. R. and A. Roussou. 1997. A minimalist theory of control. Ms., Università di Firenze/ University College London and University of Wales, Bangor. [Revised version published as: A minimalist theory of A-movement and control, *Lingua* 110: 409–47, 2000.]

Martin, R. 1996. *A minimalist theory of PRO and control.* Doctoral dissertation, University of Connecticut, Storrs.

Nunes, J. 1995. *The copy theory of movement and linearization of chains in the Minimalist Program.* Doctoral dissertation, University of Maryland, College Park.

O'Neil, J. 1995. Out of control. In J. N. Beckman (ed.), *Proceedings of the 25th Annual Meeting of the North East Linguistic Society*, Amherst, MA: GLSA, pp. 361–71.

Rizzi, L. 1986. On chain formation. In H. Borer (ed.), *The syntax of pronominal clitics. Syntax and semantics 19*, New York: Academic Press, pp. 65–95.

Rizzi, L. 1990. *Relativized minimality.* Cambridge, MA: MIT Press.

Rosenbaum, P. S. 1967. *The grammar of English predicate complement constructions.* Cambridge, MA: MIT Press.

Sag, I. 1976. *Deletion and logical form.* Doctoral dissertation, MIT.

Salmon, N. 1986. Reflexivity. *Notre Dame Journal of Formal Logic* 27: 401–29.

Stowell, T. 1982. The tense of infinitives. *Linguistic Inquiry* 13: 561–70.

Uriagereka, J. 1998. *Rhyme and reason.* Cambridge, MA: MIT Press.

Williams, E. 1977. Discourse and logical form. *Linguistic Inquiry* 8: 101–39.

Williams, E. 1980. Predication. *Linguistic Inquiry* 11: 203–38.

2.3   Locality

From "THE THEORY OF PRINCIPLES AND PARAMETERS"
Noam Chomsky and Howard Lasnik

To make this intuitive account more precise and descriptively more accurate, we have to explain in what sense a "cost" accrues to failure to make the shortest move, and why violation of the economy condition is more severe for adjuncts than arguments, as noted throughout. Adapting mechanisms just discussed, we might suppose that when a chain link is formed by Move α, the trace created is assigned * if the economy condition [Minimize Chain Links] is violated as it is created (a version of the γ-marking operation of Lasnik and Saito 1984, 1992).

Note further that only certain entities are legitimate LF objects, just as only certain entities are legitimate PF objects (e.g. a [+high, +low] vowel, or a stressed consonant, is not a legitimate PF object, and a derivation that yields such an output fails to form a proper SD [structural description]. We therefore need some notion of legitimate LF object. Suppose that the chain C of (1) is a legitimate LF object only if C is *uniform* (see Browning 1987).

(1) $C = (\alpha_1, \ldots, \alpha_n)$

The only other legitimate LF objects are operator-variable constructions (α, β), where α is in an Ā-position and β heads a legitimate (uniform) chain.

Uniformity is a relational notion: the chain C is *uniform with respect to* P (UN[P]) if each α_i has property P or each α_i has non-P. One obvious choice for the relevant property P is L-relatedness, which we have suggested to ground the distinction between A- and Ā-positions; see section 1.3.2 of Chomsky (1995). A chain is UN[L] if it is uniform with respect to L-relatedness. Heads and adjuncts are non-L-related and move only to non-L-related positions; hence, the chains they form are UN[L]. An argument chain consists only of L-related positions, hence is UN[L]. The basic types – heads, arguments, adjuncts – are therefore uniform chains, legitimate objects at LF.

Taking this as a first approximation, we now regard the operation of deletion, like movement, as a "last resort" principle, a special case of the principle of economy of derivation (make derivations as short as possible, with links as short as possible): operations in general are permissible only to form a legitimate LF object. Deletion is impermissible in a uniform chain, since these are already legitimate. Deletion in the chain C of (1) is, however, permissible for α_i in an Ā-position, where $n > i > 1$ and α_n is in an A-position – that is, the case of successive-cyclic movement of an argument. In this case a starred trace can be deleted at LF, voiding the violation; in other cases it cannot.

An expression (an SD) is a Subjacency violation if its derivation forms a starred trace. It is an Empty Category Principle (ECP) violation if, furthermore, this starred trace remains at LF; hence, ECP violations are more severe than Subjacency violations, which leave no residue at LF. Note that the concept ECP is now a descriptive cover term for various kinds of violations that are marked at LF, among them, violations of the economy principle (Relativized Minimality).

References

Browning, M. A. 1987. *Null operator constructions.* Doctoral dissertation, MIT.
Chomsky, N. 1995. *The Minimalist Program.* Cambridge, MA: MIT Press.
Lasnik, H. and M. Saito. 1984. On the nature of proper government. *Linguistic Inquiry* 15: 235–55.
Lasnik, H. and M. Saito. 1992. *Move α.* Cambridge, MA: MIT Press.

From "A MINIMALIST PROGRAM FOR LINGUISTIC THEORY"
Noam Chomsky

There appears to be a conflict between two natural notions of economy: shortest move versus fewest steps in a derivation. If a derivation keeps to shortest moves, it will have more steps; if it reduces the number of steps, it will have longer moves. The paradox is resolved if we take the basic transformational operation to be not Move α but *Form Chain*, an operation that applies, say, to the structure (1a) to form (1b) in a single step, yielding the chain CH of (1c).

(1)   a.   *e* seems [*e* to be likely [John to win]]
        b.   John seems [*t′* to be likely [*t* to win]]
        c.   CH = (*John, t′, t*)

Similarly, in other cases of successive-cyclic movement. There is, then, no conflict between reducing derivations to the shortest number of steps and keeping links minimal ("Shortest Movement" Condition). There are independent reasons to suppose that this is the correct approach: note, for example, that successive-cyclic *wh*-movement of arguments does not treat the intermediate steps as adjunct movement, as it should if it were a succession of applications of Move α.

From "ECONOMY OF DERIVATION AND THE GENERALIZED PROPER BINDING CONDITION"
Chris Collins

1 Introduction: Economy of Derivation

Chomsky (1991, 1993) and Chomsky and Lasnik (1993) have proposed that syntactic derivations are constrained by the principle of Economy of Derivation. In this article I will show that two direct consequences follow from this proposal. First, it eliminates a class of derivations involving "chain interleaving" (section 2). Second, it prohibits certain cases of downward and sideways movement (section 3). To the extent that these consequences are easily verifiable, they provide strong support for such a principle.

Since chain interleaving and downward movement can also be blocked with the Generalized Proper Binding Condition (GPBC) (see Lasnik and Saito 1992), it will be concluded that in all known cases the GPBC is redundant.

1.1 Economy of Derivation

I will assume the following framework (modified from Chomsky 1991, 1993, and Chomsky and Lasnik 1993):[1]

(1) *Convergence*
     A derivation converges if its structural description (a pair of representations at LF and PF) contains only legitimate objects.
(2) *Legitimacy*
     An object is legitimate if all its morphological features have been satisfied (e.g. Case, [+wh]).

For example, in the sentence *John was killed*, *John* heads an A-chain that is a legitimate object since *John* has been assigned Case. As another example, in the sentence *Who left?*, *who* heads an Ā-chain that is a legitimate object since *who* occupies the Spec CP, where it satisfies its [+wh] feature.

(3) *Length of derivation*
     Derivation D_1 is longer than derivation D_2 if D_1 involves more operations or steps than D_2. (The notion of length that is relevant here will be clarified in the course of the article.)

(4) *Optimality*
     A derivation is optimal if there is no shorter derivation yielding the same legit-
     imate objects.

The principle of *Economy of Derivation* states that shorter derivations are preferred over longer derivations, or that derivations must be optimal.

1.2 Proper Binding

One goal of this article is to eliminate the Generalized Proper Binding Condition
as an independent principle of grammar. In this section I will illustrate the principle of Proper Binding (Fiengo 1977) and give several variants of it.
    Consider the following example (from Saito 1989: 191):

(5) a.   I urged Bill to find out [who$_1$ Mary saw t$_1$].
     b.   *I urged t$_1$ to find out [who$_1$ Mary saw John].

The verb *urge* takes a clausal complement and an NP complement. In (5b) the NP
complement of *urge* is moved down to the Spec CP position of the embedded clause.
This derivation must be ruled out.
    Consider the following condition (from Saito 1989):

(6) *Proper Binding Condition*
     Traces must be bound.

Two stances on this condition are found in the literature. First, it has been construed as a condition on S-Structure, LF, or both. For convenience, I will use the
term *Proper Binding Condition* (PBC) for all of these variants. Second, it has been
taken to hold at every stage in the derivation, in which case it is called the *Generalized
Proper Binding Condition* (GPBC; see Lasnik and Saito 1992).
    The PBC rules out (5b) easily, at either S-Structure or LF, since the trace in
the object position of *urge* is not bound.

2 The interleaving of A- and Ā-chains

2.1 Introduction

Chomsky (1993) notes that the Economy framework raises a question for long-
distance Ā-movement (in the framework in Chomsky 1986). Consider the following example:

(7) [$_{CP}$ Who$_1$ [$_{C'}$ did [$_{IP}$ John [$_{VP}$ t$_1'$ [$_{VP}$ kill t$_1$]]]]]?

Here the object of *kill* undergoes Ā-movement to the Spec CP position. First, the
wh-phrase *who$_1$* moves to adjoin to VP, since VP is a barrier. Second, *who$_1$* moves from
the adjoined position to the Spec CP. This movement yields the following chain:

(8)   (who$_1$, t$_1'$, t$_1$)

The question is whether the formation of this chain should count as two operations (two instances of Move α) or as one. There is an argument in favor of the latter solution. If the formation of this Ā-chain counted as two operations, there would be a less costly derivation that did not involve adjunction to VP. Since there is a less costly derivation that does not involve adjunction to VP, it must be chosen by Economy of Derivation. Therefore, only the following chain should be formed:

(9)   (who$_1$, t$_1$)

But this chain crosses the VP barrier, and therefore the sentence should be unacceptable, which it is not.

Chomsky's (1993) answer to this question is that the formation of a chain, even if it has a large number of links, is a single operation (called *Form Chain*). Therefore, the relevant notion of length of derivation is the number of operations, such as the number of times a chain is formed, and not the number of links in a chain.[2]

In this section I will offer another argument for the view that chain formation counts as a single operation. The structure of the argument will be as follows: There are a number of unacceptable sentences that have a certain type of derivation that must be ruled out. This type of derivation involves A-/Ā-chain interleaving. Two chains, X and Y, are interleaved if during a derivation, part of X is formed, then part of Y is formed, then part of X is formed, and so on. These derivations can be naturally ruled out by assuming that chain formation takes place in a single operation and that derivations are constrained by Economy of Derivation.

2.2   Extraction from the Object

Consider the following sentences:

(10)   a.   Who did you say that John stole pictures of?
       b.   ??Who did you say that pictures of were stolen?

[. . .]

If what I have called "chain interleaving" is allowed, the (b) sentence of (10) has an acceptable derivation. Consider first the D-Structure representation of (10b) (where *e* represents a vacuous empty element):

(11)   *D-Structure representation*
       [$_{CP}$ you said [$_{CP}$ that e were [$_{VP}$ stolen [$_{NP}$ pictures of who]]]]

From this D-Structure representation, (10b) can be derived as in (12)–(14).

(12)   Wh-*phrase adjoins to VP*
       [$_{CP}$ you said [$_{CP}$ that e was [$_{VP}$ who$_1$ [$_{VP}$ stolen [$_{NP}$ pictures of t$_1$]]]]]

I will assume that this operation must be permissible because of sentences like (10a) where the *wh*-phrase has been extracted from an NP (i.e. the object is not a barrier). Note that at this point of the derivation the trace t_i is γ-marked, assuming that γ-marking is done during the course of the derivation.[3]

(13)   *NP-movement*
       $[_{CP}$ you said $[_{CP}$ that $[_{NP}$ pictures of $t_1]_2$ were $[_{VP}$ who$_1$ $[_{VP}$ stolen $t_2]]]]]$

In this second step the object of *stolen* undergoes NP-movement to the subject position (to get Case). Note that in this derivation the Strict Cycle Condition (SCC) is not violated.[4] Furthermore, since t_i is already assigned $[+\gamma]$, it will not violate the Empty Category Principle (ECP).

(14)   *Ā-movement of* who$_1$ *to matrix Spec CP*
       $[_{CP}$ who$_1$ you $[_{VP}$ t_1''' $[_{VP}$ said $[_{CP}$ t_1'' that $[_{NP}$ pictures of $t_1]_2$ were $[_{VP}$ t_1'
       $[_{VP}$ stolen $t_2]]]]]]]$

The above derivation violates neither the SCC nor the ECP. The step in (13) might be construed as violating the GPBC, but since one goal of this study is to eliminate the PBC, I will not appeal to this solution here. Rather, I will show that Economy of Derivation and the notion of Form Chain as a single operation will rule the derivation out.

To see what the problem is with the derivation in (11)–(14), consider the chains that must result:

(15)   a.   (who$_1$, t_1''', t_1'', t_1', t_1)
       b.   ([pictures of $t_1]_2$, t_2)

I would like to propose that the problem is that the chains in (15) are interleaved. In other words, the chains in (15) were formed in this order: the first link of (15a), then (15b), then the rest of the links of (15a).

Let us assume that chains cannot be interleaved, as they are in (11)–(14). This would follow naturally on an account where chain formation was a single operation. If this assumption is correct, then it follows that a chain must be formed all at one time. It is not possible to form part of a chain, and then the rest.[5] Given this assumption, there are only two derivations that yield the chains in (15), both of which can be ruled out. First, if (15a) were formed first (i.e. *who$_1$* moves directly to the matrix Spec CP from the object position of *pictures of*), then (15b) could not be formed, since that would violate the SCC (both the version in Chomsky 1973 and the one in Chomsky 1993). Second, if (15b) were formed first (i.e. the constituent [pictures of who] is A-moved to the embedded Spec IP), then the chain in (15a) would represent an extraction from subject, violating Subjacency (see Chomsky 1986).

Note that both alternatives involve only two operations of Form Chain, since only two chains result (those in (15)).

Another possibility is that the chains involved in the derivation are not the ones represented in (15), but the ones given here:

(16) a.   (who$_1$, t$_1'''$, t$_1''$, t$_1'$), (t$_1'$, t$_1$)
      b.   ([pictures of t$_1$]$_2$, t$_2$)

These chains correspond to the derivation in (11)–(14), where there are three operations of Form Chain. This derivation is ruled out by Economy, since there is a more economical derivation (i.e. either derivation described above yielding the chains in (15), which involve only two operations of Form Chain).[6]

There are other cases of this type as well, involving the interleaving of Ā-chains. Consider the following example (Lasnik and Saito 1992 claim that sentences like (17) are not as fully unacceptable as ones like (10b)):

(17)   ??Who do you believe that [$_{IP}$ pictures of, John likes]?

This case and the others treated above have been discussed by Browning (1991). Browning claims that if Subjacency is a condition on representations, then (10b) is ruled out. My account of (10b) (in terms of Economy of Derivation) is an alternative to Browning's, which maintains Subjacency as a condition on derivations (see Browning 1991 for clarifications of these two construals of Subjacency).

There are empirical reasons to doubt that Subjacency is a condition on representations. Consider the following examples (discussed extensively in Johnson 1985: 110):

(18)   The case was judged.
       a.   Then a lawyer with green eyes appeared.
       b.   Then a lawyer appeared with green eyes.
       c.   Then a lawyer with green eyes appealed.
       d.   *Then a lawyer appealed with green eyes.

As shown in (18d), extraposition is blocked from the subject position with unergative verbs. On the other hand, extraposition is not blocked from the subject of an unaccusative verb, as shown in (18b). If Subjacency is construed as a condition on representations, then it cannot account for the difference between these two examples.

If Subjacency is construed as a condition on derivations, the difference between (18b) and (18d) can be accounted for. In (18b) the modifier *with green eyes* can be extraposed at D-Structure, since at that level the NP *a lawyer with green eyes* will not be a barrier. On the other hand, there is no level at which the subject NP in (18b) will be L-marked (see Chomsky 1986: 40–1 for a different view of extraposition).[7,8]

        [. . .]

In considering the alternative shorter derivation in (10b) it is important to note that the shorter derivation (which blocks the longer derivation) is actually not grammatical. It is ruled out by Subjacency. This is irrelevant for the calculation of Economy. The only thing that matters is that there is a shorter derivation that satisfies the morphological properties of the moved *wh*-phrase (i.e. that it must be in Comp at LF).

        [. . .]

2.5 Summary

In summary, postulating the operation Form Chain allows us to block a number of previously undiscussed derivations that need to be blocked.[9]

3 Downward movement

3.1 Reflexes of successive-cyclic movement

Many languages show reflexes of successive-cyclic movement: complementizer selection in Irish (McCloskey 1979), stylistic inversion in French (Kayne and Pollock 1978), and tonal morphology in Kikuyu (Clements 1984). Ewe provides a unique diagnostic of successive cyclicity: if Spec CP is filled during the derivation by a trace of Ā-movement, the morphological form of the third person singular subject pronoun changes.[10] The following sentences illustrate the basic distribution of é/wo:[11]

(19) [É/*Wo] fo Kɔsi.
        he   hit Kɔsi

(20) Kofi gblɔ be [é/*wo] fo Kɔsi.
        Kofi said that he   hit Kɔsi

(21) Kofi biɛ be lamata [*é/wo] fo Kɔsi.
        Kofi asked that why   he   hit Kɔsi

(19) indicates that é occurs in matrix indicative clauses and wo does not. (20) indicates that the third singular subject of an embedded clause can also only be é, not wo. (21) indicates that if there has been movement into Spec CP in the embedded clause, then wo is obligatory. This can be analyzed in the following way. If Spec CP is occupied (as in (21), but not (19) and (20)), a special form of nominative Case is assigned to the subject of the associated IP. It is this special form of nominative Case that accounts for the appearance of wo in (21).

This account extends to successive-cyclic movement. Consider (22)–(23).

(22) Kofi ɛ me gblɔ be [é/wo] fo.
        Kofi FOC I said that he   hit
        'It was Kofi₁ that I said that he hit t₁.'

(23) Kofi ɛ me gblɔ na be [é/*wo] fo Kɔsi.
        Kofi FOC I said to that he   hit Kɔsi
        'It was Kofi₁ that I told t₁ that he hit Kɔsi.'

As (22) illustrates, if long-distance extraction has taken place out of the embedded clause, then either é or wo is possible. (23) shows that if the extraction takes place from the matrix clause (the object of the preposition na), then only é is possible. I will assume that in (22) there is movement through the embedded Spec CP (I will not treat the optionality of the selection of wo in (22); see Collins 1993 for an analysis of this). Therefore, the special form of nominative Case is assigned to the subject pronoun and wo is used. In (23) there has been no movement through the embedded Spec CP, and therefore wo is not used.

3.2 Downward movement and successive cyclicity

The relevance of the Ewe data for Economy of Derivation is revealed by an analysis of (23). (In any language with overt reflexes of successive-cyclic movement, there will be sentences analogous to (23); see McCloskey 1979: 151.) In this analysis I assumed that there is no movement through the embedded Spec CP. This assumption may be questioned. Consider the derivation in (24)–(27) (to simplify the exposition, I give only the glosses).

(24) *Adjoin* Kofi *to the matrix VP*
    FOC [$_{IP}$ I [$_{VP}$ Kofi [$_{VP}$ said [to t] [$_{CP}$ that [he hit Kɔsi]]]]]

In this step the trace of *Kofi* will be γ-marked at the time of movement.

(25) *Lower* Kofi *to the embedded Spec CP*
    FOC [$_{IP}$ I [$_{VP}$ t [$_{VP}$ said [to t] [$_{CP}$ Kofi that [he hit Kɔsi]]]]]

In (25), as soon as *Kofi* is lowered from the position adjoined to VP, its trace will be deleted,[12] so that the ECP is not violated. Furthermore, the Strict Cycle Condition is not violated.[13] However, (25) does violate the GPBC. If the trace adjoined to the VP is deleted, the object of *to* will not be properly bound. Since I am trying to eliminate the GPBC, I will not appeal to it here. Rather, I will show that this lowering is blocked by Economy of Derivation.

(26) *Readjoin* Kofi *to matrix VP*
    FOC [$_{IP}$ I [$_{VP}$ Kofi [$_{VP}$ said [to t] [$_{CP}$ t that [he hit Kɔsi]]]]]

After *Kofi* is readjoined to the matrix VP, a trace is left in the embedded Spec CP. This embedded trace then triggers the selection of *wo*.

(27) *Move* Kofi *to matrix Spec CP*
    Kofi FOC [$_{IP}$ I [$_{VP}$ t [$_{VP}$ said [to t] [$_{CP}$ t that [he hit Kɔsi]]]]]

Note that the Bijection Principle (see Chomsky 1986: 6) holds of the representation in (26) since the operator *Kofi* binds only one variable (the trace in the object position of *to*). The trace in the embedded Spec CP is merely an intermediate trace, not a variable.[14]

Since (23) is unacceptable with *wo* as the embedded subject pronoun, the derivation in (24)–(27) must be blocked. We can account for this in terms of Economy of Derivation by noting that alongside the derivation proposed above, there is a shorter one in which *Kofi* moves directly from the object position of *to* to the matrix Spec CP (via adjunction to the matrix VP). The direct derivation (illustrated in (28)) takes two steps, whereas the derivation involving downward movement takes four steps. The latter is therefore excluded by Economy of Derivation.

(28)   *Direct derivation*
       Kofi FOC [$_{IP}$ I [$_{VP}$ t [$_{VP}$ said [to t] [$_{CP}$ that [he hit Kɔsi]]]]]

At this point, we have something of a dilemma. Clearly, we would like to rule out the derivation in (24)–(27) by Economy of Derivation. The problem is that all of the steps in (24)–(27) constitute only one instance of Form Chain. Therefore, in one sense the derivation in (24)–(27) is no longer than the one in (28), which also involves only one instance of Form Chain.

To resolve this dilemma, I propose that internal to the operation of Form Chain, the length of the derivation is to be measured in terms of the number of nodes traversed during the derivation. The following paragraphs will make this proposal more explicit. First, I will define *path* as follows (this definition differs from the one used in Pesetsky 1982):[15]

(29)   *Path*
       Let P_1 and P_2 be two categories in a tree.[16] Let S_1 be the set of categories dominating P_1 and let S_2 be the set of categories dominating P_2. The path between P_1 and P_2 is defined as follows:
       Path(P_1, P_2) = ($S_1 \cup S_2$) − ($S_1 \cap S_2$)

This definition has the effect of counting the nodes on the shortest "route" that goes from P_1 to P_2 in a tree. The number of nodes traversed in a derivation can now be defined in terms of the sum of the length of the links in the derivation, as follows:

(30)   *Nodes traversed*
       Let D be a derivation, and $\{L_i\}_D$ its links. Let π_i be the path associated with L_i, and N_i be the cardinality of π_i. The number of nodes traversed is defined as follows:
       N_D = the sum of N_i for L_i in $\{L_i\}_D$
(31)   *Length of derivation (revised)*
       Derivation D_1 is longer than derivation D_2 if
       a. D_1 involves more operations (e.g. Form Chain) than D_2 or
       b. D_1 traverses more nodes than D_2.

Considering the above derivations again, we see that N_D for the derivation in (24)–(27) is much larger than N_D for (28). To be concrete, for the derivation in (24)–(27) the nodes traversed are (in order of traversal) {PP, VP, VP, CP, CP, VP, I', IP, C'}, and $N_D = 9$. For the direct derivation in (28) the nodes traversed are {PP, VP, I', IP, C'}, and $N_D = 5$.[17] (I assume that nonmaximal projections such as I' and C' are counted.) [. . .] Clearly, given (31), the derivation in (24)–(27) blocks the derivation in (28).

It might be asked whether the number of nodes traversed can supplant other measures of Economy, such as number of operations or steps in a derivation. This will not be possible. For example, the derivation in (11)–(14) yielding the three chains in (16) must be blocked by a derivation that traverses the same number of nodes but involves only two operations of Form Chain (see paragraph following (15)).

As another example, consider the following sentence discussed by Epstein (1992):

(32) a.   *S-Structure*
           *Who thinks [$_{CP}$ what$_1$ John likes t$_1$]?
      b.   *LF*
           what$_1$ who thinks [$_{CP}$ t$_1'$ John likes t$_1$]

Epstein points out that the representation in (32a) is ruled out by a filter that prohibits a *wh*-phrase in a [−wh] Comp at S-Structure. Alternatively, it can be ruled out by Economy of Derivation. The ultimate derivation of (32b) will involve two operations, one to move *what* to the embedded Spec CP at S-Structure (32a) and another to move *what* to the matrix Spec CP at LF (32b). According to Epstein, there is a shorter derivation of (32b) involving a one-step movement of *what* from the object position of *likes* to the matrix Spec CP at LF (assuming no Subjacency at LF). This shorter derivation blocks the longer derivation presented in (32), by Economy of Derivation.

For present purposes, the important thing to recognize is that both derivations of the LF representation in (32b) cross the same number of nodes. Therefore, if the number of nodes traversed was the only measure of Economy, both derivations of (32b) would be equally economical.

In conclusion, there must be at least two measures of Economy: the number of nodes traversed and the number of operations of Form Chain.

Notes

1   The background theory that I adopt is that of Chomsky 1986 and Lasnik and Saito 1992. Any relevant differences between these works and any assumptions that differ from those made in these works will be pointed out in the text.

2   The same point can be made using Comp-to-Comp movement as an example, instead of VP adjunction. See Chomsky (1993).

3   See Chomsky and Lasnik (1993) for a strong argument that γ-marking must be done during the course of the derivation. Their argument is stated not in terms of γ-marking but in terms of "locality conditions."

4   I will assume the standard version of the SCC given by Chomsky (1973): "No rule can apply to a domain dominated by a cyclic node A in such a way as to affect solely a proper su domain of A dominated by a node B which is also a cyclic node." This version of the SCC is also assumed implicitly by Lasnik and Saito (1992). I will assume that any maximal projection can be a cyclic node.

    Chomsky (1993) derives the effects of the SCC from his "extension condition" on generalized transformations.

    Neither version of the SCC (Chomsky 1973 or Chomsky 1993) would prevent (13).

    Following a suggestion of Hiroaki Tada, it may be that the SCC is really a subcase of Economy of Derivation. A countercyclic step crucially involves going back to structure created earlier in the derivation. Such repetition would be avoided on a purely cyclic derivation. The formalization of this idea is not trivial.

5   The one exception to this seems to be the case of chain linking discussed by Chomsky and Lasnik (1993).

6   One reviewer suggests that ruling out this derivation (as well as the others in this study) with the GPBC is actually preferable, since the GPBC is comparatively local: "At any given point in any given derivation one can look only at the representation in question and decide whether the GPBC is satisfied or not." In the case of the derivation in (11)–(14), there is also a "local" way to construe Economy of Derivation.

It may be that the formation of the chain (t_1', t_1) in (16a) is blocked by the principle of Last Resort (see Chomsky and Lasnik 1993), since the formation of this chain does not satisfy any morphological properties. This account is more "local" than the account of (16a–b) that I propose in the text. It is an open question whether all uses of Economy of Derivation can be restated in such a local fashion (thanks to Tony Bures and Akira Watanabe for discussing this issue with me).

7   It should be noted that some of the phenomena that Economy of Derivation accounts for could also be accounted for if one adopted the view that chains were read off S-Structure representations. For example, on such a representational view of structure, "chain interleaving" would be impossible. The trade-off between Economy of Derivation and a more representational view of chains needs to be considered in greater detail.

8   A reviewer suggests that the data in (18) could be accounted for if extraposition was analyzed in a way analogous to Sportiche's (1988) analysis of floating quantifiers. In other words, (18b) would be a case of stranding the PP adjunct *with green eyes*, which would not be possible with the unergative verb in (18d). There are two problems with this approach. First, neither unaccusatives nor unergatives allow postverbal floating quantifiers, for reasons discussed by Sportiche (1988: 444):

(i)   The men have (all) appealed (*all).
(ii)   The men have (all) appeared (*all).

If it is the case that the mechanisms underlying quantifier floating and PP extraposition are the same, then (i) with postverbal *all* should be unacceptable and (ii) should be acceptable.

Second, it does not seem possible for a PP to appear in any intermediated A-positions:

(iii)   The men will ˆ appear ˆ to ˆ leave at six.

Whereas *both* is permissible in any of the positions marked with ˆ, *with green eyes* is not.

9   This approach should more generally block operation interleaving. Thus, it should not be possible to form part of a chain, then extract (as, e.g. in clitic movement) from the head of the partial chain, and then form the rest of the chain. I will leave the investigation of such cases for further research.

10   Ewe is a Kwa language spoken in West Africa. The data are taken from the Kpele dialect of Ewe, spoken north of Kpalimé in Togo.

11   This pronoun alternation is analyzed in much greater detail in Collins (1993).

12   Trace deletion is allowed by both Chomsky (1986: 21) and Lasnik and Saito (1992).

13   The lowering in (25) would appear to violate Chomsky's (1993) extension condition. However, because on Chomsky's theory all the movements in (24)–(27) constitute one occurrence of Form Chain, the derivation (recast in terms of generalized transformations) does not violate this condition.

14   The type of derivation given in (24)–(27) not only is admitted by the system of Lasnik and Saito (1992), but also resembles some of the actual derivations that they propose. This type of movement (downward followed by upward) has come to be called "yo-yo" movement.

15 The definition of path that Pesetsky gives is this:

    (i)   Suppose t is an empty category locally $\bar{\text{A}}$-bound by b. Then:
        a.   for α = the first maximal projection dominating t
        b.   for β = the first maximal projection dominating b
        c.   the path between t and b is the set of nodes P such that P = {x | (x = α) or
           (x = β) or (x dominates α and x does not dominate β)}

    This definition of path would not work for downward movement, since the length of the
    path for any link that involved downward movement would be two.

16 *Category* is used in the sense of Chomsky (1986), in order to prevent segments from being
    counted in measuring the length of a derivation. If segments were counted, adjunction to
    XP would never be allowed by Economy of Derivation. For example, the derivation in (7)
    would be blocked, since it traverses two VP segments. If no adjunction took place, only
    one VP category would be traversed.

    For the purposes of this definition, I will assume that categories do not dominate them-
    selves. See Barss (1984) for a discussion of this assumption.

17 Note that the revised definition of length of derivation has nothing to say about examples
    like (i).

    (i)   Who wonders where we bought what?

    There are two possibilities for interpreting (i): *what* can be construed either with *where* or
    with *who*. It might be thought that movement of *what* to *where* at LF would block a deriva-
    tion where *what* moves to *who*, since in moving to *who*, *what* would have to traverse a greater
    number of nodes. The reason why this is not the case is that movement of *what* to *where*
    forms an $\bar{\text{A}}$-chain that is different from the $\bar{\text{A}}$-chain formed by movement of *what* to *who*,
    and Economy of Derivation does not choose between these possibilities. In other words,
    Economy of Derivation chooses the shortest derivation leading to a *given set* of legitimate
    objects.

References

Barss, A. 1984. Adjunction and reflexive hierarchical relations. Ms., MIT.

Browning, M. A. 1991. Bounding conditions on representation. *Linguistic Inquiry* 22: 541–62.

Chomsky, N. 1973. Conditions on transformations. In S. Anderson and P. Kiparsky (eds.), *A Festschrift for Morris Halle*, New York: Holt, Rinehart, and Winston, pp. 232–86.

Chomsky, N. 1986. *Barriers*. Cambridge, MA: MIT Press.

Chomsky, N. 1991. Some notes on economy of derivation and representation. In R. Freidin (ed.), *Principles and parameters in comparative grammar*, Cambridge, MA: MIT Press, pp. 417–54. [Reprinted in Chomsky (1995), *The Minimalist Program*, Cambridge, MA: MIT Press, pp. 128–66.]

Chomsky, N. 1993. A minimalist program for linguistic theory. In K. Hale and S. J. Keyser (eds.), *The view from Building 20: Essays in linguistics in honor of Sylvain Bromberger*, Cambridge, MA: MIT Press, pp. 1–52. [Reprinted in Chomsky (1995), *The Minimalist Program*, Cambridge, MA: MIT Press, pp. 167–217.]

Chomsky, N. and H. Lasnik. 1993. The theory of principles and parameters. In J. Jacobs, A. von Stechow, W. Sternefeld and T. Vennemann (eds.), *An international handbook of contemporary research*, Berlin/New York: Walter de Gruyter, pp. 506–69. [Reprinted in Chomsky (1995), *The Minimalist Program*, Cambridge, MA: MIT Press, pp. 13–127.]

Clements, G. N. 1984. Binding domains in Kikuyu. *Studies in Linguistic Science* 14: 37–56.

Collins, C. 1993. *Topics in Ewe syntax*. Doctoral dissertation, MIT.

Epstein, S. D. 1992. Derivational constraints on A′-chain formation. *Linguistic Inquiry* 23: 235–60.

Fiengo, R. 1977. On trace theory. *Linguistic Inquiry* 8: 35–61.

Johnson, K. 1985. *A case for movement*. Doctoral dissertation, MIT.

Kayne, R. S. and J.-Y. Pollock. 1978. Stylistic inversion, successive cyclicity, and Move NP in French. *Linguistic Inquiry* 9: 595–621.

Lasnik, H. and M. Saito. 1992. *Move α*. Cambridge, MA: MIT Press.

McCloskey, J. 1979. *Transformational syntax and model theoretic semantics: A case study in modern Irish*. Dordrecht: Reidel.

Pesetsky, D. 1982. *Paths and Categories*. Doctoral dissertation, MIT.

Saito, M. 1989. Scrambling as semantically vacuous A′-movement. In M. Baltin and A. Kroch (eds.), *Alternative conceptions of phrase structure*, Chicago: University of Chicago Press, pp. 182–200.

Sportiche, D. 1988. A theory of floating quantifiers and its corollaries for constituent structure. *Linguistic Inquiry* 19: 425–49.

From *ELEMENTARY OPERATIONS AND OPTIMAL DERIVATIONS*
Hisatsugu Kitahara

3.3   Deriving the Proper Binding Condition

In this section, I show that the two central cases motivating the Proper Binding Condition can be explained: the one involving lowering is excluded by the C-Command Condition, and the one involving no lowering is excluded by the MLC [Minimal Link Condition].

3.3.1   The Proper Binding Condition

The contrast exhibited by pairs such as (1a–b) has been attributed to the presence of an unbound trace (see, among others, Fiengo 1977).

(1)   a.   I wonder $[_{CP}$ who$_1$ $[_{TP}$ Mary asked t_1
             $[_{CP}$ what$_2$ $[_{TP}$ John fixed t_2]]]].
     b.   *I think $[_{CP}$ that $[_{TP}$ Mary asked t_1
             $[_{CP}$ who$_1$ $[_{TP}$ John fixed the car]]]].

Whereas t_1 and t_2 are each bound in (1a), t_1 is not in (1b). (1b) has been excluded by the *Proper Binding Condition* (PBC) (see, among others, Fiengo 1977; May 1977; Saito 1989, 1992).[1]

(2)   *Proper Binding Condition*
     Traces must be bound.

Given that a trace is bound iff it is c-commanded by its antecedent, the PBC permits (1a) while excluding (1b). The PBC further captures the deviance of examples such as (3).

(3) *[$_{CP}$ [Which picture of t$_1$]$_2$ do [$_{TP}$ you wonder
     [$_{CP}$ who$_1$ [$_{TP}$ John likes t$_2$]]]]?

In (3), the *wh*-movement of *who* to the specifier of the embedded C precedes the
wh-movement of the embedded object *wh*-phrase (containing the trace of *who*) to
the specifier of the matrix C. In the structure resulting from these two applications of *wh*-movement, t$_2$ is bound, but t$_1$ is not: the PBC is violated.

3.3.2 Deriving the central cases motivating the Proper Binding Condition

Under the Minimalist Program, the derivation of (1b) is excluded by the C-
Command Condition, repeated in (4).

(4) *C-Command Condition*
     H(K) attracts α only if H(K) c-commands α.

In (1b), the embedded C does not c-command the matrix object *who*; hence, the
C-Command Condition prohibits it from attracting *who*. Thus, the derivation of
(1b), employing an illegitimate application of Move, induces deviance. Under the
C-Command Condition analysis, therefore, the deviance of cases such as (1b) (involving lowering) is captured without any reference to the PBC.[2]
  Turning to the deviance of cases such as (3) (involving no lowering), let us consider the relevant aspects of the derivation of (3). Move first raises *who* to the specifier
of the embedded C, then the embedded object *wh*-phrase (containing the trace
of *who*) to the specifier of the matrix C, thereby inducing no violation of the C-
Command Condition. To exclude the derivation of (3) (involving no lowering but
inducing deviance), we need another principle.
  Let us first ask whether the PBC can exclude the derivation of (3) under minimalist assumptions. The PBC was originally taken to be a condition applying at
S-Structure. Such S-Structure application of the PBC would exclude the derivation of (3), which yields an S-Structure representation containing an unbound trace.
But if we adopt the minimalist assumption that eliminates S-Structure (like D-
Structure) as a level of representation (Chomsky 1993), there cannot be any
conditions applying at S-Structure. Given this assumption, the PBC must be
formulated as a condition applying at LF. But even such LF application of the
PBC fails to exclude the LF structure of (3) if we adopt the *copy theory of movement* and the *Preference Principle* (Chomsky 1993).[3]
  Given the copy theory of movement, C$_{HL}$ generates the following structure for
(3) to which Spell-Out applies:

(5) [$_{CP}$ [which picture of t(who)] do you wonder
     [$_{CP}$ who John likes t([which picture of t(who)])]]]

Later, in the LF component, the Preference Principle (requiring a minimization
of the restriction in the operator position, for example, specifier of C) converts (5)
(roughly) to the following LF structure:

(6)   [$_{CP}$ (which y) you wonder
       [$_{CP}$ (which x) John likes (y picture of (x person))]]

In (6), the variables x and y are each bound; hence, LF application of the PBC is satisfied. Given the copy theory of movement and the Preference Principle, therefore, the LF application of the PBC cannot exclude the derivation of (3).

Instead of pursuing a PBC analysis any further, I would like to argue that the MLC analysis readily extends to capture the severe deviance of (3). I first point out that the derivation of (3) involves two illegitimate applications of Move. I then discuss an implication of such multiple violations.

Consider the relevant aspects of the derivation of (3). At some point in the derivation, C_{HL} constructs the following structure:

(7)   [$_{CP}$[$_{TP}$ John likes [which picture of who]]]

Given that the C has a strong feature triggering *wh*-movement, the MLC forces it to attract the closest category that can enter into a checking relation with its sublabel, namely, *which*. Given that the raising of *which* alone causes the derivation to crash, C_{HL} can and should raise the minimal category containing *which* that allows convergence, namely, *which picture of who*. Thus, the application of Move raising *who* to the specifier of the C violates the MLC. Suppose C_{HL} employs this illegitimate application of Move. Then, C_{HL} yields (8).

(8)   [$_{CP}$ who [$_{C'}$[$_{TP}$ John likes [which picture of t(who)]]]]

At a later stage in this derivation, C_{HL} reaches the following structure:

(9)   [$_{CP}$ do [$_{TP}$ you wonder
       [$_{CP}$ who [$_{C'}$[$_{TP}$ John likes [which picture of t(who)]]]]]]

Given that the matrix C has a strong feature triggering *wh*-movement, the MLC forces it to attract the closest category that can enter into a checking relation with its sublabel, namely, *who*. Thus, the application of Move raising *which picture of t(who)* to the specifier of the matrix C violates the MLC. Suppose C_{HL} employs this illegitimate application of Move. Then, C_{HL} yields (10).

(10)   [$_{CP}$ [which picture of t(who)] [$_{C'}$ do [$_{CP}$ you wonder
       [$_{CP}$ who [$_{C'}$[$_{TP}$ John likes t([which picture of t(who)])]]]]]]

As shown above, C_{HL} employs two illegitimate applications of Move to generate (10) (i.e., the structure of (3)), to which Spell-Out applies.

Now compare the severely deviant (3) with the marginally deviant (11). The derivations of (3) and (11) are associated with the same initial numeration, and they compete in the eyes of derivational economy.[4]

(11)   ??[$_{CP}$ Who$_1$ do [$_{TP}$ you wonder
           [$_{CP}$ [which picture of t$_1$]$_2$ [$_{TP}$ John likes t$_2$]]]]?

Let us examine the relevant aspects of the derivation of (11). Notice that the structure (7) is common to the derivations of (3) and (11). In (7), the C has a strong feature triggering *wh*-movement; hence, the MLC forces it to attract the closest category that can enter into a checking relation with its sublabel, namely, *which*. Given that the raising of *which* alone causes the derivation to crash, C$_{HL}$ can and should raise the minimal category containing *which* that allows convergence, namely, *which picture of who*. Thus, the application of Move raising *which picture of who* to the specifier of the C satisfies the MLC. Suppose C$_{HL}$ employs this legitimate application of Move. Then, C$_{HL}$ yields (12) (instead of (8)).

(12)   [$_{CP}$ [which picture of who]
           [$_{C'}$[$_{TP}$ John likes t([which picture of who])]]]

At a later stage in this derivation, C$_{HL}$ reaches the following structure:

(13)   [$_{CP}$ do [$_{CP}$ you wonder [$_{CP}$[which picture of who]
           [$_{C'}$[$_{TP}$ John likes t([which picture of who])]]]]]

Given that the matrix C has a strong feature triggering *wh*-movement, the MLC forces it to attract the closest category that can enter into a checking relation with its sublabel, namely, *which*. Given that the raising of *which* alone causes the derivation to crash, C$_{HL}$ can and should raise the minimal category containing *which* that allows convergence, namely, *which picture of who*. Thus, the application of Move raising *who* to the specifier of the matrix C violates the MLC. Suppose C$_{HL}$ employs this illegitimate application of Move. Then, C$_{HL}$ yields (14).

(14)   [$_{CP}$ who [$_{C'}$ do [$_{CP}$ you wonder [$_{CP}$[which picture of t(who)]
           [$_{C'}$[$_{TP}$ John likes t([which picture of who])]]]]]]

As shown above, C$_{HL}$ employs only one illegitimate application of Move to generate (14) (i.e. the structure of (11)), to which Spell-Out applies.

Under the MLC analysis, the derivation of (3) employs two illegitimate applications of Move and induces severe deviance, whereas the derivation of (11) employs one illegitimate application of Move and induces marginal deviance. To explain why the derivation of (3) induces a greater degree of deviance than does the derivation of (11), I adopt the following (arguably natural) assumption (Chomsky 1965; Epstein 1990):[5]

(15)   A derivation employing a greater number of illegitimate steps induces a greater degree of deviance.

Given (15), the derivation of (3) (employing two illegitimate applications of Move) exhibits a greater degree of deviance than does the derivation of (11) (employing one illegitimate application of Move).[6,7] Under the MLC analysis (incorporating (15)), therefore, the severe deviance of cases such as (3) (involving no lowering) is captured without any reference to the PBC.

3.3.3 Further consequences

The MLC analysis of PBC effects further captures the following contrast, the so-called nesting effect (Pesetsky 1982, 1987):

(16) a.   ??What$_2$ did you wonder [$_{CP}$ whom$_1$ John persuaded t$_1$ to buy t$_2$]?
      b.   ?*Whom$_1$ did you wonder [$_{CP}$ what$_2$ John persuaded t$_1$ to buy t$_2$]?

Pesetsky (1982, 1987) proposes a general condition on movement that captures this contrast. He calls it the *Nested Dependency Condition* (NDC).

(17) *Nested Dependency Condition*
      If two *wh*-trace dependencies overlap, one must contain the other.

Taking *wh*-trace dependencies to be LF chain structures formed by *wh*-movement, Pesetsky assigns the chain structures (18a–b) to (16a–b), respectively:

(18) a.   what$_2$ whom$_1$ t$_1$ t$_2$

      b.   whom$_1$ what$_2$ t$_1$ t$_2$

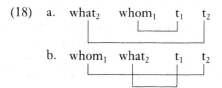

The LF structure of (16a) (assigned the nesting dependency (18a)) satisfies the NDC and the movement of *what* is therefore legitimate, whereas the LF structure of (16b) (assigned the intersecting dependency (18b)) violates the NDC and the movement of *whom* is therefore illegitimate.

   This nesting effect follows rather straightforwardly from the MLC analysis: the derivation of (16a), involving one illegitimate application of Move, induces marginal deviance, whereas the derivation of (16b), involving two illegitimate applications of Move, induces severe deviance.

   First consider the relevant aspects of the derivation of (16a). At some point in the derivation of (16a), C$_{HL}$ constructs the following structure:

(19) [$_{CP}$[$_{TP}$ John persuaded whom to buy what]]

Given that the C has a strong feature triggering *wh*-movement, the MLC forces it to attract the closest category that can enter into a checking relation with its sub-label, namely, *whom*. Thus, the application of Move raising *whom* to the specifier of the C satisfies the MLC. Suppose C$_{HL}$ employs this legitimate application of Move. Then, C$_{HL}$ yields (20).

(20) [$_{CP}$ whom [$_{C'}$[$_{TP}$ John persuaded t(whom) to buy what]]]

At a later stage in this derivation, C_{HL} reaches the following structure:

(21) [CP did [TP you wonder
[CP whom [C'[TP John persuaded t(whom) to buy what]]]]]

Given that the matrix C has a strong feature triggering *wh*-movement, the MLC
forces it to attract the closest category that can enter into a checking relation with
its sublabel, namely, *whom*. Thus, the application of Move raising *what* to the
specifier of the matrix C violates the MLC. Suppose C_{HL} employs this illegitimate
application of Move. Then, C_{HL} yields (22).

(22) [CP what [C' did [TP you wonder
[CP whom [C'[TP John persuaded t(whom) to buy t(what)]]]]]]]

As shown above, C_{HL} employs only one illegitimate application of Move to generate (22) (i.e. the structure of (16a)), to which Spell-Out applies.

Now compare the derivation of the marginally deviant (16a) with the derivation of the severely deviant (16b). The derivations of (16a–b) are associated with
the same initial numeration, and they compete in the eyes of derivational economy. Let us examine the relevant aspects of the derivation of (16b). Notice that
the structure (19) is common to the derivations of (16a–b). In (19), the C has a
strong feature triggering *wh*-movement; hence, the MLC forces it to attract the
closest category that can enter into a checking relation with its sublabel, namely,
whom. Thus, the application of Move raising *what* to the specifier of the C violates the MLC. Suppose C_{HL} employs this illegitimate application of Move. Then,
C_{HL} yields (23) (instead of (20)).

(23) [CP what [C'[TP John persuaded whom to buy t(what)]]]

At a later stage in this derivation, C_{HL} reaches the following structure:

(24) [CP did [TP you wonder
[CP what [C'[TP John persuaded whom to buy t(what)]]]]]

Given that the matrix C has a strong feature triggering *wh*-movement, the MLC
forces it to attract the closest category that can enter into a checking relation with
its sublabel, namely, *what*. Thus, the application of Move raising *whom* to the
specifier of the matrix C violates the MLC. Suppose C_{HL} employs this illegitimate
application of Move. Then, C_{HL} yields (25).

(25) [CP whom [C' did [TP you wonder
[CP what [C'[TP John persuaded t(whom) to buy t(what)]]]]]]]

As shown above, C_{HL} employs two illegitimate applications of Move to generate
(25) (i.e. the structure of (16b)), to which Spell-Out applies.

Finally, recall (15), repeated here.

(15)   A derivation employing a greater number of illegitimate steps induces a greater
degree of deviance.

Given (15), the derivation of (16b) (employing two illegitimate applications of
Move) exhibits a greater degree of deviance than does the derivation of (16a)
(employing one illegitimate application of Move). Under the MLC analysis (incorporating (15)), therefore, the nesting effect is captured without any reference
to the NDC.

The proposed analysis is further supported by the absence of deviance in examples such as (26) (see, among others, Huang 1993).

(26)   I wonder $[_{CP}[$how certain $[_{TP}$ t'_1 to $[_{vP}$ t_1 win$]]]_2$ $[_{TP}$ John$_1$ is $t_2]]$.

First recall Chomsky's (1995) version of the predicate-internal subject hypothesis
(i.e. a subject is base-generated in the specifier of a light verb).[8] Given this, the
trace of *John* occupying the specifier of the most deeply embedded T (namely, t'_1)
becomes unbound when the embedded predicate is raised to the specifier of the
embedded C; nevertheless, (26) exhibits no PBC effect.[9]

The MLC analysis correctly predicts that the derivation of (26) employs no illegitimate application of Move and converges. Consider the relevant aspects of the
derivation of (26). At some point in the derivation of (26), C_{HL} constructs the following structure (in which *John* has been raised to the specifier of the most deeply
embedded T):

(27) $[_{TP}$ is $[_{\alpha}$ how certain $[_{TP}$ John to $[_{vP}$ t(John) win$]]]]$

Given that the higher T has a strong feature triggering subject raising, the MLC
forces it to attract the closest category that can enter into a checking relation with
its sublabel, namely, *John*. Thus, the application of Move raising *John* to the specifier
of the higher T satisfies the MLC. Suppose C_{HL} employs this legitimate application of Move. Then, C_{HL} yields (28).

(28) $[_{TP}$ John $[_{T'}$ is $[_{\alpha}$ how certain $[_{TP}$ t′(John) to $[_{vP}$ t(John) win$]]]]]$

At a later stage in this derivation, C_{HL} reaches the following structure:

(29) $[_{CP}[_{TP}$ John $[_{T'}$ is $[_{\alpha}$ how certain $[_{TP}$ t′(John) to $[_{vP}$ t(John) win$]]]]]]$

Given that the C has a strong feature triggering *wh*-movement, the MLC forces
it to attract the closest category that can enter into a checking relation with its sublabel, namely, *how*. Given that the raising of *how* alone causes the derivation to
crash, C_{HL} can and should raise the minimal category containing *how* that allows

convergence, namely, α containing the traces of *John*. Thus, the application of Move raising α to the specifier of the C satisfies the MLC. Suppose C_{HL} employs this legitimate application of Move. Then, C_{HL} yields (30).

(30) $[_{CP}[_{\alpha}$ how certain $[_{TP}$ t'(John) to $[_{vP}$ t(John) win]]]
        $[_{C'}[_{TP}$ John $[_{T'}$ is t(α)]]]]]

This derivation later yields (31):

(31) $[_{CP}[_{TP}$ I wonder $[_{CP}[_{\alpha}$ how certain $[_{TP}$ t'(John) to $[_{vP}$ t(John) win]]]
        $[_{C'}[_{TP}$ John $[_{T'}$ is t(α)]]]]]]]

As shown above, C_{HL} employs no illegitimate application of Move to generate (31) (i.e. the structure of (26)), to which Spell-Out applies. In the LF component, the Preference Principle converts (31) (roughly) to the following structure:

(32) $[_{CP}[_{TP}$ I wonder $[_{CP}$ (how x) $[_{TP}$ John is
        (x certain $[_{TP}$ t'(John) to $[_{vP}$ t(John) win]])]]]]

Assuming that the LF representation of (26), given in (32) (in which the variable x and the traces of *John* are each bound), is legitimate, the derivation of (26) converges: the MLC analysis captures, without special stipulation, the absence of a PBC effect in (26).

Notes

1   For more recent discussion of PBC phenomena, see Lasnik and Saito (1992), Collins (1994).
2   Since *who* binds no variable in the LF representation resulting from this illegitimate application of Move, the derivation of (1b) crashes because of a violation of the principle of Full Interpretation (FI). [. . .]
3   The copy theory of movement is motivated (in part) to capture the absence of the coreference interpretation between *he* and *John* in the following example (Chomsky 1993):

(i)   *Which claim that John₁ was asleep was he₁ willing to discuss?

Given that Condition C of the binding theory applies solely at LF, (i) shows that the complement CP contained in the landing site of the moved *wh*-phrase is interpreted as if it were contained in the departure site of the moved *wh*-phrase. That is, reconstruction is obligatory in (i) (see, among others, Freidin 1986; Lebeaux 1988; Riemsdijk and Williams 1981). To explain such a reconstruction effect, Chomsky (1993: 35) proposes the copy theory of movement, under which a trace left by movement is a complete copy of the moved category: literal lowering operations are rendered unnecessary (and now prohibited by the C-Command Condition). Given the copy theory of movement, (i) is assigned the following structure:

(ii) $[_{CP}$ [which claim that John$_1$ was asleep] was $[_{TP}$ he$_1$ willing to discuss t([which claim that John$_1$ was asleep])]]

Chomsky (1993: 41) then proposes the Preference Principle (minimizing the restriction in the operator position, for example, specifier of C). Given this, (ii) is converted (roughly) to the following LF structure:

(iii) $[_{CP}$ (which x) was $[_{TP}$ he$_1$ willing to discuss (x claim that John$_1$ was asleep)]]

As shown in (iii), the complement CP occurs in the copy position (i.e. the departure site of the moved *wh*-phrase), ensuring a Condition C violation.

Chomsky further argues that reconstruction (i.e. a minimization of the restriction in the operator position) is essentially a reflex of the formation of operator-variable constructions. Thus, reconstruction holds only for operator chains, not for argument chains. This analysis is supported by the following example, in which coreference between *him* and *John* is permitted:

(iv) $[_α$ The claim that John$_1$ was asleep] seems to him$_1$ $[_{TP}$ t($α$) to be correct].

Given that reconstruction does not hold for the argument chain resulting from the application of Move raising $α$ to the specifier of the matrix T (in the derivation of (iv)), the complement CP in $α$ is interpreted in the specifier of the matrix T, thereby inducing no violation of Condition C. If the complement CP in $α$ were interpreted inside the embedded TP, the coreference interpretation between *John* and *him* would be prohibited, just as in (v).

(v)   *$[_α$ They] seem to him$_1$ $[_{TP}$ t($α$) to like John$_1$].

For further discussion of reconstruction effects, see Chomsky (1993, 1995), Huang (1993), Takano (1995).

4   For discussion of the contrast between (3) and (11), see, among others, Browning (1989), Chomsky (1986); Fiengo et al. (1988); Lasnik and Saito (1992); Tiedeman (1989); Torrego (1985).

5   Following Chomsky (1965) and Epstein (1990), I assume that a descriptively adequate grammar should be able to account for degrees of deviance.

6   Under minimalist assumptions, the derivations of (3) and (11) are not directly generated by the system: the derivation of (3) is generated by relaxing the MLC twice, whereas the derivation of (11) is generated by relaxing the MLC once.

7   An assumption similar to (15) has already been adopted in Chomsky and Lasnik's (1993) analysis of degrees of deviance (involving an illegitimate trace). Assuming that a trace must be properly governed (both antecedent- and head-governed by a lexical feature), Chomsky and Lasnik propose an analysis in which a trace is marked * if it fails either of these conditions, ** if it fails both or if it fails one along with the economy condition, and *** if it fails all three, with multiple starring indicating increased deviance. See also Chomsky (1986) for relevant discussion concerning degrees of deviance.

8   See also Collins and Thráinsson (1993); Fukui and Speas (1986); Kitagawa (1986); Koizumi (1993, 1995); Koopman and Sportiche (1991); and Kuroda (1988).

9   Lasnik and Saito (1992), assuming that the PBC applies at every point of the derivation (the Generalized Proper Binding Condition), propose a control analysis of nondeviant examples such as (26), in which *John* is base-generated outside the embedded predicate that undergoes *wh*-movement; consequently, the derivation of (26) induces no violation of the PBC.

Huang (1993), on the other hand, provides the contrast in (i), supporting the raising analysis of constructions such as (26) (in which *John* is raised from a position inside the embedded predicate).

(i)   a.   How certain that he$_1$ will win is John$_1$?
      b.   How certain to win is John?

Huang notes that the speaker of (ia), in which the embedded pronoun is bound by the matrix subject, presumes "John" to be certain that "John" will win, whereas the speaker of (ib) presumes the addressee to be certain that "John" will win. A unified control analysis of (ia) and (ib) would, by hypothesis, fail to make this distinction between them.

   In this study, I adopt the raising analysis of constructions such as (26) and explain why they exhibit no PBC effect. But see Lasnik and Saito (1992) for arguments supporting the control analysis.

References

Browning, M. A. 1989. ECP ≠ CED. *Linguistic Inquiry* 20: 481–91.

Chomsky, N. 1965. *Aspects of the theory of syntax*. Cambridge, MA: MIT Press.

Chomsky, N. 1986. *Barriers*. Cambridge, MA: MIT Press.

Chomsky, N. 1993. A minimalist program for linguistic theory. In K. Hale and S. J. Keyser (eds.), *The view from Building 20: Essays in linguistics in honor of Sylvain Bromberger*, Cambridge, MA: MIT Press, pp. 1–52. [Reprinted in Chomsky (1995), *The Minimalist Program*, Cambridge, MA: MIT Press, pp. 167–217.]

Chomsky, N. 1995. Categories and transformations. In Chomsky (1995), *The Minimalist Program*, Cambridge, MA: MIT Press, pp. 219–394.

Chomsky, N. and H. Lasnik. 1993. The theory of principles and parameters. In J. Jacobs, A. von Stechow, W. Sternefeld and T. Venneman (eds.), An International handbook of contemporary research, Berlin/New York: Walter de Gruyter, pp. 506–69. [Reprinted in Chomsky (1995), *The Minimalist Program*, Cambridge, MA: MIT Press, pp. 13–127.]

Collins, C. 1994. Economy of derivation and the generalized proper binding condition. *Linguistic Inquiry* 25: 45–61.

Collins, C. and H. Thráinsson. 1993. Object shift in double object constructions and the theory of Case. In C. Phillips (ed.), *Papers on Case and agreement II. MIT Working Papers in Linguistics 19*, Cambridge, MA: MITWPL, pp. 131–74.

Epstein, S. D. 1990. Differentiation and reduction in syntactic theory: A case study. *Natural Language and Linguistic Theory* 8: 313–23.

Fiengo, R. 1977. On trace theory. *Linguistic Inquiry* 8: 35–61.

Fiengo, R., C.-T. J. Huang, H. Lasnik and T. Reinhart. 1988. The syntax of wh-in-situ. In H. Borer (ed.), *The Proceedings of the 7th West Coast Conference on Formal Linguistics*, Stanford: CSLI, pp. 81–98.

Freidin, R. 1986. Fundamental issues in the theory of binding. In B. Lust (ed.), *Studies in the acquisition of anaphora*, vol. 1, Dordrecht: Reidel, pp. 151–88.

Fukui, N. and M. Speas. 1986. Specifiers and projection. In N. Fukui, T. R. Rapoport and E. Sagey (eds.), *Papers in theoretical linguistics. MIT Working Papers in Linguistics 8*, Cambridge, MA: MITWPL, pp. 128–72.

Huang, C.-T. J. 1993. Reconstruction and the structure of VP: Some theoretical consequences. *Linguistic Inquiry* 24: 103–38.

Kitagawa, Y. 1986. *Subjects in Japanese and English*. Doctoral dissertation, University of Massachusetts, Amherst.

Koizumi, M. 1993. Object agreement phrases and the split VP hypothesis. In J. D. Bobaljik and C. Phillips (eds.), *Papers on Case and agreement I. MIT Working Papers in Linguistics 18*, Cambridge, MA: MITWPL, pp. 99–148.

Koizumi, M. 1995. *Phrase structure in minimalist syntax*. Doctoral dissertation, MIT.

Koopman, H. and D. Sportiche. 1991. The position of subjects. *Lingua* 85: 211–58.

Kuroda, S.-Y. 1988. Whether we agree or not: A comparative syntax of English and Japanese. *Linguisticae Investigationes* 12.

Lasnik, H. and M. Saito. 1992. *Move α*. Cambridge, MA: MIT Press.

Lebeaux, D. 1988. *Language acquisition and the form of the grammar*. Doctoral dissertation, University of Massachusetts, Amherst.

May, R. 1977. *The grammar of quantification*. Doctoral dissertation, MIT.

Pesetsky, D. 1982. *Paths and categories*. Doctoral dissertation, MIT.

Pesetsky, D. 1987. Wh-in-situ: Movement and unselective binding. In E. Reuland and A. ter Meulen (eds.), *The representation of* (in)definiteness, Cambridge, MA: MIT Press, pp. 98–129.

Riemsdijk, H. van and E. William. 1981. NP-structure. *The Linguistic Review* 1: 171–218.

Saito, M. 1989. Scrambling as semantically vacuous A-movement. In M. Baltin and A. Kroch (eds.), *Alternative conceptions of phrase structure*, Chicago: University of Chicago Press, pp. 182–200.

Saito, M. 1992. Long-distance scrambling in Japanese. *Journal of East Asian Linguistics* 1: 69–118.

Takano, Y. 1995. Predicate fronting and internal subjects. *Linguistic Inquiry* 26: 327–40.

Tiedeman, R. C. 1989. *Government and locality conditions on syntactic relations*. Doctoral dissertation, University of Connecticut, Storrs.

Torrego, E. 1985. Empty categories in nominals. Ms., University of Massachusetts, Boston.

From "CATEGORIES AND TRANSFORMATIONS"
Noam Chomsky

4.4.4   Move F

[. . .]

So far I have kept to the standard assumption that the operation Move selects α and raises it, targeting K, where α and K are categories constructed from one or more lexical items. But on general minimalist assumptions, that is an unnatural interpretation of the operation. The underlying intuitive idea is that the operation Move is driven by morphological considerations: the requirement that some feature F must be checked. The minimal operation, then, should raise just the feature F: we should restrict α in the operation Move α to lexical features. Let us investigate what happens if we replace the operation Move α by the more principled operation Move F, F a feature.

We now extend the class of syntactic objects available to the computational system. Along with those permitted by the procedure (1), we allow also (2).

(1)   a.   lexical items
      b. $K = \{\gamma, \{\alpha, \beta\}\}$, where α, β are objects and γ is the label of K

(2) $K = \{\gamma, \{\alpha, \beta\}\}$, where α, β are features of syntactic objects already formed.

The extension holds only for Move; it is vacuous for Merge. So far we have considered only one case of the form (2), namely, $K = \{\gamma, \{F, \beta\}\}$, where F is raised to target β. We will see that the extension is even narrower: if α raises to target β, then β must be a full-fledged category and α may (and in a certain deeper sense *must*) be a feature.

One question arises at once: when F is raised to target K, why does F not raise alone to form {γ, {F, K}}? Suppose that the subject raises to [Spec, IP]. The simplest assumption would be that only the formal features of the head involved in feature checking raise to this position, leaving the rest of the DP unaffected. Why is this not the case? The answer should lie in a natural economy condition.

(3)   F carries along just enough material for convergence.

The operation Move, we now assume, seeks to raise just F. Whatever "extra baggage" is required for convergence involves a kind of "generalized pied-piping." In an optimal theory, nothing more should be said about the matter; bare output conditions should determine just what is carried along, if anything, when F is raised.

For the most part – perhaps completely – it is properties of the phonological component that require such pied-piping. Isolated features and other scattered parts of words may not be subject to its rules, in which case the derivation is canceled; or the derivation might proceed to PF with elements that are "unpronounceable," violating FI. There may be a morphological requirement that features of a single lexical item must be within a single X^0 (see McGinnis 1995). In any event, properties of the phonological component have a major (perhaps the total) effect on determining pied-piping.

To take a concrete example, suppose that the words *who*, *what* have three components: the *wh*-feature, an abstract element underlying indefinite pronouns, and the feature [±human].[1] Suppose interrogative C (= Q) is strong, as in English. The *wh*-feature cannot overtly raise alone to check Q because the derivation will crash at PF. Therefore, at least the whole word *who*, *what* will be pied-piped in overt raising. Suppose that *who* appears in the phrase *whose book*, which we assume to have the structure (4), with D the possessive element and *book* its complement.

(4)

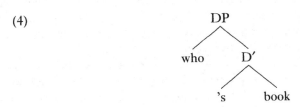

Suppose that Move F seeks to raise the *wh*-feature to check strong Q, pied-piping *who* and leaving the residue -*'s book*. That too crashes at PF (at least). And *whose* cannot raise because it is not a syntactic object at all, hence not subject to movement. Therefore, the smallest category that can be raised by the operation Move [*wh*-] in this case is the phrase *whose book* – though as far as the computational procedure is concerned, it is only the feature [*wh*-] that is raising; the rest is automatically carried along by virtue of the economy condition (3).

PF convergence is determined in this case by a morphological property of the determiner D = Possessive. Suppose that these properties of D did not bar extraction of the *wh*-phrase. Then violation of the Left-Branch Condition should be permitted. Uriagereka (1988) found a correlation between left-branch extraction and "richness" of D, in a sense he characterizes: the Left-Branch Condition holds for languages with D rich. The correlation follows, he observes, if the reasoning outlined here is correct.

Just how broadly considerations of PF convergence might extend is unclear, pending better understanding of morphology and the internal structure of phrases. Note that such considerations could permit raising without pied-piping even overtly, depending on morphological structure, as in the theory of overt raising of empty operators in Japanese developed by Watanabe (1992).

Pied-piping might in principle depend as well on factors that constrain movement: barriers, Empty Category Principle (ECP) considerations, the Minimal Link Condition (MLC) that requires "shortest moves," or whatever turns out to be the right story for this much-studied but still murky area. In the case of all such principles, one open question has been whether violation causes a derivation to crash or allows it to converge as deviant (say, a Subjacency violation vs. an ECP violation). The question could have an answer in the terms now being considered. Thus, if pied-piping is forced by the need to satisfy some principle P, we conclude that violation of P causes the derivation to crash so that it does not bar less economical derivations without pied-piping – for example, the principle P that sometimes bars preposition stranding.

Any further elaboration would be a departure from minimalist assumptions, hence to be adopted only insofar as that is forced on empirical grounds: never, in the best case. A host of problems arise that look difficult. The basic task is to determine how much of a departure (if any) is required from these optimal assumptions to account for "generalized pied-piping"; how PF and LF considerations enter into the picture; what these considerations imply about the structure of phrases and the status and nature of conditions on movement; and how language variation is determined.

As noted by Hisa Kitahara and Howard Lasnik, the proposed economy principle provides a further rationale for the principle Procrastinate: nothing at all is the least that can be carried along for convergence, and that is possible only if raising is covert, not entering the phonological component.

Consider now the case of covert movement. Questions of PF convergence do not arise, so generalized pied-piping could only be required by conditions on movement. Earlier discussion of Move α assumed that the principles that govern the operation hold only for categories, since only categories were assumed to move. If that happens to be true, then these principles hold only of overt movement, which has to carry along whole categories for PF convergence. The conclusion could well be true for other reasons even if the assumption is false. If the conclusion is true (for whatever reason), then covert raising is restricted to feature raising. The operation Move F carries along "excess baggage" only when it is "heard" in the phonetic output. I will assume that to be the case. The assumption accords well with the general minimalist perspective, and it has no obvious empirical flaw.

We tentatively assume, then, that only PF convergence forces anything beyond features to raise. If that turns out to be the case, or to the extent that it does, we have further reason to suspect that language "imperfections" arise from the external requirement that the computational principles must adapt to the sensorimotor apparatus, which is in a certain sense "extraneous" to the core systems of language as revealed in the N → λ computation.

When the feature F of the lexical item LI raises without pied-piping of LI or any larger category α, as always in covert raising, does it literally raise alone or does it automatically take other formal features along with it? There are strong empirical reasons for assuming that Move F automatically carries along FF(LI), the set of formal features of LI. We therefore understand the operation Move F in accord with (5), where FF[F] is FF(LI), F a feature of the lexical item LI.

(5)   Move F "carries along" FF[F].

This much pied-piping is automatic, reflecting the fact that Move relates to checking of formal features. Broader pied-piping is as required for convergence – "extraneous," insofar as PF convergence is the driving factor, which we tentatively assume to mean "always."

Applied to the feature F, the operation Move thus creates at least one and perhaps two "derivative chains" alongside the chain $CH_F = (F, t_F)$ constructed by the operation itself. One is $CH_{FF} = (FF[F], t_{FF[F]})$, consisting of the set of formal features FF[F] and its trace; the other is $CH_{CAT} = (\alpha, t_\alpha)$, α a category carried along by generalized pied-piping and including at least the lexical item LI containing F. CH_{FF} is always constructed, CH_{CAT} only when required for convergence. The computational system C_{HL} is really "looking at" CH_F, but out of the corner of its eye it can "see" the other two as well. Each enters into operations. Thus, CH_{CAT} determines the PF output, and CH_{FF} enters into checking operations in a manner to which we will return. As noted, CH_{CAT} should be completely dispensable, were it not for the need to accommodate to the sensorimotor apparatus.

[. . .]

Assuming this, we conclude that pure feature raising – hence all covert raising – is adjunction of a feature to a head, which projects.

[. . .]

4.5.1 Types of features

[. . .]

Evidently, certain features of FF(LI) enter into interpretation at LF while others are uninterpretable and must be eliminated for convergence. We therefore have a crucial distinction ±interpretable. Among the Interpretable features are categorial features and the φ-features of nominals.[2] The operations that interpret an example like *we build airplanes* at the LF interface will have to know that *build* is a V and *airplanes* an N with the φ-features [plural], [–human], [3 person]. On the other hand, these operations have no way to interpret the Case of *airplane* or the agreement features of *build*, which must therefore be eliminated for LF convergence.

[. . .]

4.5.2 Checking theory

[. . .]

Some features remain visible at LF even after they are checked: for example, φ-features of nouns, which are interpreted. And some plainly are not accessible to the computational system when checked: the Case feature of nouns, for example, which cannot be accessed after checking.

We therefore have to give a more nuanced analysis of the relation between visibility at LF and accessibility to the computational system. The two properties are related by the descriptive generalization (6).

(6) a. Features visible at LF are accessible to the computation C_{HL} throughout, whether checked or not.
     b. Features invisible at LF are inaccessible to C_{HL} once checked.

[. . .]

Case (6a) is true without exception: Interpretable features cannot be deleted (a fortiori, erased) and therefore remain accessible to the computation and visible at LF. Case (6b) holds unless erasure of the − Interpretable checked feature erases a term or is barred by a parametrized property P of the feature. Though examples exist, they are few; thus, case (6b) holds quite generally. For expository purposes, I will speak of deletion as erasure except when the issue arises.

The revision of checking theory is without effect for − Interpretable features in the checking domain, such as Case of an argument. It is these features that must be inaccessible after checking; the examples discussed are typical in this regard.

4.5.5 The Minimal Link Condition

Consider (7).

(7) they remember [which book Q [John gave t to whom]]

Suppose that (7) is interrogative, with the complementizer Q′. If it is a root construction, the strong feature of Q′ can be eliminated by adjunction of I to Q′ or substitution of a *wh*-phrase in [Spec, Q′]; if it is embedded, as in (8), only the latter option is available.

(8) guess [Q′ they remember [which book Q [John gave t to whom]]]

Embedded or not, there are two *wh*-phrases that are candidates for raising to [Spec, Q′] to check the strong feature: *which book* and *(to-)whom*, yielding (9a) and (9b).

(9) a. (guess) [which book Q′ [they remember [$t′$ Q [to give t to whom]]]]
     b. (guess) [[to whom]$_2$ Q′ [they remember [[which book]$_1$ Q [to give t_1 t_2]]]]

(9b) is a *Wh*-Island violation. It is barred straightforwardly by the natural condition that shorter moves are preferred to longer ones – in this case, by raising of *which book* to yield (9a). This operation is permissible, since the *wh*-feature of *which book* is Interpretable, hence accessible, and the raising operation places it in a checking relation with Q′, erasing the strong feature of Q′. The option of forming (9a) bars the "longer move" required to form (9b). But (9a), though convergent, is deviant.

Let us interpret the Minimal Link Condition (MLC) as requiring that at a given stage of a derivation, a longer link from α to K cannot be formed if there is a shorter legitimate link from β to K. In these terms, the Ā-movement cases of relativized minimality can be accommodated (to a first approximation; we will return to further comment). It is not that the island violation is deviant; rather, there is no such derivation, and the actual form derived by the MLC is deviant.

What about the A-movement cases (superraising)? Suppose we have constructed (10).

(10)   seems [$_{IP}$ that it was told John [$_{CP}$ that IP]]

Raising of *John* to matrix subject position is a Relativized Minimality (ECP) violation, but it is barred by the "shorter move" option that raises *it* to this position. Raising of *it* is a legitimate operation: though its Case feature has been erased in IP, its D-feature and ϕ-features, though checked, remain accessible.

There are differences between the A- and Ā-movement cases that have to be dealt with, but these aside, both kinds of Relativized Minimality violation fall together naturally under the MLC.[3]

Closer analysis of formal features thus allows us to resurrect an idea about island violations that has been in the air for some years: they involve a longer-than-necessary move and thus fall under an approach that has sometimes been suggested to account for superiority phenomena.[4] The idea ran into two problems. Suppose a derivation had reached the "intermediate stage" Σ of (8) and (10), with an intermediate category (*which book, it*) closer to the intended target than the one we hope to prevent from raising. The first problem is that the intermediate category has its features checked, so it should be frozen in place. The second problem has to do with the range of permissible operations at stage Σ: there are so many of these that it is hard to see why raising of the intermediate category is the "shortest move." That problem was in fact more general: thus, it was far from clear why raising of *John* to [Spec, I] in (11) is the "shortest move."[5]

(11)   I(nfl) was told John (that IP)

Both problems are now overcome, the first by attention to interpretability of features, the second by a radical narrowing of the class of permissible operations under Last Resort [Move F raises F to target K only if F enters into a checking relation with a sublabel of K].

Let us turn now to the differences between the Ā- and A-movement violations (*Wh*-Island, superraising). In the former case, the derivation satisfying the
MLC converges; in the latter, it does not. Raising of embedded *it* to matrix
subject satisfies the EPP [Extended Projection Principle] and the φ-features of
[I, seem], but not the Case feature. But matrix T has a –Interpretable Case feature, which, unless checked and erased, causes the derivation to crash.[6] In the
case of A-movement, unlike Ā-movement, the "shortest move" does not yield a
convergent derivation.

For the account of the superraising violation to go through, we must take the
MLC to be part of the definition of Move, hence inviolable, not an economy condition that chooses among convergent derivations: "shortest moves" are the only
ones there are. As noted earlier, that has always been the preferred interpretation
of the MLC for purely conceptual reasons, and perhaps the only coherent interpretation. We are now in a position to adopt it, having eliminated many possible
operations that would appear to undermine the condition.

We therefore add to the definition of Move the condition (12), expressing the
MLC, where *close* is (tentatively) defined in terms of c-command and equidistance.

(12)   α can raise to target K only if there is no legitimate operation Move β
       targeting K, where β is closer to K.

A "legitimate operation" is one satisfying Last Resort.

Before proceeding, let us review the status of the superraising violation (10)
in the light of economy considerations. Suppose that the derivation D with the
initial numeration N has reached stage Σ. The reference set within which relative
economy is evaluated is determined by (N, Σ): it is the set R(N, Σ) of convergent
extensions of the derivation N → Σ, using what remains of N. At Σ, the operation OP is blocked if OP′ yields a more economical derivation in R(N, Σ).

Considerations of economy arise at stage Σ of the derivation only if there is a
convergent extension. But in the case of (10), there is none. The problem is not
with the initial numeration N: there is a convergent derivation that takes a different path from N, leading to (13), with *it* inserted in matrix subject position.

(13)   it seems [that John was told *t* [that IP]]

Superraising from (10) is not barred by economy considerations that reject the outcome in favor of (13), because (10) is not a stage on the way to a convergent derivation at all. Unless the shortest-move requirement is part of the definition of Move,
there will be a convergent derivation from (10), namely, the one that involves superraising. But things work out as desired if the MLC is part of the definition of Move,
as preferred for other reasons.[7]

As is well known, the superraising violation is far more severe than the *Wh*-
Island violation involving arguments, and there are many related problems that
have been the topic of much investigation.[8] The conclusions here shed no further
light on them.

4.5.6 Attract/move

The formulation of the MLC is more natural if we reinterpret the operation of movement as "attraction": instead of thinking of α as raising to target K, let us think of K as attracting the closest appropriate α.[9] We define *Attract F* in terms of the condition (14), incorporating the MLC and Last Resort.

(14)   K *attracts* F if F is the closest feature that can enter into a checking relation with a sublabel of K.

If K attracts F, then α merges with K and enters its checking domain, where α is the minimal element including FF[F] that allows convergence: FF[F] alone if the operation is covert. The operation forms the chain (α, t).
   [. . .]
   The operation Attract/Move can "see" only the head of a chain, not its second or later members. Though it is not forced, the natural more general principle is that traces also cannot be targets, so that we have (15), with the qualifications already noted.

(15)   Only the head of a chain CH enters into the operation Attract/Move.

   If (15) holds, we settle a question that was left unresolved in the case of V-raising: do the features of the object Obj adjoin to the head of the V-chain or to its trace? Suppose, say, that V-raising is overt, as in French-type languages. Do the features FF(Obj) adjoin to the trace of [V, Agr_O], a copy of the raised V–Agr complex, or to the I complex of which V is a part? The latter must be the case if (15) is correct, as I will assume.
   [. . .]
   A problem is posed, once again, by such constructions as [*they seemed to each other [*t to have been angry*]*], which appear in preraising form as (16).

(16)   I(nfl) seem [$_{\mathrm{pp}}$ to γ] Cl

There is good evidence that γ c-commands into the infinitival clause Cl. Suppose that γ = *him* and Cl = *they to like John*, so that the preraising structure is (17), yielding *they seem to him to like John* after raising.

(17)   I(nfl) seem [to him] [$_{\mathrm{Cl}}$ they to like John]

Then a Condition C violation results if γ (= *him*) takes *John* as antecedent. It follows that γ must also c-command *they*.
   Why, then, does I in (16) attract the subject *they* of Cl rather than γ, which c-commands it, an apparent Relativized Minimality violation?
   In (16) *seem* has two internal arguments: PP and Cl. On present assumptions, that requires an analysis as a Larsonian shell, with *seem* raising to the light verb v and subsequent operations yielding (18) (internal structure of I omitted).

(18)

```
              I
           /     \
          I       VP₁
               /      \
              υ        VP₂
                    /      \
                  XP        V′₂
                         /      \
                      seem      YP
```

Since PP is the optional argument and Cl the obligatory one in (16), it is likely that Cl is the complement YP and PP the specifier XP, which yields the observed order directly.[10]

When *seem* raises to adjoin to v, it forms the chain CH = (*seem*, t). PP is in the minimal domain of CH, but this does not suffice to place PP within the neighborhood of I that can be ignored when we ask whether *they* in (17) is close enough to IP to be attracted by IP. It is not, because nothing has adjoined to I at the point when *they* raises.[11] Therefore, γ = *him* is closer to IP and has features that can enter into a checking relation with I (e.g. its D-feature). We expect, then, that *they* should not raise in (17), contrary to fact.

In some languages, the facts generally accord with these expectations. In French, for example, raising is barred in the counterpart to (17), unless PP is a clitic, which raises, presumably leaving a trace.[12]

(19) a.   *Jean semble à Marie [t_j avoir   du talent]
           Jean seems to Marie   to.have talent
      b.   Jean lui   semble t_1 [t_j avoir   du talent]
            Jean to.her   seems   to.have talent
            'Jean seems to her to have talent'

The results are as predicted. *Marie* is closer to IP than the embedded subject *Jean* in the position t_j of (19a) and therefore bars raising. The Case of *Jean* is not checked and erased, so the derivation crashes. In (19b) the trace of the clitic cannot be attracted, by (15). Therefore, raising is permitted and the derivation converges.

If PP in such structures could be raised by Ā-movement (topicalization, *wh*-movement), it would leave the structure (20).

(20)   V t Cl

According to the principle (15), the effects should be as in (19b). The evidence appears to be partial and somewhat obscure, however. The status of the English constructions still remains unexplained, along with many other related questions.

[. . .]

I will therefore strengthen [the claim that features cannot be checked under feature mismatch] to (21).

(21)   Mismatch of features cancels the derivation.

A configuration with mismatched features is not a legitimate syntactic object.[13] We distinguish mismatch from nonmatch: thus, the Case feature [accusative] mismatches F' = [assign nominative], but fails to match F' = I of a raising infinitival, which assigns no Case. I have left the notion "match" somewhat imprecise pending a closer analysis. But its content is clear enough for present purposes: thus, the categorial feature D of DP matches the D-feature of I; ϕ-features match if they are identical; and so on.

Notice that cancellation of a derivation under mismatch should be distinguished from nonconvergence. The latter permits a different convergent derivation to be constructed, if possible. But the point here is literally to bar alternatives. A canceled derivation therefore falls into the category of convergent derivations in that it blocks any less optimal derivation; mismatch cannot be evaded by violation of Procrastinate or other devices. If the optimal derivation creates a mismatch, we are not permitted to pursue a nonoptimal alternative.

Suppose, for example, that a series of applications of Merge has formed a verb phrase α with DP_1 as specifier and DP_2 as complement, bearing accusative and nominative Case, respectively. We will see that the optimal derivation from that point leads to mismatch. Since mismatch is equivalent to convergence from an economy-theoretic point of view, we cannot construct a less optimal derivation from α that might converge, with the thematic subject bearing accusative Case and the thematic object nominative Case. The interpretation is motivated on purely conceptual grounds: it sharply reduces computational complexity. Again, conceptual and empirical considerations converge.

[. . .]

4.10.2   Core concepts reconsidered

To accommodate the change from an Agr-based to a multiple-Spec theory, we have to simplify the notions of equidistance and closeness that entered into the definition of Attract/Move. These were expressed in principle (22).

(22)   β is *closer to* K than α if β c-commands α and is not in the minimal domain of CH, where CH is the chain headed by γ, γ adjoined within the zero-level projection $H(K)^{0max}$.

But this no longer works: with the elimination of intervening heads, minimal domains collapse. We therefore have to exclude nontrivial chains from the account of equidistance, relying instead on the much more differentiated analysis of features now available and the immobility of traces – that is, on the fact that only the head of a chain can be "seen" by K seeking the closest α to attract.

In the earlier formulation, the basic case is (23), which accommodates adjunction of α to X as well as substitution of α in [Spec, X] (where X may already be the head of a complex zero-level projection).

(23)

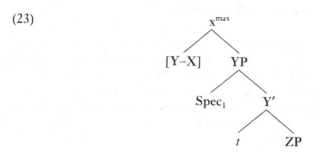

When α raises, targeting x^{max}, it creates a new position $\tau(X)$, which may either be [Spec, X] or adjoined to [Y–X] (= X^{0max}); call $\tau(X)$ the *target* in either case. The minimal domain of the chain CH = (Y, t) includes $Spec_1$ and ZP along with $\tau(X)$ formed by raising of α, which is within ZP or is ZP. Crucially, $Spec_1$ is within the "neighborhood of X" that is ignored in determining whether α is close enough to be attracted by X (technically, by its projection). That assumption was necessary in order to allow α to cross $Spec_1$ to reach $\tau(X)$. In a transitive verb construction, for example, it was assumed that X = Agr, $Spec_1$ = Subj, Y is the verbal element that adjoins to Agr, and Obj is within its ZP complement. Obj has to raise to the checking domain of Agr for feature checking either overtly or covertly, requiring that it be "as close" to the target as $Spec_1$.

Most of this is now beside the point. We have eliminated Agr and its projection from the inventory of elements. For the case of overt object raising, the structure formed is no longer (23) with X = Agr and $\tau(X)$ = [Spec, Agr], but (24), with an extra Spec in YP.

(24)

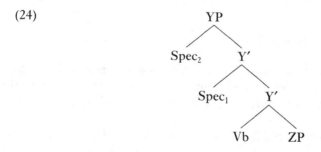

Vb is the verbal element (or its trace, if the complex has raised further to adjoin to T); Y' and YP are projections of the light verb v to which V has adjoined to form Vb; ZP = [t_V Obj], t_V the trace of V; and $Spec_2$ is the target $\tau(v)$ created by the raising operation. $Spec_1$ is Subj, and it is only necessary that it be no closer to the target $Spec_2$ than α in ZP. For this purpose, it suffices to simplify (22), keeping just to the trivial chain CH = H(K) (the head of K) and its minimal domain. We therefore restate (22) as (25).

(25)   γ and β are equidistant from α if γ and β are in the same minimal domain.

Hence, γ = Spec$_2$ and β = Spec$_1$ are equidistant from α = Obj in the illustrative example just discussed.

We now define "close" for Attract/Move in the obvious way: if β c-commands α and τ is the target of raising, then

(26)   β is *closer to* K than α unless β is in the same minimal domain as (a) τ or (b) α.

We thus have two cases to consider. We ask (case (26a)) whether β and τ are equidistant from α, and (case (26b)) whether β and α are equidistant from τ. If either is true, then β does not bar raising of α to τ. In case (26a), β and τ are in the minimal domain of H(K); and in case (26b), β and α are in the minimal domain of *h*, for some head *h*. In case (26a), β is in the "neighborhood" of H(K) that is ignored, in the sense of earlier exposition.

By case (26a), Obj within ZP in (24) is close enough to be attracted by Y′ (= YP, at this point), since Spec$_1$ is in the minimal domain of H(Y′) and is therefore not closer to Y′ than Obj; Spec$_1$ and Spec$_2$ (= τ) are equidistant from Obj. Therefore, either Subj in Spec$_1$ or Obj (in ZP) can raise to the new outer Spec, Spec$_2$, required by the strong feature of *v*. Both Obj and Subj must raise for Case checking, and something must raise to check the Case feature of T (or of some higher category if T is a raising infinitival, as already discussed). By case (26b), overt object raising to Spec$_2$ does not prevent subject raising from Spec$_1$, because Spec$_2$ and Spec$_1$ are equidistant from any higher target; both are in the minimal domain of *v*. How about direct raising of Obj from within ZP, targeting T, crossing Subj and Spec$_1$? That is barred by the MLC, since Subj and Obj are not equidistant from T, given the *v*–VP analysis of transitives; they are in different minimal domains. We will return to a closer analysis, reviewing other options skirted here.

Consider the following counterargument. Suppose the language has the EPP and optional object raising: T requires [Spec, T] and *v* permits an outer Spec, Spec$_2$, beyond Subj in Spec$_1$ (both overt). Suppose that Obj raises to [Spec$_2$, *v*], then raises again to [Spec, T], satisfying the EPP. That much is permitted. Subj and T have not had Case features checked, but that can be overcome by covert raising of Subj, targeting T, which is also permitted. So the derivation converges, incorrectly. But this derivation is blocked by economy conditions. It involves three raising operations, and two would suffice for convergence: object raising followed by subject raising to [Spec, T] (in both cases, with two violations of Procrastinate, the minimal number with two strong features). So the unwanted series of steps, though permitted, is barred by economy considerations: shorter derivations block longer ones.

The computation is local: after raising the object, we choose the operation that will lead to the shortest convergent derivation: raising of Subj to [Spec, T]. We also have empirical support for the tentative assumption made earlier that shorter derivations, locally determined in this sense, block longer ones.

Note that we have lost Holmberg's generalization and other effects of V-raising on extension of chains; that is a consequence of excluding chains from the definition of "closeness." Such generalizations, if valid, would now have to be stated in terms of a property of Vb in (24): it can have a second outer Spec only if it is a trace. There is no obvious reason why this should be so.

[. . .]

The conclusion that equidistance is still needed relies on a tacit assumption that could be challenged: that the strong feature of v must be satisfied by the outer Spec, $Spec_2$ of (24), not the inner Spec, $Spec_1$. All we know, however, is that *some* Spec of v is motivated by considerations of θ-theory (to host the external argument) and is therefore independent of the strength of v; the other Spec is present only to check the strength feature. But both Specs are within the minimal domain of v, so either is available for θ-marking of the external argument of a transitive verb. Suppose we allow this possibility, so that the outer Spec can host the external argument. In that case we can drop the notion of equidistance entirely, simplifying (26) to the statement that β is *closer* to the target K than α if β c-commands α. It follows, then, that Obj can only raise to the inner Spec, $Spec_1$ of (24), to check the strength feature and undergo overt Case marking. If overt object raising takes place, then Subj will be merged in the outer Spec to receive the external θ-role provided by the configuration. With "closer than" restricted to c-command, only Subj in the outer Spec can be attracted by T (note that Subj always has features that will check sublabels of T). Therefore, Obj is frozen in place after overt object raising, and the conclusions reached above follow directly.[14]

Notes

1   See Chomsky (1964), and recent work based on much richer typological and morphological evidence (in particular, Tsai 1994 and work summarized there).
2   Given the relation to semantic content, we might expect that a categorial feature associated with no such content, in a pure expletive, should be eliminated at LF. We will return to this matter.
3   No link of the *there*-associate type holds between *it* and CP in (10); see McCloskey (1991).
4   See Chomsky (1994: note 59), Ura (1995), and references cited. For recent discussion of superiority, see several papers in Thráinsson, Epstein, and Kuno (1993). The status of the phenomenon is not entirely clear. Standard examples, such as the contrast between (ia–b) and (ic–d) prove little.

(i)   a.   who saw what
      b.   whom did you persuade to do what
      c.   *what did who see
      d.   *what did you persuade whom to do

In the acceptable cases, the *wh*-phrase in situ has focal stress and could be taking clausal scope for this reason alone; the preferred cases degrade when that property is removed. Other properties that have been studied also raise questions. Thus, considerable ingenuity has been expended to explain why in (ii), the embedded *who* takes matrix rather than embedded scope.

(ii)   who wonders what who bought

That could be an artifact, however, reflecting a preference for association of likes. Thus, the opposite association holds in (iii).

(iii)   what determines to whom who will speak

There are many other problems.

5   See Chomsky (1986) for attempts to deal with this problem, now unnecessary.

6   The derivation of (10) crashes for two reasons: *John* lacks Case, and matrix T fails to assign Case. [. . .]

7   If the local interpretation of reference sets is abandoned, the same approach to superraising might be feasible on the assumption that a derivation that involves shorter moves blocks one with longer moves, so that (13) blocks the application of superraising in (10). [. . .]

8   [. . .] It is possible that the "weak islands" for arguments have to do with the option of multiple Specs, adapting ideas of Reinhart (1981) more generally along lines already indicated.

9   I follow here a suggestion of John Frampton's.

10   The surface order is not a clear criterion because of ordering effects involving "heaviness" and other poorly understood properties. The relation of obligatoriness to specifier-complement choice also leads into mainly uncharted territory. But the conclusions are reasonable and are supported empirically by the fact that α c-commands into Cl, assuming the PP to function as a DP with P adjoined, as a kind of Case marker, so that it does not affect c-command.

11   Even if the light verb v to which *seem* has adjoined raised overtly to adjoin to I, as in French-type languages, that would not affect the matter. The minimal domain of the chain it heads, which determines the "neighborhood of I" relevant for determining closeness, does not contain PP.

12   See preceding note. Thanks to Viviane Déprez for examples and for clarification of the general issue, which, she observes, is considerably more complex than indicated here, with graded judgments and many other factors involved, among them choice of clitic, infinitive versus small clause, ordering of PP and clausal complement, and idiom chunks (which give sharper distinctions) versus other phrases. Esther Torrego (forthcoming, and personal communication) points out that where the clitic is doubled, as in Spanish, the analogue of (19b) is barred, again as expected if (as she assumes) the doubled element is present as *pro*, so that there is no clitic chain but rather a structure analogous to (19a).

13   A qualification is needed for multiple-Spec constructions, restricting mismatch to the inner Spec.

14   We need not be concerned that Merge is favored over Move at a given point in a derivation, because the derivation will now crash if the favored option is selected, inserting Subj before raising Obj.

References

Chomsky, N. 1964. *Current issues in linguistic theory*. The Hague: Mouton.

Chomsky, N. 1986. *Barriers*. Cambridge, MA: MIT Press.

Chomsky, N. 1994. *Bare phrase structure. MIT Occasional Papers in Linguistics 5*. Cambridge, MA: MITWPL. [Published in P. Kempchinsky (ed.) (1994), *Evolution and revolution in linguistic theory: Essays in honor of Carlos Otero*. Washington, DC: Georgetown University Press, pp. 51–109. Also published in G. Webelhuth (ed.) (1994), *Government and binding theory and the minimalist program*. Cambridge, MA: MIT Press, pp. 383–439.]

McCloskey, J. 1991. *There, it*, and agreement. *Linguistics Inquiry* 22: 563–7.

McGinnis, M. 1995. Fission as feature-movement. In R. Pensalfini and H. Ura (eds.), *Papers on Minimalist Syntax. MIT Working Papers in Linguistics 27*, Cambridge, MA: MITWPL, pp. 165–87.

Reinhart, T. 1981. A second COMP position. In A. Belletti, L. Brandi and L. Rizzi (eds.), *Theory of markedness in generative grammar: Proceedings of the 1979 GLOW conference*. Pisa: Scuola Normale Superiore di Pisa, pp. 515–57.

Thráinsson, H., S. D. Epstein and S. Kuno (eds.) 1993. *Harvard Working Papers in Linguistics 3*, Department of Linguistics, Harvard University.

Torrego, E. forthcoming. Experiencers and raising verbs. [Published in R. Freidin (ed.) (1996), *Current issues in comparative grammar*. Dordrecht: Kluwer, pp. 101–20.]

Tsai, D. W.-T. 1994. *On economizing the theory of A-bar dependencies*. Doctoral dissertation, MIT.

Ura, H. 1995. Towards a theory of "strictly derivational" economy condition. In R. Pensalfini and H. Ura (eds.), *Papers on minimalist syntax. MIT Working Papers in Linguistics 27*. Cambridge, MA: MITWPL, pp. 243–67.

Uriagereka, J. 1988. *On government*. Doctoral dissertation, University of Connecticut, Storrs.

Watanabe, A. 1992. Subjacency and S-structure movement of wh-in-situ. *Journal of East Asian Linguistics* 1: 255–91.

From LOCAL ECONOMY
Chris Collins

We can define local economy as in (1).

(1)   Given a set of syntactic objects Σ which is part of derivation D,[1] the decision about whether an operation OP may apply to Σ (as part of an optimal derivation[2]) is made only on the basis of information[3] available in Σ.

This definition is very abstract, but it is based on a very simple intuition. During a derivation, at any step the decision about whether to apply an operation (in an optimal derivation) is based on the syntactic objects to which the operation is applying. In other words, the decision about whether to apply OP may not refer to another set of syntactic objects Σ' that is in D, or to what happens at LF and PF, nor to another set of syntactic objects Σ' that is in another derivation D'.

Perhaps the best way to grasp the definition of local economy is to compare it with one particular form of global economy, given in (2). (Here I follow Kitahara's (1995) convenient formulation.)

(2)   *Shortest Derivation Requirement (SDR)*
      Minimize the number of operations necessary for convergence.

This definition is global in two very different ways. First, in order to decide whether an operation OP applying to a set Σ is in the optimal derivation, we must evaluate the number of steps in other derivations. This kind of comparison clearly does not fall under local economy. Note that in order to make this definition work, there must be some way of comparing derivations. A number of different approaches have been tried. For example, Collins (1994) and Kitahara (1995) suggest that the two derivations must have the same LF objects. Chomsky (1994, 1995) assumes that two derivations are comparable if they have the same Numeration. In Chomsky's (1995: 227) terminology, the Numeration determines the reference set, and the only derivations that are considered are ones with the same Numeration. [. . .]

The other way in which this definition is global is that it involves a reference to the notion of convergence. A derivation is convergent if it leads to representations at PF and LF that satisfy Full Interpretation (FI). Minimally, a representation at PF satisfies FI only if all the strong features have been deleted. A representation at LF satisfies FI only if all the uninterpretable features have been deleted. [. . .] Crucially, in order to know if a derivation is convergent, it is necessary to verify the status of the final LF and PF representations of the derivation. This entails that (2) is not a local economy condition. In order to decide whether an operation OP applying to a set Σ is in the optimal derivation, we must verify that the derivation D (of which OP is an operation) leads to LF and PF representations satisfying Full Interpretation. This decision clearly does not conform to the definition of local economy.[4]

The definition of SDR in (2) is global in two ways: it refers to the number of steps in an alternative derivation and it refers to convergence. As we will see in this book, most of the global economy conditions that have been presented in the literature have these properties.

There are a number of reasons why local economy is superior to global economy. First, it is empirically superior [. . .]. Second, it tends to allow a more natural analysis of optionality [. . .]. Third, as was originally pointed out to me by Akira Watanabe, if global economy chooses the derivation with fewest steps, this is a case where the grammar is able to count. To evaluate the SDR, the number of operations in two different derivations must be counted and compared. This kind of comparison does not seem to be necessary in other parts of the grammar. For example, there is no condition that makes reference to the checking of exactly three features, or to comparing the number of violations of some condition against the number of violations of some other condition, or whatever.[5] What the grammar appears to be able to do is verify whether some simple condition (such as Last Resort or Minimality, as they are defined below) holds.

Perhaps the strongest reason to adopt local economy is that it places a strong constraint on possible economy conditions. This sharply limits the theoretical possibilities in giving an economy analysis of any particular phenomenon, which is desirable. Note that there is no question of learnability or explanatory adequacy. Whether or not local economy is adopted, the economy conditions are part of UG and therefore do not have to be acquired.[6]

[. . .]

The final result of this book will be that there are only two real economy conditions, both of which are local:

(3) *Last Resort*
     An operation OP involving α may apply only if some property of α is satisfied.
(4) *Minimality*
     An operation OP (satisfying Last Resort) may apply only if there is no smaller operation OP′ (satisfying Last Resort).

Most other conceivable economy conditions are global and are therefore ruled out.
     [. . .]

I speculate that (3) and (4) above are the only real economy conditions, therefore giving economy a limited but important role in grammatical theory. In this book I will address many questions about these two conditions. For example, is there any interaction between them? I assume that there is no interaction, in the sense that every operation must meet both of the conditions. In this sense the economy conditions are independent. However, there is a natural hierarchy that can be imposed on the conditions: Last Resort determines when an operation is possible. If the operation is possible, Minimality determines the smallest one. Therefore, Minimality could be restated as a requirement that operations satisfying Last Resort be minimal.

I will also assume in this book that (3) and (4) are inviolable – in other words, that they can never be overridden. To clarify, consider the assumption (Chomsky 1994: 428) that Procrastinate selects among convergent derivations. We could make the same assumption about Minimality and Last Resort. In other words, we could rephrase Minimality as in (5).

(5) *Minimality*
     An operation OP in derivation D may apply only if there no smaller operation OP' in D', and both D and D' converge.

Clearly this is unacceptable from the standpoint of local economy. It would mean that, in order to decide whether an operation OP (applying to Σ) is part of the optimal derivation, we would have to know whether OP is part of a convergent derivation. To know this, we would have to look at the PF and LF representations of the derivation.

It may be asked whether local economy throws any light on the question of optionality. To a certain extent it does. [. . .] [A]pparent cases of optional inversion are allowed by local economy and disallowed by global economy. As a general assessment, global economy tends to eliminate most cases of optionality, since an optional movement always results in a longer derivation. [. . .] From a local perspective, the only thing that matters is that each step satisfies the local economy conditions of Minimality and Last Resort (and perhaps others). To the extent that local economy is satisfied, optional movements are allowed.[7]

[. . .]

2.5 Attract versus Move

Chomsky (1995) postulates that Last Resort and Minimality are part of the definition of the operation he calls Attract (which is meant to supplant Move). This definition is given in (6).

(6) K attracts F if F is the closest feature that can enter into a checking relation with a sublabel of K.

Before addressing Chomsky's reasons for incorporating Last Resort and Minimality into the definition of Attract (replacing movement), I will give a number of reasons why such a definition is not desirable.

First, in the system I am developing, there are very simple operations, such as Merge, Copy (which is always a reflex of Merge), and Delete. The complicated facts concerning movement are the results of these very simple operations inter-acting with general principles, such as Last Resort and Minimality. Under this way of looking at things, we may expect the general principles to apply not only to movement but also to cases of pure Merge. [. . .] [P]ure Merge then satisfies Last Resort and Minimality. If Last Resort and Minimality were parts of the definition of Attract (supplanting Move), then they would independently have to be part of the definition of pure Merge. Such a result would be odd. Both Attract and Merge would have exactly the same conditions built into them.

Second, we may expect conditions like Last Resort and Minimality to operate in morphology (governing the placement of second-position clitics and the rear-rangement of affixes) and phonology (governing deletion and epenthesis and the placement of prosodically determined affixes). This would be the optimal result: very general conditions, restricting all linguistic systems. However, if Last Resort and Minimality were part of the definition of Attract, we would not necessarily expect to see these conditions operate outside the domain of syntactic movement.

Now let us consider Chomsky's reasons for defining Attract as incorporating Last Resort and Minimality. First, Chomsky (1995: 296) says that the Minimal Link Condition (our Minimality) has the property that it is inviolable. In other words, it does not choose the optimal derivation from among just the convergent derivations. This means that we do not expect a situation where a violation of the MLC is allowed, if otherwise the derivation would crash. If the MLC was part of the definition of Attract/Move, this property would be explained. Every opera-tion would obey the MLC as a matter of definition. However, on the theory of economy that I am developing here, no economy condition selects the optimal deriva-tion from among convergent derivations (this type of selection being a global notion).

Chomsky (1995: 268) raises the question of how two derivations could be compared if they had shorter links in different places. [. . .] If MLC was part of the definition of Attract/Move, no such comparison would ever be possible. Similarly, under the definition of local economy, if Minimality is a local economy condition, it could never compare operations that apply in two different derivations at all.

Chomsky (1995: 253) lists several properties that he assumes are part of the definition of Move. These include c-command, uniformity and Last Resort. According to Chomsky, these conditions will never be overridden for convergence, since they are not economy conditions, rather they are part of the definition of Move. As far as Last Resort is concerned, in the system of this book, no economy condition may be overridden for the sake of convergence, since that is a global notion. Thus, there is no difficulty in maintaining Last Resort as an economy con-dition from this point of view.

Now consider c-command. It seems to be the case that a moved α always c-commands its trace. This generalization has variously been called the Proper Binding Condition, or has been incorporated into the Empty Category Principle. One way to account for this fact is to assume that c-command is part of the definition of Move. However, this would clearly be missing the generalization that most cases of downward and sideways movement are ruled out by completely independent conditions. For example, overt downward movement would violate the strict cycle (which reduces to the LCA). [. . .] A quantifier-like expression (such as *which man*) always moves to a c-commanding position, presumably for reasons of interpretation. The only remaining cases are covert downward head movement and covert downward A-movement. However, it is extremely difficult to find genuine examples of this kind of movement that are not ruled out by completely independent conditions. Therefore, I assume that c-command is not part of the definition of Move.[8]

Therefore, it is reasonable to maintain the simplest definition of Move (Copy + Merge) and to derive the properties of Move (such as c-command, Last Resort and Minimality) from general principles.

Notes

1   Here D is the derivation up to Σ.

2   This definition is not an economy condition; rather, it forces economy conditions to be defined locally. More generally, this definition limits all conditions on operations to be defined locally. The definition says "an optimal derivation," since in the usual case there will be many possible operations at a given point in the derivation that satisfy local economy.

3   I use the word "information" in a broad sense to include at least the unchecked features and the dominance relations that exist. The question is really what types of information a syntactic operation such as Move or Merge may be sensitive to.

4   Ura (1995) also comes to the conclusion that economy operations are not limited to selecting among convergent derivations.

5   See, for example, Chomsky (1986: 30). Consider the following alternative to counting for implementing the Shortest Derivation Requirement: form the set of operations in D_1 {OP_1, OP_2, OP_3), then form the set of operations in derivation D_2 {OP_1', Op_2', OP_3', OP_4'}. Now match up the first members in each set, and eliminate them from D_1 and D_2. Repeat this process for the second members, and continue until there are no more matches left to be made. Whichever derivation ends up with an operation left is the longest. Even this alternative to counting does not seem to necessary in other parts of the grammar, and so it should be excluded for the same reasons counting is.

6   A natural generalization of (1) might be to restrict the evaluation of whether a predicate P holds of Σ to information in Σ. This would exclude the definition of A-position as a potential θ-position. Evaluating whether position X is an A-position would necessitate finding another verb (and therefore a different Σ), and seeing if X is a θ-position with respect to that verb. Similarly, it seems that OT phonology/syntax would be ruled out by this generalization of (1). Evaluating whether Σ is "optimal" involves a comparison to Σ'. Whether OT could be reformulated to make it consistent with this kind of locality is not clear. On a general note, any use of the word "potential" in a syntactic condition would give rise to similar considerations.

7   The empirical question of whether a particular operation is optional is usually not so clear. If some feature F may be either strong or weak, the operation resulting in the checking of the feature will appear to be optional. If two derivations (with the same Numeration) have the same number of steps, then global economy allows both derivations. Some cases of apparent optionality may be naturally analyzed in these terms (see, e.g. Chomsky 1991: 431).

8   I will leave consideration of how to explain the uniformity condition on Move for further work. Clearly, the logic of my system requires that uniformity either be an independent condition (not part of the definition of Move) or reducible to other conditions (like Last Resort).

References

Chomsky, N. 1986. *Barriers*. Cambridge, MA: MIT Press.

Chomsky, N. 1991. Some notes on economy of derivation and representation. In R. Freidin (ed.), *Principles and parameters in comparative grammar*. Cambridge, MA: MIT Press, pp. 417–54. [Reprinted in Chomsky (1995), *The Minimalist Program*. Cambridge, MA: MIT Press, pp. 128–66.]

Chomsky, N. 1994. Bare phrase structure. *MIT Occasional Papers in Linguistics 5*. Cambridge, MA: MITWPL. [Published in P. Kempchinsky (ed.) (1994), *Evolution and revolution in linguistic theory: Essays in honor of Carlos Otero*, Washington, DC: Georgetown University Press, pp. 51–109. Also published in G. Webelhuth (ed.) (1994), *Government and binding theory and the minimalist program*, Cambridge, MA: MIT Press, pp. 383–439.

Chomsky, N. 1995. *The Minimalist Program*. Cambridge, MA: MIT Press.

Collins, C. 1994. Economy of derivation and the generalized proper binding condition. *Linguistic Inquiry* 25: 45–61.

Kitahara, H. 1995. Target α: Deducing strict cyclicity from derivational economy. *Linguistic Inquiry* 26: 47–77.

Ura, H. 1995. Towards a theory of "strictly derivational" economy condition. In R. Pensalfini and H. Ura (eds.), *Papers on minimalist syntax. MIT Working Papers in Linguistics 27*. Cambridge, MA: MITWPL, pp. 243–67.

From "MOVE OR ATTRACT?"
Masao Ochi

1 Introduction

The aim of this paper is to explore some consequences of Chomsky's (1995) recent proposal under the minimalist program that what is actually affected by the movement operation is a feature rather than a category. Chomsky (1995) further argues that what triggers movement is a morphological requirement of the target rather than the category which moves: a target K which has a formal feature to be checked off attracts some relevant feature(s). This so-called 'Attract F' theory, despite its conceptual elegance and empirical adequacy for certain constructions, raises nontrivial questions for the theory of Universal Grammar. For instance, is feature movement subject to the same set of constraints as category movement? Also, how is it possible to reconcile Attract F with apparent empirical evidence for Move? The theory of Attract raises some technical questions as well. For instance, how are the previous accounts of the CED [Condition on Extraction Domain] effects such as Takahashi (1994), which are based on Move, maintained under Attract? Or do we need a new account once Attract is adopted? This paper attempts to answer some of those puzzles surrounding the theory of Attract F. I will argue, building on Chomsky (1995), that category movement in fact involves two formal chains of different nature, one of which has the characteristics of Move, which offers a way to reconcile Attract with apparent evidence for Move. Some theoretical consequences of the proposed analysis will also be discussed.

The organization of this paper is as follows. In section 2, I first review Takahashi's (1994) approach to island effects, in particular CED effects, based on the theory of Move. In section 3, I will propose a way to preserve Takahashi's insight under the theory of Attract F. I also demonstrate how the proposed analysis accounts for (the lack of) certain island effects in English and Japanese.

2   Previous approaches

2.1   Takahashi (1994)

Various attempts have been made within the principles-and-parameters approach to provide a principled account of the island effects shown below (cf. Huang 1982; Chomsky 1986). (la) and (1b) show Adjunct Condition and Subject Condition effects, respectively. (2) is an instance of *wh*-island Condition effect.

(1)   a.   ?*What$_i$ did John leave [after Mary bought t$_i$]?
      b.   ?*What$_i$ did [a picture of t$_i$] irritate John?
(2)   ?*What$_i$ did John wonder [whether Mary bought t$_i$]?

Under the minimalist approach (Chomsky 1993, 1995), Takahashi (1994) argues that these island effects are derived through the interaction of the following two principles.[1]

(3)   Uniformity Corollary on Adjunction (UCA)
      Adjunction is impossible to a proper subpart of a uniform group, where a uniform group is a non-trivial chain or a coordination.
(4)   Shortest Movement Condition (SMC)
      Make the shortest movement.

Before examining how those principles exclude (1–2), let us follow Takahashi and motivate the UCA (3). One thing to notice is that the statement in (3) includes disjunction. As we will see below, however, this disjunction is well-motivated within the minimalist framework. The UCA is essentially based on the following idea, which is due to Chomsky (1991, 1994).

(5)   Chains are uniform.

Given this, Takahashi (1994) suggests that uniformity is violated if some element adjoins only to some (but not all) members of the chain. This makes sense especially under the conception of movement as a copying operation. Suppose that the category α has formed a non-trivial chain as a result of movement, as shown in (6a). Now, suppose that an element β, which is contained in α, adjoined to the head of the chain α_1. This is shown in (6b).

(6)   a. (α_1, α_2)
      b. $([_\alpha \beta [_\alpha \alpha_1]], \alpha_2)$

Apparently, uniformity is not observed in (6b). The UCA derives a ban on adjunction to subjects (cf. Chomsky 1986), if we assume the VP-internal subject hypothesis (cf. Kuroda 1988; Fukui and Speas 1986). According to this hypothesis, the subject in English raises from a VP-internal position and heads a non-trivial chain, which must observe the UCA (3). Hence, if an element contained in the subject adjoins to the subject, the UCA is violated. One question we may address at this point is: what exactly goes wrong if uniformity is violated? One conceivable answer is the following. At PF, chains created via movement are subject to deletion of copies (i.e. non-head members), since copies are not pronounced. Assuming this, we might say that PF cannot delete non-head members of a chain if uniformity is not observed. In (6a), for instance, α_2 is deleted at PF under identity with α_1. PF cannot perform such an operation in (6b), since the two members of the chain are not identical. Then, an illegitimate PF object results, in the sense that the articulatory and perceptual (A–P) interface cannot interpret it. Thus, "uniformity" required on a non-trivial chain may be reducible to a bare output condition imposed by the A–P interface.

How about the uniformity required for coordination? One crucial ingredient for Takahashi's (1994) analysis is the following. He follows Higginbotham (1985) and assumes that adjuncts involve coordination. For instance, the example in (7a) has the semantic representation in (7b), which is roughly paraphrased as "there is an event such that it was a walking by John and it is slow," where adjuncts like *quickly* are analyzed as predicated of events. Takahashi (1994) suggests that this mapping from syntax to semantics is transparently obtained by assuming the LF representation in (7c), in which the sisters, VP_2 and the adjunct *slowly*, are predicated of the event argument which is generated under I.

(7) a. John walks slowly.
     b. $\exists e$ [walk (John, e) & slow (e)]
     c. $[_{IP}$ John$_i$ $[_{I'}$ I (e) $[_{VP1}$ $[_{VP2}$ t$_i$ walks] slowly]]]

Takahashi (1994) argues that the UCA (3), coupled with the assumption that adjuncts involve coordination, derives the ban on adjunction to adjuncts (cf. Chomsky 1986) in a principled manner. The UCA states that adjunction is not possible to a subpart of a uniform group, such as coordination. If an adjunct is a subpart of coordination, as suggested above, then, adjunction to an adjunct violates the UCA. Thus, it is crucial for Takahashi's analysis that adjuncts are regarded as part of coordination. Yet, as Howard Lasnik (p.c.) points out, this holds only under semantic considerations. In purely syntactic terms, adjunct structures need to be distinguished from coordinated structures. In order for the above argument to go through, therefore, we would have to regard this aspect of "uniformity" as a requirement on mapping to LF. If "uniformity" on (semantic) coordinated structure is lost in LF representations, then presumably the conceptual–intentional (C–I) interface cannot interpret such an object. In this sense, the effect the UCA imposes on coordination might be reducible to a bare output condition by the C–I interface. To summarize, the disjunctiveness in (3) may be attributed to distinct output conditions by two interfaces, A–P and C–I.

Let us now return to the examples in (1–2). The sentences in (1) are excluded by (3) and (4) in the following way. Consider (1a) first. Recall that if an element is adjoined to an adjunct, then the UCA is violated as the adjunct clause is a sub-part of a uniform group (i.e. coordination in this case). Thus, the derivation shown in (8a), in which the movement of *what* makes use of an adjunction to the adjunct clause, violates the UCA (3).[2] If, on the other hand, *what* does not adjoin to the adjunct clause on its way to its target as shown in (8b), then the SMC (4) is violated (although the UCA is not), and the example (1a) is excluded in this manner.

(8)   a.   What$_i$ did [$_{IP}$ t$_i$ [John [$_{VP}$ t$_i$ [$_{VP}$ leave [$_{CP}$ *t$_i$ [$_{CP}$ after [$_{IP}$ t$_i$ [$_{IP}$ Mary [$_{VP}$ t$_i$ [$_{VP}$ bought t$_i$]]]]]]]]]]]

       b.   What$_i$ did [$_{IP}$ t$_i$ [John [$_{VP}$ t$_i$ [$_{VP}$ leave [$_{CP}$ after [$_{IP}$ *t$_i$ [$_{IP}$ Mary [$_{VP}$ t$_i$ [$_{VP}$ bought t$_i$]]]]]]]]]]

As for (1b), recall that the VP-internal Subject Hypothesis plays a role here. According to this hypothesis, the subject in English heads a non-trivial chain, which must observe the UCA (3). This has the effect of barring adjunction to the subject. Thus, the derivation in (9a) violates the UCA (3). If the movement of *what* does not make use of adjunction to the subject (so that the UCA is observed) as shown in (9b), the SMC (4) is violated. Hence the example (1b) is ruled out.[3]

(9)   a.   What$_i$ did [$_{IP}$ t$_i$ [$_{IP}$ [$_{NP}$ *t$_i$ [$_{NP}$ a picture of t$_i$]]$_j$ [$_{VP}$ t$_j$ irritate John]]]

       b.   What$_i$ did [$_{IP}$ *t$_i$ [$_{IP}$ [$_{NP}$ a picture of t$_i$]$_j$ [$_{VP}$ t$_j$ irritate John]]]

Now, let us turn to *wh*-island effects in (2). Consider a step in a derivation shown in (10a), in which *what* adjoined to the matrix VP from the position adjoined to the embedded IP. This step violates the SMC, since the movement here does not adjoin to (or move through the specifier of) CP.[4]

(10)   a.   . . . [$_{VP}$ what [$_{VP}$ . . . [$_{CP}$ whether [$_C$ C [$_{IP}$ t [$_{IP}$ . . . .

       b.   . . . [$_{VP}$ what [$_{VP}$ . . . [$_{CP}$ t′ [$_{CP}$ whether [$_{C'}$ C [$_{IP}$ t [$_{IP}$ . . . .

Still, another derivation shown in (10b) does not violate the SMC, given the definition of *equidistance* in Chomsky (1993).[5] Under Chomsky's (1993) framework, the position adjoined to CP and Spec-CP are equidistant from the position of t in (10b). This is because the CP-adjoined position and the Spec-CP position are in the same minimal domain.[6] This means that the derivation shown in (10b) does not violate the SMC. Nor does it violate the UCA, since the CP here is neither a member of a non-trivial chain nor a member of the coordinated structure.

     Takahashi's solution is to modify the definition of *Domain* in such a way that the CP-adjoined position and the Spec-CP position are not equidistant from the position of *t* in (10b).[7] His revised definition of *Domain* is shown below.

(11)   The domain of a head A (DOM (A)) is the set of nodes dominated by the least full category maximal projection dominating A that are distinct from and do not contain A.

It follows from this revision that the minimal domain of a head is limited to its specifier, its complement, and a head adjoined to it.[8] Crucially, the CP-adjoined position and the Spec-CP position are not in the same minimal domain. As a result, the derivation illustrated in (10b) is ruled out as a violation of the SMC.

There is one crucial respect in which *wh*-island effects differ from other island effects under Takahashi's account. While other islands are accounted for by the interaction of the two principles, the UCA and the SMC, the UCA is irrelevant for *wh*-island effects. The latter is accounted for solely by the SMC.[9] This divorce between the two types of islands will be made even clearer in section 3.

2.2   Chomsky (1995)

More recently, however, Chomsky (1995) advances the hypothesis that movement is triggered solely by the need for the target K to check off its formal feature(s) by attracting the closest relevant feature F. Let us call this approach Attract F, following Chomsky (1995: 297).

(12)   Attract F
       K attracts F if F is the closest feature that can enter into a checking rela-
       tion with a sublabel of K.

One immediate theoretical consequence of Attract F is that the effect of the SMC (4) is directly incorporated into the definition of the operation Attract. That is, the target K can attract only the closest relevant feature F. Thus, the SMC (or Minimal Link Condition for Chomsky) is reformulated as follows in Chomsky (1995: 311).

(13)   K attracts α only if there is no β, β closer to K than α, such that K
       attracts β.

Consequently, nothing forces the attracted feature F to adjoin to every XP on its way to the target K. Rather, the feature F should be attracted in one step to the position of K. Notice now that Takahashi's (1994) UCA (3) virtually loses its force under Attract F, given that there is no need for a movement to make use of inter-mediate adjunctions.

As Chomsky (1995) observes, *wh*-island effects follow rather naturally from Attract F. Consider the following example.

(14)   ?*What$_i$ did John wonder [$_{CP}$ whether Mary bought t$_i$]?

The matrix C attracts the closest relevant feature in accordance with the nature of Attract. The wh-feature of *What* is not the closest relevant feature, that of *whether* being the closest, so the derivation for (14) is barred by the following derivation.

(15)   *Whether$_i$ did John wonder t$_i$ Mary bought what?

This derivation, in which the relevant feature of *whether* is attracted to the matrix C, does not run afoul of the requirement of Attract F. But Chomsky (1995) (also

Maki 1995) suggests that this structure is not interpretable because the matrix C, which indicates a *wh*-question, and *whether*, a yes-no question operator, are not semantically compatible. In short, the Attract F hypothesis captures the effect of *wh*-island Condition rather nicely.[10]

However, other island effects such as the Adjunct Condition effects do not follow immediately under Attract F. Recall that under Takahashi's (1994) approach, those island effects are accounted for through the interaction of the SMC in (4) and the UCA (3), but neither is relevant for the theory of movement under Attract.

Further, there is a rather strong empirical argument, originally due to Barss (1986), that movement drops by some intermediate positions on its way to the final landing site, in accordance with the spirit of the SMC (4). (16a) is a grammatical sentence, although as (16b) shows, the anaphor *himself* is not licensed in its original position. According to Belletti and Rizzi's (1991) analysis, which claims that Condition A can be met anywhere in the derivation, the anaphor is licensed in the intermediate stage of the derivation (17) in which the *wh*-phrase containing *himself* lands in the specifier position of the embedded CP.[11] That the anaphor is licensed in this configuration is supported by the grammaticality of (18).

(16) a.   Which picture of himself$_i$ does John$_i$ think that Mary likes t?
      b.   *John$_i$ thinks that Mary likes a picture of himself$_i$.
(17) __ does John$_i$ think [$_{CP}$ [Which picture of himself$_i$]$_j$ that Mary likes t$_j$].
(18) John$_i$ wonders [$_{CP}$ [which picture of himself$_i$]$_j$ Mary likes t$_j$].

Thus there seems to be a discrepancy between the spirit of Attract and its empirical adequacy.[12]

In what follows, I will pursue an approach which reconciles Attract F with apparent evidence for Move. As will be demonstrated, the proposal has interesting theoretical consequences.

3   Proposal: two chain hypothesis

My proposal is based on a particular view of category movement, adopted by Chomsky (1995). He suggests that when the whole category moves, (at least) two chains are created. This is shown below.

(19) a. $CH_{FF} = (FF[F], t_{FF})$
      b. $CH_{CAT} = (\alpha, t_\alpha)$

When the relevant feature F of the category α is attracted by the target K, the whole set of formal features (FF) of α is carried along, forming the chain CH_{FF} in (19a). Further, if the operation is overt, then the generalized pied-piping is required for PF convergence: sensorimotor systems cannot interpret a word whose features are scattered. This pied-piping chain is shown in (19b).

We notice that the two chains in (19) have quite different characters. CH_{FF} is created by Attract. On the other hand, it is clear that CH_{CAT} is not formed via Attract: in fact, it does not even involve feature checking. Thus, we find a formal chain which is not formed via Attract under Chomsky's (1995) Attract theory. Then, what is the driving force for the formation of CH_{CAT}? Chomsky (1995) does not elaborate on this question, merely stating that CH_{CAT} is necessary (solely) for PF convergence. Building on Chomsky's idea that (only) PF convergence is relevant for the formation of CH_{CAT}, I suggest that the driving force for the formation of CH_{CAT} lies in the PF deficiency of the category α whose feature is attracted away from it. That is, the category α, being defective for the PF interface, 'moves' to the position where its missing feature is located. If this is the case, then it follows that CH_{CAT} is motivated by (something like) "Greed": α moves to overcome its own PF inadequacies. Suppose that this chain therefore has the property of Move (as opposed to Attract), thus being subject to the SMC. Let us consider this in more detail by looking at examples like the following.

(20) a. What did John eat?

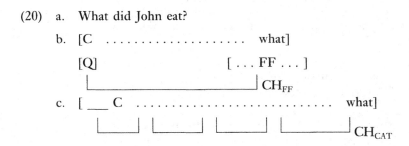

Assuming that the interrogative C in English has a strong feature to be checked off, overt movement is involved here. More specifically, two chains are formed as shown in (20b) and (20c). I assume that CH_{FF} in (20b) is a two-member chain, in accordance with the spirit of Attract: all that is required here is that the target C attracts the 'closest' relevant feature, and hence the feature (or FFs) of *what* need not move in a successive cyclic fashion. In addition to CH_{FF}, since the operation is overt, CH_{CAT} is necessary to ensure PF convergence. Under the proposed hypothesis, the category *what* in (20), being defective for the PF interface, moves to the position where its missing feature is located: otherwise, the derivation would crash at PF.

Let us reexamine (16a) under the proposed analysis, repeated below.

(21)   Which picture of himself$_i$ does John$_i$ think that Mary likes t?

As shown in (22a), the matrix C attracts the closest relevant feature, the wh-feature of *which*. Then, the whole phrase *which picture of himself*, being defective for PF interface, moves to the position where its missing feature is located. If this pied-piping movement is successive cyclic in accordance with the SMC (4), then Barss's (1986) or Belletti and Rizzi's (1991) account (cf. discussion in 2.2) can be maintained under Attract theory.

(22) a. [C . . . . [which picture of himself]]

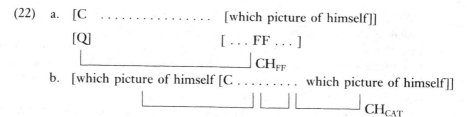

   b. [which picture of himself [C . . . . which picture of himself]]

Further, the proposed analysis has an interesting implication for the issue concerning the content of formal features. Let us take as an example features relevant
for anaphor licensing. There are two contrasting views in the recent literature;
Chomsky (1995) and Lasnik (1995). Chomsky (1995) claims that the property of
a lexical item (LI) which is relevant for anaphor licensing resides in the formal
features of LI. Lasnik (1995), on the other hand, argues that such properties are
not part of the formal features of a lexical item. For Lasnik, when only formal features are raised (as in LF movement), the properties relevant for anaphor licensing
remain below. Keeping these two contrasting views in mind, let us consider the
following example.[13] It is fine, with the anaphor taking the matrix subject as its
antecedent.[14]

(23)   Himself$_i$, John$_i$ thinks that Mary likes t$_i$.
        cf. *John$_i$ thinks that Mary likes himself$_i$.

(24) illustrates the derivation of (23) under the proposed analysis. Suppose for the
sake of discussion that what drives the movement here is the need for a functional
head, call it Top, to check off its strong [+Top] feature, although the exact nature
of topicalization does not concern us. CH$_{FF}$ is formed as a result of Attract, as shown
in (24a). Further, CH$_{CAT}$ is required for PF convergence, as in (24b).

(24) a. [Top . . . John . . . . [himself]]

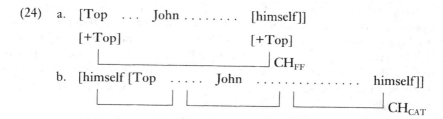

   b. [himself [Top . . . . John . . . . himself]]

The fact that the anaphor is licensed in (23) is not expected under Chomsky's (1995)
view. As shown in (24a), raising of the FFs of *himself* is in one step, which is due to
the nature of Attract. If the FFs are relevant for anaphor licensing as Chomsky (1995)
argues, then (23) is predicted to be ungrammatical, since the relevant property of the
anaphor *himself* never occupies a position which is close enough to *John* (i.e. intermediate landing sites under Barss's (1986) analysis). On the other hand, Lasnik's (1995)
hypothesis about anaphor licensing is compatible with the grammaticality of (23).
The features relevant for anaphor licensing, whatever they may be, are affected
only by the pied-piping chain CH$_{CAT}$. This chain is formed in a successive cyclic

fashion, which means that the movement stops by some intermediate position close to *John*, hence creating the necessary configuration for licensing *himself* (whatever the exact nature of the licensing configuration is). Thus, to the extent that the proposed hypothesis is justified, it lends a strong empirical support for Lasnik's (1995) view on anaphor licensing.

In the following subsections, I will demonstrate that the proposed hypothesis also helps us to explain why CED effects are observed in English, but not in Japanese.

3.1 Adjunct Condition effects

As reported in the literature (cf. Nishigauchi 1986), English *wh*-movement, but not its Japanese counterpart, is constrained by the Adjunct Condition.[15]

(25) a. John-wa   [Mary-ga   nani-o   katta   ato] kaetta no?
          John-TOP Mary-NOM what-ACC bought after left   Q
          '?*What$_i$ did John leave [after Mary bought t$_i$]?'
      b. ?*What$_i$ did John leave [after Mary bought t$_i$]?

Let us consider the Japanese case first. Assuming that the wh-feature of *nani* 'what' is attracted at LF, only CH$_{FF}$ is formed: crucially, CH$_{CAT}$ is not formed.[16] There is no problem with this attraction, since there is no relevant feature closer than the feature of *nani* 'what' from the viewpoint of the C. Hence, a two-member chain is formed and the derivation converges without any problem.

(26) [C .... [$_\alpha$ ...... nani ...]]   (α = adjunct clause)

      [Q]   [... FF ...]
      └_____┘ CH$_{FF}$

This accounts for the absence of Adjunct Condition (or, more generally, CED) effects in Japanese *wh*-movement. Let us now turn to the English case. As the movement is overt in English, two chains are formed. As far as CH$_{FF}$ is concerned, no problem arises. The feature of *what* is the closest from the matrix C, and attraction is therefore successful. However, the remnant movement, which is constrained by the SMC, causes a violation of the UCA (27b) or the SMC (27c), since this chain would necessarily involve a step out of the adjunct clause.

(27) a. [C .... [$_\alpha$ ...... what ...]]

          [Q]   [... FF ...]
          └_____┘ CH$_{FF}$
      b. [$_{CP}$ ___ C .... [$_\alpha$ [$_\alpha$ ...... WH ...]]]   (α = adjunct)
          └_____┘└_____┘ └_____┘ CH$_{CAT}$
      c. [$_{CP}$ ___ C .... [$_\alpha$ .. WH ...]]   (α = adjunct)
          └_____┘ └_____┘└_____┘ CH$_{CAT}$

Thus, under the proposed analysis, a CED effect obtains when the pied-piping chain (i.e. CH_{CAT}) is formed across an adjunct domain.

3.2 *wh*-island effects

Finally, the fact that the *wh*-island effect is detected in Japanese (cf. Nishigauchi 1986) as well as in English follows from the definition of Attract (12).[17]

(28) a. ??John-wa   [Mary-ga   nani-o   katta   kadooka]
        John-TOP Mary-NOM what-ACC bought whether
        siritai   no?
        want-to-know Q
        '?*What does John want to know [whether Mary bought t]?'
     b. ?*What; did John wonder [whether Mary bought t;]?

Since the relevant feature of *whether/kadooka* is closer to the matrix C than that of the *wh what/nani*, it is impossible for the latter to be attracted by the matrix C.

(29)   [C .... [whether .... *wh*]]
             | | |

            [Q]   [*wh*]   [*wh*]

To summarize this section, I proposed that movement operation involves both Move and Attract in the sense that two chains of different nature are involved when the category moves, an idea which stems from Chomsky's (1995) view of category movement. Note that in the proposed analysis, the *wh*-island Condition and the CED-type islands (Adjunct Condition and Subject Condition) are clearly given a separate treatment. While the former is about CH_{FF} (i.e. the definition of Attract), the latter arise only when CH_{CAT} is formed across an adjunct domain.

4 Concluding remarks

This paper was an attempt to provide answers and solutions to problems arising under the theory of Attract F. Building on Chomsky's (1995) conception of movement, I argued that category movement consists of two chains of different nature, one of which has properties of Move. This enables us to solve apparent empirical problems for Attract. It was also demonstrated that feature movement, as it is via Attract, is not subject to Huang's (1982) CED. According to the proposed hypothesis, CED effects show up only when the pied-piping chain CH_{CAT} is formed out of an adjunct domain. This accounts for the lack of CED effects with Japanese *wh*-movement: since the relevant movement is covert in Japanese, CH_{CAT} is not necessary. As a consequence, locality of feature movement is looser than category movement under this analysis.

Finally, this paper did not touch on the issue of argument/adjunct asymmetries with respect to *wh*-movement in both English and Japanese. As noted in the literature (cf. Lasnik and Saito 1984), Japanese as well as English exhibits an asymmetry between argument and adjunct *wh*-phrases, which would be surprising if all that is involved in Japanese *wh*-movement is the attraction of the [+Q] feature of a *wh*-phrase. Similarly, it is not clear at all how to account for the asymmetry in English. This remains as a serious problem for the current framework, and I must leave it as a topic for future research.

Notes

1   See also Uriagereka (in press) for an illuminating attempt to derive the effects of the CED within the minimalist framework.

2   Takahashi (1994) does not use * to indicate a violation of the UCA, as I do in (8a). I use it simply for expository purposes.

3   There is an alternative derivation which does not violate either the SMC or the UCA. Suppose that the movement of *what* takes place before the subject NP moves to the specifier position of IP. Then, nothing prevents the adjunction of *what* to the subject NP, since the latter has not formed a non-trivial chain at this point of derivation. See Takahashi (1994) and Collins (1994) for discussion on how Economy rules out this derivation independently.

4   Under Takahashi's framework, substitution into the specifier position of XP is regarded as an instance of adjunction to XP.

5   Two targets of movement are *equidistant* if they are in the same minimal domain (cf. Chomsky 1993).

6   *Domain* and *Minimal Domain* are defined as follows.

   (i)   The *domain* of a head A (DOM (A)) is the set of nodes contained in the least full category maximal projection dominating A that are distinct from and do not contain A.

   (ii) The *minimal domain* of a head A (MIN (A)) is the smallest subset K of DOM (A) such that for any G, G is a member of DOM (A), some B, a member of K, reflexively contains it.

7   See Takano (1994) for an alternative approach to the *wh*-island condition effect under the theory of Move.

8   Takahashi uses French participial agreement facts as an empirical support for this modification. See Takahashi (1994) for details.

9   This situation is reminiscent of the analysis presented by Huang (1982). For Huang, islands such as the Subject Condition and Adjunct Condition are due to the Condition on Extraction Domain (CED), but *wh*-island effects do not fall under the CED, since the CP whose specifier position is filled by a *wh*-phrase is typically a complement and hence is properly governed. Therefore, Subjacency was independently called for in order to explain *wh*-island effects.

10   Problematic cases are those like the example in (i). It is not clear what prevents a single *wh*-phrase from checking strong features of C more than once. Descriptively, an element moved into an operator position (such as specifier of CP) cannot be further attracted. See Maki (1995) for discussion.

   (i)   *Who$_i$ do you wonder [$_{CP}$ t$_i$ [t$_i$ bought what]]?

11   For Barss (1986), the anaphor *himself* in (16a) satisfies Condition A as its antecedent *John* 'chain binds' it in a local domain. The following definition of chain binding is from Saito (1989).

   (i)   X chain binds Y = df X and Y are coindexed, and
       (a)   X c-commands Y, or
       (b)   X c-commands a trace of Z, where Z = Y or Z contains Y.

The exact choice between Belletti and Rizzi's (1991) and Barss's (1986) accounts of the relevant data does not matter for our discussion.

12 The following example further illustrates the point.

(i)   ??Which picture of himself$_i$ does John wonder [whether Mary likes t$_i$]?

This example has the status of a typical *wh*-island violation, but is no worse than that. This suggests that the anaphor *himself* is indeed licensed in this example, just as in (16a) in the text. Takahashi (1994) claims that this provides strong empirical support for the SMC. The anaphor is licensed in (i) because the *wh*-phrase moves in a cyclic fashion as required by the SMC, adjoining to the embedded CP (and the matrix VP) among others, which would create a configuration for licensing *himself*. This type of example poses a serious problem for Attract.

13 I thank Željko Bošković (p.c.) for the following discussion.

14 See Uchibori (1996) for an extensive discussion of examples similar to (23).

15 I will not discuss the Subject Condition in Japanese in the text. As reported in the literature (cf. Lasnik and Saito 1992), Japanese lacks Subject Condition effects for movement operations in general (including scrambling). Thus, it is not surprising that (i) with *nani* 'what' in the domain of subject is grammatical.

(i)   [John-ga   nani-o   katta   koto]-ga   minna-o   odorokaseta no?
      John-NOM what-ACC bought fact-NOM everyone-ACC surprised   Q
      '?*What did [the fact that John bought t] surprise everyone?'

According to Takahashi (1994), this is because the subject in Japanese may stay within VP overtly. Then, since the subject in this language does not form a non-trivial chain, it is correctly predicted that extraction out of such a domain is possible without violating either the UCA or the SMC.

16 According to Watanabe (1992), examples with *nani* 'what' involve an overt movement of a null operator from the position of *nani* 'what'. This achieves the same desired result. Since phonology is irrelevant for null operators, the pied-piping of the whole category should be unnecessary (cf. Takahashi 1995, 1996). In the text, I simple assume that Japanese *wh*-movement takes place covertly.

17 Here are additional data to illustrate the same point. (i) allows only the matrix yes-no question reading (cf. Nishigauchi 1986).

(i)   John-wa   [dare-ga   nani-o   katta   ka] siritai   no?
      John-TOP who-NOM what-ACC bought Q   want-to-know Q
      'Does John want to know who bought what?'
      Not 'For which x, x a person, does John want to know what x bought?'
      Not 'For which y, y a thing, does John want to know who bought y?'

References

Barss, A. 1986. *Chains and anaphoric dependence*. Doctoral dissertation, MIT.

Belletti, A. and L. Rizzi. 1991. Notes on psych-verbs, THETA-theory, and binding. In R. Freidin (ed.), *Principles and parameters in comparative grammar*, Cambridge, MA: MIT Press, pp. 132–62.

Chomsky, N. 1986. *Barriers*. Cambridge, MA: MIT Press.

Chomsky, N. 1991. Some notes on economy of derivation and representation. In R. Freidin (ed.), *Principles and parameters in comparative grammar*, Ccambridge, MA: MIT Press, pp. 417–54. [Reprinted in Chomsky (1995), *The Minimalist Program*, Cambridge, MA: MIT Press, pp. 128–66.]

Chomsky, N. 1993. A minimalist program for linguistic theory. In K. Hale and S. J. Keyser (eds.), *The view from Building 20: Essays in linguistics in honor of Sylvain Bromberger*, Cambridge, MA: MIT Press, pp. 1–52. [Reprinted in Chomsky (1995), *The Minimalist Program*, Cambridge, MA: MIT Press, pp. 167–217.]

Chomsky, N. 1994. *Bare phrase structure. MIT Occasional Papers in Linguistics 5.* Cambridge, MA: MITWPL. [Published in P. Kempchinsky (ed.) (1994), *Evolution and revolution in linguistic theory: Essays in honor of Carlos Otero*, Washington, DC: Georgetown University Press, pp. 51–109. Also published in G. Webelhuth (ed.) (1994), *Government and binding theory and the minimalist program*, Cambridge, MA: MIT Press, pp. 383–439.]

Chomsky, N. 1995. *The Minimalist Program.* Cambridge, MA: MIT Press.

Collins, C. 1994. Economy of derivation and the generalized proper binding condition. *Linguistic Inquiry* 25: 45–61.

Fukui, N. and M. Speas. 1986. Specifiers and projection. In N. Fukui, T. R. Rapoport and E. Sagey (eds.), *Papers in theoretical linguistics. MIT Working Papers in Linguistics 8.* Cambridge, MA: MITWPL, pp. 128–72.

Higginbotham, J. 1985. On semantics. *Linguistic Inquiry* 16: 547–94.

Huang, C.-T. J. 1982. *Logical relations in Chinese and the theory of grammar.* Doctoral dissertation, MIT.

Kuroda, S.-Y. 1988. Whether we agree or not: A comparative syntax of English and Japanese. In W. Poster (ed.), *Papers from the second international workshop on Japanese syntax*, CSLI, pp. 103–43.

Lasnik, H. 1995. Last resort. In S. Haraguchi and M. Funaki (eds.), *Minimalism and linguistic theory*, Tokyo: Hituzi Syobo, pp. 1–32. [Reprinted in Lasnik (1999), *Minimalist analysis*, Malden, MA/Oxford: Blackwell, pp. 120–50.]

Lasnik, H. and M. Saito. 1984. On the nature of proper government. *Linguistic Inquiry* 15: 235–55.

Lasnik, H. and M. Saito. 1992. *Move α.* Cambridge, MA: MIT Press.

Maki, H. 1995. *The syntax of particles.* Doctoral dissertation, University of Connecticut, Storrs.

Nishigauchi, T. 1986. *Quantification in syntax.* Doctoral dissertation, University of Massachusetts, Amherst.

Saito, M. 1989. Scrambling as semantically vacuous A′-movement. In M. Baltin and A. Kroch (eds.), *Alternative conceptions of phrase structure*, Chicago: University of Chicago Press, pp. 182–200.

Takahashi, D. 1994. *Minimality of Movement.* Doctoral dissertation, University of Connecticut, Storrs.

Takahashi, D. 1995. Move-F and null operator movement. Ms., Tohoku University. [Published in *The Linguistic Review* 14: 181–96, 1997.]

Takano, Y. 1994. Scrambling, Relativized Minimality and economy of derivation. In R. Aranovich, W. Byrne, S. Preuss and M. Senturia (eds.), *Proceedings of the 13th West Coast Conference on Formal Linguistics*, Stanford: CSLI, pp. 385–99.

Uchibori, A. 1996. Some asymmetries in the reconstruction effects on anaphora. In E. Laurencot, R. Lee and M.-K. Park (eds.), *University of Connecticut Working Papers in Linguistics 5*, Cambridge, MA: MITWPL, pp. 81–115.

Uriagereka, J. In press. Multiple spell-out. [Published in S. D. Epstein and N. Hornstein (eds.) (1999), *Working minimalism*, Cambridge, MA: MIT Press, pp. 251–82.]

Watanabe, A. 1992. Subjacency and S-structure movement of wh-in-situ. *Journal of East Asian Linguistics* 1: 255–91.

From "A-MOVEMENT AND THE EPP"
Željko Bošković

1 Introduction

The Extended Projection Principle (EPP) has been in the center of theorizing within
the government and binding, principles and parameters, and minimalist frameworks
ever since Chomsky (1981, 1982; see also Perlmutter 1971) proposed it, which is
not surprising given that movement to subject position plays a central role in the
theory. Chomsky proposed the EPP, which requires that all clauses have a subject, to account for the ungrammaticality of constructions like (1).[1]

(1)   *Is likely that Peter likes Mary.

The stipulatory nature of the EPP was immediately obvious and gave rise to several attempts to deduce it from deeper principles. Thus, several authors have tried
to make the EPP follow from semantic/pragmatic considerations. For example,
Rothstein (1983) argues that EPP effects completely follow from *predication* – more
precisely, the requirement that predicates be saturated (for relevant discussion,
see also Heycock 1994 and Stowell 1983). Under the standard semantic view of
predication,[2] the EPP would then follow from a deep, semantic requirement. An
obvious problem for this approach is raised by the fact that the EPP can be satisfied
by semantically null elements like the expletives *there* and *it*.[3]

(2)   a.   It is likely that Peter likes Mary.
      b.   There is someone in the garden.

[. . .]
    Among formal approaches to the EPP, which easily handle expletive constructions
like (2), stands out Chomsky's (1995) approach, in which the EPP is a result of a
feature-checking (i.e. morphological) requirement; more precisely, the requirement
that the N-feature (or D-feature) of Infl be checked overtly, formalized by considering the relevant feature to be strong in Chomsky's (1995) sense. Chomsky (1999,
2000), on the other hand, states the EPP property as a requirement to have an
overtly filled specifier, thus essentially going back to his earlier (1981, 1982) approach.
    Lasnik (2001a, 2001b) provides empirical evidence for the superiority of the filled-
specifier approach over the feature-checking approach. Lasnik's argument is
based on the pseudogapping construction, exemplified by (3).

(3)   Peter read a book and Mary did a magazine$_i$ [$_{VP}$ ~~read t_i~~].

Lasnik analyzes pseudogapping constructions like (3) as involving VP ellipsis, which
he assumes involves PF deletion, with the remnant of pseudogapping moving
out of the VP prior to the ellipsis via object shift; that is, overt movement to
[Spec, Agr$_O$P]. Lasnik's analysis is based on the assumption that English has overt
object shift, for which he provides considerable evidence (see also the discussion

below). Under the overt object-shift analysis, the verb must undergo short V-movement in English, which places it in front of the shifted object. If the verb does not raise in front of the shifted object, we get an ungrammatical construction, as illustrated by (4a,b), which contrast with (5).

(4) a. *Peter a magazine read.
      b. *Peter did a magazine read.
(5) Peter read the magazine.

Why, then, is (3) acceptable even though the verb apparently does not move in front of the shifted object, as it normally does in English? Lasnik provides two answers to the question. [. . .] The alternative analysis is based on Chomsky's Two Movements Hypothesis (1995: ch. 4; see also Ochi 1998, 1999), in which overt movement is a result of feature movement followed by pied-piping of the remnant category. Following Ochi, Lasnik assumes that the pied-piping takes place because the category from which formal features have moved is phonologically deficient. The deficiency is normally overcome by moving the category to a position in the vicinity of its formal features. Lasnik suggests that another way of dealing with the deficiency is simply to delete the deficient element in PF. This is what happens in (3). The verb undergoes formal feature movement in overt syntax. The remnant category's phonological deficiency would normally cause a PF crash. However, this does not happen in (3) because the remnant category is removed from the structure through PF deletion so that it is not present in the final PF representation.

It appears that this analysis incorrectly rules in (6).

(6) *Mary said she won't sleep, although will [$_{VP}$ ~~she sleep~~].

Assume Chomsky's (1995: ch. 4) feature-checking approach to the EPP. Suppose we raise the formal features of *she*, checking the feature responsible for the EPP effect. We then delete the VP in PF, removing the now phonologically deficient element *she* from the final PF representation. It appears that nothing goes wrong with this derivation. Lasnik interprets this as an argument that the EPP is not merely a feature-checking requirement. Rather, what the EPP requires is that [Spec, IP] be filled; in other words, that a clause have a subject. This brings us back to Chomsky's original conception of the EPP. It thus seems that twenty years of research concerning the EPP has not brought us any closer to understanding the nature of the EPP. In other words, we are back where we started. Given that no attempt to deduce the EPP from other mechanisms has worked, the next logical step seems to be to deny the EPP altogether. This is, in fact, the step taken by several authors in recent work, in particular, Boeckx (2000a), Castillo, Drury, and Grohmann (1999), Epstein and Seely (1999), Grohmann, Drury, and Castillo (2000), and Martin (1999). (The predecessors of this line of research are Borer 1986 and Fukui and Speas 1986.) This is also the approach I pursue in this article. The analysis to be endorsed is, however, quite different from the analysis argued for by the authors just cited. Although, like the authors in question, I argue that the EPP should be eliminated, I also argue that [Spec, IP] has to be filled in certain cases where it is not filled in the alternative analyses denying the EPP. As a result, several empirical problems that arise under the alternative analyses do not arise under the analysis presented in this article.

[. . .]

2 "Final EPP"

2.1 *BELIEVE*

The general strategy in this section is to examine constructions that violate the EPP and consider whether the constructions in question can be accounted for if the EPP is eliminated from the grammar.

Probably the strongest argument for the final EPP involves the *BELIEVE*-class verbs discussed in Bošković (1997a). Consider first (7).

(7)   *$[_{IP} [_{VP}$ Kissed John]].

The construction can be ruled out by appealing to the EPP. However, it can also be accounted for without invoking the EPP. The construction violates the θ-Criterion, because the subject θ-role of *kiss* is not assigned, as well as what I earlier referred to as the Inverse Case Filter (Bošković 1997a; the term is due to Howard Lasnik) – that is, the requirement that traditional Case assigners assign their Case features (Tense and nominative in (7)), which in the checking theory can be interpreted as a feature–checking requirement.[4] In (1), repeated here as (8), the θ-Criterion is not violated. However, the construction can still be ruled out independently of the EPP by appealing to the Inverse Case Filter (see also Fukui and Speas 1986).

(8)   *Is likely that Peter likes Mary.

The same holds for (9) under the Case-theoretic approach to the distribution of PRO, on which the subject position of control infinitives is a Case position. More precisely, the construction is ruled out because the null Case of the embedded infinitival Tense cannot be assigned.[5]

(9)   *John tried to seem that Peter likes Mary.

A potential problem for the Inverse Case Filter is raised by quirky subject constructions such as Icelandic (10), which appears to invalidate the Inverse Case Filter.

(10)   Okkur var hjálpað.
       us.DAT was helped
       'We were helped.'

However, a number of authors (see Belletti 1988; Chomsky 2000: 127; Cowper 1988; Frampton and Gutmann 1999; Freidin and Sprouse 1991, among others) have argued that quirky subjects have a structural Case, which is not morphologically realized, on top of the inherent case. The structural Case is checked against the nominative Case feature of T in (10). I will assume this as well.

Consider now (11).

(11) a.   *Was told Mary that Peter left.
      b.   *John believes to have been told Mary that Peter left.

The constructions in (11) can be ruled out by the Inverse Case Filter if we assume that both nominative and accusative must be checked overtly (not through Agree or Move F). This is, in fact, what the authors arguing for eliminating the EPP as an independent principle assume. (See Epstein and Seely 1999: 64–5, 72–3 and Martin 1999. Boeckx 2000a: 38 and Castillo, Drury and Grohmann 1999: 23 differ somewhat. See also Bejar and Massam 1999, who argue that covert Case checking quite generally does not exist.) It follows that English has overt object shift (i.e. overt movement of accusative NPs to their Case-checking position outside of the VP, which *Mary* in (11b) fails to undergo), a position argued for by a number of authors (see Authier 1991; Bošković 1997a, 1997b; Johnson 1991; Koizumi 1995; Lasnik 1995b, 1995c; McCloskey 2000; Runner 1998; and Ura 1993, among others).

Epstein and Seely (1999) and Boeckx (2000a) propose accounts of why Case features cannot be checked by Agree or Move F. Thus, assuming that features can be checked (i.e. probed) only under c-command, Epstein and Seely observe that when elements Y and Z have to check against each other an uninterpretable feature X (i.e. a feature that is uninterpretable on both Z and Y, which is the situation with Case features), X can be checked on both Y and Z only if the two at some point undergo Spec-head agreement. Given that covert checking involves Agree (or Move F, for that matter), it follows that Case checking must be done overtly. Whereas a traditional Case assigner c-commands the traditional Case assignee and therefore can "probe" the Case assigner without category movement of the Case assignee to the specifier of the Case assigner, the traditional Case assignee does not c-command the Case assigner and hence cannot probe it without this movement. A Spec-head configuration thus needs to be established so that the Case assignee can c-command and probe the Case assigner.[6]

[. . .]

3 "Intermediate EPP"

3.1 Quantifier float

The first argument for the intermediate EPP is provided by quantifier-float constructions like (12).

(12)   The students$_i$ seem [all t_i] to know French.

Under Sportiche's (1988) analysis of quantifier float, in which the element a floating quantifier modifies is generated as a constituent with the quantifier, the quantifier being subsequently stranded under movement of the element in question, (12) provides evidence that *the students* passes through the infinitival [Spec, IP] when moving from its θ-position, [Spec, VP], to the matrix clause [Spec, IP][7]. Given that the embedded [Spec, IP] is not a Case position, movement to this position cannot be motivated by the Inverse Case Filter.

3.2 Condition A

More evidence for the intermediate EPP is provided by (13), taken from Castillo, Drury, and Grohmann (1999), who attribute the data to Danny Fox.

(13) a. Mary seems to John [$_{IP}$ to appear to herself to be in the room].
      b. *Mary seems to John [$_{IP}$ to appear to himself to be in the room].

Whereas in (13a) the anaphor in the embedded clause can take a matrix-clause NP as its antecedent, in (13b) this is not possible. Why is the anaphor in (13b) unable to take the experiencer as its antecedent? Notice that there is evidence that the experiencer NP can c-command outside of the experiencer PP, so we cannot attribute the ungrammaticality of (13b) to the failure of the potential antecedent to c-command the anaphor. Example (14a) shows that the experiencer NP can induce a Condition C violation, and (14b,c) show that it can license a negative polarity item and an anaphor in a position outside of the experiencer.

(14) a. *It seems to him$_i$ that John$_i$ is in the room.
      b. Pictures of any linguist seem to no psychologist to be pretty.
      c. Pictures of himself seem to John to be cheap.

The ungrammaticality of (13b) immediately follows if the matrix subject passes – in fact, must pass – through the embedded clause [Spec, IP] on its way to the matrix [Spec, IP]. Example (13b) then exhibits a Specified Subject Condition effect. The experiencer is attempting to bind the anaphor across a closer binder, namely the trace in [Spec, IP] (see (15b)). The problem does not arise in (13a), where the anaphor is bound by the closest subject (see (15a)).[8]

(15) a. Mary$_i$ seems to John [$_{IP}$ t_i to appear to herself$_i$ to be the room].
      b. *Mary$_i$ seems to John$_i$ [$_{IP}$ t_i to appear to himself$_i$ to be in the room].

3.3 Reconstruction effects

Consider now the following data from Lebeaux (1991: 234), which were also discussed by Nunes (1995: 200–2).

(16) *[His$_i$ mother's$_j$ bread] seems to her$_j$ ___ to be known by every man$_i$ to be ___ the best there is.
(17) [His$_i$ mother's$_j$ bread] seems to every man$_i$ ___ to be known by her$_j$ to be ___ the best there is.

The data in question can be easily accounted for if the matrix-clause subject passes through the embedded [Spec, IP]s, which can then serve as reconstruction sites.[9]

In (16), the matrix-clause subject has to be reconstructed into the most embedded clause to license the bound-variable reading. However, the construction is then ruled out as a Condition C violation. (Notice that the construction is acceptable if *her* and *his mother* are not coindexed, which indicates that the quantifier can bind a variable outside of the *by*-phrase.) On the other hand, in (17) we can reconstruct the matrix subject to the higher infinitival [Spec, IP], a position where the bound-variable reading can be licensed without inducing a Condition C violation.

Similar arguments can be constructed with respect to other phenomena where reconstruction is relevant. I believe, however, that there is already enough evidence to conclude that the "intermediate EPP" holds. Intermediate subject positions can be, and in fact must be, there. The Inverse Case Filter cannot help in this case, as it did in the case of the "final EPP," given that we are not dealing with Case-licensing positions. So, do we have here evidence for the EPP? That is, do we need to conclude that the EPP is needed based on the "intermediate EPP" effects discussed in this section? Not necessarily. The next section shows that the data in question can be captured without positing the EPP.

4 Accounting for "intermediate EPP" effects: successive cyclicity

It is standardly assumed that the *wh*-phrase in (18) passes (more precisely, must pass) through the intermediate [Spec, CP] as a result of successive cyclicity.

(18)   What$_i$ do you think [t_i that Mary bought t_i]?

Note that there is no requirement that the specifier of the CP headed by *that* be filled, as shown by the grammaticality of (19), where the specifier of the embedded CP remains empty.

(19)   You think [that Mary bought a car].

Apparently, *what* must pass through the embedded [Spec, CP] in (18) for a reason independent of any property of *that*, which does not require a specifier. In other words, creation of the embedded [Spec, CP] in (18) is a reflex of successive cyclic movement. It is required by a property of this movement, not by a property of *that*. I would like to suggest that the same holds for the movement of *the students* to the embedded [Spec, IP] in (20).

(20)   The students$_i$ seem [t_i to have t_i liked French].

Departing from standard assumptions, I would like to suggest that just like *what* in (18), whose final landing site is [Spec, CP], passes through the embedded [Spec, CP] as a result of successive cyclic movement (not a property of C), *the students* in (18), whose final landing site is [Spec, IP], passes through the embedded [Spec, IP] as a result of successive cyclic movement, not a property of Infl, which, like *that*, does not require a specifier. In other words, I suggest that (18) and (20) should be treated in the same way in the relevant respect. In particular, the successive cyclic movement treatment of (18) should be extended to (20).

Let us see what this suggestion would imply when plugged into some recent accounts of the constructions in question. Chomsky (2000) follows standard assumptions in making a distinction between (18) and (20) in the relevant respect (see, however, Chomsky 1999, which also explores an alternative analysis). Following standard assumptions, Chomsky (2000) assumes that Infl always requires a filled specifier. In other words, it is subject to the EPP. As for *that*, Chomsky assumes that *that* may, but does not have to, have the EPP property.[10] Example (19) instantiates the no EPP property option. As for (18), although in principle *that* does not have to have the EPP property, according to Chomsky the no-EPP option for *that* is ruled out in (18) by the Phase-Impenetrability Condition, which says that only the head and specifier of a phase are accessible for movement to a position outside of the phase.[11] Because for Chomsky CP is a phase, it is necessary to move *what* in (18) to the embedded [Spec, CP] so that *what* can later be moved outside of the CP. This is accomplished by giving *that* the EPP option. If *that* is not given the EPP option, *what* would not move to the embedded [Spec, CP], as a result of which it could not move outside of the embedded CP due to the Phase-Impenetrability Condition. Technically, it would be easy to extend Chomsky's account of (18) to (20). We would just need to assume that Infl may, but need not, have the EPP property and that IP is a phase.[12] Chomsky argues that IP is not a phase. Interestingly, the criterion for phasehood he adopts – propositionality – would classify the embedded IP in (20), and in fact, all raising IPs, as a phase. The embedded clause in (20) seems to be a complete proposition and should therefore count as a phase.[13] We could also relativize the notion of phasehood for locality of movement following the line of research that originated with Rizzi (1990), who shows that in a number of respects, relativized barrierhood is superior to rigid barrierhood. (Chomsky's conception of phase-based locality corresponds to rigid barrierhood.) In particular, one could easily develop a relativized phase system, where CP would be a phase for elements undergoing movement to CP, and IP for elements undergoing movement to IP. The Phase-Impenetrability Condition would then again force movement through the infinitival [Spec, IP] in (20).

The upshot of this discussion is that my proposal concerning the "intermediate EPP" can be incorporated into Chomsky's (2000) system. In fact, the incorporation would not face any of the problems for the true intermediate EPP discussed in the next section. However, I hesitate to endorse this analysis here because Chomsky's (2000) approach to successive cyclic movement seems to me to be on the wrong track. The problem with the approach is that it relates the successive cyclic movement of *what* in (18) to a property of *that*. As a result, it is difficult to rule out constructions like (21) in a principled way, given the derivation on which we have chosen the EPP option for *that*, which results in the movement of *what* to the embedded [Spec, CP], just as it does in (18) (see the discussion of (23) and section 5.2 for additional problems).[14]

(21)   *Who thinks what that Mary bought?

The most principled way of accounting for (21) seems to be to divorce movement through intermediate [Spec, CP]s from C – that is, not to consider it to be a result of a property of C but of the movement itself. This was actually the standard assumption until very recently. For example, this was the case with Takahashi's (1994) system, the most comprehensive account of locality of movement in early minimalism, based on Chomsky and Lasnik's (1993) Minimize Chain Links Principle (MCLP).[15] For Takahashi, successive cyclic movement is not a result of feature checking. Rather, it is a result of the requirement that all chain links be as short as possible.[16] The requirement forces element X undergoing movement of type Y to stop at every position of type Y on the way to its final landing site, independently of feature checking. The MCLP thus forces *what* in (18) to pass through the embedded [Spec, CP] on its way to the matrix [Spec, CP]. It also forces *the students* in (20) to pass through the embedded [Spec, IP] on its way to the matrix [Spec, IP]. The intermediate [Spec, CP] and [Spec, IP] in the constructions in question are filled as a result of the property of the movements involved. We do not need to invoke a property of the embedded C and Infl to drive the movement to these positions. Notice also that, because no feature checking is posited between a *wh*-phrase and declarative C, both (21) and (19) are easily accounted for. In particular, (21) violates Last Resort.

The old problem of the impossibility of intermediate preposition (P) stranding provides further evidence for the superiority of the MCLP approach. Consider (22) and (23).

(22)   a.   In which garage did you find that car?
        b.   Which garage did you find that car in?
(23)   *Which garage do you think in (that) John found that car?

Although pied-piping of the P is in principle optional in the constructions under consideration, it cannot take place in an intermediate position, as shown in (23). Under Chomsky's (2000) approach to successive cyclicity, which ties successive cyclic movement to a property of intermediate heads and considers each step of successive cyclic movement a separate operation, it is very difficult to account for the contrast between (22b) and (23). It seems that (23) is incorrectly ruled in.[17] On the other hand, accounting for these facts under the MCLP approach is straightforward, given that, as discussed earlier and argued for extensively in section 5.2, the embedded declarative C does not establish a feature-checking relation (i.e. it does not undergo Spec-head agreement) with a *wh*-phrase. In (22), *wh*-movement takes place after the matrix C, which drives the movement, enters the structure (see n. 16). The chain starting in the original position of the *wh*-elements (PP in (22a) and NP in (22b)) and finishing in the matrix [Spec, CP] is then formed, formation of the chain being driven by a formal inadequacy of the matrix C – that is, checking its strong [+wh] feature – thus conforming with Last Resort. The MCLP forces the movement to proceed via the intermediate [Spec, CP], but no feature checking takes place in this position. In contrast to (22), (23) does not involve a single chain formation. Rather, there are two separate chains: one involving movement of a PP to the embedded [Spec, CP], and the other involving movement of

the *wh*-phrase, an NP, from inside the PP to the matrix [Spec, CP].[18] Given my
contention that no feature checking (i.e. Spec-head agreement) with the embedded declarative C takes place in the constructions under consideration (C does
not require movement of a *wh*-element to [Spec, CP]), formation of the first chain
violates Last Resort. The contrast between (22b) and (23) is thus accounted for.
The impossibility of intermediate P-stranding provides further evidence that
successive cyclic movement is not driven by a requirement on intermediate heads.

It is also worth noting in this respect the following quantifier-float construction
from Sportiche (1988).[19]

(24)   The carpets (all) will (all) have (all) been (all) being (all) dusted for two hours.

Under Sportiche's account of quantifier float we are led to the conclusion that *the
carpets* in (24) passes through all the positions in which *all* can be placed. It is unlikely
that all the positions in question involve the feature-checking/EPP property. On
the other hand, Takahashi's (1994) analysis can be easily extended to (24). What
is important here is that, under a Takahashi-style analysis, A-movement can be
forced to proceed via intermediate [Spec, IP]s independently of the EPP. As a result,
we can account for "intermediate EPP" effects without appealing to the EPP itself.

There is a suggestion in Chomsky (2000: 109), more fully worked out in Chomsky
(1999: 29), which has the effect of making the movement to the specifier of a phase
head that does not obligatorily have the EPP property essentially independent
in terms of the driving force from the phase head itself, even in a phase-based
locality system. The suggestion is to make the assignment of an EPP property to
nontrue EPP heads conditioned on it being required to permit successive cyclic
movement (see Chomsky 1999: 29 for another possibility). The embedded clause
heads in (18) and (20) can then be assigned an EPP feature (given the above
suggestion to extend phasehood to the infinitive in (20)), since the assignment is
necessary to permit successive cyclic movement. On the other hand, the embedded clause heads in (19) and (21) cannot be assigned an EPP feature, because the
assignment is not necessary to permit successive cyclic movement. Under this
analysis, movement through the specifier of a nontrue EPP phase head is really a
reflex of successive cyclic movement. The phase head is essentially a bystander.
By itself, it cannot induce movement to its specifier, hence the ungrammaticality
of (21). In other words, we are not dealing here with true intermediate EPP, which
this work is attempting to eliminate. (Note, however, that the data in (22) and (23),
particularly the ungrammaticality of (23), appear to remain unaccounted for
even under this version of the phase analysis. The same holds for the phenomena
discussed in section 5.2.)

There are other ways of instantiating the idea that movement to the embedded-
clause specifier in both (18) and (20) takes place because of locality, not because
the embedded clause head always requires a specifier. Thus, we can implement
the idea by appealing to the old notion of a phrase boundary breaking a chain (see
Aoun 1986: 72), now relativized in such a way that CP breaks an A'-movement
chain, and IP an A-movement chain, which is relatable to the final landing sites
of these movements. Consider the condition in (25).[20]

(25)   The Successive Chain Links Condition
       *A$_i$ [$_\alpha$ A$_j$], where α dominates A$_j$ and excludes A$_i$, A$_i$ and A$_j$ successive links of
       a chain β and α = CP if A$_i$ is in an A'-position, α = IP if A$_i$ is in an A-position.

Given (25), A'-movement is not allowed to cross a CP boundary, and A-movement
is not allowed to cross an IP boundary. A way around the blocking effect of the CP
and IP is to adjoin to the CP and IP. Under Kayne's (1994) proposal that traditional
specifiers are actually adjuncts, this is tantamount to movement through [Spec, CP]
and [Spec, IP]. I conclude therefore that (25) forces movement through [Spec, CP]
and [Spec, IP] for A'- and A-movement, respectively. What is important for our
current purposes is that (25) gives us "intermediate EPP" effects for A-movement
without employing true EPP.[21]

Yet another possibility is to appeal to Manzini's (1994) approach to locality, which
requires movement to pass through the domain of each head. A relativized minimality version of Manzini's proposal would require movement to pass through the
domain of each head of an appropriate type, A'-head for A'-movement and A-head
for A-movement. A consequence of this is that A'-movement would have to pass
through the domain of C and A-movement through the domain of Infl. Both movement through [Spec, CP], in the case of A'-movement, and movement through
[Spec, IP], in the case of A-movement, are then forced by locality.

For ease of exposition, I will continue the discussion assuming Takahashi's (1994)
MCLP analysis of locality. The details of the analysis, however, are not essential
here. Working them out would entail giving a complete account of successive cyclicity and locality of movement, notorious issues that go well beyond the scope of
this article. The main goal of the preceding discussion of successive cyclicity was
to point out an important ingredient that a successful theory of successive cyclic
movement should have, which the current phase-based theory of successive
cyclicity is missing. This lack is due to a change in the perspective concerning the
driving force of successive cyclic movement that was made in a departure from a
long-standing tradition. (Note, for example, that in the *Barriers* system, successive cyclic movement was considered a result of a property of movement [or the
resulting chain], not intermediate landing sites.)

Returning to the main topic, the most important point made in section 4 is the
proposal that movement through intermediate [Spec, IP]s should be treated on a
par with movement through intermediate [Spec, CP]s. The best way of dealing with
the latter is to consider it a reflex of successive cyclic movement – more precisely,
a result of the property of the movement itself rather than a property of the C
head, which clearly independently does not require a specifier. The suggestion is
to treat passing through intermediate [Spec, IP]s in the same way, which means
that an intermediate Infl does not require a filled specifier. This way, we can capture "intermediate EPP" effects without the EPP. In the next section I show that
the successive cyclic movement approach to "intermediate EPP" effects is empirically superior to the EPP approach (i.e. the approach on which intermediate
[Spec, IP]s are filled as a result of the requirement that every sentence have a subject). I will show that in a number of configurations intermediate [Spec, IP]s remain
empty (i.e. are not created), which raises an insurmountable problem for the EPP.

I will also show that exactly in these configurations [Spec, IP] does not have to be filled as a result of successive cyclic movement.[22]

5   Arguments against the intermediate EPP

5.1   Merge over Move

Consider the data in (26).

(26)   a.   There seems to be a man in the garden.
      b.   *There seems a man$_i$ to be t_i in the garden.

Chomsky (1995) gives an account of (26) that assumes the EPP. The account is based on the Merge-over-Move preference. According to Chomsky, at the point when the embedded clause is built we need to insert something into the infinitival [Spec, IP] to satisfy the EPP, an overt syntax requirement. We have two possibilities for doing this in (26). We can either insert *there*, which is present in the numeration, into [Spec, IP], or we can move the indefinite to this position. Chomsky argues that lexical insertion is a simpler operation than movement. Therefore, the possibility of expletive insertion into the embedded [Spec, IP], which for Chomsky takes place in (26a), blocks the indefinite movement to the embedded [Spec, IP], which takes place in (26b). Castillo, Drury, and Grohmann (1999) and Epstein and Seely (1999), however, observe several problems with the Merge-over-Move account. Consider first the following construction from Castillo, Drury, and Grohmann, attributed to Juan Romero and Alec Marantz (see also Epstein and Seely 1999; Frampton and Gutmann 1999; Nunes and Uriagereka 2000), where the indefinite has apparently moved to [Spec, IP] although an expletive was available for lexical insertion.

(27)   There was a rumor that a man$_i$ was t_i in the room.

To deal with this type of construction Chomsky (2000) introduces the concept of subnumeration, defined on phases. More precisely, Chomsky proposes that each phase has its own subnumeration. Given that the expletive is not present in the subnumeration corresponding to the embedded clause, the option of expletive insertion is not available.

A serious problem for this analysis is raised by (28).

(28)   a.   There has been a book$_i$ put t_i on the table.
      b.   *There has been put a book on the table.

Lasnik (1995a) argues that the indefinite in (28a) moves overtly to satisfy the EPP.[23] Under Chomsky's definition of phase, the constructions in (28) contain only one phase (passive VP is not a phase for Chomsky). As a result, the expletive should be available for lexical insertion at the point when the indefinite undergoes movement in (28a). Given the Merge-over-Move preference, the possibility of expletive insertion should block the indefinite movement. As a result, (28b) should block (28a).

Consider now (29).

(29) Mary believes John$_i$ to t_i know French.

At the point when the embedded clause is built in (29), there are two possibilities for satisfying the EPP. We can either move *John* or Merge *Mary* into that position. Given the Merge-over-Move preference, the latter should block the former. As a result, we cannot derive (29). Chomsky (1994) observes that the derivation on which *Mary* is introduced into the embedded [Spec, IP] eventually violates the θ-Criterion.[24] However, we need look-ahead to take advantage of this to rule out the derivation in question. To avoid look-ahead, Chomsky (2000) proposes the condition that arguments can be merged only in θ-positions. The condition blocks the unwanted derivation for (29) without look-ahead. However, Epstein and Seely (1999: 48–50) point out several problems with this condition. For one thing, the condition is massively redundant. For example, the condition unnecessarily rules out (30), which is plausibly already ruled out because it is uninterpretable (i.e. because the presence of *John* induces a Full Interpretation violation).

(30) *John seems that Peter likes Mary.

Based on these problems, Epstein and Seely (1999) and Castillo, Drury, and Grohmann (1999) argue that the Merge-over-Move preference should be abandoned. If the preference is abandoned, a question arises how the data in (26), especially the ungrammaticality of (26b), can be accounted for. Notice, however, that (26b) raises a problem only if there is EPP. If there is no EPP (more precisely, if the only [Spec, IP] positions that need to be filled are those that are required by the Inverse Case Filter or the MCLP; i.e. the requirement of successive cyclic movement), the ungrammaticality of (26b) can be easily accounted for. There is no reason to move the indefinite to the embedded [Spec, IP], hence the movement is blocked by the Last Resort Condition.

5.2 Ellipsis

Certain facts concerning ellipsis in infinitival constructions provide another argument against the EPP. Lobeck (1990) and Saito and Murasugi (1990) note that functional heads can license ellipsis of their complement only when they undergo Spec-head agreement (SHA); that is, feature checking. Thus, (31) shows that tensed Infl, *'s*, and [+wh] C, which according to Fukui and Speas (1986) undergo SHA, license ellipsis, whereas the nonagreeing functional categories *the* and *that* do not.

(31) a. John liked Mary and [$_{IP}$ Peter$_i$ [$_{I'}$ did t_i ~~like Mary~~]] too.
   b. John's talk about the economy was interesting but [$_{DP}$ Bill [$_{D'}$'S ~~talk about the economy~~]] was boring.
   c. *A single student came to the class because [$_{DP}$ [$_{D'}$ the ~~student~~]] thought that it was important.
   d. John met someone but I don't know [$_{CP}$ who$_i$ [$_{C'}$ C ~~John met t_i~~]].
   e. *John believes that Peter met someone but I don't think [$_{CP}$ [$_{C'}$ that ~~Peter met someone~~]].

As discussed by Martin (1996, 2001; see also Bošković 1997a and Koizumi 1995), VP ellipsis is also possible in control infinitives, which is expected under the Case-theoretic approach to the distribution of PRO, in which PRO in (32) is checked for null Case by the infinitival Infl, *to*, hence must undergo SHA with *to*.

(32)   John was not sure he could leave, but he tried [$_{IP}$ PRO$_i$ [$_{I'}$ to ~~t_i leave~~]].

Significantly, Martin (1996, 2001; see also Bošković 1997a and Koizumi 1995) observes that VP ellipsis is not possible in ECM infinitives.

(33)   *John believed Mary to know French but Peter believed [$_{AgroP}$ Jane$_i$ [$_{IP}$ t_i [$_{I'}$ to ~~t_i know French~~]]].

Epstein and Seely (1999: 81) interpret this as indicating that, in contrast with *to* in (32), *to* in (33) does not undergo SHA. This in turn provides evidence against the feature-checking approach to the EPP; more precisely, the intermediate EPP given overt object shift. Under the analysis proposed here, which assumes overt object shift, *Jane* passes through the infinitival [Spec, IP] in (33). However, the movement is forced by the MCLP, not a feature-checking requirement. As a result, no SHA with *to* takes place in (33) in spite of *Jane* passing through the embedded [Spec, IP]. In this respect, note the possibility of quantifier float in (34), which under Sportiche's (1988) analysis indicates that the ECM subject indeed passes through the infinitival [Spec, IP].[25]

(34)   I believe the students all to know French.

The ungrammaticality of (35), taken from Bošković (1997a), is also relevant to the current discussion.

(35)   *John met someone but I don't know who$_i$ Peter said [$_{CP}$ t_i [$_{C'}$ C ~~John met t_i~~]].

Apparently, IP ellipsis is not licensed in (35). This can be readily accounted for if passing through an intermediate [Spec, CP] does not imply feature checking (i.e. SHA with C), as I argue. In fact, the ungrammaticality of (35) should be taken as additional evidence against the feature-checking view of successive cyclic movement, on which C would undergo SHA in (35). Under this view, (35) is incorrectly expected to pattern with (31d) rather than (31e).

   Notice that in Chomsky's (2000) system, the SHA requirement on ellipsis would be restated as an EPP requirement (see also the discussion of the EPP with respect to selection and agreement in n. 6). The facts under consideration, both those concerning C and those concerning Infl, thus also provide evidence against Chomsky's (2000) system. In this system, (33) and (35) are incorrectly predicted to be acceptable because *to* and the declarative C take a specifier.

   Note also that the feature-checking approach to successive cyclic movement forces on us a rather perverse assumption that in constructions like *What do you think that Mary bought* (i.e. (18)), the *wh*-phrase, a [+wh] element, undergoes SHA with the declarative complementizer *that*, which is specified as [−wh] (see Lasnik and Saito 1992).[26] The assumption is not necessary under Takahashi's (1994) approach to successive cyclic movement, where the movement to the intermediate [Spec, CP] is forced by the MCLP, not a feature-checking requirement; therefore no SHA between the *wh*-phrase and *that* has to take place in the construction in question. This should be taken as another argument for the superiority of the MCLP approach over the feature-checking approach to successive cyclic movement.

5.3 Effect on output

Returning to the central topic of the article, the EPP, another argument against the EPP is provided by (36).

(36) a. There seems to be someone in the garden.
      b. Someone seems to be in the garden.

Chomsky (1995), who treats the EPP in terms of strong feature checking, argues that an element can be present in a numeration only if it has an effect on the output. In the case of strength, the effect is reflected in PF – namely, in causing displacement (with a change in word order, not PF vacuous displacement). In other words, for Chomsky, strength can be present in the numeration only if it induces movement that has a PF effect.[27] As a result, as observed by Nunes (1995: 165), the infinitival Infl in (36) cannot have a strong feature because the feature would not have an effect on PF. In other words, the EPP cannot hold for the embedded clause in (36).

5.4 Double *there*

The notorious double-*there* construction raises another problem for the EPP, especially under the position, held by Chomsky (1995), that *there* does not have Case. It is difficult to rule out double-*there* constructions like (37) in a principled way given this assumption and the EPP.[28]

(37) *There seems there to be someone in the garden.

On the other hand, (37) can be easily ruled out if there is no EPP. If we assume with Chomsky (2000: 132–3; see also Hornstein 2001: 55–6) that even pure Merge is subject to Last Resort,[29] (37) is straightforwardly ruled out because there is no reason to merge *there* in the infinitival [Spec, IP].

To summarize the discussion so far, we have seen that there is empirical evidence for the "intermediate EPP" (i.e. that A-movement proceeds via intermediate [Spec, IP]s). However, I have argued that this happens because of the MCLP (i.e. as a reflex of successive cyclicity), not the EPP. We have already seen some evidence against the intermediate EPP. In the next section I examine several contexts in which I will argue intermediate [Spec, IP]s have to remain empty (more precisely, they cannot be created), which will provide us with conclusive evidence against the intermediate EPP. I will furthermore show that exactly in these contexts intermediate [Spec, IP]s are expected not to be created under the MCLP view of passing through intermediate [Spec, IP]s, which will provide evidence for the MCLP analysis of "intermediate EPP" effects. The contexts in question concern expletive constructions.[30]

5.5 Expletives don't move

In this section, I show that the MCLP approach and the EPP approach make different predictions concerning "intermediate EPP" effects in expletive constructions. Under the EPP approach, intermediate [Spec, IP]s must be created in such constructions, which is not the case under the MCLP approach. Whereas the EPP forces filling of intermediate [Spec, IP]s in both expletive and nonexpletive constructions, the MCLP does not do so in expletive constructions, in contrast to nonexpletive constructions. Under the MCLP approach, the structures in (38) are permitted for the constructions in question.

(38)   a.   Someone$_i$ is likely [$_{IP}$ t_i to be t_i in the garden].
       b.   There is likely [$_{IP}$ to be someone in the garden].

In the following subsections, I provide a number of arguments that expletives quite generally do not move – they are indeed inserted directly into their surface positions.[31] As a result, intermediate [Spec, IP]s in expletive constructions remain empty, in contrast to intermediate [Spec, IP]s in nonexpletive constructions. This state of affairs provides strong evidence against the EPP and for the MCLP account of "intermediate EPP" effects. The arguments for the immobility of expletives also provide evidence against analyses of expletive constructions such as those developed by Moro (1997), Hoekstra and Mulder (1990), and Sabel (2000), among others, which crucially rely on expletive movement. (Under these analyses, expletives are introduced into the structure lower than [Spec, IP] and then move to [Spec, IP].)

5.5.1 Wager-class verbs

My central argument that expletives do not move concerns locality restrictions on movement. The first locality argument concerns *wager*-class verbs.

Pesetsky (1992) establishes the descriptive generalization that agentive verbs cannot ECM lexical NPs, as illustrated in (39).

(39)   a.   *John wagered the woman to know French.
       b.   *Mary alleged the students to have arrived late.

In Bošković (1997a), I deduce Pesetsky's generalization from the proposal that agentive verbs have an additional VP shell (see Hale and Keyser 1993) and the MCLP. In short, I argue that as a result of the presence of the additional VP shell, matrix [Spec, Agr$_O$P], the accusative-checking position, is too far from the embedded-clause subject.[32]

(40)   *John$_i$ wagered [$_{AgroP}$ the woman$_j$ [$_{VP}$ t_i [$_{VP}$ t_i [$_{IP}$ t_j to t_i know French]]]].

What is important for our current purposes is that (39) involves a locality violation.

Significantly, Postal (1974, 1993) shows that expletives can be ECMed by the verbs in question, as shown by (41). (Examples (41a–c) are from Postal 1993 and (41d) from Ura 1993. Recall that expletives are Case marked, hence must get to the matrix [Spec, Agr$_O$P] in (41).)

(41)   a.   He alleged there to be stolen documents in the drawer.
       b.   *He alleged stolen documents to be in the drawer.
       c.   He acknowledged it to be impossible to square circles.
       d.   John wagered there to have been a stranger in that haunted house.
       e.   *John wagered a stranger to have been in that haunted house.

Why is it that the locality violation that arises in the nonexpletive constructions does not arise in their expletive counterparts? My answer is straightforward, following the general logic of dealing with this type of a situation: there is no locality violation because there is no movement. More precisely, the locality violation does not arise in the expletive constructions because the expletives do not move. They are inserted right into their Case-checking position.

Consider how the data in (39) and (41) would be treated in the current system, which dispenses with the EPP. Given that there is no EPP, in contrast to the ECMed NPs in (39) and (41b,e), which have to be generated within the infinitival clause for θ-theoretic reasons, the expletive in (41a,c,d) can be merged directly into the matrix-clause [Spec, Agr$_O$P], where it satisfies the Inverse Case Filter. Because, in contrast to (39) and (41b,e), no A-movement out of the infinitival clause takes place in the expletive constructions in (41), the locality violation induced by A-movement out of the infinitive in (39) and (41b,e) does not arise in (41a,c,d). The expletive/nonexpletive contrast with respect to the possibility of ECM by agentive verbs is thus accounted for. The crucial ingredient of the analysis is that the infinitival [Spec, IP] is not created in (41a,c,d). We thus have an argument against the "intermediate EPP" in expletive constructions.

       [. . .]

5.5.2   Extraposition

Consider now the following contrast from Baltin (1985):

(42)   a.   *John is believed to be certain by everybody that Fred is crazy.
       b.   It is believed to be obvious by everybody that Fred is crazy.

How can we rule out (42a) while still allowing (42b)? There is a rather straightforward way of accounting for the otherwise puzzling contrast in (42) whose crucial ingredient is the assumption, argued for in this work, that *John* in (42a), but not *it* in (42b), moves to the matrix [Spec, IP] from the infinitival clause. Because the extraposed clause follows the matrix *by*-phrase in (42), I assume that it is located in the matrix clause. I further assume that extraposed elements are quite generally base-generated in their surface positions, as in Culicover and Rochemont (1990; see also Bennis 1986, Jackendoff 1990, and Zaring 1994). A strong argument for this assumption and against the movement analysis of extraposition, in which extraposition involves movement of the extraposed element, is provided by split-antecedent constructions noted by Perlmutter and Ross (1970; see also Gazdar 1981), where there is no plausible source for the base-generation of the extraposed element within an NP. (The following constructions are taken from Gazdar 1981).

(43)   a.   A man came in and a woman left who were quite similar.
       b.   A man came in and a woman left who know each other well.

Returning to (42a), we can rule out the construction by assuming that *John* is not allowed to cross the extraposed clause when moving from the infinitive to the matrix [Spec, IP], the extraposed clause being closer to the matrix Infl than *John*. In other words, (42a) is a straightforward locality (more precisely, Attract Closest/relativized minimality) violation.[33] It follows then that *it* in (42b) does not move to its S-structure position from inside the infinitival clause. Rather, it is base-generated in the matrix [Spec, IP], which means that the infinitival [Spec, IP] remains empty throughout the derivation. Under the current analysis, the contrast in (42) provides another argument against the EPP as well as additional illustration of the insensitivity of expletives to locality restrictions on movement, which immediately follows if expletives do not move.

5.5.3   The experiencer blocking effect in French and Icelandic
Probably the strongest piece of evidence that expletives indeed do not move is provided by the experiencer blocking effect in French.
    It is well known that English allows raising across an experiencer, as shown by (44).

(44)   John seems to Mary to be smart.

Some languages, however, do not allow NP raising across an experiencer. French is such a language, as observed by Chomsky (1995: 305) and McGinnis (1998, 2001) and illustrated in (45).[34]

(45)   a.   *Deux soldats semblent au   général manquer (être   manquants)
            two   soldiers seem   to-the general to-miss   to-be missing
            à la   caserne.
            at the barracks
            'Two soldiers seem to the general to be missing from the barracks.'
       b.   *Deux soldats semblent au   général être   arrivés en ville.
            two   soldiers seem   to-the general to-be arrived in town
            'Two soldiers seem to the general to have arrived in town.'

According to Chomsky and McGinnis, (45) contains a violation of locality restrictions on movement; more precisely, relativized minimality. The constructions involve A-movement across an A-specifier.[35]

Significantly, the expletive counterparts of (45) are acceptable, as shown in (46).

(46) a. Il   semble au   général y avoir deux soldats manquants à
          there seems to-the general to-have two   soldiers missing   at
          la   caserne.
          the barracks
          'There seem to the general to be two soldiers missing from the barracks.'
     b. Il   semble au   général être arrivé deux soldats en ville.
          there seems to-the general to-be arrived two   soldiers in town
          'There seem to the general to have arrived two soldiers in town.'

There is an obvious, principled account of the contrast between (45) and (46) that is available under the current analysis. In contrast to (45a,b), (46a,b) do not involve A-movement across an A-specifier. In other words, the expletive is generated in its surface position. As a result, it does not cross the experiencer, hence its presence does not induce a locality violation.[36] The contrast between (45) and (46), or more precisely, the absence of a locality violation in (46), provides strong evidence that expletives do not move, which in turn provides evidence against the EPP. The infinitival subject position remains unfilled (i.e. it is not created) in the expletive constructions in (46).[37]

It is worth noting here that, as pointed out to me by Halldór Á. Sigurðsson (personal communication), Icelandic, which like French has the experiencer blocking effect (see Boeckx 2000b; McGinnis 1998, 2001; Holmberg and Hróarsdóttir 2002; Stepanov 2002; and Thráinsson 1979, among others), patterns with French in that the blocking effect disappears in expletive constructions. This is illustrated in (47). (Note that (47a) is acceptable if the experiencer is dropped.)[38]

(47) a. *Við töldum myndir   hafa   einhverjum stúdentum
          we believed photos.NOM to-have some   students.DAT
          virst   hafa   verið teknar.
          seemed to-have been taken
          'We believed photos to have seemed to some students to have been taken.'
     b. ??Við töldum það hafa   einhverjum stúdentum   virst
          we believed there to-have some   students.DAT seemed
          hafa   verið teknar myndir.
          to-have been taken photos.NOM
          'We believed there to have seemed to some students to have been photos taken.'

The absence of a relativized minimality violation in (47b) confirms that expletives do not move – that is, that they are base-generated in their surface positions. Given that the expletive is not base-generated in the most embedded infinitival subject position in (47b), the position in question must remain unfilled. Like French (46), Icelandic (47b) thus also provides evidence against the EPP.

[. . .]

To summarize the discussion in section 5.5, I presented a number of arguments that expletive constructions (i.e. constructions where the highest [Spec, IP] is filled by an expletive) and nonexpletive constructions (i.e. constructions where the high-est [Spec, IP] is filled by a nonexpletive NP) differ with respect to the creation of intermediate [Spec, IP]s. I argued that expletives do not move – they are inserted directly into their surface positions. The conclusion that expletives do not move has a number of important consequences. First, Moro (1997)-style and Sabel (2000)-style analyses of expletive constructions, where expletives are introduced into the structure lower than [Spec, IP] and then move to [Spec, IP], cannot be maintained.[39] There is also evidence here against the EPP. Given that expletives do not move, intermediate [Spec, IP]s do not exist in expletive constructions – a straightforward argument against the EPP.

Based on the discussion so far, I conclude that the EPP is to be eliminated from the grammar. In certain constructions, the EPP simply does not hold – that is, there are clauses whose subject position remains empty. In the cases where the EPP does appear to hold, its effects are derivable from independent mechanisms, namely the Inverse Case Filter and the MCLP.

Notes

1   The term *Extended Projection Principle* is a misnomer, because the EPP seems quite dif-ferent from the Projection Principle, which requires that lexical properties of lexical items be satisfied at all levels.

2   Rothstein does not confine herself to this view.

3   Some of the standard arguments in support of the semantically dummy status of these elements concern the fact that these elements cannot be questioned and contrastively focused, which immediately follows if the elements in question are semantically dummy.

4   See Bošković (1997a) for arguments for the Inverse Case Filter. One argument for the Inverse Case Filter not noted there concerns constructions like (ia,b), which contrast with (iia–d). (For discussion of constructions like (i), see also Kayne 2000 and Larson 1985.)

   (i)   a.   *Mary loves here/there.
          b.   *Mary finds here/there interesting.
   (ii)   a.   Mary loves it here/there.
          b.   Mary loves this/that place.
          c.   Mary finds it interesting here/there.
          d.   Mary finds this/that place interesting.

   Given the natural assumption that *here* and *there* are not Case marked, (ia,b) are ruled out by the Inverse Case Filter because the accusative Case feature of the verb cannot be assigned. The Inverse Case Filter problem does not arise in (ii) (see also Authier 1991 for an Inverse Case Filter approach to object expletives).

5   For the null Case approach, see Bošković (1997a), Chomsky and Lasnik (1993), Martin (1996, 2001), and Ormazabal (1995), among others. I assume that, as discussed in Martin (1996, 2001), the control infinitival Infl is specified as [+Tense] and assigns null Case. (This is not the case with the ECM infinitival Infl, which is specified as [–Tense].)

   The infinitival [Spec, IP] position in (9) could actually be filled by PRO, in which case neither the EPP nor the Inverse Case Filter would be violated in (9). However, on this derivation, (9) is ruled out by whatever is responsible for the well-known ban on expletive PRO. (See also Hornstein 2001 for an account of (9) under the movement into a θ-position approach to control.)

6   As I will discuss, expletive *there* is involved in Case checking upon merger in [Spec, IP].
    Given that upon merger, a projection of Infl, whose Case feature *there* checks, c-commands
    there, I assume that Infl can probe *there*. It is worth noting here that the system I develop
    does not necessarily require banning Case licensing without overt movement for all lan-
    guages (which the Epstein and Seely proposal summarized in the text appears to do); that
    is, there could still be crosslinguistic variation in the relevant respect.

    Notice that I will remain silent in this article on φ-feature licensing. I assume that if it
    is done through feature checking it is done through Agree (or LF Move F), hence
    does not induce overt movement, which is what I am concerned with in this article. (φ-
    feature licensing clearly does not require a Spec-head configuration, as can be seen in explet-
    ive constructions like *There are some women in the garden*.)

    It is also worth noting here that the EPP must involve some kind of feature check-
    ing/matching/agreement, given that it is not the case that anything can satisfy it, as shown
    by the ungrammaticality of (i).

    (i)   *[IP [Because Mary had left] [I' arrived someone]].

7   See McCloskey (2000) for very strong evidence for Sportiche's approach. It is often noted
    that the ungrammaticality of passive and ergative constructions in (i) provides evidence against
    Sportiche's analysis, because the surface subject should be generated next to the floating
    quantifier.

    (i)   a.   *The students arrived all.
          b.   *The students were arrested all.

    However, in Bošković (2001, 2002), I provide an account of these constructions that is fully
    compatible with Sportiche's analysis of quantifier float. More precisely, I show that quan-
    tifiers quite generally cannot be floated in θ-positions [. . .] and demonstrate that the ban
    on floating quantifiers in θ-positions follows from independently motivated mechanisms;
    in other words, it is a theorem.

8   It is worth noting here that Castillo, Drury, and Grohmann (1999) argue that the experi-
    encer cannot bind outside of its PP, based on the lack of a Condition B effect in (i).

    (i)   Mary_j seems to John_i [IP t_j to appear to him_i to be in the room].

    Notice, however, that the experiencer is quite plausibly too far away from the pronoun to
    induce a Condition B violation in (i). In fact, there is a subject intervening between the
    experiencer and the pronoun – namely, the trace in the embedded [Spec, IP] – which plaus-
    ibly saves (i) from violating Condition B.

9   I use the term *reconstruction* throughout this section informally to refer to interpretation
    of intermediate positions in nontrivial chains. The process in question can either involve
    activation of lower copies of chains in LF or a derivational, online application of relevant
    conditions at the point when the intermediate positions are actually heads of chains.

10 I refer to heads that always require a specifier, which is not the case with *that*, as true EPP
    heads. Note that this article is concerned with eliminating the true EPP, which holds inde-
    pendently of successive cyclic movement.

11 In what follows I ignore vP as a phase.

12 It is worth noting in this respect that Ormazabal (1995) argues that raising and ECM infinitives
    are actually CPs.

    One possibility that I will not explore here would be to assume that each phrase is a
    phase, which seems to be the null hypothesis, essentially importing Manzini's (1994) pro-
    posal that movement must proceed through the domain of each head into a phase-based

system. Under this analysis, each head would have to be assigned an EPP property when movement takes place out of its maximal projection from its complement.

13　Compare also the infinitive in *There seemed to have arrived someone* with the embedded finite clause in *It seemed there had arrived someone* or *It seemed someone had arrived.* The embedded finite clause seems to be no more of a proposition than the infinitive.

Chomsky (2000) gives two empirical arguments that IPs are not phases (see Franks and Bošković 2001 for an additional argument that is not discussed here). First, he claims that, in contrast to CPs, IPs are not phonologically isolable, which is supposed to follow from them not being phases. Second, the assumption that IPs are not phases is supposed to provide us with an account of the fact that partial raising of the associate in expletive constructions is generally not possible, as shown by the ungrammaticality of *There seems someone to have arrived.* I discuss the latter property in section 5.1, where I argue, following Castillo, Drury, and Grohmann (1999) and Epstein and Seely (1999) that Chomsky's account of that property cannot be maintained. As for the former, the claim that IPs are not isolable cannot be maintained. Thus, IPs can undergo right-node raising, as shown by (i).

(i)　Mary wonders when, and John wonders why, Peter left.

For problems with Chomsky's approach to phases, see also Epstein and Seely (1999: 44–6) and Bošković, [2005].

14　Notice that it is not possible to appeal to the Doubly Filled Comp Filter, because nothing changes if *that* is replaced by a null C, as in *Who thinks what Mary bought?* See, however, the following discussion for a way of handling (21) hinted at in Chomsky (2000). For much relevant discussion, see also Saito (2000).

15　Takahashi's approach is revived by Boeckx (2001), who also provides convincing new arguments for this approach to locality of movement.

16　Takahashi assumes the Form Chain operation. Under this approach, Last Resort is relevant to the formation of a chain, not links of a chain. In other words, formation of a chain must have a feature-checking motivation, not formation of chain links. Notice also that because Form Chain is a single operation, formation of a chain cannot be interleaved with another operation (in this respect, see also Collins 1994). Thus, in the structure X_i Y t_i t_i, with X_i t_i t_i a three-member chain and Y the target of movement, no movement of X takes place until Y enters the structure.

17　Notice that movement out of [Spec, CP] is in principle possible, yielding at worst a very weak violation. In this respect, notice the contrast between? *Who do you wonder which picture of Jane bought* and (23), both of which involve extraction of a complement of P from [Spec, CP].

18　Form Chain being a single operation, we cannot drop the P, thus changing the categorial status of the element undergoing movement, without breaking chain formation. (Note that, as discussed in Bošković 2001, 2002, in quantifier-float constructions stranding of the quantifier does not lead to changing the categorial status of the element undergoing movement.)

19　The last *all* actually seems to be an instance of *all* meaning 'entirely' (Bobaljik's [1995] completive *all*) rather than a floating-quantifier *all*.

20　See also n. 21 for a version of the analysis based on (25) that does not require appealing to the notion of chain.

21　A version of this analysis that would not require an appeal to the notion of chain would make the step of crossing a CP boundary, in the case of A′-movement, and an IP boundary, in the case of A-movement, in itself illegitimate, requiring adjunction to CP and IP (i.e. movement to [Spec, CP] and [Spec, IP] under Kayne's proposal). In its spirit, this analysis would be close to the *Barriers* system (Chomsky 1986), with "relativized barriers" CP and IP being voided through adjunction.

22 It is worth noting here that the arguments against the EPP given in section 5 can also be accommodated in EPP-less analyses that do not assume "intermediate EPP" effects (i.e. passing through intermediate [Spec, IP]s), as in Boeckx (2000a); Castillo, Drury, and Grohmann (1999); Epstein and Seely (1999); Grohmann, Drury, and Castillo (2000); Martin (1999).

23 Under the partitive Case hypothesis, to be discussed, the indefinite may be located in its Case-checking position.

24 It would also yield a Case violation if we assume that the trace of *Mary* in the infinitival [Spec, IP] blocks Case licensing of *John*. [. . .]

25 Following Lasnik and Saito (1992), Martin (1996, 2001) argues convincingly that some traditional raising predicates have control variants. As expected, given the discussion of (32), the control variants, whose infinitival complement [Spec, IP] is filled by PRO, allow VP ellipsis. The reader is referred to Martin (1996, 2001) for convincing arguments that (i), where VP ellipsis is allowed, instantiates the control variant. Where the control option is ruled out, as in (ii) (expletive *there* cannot control PRO), VP ellipsis is disallowed, as expected.

(i)   Kim may not leave, but Sarah is likely to ~~leave~~.
(ii) *It was announced that there may be a riot, so everyone believes there is likely to ~~be a riot~~.

26 A similar problem also seems to arise in Chomsky's (2000) system, given that Agree is a component of Move (see n. 6). Notice that in the preminimalist trace theory of movement, a solution to the problem in question was available. Thus, Lasnik and Saito (1992) proposed that a *wh*-phrase in [Spec, CP] and its trace in an intermediate [Spec, CP] differ with respect to the specification for the [wh] feature, the *wh*-phrase, but not its trace, being specified as [+wh]. They furthermore assumed that the trace in an intermediate [Spec, CP] (not the head of the *wh*-chain) undergoes SHA with the intermediate C. Under these assumptions, (18) would not have to involve SHA between a [+wh] and a [−wh] element. However, the analysis cannot be maintained under the copy theory of movement, where it is impossible to maintain the assumption that in a construction like (18), the *wh*-phrase in the matrix interrogative [Spec, CP], but not the element in the intermediate [Spec, CP] (actually a copy of the *wh*-phrase), is specified as [+wh]. (In addition, in the current system, under the feature-checking approach to successive cyclic movement the head of the *wh*-chain itself would undergo SHA with *that* since the SHA would take place before the root-clause structure is built.)

27 See also Chomsky (2000: 109) concerning the filled-Spec EPP requirement. The argument given in the text can thus be extended to this view of the EPP.

28 Chomsky (1995) gives an account of the double-*there* construction that I have shown (Bošković 1997a: 98–9) to cause very serious problems for his analysis of expletive constructions, hence cannot be maintained (see, however, Chomsky 2000 for an alternative analysis).

29 On this view, satisfying a selectional requirement counts as a legitimate driving force with respect to Last Resort.

30 The reader should bear in mind that with respect to Case licensing in expletive constructions, I will be adopting the line of research that originated with Belletti (1988) and was extensively argued for in a number of articles by Howard Lasnik (see, e.g. Lasnik 1995a, 1995b) as well as Bošković (1997a), Epstein and Seely (1999), and Martin (1992), among others, on which expletive *there* has structural Case, its associate being licensed for partitive Case by the verb. I therefore depart from Chomsky (1995), for whom *there* in constructions like *there is a woman in the garden* is Caseless, the associate bearing nominative Case. Constructions like (i), however, provide strong evidence against Chomsky's position. (See Lasnik 1995a, 1995b and Bošković 1997a for a number of additional arguments against Chomsky's position.) [. . .]

(i)   There's always him/*he.

31   Recall that, given that pure Merge is subject to Last Resort, *there* cannot be inserted in the
     infinitival [Spec, IP] position if the EPP does not hold. Note also that I confine the discussion
     below to A-movement. I do not discuss the possibility of A′-movement of expletives.
32   See Bošković (1997a) for details of the analysis and justification of the structure in (40).
     The upshot of the analysis is that equidistance allows skipping of one but not two
     specifiers, which is what would have to happen with agentive ECM constructions (see
     Bošković 1997a for discussion of simple transitives). I also argue there that the additional
     agentive shell, which is responsible for the ungrammaticality of (39), is not present in
     passive constructions, which provides a straightforward account of the contrast between
     active (39) and passive (i).

     (i)   a.   The woman was wagered to know French.
           b.   The students were alleged to have arrived late.

     The additional agentive shell is also not present with verbs like *believe*, which can ECM.
33   Under the base-generation approach to extraposition, it is natural to consider the extra-
     posed clause in (42) an argument in its S-structure position (with an interpretative process
     that would treat it as if it were located within the AP; see Culicover and Rochemont 1990
     and Guéron and May 1984), so that movement of *John* to the matrix [Spec, IP] in (56a)
     involves A-movement across an A-element. The reader is also referred to Bošković (1995)
     for arguments that finite CPs can occur in subject position (i.e. [Spec, IP]), contra Koster
     (1978), which means that the extraposed CP is clearly a candidate for attraction to the matrix
     [Spec, IP] in (42). (I argue in Bošković 1995 that finite CPs can even bear Case; see also
     McCloskey 1991 for evidence that they have φ-features.)
34   There is apparently some disagreement among French speakers with respect to construc-
     tions like (45). For relevant discussion, see, among others: Boeckx (2000b); Chomsky (1995);
     McGinnis (1998, 2001); and Rouveret and Vergnaud (1980). I am focusing here on the dialect
     in which (45a,b) are unacceptable.
35   See references given previously and Boeckx (2000b), Stepanov (2002), and Torrego (1996)
     for discussion why English (44) is acceptable.
36   Would the experiencer still block the agreement relation between the indefinite and
     Infl? The question does not arise in French, where Infl does not agree with the indefinite.
     For relevant discussion of English, see Boeckx (1999), which shows that in English the
     experiencer can interfere with establishing an agreement relation between Infl and a lower
     associate.
37   A question arises concerning what happens with the quasi-argument expletive with respect
     to the experiencer blocking effect. Interestingly, (i) seems worse than (46).

     (i)   ?*Il   semble au   général avoir   plu.
            there seems   to-the general to-have rained
            'It seems to the general to have rained.'

     This is not surprising. Under the quasi-argument hypothesis, *il* is actually θ-marked by
     plu in (i). As a result, it must be generated within the infinitive, which means that it under-
     goes movement to the matrix [Spec, IP] across the experiencer, hence the contrast with
     (46). The contrast between (i) and (46) thus confirms the quasi-argument hypothesis. It
     also confirms that only elements that are θ-marked in a position lower than the experiencer
     are subject to the experiencer blocking effect, as expected under the current analysis.
38   I thank Halldór Á. Sigurðsson for help with the Icelandic data. Note that I use an ECM
     structure to exclude the possibility of topicalization of the embedded-clause subject.

(Sigurðsson informs me that the expletive is always somewhat degraded as a subject of ECM infinitives. In spite of that, (47b) is clearly better than (47a).)

Notice also that not all languages that exhibit the experiencer blocking effect with respect to constructions like (45) are necessarily expected to pattern with French with respect to (46). Ausín and Depiante (2000) investigate the experiencer blocking effect in Spanish, which also disallows constructions like (45). They argue that in Spanish, *seem*+experiencer is a control construction; in particular, it involves subject control. Obviously, a language that treats the *seem*+experiencer construction as a subject-control construction is not expected to allow an expletive in this construction for reasons independent of the current concerns.

39 Both Moro's (1997) and Sabel's (2000) analyses crucially involve expletive movement. For Moro, the expletive undergoes predicate raising to [Spec, IP]. Sabel, on the other hand, generates the expletive as a constituent with its associate and then moves it to [Spec, IP].

References

Aoun, J. 1986. *Generalized binding: The syntax and logical form of Wh-interrogatives.* Dordrecht: Foris.

Ausín, A. and M. A. Depiante. 2000. On the syntax of *parcer* with and without experiencer. In H. Campos, E. Herburger, A. Morales-Font and T. J. Walsh (eds.), *Hispanic linguistics at the turn of the millennium: Papers from the 3rd Hispanic Linguistic Symposium.* Somerville, MA: Cascadilla Press, pp. 155–70.

Authier, J.-M. 1991. V-governed expletives, case theory, and the projection principle. *Linguistic Inquiry* 22: 721–40.

Baltin, M. R. 1985. *Toward a theory of movement rules.* New York: Garland.

Bejar, S. and D. Massam. 1999. Multiple case checking. *Syntax* 2: 66–79.

Belletti, A. 1988. The case of unaccusatives. *Linguistic Inquiry* 19: 1–34.

Bennis, H. 1986. *Gaps and dummies.* Dordrecht: Foris.

Bobaljik, J. D. 1995. *Morphosyntax: The syntax of verbal inflection.* PhD dissertation, MIT.

Boeckx, C. 1999. Conflicting c-command requirements. *Studia Linguistica* 53: 227–50.

Boeckx, C. 2000a. EPP eliminated. Ms., University of Connecticut, Storrs.

Boeckx, C. 2000b. Raising over experiencers, crosslinguistically. Ms., University of Connecticut, Storrs.

Boeckx, C. 2001. *Mechanisms of chain formation.* Doctoral dissertation, University of Connecticut, Storrs.

Borer, H. 1986. I-subjects. *Linguistic Inquiry* 17: 375–416.

Bošković, Ž. 1995. Case properties of clauses and the Greed Principle. *Studia Linguistica* 49: 32–53.

Bošković, Ž. 1997a. *The syntax of nonfinite complementation: An economy approach.* Cambridge, MA: MIT Press.

Bošković, Ž. 1997b. Coordination, Object Shift, and V-movement. *Linguistic Inquiry* 28: 357–65.

Bošković, Ž. 2001. Floating quantifiers and THETA-role assignment. In M. Kim and U. Strauss (eds)., *Proceedings of the 31st Annual Meeting of the North East Linguistic Society,* Amherst, MA: GSLA, pp. 59–78.

Bošković, Ž. 2002. Be careful where you float quantifiers. *Natural Language and Linguistic Theory* 22: 681–742.

Bošković, Ž. 2003. On left branch extraction. In P. Kosta, J. Blaszczak, J. Frasek, L. Geist and M. Zygis (eds.), *Investigations into formal Slavic linguistics. Contributions of the Fourth European Conference on Formal Description of Slavic Language – FDSL IV,* Frankfurt am Main: Peter Lang, pp. 543–77.

Bošković, Ž. 2005. On the locality of left branch extraction and the structure of NP. *Studia Linguistica* 59: 1–45.

Castillo, J. C., J. Drury and K. K. Grohmann. 1999. The status of the merge over move preference. Ms., University of Maryland, College Park.

Chomsky, N. 1981. *Lectures on government and binding*. Dordrecht: Foris.

Chomsky, N. 1982. *Concepts and consequences of the theory of government and binding*. Cambridge, MA: MIT Press.

Chomsky, N. 1986. *Barriers*. Cambridge, MA: MIT Press.

Chomsky, N. 1994. Bare phrase structure. *MIT Occasional Papers in Linguistics 5*. Cambridge, MA: MITWPL. [Published in P. Kempchiusky (ed.) (1994), *Evolution and revolution in linguistic theory: Essays in honor of Carlos Otero*, Washington, DC: Georgetown University Press, pp. 51–109. Also published in G. Webelhuth (ed.) (1994), *Government and binding theory and the minimalist program*, Cambridge, MA: MIT Press, pp. 383–439.

Chomsky, N. 1995. *The Minimalist Program*. Cambridge, MA: MIT Press.

Chomsky, N. 1999. *Derivation by phase. MIT Occasional Papers in Linguistics 18*. Cambridge, MA: MITWPL.

Chomsky, N. 2000. Minimalist inquiries: The framework. In R. Martin, D. Michaels and J. Uriagereka (eds.), *Step by step: Essays on minimalism in honor of Howard Lasnik*, Cambridge, MA: MIT Press, pp. 89–155.

Chomsky, N. and H. Lasnik. 1993. The theory of principles and parameters. In J. Jacobs, A. von Stechow, W. Sternefeld and T. Vennemann (eds.), *An international handbook of contemporary research*, Berlin/New York: Walter de Gruyter, pp. 506–69. [Reprinted in Chomsky (1995), *The Minimalist Program*, Cambridge, MA: MIT Press, pp. 13–127.]

Collins, C. 1994. Economy of derivation and generalized proper binding condition. *Linguistic Inquiry* 25: 45–61.

Cowper, E. A. 1998. What is a subject? In J. Blevins and J. Carter (eds.), *Proceedings of the 18th Annual Meeting of the North East Linguistic Society*, Amherst, MA: GLSA, pp. 94–108.

Culicover, P. W. and M. S. Rochemont. 1990. Extraposition and the Complement Principle. *Linguistic Inquiry* 21.

Epstein, S. D. and T. D. Seely. 1999. SPEC-ifyng the GF subject: Eliminating A-chains and the EPP within a derivational model. Ms., University of Michigan and Eastern Michigan University.

Frampton, J. and S. Gutmann. 1999. Cyclic computation: A computationally efficient minimalist syntax. *Syntax* 2: 1–27.

Franks, S. and Željkó Bošković. 2001. An argument for multiple Spell-out. *Linguistic Inquiry* 32: 174–83.

Freidin, R. and R. Sprouse. 1991. Lexical case phenomena. In R. Freidin (ed.), *Principles and parameters in comparative grammar*, Cambridge, MA: MIT Press, pp. 392–416.

Fukui, N. and M. Speas. 1986. Specifiers and projection. In N. Fukui, T. R. Rapoport and E. Sagey (eds.), *Papers in Theoretical Linguistics. MIT Working Papers in Linguistics 8*, Cambridge, MA: MITWPL, pp. 128–72.

Gazdar, G. 1981. Unbounded dependencies and coordinate structure. *Linguistic Inquiry* 12: 155–84.

Grohmann, K. K., J. Drury and J. C. Castillo. 2000. No more EPP. In R. Billerey and B. D. Lillehaugen (eds.), *Proceedings of the 19th West Coast Conference on Formal Linguistics*, Somerville, MA: Cascadilla Press, pp. 139–52.

Guéron, J. and R. May. 1984. Extraposition and logical form: *Linguistic Inquiry* 15.

Hale, K. and S. J. Keyser. 1993. On argument structure and the lexical expression of grammatical relations. In K. Hale and S. J. Keyer (eds.), *The view from Building 20: Essays in linguistics in honor of Sylvain Bromberger*, Cambridge, MA: MIT Press, pp. 53–109.

Heycock, C. 1994. *Layers of predication*. New York: Garland Publishing.

Hoekstra, T. and R. Mulder. 1990. Unergatives as copular verbs: Locational and existential predication. *The Linguistic Review* 7: 1–79.

Holmberg, A. and T. Hróarsdóttir. 2002. Agreement and movement in Icelandic raising constructions. *Working Papers in Scandinavian Syntax* 69: 147–68.

Hornstein, N. 2001. *Move! A minimalist theory of construal*. Malden, MA: Blackwell.

Jackendoff, R. 1990. *Semantic structures*. Cambridge, MA: MIT Press.

Johnson, K. 1991. Object positions. *Natural Language and Linguistic Theory* 9: 577–636.

Kayne, R. 1994. *The antisymmetry of syntax*. Cambridge, MA: MIT Press.

Kayne, R. S. 2000. Here and there. Ms., New York University.

Koizumi, M. 1995. *Phrase structure in minimalist syntax*. Doctoral dissertation, MIT.

Koster, J. 1978. Why subject sentences don't exist? In S. J. Keyser (ed.), *Recent transformational studies in European languages*, Cambridge, MA: MIT Press. pp. 53–64.

Larson, R. 1985. Bare-NP adverbs. *Linguistic Inquiry* 16: 595–621.

Lasnik, H. 1995a. Case and expletives revisited: On Greed and other human failings. *Linguistic Inquiry* 26: 615–33.

Lasnik, H. 1995b. Last resort. In S. Haraguchi and M. Funaki (eds.), *Minimalism and linguistic theory*, Tokyo: Hituzi Syobo, pp. 1–32. [Reprinted in Lasnik (1999), *Minimalist analysis*, Malden, MA/Oxford: Blackwell, pp. 120–50.]

Lasnik, H. 1995c. Notes on pseudogapping. In R. Pensalfini and H. Ura (eds.), *Papers on minimalism. MIT Working Papers in Linguistics 27*, Cambridge, MA: MITWPL, pp. 143–63.

Lasnik, H. 2001a. A note on the EPP. *Linguistic Inquiry* 32: 356–62.

Lasnik, H. 2001b. When can you save a structure by destroying it? In M. Kim and U. Strauss (eds.), *Proceedings of the 31st Annual Meeting of the North East Linguistic Society*, Amherst, MA: GLSA, pp. 301–20.

Lasnik, H. and M. Saito. 1992. *Move α*. Cambridge, MA: MIT Press.

Lebeaux, D. 1988. Relative clauses, licensing, and the nature of the derivation. In S. Rothstein (ed.), *Perspectives on phrase structure. Syntax and semantics 25*, New York: Academic Press, pp. 209–39.

Lebeaux, D. 1991. Relative clauses, licensing, and the nature of the derivation. In S. Rothstein (ed.), *Perspectives on phrase structure. Syntax and Semantics 25*, New York: Academic Press, pp. 209–39.

Lobeck, A. 1990. Functional heads as proper governors. In J. Carter, R.-M. Dechaine, B. Philip and T. Sherer (eds.), *Proceedings of the 20th Annual Meeting of the North East Linguistic Society*, Amherst, MA: GLSA.

McCloskey, J. 1991. *There, it*, and agreement. *Linguistic Inquiry* 22: 563–67.

McCloskey, J. 2000. Quantifier float and wh-movement in an Irish English. *Linguistic Inquiry* 31: 57–84.

McGinnis, M. 1998. Locality and inert case. In P. Tamanji and K. Kusumoto (eds.), *Proceedings of 28th Annual Meeting of the North East Linguistic Society*, Amherst, MA: GSLA, pp. 267–81.

McGinnis, M. 2001. Variation in the phrase structure of applicatives. Ms., University of Calgary.

Manzini, M. R. 1994. Locality, minimalism, and parasitic gaps. *Linguistic Inquiry* 25: 481–508.

Martin, R. 1992. On the distribution and Case features of PRO. Ms., University of Connecticut, Storrs.

Martin, R. 1996. *A minimalist theory of PRO and control*. Doctoral dissertation, University of Connecticut, Storrs.

Martin, R. 1999. Case, the Extended Projection Principle, and minimalism. In S. D. Epstein and N. Hornstein (eds.), *Working minimalism*, Cambridge, MA: MIT Press, pp. 1–25.

Martin, R. 2001. Null Case and the distribution of PRO. *Linguistic Inquiry* 32: 141–66.

Moro, A. 1997. *The raising of predicates*. Cambridge: Cambridge University Press.

Nunes, J. 1995. *The copy theory of movement and linearization of chains in the Minimalist Program*. Doctoral dissertation, University of Maryland, College Park.

Nunes, J. and J. Uriagereka. 2000. Cyclicity and extraction domains. *Syntax* 3: 20–43.

Ochi, M. 1998. Move or attract? In E. Curtis, J. Lyle and G. Webster (eds.), *Proceedings of the 16th West Coast Conference on Formal Linguistics*, Stanford: CSLI, pp. 319–33.

Ochi, M. 1999. Some consequences of Attract F. *Lingua* 109: 81–107.

Ormazabal, J. 1995. *The syntax of complementation: On the connection between syntactic structures and selection*. Doctoral dissertation, University of Connecticut, Storrs.

Perlmutter, D. M. 1971. *Deep and surface structure constraints in syntax*. New York: Holt, Rinehart, and Winston.

Perlmutter, D. M. and J. R. Ross. 1970. Relative clauses with split antecedents. *Linguistic Inquiry* 1: 350.

Pesetsky, D. 1992. Zero syntax, vol. 2. MS., MIT.

Postal, P. M. 1974. *On raising*. Cambridge, MA: MIT Press.

Postal, P. M. 1993. Some defective paradigms. *Linguistic Inquiry* 24: 347–64.

Rizzi, L. 1990. *Relativized minimality*. Cambridge, MA: MIT Press.

Rothstein, S. 1983. *The syntactic forms of predication*. Doctoral dissertation, MIT.

Rouveret, A. and J.-R. Vergnaud. 1980. Specifying the reference to the subject: French causatives and conditions on representations. *Linguistic Inquiry* 11.

Runner, J. 1998. *Noun phrase licensing and interpretation*. New York: Garland.

Sabel, J. 2000. Expletives as features. In R. Billerey and B. D. Lillehaugen (eds.), *Proceedings of the 19th West Coast Conference on Formal Linguistics*, Somerville, MA: Cascadilla Press, pp. 101–14.

Saito, M. 2000. Scrambling in the Minimalist Program. Ms., Nanzan University.

Saito, M. and K. Murasugi. 1990. N′ deletion in Japanese. In J. Ormazabal and C. Tenny (eds.), *University of Connecticut Working Papers in Linguistics 3*, University of Connecticut, pp. 86–107.

Sportiche, D. 1988. A theory of floating quantifiers and its corollaries for constituent structure. *Linguistic Inquiry* 19: 425–49.

Stepanov, A. 2002. Derivational properties of inherent Case. Ms., University of Connecticut, Storrs.

Stowell, T. 1983. Subject across categories. *The Linguistic Review* 2: 285–312.

Takahashi, D. 1994. *Minimality of movement*. Doctoral dissertation, University of Connecticut, Storrs.

Thráinsson, H. 1979. *On complementation in Icelandic*. New York: Garland.

Torrego, E. 1996. Experiencers and raising verbs. In R. Freidin (ed.), *Current issues in comparative grammar*, Dordrecht: Kluwer, pp. 101–20.

Ura, H. 1993. On feature-checking for wh-traces. In J. D. Bobaljik and C. Phillips (eds.), *Papers on Case and agreement I. MIT Working Papers in Linguistics 18*, Cambridge, MA: MITWPL, pp. 215–42.

Zaring, L. 1994. On the relationship between subject pronouns and clausal arguments. *Natural Language and Linguistic Theory* 12: 515–69.

2.3.1   Recent Developments: Phases

From "MINIMALIST INQUIRIES: THE FRAMEWORK"
Noam Chomsky

Each core functional category (CFC) also allows an extra Spec beyond its s-selection: for C, a raised *wh*-phrase; for T, the surface subject; for *v*, the phrase raised by object shift (OS). For T, the property of allowing an extra Spec is the Extended Projection Principle (EPP). By analogy, we can call the corresponding properties of C and *v EPP-features*, determining positions not forced by the Projection Principle. I will restrict attention to XP positions, though a fuller picture might add X^0 as another case of the EPP. EPP-features are uninterpretable (nonsemantic, hence the name), though the configuration they establish has effects for interpretation.

[. . .]

The next step is to characterize the subarrays LA_i that can be selected for active memory. LA_i should determine a natural syntactic object SO, an object that is relatively independent in terms of interface properties. On the "meaning side," perhaps the simplest and most principled choice is to take SO to be the closest syntactic counterpart to a proposition: either a verb phrase in which all θ-roles are assigned or a full clause including tense and force. Call these objects *propositional*. [. . .]

LA$_i$ can then be selected straightforwardly: LA$_i$ contains an occurrence of C or of v, determining clause or verb phrase – exactly one occurrence if it is restricted as narrowly as possible, in accordance with the guiding intuitions. Take a *phase* of a derivation to be an SO derived in this way by choice of LA$_i$. A phase is CP or vP, but not TP or a verbal phrase headed by H lacking φ-features and therefore not entering into Case/agreement checking: neither finite TP nor unaccusative/passive verbal phrase is a phase. Suppose phases satisfy a still stronger cyclicity condition:

(1)   The head of a phase is "inert" after the phase is completed, triggering no further operations.

A phase head cannot trigger Merge or Attract in a later phase, and we can restrict attention to phases in which all selectional requirements are satisfied, including the EPP for T (by virtue of cyclicity) and for v/C, and selection of EA [external argument] for v if required; otherwise, the derivation crashes at the phase level.

Derivations proceed phase by phase: (2), for example, has the four phases shown in brackets.

(2)   [John [t thinks [Tom will [t win the prize]]]]

[. . .]

The descriptive typology of movement, a leading research topic for years,[1] offers other reasons to suspect that phases are real. [. . .] There are several categories: movement can be feature-driven or not, and in the former case can be directly or indirectly feature-driven. Typical cases include raising to subject (directly feature-driven), the nonfinal stages of successive-cyclic movement (indirectly feature-driven), and QR and "stylistic movement" (perhaps not feature-driven).[2]

Indirect feature-driven movement (IFM) subdivides into types depending on the attracting head H in the final stage: (a) A-movement when H has φ-features (yielding the Case/agreement system), or (b) Ā-movement when H has *P-features* of the peripheral system (force, topic, focus, etc.).[3] The intuitive argument for IFM has always been that locality conditions require "short movement" in successive stages, leading to convergence in the final stage. We can express a version of this idea as a "phase-impenetrability condition," strengthening further the notion of cyclic derivation. Given HP = [α [H β]], take β to be the *domain* of H and α (a hierarchy of one or more Specs) to be its *edge*. The thesis under consideration is (3).

(3)   *Phase-Impenetrability Condition*
    In phase α with head H, the domain of H is not accessible to operations outside α, only H and its edge are accessible to such operations.

The cycle is so strict that operations cannot "look into" a phase α below its head H. H itself must be visible for selection and head movement; hence, its Specs must be as well. The Phase-Impenetrability Condition yields a strong form of Subjacency.[4] For A-movement, it should follow from the theories of Case/agreement and locality.[5] The stipulation is for clausal Ā-movement, the basic question from the earliest study of these topics. [. . .]

The Phase-Impenetrability Condition requires that Ā-movement target the edge of every phase, CP and vP. There is evidence from reconstruction effects and parasitic gap constructions that this may be true.[6]

The idea that IFM applies only if needed to guarantee eventual convergence appears to raise questions of look-ahead. These are obviated if the Phase-Impenetrability Condition holds. Local determination is straightforward, and an uninterpretable feature in the domain determines at the phase level that the derivation will crash.[7]

[. . .]

Phases are determined by a choice of C/v, not T, which suggests a basis for the similarities and asymmetry. The fact that the EPP-feature when available is optional for C/v suggests that it is a property of the phase Ph.

(4)   The head H of phase Ph may be assigned an EPP-feature.[8]

Once Ph is completed, exhausting the lexical subarray from which it is derived, (4) may optionally apply, assigning an EPP-feature to H. From the strong cyclicity condition that renders H inert beyond the phase itself (see (1)), it follows that the EPP must be satisfied by raising within Ph: pure Merge from outside Ph is barred.

[. . .]

(4) yields A- or Ā-movement depending on whether the phase head has ϕ- or P-features. It might have both. Suppose that in the construction (5) all four phase heads are assigned an extra Spec by (4), associated with P-features for C and v_2 but not for v_1.

(5)   [Spec, C_2] . . . [Spec, v_2] . . . [Spec, C_1] . . . [Spec, v_1] . . . XP

XP raises through the Specs in succession, landing finally in [Spec, C_2]. The result is the four-membered Ā-chain ([Spec, C_2], [Spec, v_2], [Spec, C_1], [Spec, v_1]) and the two-membered A-chain ([Spec, v_1], XP) (formed by OS). [Spec, v_2] is an Ā-position, by virtue of the P-feature associated with the extra Spec introduced by (4); v_2 also had ϕ-features involved in object Case/agreement but these would have been deleted phase-internally before (4) assigns the extra Spec.[9]

Notes

1   Early work sought to establish the categories of A- and Ā-movement ("Move NP," "Move *Wh*"), later head movement, while parallel inquiries sought commonalities. Important

outcomes were Rizzi's (1990) theory of Relativized Minimality and Lasnik and Saito's (1992) Move α theory. The distinctions mentioned here crosscut these categories.

2   "Stylistic" operations might fall within the phonological component (see *MP* [*The Minimalist Program*], sec. 4.7.3, Kidwai 1996). Operations lacking overt counterparts and apparently not interacting with C_{HL} might be among the principles of interpretation of LF, hence "postcyclic," inspecting a representational level in the manner of many other systems (including binding theory, on the assumptions of *MP*). If so, much of the very enlightening recent work on ellipsis and antecedent-contained deletion (along with event structure and other topics) could be understood as an exploration of the language-external systems at the border of the language faculty, roughly analogous to acoustic and articulatory phonetics on the sound side.

3   The categories might overlap, but unproblematically it seems. System design should preclude unwanted cases of improper movement. That seems attainable, but must be demonstrated. I will continue to restrict attention to raising of XP.

4   It also suggests a new approach to some Empty Category Principle (ECP) issues, such as subject extraction (Idan Landau, personal communication).

5   To clarify this and related conclusions and establish them in full generality requires a far more comprehensive review and analysis than is undertaken below. Similar qualifications hold throughout.

6   See Fox (1998) and Nissenbaum (1998). If adjunction is restricted as suggested in *MP* (sec. 4.7.3), then movement to the edge will be to a Spec position for *v*P as well as CP. Phases might also be the target for QR, if this noncyclic operation targets C′, merging the raised quantifier phrase between C and [Spec, C].

7   Convergence is not guaranteed, of course (it can fail in many ways) – only permitted without look-ahead, the desideratum we are exploring. Conditions could be added to restrict crash, but they are redundant, simply restating properties of convergence, unless motivated in some other way. Questions arise about operations that appear to violate Subjacency. Note the restriction to uninterpretable features *in the domain*. Legitimacy of those at the edge (specifically, EA) will be determined at the next higher phase, a matter that opens interesting questions, put aside here.

8   Parametrically varying properties of H enter into the application of (4), which might be extended to head movement. I will call the EPP-feature a *P-feature* (*periphery feature*) if H does have an appropriate EPP-feature by virtue of its inherent properties (e.g. the Case/agreement properties of *v*, the Q-feature of interrogative C). The device is introduced to extend the general theory of movement beyond A-movement, but should raise warning flags.

9   On some assumptions, though not here, IFM passing through [Spec, v_2] is improper movement.

References

Chomsky, N. 1995. Categories and transformations. In Chomsky (1995), *The Minimalist Program*, Cambridge, MA: MIT Press, pp. 219–394.

Fox, D. 1998. *Economy and semantic interpretation*. Doctoral dissertation, MIT. [Published by MIT Press and MITWPL, Cambridge, MA, 2000.]

Kidwai, A. 1996. Word order and focus positions in Universal Grammar. Ms., Jawaharlal Nehru University.

Lasnik, H. and M. Saito. 1992. *Move α*. Cambridge, MA: MIT Press.

Nissenbaum, J. W. 1998. Movement and derived predicates: Evidence from parasitic gaps. In U. Sauerland and O. Percus (eds.), *The interpretive tract. MIT Working Papers in Linguistics 25*, Cambridge, MA: MITWPL, pp. 247–95.

Rizzi, L. 1990. *Relativized minimality*. Cambridge, MA: MIT Press.

From "DERIVATION BY PHASE"
Noam Chomsky

The evidence reviewed in MI [Chomsky 2000] suggested that the phases are "propositional": verbal phrases with full argument structure and CP with force indicators, but not TP alone or "weak" verbal configurations lacking external arguments (passive, unaccusative). Assume that substantive categories are selected by functional categories: V by a light verb, T by C. If so, phases are CP and $v*$P, and a subarray contains exactly one C or $v*$.

The choice of phases has independent support: these are reconstruction sites, and they have a degree of phonetic independence (as already noted for CP vs. TP). The same is true of vP constructions generally, not just $v*$P.[1] If these too are phases, then PF and LF integrity correlate more generally.

Suppose, then, we take CP and vP to be phases. Nonetheless, there remains an important distinction between CP/$v*$P phases and others; call the former *strong* phases and the latter *weak*. The strong phases are potential targets for movement; C and $v*$ may have an Extended Projection Principle (EPP)-feature, which provides a position for XP-movement, and the observation can be generalized to head movement of the kind relevant here.[2]

The special role of strong phases becomes significant in the light of another suggestion of MI that I will adopt and extend here: cyclic Spell-Out, necessary for reasons already discussed, takes place at the strong phase level. The intuitive idea, to be sharpened, is that features deleted within the cyclic computation remain until the strong phase level, at which point the whole phase is "handed over" to the phonological component. The deleted features then disappear from the narrow syntax, allowing convergence at LF, but they may have phonetic effects.

Spell-Out seeks formal features that are uninterpretable but have been assigned values (checked); these are removed from the narrow syntax as the syntactic object is transferred to the phonology. The valued uninterpretable features can be detected with only limited inspection of the derivation if earlier stages of the cycle can be "forgotten" – in phase terms, if earlier phases need not be inspected. The computational burden is further reduced if the phonological component too can "forget" earlier stages of derivation. These results follow from the Phase Impenetrability Condition (PIC), for strong phase HP with head H,

(1)   The domain of H is not accessible to operations outside HP; only H and its *edge* are accessible to such operations.

the *edge* being the residue outside of H′, either specifiers (Specs) or elements adjoined to HP.

H and its edge are accessible only up to the next strong phase, under the PIC: in (2), elements of HP are accessible to operations within the smallest strong ZP phase but not beyond.

(2) $[_{ZP}$ Z . . . $[_{HP}$ α [H YP]]]

Local head movement and successive-cyclic A- and Ā-movement are allowed, and both Spell-Out and the phonological component can proceed without checking back to earlier stages. The simplest assumption is that the phonological component spells out elements that undergo no further displacement – the heads of chains – with no need for further specification.[3]

In effect, H and its edge α in (2) belong to ZP for the purposes of Spell-Out, under the PIC. YP is spelled out at the level HP. H and α are spelled out if they remain in situ. Otherwise, their status is determined in the same way at the next strong phase ZP. The question arises only for the edge α, assuming that excorporation is disallowed.

The picture improves further if interpretation/evaluation takes place uniformly at the next higher phase, with Spell-Out just a special case. Assuming so, we adopt the guiding principle (3) for phases Ph_i.

(3) Ph_1 is interpreted/evaluated at the next relevant phase Ph_2.

What are the relevant phases? As noted, because of the availability of EPP, the effects of Spell-Out are determined at the next higher *strong* phase: CP or v^*P. For the same reason, a strong-phase HP allows extraction to its outer edge, so the domain of H can be assumed to be inaccessible to extraction under the PIC: an element to be extracted can be raised to the edge, and the operations of the phonological component can apply to the domain at once, not waiting for the next phase. Keeping to the optimal assumption that all operations are subject to the same conditions, we restate (3) as (4), where Ph_1 is strong and Ph_2 is the next highest strong phase.

(4) Ph_1 is interpreted/evaluated at Ph_2.

On similar grounds, the PIC should fall under (4). We therefore restate the PIC as (5), for (2) with ZP the smallest strong phase.

(5)   The domain of H is not accessible to operations at ZP; only H and its edge are accessible to such operations.

We can henceforth restrict attention to phases that are relevant under (4), that is, the strong phases. For the same reason, we restrict attention to v^* rather than light verb v generally, unless otherwise indicated.

Considerations of semantic-phonetic integrity, and the systematic consquences of phase identification, suggest that the general typology should include among phases nominal categories, perhaps other substantive categories. If categorial features are eliminated from roots, then a plausible typology might be that phases are configurations of the form F-XP, where XP is a substantive root projection, its category determined by the functional element F that selects it. CP falls into place as well if T is taken to be a substantive root, as discussed earlier. Phases are then (close to) functionally headed XPs. Like TP, NP cannot be extracted, stranding its functional head. The same should be true of other nonphases.[4] Some phases are strong and others weak – with or without the EPP option, respectively, hence relevant or not for Spell–Out and the general principle (4).[5]

Let us return to (2), repeated as (6) (HP and ZP strong).

(6) $[_{ZP} Z \ldots [_{HP} \alpha [H\ YP]]]$

Suppose that the computation L, operating cyclically, has completed HP and moves on to a stage Σ beyond HP. L can access the edge α and the head H of HP. But the PIC now introduces an important distinction between $\Sigma = ZP$ and Σ within ZP, for example, $\Sigma = TP$. The probe T can access an element of the domain YP of HP; the PIC imposes no restriction on this. But with $\Sigma = ZP$ (so that $Z = C$), the probe Z cannot access the domain YP.[6]

If Z is C in (6), then its complement TP is immune to extraction to a strong phase beyond CP, and only the edge or head of HP (a strong-phase CP or v*P) is accessible for extraction to Z. The same holds for $Z = v$*, and the observations extend to Agree. But T in the domain of Z can agree with an element within its complement, for example, with the in-situ quirky nominative object of its v*P complement.[7]

Notes

1   See Legate (1998) and, for the broader picture with regard to reconstruction in such cases, Fox (2000).

2   Namely, head movement involving inflectional categories: to C, or to T (hence to a position between the vP and CP phases). We will return to the status of head movement.

3   The idea that the phonological component can choose which element of a chain to spell out has been investigated since Groat and O'Neil (1996). Any such approach requires either new UG principles or language-specific rules to determine how the choice is made.

4   For VP, testable only with a nonaffixal light verb. One might consider treating preposition stranding within the same context.

5   Head movement aside; see note 4. For conclusions about next-higher-phase evaluation drawn from the theory of control, see Landau (1999).

6   It is accessibility of the domain of weak phases at Σ, under (4), that permits the extension of phases to weak phases, yielding the preferred result of relative phonetic-semantic integrity of phases, an extension barred in MI.

7   The consequences include some barrier/Relativized Minimality–type phenomena (Empty Category Principle, Subjacency, and Head Movement Constraint effects). They extend partially to Huang's (1982) Condition on Extraction Domain if phases include DPs, as just suggested. For A-movement, (i) is not obviated; thus, the PIC prevents access to an inactive subject of CP from the next strong phase, but not from a higher T with no intervening strong phase (as in *T be believed [that John is intelligent], with Agree (T, John) barred by (i) but not the PIC).

(i)   Goal as well as probe must be active for Agree to apply.

For Ā-movement, questions arise of the kind mentioned earlier, along with others, among them the issue of Slavic-style multiple wh-movement violating Subjacency.

References

Chomsky, N. 2000. Minimalist inquiries: The framework. In R. Martin, D. Michaels and J. Uriagereka (eds.), *Step by step: Essays on minimalism in honor of Howard Lasnik*, Cambridge, MA: MIT Press, pp. 89–155.

Fox, D. 2000. *Economy and semantic interpretation*. Cambridge, MA: MIT Press.

Groat, E. and J. O'Neil. 1996. Spell-out at the LF interface. In W. Abraham, S. D. Epstein, H. Thráinsson and J.-W. Zwart (eds.), *Minimal ideas: Syntactic studies in the Minimalist framework*, Amsterdam: John Benjamins, pp. 113–39.

Huang, C.-T. J. 1982. *Logical relations in Chinese and the theory of grammar*. Doctoral dissertation, MIT.

Landau, I. 1999. *Elements of control*. Doctoral dissertation, MIT.

Legate, J. 1998. Verb phrase types and the notion of a phase. Ms., MIT. [Revised version published as "Some interface properties of the phase," *Linguistic Inquiry* 34: 506–16, 2003]

From *SUCCESSIVE CYCLICITY, ANTI-LOCALITY, AND ADPOSITION STRANDING*
Klaus Abels

The Stranding Generalization can be stated as in (1). What (1) says is that for a particular class of heads, the phase heads, some (modalized) general statement is true. The diamond symbol ($\lozenge$) is used here with its usual interpretation in modal logic. Thus a structure like (1a) is possibly acceptable, a structure like (1b) is never acceptable. The Stranding Generalization is a new generalization. Deriving and defending it is the main goal of this thesis.

(1)   *Stranding Generalization*
      Given a phase head $\alpha°$ and a constituent X in $\alpha°$'s c-command domain
      a. $\lozenge\checkmark[X \ldots [\alpha° [\ldots t_X \ldots]] \ldots]$ and
      b. $\neg\lozenge\checkmark[X \ldots [\alpha° t_X] \ldots]$

You can think of the phase heads in my system in a first approximation as the same heads that project a phase in Chomsky (2000). In other words $v°$ and $C°$ and maybe some others are 'phase heads'. The Stranding Generalization says that a phase head may – when all the right conditions come together, which often they don't – allow a constituent to move out of its c-command domain. That's (1a). But what a phase head will never – never ever! – allow to happen is for its own complement to escape and move away out from under it.[1] And that's (1b).

Let me illustrate with an example from Icelandic what I mean. The complementizer *að* in Icelandic allows extraction across it in principle (2a). Icelandic also has a process that topicalizes clauses. Thus a CP complement of a verb like *think* can be topicalized without any major problems (2b–2c). But the TP, which is embedded under the complementizer *að* cannot be so topicalized. This is shown in (2d), which is totally unacceptable.

(2)   Icelandic (Halldór Sigurðsson, p.c.)

    a.   ✓Hver heldur þú að hafi lesið þessa bók?
       who think you that has$_{SUBJ}$ read this book
       lit: 'Who do you think that has read this book?'

    b.   ✓Jón heldur að María sé að lesa.
       Jon thinks that Maria is$_{SUBJ}$ to read$_{INF}$
       'Jon thinks that Maria is reading.'

    c.   ?Að María sé að lesa heldur Jón.
       that Maria is$_{SUBJ}$ to read$_{INF}$ thinks Jon
       'That Maria is reading, John thinks.'

    d.   *María sé að lesa heldur Jón að.
       Maria is$_{SUBJ}$ to read$_{INF}$ believes Jon that

(3) a.   ✓What do you think that Mary has read?

    b.   ✓Nobody thought that anything would happen.

    c.   ✓That anything would happen, nobody thought.

    d.   *Anything would happen, nobody thought that.

    e.   *Who do you think that has read this book?

The same is also true in English. Extraction past the complementizer *that* is possible (3a), topicalization of a CP is allowed (3c), but similar topicalization of TP is not allowed (3d). But whereas English is subject to the that-trace effect (3e) which may rule out example (3d), Icelandic is not subject to the that-trace effect (Maling and Zaenen 1978) as (2a) illustrates. What rules out example (2d) is not the that-trace effect on any interpretation, but rather the second part of the Stranding Generalization (1b). Stranding of complementizers seems to be universally banned.

In chapter 3 I investigate v° and C° and spend a considerable effort to show that the Stranding Generalization is a surprising property of phase heads. It's surprising, because the complements of phase heads are in principle movable categories. It's the phase head above that immobilizes them!

In chapter 4 I pursue Emonds' (1985) idea that prepositions and complementizers are really the same thing, or at least almost, or at least the same kind of thing: phase heads. I claim that the ban against adposition-stranding, operative in most languages, is really just an instance of the Stranding Generalization. [. . .]

[. . .] When a phase head allows movement across it as in (1a), the moving phrase must make a stop-over in the specifier projected by the phase head. If it is true that all phase heads require this stop-over and obey the Stranding Generalization, then we would surely want to know why.

The answer is given in chapter 2, which provides the theoretical lineage of the Stranding Generalization. [. . .] Assume a condition, call it Last Resort, that says that movement is allowed only if there is a good reason for doing it – and the only thing that counts as a good reason is if you immediately establish of a new feature satisfaction (or 'checking') relation. [. . .] So Last Resort is a local economy condition in the sense of Collins (1997). I claim that this categorically rules out movement of the complement of some head to the specifier of that very same head.

The reason for this is that the Head-Complement Relation is the closest relation two things can be in syntax. All features can be satisfied (or 'checked') in that relation. But if movement needs to give rise to some new feature satisfaction immediately, then there can never be any reason to move a phrase from the complement to the specifier position of the same head. This is really a corollary of Last Resort and some assumptions about what it means to 'establish a feature satisfaction relation', i.e. feature checking, but I call it the Anti-locality Constraint (4) anyway. The Anti-locality Constraint is totally general. It applies to all heads and their complements and is not limited to phase heads.

(4)   *Anti-locality Constraint*

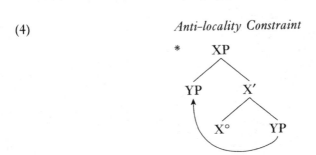

But let's apply the Anti-locality Constraint to phase heads now. Movement out of the domain of a phase head requires movement through the specifier of that phase head. If you wanna get out, you absolutely must go through the specifier position. But since complements can never get to the specifier position in the phrase where they are complements, the complement of a phase head is frozen in place. *Voilà*, the Stranding Generalization: The complement of a phase head can never get out, because it cannot reach the specifier position, but that is an absolute requirement. The Stranding Generalization now is a corollary of the Last Resort Condition, some assumptions about feature satisfaction ('checking'), and the funky property of phase heads that movement must pass through the specifier position they project.

But now come on already, why should phase heads have this funky property? [. . .] One answer is that phase heads simply have this property – period. Chomsky (2000) calls that the Phase Impenetrability Condition. But we want to do better, don't we? So the idea is that movement through the specifier of a phase head is enforced by general considerations of Locality. Here's the idea in a nutshell: nobody of the higher ups can see you (and if they can't see you, hell, they can't attract you!) if you are c-commanded by a phase head.

Note

1   Since theses require footnotes, I will acknowledge that the last sentence was inspired by Jackendoff (1973) – in its form, not in its content.

References

Chomsky, N. 2000. Minimalist inquiries: The framework. In R. Martin, D. Michaels and J. Uriagereka (eds.), *Step by step: Essays on minimalism in honor of Howard Lasnik*, Cambridge, MA: MIT Press, pp. 89–155.

Collins, C. 1997. *Local economy*. Cambridge, MA: MIT Press.

Emonds, J. 1985. *A unified theory of syntactic categories*. Dordrecht: Foris.

Jackendoff, R. 1973. The base rules for prepositional phrases. In S. R. Anderson and P. Kiparsky (eds.), *A Festschrift for Morris Halle*, New York: Holt, Rinehart, and Winston, pp. 345–56.

Maling, J. and A. Zaenen. 1978. The nonuniversality of a surface filter. *Linguistic Inquiry* 9: 475–97.

3

Structure Building and Lexical Insertion

3.1 Bare Phrase Structure

From "CATEGORIES AND TRANSFORMATIONS"
Noam Chomsky

4.3 Phrase structure theory in a minimalist framework

The development of X-bar theory in the 1960s was an early stage in the effort to resolve the tension between explanatory and descriptive adequacy. A first step was to separate the lexicon from the computations, thus removing a serious redundancy between lexical properties and phrase structure rules and allowing the latter to be reduced to the simplest (context-free) form. X-bar theory sought to eliminate such rules altogether, leaving only the general X-bar-theoretic format of UG [Universal Grammar]. The primary problem in subsequent work was to determine that format, but it was assumed that phrase structure rules themselves should be eliminable, if we understood enough about the matter – which, needless to say, we never do, so (unsurprisingly) many open questions remain, including some that are quite central to language.[1]

In earlier papers on economy and minimalism ([Chomsky 1995: chs. 1–3]). X-bar theory is presupposed, with specific stipulated properties. Let us now subject these assumptions to critical analysis, asking what the theory of phrase structure should look like on minimalist assumptions and what the consequences are for the theory of movement.

At the LF interface, it must be possible to access a lexical item LI and its nonphonological properties LF(LI): the semantic properties and the formal properties that are interpreted there. Accordingly, LI and LF(LI) should be available for C_{HL}, on the natural minimalist assumption, discussed earlier, that bare output conditions determine the items that are "visible" for computations. In addition, C_{HL} can access the formal features FF(LI), by definition. It is also apparent that some larger units constructed of lexical items are accessed, along with their types: noun phrases and verb phrases interpreted, but differently, in terms of their type, and so on. Of the larger units, it seems that only maximal projections are relevant to LF interpretation. Assuming so,[2] bare output conditions make the concepts "minimal and maximal projection" available to C_{HL}. But C_{HL} should be able to access no other projections.

Given the inclusiveness condition, minimal and maximal projections are not identified by any special marking, so they must be determined from the structure in which they appear; I follow Muysken (1982) in taking these to be relational properties of categories, not properties inherent to them. There are no such entities as XP (X^{max}) or X^{min} in the structures formed by C_{HL}, though I continue to use the informal notations for expository purposes, along with X' (X-bar) for any other category. A category that does not project any further is a maximal projection XP, and one that is not a projection at all is a minimal projection X^{min}; any other is an X', invisible at the interface and for computation.[3] As we proceed, I will qualify the conclusion somewhat for X^0 categories, which have a very special role.

A further goal is to show that computation keeps to local relations of α to terminal head. All principles of UG should be formulated in these terms – which have to be made precise – and only such relations should be relevant at the interface for the modules that operate there.[4]

Given the numeration N, C_{HL} may select an item from N (reducing its index) or perform some permitted operation on the syntactic objects already formed. As discussed earlier, one such operation is necessary on conceptual grounds alone: an operation that forms larger units out of those already constructed, the operation Merge. Applied to two objects α and β, Merge forms the new object K, eliminating α and β. What is K? K must be constituted somehow from the two items α and β; the only other possibilities are that K is fixed for all pairs (α, β) or that it is randomly selected, neither worth considering. The simplest object constructed from α and β is the set {α, β}, so we take K to involve at least this set, where α and β are the *constituents* of K. Does that suffice? Output conditions dictate otherwise; thus, verbal and nominal elements are interpreted differently at LF and behave differently in the phonological component. K must therefore at least (and we assume at most) be of the form {γ, {α, β}}, where γ identifies the type to which K belongs, indicating its relevant properties. Call γ the *label* of K.

For the moment, then, the syntactic objects we are considering are of the following types:

(1) a. lexical items
     b. K = {γ, {α, β}}, where α, β are objects and γ is the label of K

Objects of type (1a) are complexes of features, listed in the lexicon. The recursive step is (1b). Suppose a derivation has reached state $\Sigma = \{\alpha, \beta, \delta_i, \ldots, \delta_n\}$. Then application of an operation that forms K as in (1b) converts Σ to $\Sigma' = \{K, \delta_i, \ldots, \delta_n\}$. including K but not α, β. In a convergent derivation, iteration of operations of C_{HL} maps the initial numeration N to a single syntactic object at LF.

We assume further that the label of K is determined derivationally (fixed once and for all as K is formed), rather than being derived representationally at some later stage of the derivation (say, LF). This is, of course, not a logical necessity; Martian could be different. Rather, it is an assumption about how *human* language works, one that fits well with the general thesis that the computational processes are strictly derivational, guided by output conditions only in that the properties available for computational purposes are those interpreted at the interface. The proper question in this case is whether the assumption (along with the more general perspective) is empirically correct, not whether it is logically necessary; of course it is not.

Suppose that the label for $\{\alpha, \beta\}$ happens to be determined uniquely for α, β in language L, meaning that only one choice yields an admissible convergent derivation. We would then want to deduce that fact from properties of α, β L – or, if it is true for α, β in language generally, from properties of the language faculty. Similarly, if the label is uniquely determined for arbitrary α, β L, or other cases. To the extent that such unique determination is possible, categories are representable in the more restricted form $\{\alpha, \beta\}$, with the label uniquely determined. I will suggest below that labels are uniquely determined for categories formed by the operation Move α, leaving the question open for Merge, and indicating labels throughout for clarity of exposition, even if they are determined.

The label γ must be constructed from the two constituents α and β. Suppose these are lexical items, each a set of features.[5] Then the simplest assumption would be that γ is either

(2) a.   the intersection of α and β
     b.   the union of α and β
     c.   one or the other of α, β

The options (2a) and (2b) are immediately excluded: the intersection of α, β will generally be irrelevant to output conditions, often null; and the union will be not only irrelevant but "contradictory" if α, β differ in value for some feature, the normal case. We are left with (2c): the label γ is either α or β; one or the other *projects* and is the *head* of K. If α projects, then K = $\{\alpha, \{\alpha, \beta\}\}$.

For expository convenience, we can depict a constructed object of type (1b) as a more complex configuration involving additional elements such as nodes, bars, primes, XP, subscripts and other indices, and so on. Thus, we might represent K = $\{\alpha, \{\alpha, \beta\}\}$ informally as (3) (assuming no order), where the diagram is constructed from nodes paired with labels and pairs of such labeled nodes, and labels are distinguished by subscripts.

(3)

This, however, is informal notation only: empirical evidence would be required to postulate the additional elements that enter note (3) beyond lexical features, and the extra sets. I know of no such evidence and will therefore keep to the minimalist assumption that phrase structure representation is "bare," excluding anything beyond lexical features and objects constructed from them as in (1) and (2c), with some minor emendations as we move toward a still more principled account.

The terms *complement* and *specifier* can be defined in the usual way, in terms of the syntactic object K. The head–complement relation is the "most local" relation of an XP to a terminal head Y, all other relations within YP being head–specifier (apart from adjunction, to which we turn directly). In principle, there might be a series of specifiers, a possibility with many consequences to which we return. The principles of UG, we assume, crucially involve these local relations.

Further projections satisfy (2c), for the same reasons. Any such category we will refer to as a *projection* of the head from which it ultimately projects, restricting the term *head* to terminal elements drawn from the lexicon, and taking complement and specifier to be relations to a head.

To review notations, we understand a *terminal element* LI to be an item selected from the numeration, with no parts (other than features) relevant to C_{HL}. A category X^{min} is a terminal element, with no categorial parts. We restrict the term *head* to terminal elements. An X^0 (zero-level) category is a head or a category formed by adjunction to the head X, which projects. The head of the projection K is H(K). If H = H(K) and K is maximal, then K = HP. We are also commonly interested in the maximal zero-level projection of the head H (say, the T head of TP with V and perhaps more adjoined). We refer to this object as H^{0max}.

If constituents α, β of K have been formed in the course of computation, one of the two must project – say, α. At the LF interface, maximal K is interpreted as a phrase of the type α (e.g. as a nominal phrase if H(K) is nominal); and it behaves in the same manner in the course of computation. It is natural, then, to take the label of K to be not α itself but rather H(K), a decision that also leads to technical simplification. Assuming so, we take K = {H(K), {α, β}}, where H(K) is the head of α and its label as well, in the cases so far discussed. We will keep to the assumption that the head determines the label, though not always through strict identity.

The operation Merge(α, β) is asymmetric, projecting either α or β, the head of the object that projects becoming the label of the complex formed. If α projects, we can refer to it as the *target* of the operation, borrowing the notion from the theory of movement in the obvious way. There is no such thing as a non-branching projection. In particular, there is no way to project from a lexical item α a subelement H(α) consisting of the category of α and whatever else enters into further computation, H(α) being the actual "head" and α the lexical element itself; nor can such "partial projections" be constructed from larger elements. We thus dispense with such structures as (4a) with the usual interpretation: *the*, *book* taken to be terminal lexical items and D+ , N+ standing for whatever properties of these items are relevant to further computation (perhaps the categorial information D, N; Case; etc.). In place of (4a) we have only (4b).

(4)

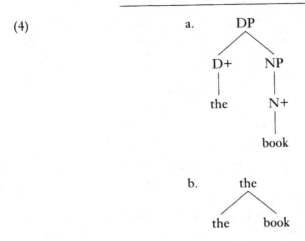

Standard X-bar theory is thus largely eliminated in favor of bare essentials.

Suppose that we have the structure represented informally as (5), with x, y, z, w terminals.

(5)

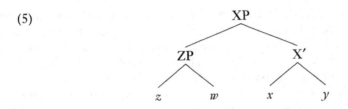

Here ZP = $\{z, \{z, w\}\}$, X′ = $\{x, \{x, y\}\}$, XP = $\{x, \{ZP, X′\}\}$; more accurately, the tree with ZP as root corresponds to $\{z, \{z, w\}\}$, and so on, the labels of the roots having no status, unlike standard phrase markers. Note that w and y are both minimal and maximal; z and x are minimal only.

The functioning elements in (5) are at most the configurations corresponding to (the trees rooted at) the nodes of the informal representation: that is, the lexical terminals z, w, x, y; the intermediate element X′ and its sister ZP; and the root element XP. Represented formally, the corresponding elements are z, w, x, y; $\{x, \{x, y\}\} = P$ and its sister $\{z, \{z, w\}\} = Q$; and the root element $\{x, \{P, Q\}\}$. These alone can be functioning elements; call them the *terms* of XP. More explicitly, for any structure K,

(6) a.   K is a term of K.
     b.   If L is a term of K, then the members of the members of L are terms of K.

For the case of substitution, terms correspond to nodes of the informal representations, where each node is understood to stand for the subtree of which it is the root.[6]

In (5) x is the head of the construction, y its complement, and ZP its specifier. Thus, (5) could be, say, the structure VP with the head *saw*, the complement *it*, and the specifier *the man* with the label *the*, as in (7).

(7)
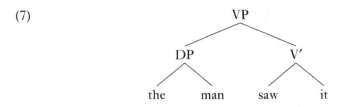

Here V′ = VP = *saw*, and DP = *the*.

Note that this very spare system fails to distinguish unaccusatives from unergatives, a distinction that seems necessary. The simplest solution to the problem would be to adopt the proposal of Hale and Keyser (1993) that unergatives are transitives; I will assume so.

We assumed earlier that Merge applies at the root only. In the bare system, it is easy to see why this is expected. Suppose that the derivation has reached stage Σ, with objects α and β. Then Merge may eliminate α and β from Σ in favor of the new object K = $\{\gamma, \{\alpha, \beta\}\}$, with label γ. That is the simplest kind of merger. We might ask whether C_{HL} also permits a more complex operation: given α and β, select K within β (or within α; it is immaterial) and construct the new object $\{\gamma, \{\alpha, K\}\}$, which replaces K within β. That would be an application of Merge that embeds α within some construction β already formed. Any such complication (which could be quite serious) would require strong empirical motivation. I know of none, and therefore assume that there is no such operation. Merge always applies in the simplest possible form: at the root.

The situation is different for Move. [. . .]

To complete the minimalist account of phrase structure, we have to answer several questions about adjunction. Let us keep to the simplest (presumably only) case: adjunction of α to β, forming a two-segment category.

That adjunction and substitution both exist is not uncontroversial; thus, Lasnik and Saito (1992) reject the former while Kayne (1993) largely rejects the latter, (virtually) assimilating specifiers and adjuncts (see Chomsky 1994). Nevertheless, I will assume here that the distinction is real: that specifiers are distinct in properties from adjuncts, and A- from Ā-positions (a related though not identical distinction).

Substitution forms L = $\{H(K), \{\alpha, K\}\}$, where H(K) is the head (= the label) of the projected element K. But adjunction forms a different object. In this case L is a two-segment category, not a new category. Therefore, there must be an object constructed from K but with a label distinct from its head H(K). One minimal choice is the ordered pair $\langle H(K), H(K)\rangle$. We thus take L = $\{\langle H(K), H(K)\rangle,$ $\{\alpha, K\}\}$. Note that $\langle H(K), H(K)\rangle$, the label of L, is not a term of the structure formed. It is not *identical* to the head of K, as before, though it is constructed from it in a trivial way. Adjunction differs from substitution, then, only in that it forms a two-segment category rather than a new category. Along these lines, the usual properties of segments versus categories, adjuncts versus specifiers, are readily formulated.

Suppose that α adjoins to K and the target K projects. Then the resulting structure is L = {⟨H(K), H(K)⟩, {α, K}}, which replaces K within the structure Σ containing K: Σ itself, if adjunction is at the root. Recall that it is the *head* that projects; the head either *is* the label *or*, under adjunction, determines it trivially.

We thus have the outlines of a "bare phrase structure" theory that derives fairly strictly from natural minimalist principles. The bare theory departs from conventional assumptions in several respects: in particular, categories are elementary constructions from properties of lexical items, satisfying the inclusiveness condition; there are no bar levels and no distinction between lexical items and "heads" projected from them (see (4)). A consequence is that an item can be both an X^0 and an XP. Does this cause problems? Are there examples that illustrate this possibility? I see no particular problems, and one case comes to mind as a possible illustration: clitics. Under the DP hypothesis, clitics are Ds. Assume further that a clitic raises from its θ-position and attaches to an inflectional head. In its θ-position, the clitic is an XP; attachment to a head requires that it be an X^0 (on fairly standard assumptions). Furthermore, the movement violates the Head Movement Constraint (HMC),[7] indicating again that it is an XP, raising by XP-adjunction until the final step of X^0-adjunction. Clitics appear to share XP and X^0 properties, as we would expect on minimalist assumptions.

If the reasoning sketched so far is correct, phrase structure theory is essentially "given" on grounds of virtual conceptual necessity in the sense indicated earlier. The structures stipulated in earlier versions are either missing or reformulated in elementary terms satisfying minimalist conditions, with no objects beyond lexical features. Stipulated conventions are derived. Substitution and adjunction are straightforward. At least one goal of the Minimalist Program seems to be within reach: phrase structure theory can be eliminated entirely, it seems, on the basis of the most elementary assumptions. If so, at least this aspect of human language is "perfect" (but see note 1).

Notes

1   For example, we still have no good phrase structure theory for such simple matters as attributive adjectives, relative clauses, and adjuncts of many different types.

2   The exact force of this assumption depends on properties of phrases that are still unclear. [. . .]

3   See Fukui (1986), Speas (1986), Oishi (1990), and Freidin (1992), among others. From a representational point of view, there is something odd about a category that is present but invisible; but from a derivational perspective, as Sam Epstein observes, the result is quite natural, these objects being "fossils" that were maximal (hence visible) at an earlier stage of derivation, targeted by the operation that renders them invisible.

4   In present terms, selection of complement CM by head H is a head–head relation between H and the head H_{CM} of CM, or the reflex of adjunction of H_{CM} to H; and chain links are reflexes of movement. Further questions arise about binding theory and other systems. Optimally, these too should reduce to local relations (see Chomsky 1986: 175 f.), a topic of much important work in recent years.

5   Nothing essential changes if a lexical entry is a more complex construction from features.

6   As pointed out by Chris Collins, a technical question arises if heads are understood as sets $\{\alpha_i\}$, where each element is again a set; then the members of α_i will be terms, as the notion is defined – an unwanted result, though it is unclear that it matters. We can leave the issue unresolved, pending some answer to questions left open about the nature of lexical items.

7   Assuming that the HMC is a valid principle, which is not obvious. We will return to this question.

References

Chomsky, N. 1986. *Knowledge of language: Its nature, origin, and use*. New York: Praeger.

Chomsky, N. 1994. *Bare phrase structure. MIT Occasional Papers in Linguistics 5*. Cambridge, MA: MITWPL. [Published in P. Kempchinsky (ed.) (1994), *Evolution and revolution in linguistic theory: Essays in honor of Carlos Otero*, Washington, DC: Georgetown University Press, pp. 51–109. Also published in G. Webelhuth (ed.) (1994), *Government and binding theory and the minimalist program*, Cambridge, MA: MIT Press, pp. 383–439.]

Chomsky, N. 1995. *The Minimalist Program*. Cambridge, MA: MIT Press.

Freidin, R. 1992. *Foundations of generative syntax*. Cambridge, MA: MIT Press.

Fukui, N. 1986. *A theory of category projection and its applications*. Doctoral dissertation, MIT. [Revised version published as *Theory of projection in syntax*, Stanford: CSLI/Tokyo: Kuroshio, 1995.]

Hale, K. and S. J. Keyser. 1993. On argument structure and the lexical expression of grammatical relations. In K. Hale and S. J. Keyser (eds.), *The view from Building 20: Essays in linguistics in honor of Sylvain Bromberger*, Cambridge, MA: MIT Press, pp. 53–109.

Kayne, R. 1993. The antisymmetry of syntax. Ms., CYNY Graduate Center. [Published as *The antisymmetry of syntax*, Cambridge, MA: MIT Press, 1994.]

Lasnik, H. and M. Saito. 1992. *Move α*. Cambridge, MA: MIT Press.

Muysken, P. 1982. Parameterizing the notion "head." *Journal of Linguistic Research* 2: 57–75.

Oishi, M. 1990. Conceptual problems of upward X-bar theory. Ms., Tohoku Gakuin University.

Speas, M. 1986. *Adjunction and projection in syntax*. Doctoral dissertation, MIT.

From "BEYOND EXPLANATORY ADEQUACY"
Noam Chomsky

In standard terminology, the first element merged to a head is its complement, later ones its specifiers (Spec). In the best case, there should be no further restrictions on Merge; in particular, no stipulation on the number of Specs, as in X-bar theories. There are further reasons to be skeptical about such stipulations. Typically, they are redundant; the limitations on Merge follow from selectional and other conditions that are independent. If empirical arguments are offered in support of restrictions on Merge, one must be careful to ensure that they do not follow from these independent considerations. It is sometimes supposed that stipulated restrictions have a conceptual advantage in that they reduce the number of possible configurations, but that is a dubious argument. Suppose we have a head

H and three elements K, L, M to be successively merged to it. Free Merge yields the syntactic object $SO_1 = \{M, \{L, \{H, K\}\}\}$ (L, M Specs of H). Stipulation that Merge can apply only twice yields $SO_2 = \{M, \{H', \{L, \{H, K\}\}\}\}$ (L the Spec of H, M the Spec of a new head H'). Stipulation that Merge can apply only once yields $SO_3 = \{M, \{H'', \{L, \{H', \{H, K\}\}\}\}\}$, with two new heads H' and H''. Each more restrictive stipulation reduces the types of possible configurations (under some interpretations), but there is no clear sense in which requiring SO_3 is preferable to SO_2 or either is preferable to SO_1; if anything, the opposite would appear to be the case. Empirical arguments might be offered to show that H' and H'' really exist, but if so, no restriction of Multiple Merge is necessary.

3.2   Numeration and the Merge-over-Move Preference

From "MINIMALIST INQUIRIES: THE FRAMEWORK"
Noam Chomsky

Is it also possible to reduce access to Lex [the lexicon], the second component of the domain of L? The obvious proposal is that derivations make a one-time selection of a *lexical array* LA from Lex,[1] then map LA to expressions, dispensing with further access to Lex. That simplifies computation far more than the preceding steps. If the derivation accesses the lexicon at every point, it must carry along this huge beast, rather like cars that constantly have to replenish their fuel supply.[2] Derivations that map LA to expressions require lexical access only once, thus reducing operative complexity in a way that might well matter for optimal design.

[. . .]

First, what operations enter into this component of C_{HL}? One is indispensable in some form for any language-like system: the operation *Merge*, which takes two syntactic objects (α, β) and forms K(α, β) from them. A second is an operation we can call *Agree*, which establishes a relation (agreement, Case checking) between an LI [lexical item] α and a feature F in some restricted search space (its *domain*). Unlike Merge, this operation is language-specific, never built into special-purpose symbolic systems and apparently without significant analogue elsewhere. We are therefore led to speculate that it relates to the design conditions for human language. A third operation is *Move*, combining Merge and Agree. The operation Move establishes agreement between α and F and merges P(F) to αP, where P(F) is a phrase determined by F (perhaps but not necessarily its maximal projection) and αP is a projection headed by α. P(F) becomes the specifier (Spec) of α ([Spec, α]). Let us refer to Move of P to [Spec, ϕ] as *A-movement*, where ϕ is an agreement feature (ϕ-feature); other cases of Move are $\bar{\text{A}}$-movement.

Plainly Move is more complex than its subcomponents Merge and Agree, or even the combination of the two, since it involves the extra step of determining P(F) (generalized "pied-piping"). Good design conditions would lead us to expect that simpler operations are preferred to more complex ones, so that Merge or Agree (or their combination) preempts Move, which is a "last resort," chosen when nothing else is possible. Preference for Agree over Move yields much of the empirical basis for Procrastinate and has other consequences, as do the other preferences.

[. . .]

The examples in (2)/(3) contrast with those in (1).

(1) a. *there is likely [$_\alpha$ a proof to be discovered]
     b. *I expected [$_\alpha$ t to be a proof discovered]
     c.   I expected [$_\alpha$ a proof to be discovered]
(2) a. T$_\beta$-is likely [$_\alpha$ there to be a proof discovered]
     b. T$_\beta$ [$_{vP}$ I expected [$_\alpha$ there to be a proof discovered]]
(3) a. there is likely to be a proof discovered
     b. I expected there to be a proof discovered

Suppose the derivation has reached reached the stage (4)

(4) [T$_\alpha$ [be a proof discovered]]

The EPP [Extended Projection Principle] requires that something occupy [Spec, T$_\alpha$]. Two options are available: merge *there* or move *a proof*. Preference of Merge over Move selects the former. Accordingly, (2a)/(3a) is permitted and (1a) is barred. But Merge of an argument in [Spec, T$_\alpha$] violates the θ-theoretic condition that Pure Merge in θ-position is required of (and restricted to) arguments. Therefore, (1b) is barred.

[. . .]

Suppose we select LA as before; after selection of LA from the lexicon, the computation need no longer access the lexicon. Suppose further that at each stage of the derivation a subset LA$_i$ is extracted, placed in active memory (the "workspace"), and submitted to the procedure L. When LA$_i$ is exhausted, the computation may proceed if possible; or it may return to LA and extract LA$_j$, proceeding as before. The process continues until it terminates. Operative complexity in some natural sense is reduced, with each stage of the derivation accessing only part of LA. If the subarray in active memory does not contain Expl, then Move can take place in the corresponding stage; if it does, Merge of Expl preempts Move.[3]

Notes

1 Or, if we distinguish independent selections of a single lexical item, a numeration Num (as in Chomsky 1995), an extension I will put aside until it becomes relevant.
2 It would not suffice to say that constant memory can be accessed throughout the derivation. The lexicon is a distinct component of memory; for C$_{HL}$, our beliefs about the stars don't matter, but the lexical properties of *star* do. However hard it may be to make the distinction properly, there is good reason to believe that it is real.

3   Why not dispense with LA, just selecting subarrays cyclically? Apart from the general considerations about access reduction already discussed, there is a more specific reason: chain properties can be reduced in significant part to identity if lexical arrays are enriched to numerations. To achieve the same result with cyclic choice of successive subarrays requires continual access to the full lexicon and memory of how many times each item has been selected.

Reference

Chomsky, N. 1995. Categories and transformations. In Chomsky (1995), *The Minimalist Program*, Cambridge, MA: MIT Press, pp. 219–394.

3.3   Cycle

From *MOVEMENT IN LANGUAGE: INTERACTIONS AND ARCHITECTURES**
Norvin Richards

Chomsky (1995) suggests that we derive cyclicity by assuming something like the following principle:

(1)   A strong feature must be checked as soon as possible after being introduced into the derivation.

Together with the assumptions that (a) Merge always expands the tree and (b) overt movement can only take place in response to a strong feature, this principle derives cyclicity in a pleasingly minimalist way. Consider the derivations in (2, 3). Both (2) and (3) involve a ZP with specifier AP and complement BP, to which are added the heads Y° and X°, both of which bear a strong feature which might in principle attract either AP or BP:

(2)   a.

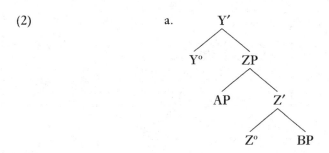

*The theory developed here was independently developed in Mulders (1996, 1997), and I would like to thank Iris Mulders for much helpful discussion of the issues in this chapter.

b.

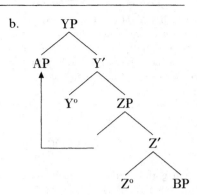

c.

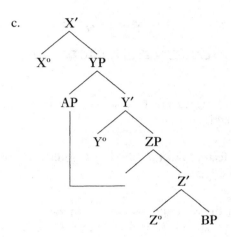

d.

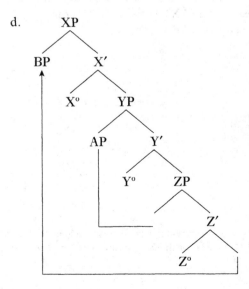

(2) is a derivation that obeys Cyclicity. As each of the heads X° and Y° is introduced into the structure, the strong feature that the head bears is checked immediately, as (1) requires.

(3)   a.

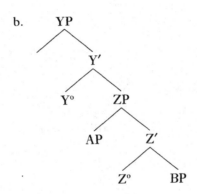

                       b.

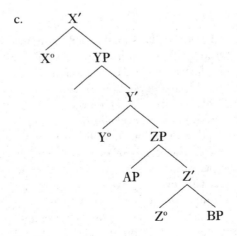

                       c.

d.
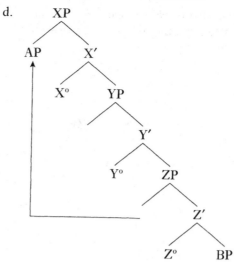

e.
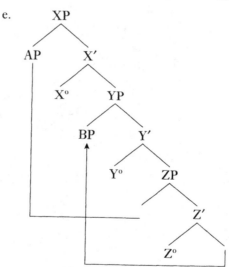

In (3), by contrast, Cyclicity is disobeyed, as BP moves to Spec YP after XP has already been projected (in step (e)). The principle in (1) correctly distinguishes between the two derivations. In the well-formed derivation in (2), the strong features introduced in the heads Y^o and X^o are checked off in the steps immediately after the features are introduced, as (1) requires. In (3), on the other hand, the strong feature introduced in Y^o in step (a) is not checked off until step (e). Cyclicity thus correctly rules out the derivation. As Kitahara (1994, 1997) observes, Cyclicity, along with Shortest Move, yields the effects of Pesetsky's (1982) Path Containment Condition: intersecting paths are forced to nest, rather than cross, as we have seen.

This way of deriving cyclicity avoids problems raised by head-movement for Chomsky's (1993) definition of cyclicity. Chomsky suggested that all operations must necessarily expand the tree. This requirement successfully distinguishes between the derivations in (2, 3), but it is always violated by head-movement, which apparently never expands the tree. The definition of cyclicity in terms of strong features, on the other hand, can be satisfied by head-movement, as long as the head-movement is checking a strong feature.

The two versions of cyclicity might also make different predictions in cases of movement to multiple specifiers of a single head. Suppose a head is generated with two strong features[1] and attracts two XPs, as in (4):

(4)   a.

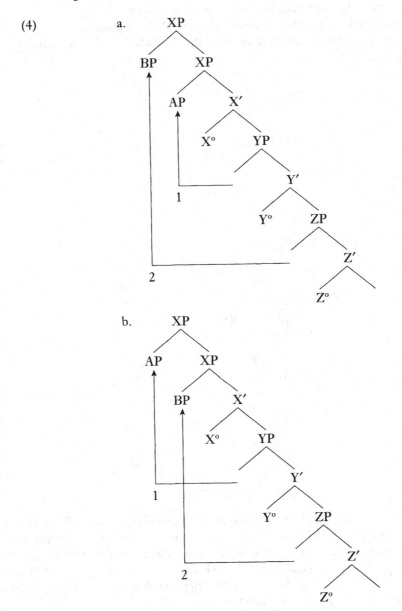

In (4a) the two specifiers are treated just like specifiers of two separate heads; the landing-site of the first movement is a specifier which is lower than the landing site of the second movement. In (4b), on the other hand, the two paths cross, and the second move lands closer to the head than the first move. Chomsky's (1993) derivation of cyclicity from a requirement that every operation expand the tree would rule out the derivation in (4b); the second move here does not expand the tree. Chomsky's (1995) version of cyclicity, on the other hand, fails to distinguish between the two derivations. As long as both XPs are moving to check a strong feature, either derivation ought in principle to be possible.[2]

In fact, depending on what version of Shortest Move we assume, we might expect the derivation in (4b) to be preferred over that in (4a). Consider the derivation in (4b) again, step by step:

(5)

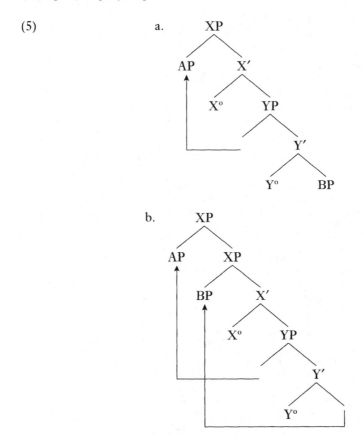

In (5a), we first move AP into a specifier of XP. In (5b), we move BP, and must decide where to move it to; does it go to a specifier outside AP, or one inside AP? Featural cyclicity, as we have seen, allows both options. On the other hand, if the specifier inside the one containing AP is closer, in the relevant sense, to the base position of BP than is the one outside AP, then Shortest Move will require us to move to the lower specifier, as shown in (5a).

A feature-based notion of cyclicity, then, along with a certain conception of Shortest Move, predicts that multiple specifiers of a single head will be treated

very differently from specifiers of multiple heads. Paths to such specifiers ought
to cross, rather than nesting, thus maintaining the base c-command relations (and,
in principle, the base order) among XPs which move to them. In this chapter I
will argue that this is a correct result; paths to multiple specifiers of a single head
do indeed cross, all other things being equal.

1   Multiple wh-movement

Suppose we consider the case of multiple wh-movement, one case in which movement to multiple specifiers is arguably involved. Multiple wh-movement is subject
in some languages to a restriction on the order of movement; the highest wh-word
must be moved first:

(6)   a.   Who __ bought what?

      b.   *What did who buy __?

This is plausibly viewed as an effect of Shortest Attract; the C° which attracts the
wh-words prefers to attract *who* rather than *what*, since *who* moves a shorter distance. Movement of *what* must then follow anyway, but on the assumption that
the grammar cannot look ahead in the derivation, this is irrelevant to the choice
of which wh-word to move first.

   In certain other languages, Superiority phenomena seem to take on a rather different form. Our standard assumptions seem to make precisely the wrong predictions
for wh-movement in certain multiple overt wh-movement languages. As we saw in
the last chapter, Rudin (1988) shows that such languages can be divided into two groups:
those which impose no ordering on multiple fronted wh-words (Serbo-Croatian,
Polish), and those which do (Bulgarian, Romanian). For those languages which do
impose such an ordering, the order essentially preserves the base c-command order:

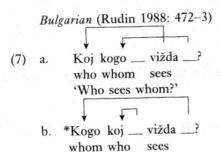

Bulgarian (Rudin 1988: 472–3)

(7)   a.   Koj kogo __ vižda __?
           who whom   sees
           'Who sees whom?'

      b.   *Kogo koj __ vižda __?
            whom who   sees

Here we must apparently give up one of our standard assumptions. If we wish to
maintain the idea that movement always expands the tree, creating a specifier
higher than all the existing structure, we must apparently conclude here that a kind
of "Anti-Superiority" is at work; the lower of the two wh-words (*kogo* 'whom' in

(7a)) must move first. Another possibility, of course, would be to say that the order of wh-movements in this case is just as in English; *koj* 'who' moves first, followed by movement of *kogo* 'what' to a lower specifier. On this account, the paths of these multiply fronted wh-words must obligatorily cross, rather than nest.

Notes

1   Or, equivalently, with a single strong feature that can be checked multiple times; I will not have anything to say about possible differences between these two approaches.
2   The case of movement to multiple specifiers raises another potential question about this version of Cyclicity. Assuming that the two movements are not simultaneous, how can a derivation in which two strong features are introduced at the same time satisfy Cyclicity at all? Whichever feature is checked first, the other feature must presumably "wait" for the first feature-checking operation to take place before it can itself be checked. One can imagine a number of ways out of this problem, which I will not try to discuss here: one would be to understand the requirement that strong features be checked "immediately" as meaning that they must be checked "as soon as possible"; in particular, before any operations which do not check strong features are performed. Another approach, following Chomsky (1995: 234 ff.), would be to state the condition on strong features as one which cancels the derivation if at any point a strong feature is present on a head which is not the head of the structure in which it is contained.

References

Chomsky, N. 1993. A minimalist program for linguistic theory. In K. Hale and S. J. Keyser (eds.), *The view from Building 20: Essays in linguistics in honor of Sylvain Bromberger*, Cambridge, MA: MIT Press, pp. 1–52. [Reprinted in Chomsky (1995), *The Minimalist Program*, Cambridge, MA: MIT Press, pp. 167–217.]

Chomsky, N. 1995. Categories and transformations. In Chomsky (1995), *The Minimalist Program*, Cambridge, MA: MIT Press, pp. 219–394.

Kitahara, H. 1994. *Target α: A unified theory of movement and structure building*. Doctoral dissertation, Harvard University.

Kitahara, H. 1997. *Elementary operations and optimal derivations*. Cambridge, MA: MIT Press.

Mulders, I. 1996. Multiple checking and mirrored specifiers: The structure of CP. MA thesis, Utrecht University.

Mulders, I. 1997. Mirrored specifiers. In H. de Hoop and J. Coerts (eds.), *Linguistics in the Netherlands 1997*, Amsterdam: John Benjamins, pp. 135–46.

Pesetsky, D. 1982. *Paths and categories*. Doctoral dissertation, MIT.

Rudin, C. 1988. On multiple questions and multiple WH fronting. *Natural Language and Linguistic Theory* 6: 445–501.

From "MINIMALIST INQUIRIES: THE FRAMEWORK"
Noam Chomsky

It follows that derivations meet the condition (1).

(1)   Properties of the probe/selector α must be satisfied before new elements of the lexical subarray are accessed to drive further operations.

If the properties of α are not satisfied, the derivation crashes because α can no longer be accessed.

[...]

The new object K formed by Merge of β to α retains the label L of α, which projects. There are two reasonable possibilities, illustrating the ambiguity of cyclicity mentioned earlier:

(2)   a.   α is unchanged.
       b.   β is as close to L as possible.

Suppose we have the LI H with selectional feature F, and XP satisfying F. Then first Merge yields α = {XP, H}, with label H. Suppose we proceed to second Merge, merging β to α. In this case β is either extracted from XP (Move) or is a distinct syntactic object (pure Merge). There are two possible outcomes, depending on choice of K in (2).

(3)   a.   {β, {XP, H}} (as in (2a))
       b.   {XP, {β, H}} (as in (2b))

In tree notation the equivalents are (4a,b), respectively.

(4)

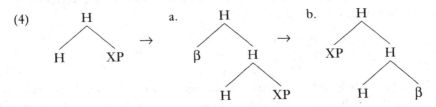

The desired outcome is (4a), not (4b); that has always been assumed without discussion. Thus, if H = T, XP = VP, and β is either an expletive merged to TP or a DP raised from XP, the result of Merge would be (5a), with β the Spec of T and VP remaining its complement, not (5b), with β becoming the complement of T and VP its Spec.

(5)   a.   [_T β [T VP]]
       b.   [_T VP [T β]]

But the reasons are not entirely obvious. Each outcome satisfies a reasonable condition: (5a) satisfies the familiar *Extension Condition* (2a); (5b) satisfies the condition of *Local Merge* (2b).

One possibility is to stipulate that the Extension Condition always holds: operations preserve existing structure. Weaker assumptions suffice to bar (4b) but still allow Local Merge under other conditions. Suppose that operations do not tamper with the basic relations involving the label that projects: the relations provided by Merge and composition, the relevant ones here being sisterhood and c-command.[1] Derivations then observe the condition (6), a kind of economy condition, where R is a relevant basic relation.

(6)   Given a choice of operations applying to α and projecting its label L, select one that preserves R(L, γ).

In the case of (3)–(4) the principle (6) selects (a) over (b). Basic relations of H are preserved in (a), but not in (b), which modifies sisterhood and c-command for H (in fact, the category α = {XP, H} disappears altogether).

    One case permitted under (6) but barred by strict adherence to the Extension Condition is head adjunction. The standard assumption is that in this case Local Merge takes precedence over the Extension Condition. Thus, in (3)–(4), (b) is chosen over (a) for β a head H′. Adherence to the Extension Condition would change the status of H′ to an XP; V-raising to T, for example, would create a VP-TP structure, with VP the Spec of T, contrary to intention. The uniformity condition for chains (Chomsky 1995: sec. 4.1, (17)) bars that choice, leaving as the only option head adjunction yielding (b), in violation of the Extension Condition. (6) is satisfied vacuously.[2] Head adjunction thus provides some reason to weaken the Extension Condition as proposed, permitting Local Merge if (6) is satisfied.

    For XP-merger, (6) eliminates the ambiguity of choice of K for second Merge, imposing the Extension Condition (2a) rather than Local Merge (2b). But the choice remains open for third Merge. Suppose we have the outcome (a) of (3)–(4), as required, and now merge γ to it (either by pure Merge, or with γ extracted from XP). The two possible outcomes are (7a) (satisfying the Extension Condition) or (7b) (satisfying Local Merge).

(7)   a.   {γ, {β, {XP, H}}}
       b.   {β, {γ, {XP, H}}}

In (7a) the newly merged phrase γ is the outer Spec; in (7b) it is the inner Spec. Either way, sisterhood and c-command are preserved for H, satisfying condition (6). The discussion so far has kept to the Extension Condition (2a). The question becomes more intricate when we cast a wider net, another issue deferred here.[3]

Notes

1   New containment relations are defined whichever choice we make, in incommensurable ways; identity is irrelevant.
2   Whether sisterhood (hence c-command) is preserved depends on how (or if) the notion is defined for head adjunction.
3   See Richards (1997) for evidence in support of Local Merge in the important case of multiple Move. The proposal there falls under Local Merge, with the Extension Condition obviated vacuously for "postcyclic" QR.

References

Chomsky, N. 1995. *The Minimalist Program.* Cambridge, MA: MIT Press.
Richards, N. 1997. *What moves where when in which language?* Doctoral dissertation, MIT. [Revised version published as *Movement in language*, Oxford/New York: Oxford University Press, 2001.]

3.4   Covert Lexical Insertion

From "LF MOVEMENT AND THE MINIMALIST PROGRAM"
Željko Bošković

Huang (1982) argues that LF movement is less constrained than overt movement. In particular, he argues that subjacency constrains overt movement but not LF movement. Evidence for his claim is provided by the contrasts in (1) under his assumption that wh-phrases that are located in situ at SS undergo LF wh-movement.

(1)   a.   ??What does John wonder whether Peter bought?
      b.   Who wonders whether Peter bought what?
      c.   ?*What did you see the woman that bought?
      d.   Who saw the woman that bought what?

Tsai (1994) and Reinhart (1995) propose an alternative analysis of (1a–d) that does not require stipulating a difference between LF and overt movement with respect to locality restrictions on movement. Essentially following work by Higginbotham (1983, 1985), where N is generated with an index-argument that must be bound, they argue that wh-NPs have an open position and therefore can introduce variables in situ. As a result, they can be unselectively bound by C.[1] Under their analysis *what* in (1b) and (1d) does not have to undergo LF movement. Subjacency is then trivially satisfied. They furthermore argue that wh-adverbs do not have an open position and therefore cannot introduce variables in situ.[2] As a result, wh-adverbs cannot be unselectively bound, hence still need to undergo LF wh-movement. This is supposed to account for the ungrammaticality of constructions such as (2a–c), which are under traditional assumptions ruled out via the ECP.[3]

(2)   a.   *Who wonders whether Peter left why?
      b.   *Who saw the woman that left why?
      C.   *Who left why?

In this paper I will show that there are constructions in which wh-NPs in situ must undergo LF wh-movement in spite of the possibility of unselective binding. I will use such constructions to investigate locality restrictions on LF wh-movement. While I will argue, along with Huang and contra Tsai and Reinhart, that there is a difference between LF and overt movement with respect to locality restrictions on movement, the conclusion I reach is very different from Huang's. In particular, I will argue that LF movement is more local than overt movement. I will show that this state of affairs can be accounted for by adopting Chomsky's (1995) Move F Hypothesis.

1   French wh-in-situ constructions

I will start by examining French wh-in-situ, in particular, the paradigm in (3–5).[4]

(3)　a.　Tu as　vu　qui?
　　　　you have seen whom
　　　　'Who did you see?'

　　　b.　Qui as-tu vu?

(4)　a.　Pierre a demandé qui　tu as　vu.
　　　　Pierre has asked　　　whom you have seen

　　　b.　*Pierre a demandé tu as vu qui.

(5)　a.　Qui　que tu as　vu?
　　　　whom C　you have seen
　　　　'Who did you see?'

　　　b.　*Que tu as vu qui?

In Bošković (1996c) I show that the above paradigm can be accounted for rather straightforwardly in the Minimalist system. I will briefly summarize here the necessary mechanisms from Chomsky (1995).

Chomsky argues that Merge, which includes lexical insertion, must expand the tree, i.e. it cannot take place in embedded positions. Merger generally takes place in overt syntax. This follows without stipulation. Thus, if an NP such as *John* is inserted in LF the derivation crashes because LF cannot interpret the phonological features of *John*. If, on the other hand, *John* is inserted in PF. PF will not know how to interpret the semantic features of *John*. The only way to derive a legitimate PF and a legitimate LF is for *John* to be inserted before the level of SS is reached. PF will then strip off the phonological features of *John* and the semantic features of *John* will proceed into LF. This line of reasoning allows lexical insertion to take place in PF and LF under certain conditions. To be more precise, it allows PF insertion of semantically null elements and LF insertion of phonologically null elements. We are interested in this second possibility here.

The last mechanism relevant to the account of the paradigm in (3) is the notion of *strength*. Chomsky (1995) offers a derivational definition of strength, where strong features are defined as elements that cannot be tolerated by the derivation and therefore must be eliminated through checking from the structure immediately upon insertion. In Chomsky's words: "A strong feature . . . triggers a rule that eliminates it: [strength] is associated with a pair of operations, one that introduces it into the derivation . . . a second that (quickly) eliminates it" (p. 233).[5] Under this view, insertion of an element with a strong feature F must be immediately followed by an operation that checks F.

In this system, it is possible to insert even an element with a strong feature in LF as long as the element is phonologically null, the insertion takes place at the top of the tree, and the strong feature is checked immediately upon insertion. In Bošković (1996c) I argue that this is exactly what happens in French wh-in-situ constructions. I argue that C with a strong +wh-feature is inserted in the LF of (3a). Wh-movement then does not take place in (3a) overtly for a trivial reason: its trigger is not present overtly. The LF insertion of the strong +wh C triggers LF wh-movement, which checks the strong +wh-feature of C. In (4b) the LF C-insertion derivation fails because it involves merger in an embedded position, and in (5b) because the complementizer is not phonologically null. In (3b), (4a), and

(5a) the strong +wh C is inserted overtly, which triggers overt wh-movement given that strong features must be checked immediately upon insertion.[6]

Notice now that, in contrast to English (1b,d), unselective binding is not an option for the wh-phrase in situ in French (3a), because it would leave the strong +wh-feature of C unchecked. In (1b,d), the strong +wh-feature of C, which is standardly assumed to be the trigger for wh-movement, is checked in overt syntax, which is not the case in (3a). As a result, LF C-insertion of the complementizer must be followed by wh-movement of the wh-phrase in situ. French wh-in-situ constructions thus provide us with a tool for investigating locality restrictions on LF wh-movement.

1.1 Questioning out of finite and negative clauses in French

In Bošković (1996c) I show that French in situ questions have a very limited distribution. For example, long-distance in situ questions are unacceptable in French even when the interrogative complementizer is null and located at the top of the tree. According to my informants, (6a) is good only on the irrelevant echo question reading. Recall now that French in situ questions such as (3a) or (6a) involve LF insertion of a strong +wh-complementizer followed by wh-movement motivated by checking the strong +wh-feature of the complementizer. Given this, the contrast between (3a) and (6a) should be interpreted as indicating that French LF wh-movement is clause-bounded. Significantly, this is not true of overt wh-movement in French, As (6b) shows, overt wh-movement in French is not clause-bounded.

(6) a. *Jean et   Pierre croient que Marie a   vu   qui?
         Jean and Pierre believe that Marie has seen whom
         'Whom do Jean and Pierre believe that Marie saw?'
     b. Qui Jean et Pierre croient-ils que Marie a vu?

A similar contrast between overt and LF wh-movement is found with long-distance questioning out of interrogative clauses. (7b), involving overt wh-movement, is somewhat degraded; it has the status of a subjacency violation. (7a), however, is even worse on the true question reading, on which *qui* is interpreted in the matrix SpecCP. This derivation must involve LF wh-movement, given the above discussion.[7]

(7) a. *Jean et   Marie se demandent si Pierre aime qui?
         Jean and Marie wonder   if Pierre loves whom
         'Whom do Jean and Marie wonder if Peter loves?'
     b. ?Qui Jean et Marie se demandent-ils si Pierre aime?

The contrasts in (6–7) lead me to conclude that LF wh-movement is actually more local than overt wh-movement. This is confirmed by the contrast in (8), also noted in Bošković (1996c). (8a–b) show that wh-movement can take place across negation in overt syntax, but not in covert syntax. We thus have another context with respect to which LF wh-movement is more local than overt wh-movement.

(8) a.   ?*Jean ne mange pas quoi?
          Jean neg eats   neg what
          'What doesn't John eat?'
     b.   Que ne mange-t-il pas?

Notice also that there is independent evidence that LF wh-movement is responsible for the ungrammaticality of negative and long-distance in situ questions in
French.[8] Consider (9).[9]

(9) a.   Qui croit   que Marie a   vu qui?
          who believes that Marie has seen whom
     b.   Qui ne mange pas quoi?
          who neg eats   neg what

(9a–b) are acceptable on the true question, pair-list reading. They crucially differ
from (6a) and (8a), which are degraded on the true question reading, in that they
contain another wh-phrase that is located overtly in the interrogative SpecCP. This
wh-phrase can check the strong +wh-feature of C, so that there is no need for the
wh-phrase in situ to move in LF. The wh-phrase in situ can then be unselectively
bound. In (6a) and (8a), on the other hand, the wh-phrase in situ is the only
element that can check the strong +wh-feature of C and, is therefore, forced to
undergo LF wh-movement. Unselective binding by C is not an option in these
constructions, since it would leave the strong +wh-feature of C unchecked. (The
wh-phrase would never enter the checking domain of the C.) The contrasts under
consideration indicate that movement to SpecCP is driven by an inadequacy of
the interrogative C, as suggested by Chomsky (1995). When this inadequacy is taken
care of, as in (9a,b), the wh-phrase in situ does not have to move in LF. When
the inadequacy of C is not taken care of ((6a) and (8a)), the wh-phrase must move
in LF. Given that the wh-phrase in situ needs to undergo LF wh-movement in
(6a, 8a) but not in (9a,b) it seems plausible to attribute the ungrammaticality of
(6a) and (8a) to locality restrictions on movement. (8a) indicates that negation has
a blocking effect on LF wh-movement.[10] (6a) appears to indicate that C also has
a blocking effect on LF wh-movement. Another potential trouble maker here could
be the finiteness of the embedded clause. Certain facts concerning infinitival complementation in French, however, strongly indicate that finiteness is irrelevant and
that C indeed has a blocking effect on LF wh-movement.

1.2 Infinitival in situ questions

It is well-known that French differs from English in that it allows PRO even in propositional infinitivals. I will not be interested in this difference between English
and French here (for a recent minimalist account of the difference, see Bošković
1996a, 1997). What I will be interested in is Huot's (1981) observation that the infinitival complement of propositional verbs such as *croire* 'believe' cannot be dislocated.
In this respect *croire* differs from, for example, *vouloir* 'want', whose infinitival complement can be dislocated.

(10) a. Pierre croit   avoir   convaincu ses amis.
          Pierre believes to have convinced his friends
      b. (*)Avoir convaincu ses amis, Pierre le croit.
          'To have convinced his friends, Pierre believes it'
(11) a. Il a   toujours voulu   revenir   mourir en France.
          he has always   wanted to return to die in France
      b. Revenir mourir en France, il l'a toujours voulu.
          'To return to die in France, he has always wanted it'

In Bošković (1996a, 1997) I showed that the paradigm in (10–11) can be accounted for if the infinitival complement of *croire* is a CP, and that of *vouloir* an IP.
The ungrammaticality of (10b), and the contrast between (10a) and (10b), is reminiscent of the following English constructions:

(12) a. Everyone believes (that) John likes Mary.
      b. *John likes Mary is believed by everyone.
      c. cf. That John likes Mary is believed by everyone.
      d. *John likes Mary Peter never believed.
      e. cf. That John likes Mary Peter never believed.

Stowell (1981) observes that it is not possible to passivize or topicalize complements headed by a null C in English. He argues that doing this results in violation of licensing requirements on the null complementizer (in particular, the ECP
[Empty Category Principle]). That the null C is indeed to blame for the ungrammaticality of (12b,d) is confirmed by the fact that the constructions become good
if we use the lexical complementizer *that* (cf. (12c,e)). Returning now to (10b),
we can account for Huot's observation concerning the dislocatability of the
infinitival complement of *croire* if the infinitival is a CP. The ungrammaticality
of (10b) then reduces to (12b,d). The grammaticality of (11b) should then be
interpreted as indicating that the infinitival complement of *vouloir* is an IP, which
is what I concluded in Bošković (1996a, 1997). The conclusions reached there,
however, need to be slightly modified. Whereas all my informants agree on the
acceptability of (11b), the status of (10b) is less clear: some of my informants accept,
and some reject, (10b). This suggests that there is a variation with respect to the
categorial status of the infinitival complement embedded under *croire* (and propositional verbs in general). For some speakers, the infinitival is a CP. For other
speakers, it is an IP (for an interesting discussion of this variation and its consequences, see Boeckx in preparation).
    Returning now to wh-in-situ, all the speakers I consulted allow long–distance
wh-in-situ questions with the infinitival embedded under *vouloir*, which uniformly
has IP status. As for the infinitival embedded under *croire*, the speakers for whom
the infinitival is a CP (i.e. the speakers who reject (10b)) do not accept (13a)
on the true, non-echo question reading. The speakers for whom the infinitival is
an IP (i.e. the speakers who accept (10b)), accept (13a) on the true question reading. This state of affairs strongly indicates that C has a blocking effect on LF
wh-movement, finiteness being irrelevant.

(13) a. (*)Tu crois   avoir   vu   qui?
          you believe to have seen whom
      b. Tu veux faire quoi aujourd'hui?
          you want to do what today

To summarize the discussion so far, I have shown that when we exclude the possibility of unselective binding of wh-NPs, we can see that, contrary to what is standardly assumed, LF movement is more local than overt movement. In particular, C and Neg block LF wh-movement even in the contexts in which they do not block overt wh-movement. V and INFL, on the other hand, do not block LF wh-movement, as indicated by the grammaticality of (3a).

2   German wh-adverbs in situ

This conclusion is confirmed by certain facts from German. It is well-known that constructions involving wh-adverbs in situ are unacceptable in English (14). They are, however, not universally unacceptable. Thus, it is well-known that such constructions are acceptable in German, as illustrated in (15a–b). I will not be interested here in what is responsible for this difference between German and English. For an account of this difference, the reader is referred to Bošković (1996c). I will put aside here English (14) and concentrate on German questions containing wh-adverbs in situ.

(14) *Who left why?
(15) a. Wer hat es wie repariert?   (Haider 1996)
          who has it how fixed
          'Who fixed it how?'
      b. Wer is warum gekommen?   (Müller and Sternefeld 1996)
          who is why   come
          'Who came why?'

Notice first that, given that, as argued by Tsai (1994) and Reinhart (1995), wh-adverbs cannot be unselectively bound due to the lack of an open position, wh-adverbs in situ will have to undergo LF wh-movement even in the constructions in which a wh-phrase is present in the interrogative SpecCP. Given the French data discussed above, we would then expect that, in contrast to short-distance questions such as (15), wh-adverbs will not be able to occur in long-distance in situ questions. The prediction is borne out.[11]

(16) a. *Wer hat gesagt daß Fritz warum ein Buch gelesen hat?
          who has said   that Fritz why   a   book read   has
          'Who has said that Fritz has read a book why?'
      b. *Wen   hast du empfohlen   daß man wie bestrafen soll?
          whom have you recommended that one how punish   should
          'Who have you recommended that one should punish how?'
          (Müller and Sternefeld 1996)

The contrast between (15) and (16) confirms that C has a blocking effect on LF wh-movement. Significantly, as shown in (17), in contrast to LF, adverbs can undergo long-distance wh-movement in overt syntax. The contrast between (17) and (16) confirms the conclusion reached above with respect to French wh-in-situ constructions that LF wh-movement is more local than overt wh-movement.[12]

(17) a. Warum hat Hans gesagt daß Fritz t ein Buch gelesen hat?
      b. Wie hast du empfohlen daß man t Hans bestrafen soll?

The data examined so far indicate that there is a difference between LF and overt movement with respect to locality, the former being more local than the latter. A question that arises now is whether this difference needs to be stipulated or whether it follows from independently motivated mechanisms of the grammar. In the next section I will show that the difference can be deduced given the Move F Hypothesis. Before doing that, I will make a brief digression to discuss the syntax of the *either* construction or, more precisely, the locality restrictions on *either*-movement, proposed by Larson (1985). I will show that *either*-movement exhibits the same locality restrictions as LF wh-movement, which will provide us with a clue where to look for an explanation for the locality effects with LF wh-movement. In what follows, for ease of exposition I will use relativized minimality and the A/A′ distinction. Following Rivero (1991) and Roberts (1992), I assume that relativized minimality applies to head as well as phrasal movement, the status of heads with respect to the A/A′ distinction being determined in the same way as the status of the corresponding specifiers (i.e. an A′-Spec implies an A′-head, and an A-Spec implies an A-head). It is my belief that any fully successful way of deriving the effects of relativized minimality and the A/A′ distinction from independently motivated principles of the grammar will extend to the cases discussed below.[13]

3 Either-movement

Consider the following constructions:

(18) a. John likes either football or chess.
      b. Either John likes football or chess.

Larson (1985) argues that (18a) and (18b) have the same structure at some point. In particular, he argues that (18b) is generated with the same structure as (18a) after which *either* undergoes overt movement (for scopal reasons) to an A′-position.

(19) Either$_i$ John likes t$_i$ football or chess.

I will adopt here Larson's analysis with a slight modification. Whereas Larson assumes that the movement in question can be either XP or head movement, I assume that the movement in question is uniformly head movement. Following

Larson, I assume that we are dealing here with A′-movement.[14] Since the only heads
either-movement crosses in (19) are A-heads (V and INFL), relativized minimality
is then obeyed in (19). This analysis enables us to straightforwardly capture a number
of facts concerning the distribution of *either*. Consider the following constructions. (Most of the relevant restrictions on the distribution of *either* are noted in
Larson 1985.)

(20) a.   Peter believes that John likes either football or chess.
     b.   *Either$_i$ Peter believes that John likes t$_i$ football or chess.
(21) a.   John wanted to play either football or chess.
     b.   Either$_i$ John wanted to play t$_i$ football or chess.
(22) a.   John wanted for Mary to play either football or chess.
     b.   ?*Either$_i$ John wanted for Mary to play t$_i$ football or chess.
(23) a.   John does not like either football or chess.
     b.   ?*Either$_i$ John does not like t$_i$ football or chess.

(20b) is ruled via relativized minimality: *either* undergoes A′-head movement across
another A′-head, namely C. The problem does not arise in (21b) given that, as
argued extensively in Bošković (1996b, 1997), English control infinitivals are IPs.
The only heads *either* crosses in (21b) are the A-heads V and INFL, just as in
(19). (22b), on the other hand, is ruled out for the same reason as (20b), *either* again
crosses C, an A′-head.[15] Finally, (23b) can also be ruled out via relativized minimality: *either* undergoes A′-head movement across an A′-head, this time negation.
The relativized minimality head movement analysis thus straightforwardly captures the locality effects on *either*-movement.

Returning now to French wh-in-situ constructions, notice that LF wh-movement
in French exhibits the same locality restrictions as *either*-movement. Like *either*-
movement, LF wh-movement in French is blocked by C and negation, but not
by V and INFL. This strongly indicates that a uniform account for the movements in question is in order. Chomsky's (1995) Move Hypothesis makes such an
account possible.

Chomsky (1995) observes that a natural consequence of the standard minimalist assumption that movement is driven by feature checking is that, all else
being equal, the operation Move should apply to features and not to syntactic
categories. Overt movement, which feeds PF, still has to apply to whole categories,
given the natural assumption that lexical items with scattered features cannot
be interpreted/pronounced at PF. Since the considerations of PF interpretability
are not relevant to LF, in LF the operation Move should apply only to features.
Chomsky instantiates this feature movement as adjunction to X^0-elements. He argues
that in LF formal features move to heads bearing matching features. Under a
natural interpretation of this analysis, all LF movement necessarily involves
head movement. Given this, LF wh-movement involves movement to C, and not
to SpecCP. In other words, it is movement to an A′-head position, just like
either-movement. It is then no surprise that it is subject to the same locality restrictions as *either*-movement. The analysis of locality restrictions on *either*-movement
given above straightforwardly extends to LF wh-movement: being movement to

an A′-head position (C), it is blocked by A′-heads C and Neg, but not by A-heads V and INFL.[16]

4 Quantifier raising

The analysis can be extended in an interesting way to other putative instances of LF movement. For example, it enables us to finally explain the mysterious (almost) clause boundedness of quantifier raising (QR). The clause boundedness of QR has always been an embarrassment for QR analyses, since it required positing different locality restrictions for QR and what was believed to be LF wh-movement. In the current system, however, QR displays the same locality constraints as LF wh-movement. Consider (24–25):

(24) a. Someone believes that John hates everyone.
      b. Someone believes John to hate everyone.
(25) a. Someone wants for John to hate everyone.
      b. Someone wants to hate everyone.

Although QR is traditionally considered to be clause-bounded it has often been noted that certain infinitival clauses allow quantifiers to scope out of them more easily than finite clauses. Thus, it appears that it is easier for the embedded clause quantifier to take wide scope with respect to the matrix quantifier in (24b) than in (24a). (25a) and (25b) also contrast in the relevant respect, the wide scope reading of the embedded clause quantifier being much more salient in (25b) than in (25a).[17] These facts can be straightforwardly explained given that, as argued in Bošković (1996b, 1997), English ECM and control infinitivals are IPs. (24–25) then simply indicate that C, but not V and INFL, have a blocking effect on QR. QR then behaves in the same way as LF wh-movement in the relevant respect. The analysis of locality restrictions on LF wh-movement proposed above can be readily extended to account for the almost clause boundedness of QR, given the standard assumption that QR is A′-movement. (Being an LF operation, it would also have to involve Move F.)

Another similarity between QR and LF wh-movement is that negation has a blocking effect on both. Aoun and Li (1993) note that, in contrast to (26a), the direct object quantifier cannot take wide scope in (26b). Assuming that in order to take wide scope in (26b), the direct object must QR past negation, the unavailability of the reading in question reduces to the ungrammaticality of French (8a). The analysis of (8a) proposed above straightforwardly extends to (26b).

(26) a. Someone likes everyone.
      b. Someone does not like everyone.

The most interesting parallelism between Q-scope and wh-in-situ concerns French *croire*-class infinitivals. Recall that there is a variation with respect to the categorial status of such infinitivals. For some speakers such infinitivals are IPs, and for other speakers they are CPs. (The relevant test is the possibility of dislocation of the infinitivals in question, see section 1.2.). Significantly, among my informants, the lower quantifier in (27) can have wide scope in the IP dialect, but not in the CP dialect.

(27)   Quelqu'un croit   avoir   aidé   chaque enfant.
            someone   believes to have helped each   child

Recall now that the same split obtains with respect to long-distance in situ questions with this type of infinitivals. Such questions are acceptable in the IP dialect, but not in the CP dialect (see section 1.2.). Notice finally that none of my informants allows a quantifier contained within a finite complement of *croire* to scope over a matrix quantifier. This further confirms the parallelism between QR and LF wh-movement since, as discussed in section 1.1., long-distance in situ questions are not possible with the finite complement of *croire*.[18]

(28)   Quelqu'un croit   que Jean a   aidé   chaque enfant.
            someone   believes that Jean has helped each   child

To summarize, we have seen in this section that the almost clause boundedness of QR and the blocking effect of negation on QR receive a principled account under the current analysis. What is particularly important is that QR is now brought in line with other instances of LF A'-movement, in particular, LF wh-movement. The locality of QR is the same as that of LF wh-movement, which eliminates one of the biggest obstacles for the QR analysis of quantifier scope interpretation. In fact, the discussion in this section can be interpreted as an argument in favor of QR. It is certainly possible to account for scopal interpretation and interaction of QNPs without movement. However, the algorithm for scope interpretation having to mimic locality restrictions on movement would be a strong indication that non-movement analyses of quantifier scope interaction are on the wrong track.[19]

5 Conclusion

I have argued in this paper based on a variety of constructions that LF movement is more local than overt movement. I have shown that there is no need to make any stipulations à la Huang (1982) to account for the difference between overt and covert movement. The difference follows in the Move F system. I have shown that LF movement exhibits locality restrictions of head movement, which can be captured given Move F.

Notes

1   In Reinhart's analysis wh-NPs are interpreted in situ via choice functions. (The function variable is bound by the question operator.)

2   Under Reinhart's analysis, the lack of the N variable with wh-adverbs ultimately leads to their inability to be interpreted in situ via choice functions.

3 While (2a,b) are more or less straightforward, accounting for the ungrammaticality of (2c) is actually rather tricky. For relevant discussion, see Bošković (1996c).

4 Note that overt C questions like (5a) are not acceptable in all dialects of French.

5 Chomsky formulates strength somewhat differently on p. 234: "Suppose that the derivation D has formed Σ containing α with a strong feature F. Then D is canceled if α is in a category not headed by α." I will not adopt this formulation here since, as noted in Lasnik (1997) and credited to Máire Noonan, the formulation has an undesirable consequence in that it does not force checking of strong features of elements that are not embedded (i.e. that are located at the top of the tree). To do that it is necessary to assume that strength must be removed for convergence, even if not embedded (see Chomsky 1995: 382, n. 16).

6 Notice that we cannot assume that the interrogative C in French is always inserted overtly but that its +wh-feature can be either strong or weak. If we were to do that we would not be able to ever enforce the +wh-movement option, which would leave the ungrammaticality of (4b) and (5b) (see also (6–8) below) unaccounted for. There are a number of interesting questions that the LF C-insertion analysis raises (e.g. why are both LF and overt C-insertion derivations in principle available in French, why is the LF C-insertion derivation blocked in English, etc.) that I cannot go into here due to space limitations. They are discussed in detail in Bošković (1996c).

7 Notice also that (i) is acceptable only as an embedded question. The direct object wh-phrase cannot take matrix scope in (i) on the true question, non-echo reading.

(i) Jean et Marie se demandent qui a   vu   qui?
     Jean and Marie wonder   who has seen whom

8 In what follows I take (6a) to be the representative of the latter class of questions.

9 Note that in the relevant respect French crucially differs from Iraqi Arabic, which never allows wh-phrases in situ within finite clauses (the counterparts of both (6a) and (9a) are bad in Iraqi Arabic; see Wahba 1991). As a result, Ouhalla's (1996) analysis of Iraqi Arabic that treats Iraqi Arabic wh-phrases as wh-anaphors, subject to Condition A (this is the reason why wh-phrases in Iraqi Arabic must *all* be close to their antecedent, +wh C), cannot be extended to French. Notice also that Ouhalla's analysis of Iraqi Arabic was prompted by a similarity in the morphological make-up of Iraqi Arabic wh-phrases and reflexive anaphors, which is not found in French.

   Note also that French is very different in the relevant respect from typical wh-in-situ languages such as Japanese, where both (6a) and (9a) are acceptable. The Japanese counterparts of unacceptable French constructions in (4–5) and (8) are also grammatical, which strongly indicates that French wh-in-situ is different from Japanese wh-in-situ. The LF insertion of a strong +wh C analysis is clearly inappropriate for Japanese. In Bošković (1996c), following Watanabe (1992) and Aoun and Li (1993), I argue that wh-in-situ languages like Japanese actually involve overt null operator movement to SpecCP, which makes such languages uninformative in investigations of locality restrictions on LF wh-movement.

10 Beck (1996) reaches the same conclusion with respect to German. However, her test gives an opposite result when applied to English and French. Beck's claim is based on the unacceptability of constructions such as (9b) in German. It does not carry over to English and French, where such constructions are acceptable. The German data Beck examines also lead her to conclude that all in situ wh-phrases move in LF (at least in German), a position I am arguing against here based on the French data under consideration. Wh-movement is driven by a formal inadequacy of the interrogative C. Once this inadequacy is taken care of, there is no need for LF wh-movement. (At least not with wh-NPs. See below for discussion of wh-adverbs.)

11 Müller and Sternefeld observe that, in contrast to wh-adverbs, wh-NPs can remain in situ in long-distance questions.

(i)   Wer hat gesagt daß Fritz was   lesen soll?
      who has said   that Fritz what read   should

This is expected given that, as argued by Tsai and Reinhart, wh-NPs can be unselectively bound and therefore do not need to move in LF.

12   I ignore here negative questions containing wh-adverbs since they are not informative in the relevant respect due to two interfering factors: (i) even constructions involving overt movement of wh-adverbs from a position below negation are bad due to Inner Islands effects (see Ross 1983 and Rizzi 1990). (ii) As shown in Beck (1996), constructions containing wh-phrases in situ within the scope of negation are quite generally unacceptable in German, regardless of whether we are dealing with wh-NPs or wh-adverbs.

13   Chomsky (1995) proposes one way of doing this based on feature-checking and the operation Attract. The analysis is, however, empirically problematic since it does not cover the full range of relativized minimality effects. In fact, the analysis fails to account even for the full range of Wh-Island effects, which are supposed to be its show-case. Under this analysis, the Wh-Island effect is captured by appealing to feature-checking instead of the A/A' distinction. Thus, (i) is ruled out because the matrix C, which needs to check its +wh-feature, fails to attract the closest +wh-feature bearing element (*where*).

(i)   ??Which book$_i$ do you wonder where$_j$ John put t$_i$ t$_j$?

This seems to leave (ii) unaccounted for.

(ii)   ??(Peter thinks that) That book$_i$ you wonder where$_j$ John put t$_i$ t$_j$.

It is not at all clear why an intervening +wh-feature should be relevant in the attraction of topics. A similar problem arises with respect to a number of other constructions, for example, relativization out of wh-islands (cf. *??The book that you wonder where John put* and *??The book, which you wonder where John put*) and *tough*-movement and *enough*-movement out of wh-islands (cf. *??This car is tough to ask Peter when to repair* and *??This car is old enough for us to wonder whether we should buy*). Notice that positing some kind of an operator feature that would be involved in the attraction here would not work, given Lasnik and Stowell's (1991) arguments that, in contrast to questions, appositive relatives, *tough*-movement, and *enough*-movement do not involve true operators (or variables for that matter). Under the operator feature attraction analysis we might also incorrectly predict that QNPs, which should bear the +op feature, will have a blocking effect on wh-movement (cf. *What did everyone buy*). Chomsky's (1995) system, which is based on Attract and in which feature-checking is intended to do the job of the A/A' distinction with respect to relativized minimality, thus fails to account for the full range of wh-island effects. Several other types of relativized minimality effects with A'-movement also remain unaccounted for in this system, for example, Rizzi's (1990) Pseudo-Opacity effects and Inner Island effects.

As shown in Takahashi (1994), in contrast to Attract, which considers movement from the point of view of the target, a conception of the Shortest Move Principle (SMP) that considers movement from the point of view of the moved element can readily accommodate the full range of relativized minimality effects. Takahashi shows that it can also accommodate the full range of Huang's (1982) CED phenomena and the Coordinate Structure Constraint, which remain mysterious under Attract. There thus may still be a need for the conception of the SMP that considers movement from the point of view of the moved element.

14   I will not be interested here in the question of exactly where *either* lands.

15   Throughout the paper I ignore superficial examples of ECM with *want*-class verbs (clauses containing a lexical infinitival subject without the complementizer *for*) since, due to the unclear

status of constructions that would provide the relevant tests, it is not quite clear whether such constructions involve true ECM (in which case the relevant infinitivals could be IPs) or Case-marking by a null complementizer within the infinitival, which would then have to be a CP. For relevant discussion, see Bach (1977), Bošković (1996b, 1997), Larson et al. (1997), Lasnik and Saito (1991), Martin (1996), Ormazabal (1995), Pesetsky (1992), and Postal (1974), among others.

16 It is worth noting here that Chomsky (MIT Lectures 1995) suggests that when X undergoes overt phrasal movement to SpecYP there are actually two movements involved: Move F first adjoins formal features of X to Y for feature checking and then the rest of X undergoes phrasal movement to SpecYP ('pied-piping') followed by a repair strategy that makes X pronounceable. Under this analysis, it is not possible to make LF movement more constrained than overt movement by appealing to Move F, which I attempt to do here based on the data under consideration. Therefore, if the discussion here is on the right track the two separate movements analysis cannot be correct: the decision to 'pied-pipe' must be made immediately so that only one *actual* movement takes place (XP moves to SpecYP), as originally suggested by Chomsky (MIT Lectures 1994) and Chomsky (1995). (Chomsky 1995 is somewhat ambivalent on this issue. However, he crucially assumes throughout chapter 4 that the checking configuration is Spec-head for overt syntax and FF (adjoined to head)-head for covert syntax, which goes against the spirit of the two movements analysis.)

It is also worth noting here that Chomsky (MIT Lectures 1997) develops a system that dispenses with the covert/overt syntax distinction, traditional LF movement being reanalyzed in this system as pure feature movement, i.e. Move F without category movement. As noted by Noam Chomsky (personal communication), the instances of LF movement discussed above are amenable to the same reanalysis.

17 Although the relevant contrasts seem pretty clear the wide scope reading is not straightforward (the most salient reading) even in (24b) and (25b). As pointed out by William Snyder (personal communication), one needs to be careful about the intonation of the relevant sentences. In particular, the wide scope reading of the embedded quantifier is more salient when both the matrix and the embedded quantifier are stressed. (Notice, however, that even under this intonational pattern, the relevant contrasts can be observed.)

18 See Déprez (1997) for additional data concerning QR in French, which can be readily accommodated under the current analysis.

19 The discussion in this section is necessarily very sketchy. I am glossing over a number of complexities involved in scopal phenomena that need to be carefully examined and accounted for before we can safely conclude that either QR or some of the non-movement approaches (or perhaps a mixture of the two) is the right way to handle scope. Probably the most serious issue that still remains to be resolved under the QR analysis concerns the motivation for QR. In the current system QR would have to be feature-driven. It is unclear what the relevant feature is. For some discussion, see Beghelli (1995) and Watanabe (1997).

References

Aoun, J. and Y.-H. A. Li. 1993. *Syntax of scope*. Cambridge, MA: MIT Press.

Bach, E. W. 1977. Review article *On raising: One rule of English grammar and its implications*. *Language* 53: 621–54.

Beck, S. 1996. Quantified structures as barriers for LF movement. *Natural Language Semantics* 4: 1–56.

Beghelli, F. 1955. *The phrase structure of quantifier scope*. University of California, Los Angeles.

Boeckx, C. In preparation. Raising(:) differences between French and English. ECM in French. Ms., University of Connecticut, Storrs.

Bošković, Ž. 1996a. Null Case and certain differences between French and English. In M. Przezdziecki and L. Whaley (eds.), *Proceedings of ESCOL '95*, pp. 13–24.

Bošković, Ž. 1996b. Selection and the categorial status of infinitival complements. *Natural Language and Linguistic Theory* 14: 269–304.

Bošković, Ž. 1996c. Sometimes in [Spec, CP], sometimes in-situ. [Published in R. Martin, D. Michaels and J. Uriagereka (eds.) (2000), *Step by step: Essays on minimalism in honor of Howard Lasnik*, Cambridge, MA: MIT Press, pp. 53–87.]

Bošković, Ž. 1997. *The syntax of nonfinite complementation: An economy approach*. Cambridge, MA: MIT Press.

Chomsky, N. 1995. Categories and transformations. In Chomsky (1995), *The Minimalist Program*, Cambridge, MA: MIT Press, pp. 219–394.

Déprez, V. 1997. Two types of negative concord. *Probus* 9: 103–43.

Haider, H. 1996. Towards a superior account of superiority. In U. Lutz and G. Muller (eds.), *Papers on wh-scope marking*, Stuttgart, Tübingen, and Heidelberg: Universität Stuttgart, Universität Tübingen, and IBM Deutschland GmbH, pp. 317–29.

Higginbotham, J. 1983. Logical form, binding, and nominals. *Linguistic Inquiry* 14: 395–420.

Higginbotham, J. 1985. On semantics. *Linguistic Inquiry* 16: 547–94.

Huang, C.-T. J. 1982. Logical relations in Chinese and the theory of grammar. Doctoral dissertation, MIT.

Huot, H. 1981. *Constructions infinitives du français: Le subordonnant* de. Genève: Librairie Droz.

Larson, K. R. 1985. On the syntax of disjunction scope. *Natural Language and Linguistic Theory* 3: 217–64.

Larson, K. R., M. den Dikken and P. Ludlow. 1997. Intensional transitive verbs and abstract clausal complementation. Ms., SUNY, Stony Brook and Vrije Universiteit Amsterdam.

Lasnik, H. 1997. On feature strength: Three minimalist approaches to overt movement. Ms., University of Connecticut, Storrs. [Published in *Linguistic Inquiry* 30: 197–217.]

Lasnik, H. 1999. On feature strength: Three minimalist approaches to overt movement. *Linguistic Inquiry* 30: 197–217.

Lasnik, H. and M. Saito. 1991. On the subject of infinitives. In L. Dobrin, L. Nichols and R. Rodriguez (eds.), *Papers from the 27th Regional Meeting of the Chicago Linguistics Society*, Chicago: Chicago Linguistics Society, pp. 324–43. [Reprinted in Lasnik (1999), *Minimalist Analysis*, Malden, MA/Oxford: Blackwell, pp. 7–24.]

Lasnik, H. and T. Stowell. 1991. Weakest crossover. *Linguistic Inquiry* 22: 687–720.

Martin, R. 1996. *A minimalist theory of PRO and control*. Doctoral dissertation, University of Connecticut, Storrs.

Müller, G. and W. Sternefeld. 1996. A′-chain formation and economy of derivation. *Linguistic Inquiry* 27: 480–511.

Ormazabal, J. 1995. *The syntax of complementation: On the connection between syntactic structures and selection*. Doctoral dissertation, University of Connecticut, Storrs.

Ouhalla, J. 1996. Remarks on the binding properties of *wh*-pronouns. *Linguistic Inquiry* 27: 676–707.

Pesetsky, D. 1992. Zero syntax, vol. 2. Ms., MIT.

Postal, P. M. 1974. *On raising: One rule of English grammar and its implication*. Cambridge, MA: MIT Press.

Reinhart, T. 1995. *Interface strategies. OTS Working Papers*. Research Institute for Language and Speech, Utrecht University.

Rivero, M.-L. 1991. Long head movement and negation: Serbo-Croatian vs. Slovak and Czech. *The Linguistic Review* 8: 319–51.

Rizzi, L. 1990. *Relativized minimality*. Cambridge, MA: MIT Press.

Roberts, I. 1992. *Verbs and diachronic syntax*. Dordrecht: Kluwer.

Ross, J. R. 1983. Inner islands. Ms., MIT.

Stowell, T. 1981. *Origins of phrase structure*. Doctoral dissertation, MIT.

Takahashi, D. 1994. *Minimality of movement*. Doctoral dissertation, University of Connecticut, Storrs.

Tsai, D. W.-T. 1994. *On economizing the theory of A-bar dependencies*. Doctoral dissertation, MIT.

Wahba, W. A.-F. B. 1991. LF movement in Iraqi Arabic. In C.-T. J. Huang and R. May (eds.), *Logical structure and linguistic structure*, Dordrecht: Kluwer, pp. 253–76.

Watanabe, A. 1992. Subjacency and S-structure movement of wh-in-situ. *Journal of East Asian Linguistics* 1: 255–91.

Watanabe, A. 1997. Absorption as feature checking. Ms., Kanda University of International Studies.

3.5   Eliminating Agr

From "CATEGORIES AND TRANSFORMATIONS"
Noam Chomsky

4.10.1   The status of Agr

Functional categories have a central place in the conception of language we are investigating, primarily because of their presumed role in feature checking, which is what drives Attract/Move. We have considered four functional categories: T, C, D, and Agr. The first three have Interpretable features, providing "instructions" at either or both interface levels. Agr does not; it consists of −Interpretable formal features only. We therefore have fairly direct evidence from interface relations about T, C, and D, but not Agr. Unlike the other functional categories, Agr is present only for theory-internal reasons. We should therefore look more closely at two questions.

(1)   a.   Where does Agr appear?
       b.   What is the feature constitution of Agr?

[Earlier] we tentatively assumed that Agr lacks φ-features, just as it (fairly clearly) lacks an independent Case-assigning feature, that being provided by the V or T that adjoins to it. If Agr indeed lacks φ-features as well, we would expect that the φ-features of a predicate Pred (verb or adjective) are added to Pred (optionally) as it is selected from the lexicon for the numeration. We had little warrant for the assumption about φ-features, and so far it has had little effect on the analysis. But it becomes relevant as we attempt more careful answers to the questions of (1). I will continue to assume that the original assumption was correct, returning to the question at the end, after having narrowed significantly the range of considerations relevant to it.

We have evidence bearing on question (1a) when Agr is strong, so that the position is phonetically indicated by the overt categories that raise to it: V and T by adjunction, DP by substitution in [Spec, Agr]. The richest example is an MSC [multiple subject construction] with object raising, as in the Icelandic TEC [transitive expletive construction] construction (2).

(2)   [$_{AgrP}$ there painted [$_{TP}$ a student t_T [$_{AgrP}$ [the house VP]]]]

Here three pre-VP positions are required within IP for nominal expressions: expletive, subject, and object. One position is provided by T. We therefore have evidence for two noninterpretable functional categories, the ones we have been calling Agr (Agr_S and Agr_O). In MSCs, Agr_S is strong, providing a specifier and a position for V-raising above the domain of strong T: in effect, a "double EPP" configuration. Another VP-external position is provided between T and VP by strong Agr_O. That is the basic rationale behind the analyses just outlined. It accords with the general minimalist outlook, but the anomalous status of Agr raises questions.

The background issues have to do with the strong features of T and Agr, and what appears in the overt specifier positions they make available. In the I position, preceding all verb phrases (main or auxiliary), we have postulated two functional categories: T and Agr_S. In MSCs the specifier position of each is nominal, DP or NP; hence, the strong feature must at least be [nominal-], meaning satisfied by the nominal categorial feature [D] or [N]. At most one nominal can have its Case and ϕ-features checked in this position, which suggests that one of the two nominals must be the pure expletive Exp, a DP. Let us assume this to be the case, though it is not as yet established. The observed order is Exp-nominal rather than nominal-Exp, a fact yet to be explained.

The best case is for Agr_O to have the same constitution as Agr_S. Since Agr_S allows and perhaps requires a D-feature, the same should be true of Agr_O. Hence, both Agrs attract DPs: nominals that are definite or specific. As noted, it follows that expletive-associate constructions observe the definiteness effect and that object raising is restricted to definite (or specific) nominals. This is close enough to accurate to suggest that something of the sort may be happening.

Recall, however, that the definiteness effect for object raising is at best a strong tendency, and that for expletive constructions its status is unclear. It does not rule out any derivations, but rather describes how legitimate outputs are to be interpreted: either as expletive constructions with at most weakly existential implicatures, or as list constructions with strong existential interpretation. We therefore have no strong reason to suppose that the associate *cannot* be a DP – only that if it is, a certain kind of interpretation is expected.

With strong features, Agr provides a position for T- or V-raising (adjunction) and DP-raising (substitution), so there is evidence that it appears in the numeration. If Agr has no strong feature, then PF considerations, at least, give no reason for it to be present at all, and LF considerations do not seem relevant. That suggests an answer to question (1a): Agr exists only when it has strong features. Agr is nothing more than an indication of a position that must be occupied at once by overt operations.[1] Substitution can be effected by Merge or Move. If by Merge, it is limited to expletives, for reasons already discussed.

Pursuit of question (1b) leads to a similar conclusion. The function of Agr is to provide a structural configuration in which features can be checked: Case and ϕ-features, and categorial features ([V-] and [T-] by adjunction, [D-] by substitution). The Case-assigning feature is intrinsic to the heads (V, T) that raise to Agr for checking of DP in [Spec, Agr], so there is no reason to assign it to Agr as well. With regard to ϕ-features, as already discussed, the matter is much less clear. If Agr has ϕ-features, they are –Interpretable, but there might be empirical effects anyway, as noted earlier. Continuing tentatively to assume that ϕ-features are (optionally) assigned to lexical items as they are drawn from the lexicon, we conclude that Agr consists only of the strong features that force raising.

Certain problems that arose in earlier versions now disappear. There is no need to deal with optionally strong Agr, or with the difference in strength of Agr_S and Agr_O. Since Agr is strong, the first problem is just a matter of optional selection of an element ([strength of F]) from the lexicon for the numeration, the irreducible minimum; and difference in strength is inexpressible. There still remains, however, a conflict between the θ-theoretic principle that transitive verbs have a v–VP structure and the assumption that overt object raising is internal to this construction.

Let us turn to the properties that remain.

Since Agr consists solely of strong features, it cannot attract covert raising.[2] We have so far assumed that Subj (subject) and Obj (object) raise to the checking domain of Agr, entering into a checking relation with features of T or V adjoined to Agr (technically, adjoined within Agr^{0max}, the X^0 projection headed by Agr). But with weak Agr gone, covert raising must target T and V directly.[3]

There is now no reason to postulate Agr_O unless it induces overt raising of DP to [Spec, Agr_O]. What about Agr_S? It appears in MSCs, but lacks independent motivation elsewhere, as matters now stand. For languages of the French-English type, then, Agr is not in the lexicon (unless MSCs appear marginally, with extraposition). Agr therefore occurs in highly restricted ways.

The next question is to inquire into the justification for Agr with strong features. Let us first look at Agr_O, then turn to Agr_S.

We restrict attention now to transitive verb constructions, which we continue to assume to be of the form (3), ignoring [Spec, V] (the case of a complex internal domain).

(3)

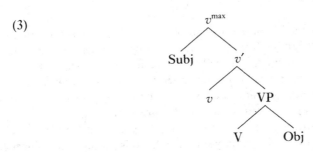

V raises overtly to the light verb v, forming the complex Vb = $[_v\ V\ v]$. Assuming unergatives to be concealed accusatives, the only other VP construction is that of unaccusatives lacking the v-shell, not relevant here.

Suppose that a derivation has formed (3) and Agr is merged with it. Agr is a collection of strong features, either [D-] or [V-] or both. As noted, we need not postulate Agr_O except for object raising; it does not consist only of strong [V-]. Holmberg's generalization states, in effect, that it cannot be just strong [D-]. Let us tentatively assume, then, that Agr_O is {strong [D-], strong [V-]}. The effect of adding Agr_O is to compel overt raising of DP to [Spec, Agr] and of Vb to Agr.

Consider the first property. There is a simple way to force overt DP-raising without the functional category Agr: namely, by adding to v itself a strong D-feature (or perhaps, the more neutral strong [nominal-] feature) that requires overt substitution in the "outer Spec" of a multiple-Spec configuration. If Obj raises to this position to form a chain (Obj, t), it will be in the checking domain of V and therefore able to check its Case and (object agreement) ϕ-features. Recall that Subj inserted by Merge in [Spec, v] is not in the checking domain of v, because it does not head a nontrivial chain.

Object raising, then, takes place when the light verb v that heads the transitive verb construction (3) is assigned the strong feature as it is drawn from the lexicon and placed in the numeration. The choice is arbitrary, forced, or unavailable as the language has optional, obligatory, or no overt object raising, respectively. Since Subj is not in the checking domain, as just noted, it does not check this strong feature, so an outer Spec must be constructed for that purpose. One way is raising of Obj; I hope to show that all others are excluded.

Suppose that an adverbial phrase Adv is adjoined to v^{max} and object raising crosses it, yielding the construction Obj–Ady–v^{max}. That provides no reason to postulate an Agr position outside of v^{max}: a strong feature need only be satisfied before a *distinct* higher category is created.[4]

Overt object raising therefore seems to provide no compelling reason for assuming the existence of Agr_O. The other property of Agr_O is that it forces overt V-raising – actually to T outside of VP, so the effects are never directly visible. The motivation was theory-internal, but it disappears within the more restricted framework, as we will see. The property was a crucial part of the expression of Holmberg's generalization that object raising is contingent on V-raising, but to introduce that consideration to justify postulation of Agr_O is circular. For VP, at least, it seems that we should dispense with Agr_O.

[. . .]

If all of this turns out to be correct, we can eliminate Agr_O from the lexical inventory entirely, for any language. Turning to Agr_S, we need to consider only MSCs, which have the surface order [Exp–V–Subj]. Our assumption so far is that the subject Subj is in [Spec, T] and the expletive in [Spec, Agr_S], and that V has raised to Agr_S. Suppose, instead, we follow the line of reasoning suggested for Agr_O, eliminating Agr and adding an optional strong feature that assigns an outer Spec to T. The situation differs from the case of Agr_O. [Spec, v] in (3) is required for independent θ-related reasons, so only one new Spec is required for object raising. In contrast, T requires no Spec, so we have to accommodate two Specs that are induced only by feature strength. Independently, we have to account for the fact that the order is not the expected (4a) but rather (4b), along with other observed properties.

(4) a. Exp [Subj [T^{0max} XP]]
     b. Exp T^{0max} Subj XP

MSCs appear only when the EPP holds. The question of their nature arises, then, only when T already has a strong [nominal-] feature, which is deleted when checked by DP or NP in [Spec, T]. Suppose that the derivation has reached the stage TP with T strong, and the numeration contains an unused expletive Exp. Then Exp can be inserted by Merge to satisfy the EPP, and we have an ordinary expletive-associate construction. The strong feature of T deletes and furthermore erases, since the derivation converges. Hence, overt MSCs exist only if T has a parameterized property of the kind discussed earlier, which allows a −Interpretable feature (in this case, the strong [nominal−] feature) to escape erasure when checked. If the option is selected, then there must be a multiple-Spec construction, with $n + 1$ specifiers if the option is exercised n times. In a language with the EPP but no MSCs, the strong nominal feature of T is introduced into the derivation with $n = 0$, hence erased when checked. In Icelandic, the descriptive facts indicate that $n = 0$ or $n = 1$; in the latter case, T has two Specs.

Let us see where this course leads, eliminating Agr from UG entirely − and, at least for our purposes here, keeping to functional categories with intrinsic properties that are manifested at the interface levels. The questions that arise are again rather delicate.

[. . .]

The first problem that arises is that we are predicting the wrong order of elements for MSCs. As noted, the observed order is (5b) instead of the predicted (5a).

(5)   a.   Exp [Subj [T^{0max} XP]]
       b.   Exp T^{0max} Subj XP

The best answer would be that the order really is (4a) throughout the $N \rightarrow \lambda$ computation. If the expletive is null, we do not know its position, though (4a) is expected by analogy to the overt case. [. . .] [w]e noted the possibility that the expletive in MSCs is overt in order to satisfy the V-second property, which may belong to the phonological component. If that is the case, the observed order is formed by phonologic operations that are extraneous to the $N \rightarrow \lambda$ computation and may observe the usual constraints (V → C), but need not, as far as we know: T^{0max}-adjunction to expletive or to TP, for example. Let us assume the best case and see where that leads. We thus take the order to be really (4a), irrespective of what is observed at the PF output.

Notes

1   Partially similar conclusions are reached on different grounds by Iatridou (1990) and Thráinsson (1994). See also Fukui (1992).

2   I put aside the question of covert insertion of strong features at the root which is not pertinent here.

3   Recall Baker's (1988) observation that incorporation is one of the ways of satisfying the Case Filter, here placed in a more general context.

4   The relevant condition is the following: Derivation is cancelled if α is in a category not headed by α. Note that there are implications with regard to the status of negation and other elements that might appear in this position, which may be significant.

References

Baker, M. 1988. Incorporation: A theory of grammatical function changing. Chicago: University of Chicago Press.

Fukui, N. 1992. The principle-and-parameters approach: A comparative syntax of English and Japanese. [Published in M. Shibatani and T. Bynon (eds.) (1995), *Approaches to language typology*, Oxford: Oxford University Press, pp. 327–71.]

Iatridou, S. 1990. About Agr(P). *Linguistic Inquiry* 21: 551–77.

Thráinsson, H. 1994. On the (non-)universality of functional categories. Ms., Harvard University and University of Iceland.

4

Verbal Morphology

4.1 Head Movement and/or Affix Hopping?

From "VERBAL MORPHOLOGY: *SYNTACTIC STRUCTURES* MEETS
THE MINIMALIST PROGRAM"
Howard Lasnik

1 Introduction

One of the major breakthroughs in the history of generative transformational grammar was the discovery by Chomsky (1955, 1957) of the regularities underlying
English verbal morphology. Much of the apparent chaos of this central portion of
English morphosyntax was rendered systematic by the fundamental insight that
the tense-agreement inflectional morpheme ("C") is syntactically independent, even
though always a bound morpheme superficially. The analysis was brilliantly successful and paved the way for numerous refinements and extensions over the following forty years, the large majority of them sharing the same fundamental insight.
The refinements can be viewed as attempts to maintain the leading ideas of the
analysis but to reconcile them with the growing concern for explanatory adequacy.

For example, Lasnik (1981) was particularly concerned with the stipulated
rule ordering and the arbitrary marking of particular transformations as obligatory
or optional in Chomsky's early system and proposed that these problematic
language-particular formal mechanisms can be eliminated in favor of the general
filter in (1):

(1) The "stranded affix" filter: A morphologically realized affix must be a syn-
    tactic dependant of a morphologically realized category, at surface structure.
    (Lasnik 1981)

Notice that this filter crucially assumes, along with Chomsky (1955, 1957) and many
succeeding analyses, that the inflectional material on a verb is a morphological affix,

even though it begins its syntactic existence as an autonomous entity. Given this assumption and given (1) and the restrictive theory of transformations it presupposes, a typical analysis of the English verb system of the early 1980s looks something like (2):

(2) a. S is the maximal projection of the inflectional morpheme Infl (= C of Chomsky 1957).
     b. Infl takes VP as its complement.
     c. When the head of VP is *have* or *be* it raises to Infl, the next head up.
     d. Otherwise Infl lowers to V: Affix Hopping.
     (e. Otherwise *do* adjoins to Infl.)

[. . .]

Emonds (1978), based on a similar model, insightfully explored certain differences between English and French.
     [. . .]
Emonds proposed that the basic difference between English and French is that in the latter language verb raising is not limited to auxiliaries. Then, given the priorities in (2), Affix Hopping will never be necessary in French.
     [. . .]

4   A minimalist-lexicalist approach

Chomsky (1993) departs in an important respect from his earlier treatments of verbal morphology by adopting a strictly lexicalist view under which verbs are taken from the lexicon already fully inflected. They still must associate syntactically with the appropriate functional heads, but only in order for their inflectional properties to be checked against abstract features of the functional heads (rather than acquired as affixes). This checking approach mirrors Chomsky's checking view of Case, which holds that Case features are already associated with (the heads of) DPs as they are first inserted into syntactic structures. These DPs must wind up in positions where the Case they already have can be suitably licensed.[1] Note that in this view there is no obvious need for Affix Hopping. The fact that verbs overtly appear with their inflectional morphology even in English is no longer a relevant consideration in determining exactly how the derivation proceeded.

Intrinsic to this checking theory is that the features of verbs and functional heads must be checked against each other, but that this checking can in principle take place anywhere in a derivation on the path to LF. Chomsky also proposes, as a matter of execution, that once a feature of Agr has done its checking work it disappears.

From this point of view the difference between French and English is not verb raising versus affix lowering. Rather, it is whether verb raising takes place in overt syntax (French) or in the LF component (English). Further, since Chomsky argues that LF and PF are the only levels of linguistic representation, this difference cannot be attributed, as it might have been in previous theories, to any S-structure property. Chomsky thus proposes (3) as the core difference between French and English. The relevant notions are explicated in (4):

(3) a. In French the V-features of Agr (i.e. those that check features of a V) are strong.
     b. In English the V-features of Agr are weak.
(4) a. V-features are not legitimate PF objects.
     b. Strong features are visible at PF; weak features are not.
     c. Surviving strong features cause the derivation to crash at PF.

In French, since the V-features of Agr are strong, if V raises to Agr overtly, the V-features of Agr check the features of the V in overt syntax and disappear. Both LF and PF are thus well formed. If on the other hand V were to delay raising until LF, the V-features of Agr would survive into PF, causing the derivation to crash at that level, even though LF requirements would be satisfied. This correctly forces overt V-raising in French.

In English delaying V-raising until LF does not result in an ill-formed PF object, so such a derivation is possible. What makes it necessary is

(5) PROCRASTINATE: Delay an operation until LF whenever possible, that is, whenever delaying would not cause the derivation to crash.

(5) thus plays a central role in excluding (6):

(6) *John likes not Mary

But, as already discussed, *have* and *be* do raise overtly. Chomsky proposes that this happens because *have* and *be* are semantically vacuous, hence not visible to LF operations. Thus, if they have not raised overtly, they will not be able to raise at all. Their unchecked features will cause the LF to crash.

This proposal raises certain questions. First, it is not clear that *be* is always semantically vacuous, yet the syntactic behavior of *be* in finite clauses is always the same. For example, it is reasonable to assume that in (7), *is* has the meaning of *exists*. Yet, as seen in (9), it raises overtly nonetheless:

(7) There is a solution
(8) a. There is not a solution
     b. Is there a solution

Second, even apart from the empirical considerations just mentioned, there is the conceptual question of whether syntactic operations, even those in the LF component, should be sensitive to purely semantic properties. LF is after all a syntactic rather than a semantic component. Finally, there is reason to believe that even instances of *have* and *be* that are vacuous in Chomsky's sense can undergo LF raising. For example, if the functional head in an English subjunctive clause has a V-feature to be checked,[2] *have* and *be* evidently can raise in LF (and, along with main verbs, do so across negation):

(9) a. I desire that John not leave
     b. I desire that John not be here

As noted by Wexler (1994), the potential problem in (9) does arise in other
languages, such as Swedish, where auxiliary verbs pattern exactly with main verbs
in remaining *in situ* in embedded clauses, even though they are undoubtedly
inflected:[3]

(10) a.   ..., om   hon inte ofte har sett honom
                        whether she not often has seen him
      b.   *om hon har inte ofte sett honom
      c.   *om hon inte har ofte sett honom

Note incidentally that Chomsky (1993) does not provide an account of (11):

(11)   *John not likes Mary

[...]

3 A hybrid approach

We have seen that Chomsky's lexicalist-Minimalist account of verbal morphology
demands that Agr and T are just abstract features that check against features of
fully inflected verbs that raise to them. The earlier accounts treated such Infl items
exclusively as bound morphemes that had to become affixes on otherwise bare verbs.
We have seen that each approach has substantial problems. I will argue that the
most important of these problems can be overcome under a hybrid approach that
allows both mechanisms to coexist. (12) sketches such a possibility, where the fundamental difference between French and English (and between English auxiliary
and main verbs) is with respect to choice of mechanism, that is, with respect to
lexical representation.

(12) a. French verbs are fully inflected in the lexicon (possibly correlating with
          the fact that there are no bare forms; even the infinitive has an ending).
      b. *Have* and *be* are fully inflected in the lexicon (possibly correlating with
          the fact that they are highly suppletive, but see below).
      c. All other English verbs are bare in the lexicon.

With the lexical properties of verbs outlined in (12) no further stipulations are
needed for Infl, at least for the core phenomena. As I will show momentarily, (13),
the null hypothesis under the theory I advocate, suffices for French and English
finite clauses:

(13)   Infl is freely an affix or a set of abstract features.

Given that English *have* and *be* behave just like French verbs and given that English main verbs are not lexically represented with inflectional features ((12c)), the Infl feature strength difference posited by Chomsky ((3), (4) above) becomes superfluous. Instead, we have (14):

(14)   Finite featural Infl is strong in both French and English.

The final necessary mechanism is for all intents and purposes the original one: Affix Hopping. Further, as conjectured by Lasnik (1981) and developed further by Halle and Marantz (1993) and Bobaljik (1994), the rule is a morphophonemic one rather than a syntactic one:

(15)   Affixal Infl must merge with a V, a PF process (distinct from head movement) demanding adjacency.

Consider now the various combinations made available by this theory. First, suppose that we select a verb with inflectional features (notated here as +F) and a featural (as opposed to affixal) Infl:

(16)   ... Infl ... V ...
          +F   +F

This configuration is, of course, well formed. V raises (overtly) to Infl, and all relevant features are checked. This is the situation with all French verbs, as well as with English *have* and *be*.
   Next, consider the case of a bare verb and an affixal (as opposed to featural) Infl:

(17)   ... Infl ... V ...
          Af   bare

This is the situation with English main verbs. In this configuration PF merger takes place as long as adjacency obtains, and the PF affixal requirement of Infl is satisfied.
   Given (13), two other configurations could potentially arise, but, since both of them will ultimately crash, there is no need to replace (13) with a stipulation. The first such mismatched configuration is shown in (18):

(18)   ... Infl ... V ...
          +F   bare

Here, the features of Infl will not be checked, so the derivation crashes at LF. And under the assumption that the features are strong, there is a PF crash as well.
   Finally, consider (19), the reverse of (18):

(19)   ... Infl ... V ...
          Af   +F

This time the features of V will fail to be checked, causing an LF crash. Additionally, if in principle affixal Infl cannot attach to an already inflected verb, this failure leads to a PF crash.

(20) summarizes the immediately preceding discussion:

(20) a.   . . . Infl . . . V . . . OK. V will overtly raise.
           +F   +F

      b.   . . . Infl . . . V . . . OK. PF merger.
           Af   bare

      c.   . . . Infl . . . V . . .   *at LF. +F of Infl will not be checked;
           +F   bare   *at PF as well, since +F is strong.

      d.   . . . Infl . . . V . . .   *at LF. +F of V will not be checked.
           Af   F+   *at PF also, if merger fails.

Thus, it follows from the lexical properties of French verbs that French Infl will always have to be featural, just as it follows from the lexical properties of *be* and auxiliary *have* that English Infl will always have to be featural when the verb is *have* or *be*. The parallelism in behavior between French verbs and English auxiliaries has a unified account in this theory, following from a parallelism in morphological properties. With a main verb in English, on the other hand, English Infl will always have to be affixal, and this follows straightforwardly.

Consider now the ill-formed negative sentences in English. (21) involves an apparently inflected verb *in situ* in overt syntax:

(21)   *John not walked

[. . .]

My account of (21) is that of Chomsky (1957).[4] *Walked* is not in the lexicon of English: all main verbs are "bare." Hence, (22) must arise from the merger of affixal Infl with *walk*. But *not* intervenes between Infl and *walk* so the former cannot merge with the latter.[5] Crucially, then, the Swedish example (10) must not involve merger. Rather, it must involve the covert analogue of the overt raising seen in French or with English *have* and *be*. That is, the verb is pulled from the lexicon fully inflected. Infl, then, is necessarily featural, so the verb must raise to Infl for the matching features to be checked. The different property of Swedish is that the V-features of Infl are weak, while those in French and English are strong. Procrastinate dictates that the Swedish verb will remain *in situ* in overt syntax. (22) is fundamentally similar:

(22)   *John walked not

Walked is not in the lexicon, so even though featural Infl exists in English and even though its V-features are strong, *walked* could never be created by raising.[6]

We have seen that raising across negation overtly, as in (23) and (24), and covertly, as in (25), is available:

(23)   Jean (n')aime pas Marie
(24)   John has not left
(25)   . . . , om hon inte ofte har sett honom

[. . .]

   The first further possibility, along the lines of Roberts (1992, 1994), is that Neg
and V are heads of different sorts (A' vs. A) and that relativized minimality is even
more relativized than in the original proposal of Rizzi (1990). If a head only blocks
movement of a head of the same type, Neg would then not block movement of V.
The second possibility is that Neg is not a head, but a modifier. [. . .]

6 Further evidence from VP ellipsis

I have argued that there is a fundamental morphological difference between French
verbs and English main verbs and that this difference is mirrored internal to English
by one between English auxiliary and main verbs. Certain surprising facts about
VP ellipsis first discussed by Warner (1986) provide interesting evidence bearing
on the English internal claim.
   It has long been known that VP ellipsis can ignore certain inflectional differences between antecedent verb and elided verb. For example, Quirk et al. (1972),
reported by Sag (1976), observe that a finite form of a verb can antecede the
deletion[7] of the bare form that follows a modal, as in the following example:

(26)   John slept, and Mary will too
(27)   a.   *John *slept*, and Mary will *slept* too
       b.   John *slept*, and Mary will *sleep* too

In (26) the past tense form *slept* serves as antecedent for the deletion of the bare
form *sleep*.
   As expected, given (26) and (27), the present tense form can also antecede the
bare form:

(28)   John sleeps (every afternoon), and Mary should too
(29)   a.   *John *sleeps*, and Mary should *sleeps* too
       b.   John *sleeps*, and Mary should *sleep* too

Similarly, the progressive and perfect forms can antecede the bare form:

(30)   ?John was sleeping, and Mary will too
(31)   a.   *John was *sleeping*, and Mary will *sleeping* too
       b.   John was *sleeping*, and Mary will *sleep* too
(32)   John has slept, and Mary will too
(33)   a.   *John has *slept*, and Mary will *slept* too
       b.   John has *slept*, and Mary will *sleep* too

It appears that a sort of sloppy identity is at work here, permitting tense and aspectual differences to be ignored in the same way that φ-feature differences typically can be. But, as Warner notes, there are certain exceptions to this general pattern. (34) is seemingly parallel to (26), but surprisingly, it is unacceptable:

(34)   *John was here, and Mary will too
(35)   a.   *John *was here* and Mary will *was here* too
       b.   John *was here* and Mary will *be here* too

Evidently *was* cannot antecede *be*; nor can *is* antecede *be*:

(36)   *John is here, and Mary will too

There is no general prohibition on VP ellipsis of a VP headed by *be* following a modal. (37) is virtually perfect and far better than (34) and (36):

(37)   John will be here, and Mary will too

Note that the failed antecedent in (34) and (36) has undergone raising out of the VP while the target V has not, unlike the situation in the successful examples among (26) through (32) and (37), where neither target nor antecedent V has undergone raising. One might therefore conjecture that a trace cannot serve as (part of) an antecedent for VP deletion. There is reason to doubt that conjecture, however. In (38) the antecedent of the elided VP in the second conjunct contains the trace of topicalization:

(38)   Linguistics$_1$, I like t_1, and you should too

Further, the trace of raising to subject position can, to a reasonably acceptable extent, antecede an NP *in situ*:

(39)   a.   Someone$_1$ is t_1 in the garden, isn't there
       b.   Someone$_1$ will be t_1 in the garden, won't there

Finally, even a form of *be* that presumably has not raised has difficulty anteceding a distinct form of *be*, as in (40), from Warner (1986), or (42):

(40)   ?*The children have been very good here. I wish they would at home

Compare (42), with *behave* instead of *be*:

(41)   ?The children have behaved very well here. I wish they would at home
(42)   *John was being obnoxious, and Mary will too

Similar effects obtain with auxiliary *have*. Ellipsis is markedly better in (43) with identical forms of *have* than in (44) with distinct ones:

(43) a.   John should have left, but Mary shouldn't ~~have left~~
      b.   ?John should have left, but Mary shouldn't
(44) a.   John has left, but Mary shouldn't have left
      b.   *John has left, but Mary shouldn't ~~have left~~

Note that, as might be expected, the ellipsis site in (44b) is fine when interpreted as *leave*. That is roughly the situation we have seen before, with one form of a main verb anteceding a distinct form of that verb (in this case perfect *left* anteceding bare *leave*).[8] Note too that the identity of form demanded for ellipsis of auxiliary *have* is somewhat abstract, making reference to morphological features and not just phonetic ones. (45) is no better than (44b):

(45) *The men have left, but the women shouldn't ~~have left~~

The present plural of auxiliary *have* cannot antecede the bare form, even though they are both superficially *have*. Note too that main verb *have* patterns with other main verbs and not with auxiliary *have*:

(46) John has a driver's license, but Mary shouldn't

The descriptive generalization covering the data considered so far is stated in (47):

(47) The bare form of a verb V other than *be* or auxiliary *have* can be deleted under identity with any other form of V. *Be* or auxiliary *have* can only be deleted under identity with the very same form.

As Warner observes, this difference does not follow directly from (degree of) suppletion. The paradigm of *go* is highly suppletive, yet that verb patterns with all the other main verbs considered above:

(48) John went, and now Mary will ~~go~~

The progressive form of all verbs (even including *be*) is also completely regular, yet such deletion under partial identity is disallowed:

(49) a.   *John slept, and Mary was too
      b.   John slept, and Mary was sleeping too
(50) a.   *John will sleep. Mary is now
      b.   John will sleep. Mary is sleeping now

Thus, the relevant difference seems to be between main verbs and auxiliaries[9] where the latter category includes *be* and certain instances of *have*. Interestingly, as Chomsky (1957) observed, main verb *have* sometimes marginally behaves like an auxiliary:

(51) ?John hasn't a driver's license
      (cf. John doesn't have a driver's license)

It is significant that when it does behave like an auxiliary it patterns with auxiliary *have* with respect to ellipsis:

(52)   ?*John hasn't a driver's license, but Mary should
       (cf. John doesn't have a driver's license, but Mary should)

The inflectional features that cause it to raise make it distinct from the bare form for the purposes of deletion under identity.

Sag (1976) briefly discusses the main verb phenomena, taking them to be representative. He observes that these cases could be accounted for by ordering verb phrase deletion before Affix Hopping. Note that on the strictly lexicalist view discussed above there is no such point in a derivation. However, on the analysis of Chomsky (1957), adopted in its essentials here, there is indeed such a point. I have departed from Chomsky (1957) in just one major respect: for him **all** verbs are introduced into syntactic structures bare and achieve their inflectional form via Affix Hopping, while I have argued that auxiliaries are pulled from the lexicon fully inflected.[10] This difference between English main and auxiliary verbs was part of my explanation of the verb-raising asymmetries. Strikingly, the very same difference can explain the ellipsis asymmetries along essentially the lines suggested by Sag:

(53)   a.   A form of a verb V can only be deleted under identity with the very same form.
       b.   Forms of *be* and auxiliary *have* are introduced into syntactic structures already fully inflected. Forms of "main" verbs are created out of lexically introduced bare forms and independent affixes.

Given (53), deletion under apparent incomplete identity is actually deletion under full identity but at a point in the derivation before the bare stem has associated with the inflectional affix. This is schematically illustrated in (54), a structure for *John slept, and Mary will too*:

(54)   John Infl sleep, and Mary will ~~sleep~~ too

We have seen numerous instances in which the finite form of a main verb antecedes a bare form. Quirk et al. (1972), cited by Sag (1976), give several examples where the progressive and perfect forms likewise antecede the bare form. This possibility indicates on the present account that the Chomsky (1957) Affix Hopping analysis is in order for these forms as well. Schematically, we have the following:

(55)   a.   John was sleeping, and now Mary will
       b.   John was ing sleep, and now Mary will ~~sleep~~
(56)   a.   John has slept, and now Mary will
       b.   John has en sleep, and now Mary will ~~sleep~~

Quirk et al. (1972) indicate that the reverse situation from (55), with bare form anteceding progressive, is not possible. They give (57), which is parallel in structure and behavior to (58):

(57)   ?*John won't enter the competition, but Peter is
(58)   ?*John slept, and Mary was too

A consideration of the structure of (58) suggests an immediate solution to this puzzle:

(59)   John Infl sleep, and Mary was *ing* ~~sleep~~ too

The progressive affix *ing* is stranded. Hence, (58) and (59) run afoul of the stranded affix filter. These examples thus provide additional evidence for the Chomsky (1957) type analysis of main verbs that I advocate. For reasons that I do not understand, though, the perfect affix diverges in behavior from the progressive, the perfect form of a main verb being deletable in just the same circumstances that the bare form is. Quirk et al. give (60) and (61), which are far better than the progressive examples just considered:

(60)   John may be questioning our motives, but Peter hasn't
(61)   Peter saw your parents last week, but he hasn't since

These ought to involve a stranded *en*. I will have to leave their acceptability as an open problem.[11]

   The conclusions about the negation and ellipsis phenomena reviewed thus far potentially provide a microscope for the examination of additional inflectional forms of verbs. Consider simple imperatives in English:

(62)   Leave

What is the morphological analysis of such a sentence? Lasnik (1981) argues that there is an imperative affix (occupying the position normally occupied by Tense) that must associate with the bare stem, based on the ungrammaticality of (64):

(63)   *Not leave

The ungrammaticality is due to the stranded affix filter, since lack of adjacency blocks the merger of Imp and *leave*. The analysis fits completely into the framework I have outlined above. Two alternatives are excluded. It cannot be that there is no Imp morpheme at all, since that would leave (63) unexplained. Nor could there be a featural Imp to which already inflected *leave* would raise, since, if the hypothesized feature were weak, (63) would be good, and if it were strong, (64) would:[12]

(64)   *Leave not

   Thus far, Imp is behaving just like finite Infl. The parallelism extends still further: (64) is salvaged (however that is to be captured in the theory) by *do*-support:

(65)   Do not leave

The parallelism breaks down with respect to auxiliary verbs, however. Not even *be* can raise:

(66)   *Be not foolish

This indicates on the present account that either (67a) or (67b) must be correct as a lexical property of English:

(67)   a.   The Imperative morpheme is strictly affixal, hence there will never be raising to it (just merger with it).
       b.   OR Imp is freely affixal or featural, and *be* and auxiliary *have* lack imperative forms in the lexicon.

On either account, in this particular construction *be* is pulled from the lexicon bare, just as main verbs are. This predicts that imperative of *be* should parallel imperative of main verbs in ellipsis behavior. (68) shows that that prediction is confirmed:[13]

(68)   a.   Leave.   I don't want to
                     I won't
       b.   Be quiet. I don't want to
                     I won't

(68) is in direct contrast with (69), the properties of the latter following from the fact that *is* never arises via affixation:

(69)   a.   Mary left. I don't want to
       b.   Mary is quiet. *I don't want to

Finally, earlier I considered the possibility that English subjunctives involve covert raising. Ellipsis facts indicate that this is incorrect:

(70)   I require that John leave, but Bill doesn't have to
(71)   I require that John be here, but Bill doesn't have to

The subjunctive form of a main verb or *be* can antecede the bare form. This indicates that the subjunctive is not a lexically inflected form at all in English. In this regard subjunctives are like imperatives. But the negative subjunctive sentences diverge from the negative imperatives, as in (72), repeated from (9):

(72)   a.   I desire that John not leave
       b.   I desire that John not be here

Thus, subjunctives cannot involve affixation either. They must be what they superficially appear: bare forms.[14] Under the standard assumption that nominative Case on a subject must be licensed by an appropriate functional head that combines with, subjunctive clauses must have a subjunctive functional head. The above argument indicates that that head is not an affix and, further, does not have V-features.

7 Conclusion

In conclusion, I have presented an analysis that, not surprisingly, differs from that of Chomsky (1957) in significant respects. For Chomsky, all of the descriptive machinery was syntactic, while I have argued, from the perspective of more recent theorizing, that Affix Hopping is a PF process rather than a syntactic one and that the differential behavior of verbs of the two sorts is stated in the lexicon and not in particular transformations. Perhaps more striking than the differences, though, are the similarities. In many respects we arrive at the end of this journey almost where we began: with an analysis of core facts of English verbal morphology highly reminiscent of the classic one in its reliance on a form of Affix Hopping and in its formal distinction between main verbs and auxiliaries. Sometimes old ideas are not merely interesting – they can even be right.

Notes

1. Interestingly, this checking view more precisely captures the insight of the earliest modern version of Case theory, that of Vergnaud (1977), than does the Case assignment approach of Chomsky (1980, 1981).
2. Later, though, we will see reason to doubt this.
3. These examples are taken from Wilder and Ćavar (1994). See also Bošković (1995) for discussion of a Serbo-Croatian construction that allows fully inflected finite auxiliary verbs to remain *in situ*.
4. See also Halle and Marantz (1993) and Bobaljik (1994).
5. One remaining question concerns the obvious grammaticality of (i):

    (i) John never left

    While *not* evidently blocks the adjacency needed for merger, adverbs in general do not. Bobaljik (1994) suggest that adverbs (or, more generally, adjuncts) are not relevant to PF adjacency, while heads and specifiers are. In fact, he assumes that *not* in English is actually a specifier. See Lasnik (in press) for another possibility.
6. I continue to assume that movement is driven solely by features of the appropriate sort. In particular, I assume that the property of being an affix is not a feature relevant to syntactic head-raising. Thus, as Roger Martin notes, under either Chomsky's (1993) Greed constraint or the weaker Enlightened Self Interest [(Lasnik 1999: ch. 4),] movement of bare V will be blocked by general economy considerations. This line of reasoning creates a problem for the analysis of *there* [in Lasnik (1999: chs. 3, 4). See Lasnik (1999: ch. 6) for an alternative.]
7. I use the term "deletion" merely for ease of exposition. As far as I can tell, all of the arguments I present are neutral between a PF deletion approach to ellipsis and an LF copying one.
8. I return to such constructions below.
9. Kayne (1989) conjectures that Universal Grammar makes available a categorial distinction between the class of lexical verbs and the class of auxiliary verbs. Such a distinction is at the core of Akmajian, Steele, and Wasow (1979) and Steele (1981). Wexler (1994) shows that a consistent pattern of inflectional errors in child language reflects a fundamental main

verb vs. auxiliary verb dichotomy. For children acquiring English his findings are reminiscent of my proposals: for main verbs, but not for auxiliaries, children would freely substitute the infinitival form for the appropriate finite form.

10   This is essentially the formal analogue of the insightful semantic proposal of Warner (1986), though he argued that such a treatment is appropriate for *be* but not for *have* (based on subtle acceptability differences that I am putting aside).

11   Descriptively, it is as if stranded *en* is spelled out as zero, much as stranded Infl is spelled out as a form of *do*. We have seen that stranded *ing* lacks the first possibility. (i) shows that it lacks the second as well:

(i)   *John slept and Mary was doing too

12   Željko Bošković points out that this conclusion does not quite follow. Suppose that negation is an A′-head in the sense of Roberts (1992) and that verb movement in imperative constructions also involves movement to an A′-head across negation. Then a simple positive imperative could involve raising, while a negative imperative could not. A special form would be needed for the negatives (*do*-support in English). Rivero (1994) shows just such a pattern for several Balkan languages. Ellipsis provides some evidence against such an approach to the English facts, however, as we will see directly.

13   (i) indicates that even in a positive imperative *be* behaves strictly like a bare verb and does not undergo raising:

(i)   a.   Should I be quiet?   Please do
      b.   *Please be

If imperative *be* could raise, (ib) could arise from raising and deletion of the residual VP, just as in (ii):

(ii)   John is

If such phenomena establish that auxiliary verbs in English have bare forms that are capable in principle of undergoing merger, the central ellipsis phenomena I have presented must be reconsidered. I showed how (37), repeated as (iii), is ruled out if *is* is necessarily taken fully inflected from the lexicon:

(iii)   *John is here, and Mary will too

But with *be* in principle able to merge with a particular inflectional affix (Imp) the question is why there cannot be an alternative merger derivation of *is*, alongside the lexicalist one. I suspect that the answer lies in the domain of what is often termed morphological blocking. If *is* exists as a word, the merger derivation will be blocked, on the assumption that inflectional slots are uniquely filled, at least in the unmarked case. See Aronoff (1976), Kiparsky (1982), and Pinker (1984) for discussion.

14   An alternative, suggested by Željko Bošković, is that the relative height of negation and subjunctive head differs from that of negation and Tense. I put that possibility aside for future research.

References

Akmajian, A., S. Steele and T. Wasow. 1979. The category AUX in Universal Grammar. *Linguistic Inquiry* 10: 1–64.

Aronoff, M. 1976. *Word formation in generative grammar*. Cambridge, MA: MIT Press.

Bobaljik, J. D. 1994. What does adjacency do? In H. Harley and C. Phillips (eds.), *The morphology–syntax connection. MIT Working Papers in Linguistics 22*, Cambridge, MA: MITWPL.

Bošković, Ž. 1995. Participle movement and second position Cliticization in Serbo-Croation. *Lingua* 96: 246–66.

Chomsky, N. 1955. The logical structure of linguistic theory. Ms., Harvard University. [Revised 1956 version published in part by Plenum, New York (1975); University of Chicago Press, Chicago (1985).]

Chomsky, N. 1957. *Syntactic structures*. The Hague: Mouton.

Chomsky, N. 1980. On binding. *Linguistic Inquiry* 11: 1–46.

Chomsky, N. 1981. *Lectures on government and binding*. Dordrecht: Foris.

Chomsky, N. 1993. A minimalist program for linguistic theory. In K. Hale and S. J. Keyser (eds.), *The view from Building 20: Essays in linguistics in honor of Sylvain Bromberger*, Cambridge, MA: MIT Press, pp. 1–52. [Reprinted in Chomsky (1995), *The Minimalist Program*, Cambridge, MA: MIT Press, pp. 167–217.]

Emonds, J. 1978. The verbal complex V′-V″ in French. *Linguistic Inquiry* 9: 151–75.

Halle, M. and A. Marantz. 1993. Distributed Morphology and the pieces of inflection. In K. Hale and S. J. Keyser (eds.), *The view from Building 20: Essays in linguistics in honor of Sylvain Bromberger*, Cambridge, MA: MIT Press, pp. 111–76.

Kayne, R. 1989. Notes on English agreement. Ms., CUNY Graduate Center.

Kiparsky, P. 1982. From cyclic phonology to lexical phonology. In H. van der Hulst and N. Smith (eds.), *The structure of phonological representations*, Dordrecht: Foris, pp. 131–75.

Lasnik, H. 1981. Restricting the theory of transformations: A case study. In N. Hornstein and D. Lightfoot (eds.), *Explanation in linguistics*, Harlow: Longman, pp. 152–73.

Lasnik, H. 1995. Case and expletives revisited: On Greed and other human failings. *Linguistic Inquiry* 26: 615–33.

Lasnik, H. 1999. *Minimalist analysis*. Malden, MA/Oxford: Blackwell.

Lasnik, H. in press. Patterns of verb raising with auxiliary "be." Paper presented at the 1995 UMass Conference on African American English, University of Massachusetts, Amherst. [Published in Lasnik (2003), *Minimalist Investigations in linguistic theory*, London and New York: Routledge, pp. 6–21.]

Pinker, S. 1984. *Language learnability and language development*. Cambridge, MA: Harvard University Press.

Quirk, R., S. Greenbaum, G. Leech and J. Svartik. 1972. *A grammar of contemporary English*. London: Seminar Press.

Rivero, M.-L. 1994. Clause structure and V-movement in the languages of the Balkans. *Natural Language and Linguistic Theory* 12: 63–120.

Rizzi, L. 1990. *Relativized minimality*. Cambridge, MA: MIT Press.

Roberts, I. 1992. *Verbs and diachronic syntax*. Dordrecht: Kluwer.

Roberts, I. 1994. Two types of head movement in Romance. In N. Hornstein and D. Lightfoot (eds.), *Verb movement*, Cambridge: Cambridge University Press, pp. 207–42.

Sag, I. 1976. *Deletion and logical form*. Doctoral dissertation, MIT.

Steele, S. 1981. *Encyclopedia of AUX*. Cambridge, MA: MIT Press.

Vergnaud, J.-R. 1977. Personal letter to Howard Lasnik and Noam Chomsky. Paris.

Warner, A. 1986. Ellipsis conditions and the status of the English copula. In *York Papers in Linguistics 12*, Heslington, England: University of York, pp. 153–72.

Wexler, K. 1994. Optional infinitives, head movement and the economy of derivations. In N. Hornstein and D. Lightfoot (eds.), *Verb movement*, Cambridge: Cambridge University Press, pp. 305–50.

Wilder, C. and D. Ćavar. 1994. Word order variation, verb movement, and economy principles. *Studia Linguistica* 48: 46–86.

4.2   Head Movement as a PF Phenomenon

From "DERIVATION BY PHASE"
Noam Chomsky

There are some reasons to suspect that a substantial core of head-raising processes, excluding incorporation in the sense of Baker (1988), may fall within the phonological component. One reason is the expectation of (near-)uniformity of LF interface representations, a particularly compelling instance of the methodological principle (1) [in the absence of compelling evidence to the contrary, assume languages to be uniform, with variety restricted to easily detectable properties of utterances], as in the case of Th/Ex [thematization/extraction rule]. The interpretive burden is reduced if, say, verbs are interpreted the same way whether they remain in situ or raise to T or C, the distinctions that have received much attention since Pollock (1989). As expected under (1), verbs are not interpreted differently in English versus Romance, or Mainland Scandinavian versus Icelandic, or embedded versus root structures. More generally, semantic effects of head raising in the core inflectional system are slight or nonexistent, as contrasted with XP-movement, with effects that are substantial and systematic. That would follow insofar as head raising is not part of narrow syntax.

A second reason has to do with what raises. Using the term *strength* for expository purposes, suppose that T has a strong V-feature and a strong nominal feature (person, we have assumed; D or N in categorial systems). It has always been taken for granted that the strong V-feature is satisfied by V-raising to T (French vs. English), not VP-raising to [Spec, T], and that the strong nominal feature is satisfied by raising of the nominal to [Spec, T] (EPP) [Extended Projection Principle], not raising of its head to T. But the theoretical apparatus provides no obvious basis for this choice. The same is true of raising to C and D. In standard cases,[1] T adjoins to C, and an XP (say, a *wh*-phrase) raises to [Spec, C], instead of the *wh*-head adjoining to C while TP raises to [Spec, C]. And N raises to D, not NP to [Spec, D]. These conclusions too follow naturally if overt V-to-T raising, T-to-C raising, and N-to-D raising are phonological properties, conditioned by the phonetically affixal character of the inflectional categories. Considerations of LF uniformity might lead us to suspect that an LF-interpretive process brings together D-N and C-T-V to form wordlike LF "supercategories" in all languages, not only those where such processes are visible.

Other considerations have to do with the nature of the head-raising rule, which differs from core rules of narrow syntax in several respects. It is an adjunction rule; it is countercyclic in ways that are not overcome along the lines discussed earlier; the raised head does not c-command its trace;[2] identification of head-trace chains raises difficulties similar to those of feature movement, since there is no reasonable notion of occurrence; it observes somewhat different locality conditions. All of this is unproblematic if overt adjunction is a phonological process reflecting affixal properties.

Note further that if excorporation is excluded, head movement is not successive-cyclic, like the rules Th/Ex and Disl, which are plausibly assigned to the phonological component. It could be, in fact, that iterability is a general property of operations of narrow syntax, but these alone.

Boeckx and Stjepanović (1999), extending and modifying work by Lasnik (1999: ch. 7), argue that some problems of pseudogapping can be accounted for by the assumption that head movement is a phonological process, also citing other recent work that finds differences between head movement and XP-movement.

The same conclusion is suggested in recent work on aphasia by Grodzinsky and Finkel (1998), extending earlier work of Grodzinsky's. They argue that a range of symptoms can be explained in terms of inability to identify XP chains, but they note that the results do not carry over to X^0 chains; the result is expected if head raising is a phonological process, creating no chains.

Notes

1   The qualification is intended to leave open other possibilities: for example, TP-raising to [Spec, C] in accord with Kayne's (1994) theory of linearity, head raising versus XP-raising as a possible distinction between *wh*-in-situ and overt raising (see [Chomsky 2000] and sources cited, particularly Watanabe 1992 and Hagstrom 1998). The N $\rightarrow$ D rule developed in Longobardi (1994) and subsequent work has crucial semantic consequences, but it seems that these might be reformulated in terms of the properties of D that do or do not induce overt raising.

2   Commonly, head movement is held to observe c-command, but with a stipulated disjunctive definition for this case, which does not fall under the "free" relation of c-command derived from Merge (see MI). The Head Movement Constraint has been assimilated to general locality conditions in various ways, but special features remain, it seems.

References

Baker, M. 1988. *Incorporation: A theory of grammatical function changing*. Chicago: University of Chicago Press.

Boeckx, C. and S. Stjepanović. 1999. Head-ing toward PF. [Published in *Linguistic Inquiry* 32: 345–55, 2001.]

Chomsky, Noam. 2000. Minimalist inquiries: the framework. In Roger Martin, David Michaels, and Juan Uriagereka (eds.), Step by step: Essays on minimalist syntax in honor of Howard Lasnik, Cambridge, MA: MIT Press, pp. 89–155.

Grodzinsky, Y. and K. Finkel. 1998. The neurology of empty categories: A phasic's failure to detect ungrammaticality. *Journal of Cognitive Neuroscience* 10: 281–92.

Hagstrom, P. 1998. *Decomposing questions*. Doctoral dissertation, MIT.

Kayne, R. 1994. *The antisymmetry of syntax*. Cambridge, MA: MIT Press.

Lasnik, H. 1999. *Minimalist analysis*. Malden, MA: Blackwell.

Longobardi, G. 1994. Reference and proper names: A theory of N-movement in syntax and logical form. *Linguistic Inquiry* 25: 609–65.

Pollock, J.-Y. 1989. Verb movement, universal grammar, and the structure of IP. *Linguistic Inquiry* 20: 365–424.

Watanabe, A. 1992. Subjacency and S-structure movement of wh-in-situ. *Journal of East Asian Liguistics* 1: 255–91.

From "HEAD-ING TOWARD PF"
Cedric Boeckx and Sandra Stjepanović

In this squib we will provide an empirical argument in favor of the PF approach to head movement. Our discussion is based on pseudogapping constructions like (1).

(1)   Debbie ate the chocolate, and Kazuko did ~~eat~~ the cookies.

[. . .]

Lasnik (1995) follows Jayaseelan (1990) in proposing that pseudogapping constructions like (1) result from VP-ellipsis, the remnant object having moved out of the VP, stranding the verb. [. . .] However, Lasnik departs from Jayaseelan in taking movement of the object not to be a case of heavy NP shift, but one of overt raising to [Spec, Agr_O], as shown in (2) (setting details aside; see Lasnik 1995 for discussion).

(2)   Debbie ate the chocolate, and Kazuko did [$_{Agr_O}$P the cookie$_i$ ~~[$_{VP}$ eat t_i]~~].

The licensing of VP-ellipsis via overt movement of the object is Lasnik's (1995) crucial piece of evidence in favor of overt object shift in English. The question that immediately arises is why the verb need not raise in pseudogapping constructions, given that in nonelliptical sentences it must (assuming overt object raising; see the papers in Lasnik 1999b for extensive discussion and motivation).

(3)   *Kazuko will the cookie$_i$ eat t_i.
       (vs. Kazuko will eat$_i$ the cookie$_j$ t_i t_j)

This question is at the core of Lasnik's (1999a) discussion of the nature of strong features. Lasnik assumes that a strong feature is involved to force movement of the verb in (3). (2) and (3) seem to show that there are two possibilities for a convergent derivation. Either V can raise, presumably checking the relevant strong feature, or it can be part of the elided constituent. Lasnik notes that this mysterious state of affairs receives a straightforward account under the PF crash theory of strong features (Chomsky 1993).

This theory in essence says that an unchecked strong feature causes the derivation to crash at PF (see Lasnik 1999a for details), under the hypothesis that the strong feature forcing V to raise overtly is a feature of the lexical V itself, rather than of the target position it raises to. Given this, Lasnik observes that if V fails to raise, and no relevant process takes place, the strong feature that is not checked overtly causes a crash at PF. But if the VP containing V is deleted in the PF component, then, patently, the strong feature cannot cause a PF crash, since the (category containing the) feature will be gone at that level.

Lasnik (1999c) shows convincingly that this result is hard to capture under the view (Chomsky 1994) that an unchecked strong feature is an illegitimate LF object (see Lasnik's article for discussion). It is also not obvious how it can be captured under the "virus" theory of strong features (Chomsky 1995), according to which a strong feature must be checked almost immediately upon insertion into the tree. But Lasnik shows that this is not impossible, under one specific construal of overt movement (which he adopts from Ochi (1999), who in turn builds upon a suggestion by Chomsky (1995)). According to Chomsky and Ochi, overt movement consists of essentially two operations: the formation of a feature chain (raising the formal features of an element to the attractor) and the formation of a category chain (Chomsky's "generalized pied-piping" approach). Chomsky and Ochi argue that the formation of a category chain is best viewed as a repair strategy, taking place because "isolated features and other scattered parts of words may not be subject to [C_{HL}'s] rules, in which case the derivation is canceled; or the derivation might proceed to PF with elements that are 'unpronounceable,' violating FI [Full Interpretation]" (Chomsky 1995: 262). Put differently, failure to pied-pipe (form a category chain) causes the derivation to crash at PF.

This is strongly reminiscent of the original PF crash conception of strong features, the more so if we adopt Ochi's (1999) interpretation of Chomsky's (1995) view on pied-piping as meaning that the inadequacy triggering the formation of a category chain lies not so much in the target/attractor (as Chomsky argues for feature movement), but in the lexical item itself: a lexical item cannot be pronounced if its features have been scattered.

Given the foregoing, Lasnik is able to maintain the essence of his 1995 explanation of why either overt movement or ellipsis leads to convergence: either the category moves and is pronounceable (its features being "united" again), or it deletes, in which case the inadequacy is eliminated.

In the next section we point out problems for Lasnik's explanation.

3   Inadequacies of Lasnik's solution

Let us start by pointing out that we assume the essential correctness of Chomsky's (1995) claim that movement (of features) is better viewed as attraction (triggered from "above" the target/attractor). It is crucial for Lasnik's (1999a) explanation above that Ochi be right in claiming that the inadequacy triggering "ancillary Move" lies in the lexical item whose formal features have just been attracted. As far as we can see, however, this conclusion does not follow from the natural ban against scattered objects/features: it could as well be the case that a feature once raised to the attractor demands movement of the category so as not to remain stranded. This is indeed what we believe Chomsky meant in suggesting (class lectures, MIT, fall 1995 and 1997) that pied-piping be viewed as reducing the "link" between scattered features. "Link reduction" is neutral with respect to the "orientation" of the operation.

The whole issue takes on another dimension under Chomsky's (2000) reinterpretation of feature movement as mere long-distance agreement (Agree), with no actual feature displacement. Assuming this view to be correct, Lasnik's argument based on Ochi (1999) becomes virtually unstatable: there is no longer any scattering of features. It seems that like Agree, pied-piping is motivated by some property of the target of movement (Chomsky's (2000) "[EP]P-feature"). If that is the case, it becomes unclear why V-movement, unlike object movement, need not take place in pseudogapping examples. Claiming that the relevant P-feature is absent is clearly not explanatory.

Since, however, the nature of overt movement is left unclear in Chomsky (2000), apart from some suggestive formulations like "Agree is not enough to satisfy the target, the category must raise to check feature P," an attempt to formulate this process precisely might turn out to offer a way out of the problems just raised regarding the source of the inadequacy driving head movement. However, in what follows we will show that the source of the inadequacy is not the only problem for Lasnik's analysis and that an alternative is needed.

To achieve a pseudogapping structure, it is crucial for Lasnik's proposal that overt object movement take place and that the verb stay put. But, as far as we can see, nothing inherent in the system Lasnik adopts forces this. What if V-movement takes place and object movement does not, yielding the ungrammatical (4)?

(4) *Debbie got chocolate, and Kazuko got ~~chocolate~~ too.

At the same time it is crucial that V-movement not be optional in standard cases like (5).

(5) Debbie ate chocolate, and Kazuko drank milk.

As Lasnik himself concedes (personal communication), there is no way to enforce this particular obligatory XP-/optional X^0-movement relation. A reviewer points out that the reasoning does not hold once we broaden the range of constructions. The reviewer notes, quite correctly, that (2) and (4) are not exactly parallel. It is a characteristic of pseudogapping (and gapping) that the remnant is contrastively focused. In (4) the remnant is patently not focused. However, there is an elliptical construction in which the verb *is* contrastively focused, namely, right node raising, illustrated in (6).

(6) Debbie bought and Kazuko ate the chocolate.

The reviewer suggests that right node raising could be derived by V-raising with the object staying put – thus offering a parallel to the pseudogapping case. Movement of either the verb or the object would then be driven by focus. There are two problems with that analysis. First, it is unclear whether focus is the driving force or the result of ellipsis (for related discussion pertaining to the interpretive consequences of object shift, see Chomsky 1999). If the latter, there is no explanation for the movement asymmetry between verb and object. Second, there is compelling evidence (Bošković 1996) that right node raising is a base-generated structure. So (6) may not be the exact parallel to (2). On the basis of this, we believe that our point still holds.

Serbo-Croatian provides an even more powerful argument that more than focus must be at stake.[1] As discussed in Stjepanović (1999), Serbo-Croatian allows

VP-ellipsis even when the verbs in the first and second conjuncts are different. This is illustrated in (7).

(7) Marko pokazuje Petra   Mariji,   a   Ivan
     Marko shows   Petar.ACC Marija.DAT and Ivan
     predstavlja_i [~~vp~~ t_i ~~Petra Mariji~~].
     introduces
     'Marko is showing Petar to Marija, and Ivan is introducing him to her.'

If mere focusing were at stake in the English cases, it would be possible to choose a different verb for the second conjunct. Here focusing on the verb is possible; hence, raising is available. Something like (8) is therefore predicted to be good, incorrectly.

(8) *Peter kissed Mary, and Tom hit_i [~~vp~~ t_i ~~Mary~~].

In light of this, we take the contrast between (2) and (4) to be genuine.

Sentences like (4) are also discussed by Matsuo (1999), who accounts for their ungrammaticality in terms of some version of Relativized Minimality. Matsuo adopts a proposal by Lasnik (1999b) for resolving a different problem in pseudogapping constructions. In particular, she assumes with Lasnik (1999b), who in turn follows Lobeck (1995) and Zagona (1982, 1988), that for VP-ellipsis to be licensed, the elided phrase (namely, VP) must be governed by an appropriate head, which for Lasnik is T^0. Furthermore, Lasnik suggests that there must not be any intervening lexical verbal heads between T^0 and the elided VP; otherwise, ellipsis will not be licensed, owing to a violation of "some version of Relativized Minimality" (p. 162). Matsuo argues that this is exactly what is wrong with (4). In (4) the lexical verbal head *got* intervenes between T^0 and VP_2, which undergoes VP-ellipsis, resulting in a violation of "some version of Relativized Minimality."

[. . .]

Neither Matsuo nor Lasnik suggests precisely how Relativized Minimality rules out these sentences – that is, why an intervening verbal head matters here. And, in fact, the generalization that there cannot be any intervening verbal heads between T^0 and the elided VP is not correct. Consider the following sentence from Serbo-Croatian.

(9) Ivan je kupio automobil, a   i   Marija je kupila ~~automobil~~.
     Ivan is bought car   and too Marija is bought car
     'Ivan bought a car, and Marija did too.'

Stjepanović (1997) provides compelling arguments that examples like (9) involve VP-ellipsis of the lowest VP after the participle raises out of that VP. Furthermore, Bošković (1997) shows that participles in Serbo-Croatian move out of their VPs, but that their landing site is not T^0. This means that participles in Serbo-Croatian constructions like (9) do intervene between T^0 and the phrase undergoing VP-ellipsis.[2]

Furthermore, even in English one finds examples where a verbal head inter-venes between T^0 and a VP undergoing VP-ellipsis, as illustrated in (10).

(10)   Debbie might have done it, but Kazuko might have ~~done it~~ also.

In (10) *have* intervenes between the modal verb *might* – standardly analyzed as being in T^0 – and the ellipsis site, and the sentence is perfectly grammatical.

Given these examples, we conclude that Matsuo's (1999) and Lasnik's (1999b) Relativized Minimality accounts of (4) and related constructions cannot be maintained. But then the only account we are left with is a stipulation that XP-movement is forced, but X^0-movement is not, which is clearly undesirable. The issue is somewhat reminiscent of Lasnik's (1981) argument against rule ordering in grammar, which he showed could be eliminated by severing affix hopping from all other transformations. In the present context one might say that XP-movement must apply first, leaving room for ellipsis to apply before head movement.

4   Head movement as a PF phenomenon

We believe that a solution to both problems – stipulating obligatory/optional move-ment, and the (at best) inconclusive evidence in favor of syntactic-feature-triggered head movement – is to assume that head movement (in our case, V-movement) takes place after Spell-Out, in the phonological component, as Chomsky has suggested in recent years.[3]

Assuming XP-movement, like object shift, to be syntactic (driven by the check-ing of some feature), it necessarily takes place in the syntax. If head movement is a PF (post-Spell-Out) phenomenon, it necessarily follows all syntactic movement operations and could be "superseded" by an ellipsis rule: not being syntactically driven, head movement and ellipsis (both PF operations, we assume) compete, the choice between them being determined by independent factors (on which, see below).

As Howard Lasnik (personal communication) points out, our PF theory so far does not exclude a third possibility: doing nothing to the verb (neither moving nor deleting it), thus incorrectly ruling in (11).

(11)   *Debbie ate chocolate, and Kazuko milk$_i$ drank t_i.

However, Lasnik's objection does not take into account the – we believe, real – possibility that V-movement is triggered in some way. We simply claim that the trigger is not featural, but may well be morphological, or prosodic, or a mixture of the two. The role of prosody in triggering head movement has recently been discussed by Holmberg (1997), Neeleman and Reinhart (1998), and Rivero (1999) (to name but a few). As for morphological triggering, it is a long-standing notion that, even though it has proven more difficult to make precise than one might have thought at first, is nonetheless well grounded. Thus, Rohrbacher (1999), Pollock (1997), and Acquaviva (to appear) account for asymmetries in V-movement by rely-ing on the morphological richness manifested in various languages.

Although we hasten to add that prosody and morphology might not be the whole story (e.g. it is unclear to us how to rule out *Debbie has the chocolate eaten*), we believe that such an approach provides a viable alternative to a purely checking account of V-movement.

To summarize, if head movement is a PF phenomenon, we have an answer to Lasnik's puzzle as to why V need not raise in the pseudogapping cases. Suppose ellipsis is a PF operation. Then head movement and ellipsis become competing operations: V either moves or is deleted, which is exactly what human language seems to require. In short, not only does the view of head movement as a PF operation remove any look-ahead and extrinsic ordering from the computational system, it also avoids the question of which head has the inadequacy that forces movement, a question we believe is doomed to remain unclear at best.

It is worth noting that the PF strategy is reminiscent of Lasnik's (1981) solution to extrinsic ordering among transformations. Lasnik achieved the desired result by factoring out the essentially morphological (PF) affix-hopping operation from the grammar. We suggest that the same be done with (most cases of) head movement.

It is also worth noting that in the approaches taken in both Lasnik (1995) and Lasnik (1999a), PF plays a crucial role in determining whether a derivation crashes or not, being tied as it is to the issue of V-raising, all other requirements being met. This role receives a much more natural explanation if head movement is a PF phenomenon.

5 Conclusion

To conclude, we have argued on the basis of pseudogapping constructions that Chomsky's recent claim that head movement is to be viewed as a PF phenomenon may well be right. We have shown that at least in the case at hand it provides a natural answer to a perennial problem for Lasnik's otherwise (we believe) correct account of pseudogapping. While a full-fledged theory of PF operations remains to be worked out before the view that head movement falls outside the core computational system can be fully endorsed, Chomsky seems right in pointing out that PF seems to be its most natural place, given otherwise well-motivated principles like Attract, the elimination of strength, and (in one form or another) the Extension Condition, all of which conflict with a syntactic view of head movement.

Notes

1 Thanks to Željko Bošković for bringing the relevance of Serbo-Croatian to our attention.

2 Bošković (in press: ch. 2) and Stjepanović (1997) argue that auxiliaries in Serbo-Croatian sentences like (9) are in T or Agr_S.

3 The solution can be traced back to a suggestion by Joe Kupin (reported in Lasnik 1981), according to which affix hopping is to be seen as an "interface operation."

References

Acquaviva, P. To appear. Uniform lexicalization: Deriving spell-out without [+/−strong] features. *Rivista di Linguistica*.

Bošković, Ž. 1996. Right-node raising as base-generation. Ms., University of Connecticut, Storrs.

Bošković, Ž. 1997. *The syntax of nonfinite complementation: An economy approach*. Cambridge, MA: MIT Press.

Bošković, Ž. in press. *On the nature of the syntax–phonology interface: Cliticization and related phenomena*. [Published by Amsterdam: Elsevier, 2001.]

Chomsky, N. 1993. A minimalist program for linguistic theory. In K. Hale and S. J. Keyser (eds.), *The view from Building 20: Essays in linguistics in honor of Sylvain Bromberger*, Cambridge, MA: MIT Press, pp. 1–52. [Reprinted in Chomsky (1995), *The Minimalist Program*, Cambridge, MA: MIT Press, pp. 167–217.]

Chomsky, N. 1994. *Bare phrase structure. MIT Occasional Papers in Linguistics 5*. Cambridge, MA: MITWPL. [Published in P. Kempchinsky (ed.) (1994), *Evolution and revolution in linguistic theory: Essays in honor of Carlos Otero*, Washington, DC: Georgetown University Press, pp. 51–109. Also published in G. Webelhuth (ed.) (1994), *Government and binding theory and the minimalist program*, Cambridge, MA: MIT Press, pp. 383–439.]

Chomsky, N. 1995. Categories and transformations. In Chomsky (1995), *The Minimalist Program*, Cambridge, MA: MIT Press, pp. 219–394.

Chomsky, N. 1999. *Derivation by phase. MIT Occasional Papers in Linguistics 18*. Cambridge, MA: MITWPL. [Reprinted in M. Kenstowicz (ed.) (2001), *Ken Hale: A Life in Linguistics*, Cambridge, MA: MIT Press, pp. 1–52.]

Chomsky, N. 2000. Minimalist inquiries: The framework. In R. Martin, D. Michaels and J. Uriagereka (eds.), *Step by step: Essays on minimalism in honor of Howard Lasnik*, Cambridge, MA: MIT Press, pp. 89–155.

Holmberg, A. 1997. The true nature of Holmberg's Generalization. In K. Kusumoto (ed.), *Proceedings of the 27th Annual Meeting of the North East Linguistic Society*, Amherst, MA: GLSA, pp. 203–17.

Jayaseelan, K. A. 1990. Incomplete VP deletion and gapping. *Linguistic Analysis* 20: 64–81.

Lasnik, H. 1981. Restricting the theory of transformations: A case study. In N. Hornstein and D. Lightfoot (eds.), *Explanation in linguistics*, Harlow: Longman, pp. 152–73.

Lasnik, H. 1995. Notes on pseudogapping. In R. Pensalfini and H. Ura (eds.), *Papers on minimalism. MIT Working Papers in Linguistics 27*, Cambridge, MA: MITWPL, pp. 143–63.

Lasnik, H. 1999a. On feature strength: Three minimalist approaches to overt movement. *Linguistic Inquiry* 30: 197–217.

Lasnik, H. 1999b. Pseudogapping puzzles. In E. Benmamoun and S. Lappin (eds.), *Fragments: Studies on ellipsis and gapping*, Oxford: Oxford University Press, pp. 141–74.

Lobeck, A. 1995. *Ellipsis: Functional heads, identification, and licensing*. Oxford: Oxford University Press.

Matsuo, A. 1999. Relativized Minimality in VP-ellipsis constructions. Ms., Université du Québec à Montréal.

Neeleman, A. and T. Reinhart. 1998. Scrambling and the PF interface. In M. Butt and W. Geuder (eds.), *The projection of arguments*, Stanford: CSLI, pp. 309–53.

Ochi, M. 1999. Constraints on feature checking. Doctoral dissertation, University of Connecticut, Storrs.

Pollock, J.-Y. 1997. Notes on clause structure. In L. Haegeman (ed.), *Elements of grammar: Handbook in generative syntax*, Dordrecht: Kluwer, pp. 237–79.

Rivero, M.-L. 1999. Prosodic trigger for head-movement. Ms., University of Ottawa.

Rohrbacher, B. W. 1999. *Morphology-driven syntax: A theory of V to I raising and pro-drop*. Amsterdam/Philadelphia: John Benjamins.

Stjepanović, S. 1997. VP-ellipsis in a V raising language: Implications for verbal morphology. In J. Austin and A. Lawson (eds.), *Proceedings of ESCOL '97*, Ithaca, NY: Cornell University, pp. 192–203.

Stjepanović, S. 1999. *What do second-position clitics, scrambling, and multiple wh-fronting have in common?* Doctoral dissertation, University of Connecticut, Storrs.

Zagona, K. 1982. *Government and proper government of verbal projections*. Doctoral dissertation, University of Washington.

Zagona, K. 1988. Proper government of antecedentless VP in English and Spanish. *Natural Language and Linguistic Theory* 6: 95–128.

5

LCA/C-command Related Issues

From *THE ANTISYMMETRY OF SYNTAX*
Richard S. Kayne

1 Introduction and proposal

1.1 Introduction

It is standardly assumed that Universal Grammar (UG) allows a given hierarchical representation to be associated with more than one linear order. For example, postpositional phrases and prepositional phrases are generally taken to be hierarchically identical, differing only in linear order. Similarly, English and Japanese phrases consisting of a verb and its complement are thought of as symmetric to one another, also differing only in linear order.

In this monograph I will propose a restrictive theory of word order and phrase structure that denies this standard assumption. I will argue that phrase structure in fact always completely determines linear order and consequently that if two phrases differ in linear order, they must also differ in hierarchical structure.

More specifically, I will propose that asymmetric c-command invariably maps into linear precedence. I will offer a particular formulation of this simple idea that will yield two major consequences. First, there will follow with few further hypotheses a highly specific theory of word order, essentially that complements must always follow their associated head and that specifiers and adjoined elements must always precede the phrase that they are sister to. I will try to show that this then leads to a series of favorable empirical results.

Second, the requirement that hierarchical structure map uniquely to linear order will turn out to yield a derivation of the essentials of X-bar theory. Put another way, I will argue that X-bar theory is not a primitive component of UG. Rather, X-bar theory in essence expresses a set of antisymmetric properties of phrase structure. This antisymmetry of phrase structure will be seen to be inherited, in effect, from the more basic antisymmetry of linear order.

Let us start from the familiar notion of phrase marker, with the usual distinction between terminal symbols and nonterminal symbols. At least in the PF wing of the grammar, the terminal symbols must be linearly ordered. A linear ordering has three defining properties.

(1)   a.   It is transitive; that is, xLy & yLz → xLz.
      b.   It is total; that is, it must cover all the members of the set: for all distinct x, y, either xLy or yLx.
      c.   It is antisymmetric, that is, not(xLy & yLx).

The familiar dominance relation on nonterminals is not a linear ordering. Although it is both transitive and antisymmetric, the dominance relation is not total; that is, there can be two nodes in a given phrase marker such that neither dominates the other.

However, the dominance relation has something significant in common with a linear ordering, beyond being transitive and antisymmetric. Consider a given nonterminal X in a phrase marker, and then consider the set of nonterminals that dominate X. For all X, that set is linearly ordered by the dominance relation, that is, for all X, Y dominates X & Z dominates X → either Y dominates Z or Z dominates Y. Although the dominance relation itself is not total, it becomes total when restricted to the set of nodes dominating a given node. Let us say that it is *locally total*, in this sense.[1] Let us further say that, although the dominance relation is not a linear ordering, it is, by virtue of being locally total, a *locally linear* ordering (in the sense that it becomes linear if one restricts oneself to the local environment of a given node).

The familiar relation of c-command is transitive, but unlike the dominance relation it is not even antisymmetric, since two sister nodes can c-command each other. However, we can add antisymmetry to c-command by simply taking the relation of asymmetric c-command:

(2)   X asymmetrically c-commands Y iff X c-commands Y and Y does not c-command X.

This relation is now both transitive and antisymmetric. It is not total, since in a given phrase marker there can be two nodes neither of which (asymmetrically) c-commands the other. But if we restrict ourselves henceforth to binary-branching phrase markers,[2] it is locally total, and hence locally linear, in the same sense as the dominance relation. This is so, since in a binary branching tree, if Y asymmetrically c-commands X and Z (distinct from Y) also asymmetrically c-commands X, then it must be the case that either Y asymmetrically c-commands Z or Z asymmetrically c-commands Y.

We now have two locally linear relations on nonterminals, dominance and asymmetric c-command. The intuition that I would like to pursue is that there should be a very close match between the linear ordering relation on the set of terminals and some comparable relation on nonterminals. By *comparable*, I now mean locally linear. Of the two locally linear relations at issue, it is natural to take asymmetric c-command to be the one that is closely matched to the linear ordering of the set of terminals.

This matching will have to be mediated by the familiar dominance relation that holds between nonterminals and terminals. To keep this relation separate from the above-discussed dominance relation between nonterminals, which I will think of as D, I will refer to the nonterminal-to-terminal dominance relation as d. This relation d is a many-to-many mapping from nonterminals to terminals. For a given nonterminal X, let us call d(X) the set of terminals that X dominates. d(X) can be said to be the "image" under d of X.

Just as we can speak of the image under d of a particular nonterminal, so we can speak of the image under d of an ordered pair of nonterminals $\langle X, Y \rangle$. What we want to say is that the image under d of $\langle X, Y \rangle$ will be based on d(X) and d(Y), specifically by taking the image to be the Cartesian product of d(X) and d(Y). Put somewhat more formally, $d\langle X, Y \rangle$ (= the image under d of $\langle X, Y \rangle$) is the set of ordered pairs $\{\langle a, b \rangle\}$ such that a is a member of d(X) and b is a member of d(Y).

If instead of simply looking at one ordered pair $\langle X, Y \rangle$ and its image, we look at a set of ordered pairs and their images under d, we can introduce the natural notion that the image of a set of ordered pairs is just the set formed by taking the union of the images of each ordered pair in the original set. For example, let S be a set of ordered pairs $\{\langle X_i, Y_i \rangle\}$ for $0 < i < n$. Then d (S) = the union for all $i, 0 < i < n$ of $d\langle X_i, Y_i \rangle$.

1.2 Proposal

To express the intuition that asymmetric c-command is closely matched to the linear order of terminals, let us, for a given phrase marker, consider the set A of ordered pairs $\langle X_j, Y_j \rangle$ such that for each j, X_j asymmetrically c-commands Y_j. Let us further take A to be the maximal such set; that is, A contains all pairs of nonterminals such that the first asymmetrically c-commands the second. Then the central proposal I would like to make is the following (for a given phrase marker P, with T the set of terminals and A as just given):

(3)   *Linear Correspondence Axiom*
      d(A) is a linear ordering of T.

2 Deriving X-bar theory

To see how the Linear Correspondence Axiom (LCA) works in practice, let us begin with the simple phrase marker in (4).

(4)

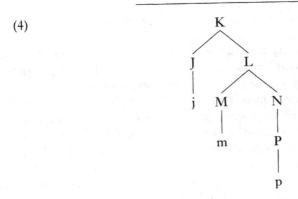

In this phrase marker the pairs that constitute the set A (i.e. the pairs of nonterminal nodes such that the first asymmetrically c-commands the second) are the following: ⟨J, M⟩, ⟨J, N⟩, ⟨J, P⟩, ⟨M, P⟩. Since in this simple case J, M, N and P all dominate just one terminal element, d (A) is easy to exhibit fully: namely, ⟨j, m⟩, ⟨j, p⟩, ⟨m, p⟩.[3] These three ordered pairs do constitute a linear ordering of the set {j, m, p}, given that (1) transitivity holds, (2) antisymmetry is respected, and (3) the ordering is total, in that for every pair of terminals an ordering is specified.

It should be noted that I am crucially taking c-command to be properly defined in terms of "first node up" and not in terms of "first branching node up." Under the latter type of definition the node P in (1) would c-command M, so that M would no longer asymmetrically c-command P, in which case no ordering between the terminals m and p would be specified at all, incorrectly.

The importance of this point can be seen further by considering the phrase marker (5), which is similar to (4) in all respects except that it lacks the node N.

(5)

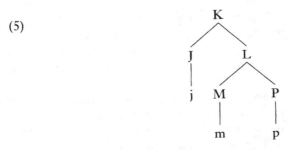

In (5) the set A of pairs such that the first nonterminal asymmetrically c-commands the second is as follows: ⟨J, M⟩, ⟨J, P⟩. Consequently, d(A) for (5) is composed of the pairs ⟨j, m⟩ and ⟨j, p⟩. Although the set d(A) consisting of these two pairs of terminals respects both transitivity (vacuously) and antisymmetry, it does not constitute a linear ordering of the set {j, m, p}, since it specifies no order at all between the two terminals m and p; that is, it fails to be total in the sense of (1b).

In other words, (5) fails to meet the requirement imposed by the LCA and is therefore not an admissible phrase marker. This has at least two desirable consequences. First, consider whether the complement of a head can itself be a head.

The usual assumption, within the context of X-bar theory, is that it cannot be. One could take that to be a basic fact of X-bar theory, but X-bar theory itself clearly provides no account of why it should hold. The LCA given in (3) does, since having a head whose complement was itself a head would yield precisely the configuration of M, P (and L) in (5), which is inadmissible.

The second desirable consequence related to (5) lies in the even more basic question of why a phrase cannot have more than one head. X-bar theory treats this as a basic fact about phrase structure but does not attempt to provide an explanation for it. The LCA does, since a phrase with two heads would again look like [L M P] in (5) and would again be excluded. Put another way, the LCA derives both the fact that a head cannot take a complement that is itself a head and the basic X-bar fact that a phrase cannot have two heads.[4]

The exclusion of (5) would not be affected if we added a nonhead sister node to M and P, as in (6).

(6)

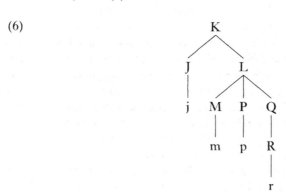

In (6) again neither M nor P asymmetrically c-commands the other (nor are m and p dominated by any other node that is in an asymmetric c-command relation). A for (6) is ⟨J, M⟩, ⟨J, P⟩, ⟨J, Q⟩, ⟨J, R⟩, ⟨M, R⟩, ⟨P, R⟩. d(A) is then ⟨j, m⟩, ⟨j, p⟩, ⟨j, r⟩, ⟨m, r⟩, ⟨p, r⟩. But again it lacks any pair involving m and p and so does not meet the totality requirement.

From this perspective, (5) and (6) are excluded essentially because the terminals m and p (and the nonterminals M and P that exhaustively dominate them) are in too symmetric a relation to one another. For that reason, they are not "seen" by the relation of asymmetric c-command and so fail to be incorporated into the required linear ordering. Another informal way to put this, reversing the vantage point, is, to say that the LCA, by virtue of requiring d (the dominance relation between nonterminals and terminals) to map A into a linear ordering, has forced the set of nonterminals to inherit the antisymmetry of the linear ordering of the terminals.

If we think of L in (5) as a VP = *see John*, with M = *see*, then the preceding discussion tells us that the complement *John* cannot be dominated (apart from VP and higher nodes) solely by N(oun), as in (7), but must also be dominated by (at least) another node NP, as in (8), in order for the phrase marker to be well formed.

(7) is not an admissible phrase marker, but (8) is (setting aside questions such as the choice between DP and NP). In (7) no linear ordering would be assigned

to *see* and *John*. In (8), on the other hand, *see* correctly is ordered with respect to (before) *John*, since V in (8) asymmetrically c-commands N.[5]

Comparing (5) with (4), we see that replacing one of the two symmetric nodes by a more complex substructure breaks the symmetry and renders

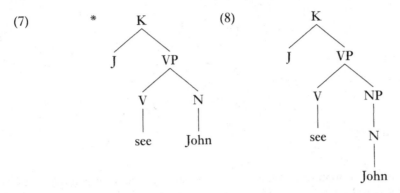

the phrase marker admissible. Now consider the result of adding structure under both M and P in (5), as in (9).

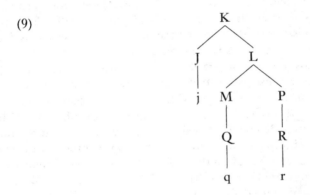

The asymmetric c–command set A for (9) is ⟨J, M⟩, ⟨J, Q⟩, ⟨J, P⟩, ⟨J, R⟩, ⟨M, R⟩, ⟨P, Q⟩. The corresponding d(A) is ⟨j, q⟩, ⟨j, r⟩, ⟨q, r⟩, ⟨r, q⟩. (⟨q, r⟩ is in d(A) since ⟨q, r⟩ = d⟨M, R⟩; ⟨r, q⟩ is in d(A) since ⟨r, q⟩ = d⟨P, Q⟩.) This d(A) for (9) is total, but it is not antisymmetric. Therefore, (9) is not an admissible phrase marker.

The problem with (9) is not exactly that M and P are symmetric in that each dominates one other nonterminal. This can be seen by adding more substructure to, for example, P, as in (10).

Concentrating just on the sub–phrase marker whose root node is L, we find that A there is ⟨M, R⟩, ⟨M, S⟩, ⟨M, T⟩, ⟨R, T⟩, ⟨P, Q⟩. But we now see that the addition of S and T, although resulting in a larger A, has not changed the heart of the problem in (9), which was the cooccurrence in A of ⟨M, R⟩ and ⟨P, Q⟩, which led to both ⟨q, r⟩ and ⟨r, q⟩ being in d(A), violating antisymmetry. Exactly the same problem arises in (10).[6]

(10)

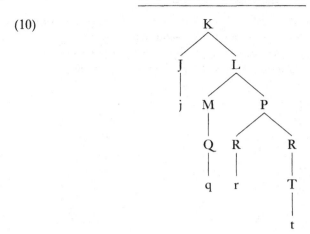

Let us call a nonterminal that dominates no other nonterminal a *head*. A nonterminal that does dominate at least one other nonterminal will be a *nonhead*. Then we can sum up the results of this chapter ((4)–(10)) in the following terms: if two nonterminals are sisters and if one of them is a head and the other a nonhead, the phrase marker is admissible ((4) and (8)). If both are heads, the phrase marker is not admissible ((5), (6), and (7)). If both are nonheads (9) and (10)), the phrase marker is again not admissible (whether or not the number of nonterminals dominated by each of those two nonheads is the same).

The prohibition against nonhead sisters has one clearly desirable and important consequence, and another consequence that will require a (familiar) refinement of the notion "nonterminal." Let me begin with the first. A basic tenet, perhaps the basic tenet, of X-bar theory is that all phrases must be headed. Thus, X-bar theory disallows a phrasal node immediately dominating two maximal projections and nothing else. X-bar theory does not, however, explain why every phrase must have a head. The LCA does. The reason that a phrasal node cannot dominate two maximal projections (and nothing else) is that if it did, there would be a failure of antisymmetry, exactly as discussed above for (9) and (10).

[. . .]

3 Adjunction

3.1 Segments and categories

The preceding discussion appears to rule out sentences such as (11), in which the subject clearly must have a sister constituent that is not a head.

(11)   The girl saw John.

Put more generally, specifiers and adjoined phrases appear to have no place in the theory being elaborated here. To allow for specifiers or adjoined phrases, I need to add a refinement to the theory of phrase structure presented so far. I will adopt the notion of segment, that is, the distinction between segment and category that was introduced by May (1985) and adopted by Chomsky (1986a). Let us return to the substructure of (10), repeated here, that was earlier argued to be inadmissible.

(12)

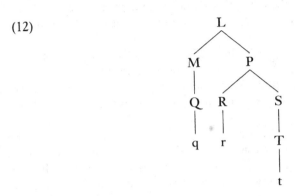

The problem arose with respect to both r and t in their relation to q. Let us look just at r. Since M asymmetrically c-commands R (i.e. *A* contains ⟨M, R⟩), it follows that d(*A*) contains ⟨q, r⟩. But d(*A*) also contains ⟨r, q⟩ by virtue of P asymmetrically c-commanding Q. As a result, d(*A*) violates antisymmetry; that is, it fails to be a linear ordering of the terminals.

This result is correct for the case in which M and P are both maximal projections dominated by another node L, and we want to maintain it. At the same time we want to allow for the case in which M is adjoined to P. The segment/category distinction leads to the statement that under adjunction L and P are two segments of one category. The question is how that makes (12) compatible with the LCA.

The solution I would like to propose is to restrict c-command to categories – that is, to say that a segment cannot enter into a c-command relation.

(13)   X c-commands Y iff *X and Y are categories* and X excludes[7] Y and every category that dominates X dominates Y.

In this light consider (14), the counterpart of (12) in which L is replaced by P, to indicate clearly the adjunction structure.

(14)

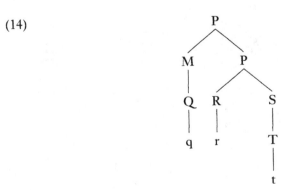

In (12) the problem was that d(A) contained both ⟨q, r⟩ and ⟨r, q⟩, the former as the image of ⟨M, R⟩, the latter as the image of ⟨P, Q⟩. The adjunction structure of (14), combined with the italicized part of (13), has the effect of eliminating ⟨P, Q⟩ from the A of (14), since the lower P is a segment and not a category.[8] Therefore, ⟨r, q⟩ does not belong to the d(A) of (14), and the potential violation of antisymmetry is eliminated.

The A associated with (14) is thus ⟨M, R⟩, ⟨M, S⟩, ⟨M, T⟩, ⟨R, T⟩.[9] The corresponding d(A) is ⟨q, r⟩, ⟨q, t⟩, ⟨r, t⟩, which constitutes a linear ordering of the set of terminals, as desired. We can now think of the segment/category distinction as being forced upon UG by the need to permit specifiers and adjoined phrases.[10]

Unless there turns out to be another natural way to permit specifiers within the theory developed here, the conclusion must be that a specifie is necessarily to be taken as an adjoined phrase, involving crucial use of the segment/category distinction.[11]

Returning to (14), note that what makes it compatible with the LCA is that (the lower) P does not c-command Q, as a result of the phrase added to the definition in (13). Strictly speaking, though, this property of (14) depends only on X in (13) being restricted to categories, the status of Y is not directly relevant. The idea that Y, too, must be a category (and not a segment) does have potential significance. If a segment cannot be c-commanded, and if antecedent government strictly has c-command as a necessary component, then a segment cannot be antecedent-governed and thus cannot be moved. In other words, a phrase that has something adjoined to it cannot be moved out by itself.

This derives the fact that a head to which a clitic (or other element) has adjoined cannot move up in such a way as to strand the clitic.[12] With respect to adjunction to a nonhead, recall that I have been led to analyze specifiers as involving adjunction. We consequently derive the prediction that the sister node of a specifier cannot be moved. This corresponds to a fairly standard assumption.[13]

3.2 Adjunction to a head

Adjunction to a head, as in the case of a clitic, is illustrated in the phrase marker (15).

(15)

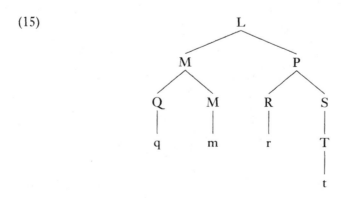

Here Q is adjoined to M. Since M does not dominate Q (only one of its segments does), the fact that M does not dominate R and S is irrelevant to Q's relation to R and S. In other words, the definition (13) of c-command has the effect that Q in (15) (asymmetrically) c-commands both R and S. The A for (15) is therefore $\langle Q, R \rangle$, $\langle Q, S \rangle$, $\langle Q, T \rangle$, $\langle M, R \rangle$, $\langle M, S \rangle$, $\langle M, T \rangle$, $\langle R, T \rangle$. (Note that although P c-commands both M and Q, it does not asymmetrically c-command either one, since M and Q both c-command P.) This yields d(A) = $\langle q, r \rangle$, $\langle q, t \rangle$, $\langle m, r \rangle$, $\langle m, t \rangle$, $\langle r, t \rangle$, which respects transitivity and antisymmetry, but appears to fail the requirement of totality, since no order is yet specified for q relative to m.

Again consider definition (13), repeated here.

(16)   X c-commands Y iff *X and Y are categories* and X excludes Y and every category that dominates X dominates Y.

By (16), M in (15) does not c-command Q because it does not exclude it. Q cannot c-command a segment of M alone, by assumption. However, Q in (15) does c-command the category M. This is so because Q excludes M and every category that dominates Q dominates M.[14]

The fact that Q in (15) c-commands, and hence asymmetrically c-commands, M means that the pair $\langle Q, M \rangle$ must be added to A: $\langle Q, R \rangle$, $\langle Q, S \rangle$, $\langle Q, T \rangle$, $\langle M, R \rangle$, $\langle M, S \rangle$, $\langle M, T \rangle$, $\langle R, T \rangle$, $\langle Q, M \rangle$. This results in the addition of $\langle q, m \rangle$ to d(A), yielding d(A) = $\langle q, r \rangle$, $\langle q, t \rangle$, $\langle m, r \rangle$, $\langle m, t \rangle$, $\langle r, t \rangle$, $\langle q, m \rangle$, which is a linear ordering of the set of terminals, as desired.[15]

The fact that Q also asymmetrically c-commands R and S as discussed three paragraphs back is an instance of a more general property of adjoined phrases, namely, that they always c-command "out of" the phrase they are adjoined to. Let us replace Q in (15) by a nonhead, as in (17).

(17)

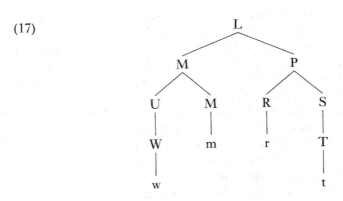

Here, U, a nonhead, has been adjoined to the head M. As before, M does not dominate U, so that U c-commands P and everything dominated by P. P itself c-commands U, so that U and P enter into no asymmetric c-command relation (as was true for Q and P in (15)).

Now consider W. W does not c-command P, because of the intervening presence of U. Therefore, P asymmetrically c-commands W. Hence, ⟨P, W⟩ is in A in (17) and ⟨r, w⟩ and ⟨t, w⟩ are in d(A). But U asymmetrically c-commands R, S, and T, so that ⟨U, R⟩, ⟨U, S⟩, and ⟨U, T⟩ are also in A, and correspondingly ⟨w, r⟩ and ⟨w, t⟩ are also in d(A). Thus, d(A) for (17) consists at least of ⟨r, w⟩, ⟨t, w⟩, ⟨w, r⟩, and ⟨w, t⟩, which violates antisymmetry, so that d(A) is not a linear ordering and (17) is excluded as a violation of the LCA.

Put another way, we have just derived without stipulation the fact that a non-head cannot be adjoined to a head, in all probability a correct result.[16]

3.3 Multiple adjunction: clitics

The phrase marker (15) represents the case of a clitic (Q) adjoined to a head (M). Now consider what happens if a second clitic (K) is adjoined to the same head (M), as in (18).

(18)

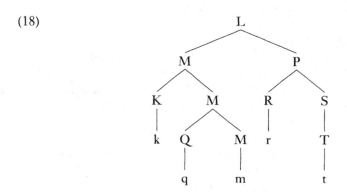

As before, Q c-commands P and everything dominated by P, and K does the same. The problem that arises for (18) instead concerns the relation between K and Q, neither of which is dominated by M. Consequently, K and Q c-command each other; that is, neither asymmetrically c-commands the other. Therefore, no linear order is specified for k and q (neither ⟨k, q⟩ nor ⟨q, k⟩ is contained in the d(A) of (18)), so that (18) is excluded by the LCA.

What we see here is that two (or more) clitics adjoined to the same head find themselves in too symmetric a relation: both clitics are dominated by segments of the same head and neither is dominated by that head as category. The required antisymmetry does not hold. The conclusion is inescapable: it is not possible to adjoin two (or more) clitics to the same head.

Run-of-the-mill French sentences like (19) appear to pose a problem.

(19) Jean vous   le donnera.
      Jean you_DAT it will-give
      'Jean will give it to you.'

However, two other structures are available for multiple clitics, both of which are compatible with the LCA. The one most likely to be appropriate for (19) is (20).

(20)

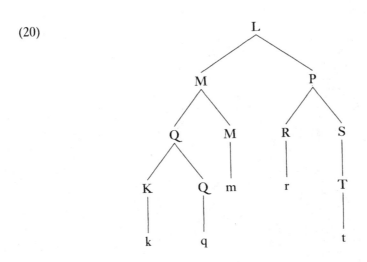

Here the clitic Q has adjoined to the head M, and the clitic K has in turn adjoined to the clitic Q. Q c-commands P and everything P dominates, as before. Since K is not dominated by Q (or by M), K c-commands P and everything P dominates, too. In other words, both K and Q asymmetrically c-command R, S, and T (but not P, since P c-commands both K and Q). The A for (20) is therefore $\langle K, Q \rangle$,[17] $\langle K, M \rangle$, $\langle Q, M \rangle$, $\langle M, R \rangle$, $\langle M, S \rangle$, $\langle M, T \rangle$, $\langle K, R \rangle$, $\langle K, S \rangle$, $\langle K, T \rangle$, $\langle Q, R \rangle$, $\langle Q, S \rangle$, $\langle Q, T \rangle$, $\langle R, T \rangle$. The corresponding d(A) is $\langle k, q \rangle$, $\langle k, m \rangle$, $\langle q, m \rangle$, $\langle m, r \rangle$, $\langle m, t \rangle$, $\langle k, r \rangle$, $\langle k, t \rangle$, $\langle q, r \rangle$, $\langle q, t \rangle$, $\langle r, t \rangle$, which is a linear ordering of the set of terminals, as desired.

The two clitics of (19) could thus be taken to form a constituent '[vous le]',[18] with *vous* adjoined to *le*.

[...]

Although no more than one clitic can be adjoined to a given head, the possibility still remains open that two adjacent clitics are to be analyzed as being adjoined to two distinct (nonclitic) heads. [...]

In summary, from the perspective of the LCA, sequences of clitics must not be analyzed as successive adjunctions to the same head but instead should be analyzed as involving either adjunctions to distinct functional heads (e.g. one clitic to Tense, one to Agr) or adjunctions of one clitic to another, or some combination thereof.

3.4 Multiple adjunctions: nonheads

The antisymmetry requirement induced by the LCA has the same consequence for adjunctions of nonheads to nonheads as it does for adjunctions of heads to heads, as discussed for clitics in the previous section. The relevant phrase marker has the form shown in (21).

(21)

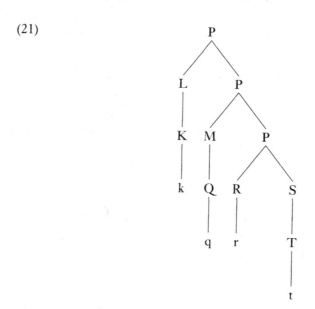

In (21) the nonhead M has been adjoined to the nonhead P, and the nonhead L has been further adjoined to the two-segment category P that was the output of the first adjunction.

In a way partially parallel to the discussion of (18), there is a problem with (21) concerning the relation between k and q. The problem here is specifically that L asymmetrically c-commands Q and at the same time M asymmetrically c-commands K. Thus, ⟨L, Q⟩ and ⟨M, K⟩ are both in the *A* of (21), so that ⟨k, q⟩ and ⟨q, k⟩ are both in d(*A*), with a consequent violation of antisymmetry.

I conclude that the adjunction of more than one nonhead to a given non-head is impossible. Since in this theory specifiers are a case of adjunction, we derive the fact (stated by X-bar theory) that a given phrase can have only one specifier.

This limitation on specifiers is not controversial (so that its derivation is clearly desirable), but the more general limitation on adjoined phrases is potentially con-troversial, since it is usually assumed that more than one phrase can be adjoined to a given projection (nonhead) and also that a phrase can be adjoined to a phrase that already has a specifier.

3.5 Specifiers

Let me begin indirectly by pointing out that the present theory does allow a cer-tain kind of multiple adjunction, parallel to that seen above in the case of clitics. More specifically, it is permissible to adjoin Y to X and Z to Y. The relevant phrase marker looks like (22).

(22)

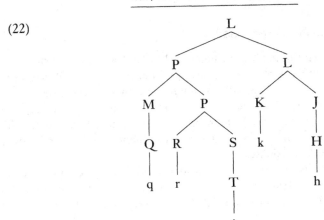

Here, the nonhead P has been adjoined to the nonhead L, and the nonhead M has been adjoined to P.

In (22) M is dominated neither by P nor by L. Consequently, M asymmetrically c-commands K, J, and H (see note 9), so that the asymmetric c-command set A contains $\langle M, K \rangle$, $\langle M, J \rangle$, and $\langle M, H \rangle$. Since M dominates q, d(A) contains $\langle q, k \rangle$ and $\langle q, h \rangle$. Similarly for $\langle M, R \rangle$, $\langle M, S \rangle$, $\langle M, T \rangle$ and $\langle q, r \rangle$, $\langle q, t \rangle$; also $\langle R, T \rangle$, $\langle K, H \rangle$ and $\langle r, t \rangle$, $\langle k, h \rangle$. The remaining pairs $\langle r, k \rangle$, $\langle r, h \rangle$, $\langle t, k \rangle$, $\langle t, h \rangle$ come into d(A) by virtue of P asymmetrically c-commanding K and J. (K and J do not c-command P, since L, which dominates K and J, does not dominate P.) (22) is thus compatible with the LCA.

This type of phrase marker takes on particular interest when we recall that in the theory being developed here specifiers are an instance of adjunction. Therefore, M in (22) could just as well be a specifier of P and P a specifier of L – in which case the specifier of the specifier of L would asymmetrically c-command K and J and everything dominated by K and J. Taking L = IP, K = I, and J = VP, we reach the conclusion that the specifier of the subject of IP asymmetrically c-commands I and VP and everything within VP.

This conclusion has some favorable consequences. First, it brings back into the fold the recalcitrant cases of pronoun binding by a quantifier phrase that are discussed by Reinhart (1983: 177). For example:

(23)   Every girl's father thinks she's a genius.

From the present perspective, the fact that *every girl* is in the specifier of the subject DP does not interfere with its binding the pronoun. Since specifiers are adjoined phrases, the definition of c-command adopted above, and repeated here, has the effect that *every girl* in (23) does in fact c-command *she*.

(24)   X c-commands Y iff X and Y are categories and X excludes Y and every category that dominates X dominates Y.

[. . .]

3.7   Adjunction of a head to a nonhead

Can a head be adjoined to a nonhead? Chomsky (1986: 73) shows that such adjunction followed by further movement back to a head position leads to an undesirable result. I will now show that the desired prohibition follows directly from the theory developed here. In its essentials, the phrase marker that corresponds to Chomsky's case is (25).

P here is the nonhead to which the head M has adjoined. K is the next higher head to which M is to move. (Note that the argument that follows holds independently of where M originates.)

To see that (25) violates the LCA, consider k and m. K c-commands M, but M also c-commands K (since M is not dominated by P). Furthermore, although K c-commands P, P also c-commands K. Therefore, A for (25)

(25)

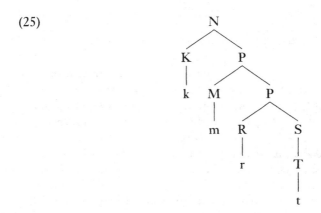

contains no pair that could lead, via the mapping d, to either ⟨k, m⟩ or ⟨m, k⟩ being in d(A). Thus, d(A) will fail the requirement of totality and hence fail to constitute the necessary linear ordering of the terminals of (25), as desired.[19]

Observe that although k and m yield a violation in (25) (essentially because they are too symmetric to one another), there is no parallel violation based on m and r. M c-commands R in (25), but R does not c-command M (since P dominates R without dominating M). Hence, M asymmetrically c-commands R, leading to ⟨m, r⟩ being in d(A), so that m and r pose no totality requirement problem.

This means that (25) without K (and N), as shown in (26), is well formed.

(26)

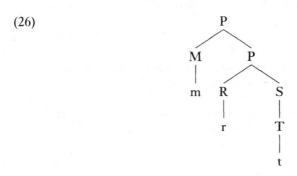

Assume, however, that the highest element of a chain of heads must have a specifier, in the sense of having a phrase that asymmetrically c-commands it within its maximal projection (or within the maximal projection of the head it is adjoined to). Then (26) is not legitimate. Furthermore, adjoining a nonhead to P in (26) would not yield a specifier of M, since M would c-command that adjoined phrase (given that M is not dominated by P). Adjunction of a head to a nonhead is thus systematically unavailable.

Since specifiers are instances of adjunction, it follows that specifiers cannot be heads.[20]

4 Word order

4.1 The specifier–complement asymmetry

I would now like to explore the relation between the LCA, repeated in (27), and the ordering, in terms of precedence/subsequence, of the terminals of a given phrase marker.

(27) *Linear Correspondence Axiom*
d(A) is a linear ordering of T.

Implicit in the earlier discussion was the assumption (not used until now) that the linear ordering of terminals constituted by d(A) must directly and uniformly provide the precedence/subsequence relation for the set of terminals.

However, nothing said so far tells us whether it is precedence itself or rather subsequence that is provided. Put another way, the question is whether asymmetric c-command is mapped (by d) to precedence or to subsequence. If it is to precedence, then the following holds:

(28) Let X, Y be nonterminals and x, y terminals such that X dominates x and Y dominates y. Then if X asymmetrically c-commands Y, x precedes y.

Were asymmetric c-command to map to subsequence, then *precedes* in (28) would have to be replaced by *follows*. I will proceed to argue that (28) is true as stated, namely, that asymmetric c-command does map to precedence.

Let us temporarily hold the choice between precedence and subsequence in abeyance, however, and consider again a phrase marker representing a head with complement and specifier, as in (29).

(29)

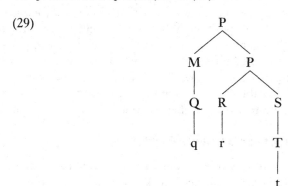

Since M asymmetrically c-commands R (the head) – that is, *A* contains ⟨M, R⟩ – it follows that d(*A*) contains ⟨q, r⟩. Similarly, since R asymmetrically c-commands T, d(*A*) contains ⟨r, t⟩. It therefore follows that with respect to the ordering of terminals, q and t are necessarily on opposite sides of the head r.

A similar conclusion would hold if M dominated a more complex phrase than just Q and if S dominated a more complex phrase than just T, as in (30).

(30)

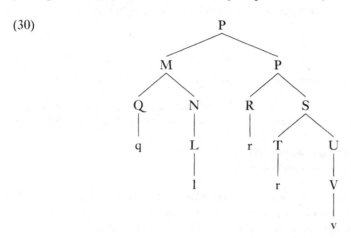

In (30) M asymmetrically c-commands R and R asymmetrically c-commands T, U, and V. Therefore, *A* for (30) contains ⟨M, R⟩, ⟨R, T⟩, ⟨R, U⟩, ⟨R, V⟩. From the fact that ⟨M, R⟩ is in *A*, it follows that ⟨q, r⟩ and ⟨l, r⟩ are in d(*A*). From the fact that ⟨R, T⟩ and ⟨R, U⟩ are in *A*, it follows that ⟨r, t⟩ and ⟨r, v⟩ are in d(*A*). In other words, all the terminals of the specifier M are on the opposite side of the head R (terminal r) from all the terminals of the complement S.

More generally put, no matter how complex the specifier or complement, it will always be the case, in any phrase marker, that specifier and complement are on opposite sides of the head. In other words, if we represent head, specifier, and complement as H, S, and C, then the conclusion so far is that of the six permutations of H, S and C, only two are permitted by the theory, namely, S-H-C and C-H-S. The other four (S-C-H, C-S-H, H-S-C, H-C-S) are all excluded by the requirement that specifier and complement be on opposite sides of the head.

The exclusion of S-C-H (e.g. of SOV) requires us to distinguish a complement position from the contents of that position. What I claim, and will return to in more detail below, is that SOV (and more generally S-C-H) is strictly impossible, in any language, if taken to indicate a phrase marker in which the sister phrase to the head (i.e. the complement position) precedes that head. On the other hand, SOV (and S-C-H) is perfectly allowable if taken to indicate a phrase marker in which the complement has raised up to some specifier position to the left of the head.

4.2   Specifier-head-complement as a universal order

We are now left with two constituent order possibilities, specifier-head-complement and complement-head-specifier. A rapid look at (a small subset of) the world's (presently existing) languages reveals that of the two orders, the former is a significantly more plausible universal than is the latter. Consideration of the relative order of head and complement alone is not sufficient to yield any firm conclusion, since both head–complement and complement-head orders are widely attested. On the other hand, the relative order of specifier and head is much more visibly asymmetric, in the following sense: although there may be some categories for which both orders are widespread, there are other categories where specifier-head order strongly predominates. (I know of no categories for which head-specifier is the cross-linguistically predominant order.)

In fact, CP is a category whose specifier, the typical landing site for moved *wh*-phrases, is visibly initial to an overwhelming degree.[21] Spec,IP (i.e. subject position) is clearly predominantly initial in its phrase.[22] That is straightforwardly true for SVO and SOV languages, and almost as obviously true for VSO languages, assuming the by now usual analysis of VSO order as deriving from SVO order by leftward V-movement.[23] According to Greenberg (1966: 76), the other types, OVS, OSV, and VOS, are "excessively rare."

From the present perspective, OSV would involve movement of the O past S to the specifier position of a higher head. OVS and VOS must not have S in a final specifier position, but must instead either have OV or VO moving as a unit leftward past S, or else V and O moving separately leftward past S,[24] with the expectation, then, that such languages should show OVSX and VOSX orders.

I conclude that specifier-head-complement, and not the reverse, is the only order available to the subcomponents of a phrase. Consider again, in this light, (30). The conclusion just stated that S-H-C order is the only one available means that the linear ordering d(A) containing, for example, $\langle q, r \rangle$ and $\langle l, r \rangle$ and $\langle r, t \rangle$ and $\langle r, v \rangle$ should be interpreted so that $\langle x, y \rangle$ means that the terminal symbol x *precedes* the terminal symbol y.

[. . .]

5 Further consequences

5.1 There is no directionality parameter

If UG unfailingly imposes S-H-C order, there cannot be any directionality parameter in the standard sense of the term. The difference between so-called head–initial languages and so-called head-final languages cannot be due to a parametric setting whereby complement positions in the latter type precede their associated heads.[25]

Instead, we must think of word order variation in terms of different combinations of movements. Note first that from the present perspective, any movement of a phrase upward to a c-commanding position must be leftward. This is so, for the simple reason that asymmetric c-command implies precedence.[26]

If syntactic theory allowed lowering a phrase to a position c-commanded by the original position, such movement would have to be rightward. If lowerings are not available at all, as Chomsky's (1993) proposals would lead one to expect, then that possibility can be set aside. (Lowerings, as well as movements to a position that neither c-commands nor is c-commanded by the original position, can be excluded by a familiar requirement to the effect that every trace of movement must be asymmetrically c-commanded by its antecedent; see Fiengo 1977.)

The picture of word order variation I arrive at, then, is the following. Languages all have S-H-C order. Languages (or subparts of languages) in which some complement precedes the associated head must necessarily have moved that complement leftward past the head into some specifier position. To take a simple example, consider prepositional phrases versus postpositional phrases. The former can be thought of as reflecting the basic order H-C. The latter cannot be. Rather, postpositional phrases must be derived by moving the complement of the adposition into the specifier position of that adposition (or of a higher functional head associated with it).

Similarly for categories other than P. In an OV language (or construction) the O must necessarily have moved leftward past the V into a higher specifier position. In a language where IP precedes C^0, IP must have moved leftward into Spec,C^0. And so on.

[. . .]

5.2   The LCA applies to all syntactic representations

The LCA imposes a tight relation between hierarchical structure and linear order. Linear order is a fundamental aspect of certain syntactic representations, in particular, those that feed into PF. However, there are other syntactic representations, notably those at LF and those at D-Structure (or the closest counterparts to D-Structure in Chomsky's (1993) framework), for which one might think that linear order is not essential. The question arises, then, whether the LCA needs to be taken to apply to all syntactic representations.

Recall that I have argued that the LCA is the source of all the major properties of phrase structure that have been attributed to X-bar theory, in other words, that X-bar theory, rather than being a primitive part of syntactic theory, actually derives from the LCA (plus the definition of c-command in terms of categories, as in (24)). It follows that to declare the LCA inapplicable to some level of representation – say, LF – would be to declare inapplicable to that level of representation all the restrictions on phrase structure familiar from X-bar theory (existence of at least one and at most one head per phrase, etc.). In the absence of compelling evidence to the contrary, the much more restrictive characterization of phrase structure is to be preferred. Since I see no such compelling evidence to the contrary, I conclude that the LCA does underlie the entire set of syntactic representations and therefore that every syntactic representation is automatically associated with a fixed linear ordering of its terminal symbols.

Notes

1   Strictly speaking, the term should be *left-locally total*.
2   See Kayne (1984: chs 6 and 7).
3   Note that $\langle j, p \rangle$ corresponds to both d$\langle J, N \rangle$ and d$\langle J, P \rangle$.
4   These two cases differ only in that in one instance M and P stand for identically labeled nodes and in the other they do not. Whether M and P are identical in category or not has no effect on the way in which the LCA applies here.

5   The question arises of what happens if *John* (or any phrase) is moved. If the result of movement is that DP (or NP) dominates just a trace, then *see* and that trace will not be ordered at all with respect to one another, since the internal structure of DP (or NP), which ensured antisymmetry, will have been lost. This might conceivably be a tolerable consequence, since traces are in any event not visible. It is notable, though, that this question does not arise if movement transformations leave a copy rather than a trace (see Chomsky 1993).

6   Where antisymmetry is in addition violated by ⟨q, t⟩ and ⟨t, q⟩.

7   In the sense of Chomsky (1986: 9): X excludes Y if no segment of X dominates Y.

8   The category P consisting of the two segments does not c-command Q by virtue of the exclusion part of the definition of c-command.

9   ⟨R, M⟩ is not in this set because P, which dominates R, does not dominate M, since only one of its segments dominates M.

   ⟨M, R⟩ is in *A* here since every category dominating M dominates R. This holds vacuously if P is the root node, nonvacuously otherwise. (The vacuous case could be eliminated by specifying in the definition of c-command ". . . and every category *or segment* that dominates X dominates Y"; but that would prevent c-command from out of adjunction configurations, in the sense discussed below.)

10 Without the segment/category distinction, and hence without specifiers or adjoined phrases, UG would be significantly less rich than we know it to be. On the other hand, it is worth noting that certain phrases, such as PP, DP, and NP, typically display no specifier (or adjoined phrase) and that if $Agr_{(S)}$ could bear a theta-role while still being a pure head of AgrP, then a verb could have a subject without having a specifier. If one were speculating about the evolution of UG, one would therefore be led to consider the possibility of a stage lacking the category/segment distinction.

11 See Fukui (1986) on Japanese. From the present perspective, there is a basic distinction between heads (categories that dominate no nonterminal) and nonheads (categories that dominate at least one nonterminal). Within the class of nonheads, a further distinction can be made between those that have a phrase adjoined to them and those that do not. See also the second paragraph of note 13.

12 See Kayne (1991: 649). The text proposal does not by itself prohibit the adjoined clitic from moving farther up; see Roberts (1991) and Kayne (1991: 661 n.).

13 See Chomsky (1986: 4). The text prediction is incompatible with the movement of *to*-VP proposed in Kayne (1985: 115) (for recent discussion of particle constructions, see den Dikken 1992) and is similarly incompatible with Riemsdijk's (1989) analysis of *Bücher habe ich keine mehr* 'books have I no more' as involving movement of X^1. Besten and Webelhuth's (1990) analysis of German remnant topicalization is compatible with the text prediction as long as the XP moved out of the to-be-topicalized VP is not adjoined to that VP (rather, the XP must move higher).

   Chomsky's (1986: 6) proposal that adjunction to an argument is prohibited (see McCloskey 1992) could perhaps be derived if arguments all had to move (by LF) and if what a specifier is adjoined to is not an argument.

14 Note that the category M does not dominate Q, so that there is no need to take M to dominate itself. On the contrary, it is in all probability preferable that dominance be irreflexive. See Chomsky (1986: n. 11). Compare also the irreflexivity of asymmetric c-command and of linear precedence itself, which I argued earlier to be significantly similar to dominance.

15 Note that the category M does not dominate q, since only one of its segments does.

16 See Chomsky and Lasnik (1993: sec. 3); also the observations in Kayne (1975: secs. 2.3, 2.4), to the effect that clitics in French are never phrasal.

   Note that if the head to which the nonhead was adjoined had no complement structure at all, then the violation displayed in the text would not occur; however, with no complement structure, there would be no source for the adjoined phrase.

17　Recall that K asymmetrically c-commands Q since every category dominating K dominates Q (so that K c-commands Q), whereas Q does not exclude K (so that Q cannot c-command K).

18　This constituent structure may turn out to be supported by the fact that Italian dative clitic doubling is facilitated by the presence of an adjacent accusative clitic; see Cinque (1990: 178, n. 4).

19　This exclusion of (25) is essentially akin to the exclusion of (6).

20　The proposal in Kayne (1991: 668), to the effect that French *de* can be in Spec, CP can now be correct only if interpreted to mean that '[PP[P de]]' can be in Spec, CP.

21　See Bach (1971: 160). Ultan (1978: 229) mentions one language (Khasi) that appears to have question words in sentence-final position. In languages like Hungarian, the interrogative phrase, although not sentence-initial, clearly seems to precede the head it is associated with.

22　This point is made by Johnson (1991: 584).

23　See Emonds (1980) and many more recent works.

24　See the convincing arguments given by Ordóñez (1994) in favor of the idea that in Spanish VOS sentences the object asymmetrically c-commands the subject.

25　Nor can the complex word orders of languages like Chinese and Kpelle be partially dependent on a directionality setting, as in Travis (1989).

26　Movement to a c-commanding but not asymmetrically c-commanding position is never possible under the present theory, most clearly if movement is copying, since the two copies would violate antisymmetry (each would asymmetrically c-command the subparts of the other).

References

Bach, E. 1971. Questions. *Linguistic Inquiry* 2: 153–66.

Besten, H. den and G. Webelhuth. 1990. Stranding. In G. Grewendorf and W. Sternefeld (eds.), *Scrambling and barriers*, Amsterdam: Academic Press, pp. 77–92.

Chomsky, N. 1986. *Barriers*. Cambridge, MA: MIT Press.

Chomsky, N. 1993. A minimalist program for linguistic theory. In K. Hale and S. J. Keyser (eds.), *The view from Building 20: Essays in linguistics in honor of Sylvain Bromberger*, Cambridge, MA: MIT Press, pp. 1–52. [Reprinted in Chomsky (1995), *The Minimalist Program*, Cambridge, MA: MIT Press, pp. 167–217.]

Chomsky, N. and H. Lasnik. 1993. The theory of principles and parameters. In J. Jacobs, A. von Stechow, W. Sternefeld and T. Vennemann (eds.), *An international handbook of contemporary research*, Berlin/New York: Walter de Gruyter, pp. 506–69. [Reprinted in Chomsky (1995), *The Minimalist Program*, Cambridge, MA: MIT Press, pp. 13–127.]

Cinque, G. 1990. *Types of A′-dependencies*. Cambridge, MA: MIT Press.

Dikken, M. den. 1992. *Particles*. Doctoral dissertation, University of Leiden.

Emonds, J. 1980. Word order in generative grammar. *Journal of Linguistic Research* 1: 33–54.

Fiengo, R. 1977. On trace theory. *Linguistic Inquiry* 8: 35–61.

Fukui, N. 1986. *A theory of category projection and its applications*. Doctoral dissertation, MIT. [Revised version published as *Theory of projection in syntax*, Stanford: CSLI/Tokyo: Kuroshio, 1995.]

Greenberg, J. H. (ed.) 1966. *Universals of language*. Cambridge, MA: MIT Press.

Johnson, K. 1991. Object positions. *Natural Languages and Linguistic Theory* 9: 577–636.

Kayne, R. S. 1975. *French syntax: The transformational cycle*. Cambridge, MA: MIT Press.

Kayne, R. S. 1984. *Connectedness and binary branching*. Dordrecht: Foris.

Kayne, R. S. 1985. Principles of particle constructions. In J. Guéron, H.-G. Obenauer and J.-Y. Pollock (eds.), *Grammatical representation*, Dordrecht: Foris, pp. 101–40.

Kayne, R. S. 1991. Romance clitics, verb movement, and PRO. *Linguistic Inquiry* 22: 647–86.

McCloskey, J. 1992. On the scope of verb movement in Irish. [Published in *Natural Language and Linguistic Theory* 14: 46–104, 1996.]

May, R. C. 1985. *Logical form*. Cambridge, MA: MIT Press.

Ordóñez Lao, F. 1994. Postverbal asymmetries in Spanish. Paper presented at the 17th GLOW Colloquium. *GLOW Newsletter* 32: 40–1.

Reinhart, T. 1983. *Anaphora and semantic interpretation*. Chicago: University of Chicago Press.

Riemsdijk, H. van. 1989. Movement and regeneration. In P. Benincà (ed.), *Dialect variation and the theory of grammar*, Dordrecht: Foris, pp. 105–36.

Roberts, I. 1991. Excorporation and minimality. *Linguistic Inquiry* 22: 209–18.

Travis, L. 1989. Parameters of phrase structure. In M. Baltin and A. Kroch (eds.), *Alternative conceptions of phrase structure*, Chicago: University of Chicago Press, pp. 263–79.

Ultan, R. 1978. Some general characteristics of interrogative systems. In J. H. Greenberg (ed.), *Universals of human language*. Vol 4: *Syntax*, Stanford CA: Stanford University Press, pp. 211–48.

From "CATEGORIES AND TRANSFORMATIONS"
Noam Chomsky

4.8 Order

Nothing has yet been said about ordering of elements. There is no clear evidence that order plays a role at LF or in the computation from N to LF. Let us assume that it does not. Then ordering is part of the phonological component, a proposal that has been put forth over the years in various forms. If so, then it might take quite a different form without affecting C_{HL} if language use involved greater expressive dimensionality or no sensorimotor manifestation at all.

It seems natural to suppose that ordering applies to the output of Morphology, assigning a linear (temporal, left-to-right) order to the elements it forms, all of them X^0s though not necessarily lexical items. If correct, these assumptions lend further reason to suppose that there is no linear order in the N → LF computation, assuming that it has no access to the output of Morphology.

The standard assumption has been that order is determined by the head parameter: languages are basically head-initial (English) or head-final (Japanese), with further refinements. Fukui has proposed that the head parameter provides an account of optional movement, which otherwise is excluded under economy conditions apart from the special case of equally economical alternative derivations. He argues that movement that maintains the ordering of the head parameter is "free"; other movement must be motivated by Greed (Last Resort). Thus, in head-final Japanese, leftward movement (scrambling, passive) is optional, while in head-initial English, such operations must be motivated by feature checking; and rightward extraposition is free in English, though barred in Japanese.[1]

Kayne (1993) has advanced a radical alternative to the standard assumption, proposing that order reflects structural hierarchy universally by means of the Linear Correspondence Axiom (LCA), which states that asymmetric c-command (ACC) imposes a linear ordering of terminal elements; any category that cannot be totally ordered by LCA is barred. From Kayne's specific formulation, it follows that there is a universal specifier-head-complement (SVO) order and that specifiers are in fact adjuncts. A head-complement structure, then, is necessarily an XP, which can be extended – exactly once, on Kayne's assumptions – to a two-segment XP.

The general idea is very much in the spirit of the Minimalist Program and consistent with the speculation that the essential character of C_{HL} is independent of the sensorimotor interface. Let us consider how it might be incorporated into the bare phrase structure theory. That is not an entirely straightforward matter, because the bare theory lacks much of the structure of the standard X-bar theory that plays a crucial role in Kayne's analysis.[2]

Kayne offers two kinds of arguments for the LCA: conceptual and empirical, the latter extended in subsequent work (see particularly Zwart 1993 and Kayne 1994). The conceptual arguments show how certain stipulated properties of X-bar theory can be derived from the LCA. The empirical arguments can largely be carried over to a reformulation of the LCA within the bare theory, but the conceptual ones are problematic. First, the derivation of these properties relies crucially not just on the LCA, but on features of standard X-bar theory that are abandoned in the bare theory. Second, the conclusions are for the most part immediate in the bare theory without the LCA.[3]

Let us ask how a modified LCA might be added to the bare theory. There is no category-terminal distinction, hence no head-terminal distinction and no associated constraints on c-command. Suppose we have the structure (1), which is the bare-theory counterpart to several of the richer structures that Kayne considers.

(1)

Here L is either m or p, K is either j or L. K may be either a separate category or a segment of either [K, j] or [K, L], depending on which projects. The heads are the terminal elements j, m, p. Assuming that L is not formed by adjunction, either m or p is its head and the other is both maximal and minimal; say m is the head, for concreteness, so L is mP.

Suppose that K is a separate category and L projects, so that j is a specifier in an A-position. ACC holds (j, m) and (j, p), so j must precede m and p. But it would hold of (m, p) only if the single-terminal p (the complement of the head m) were replaced by a complex category. Hence, we have the order specifier-head-complement, though only for nontrivial complement.

Suppose that instead of terminal j we had branching J, with constituents α, β. L is an X′, neither maximal nor minimal, so it does not c-command.[4] Therefore, the ACC relations are unchanged.

Suppose that K is a separate category and j projects, so that it is the head of K with complement L. ACC holds as before.

Suppose that K is a segment, either j or L. There is no particular problem, but adjunct-target order will depend on the precise definition of c-command.

In brief, the LCA can be adopted in the bare theory, but with somewhat different consequences. The segment-category distinction (and the related ones) can be maintained throughout. We draw Kayne's basic conclusion about SVO order directly, though only if the complement is more complex than a single terminal.

Let us return to the case of L = mP with the single-terminal complement p, both minimal and maximal. Since neither m nor p asymmetrically c-commands the other, no ordering is assigned to m, p; the assigned ordering is not total, and the structure violates the LCA. That leaves two possibilities. Either we weaken the LCA so that nontotal orderings (but not "contradictory" orderings) are admissible under certain conditions, or we conclude that the derivation crashes unless the structure N = [$_L$ m p] has changed by the time the LCA applies so that its internal structure is irrelevant; perhaps N is converted by Morphology to a "phonological word" not subject internally to the LCA, assuming that the LCA is an operation that applies after Morphology.

Consider the first possibility: is there a natural way to weaken the LCA? One obvious choice comes to mind: there is no reason for the LCA to order an element that will disappear at PF, for example, a trace. Suppose, then, that we exempt traces from the LCA, so that (1) is legitimate if p has overtly raised, leaving a trace that can be ignored by the LCA. The second possibility can be realized in essentially the same manner, by allowing the LCA to delete traces. Under this interpretation, the LCA may eliminate the offending trace in (1), if p has raised.

In short, if the complement is a single-terminal XP, then it must raise overtly. If XP = DP, then its head D is a clitic, either demonstrative or pronominal, which attaches at a higher point (determined either generally, or by specific morphological properties).[5] If XP = NP, then N must incorporate to V (and we must show that other options are blocked). Clitics, then, are bare Ds without complements, and noun incorporation must be restricted to "nonreferential NPs" (as noted by Hagit Borer), assuming the quasi-referential, indexical character of a noun phrase to be a property of the D head of DP, NP being a kind of predicate. Within DP, the N head of NP must raise to D (as argued in a different manner by Longobardi 1994).[6]

We therefore expect to find two kinds of pronominal (similarly, demonstrative) elements, simple ones that are morphologically marked as affixes and must cliticize, and complex ones with internal structure, which do not cliticize: in French, for example, the determiner D (*le*, *la*, etc.) and the complex element *lui-même* 'himself'. In Irish the simple element is again D, and the complex one may even be discontinuous, as in *an teach sin* 'that house', with determiner *an-sin* (Andrew Carnie, personal communication). A phenomenon that may be related is noted by Esther Torrego. In Spanish the Case marker *de* can be omitted in (2a), but not in (2b).

(2) a. cerca de la plaza 'near the plaza'
     b. cerca de ella 'near it'

When *de* is deleted in (2a), D = *la* can incorporate in *cerca*, satisfying the Case Filter; but that is impossible in (2b) if the complex pronominal *ella* is not D but a word with richer structure, from which the residue of D cannot be extracted.

Since the affixal property is lexical, simple pronominals cliticize even if they are not in final position (e.g. a pronominal object that is a specifier in a Larsonian shell).

If focus adds more complex structure, then focused (stressed) simple pronominals could behave like complex pronominals. If English-type pronouns are simple, they too must cliticize, though locally, not raising to I as in Romance (perhaps as a reflex of lack of overt V-raising). The barrier to such structures as *I picked up it* might follow. English determiners such as *this* and *that* are presumably complex, with the initial consonant representing D (as in *the, there*, etc.) and the residue a kind of adjective, perhaps. Various consequences are worth exploring.

Although apparently not unreasonable, the conclusions are very strong: thus, every right-branching structure must end in a trace, on these assumptions.

What about ordering of adjuncts and targets? In Kayne's theory, adjuncts necessarily precede their targets. Within the bare theory, there is no really principled conclusion, as far as I can see. Ordering depends on exactly how the core relations of phrase structure theory, *dominate* and *c-command*, are generalized to two-segment categories.

Consider the simplest case, with α attached to K, which projects.

(3)

Suppose that K_2 is a new category, α the specifier or complement, so that (3) = L = {H(K), {α, K}}. Take *dominate* to be an irreflexive relation with the usual interpretation. Then L dominates α and K; informally, K_2 dominates α and K_1.

Suppose, however, that the operation was adjunction, forming the two-segment category [K_2, K_1] = {⟨H(K), H(K)⟩, {α, K}}. Are α and K_1 dominated by the category [K_2, K_1]? As for c-command, let us assume that α c-commands outside of this category; thus, if it heads a chain, it c-commands its trace, which need not be in K_1 (as in head raising).[7] But what about further c-command relations, including those within (3) itself?

The core intuition underlying c-command is that

(4)   X c-commands Y if (a) every Z that dominates X dominates Y and (b) X and Y are disconnected.

For categories, we take X and Y to be disconnected if X ≠ Y and neither dominates the other. The notions "dominate" and "disconnected" (hence "c-command") could be generalized in various ways for segments.

These relations are restricted to *terms*, in the sense defined earlier: in the case of (3), to α, K (= K_1), and the two-segment category [K_2, K_1]. K_2 has no independent status. These conclusions comport reasonably well with the general condition that elements enter into the computational system C_{HL} if they are "visible" at the interface. Thus, K_1 may assign or receive a semantic role, as may α (or the chain it heads, which must meet the Chain Condition). But there is no "third" role left over for K_2; the two-segment category will be interpreted as a word by Morphology [...] if K is an X^0, and otherwise falls under the narrow options discussed earlier.[8]

If that much is correct, we conclude that in (3), $[K_2, K_1]$ dominates its lower segment K_1, so that the latter does not c-command anything (including α, not dominated by $[K_2, K_1]$ but only contained in it).

Turning next to c-command, how should we extend the notion "disconnected" of (4b) to adjuncts? Take adjunction to a nonmaximal head ((16) in Kayne 1993, reduced to its bare counterpart).

(5)

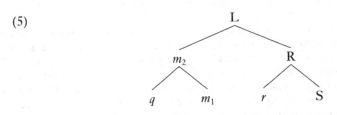

Here q is adjoined to the head m to form the two-segment category $[m_2, m_1]$, a nonmaximal X^0 projecting to and heading the category L, which has label m. R is the complement of m and r its head, and S (which may be complex) is the complement of r. What are the c-command relations for the adjunct structure?

The lowest Z that dominates q and m_1 is L, which also dominates $[m_2, m_1]$. Therefore, q and $[m_2, m_1]$ asymmetrically c-command r and S, however we interpret "disconnected." What are the c-command relations within $[m_2, m_1]$? As noted, m_1 does not c-command anything. The other relations depend on the interpretation of "disconnected" in (4b). Kayne interprets it as "X excludes Y." Then q (asymmetrically) c-commands $[m_2, m_1]$, which dominates m_1, so that q precedes m_1; and in general, an adjunct precedes the head to which it is adjoined. If X, Y are taken to be "disconnected" if no segment of one contains the other, then q c-commands m_1 but not $[m_2, m_1]$, and again q precedes m_1.[9] If "disconnected" requires still further dissociation of X, Y – say, that neither is a segment of a category that contains the other – then no ordering is determined for q, m_1 by the LCA.

I do not see any principled way to choose among the various options.

If m_1 is not a head but the complex category $[_m\ m\ P]$, so that q is an XP for reasons already discussed, then q c-commands the constituents of m_1 under all interpretations of "disconnect," and the adjunct precedes the target (whether q is internally complex or not).

Left open, then, is the case of adjunction of a head to another head, that is, ordering within words. Whether order should be fixed here depends on questions about inflectional morphology and word formation that seem rather obscure and may have no general answer.

Summarizing, it seems that Kayne's basic intuition can be accommodated in a straightforward way in the bare theory, including the major empirical conclusions, specifically, the universal order SVO and adjunct-target (at least for XP adjuncts). In the bare theory, the LCA gains no support from conceptual arguments and therefore rests on the empirical consequences. We take the LCA to be a principle of the phonological component that applies to the output of Morphology, optionally ignoring or deleting traces. The specifier-adjunct (A–Ā) distinction is maintained, along with the possibility of multiple specifiers or adjuncts, though the options for adjunction are very limited for other reasons. There are further consequences with regard to cliticization and other matters, whether correct or not, I do not know.

Notes

1   Fukui (1993); see also Ueda (1990). Note that this proposal requires that ordering be imposed within the N → LF computation.

2   I depart here from Kayne's theory in several respects, among them, by taking linear ordering to be literal precedence, not simply a transitive, asymmetric, total relation among terminals. That is the intended interpretation, but Kayne's more abstract formulation allows very free temporal ordering under the LCA. Thus, if a class of categories satisfies the LCA, so will any interchange of sisters (as Sam Epstein (personal communication) notes), meaning that consistent with the LCA a language could, for example, have any arrangement of head-complement relations (e.g. *read-books* or *books-read* freely). Kayne considers one case (fully left-to-right or fully right-to-left), but the problem is more general.

3   See Chomsky (1994) for details, along with some discussion of anomalies of the LCA that are removed when we dispense with the X-bar-theoretic notations.

4   L is part of the structure, however; otherwise, we would have a new and inadmissible syntactic object. Thus, the branching structure remains, and m, p do not c-command out of L.

5   Note that V-raising (as in French) does not affect the conclusion that the clitic must raise overtly. If D remains in situ, then whether the trace of V is ignored or deleted by the LCA, D will still be a terminal complement, either to V itself or to some intervening element, and the derivation will crash.

6   Presumably the affixal character of N is a general morphological property, not distinguishing nouns with complements from those without (which must raise).

7   The assumption is not entirely obvious; see Epstein (1989) for a contrary view. Much depends on resolution of questions involving reconstruction after adjunction and word-internal processes at LF.

8   Suppose that, as has been proposed, the upper segment enters into calculating subjacency, scope, or other properties. Then we would hope to show that these effects receive a natural expression in terms of containment and domination, notions still available even if the upper segment is "invisible" for C_{HL} and at the interface.

9   That q c-commands $[m_2, m_1]$ is required in Kayne's theory for reasons that do not hold in the bare theory, where the issue that Kayne is concerned with does not arise.

References

Chomsky, N. 1994. *Bare phrase structure. MIT Occasional Papers in Linguistics 5*. Cambridge, MA: MITWPL. [Published in P. Kempchinsky (ed.) (1994), *Evolution and revolution in linguistic theory: Essays in honor of Carlos Otero*, Washington, DC: Georgetown University Press, pp. 51–109. Also published in G. Webelhuth (ed.) (1994), *Government and binding theory and the minimalist program*, Cambridge, MA: MIT Press, pp. 383–439.]

Epstein, S. D. 1989. Adjunction and pronominal variable binding. *Linguistic Inquiry* 20: 307–19.

Fukui, N. 1993. Parameters and optionality. *Linguistic Inquiry* 24: 399–420.

Kayne, R. S. 1993. The antisymmetry of syntax. Ms., CUNY Graduate Center.

Kayne, R. S. 1994. *The antisymmetry of syntax*. Cambridge, MA: MIT Press.

Longobardi, G. 1994. Reference and proper names: A theory of N-movement in syntax and logical form. *Linguistic Inquiry* 25: 609–65.

Ueda, M. 1990. *Japanese phrase structure and parameter setting*. Doctoral dissertation, University of Massachusetts, Amherst.

Zwart, J.-W. 1993. *Morphosyntax of verb movement: A minimalist approach to the syntax of Dutch.* Dordrecht: Kluwer.

From "UN-PRINCIPLED SYNTAX: THE DERIVATION OF SYNTACTIC RELATIONS"
Samuel D. Epstein

12.3.1 Representational c-command

Consider the following representational definition of c-command (Reinhart 1979):

(1)   *The representational definition of c-command*
      A c-commands B iff
      a.   The first branching node dominating A dominates B, *and*
      b.   A does not dominate B, *and*
      c.   A ≠ B.

Four important properties of c-command should be noted here. First, (1) constitutes a *definition*, hence explanation is lacking. That is, we have no answer to the question, "Why is this particular binary relation syntactically significant?" As an illustration, consider (2).

(2)   *A schematic illustration of c-command*
      (certain irrelevant categories – e.g. AgrP and TP – are omitted)

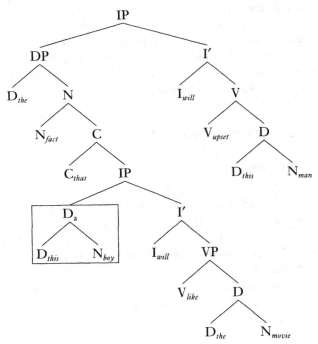

In (2), [Spec, IP] = D_a c-commands I', I_{will}, VP, V_{like}, D, D_{the}, N_{movie}, and no other categories. It is as if the other categories in (2) are inexplicably invisible with respect to D_a; hence, D_a enters into no relations with them. Why? Second, c-command is pervasive and fundamental, apparently playing a unifying role throughout the different subcomponents of the syntax. Third, it is persistent; that is, despite substantive changes in the theory of syntax, Reinhart's definition, proposed two decades ago, remains, by hypothesis, linguistically significant. Fourth, it is representational; that is, it is a relation defined on representation.

Thus, c-command faces at least these unanswered questions:

(3) a. Why does it exist at all? Why doesn't A enter into relations with all constituents in the tree?
     b. Why is the *first* branching node relevant? Why not "The first or second or third (*n*th?) node dominating A must dominate B?"
     c. Why is *branching* relevant?
     d. Why doesn't A c-command the first branching node dominating A, instead c-commanding only categories dominated by the first branching node?
     e. Why must A not dominate B?
     f. Why must A not equal B?

I will advance the hypothesis that these properties of c-command are not accidental, but are intimately related. First, I believe c-command is fundamental, pervasive, and persistent because it is, by hypothesis, indeed a syntactically significant relation. Second, I propose that it is definitional (nonexplanatory) precisely because it has been formulated or construed as a representational relation. Third, I propose that it is in fact derivational – that is, a relation between two categories X and Y established in the course of a derivation (iterative universal-rule application) when and only when X and Y are paired (concatenated) by transformational rule (i.e. Merge or Move). When c-command is construed derivationally, the unanswered questions confronting the representational definition receive natural answers.

12.3.2 The derivation of c-command

To begin with, I will assume that

(4) a. Merge and Move (Chomsky 1993, 1994) are at least partly unifiable (as proposed in Kitahara 1993, 1994, 1995, 1997) in that each pairs (concatenates) exactly two categories, A and B, rendering them sisters immediately dominated by the same (projected) mother, C (where C = the head of A or of B (Chomsky 1994)).
     b. Given (4a), there is a fundamental operation, common to or shared by Merge and Move: "Concatenate A and B, forming C (C = the head of A or of B)."

Crucially, then, each universalized transformational rule, Merge and Move, establishes a syntactic relation between two concatenated syntactic categories A and B by virtue of placing them in the "is a" relation with C, the projected category. I will also assume, with Chomsky (1994), that Merge operates bottom-up – that is, applies cyclically (cyclic application being an independently motivated universal constraint on universal-rule application) – and that Move does so as well. Consider, for example, the derivation in (5).

(5)   Merging V_{likes} and D_{it} yields, informally:

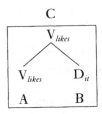

The lower V_{likes} (= A) and D_{it} (= B) are, by virtue of undergoing Merge, in a relation: they are the sister constituents of a V-phrase/projection C, labeled V_{likes}.

Thus, what Merge does is create *sisters*. Crucially, A and B cannot be or become sisters without having a common mother. Conversely, if nonbranching projection is disallowed, and only binary branching is permitted, then there cannot be a mother C without exactly two daughters (the sisters A and B). In a nutshell, both the sisterhood relation and the motherhood ("is a") relation are created simultaneously, by a single application of Merge.

Viewed in terms of Standard Theory transformations, A and B (in (5), V_{likes} and D_{it}) constitute the structural description of Merge. The structural change (perhaps deducible, given the structural description; see Chomsky 1995) specifies the categorial status of the mother or output tree/set. Since the two entities in the structural description are rendered sisters (i.e. are placed in the "is a" relation to the projected (perhaps predictable) mother C, all in one application of Merge), there is no need for a representational definition of "sister" or "mother" ("is a"); these two relations are clearly expressed (and unified) within the independently motivated, universal structure-building rules themselves. Representational definitions would therefore be redundant and (being definitions) nonexplanatory.

The tree in (5) is formally represented as $\{V_{likes}, \{V_{likes}, D_{it}\}\}$. This object (set) consists of three terms:

(6)   a.   The entire tree/set (= C)
      b. V_{likes} (= A)
      c. D_{it} (= B)

That is, following Chomsky (1994: 12; 1995), I assume:

(7)   a.   Definition of *term* ("constituent")
         i.   K is a term of K (i.e. the entire set or tree is a term).
        ii.   If L is a term of K, then the members of the members of L are
               terms of K.
      b.   The terms in (5) are as follows:
         i. $K = \{V_{likes}, \{V_{likes}, D_{it}\}\}$ = one term
        ii.   K has two members:
               member 1 = V_{likes} = "the label"
               member 2 = a two-membered set = $\{V_{likes}, D_{it}\}$
       iii.   The V_{likes} and D_{it} that are each members of member 2 are thus mem-
               bers of a member. Therefore, each is a term.

Thus, "[t]erms correspond to nodes of the informal representations, where each
node is understood to stand for the subtree of which it is the root" (Chomsky 1994:
12).

   Continuing with the derivation, suppose that concurrent with the construction
of (5), we construct the separate phrase marker (8) (recall that separate phrase markers may be constructed in parallel, as long as a single phrase marker results by
the end of the derivation (see Collins 1997)).

(8)   Merge D_{the} and N_{dog}, yielding informally:

The tree is formally represented as $\{D_{the}, \{D_{the}, N_{dog}\}\}$, similarly consisting of
three terms: the entire two-membered set and each of the two categories that
are members of a member of the two-membered set (D_{the} and N_{dog}). Now, having constructed the two three-membered trees in (5) and (8), suppose we merge
them, yielding (9) (*a*, *b*, and *c* are purely heuristic: $D_a = D_{the}$; V_b and V_c each =
V_{likes}).

(9)

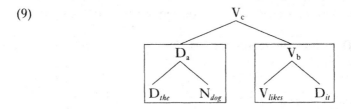

   Now notice that there exists a massive redundancy. The representational
definition of c-command (1) stipulates c-command relations between sisters in the

derived representation (9). But sisters are precisely the objects A and B that invariably undergo Merge in building the representation. Thus:

(10)   In (9):
    a.   i. D_{the} representationally c-commands N_{dog}; they were merged.
        ii. N_{dog} representationally c-commands D_{the}; they were merged.
    b.   i. V_{likes} representationally c-commands D_{it}; they were merged.
        ii. D_{it} representationally c-commands V_{likes}; they were merged.
    c.   i. D_a representationally c-commands V_b; they were merged.
        ii. V_b representationally c-commands D_a; they were merged.
    d. V_c representationally c-commands nothing; it has not been merged with any category.
    e.   In (9), the 10 binary dominance relations ("X dominates Y") are, by pure stipulation in (1b), not c-command relations; they were not merged.
    f.   By pure stipulation in (1c), no category representationally c-commands itself; no category is merged with itself.

Thus, Merge – an entirely simple, natural, minimal, and independently motivated structure-building operation (i.e. transformational rule) – seems to capture representational c-command relations. In other words, if X and Y are concatenated, they enter into (what have been called) c-command relations. Consequently, it would seem that we can eliminate the stipulated, unexplained representational definition of c-command (1).

There is a problem with this suggestion, however. When Merge pairs two categories, the pairing establishes only *symmetrical* (reciprocal) c-command relations. Consider, for example, (11).

(11)

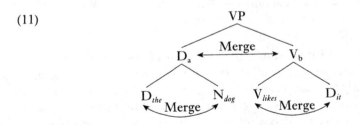

Correctly, each arrow in (11) indicates a c-command relation. But Merge does not totally subsume the representational definition of c-command, precisely because there exist c-command relations between categories that have not been merged. Thus, (12a) is true, but (12b) is false.

(12)   a.   If A and B were merged, then A c-commands B and B c-commands A.
    b.   If A c-commands B, then A and B were merged.

To see the falsity of (12b), consider (13).

(13) D_a and V_b are merged:

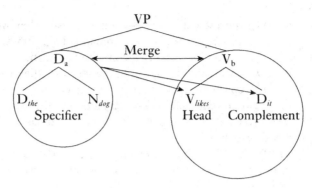

The specifier of V_{likes}, D_a, c-commands the head V_{likes} and the complement D_{it}, but D_a was not merged with either of them.

To solve this problem confronting the attempt to entirely deduce representational, definitional c-command from Merge, notice that although D_a was not merged with V_{likes} or with D_{it}, it was merged with V_b. But now recall that $V_b = \{V_b, \{V_{likes}, D_{it}\}\}$ ("each node is understood to stand for the subtree of which it is the root"). That is, V_b consists of three terms: $\{V_b, \{V_{likes}, D_{it}\}\}$ (the whole V_b subtree in (13)), V_{likes}, and D_{it}. Given that a syntactic category is a set of terms (in dominance/precedence relations), we can propose the following, natural derivational definition of c-command:

(14)   *Derivational c-command (preliminary version)*
        X c-commands all and only the terms of the category Y with which X was
        merged in the course of the derivation.

Thus, D_a ([Spec, VP]) c-commands V_b (X') and all terms of V_b.

Now recall that Move, the other structure-building operation, also pairs/concatenates exactly two categories, projecting the head of one, and in this respect is identical to Merge. Since "is a" relations are created by Move in the same manner as they are created by Merge, we can now propose the final version of the derivational definition.

(15)   *Derivational c-command (final version)*
        X c-commands all and only the terms of the category Y with which X was
        paired *by Merge or by Move* in the course of the derivation.

Given (15), consider the case of Move in (16).

(16)

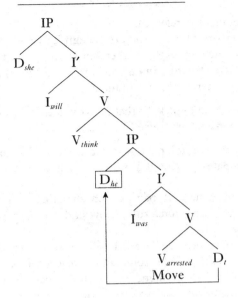

By definition (1), in (16) D_{he} representationally c-commands the five categories (subtrees) I′, I_{was}, V, $V_{arrested}$, D_t, and nothing else. This state of affairs, unexplained representationally, can be explained derivationally. D_{he} was paired/concatenated (in this case by Move) with I′, and I′ is a five-term category/tree/set consisting precisely of I′, I_{was}, V, $V_{arrested}$, and D_t. It is entirely natural then that, since D_{he} was paired with a five-term object, and since pairing/concatenation is precisely the establishment of syntactic relations, D_{he} enters into a relation (what has hitherto been called c-command) with each of these five terms, and with nothing else.

This analysis also captures a certain (correct) asymmetry. Although D_{he} c-commands each of the five terms of I′, the converse is not true. For example, I_{was} is a term of I′, but I_{was} does not c-command D_{he}; rather, since in the course of the derivation I was paired (this time by Merge) with V, the derivational analysis rightly predicts that I_{was} c-commands each of the three terms of V (V itself, $V_{arrested}$, D_t) and nothing else.

The derivational definition of c-command (15) enables us to answer questions that the representational definition (1) did not.

Q: (Really an infinite number of questions) Why is it that X c-commands Y if and only if the *first* branching node dominating X dominates Y?

A: The first (not, e.g. the fifth, sixth, or *n*th, for *n* any positive integer) node is relevant because it is the projected node created by pairing of X and Y by Merge and Move.

Q: Why doesn't X c-command the first branching node dominating X, instead of c-commanding only the categories dominated by the first branching node?

A: Merge or Move did not pair X with the first branching node dominating X.

Q: Why is branching relevant?

A: Assuming bare phrase structure (Chomsky 1994), no category is dominated by a nonbranching node. In other words, free projection (as in Chomsky 1993) is eliminated: structure building (Merge and Move) consists of pairing, hence invariably generates binary branching.

Q: Why must X not equal Y; that is, why doesn't X c-command itself?

A: X is never paired with itself by Merge or Move.

Q: Why is it that in order for X to c-command Y, X must not dominate Y?

A: If X dominates Y, X and Y were not paired by Merge or Move.

Thus, as is entirely natural, pairing/concatenating of X and Y, by application of the universal transformational rules Move and Merge, expresses syntactic relations such as c-command.

Thus far, I have provided what I believe to be strong explanatory arguments for derivational construal of c-command. However, I have provided no arguments that representational c-command is empirically inadequate. I will now present one such argument, showing that representational c-command is inconsistent with an independently motivated hypothesis (and that derivational c-command is not). (For more extensive discussion, see Epstein et al. 1998.)

Consider again a tree such as (17).

(17) V_b and V_c each $= V_{likes}$; $D_a = D_{the}$

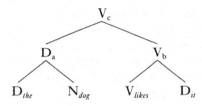

Recall that in the input to (i.e. the structural description of) Merge, there were two categories:

(18)   a. D_a = three terms:
        i. D_a itself (K is a term of K; see (7))
        ii. D_{the}
        iii. N_{dog}
   b. V_b = three terms:
        i. V_b itself
        ii. V_{likes}
        iii. D_{it}

Given that D_a and V_b were merged, derivational c-command (15) entails that

(19)   a. D_a c-commands V_b, V_{likes}, and D_{it}.
   b. V_b c-commands D_a, D_{the}, and N_{dog}.

But assuming a relational analysis of a syntactic category's phrase structure status (Muysken 1982; Freidin 1992), in the representation (17) V_b, being neither a minimal nor a maximal projection of V, is not a term (or is an "invisible term") of (17) (Chomsky 1994). Therefore, algorithmically speaking, V_b is "stricken from the record" in (19); that is, it is not a c-commander at all. Consequently, Kayne's (1994) reanalysis of the specifier as an X' adjunct is not required for Linear Correspondence Axiom compatibility, exactly as Chomsky (1994) proposed. Nor is V' (more generally, X') c-commanded by any category. Thus, the informal representation (17) includes only the following relations, a proper subset of those in (19):

(20) a. D_a asymmetrically c-commands V_{likes} and D_{it}.
      b. D_{the} symmetrically c-commands N_{dog}.
      c. V_{likes} symmetrically c-commands D_{it}.

These are, by hypothesis, the desired results. Importantly, V_b (V'), although representationally invisible (i.e. not a term in the resulting representation (17)), nonetheless blocks c-command of D_a ([Spec, VP]) by V_{likes}, the head, and by D_{it}, the complement (see (20a)). But given that V' is representationally invisible, the representational definition of c-command fails to even stipulate the apparent *fact* stated in (20a). That is, neither V_{likes} nor D_{it} is a term of some other visible term that excludes D_a ([Spec, VP]) in the resulting representation (17). By contrast, since V_{likes} and D_{it} were merged with each other, derivational c-command (15) entails that they c-command each other and nothing else. Notice that at one derivational point, V_{likes} and D_{it} were members of a term, V_b, which was a maximal term (V_{max}) that excluded [Spec, VP] immediately after merging V_{likes} and D_{it}. However, given the invisibility of X', in the resulting representation neither V_{likes} nor D_{it} is a member of a term (other than itself) that excludes D_a ([Spec, VP]); that is, there is no (visible) node (term) that dominates V_{likes} and D_{it} and also excludes D_a ([Spec, VP]). This suggests that the derivational construal of c-command proposed here is not only natural and explanatory but also empirically preferable to the extent that the representational definition wrongly predicts that categories immediately dominated by a representationally invisible single-bar projection (e.g. the complement) c-command the specifier and (worse yet) all members of the specifier.

12.3.3   Discussion

The derivational definition of c-command (15) eliminates massive redundancy (see (10)), provides principled answers to an infinite number of unanswered questions confronting the definition of representational c-command, and overcomes empirical inadequacies resulting from the interaction of the X'-invisibility hypothesis (Chomsky 1993) and representational c-command (Reinhart 1979).

Moreover, the derivational definition is an entirely natural subcase of a more general hypothesis (explored below): all syntactic relations are formally expressed by the operation "Concatenate A and B (the structural description), forming C (the structural change)" common to both structure-building operations (transformational rules), Merge and Move. Thus, Merge and Move establish relations, including "is a" and c-command, by virtue of concatenating categories. Nonetheless, despite its significant advantages over representational c-command and despite its being so natural, the derivational definition is just that: a definition. It (albeit naturally) asserts that X enters into c-command relations with all and only the terms of the category with which X is transformationally concatenated. But it still does not answer at least one very deep question: "Why does c-command exist at all? That is, why doesn't a category X simply enter into relations with *all* constituents in the tree?" I now turn to this question.

12.3.4   Toward deducing the derivational definition of c-command

First, consider the case of two categories neither of which c-commands the other, illustrated in (21).

(21) V_b and VP each = V_{likes}

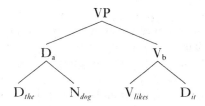

Here, neither D_{the} nor D_{it} c-commands the other, illustrating the generalization that members of the specifier do not c-command members of X′ and members of X′ do not c-command members of the specifier. The first conjunct of this generalization is illustrated by, for example, the binding violation in (22).

(22)   *[$_{Spec}$ this picture of *John*] [X′ upsets *himself*]

The derivational definition (15) correctly entails that *John* fails to c-command *himself* in (22). But the nonexistence of such c-command relations is, I think, deducible. Consider what I will call the *First Law*: The largest syntactic object is the single phrase structure tree. Interestingly, this hypothesis is so fundamental that it is usually left entirely implicit. The standard (i.e. representational) construal can be stated as follows:

(23)   *The First Law* (representationally *construed*)
         A term (tree/category/constituent) T_1 can enter into a syntactic relation with a term T_2 only if there is at least one term T_3 of which both T_1 and T_2 are member terms.

Informally, by the most fundamental definition of "syntax," there are no syntactic relations that hold between trees. In other words, the laws of syntax are intratree laws; X and Y can enter into syntactic relations only if they are both in the same tree. In (21), the Merge-derived representation, there is indeed a tree (the entire tree in (21)) such that D_{the} (a member of the specifier) and D_{it} (the complement) are both in it. But as shown in (9), derivationally prior to cyclic Merge, D_a (the specifier tree) and V_b (the X′ tree) were two unconnected trees; hence, no syntactic relation, including c-command, can hold between their members (the trees themselves can enter into a relation later, if they are merged together). Generally, there can be no relations between members of two unconnected trees.

To capture this, I reformulate the implicit First Law as a derivational law, not a representational one.

(24)   *The First Law* (derivationally *construed*)

   T_1 can enter into c-command (perhaps, more generally, syntactic) relations with T_2 only if there exists no derivational point at which

   a. T_1 is a term of K_1 ($K_1 \neq T_1$), *and*
   b. T_2 is a term of K_2 ($K_2 \neq T_2$), *and*
   c.   There is no K_3 such that K_1 and K_2 are both terms of K_3.

Informally stated: No relations hold between members of two trees that were unconnected at any point in the derivation. (For a formal explication of the First Law, making the intuition presented here explicit, see Groat 1997; Epstein et al. 1998: ch. 6.) Assuming Cyclicity (a universal constraint on universal-rule application), deducible for Move as hypothesized by Kitahara (1993, 1994, 1995), in the derivation of (21) there was necessarily a point at which D_{the} was a member of D_a ([Spec, VP]) and D_{it} was a member of V_b (X′) but there did not yet exist a tree containing both the branching D_a tree and the V_b tree. It follows from the derivational construal of the First Law that there is no relation between D_{the} and D_{it}. More generally, there are no relations between members of the specifier and members of X′. We thus at this point partially derive fundamental syntactic relations like c-command and entirely derive the nonexistence of an infinite number of logically possible but apparently nonexistent syntactic relations, each of which is representationally definable (e.g. the relation *from* X *to* X's great-great-great(. . .)aunt). We do so with no stipulations, no technicalia, nothing ad hoc – only by appeal to the First Law, derivationally construed.

Notice, incidentally, that in (25) the two merged trees, D_a and V_b themselves, *can* enter into syntactic relations even though at one derivational point they were unconnected. That is, (24) entails that since neither is a member of a term/tree other than itself (i.e. each equals a root node), neither has undergone Merge or Move. Hence, like a lexical entry, each is not yet a participant in syntactic relations.

(25)

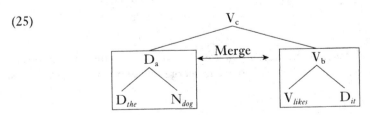

To summarize, for two nodes (trees/terms/categories) X and Y, neither of which c-commands the other, we do not need to stipulate representational c-command (1) to account for the fact that this relation does not hold. In fact, we do not even need to appeal to the far more natural (redundancy-eliminating, X′-invisibility-consistent) derivational definition of c-command (15). The derivational construal of the First Law is sufficient: no syntactic relations hold between X and Y if they were, at any derivational point, members of two unconnected trees.

As a simple illustration, again consider (22), repeated here as (26).

(26)   *[$_{Spec(=D_a)}$ this picture of *John*] [$_{X'(=V_b)}$ upsets *himself*]

This type of binding phenomenon is now easily accounted for. A reflexive requires an antecedent of a particular morphosyntactic type (by hypothesis, an irreducible lexical property). "To have an antecedent" is "to enter into a syntactic relation." However, the First Law, derivationally construed, precludes the reflexive from entering into any syntactic relation with the only morphosyntactically possible candidate, *John*, since, given cyclic Merge, there existed a point in the derivation at which *John* was a member of D_a ([Spec, VP]), *himself* was a member of V_b (X′), and D_a and V_b were unconnected trees.

This completes the discussion of deducing those aspects of the derivational definition of c-command that pertain to two categories X and Y, neither of which c-commands the other.

Next, consider the case of asymmetric c-command, illustrated by (27) – by contrast to (26), a grammatical sentence.

(27)   [$_{Spec}$ *John*], [$_{X'}$ upsets *himself*]

Here, X c-commands Y, but Y does not c-command X, as shown in the tree representation (28), where the specifier representationally c-commands the complement but not conversely.

(28)

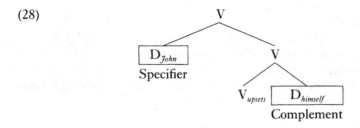

The generalization to be accounted for is that the specifier asymmetrically c-commands the complement. Given cyclic Merge, the derivation of (28) is as shown in (29).

(29) a. *First application of Merge*

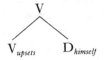

b. *Second application of Merge*

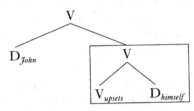

Notice that D_{John} ([Spec, V]) was never a member of a tree that did not contain $D_{himself}$; in other words, there never were two unconnected trees, one containing *John* and the other *himself*. Rather, the second application of Merge pairs/concatenates D_{John} itself (a member of the numeration) with a tree containing $D_{himself}$. Thus, correctly, the First Law allows (i.e. does not block) a c–command relation from *John* (T_1 of (24)) to *himself* (T_2 of (24)).

In fact, since there never were two unconnected trees in this derivation, the First Law, a relationship blocker, is altogether inapplicable here. Rather, the first application of Merge merges two members of the numeration (V_{likes} and $D_{himself}$), forming $\{V_{likes}, \{V_{likes}, D_{himself}\}\}$, after which the second application of Merge merges yet another element of the numeration, D_{John} (not a set/tree) with this object, yielding (30).

(30) $\{V_{likes}, \{D_{John}, \{V_{likes}, \{V_{likes}, \{D_{himself}\ \}\}\}\}$

Since the First Law is inapplicable, a problem arises: *all* relations are now allowed – not only the empirically supported (c-command) relation from the specifier to the complement, but also, incorrectly, a c-command relation from the complement to the specifier. That is, in the absence of any supplementary constraints (relationship blockers), the inapplicability of the First Law allows the complement to c-command the specifier.

As a possible solution, recall that in the Minimalist Program all concatenation/pairing is performed by either Merge or Move. As claimed above, Merge and Move express syntactic relations, including the "is a" relation. Now, if the universal rules Merge and Move are the sole relationship establishers, and in addition apply cyclically, it is altogether natural, if not necessary, that a relation between X and Y is established exactly at the derivational point at which X and Y are concatenated.

As a result, complements (and members of complements) never bear any relation to (e.g. never c-command) specifiers, because (a) when a complement (e.g. $D_{himself}$ in (29a)) is transformationally introduced, the specifier does not yet exist, and (b) an entity X can never bear a relation to a nonexistent entity (derivational preexistence).

Crucially, then, the matter of "timing" is the issue at hand; when a category X undergoes Merge/Move, it comes into a relation with everything *in the tree with which it is concatenated*. If a category Y isn't yet in the tree, the relation from X to Y does not arise. Hence, the asymmetry of the relation parallels the asymmetry of the iterative derivational procedure.

Thus, derivational c-command – and perhaps more generally the fundamental concept "syntactic relation" – appears to be deducible by appeal only to

- the independently motivated, quite simple, formal properties of two (perhaps unifiable) universalized transformational rules,
- these rules' universalized, similarly simple, and perhaps explicable mode of cyclic application, and
- the fundamental, perhaps irreducible First Law, derivationally construed.

References

Chomsky, N. 1993. A minimalist program for linguistic theory. In K. Hale and S. J. Keyser (eds.), *The view from Building 20: Essays in linguistics in honor of Sylvain Bromberger*, Cambridge, MA: MIT Press, pp. 1–52. [Reprinted in Chomsky (1995), *The Minimalist Program*, Cambridge, MA: MIT Press, pp. 167–217.]

Chomsky, N. 1994. *Bare phrase structure. MIT Occasional Papers in Linguistics 5*. Cambridge, MA: MITWPL. [Published in P. Kempchinsky (ed.) (1994), *Evolution and revolution in linguistic theory: Essays in honor of Carlos Otero*, Washington, DC: Georgetown University Press, pp. 51–109. Also published in G. Webelhuth (ed.) (1994), *Government and binding theory and the minimalist program*, Cambridge, MA: MIT Press, pp. 383–439.]

Chomsky, N. 1995. *The Minimalist Program*. Cambridge, MA: MIT Press.

Collins, C. 1997. *Local economy*. Cambridge, MA: MIT Press.

Epstein, S. D., E. Groat, R. Kawashima and H. Kitahara. 1998. *A derivational approach to syntactic relations*. New York: Oxford University Press.

Freidin, R. 1992. *Foundations of generative syntax*. Cambridge, MA: MIT Press.

Groat, E. 1997. *A derivational program for linguistic theory*. Doctoral dissertation, Harvard University.

Kayne, S. R. 1994. *The antisymmetry of syntax*. Cambridge, MA: MIT Press.

Kitahara, H. 1993. Deducing strict cyclicity from derivational economy. Paper presented at the 16th GLOW Colloquium, Lund.

Kitahara, H. 1994. *Target α: A unified theory of movement and structure building*. Doctoral dissertation, Harvard University.

Kitahara, H. 1995. Target α: Deducing strict cyclicity from derivational economy. *Linguistic Inquiry* 26: 47–77.

Kitahara, H. 1997. *Elementary operations and optimal derivations*. Cambridge, MA: MIT Press.

Muysken, P. 1982. Parameterizing the notion "head". *Journal of Linguistic Research* 2: 57–75.

Reinhart, T. 1979. The syntactic domain for semantic rules. In F. Guenther and J. Schmidt (eds.), *Formal semantics and pragmatics for natural language*, Dordrecht: Reidel.

From "MULTIPLE SPELL-OUT"
Juan Uriagereka

10.1 Deducing the base step of the LCA

A main desideratum of the Minimalist Program is reducing substantive principles to interface (or bare output) conditions, and formal principles to economy conditions. Much energy has been devoted to rethinking constraints and phenomena that appear to challenge this idea, in the process sharpening observations and descriptions. In this chapter, I attempt to reduce a version of Kayne's (1994) Linear Correspondence Axiom (LCA).

Chomsky (1995) already limits the LCA's place in the grammar. Kayne's version of the axiom is a formal condition on the shape of phrase markers. Chomsky's (for reasons that go back to Higginbotham 1983) is a condition that operates at Spell-Out, because of PF demands. Kayne's intuition is that a nonlinearized phrase marker is ill formed, in itself, whereas for Chomsky such an object is ill formed only at PF – hence the need to linearize it upon branching to this component. Chomsky's version is arguably "more minimalist" in that linearization is taken to follow from bare output conditions.

The axiom has a formal and a substantive character. The formal part demands the linearization of a complex object (assembled by the Merge operation, which produces mere associations among terms). A visual image to keep in mind is a mobile by Calder. The hanging pieces relate in a fixed way, but are not *linearly ordered* with respect to one another; one way to linearize the mobile (e.g. so as to measure it) is to lay it on the ground. The substantive part of Kayne's axiom does for the complex linguistic object what the ground does for the mobile: it tells us how to map the unordered set of terms into a sequence of PF slots. But even if Chomsky's reasoning helps us deduce the formal part of the axiom (assuming that PF demands linearization), the question remains of exactly *how* the mapping works.

Kayne is explicit about that. Unfairly, I will adapt his ideas to Chomsky's minimalist "bare phrase structure" (Chomsky avoids committing to a definition in either 1994 or 1995).

(1)   *Linear Correspondence Axiom*
   a.   Base step: If α commands β, then α precedes β.
   b.   Induction step: If γ precedes β and γ dominates α, then α precedes

I will discuss each of the steps in (1) in turn, with an eye toward deducing their substantive character from either bare output or economy considerations. Consider why command should be a sufficient condition for precedence. It is best to ask this question with a formal object in mind. I will call this object a *command unit* (CU), for the simple reason that it emerges in a derivation through the continuous application of Merge. That is, if we merge elements to an already merged phrase marker, then we obtain a CU, as in (2a). In contrast, (2b) is not a CU, since it implies the application of Merge to different objects.

(2)   a.   *Command unit: formed by continuous application of Merge to the same*
      object

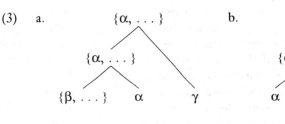

      b.   *Not a command unit: formed by discontinuous application of Merge to two*
      separately assembled objects

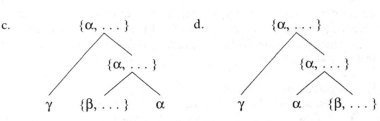

Regarding CUs, the ultimate question is why, among the possible linearizations
in (3), (3d) is chosen.

(3)   a.   b.

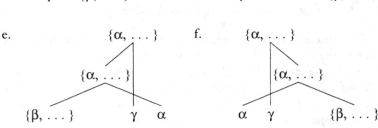

To continue with the mobile image, there are *n!* ways in which we can lay it on
the ground, for *n* the number of hanging elements. Why is it that, among all the

apparently reasonable permutations, the linguistic mobile collapses into a linearized sequence specifically in the order ⟨γ, α, {β . . . }⟩?

We may ask the question from the point of view of what syntactic relations are relevant to the terminals of the structures in (3). Concentrating on the terminals, we see that the only relation that exists between them in a CU is "I have merged with your ancestors." We can produce an order within CUs in terms of this relation, which essentially keeps track of what has merged with what when. This is, essentially, the insight behind Epstein's [1999] interpretation of command, which has the effect of ordering the terminal objects in (3) as follows: ⟨γ, α, {β . . . }⟩. If PF requirements demand that the Merge mobile collapse into a flat object, it is not unreasonable to expect that the collapse piggybacks on a previously existing relation. Indeed, minimalist assumptions lead us to expect precisely this sort of parsimony.

However, we have not yet achieved the desired results. To see this, imagine a group of people trapped inside a building, with access to a window that allows them to exit just one at a time. These people may order themselves according to some previously existing relation (e.g. age). But having found an order does not mean having decided how to leave the building. Does the youngest exit first or last – or in the middle? Likewise, a decision has to be made with regard to the ⟨γ, α, {β . . . }⟩ order. Exactly how do we map it to the PF order?

In minimalist terms, the question is not just how to map the collapsed ⟨γ, α, {β . . . }⟩ sequence to a PF order, but actually how to do it *optimally*. The hope is that mapping the collapsed ⟨γ, α, {β . . . }⟩ command order to the ⟨γ, α, {β . . . }⟩ PF order in (3d) is (one among) the best solution(s).

Another analogy might help clarify the intuition. Visualize a house of cards, and imagine how pulling out one crucial card makes it collapse. To a reasonable extent, the order in which the cards fall maps homomorphically to the order in which they were assembled, with higher cards landing on top, and cards placed on the left or right falling more or less in those directions (assuming no forces other than gravity). If Merge operations could be conceived as producing what amounts to a merge-wave of terminals, it is not unreasonable to expect such a wave to collapse into a linearized terminal sequence in a way that harmonizes (in the same local direction) the various wave states, thus essentially mapping the merge order into the PF linear order in a homomorphic way. This, of course, is hand-waving until one establishes what such a merge-wave is, but I will not go into that here (see Martin and Uriagereka, in progress, on the concept of collapsed waves in syntax).

Even if we managed to collapse the merge order into the PF sequence that most directly reflects it, why have we chosen (3d) over the equally plausible (3a)? In short, why does the command relation collapse into *precedence*, and not the opposite? The harmonized collapse problem seems to have not one optimal solution, but two.

Three different answers are possible. First, one can attribute the choice of (3d) over (3a) to something deep; it would have to be as deep as whatever explains the forward movement of time . . . (I'm not entirely joking here; physical properties are taken by many biologists to affect core aspects of the morphology of organisms, and Kayne (1994) speculates in this direction.)

Second, one can say (assuming that (3a) and (3d) are equally optimal solutions) that (3d) gave humans an adaptive edge of some sort, in terms of parsing or perhaps learnability. One could also imagine that a species that had chosen (3a) over (3d) as a collapsing technique might equally well have evolved a parser and an acquisition device for the relevant structures (but see Weinberg [1999]).

Third, one can shrug one's shoulders. So what if (3a) and (3d) are equally harmonic? Two equally valid solutions exist, so pick the one that does the work. (This view of the world would be very consistent with Stephen Jay Gould's punctuated equilibrium perspective in biology; see Uriagereka 1998.) This situation is acceptable within the Minimalist Program, or for that matter within any program that seeks to understand how optimality works in nature, which cannot reasonably seek *the* best solution to optimality problems, but instead expects *an* optimal solution; often, even mathematically optimal solutions are various.

If I am ultimately on the right track, (3d) can correctly be chosen as the actual PF ordering that the system employs; that is, we should not need to state (1a) as an axiom. In a nutshell, command maps to a PF linearization convention in simple CUs (those (1a) is designed to target) because this state of affairs is optimal. I will not claim I have proven this, for I have only indicated the direction in which a demonstration could proceed, raising some obvious questions. I have little more to say about this here and will proceed on the assumption that the base step of the LCA can be turned into a theorem.

10.2 Deducing the induction step of the LCA

Having met the demands of the Minimalist Program by showing how part of the LCA can reduce to more justifiable conditions, we should naturally ask whether the whole LCA can be deduced this way. I know of no deduction of the sort sketched above, given standard assumptions about the model.

Nonetheless, an older model provides an intriguing way of deducing the LCA.[1] For reasons that become apparent shortly, I refer to it as a *dynamically split model*. The origins of this outlook are discussions about successive cyclicity and whether this condition affects interpretation: are the interpretive components accessed in successive derivational cascades? Much of this debate was abandoned the moment a single level, S-Structure, was postulated as the interface to the interpretive components. Now that S-Structure has itself been abandoned, the question is alive again: what would it mean for the system to access the interpretation split in a dynamic way?

I want to demonstrate that the simplest assumption (i.e. nothing prevents a dynamically split access to interpretation) allows the LCA's induction step to be satisfied trivially. In effect, this would permit the deduction of (1b), albeit in a drastically changed model that neither Chomsky (1995) nor Kayne (1994) was assuming.

One way of framing the issue is to ask how many times the rule of Spell-Out should apply. If we stipulate that it applies only once, then PF and LF are accessed only once, at that point. On the other hand, liberally accessing PF and LF in successive derivational cascades entails multiple applications of Spell-Out. Surely, assuming that computational steps are costly, economy considerations favor a single application of Spell-Out. But are there circumstances in which a derivation is forced to spell out different chunks of structure in different steps?

One such instance might arise when a derivation involves more than one CU. As noted, CUs emerge as the derivational process unfolds, and they are trivially collapsible by means of the base step of the LCA. Now, what if only those trivially linearizable chunks of structure (e.g. (2a)) are in fact linearized? That is, what if, instead of complicating the LCA by including (1b), when we encounter a complex structure of the sort in (2b) we simply do not collapse it (thus linearizing it), causing a derivational crash? Only two results are then logically possible: either structures like (2b) do not exist, or they are linearized in various steps, each of which involves only CUs. The first possibility is factually wrong, so we conclude that multiple Spell-Out (MSO) is an alternative.

Before we explore whether MSO is empirically desirable, consider its possible mechanics. Bear in mind that CUs are singly spelled out – the most economical alternative. The issue, then, is what happens beyond CUs. By assumption, we have no way of collapsing them into given linearizations, so we must do the job prior to their merger, when they are still individual CUs. What we need, then, is a procedure to relate a structure that has already been spelled out to the still "active" phrase marker. Otherwise, we cannot assemble a final unified *and linearized* object.

The procedure for relating CUs can be conceived in conservative or radical terms, either solution being consistent with the program in this chapter. The conservative proposal is based on the fact that the collapsed Merge structure is no longer phrasal, after Spell-Out; in essence, the phrase marker that has undergone Spell-Out is like a giant lexical compound, whose syntactic terms are obviously interpretable but are not accessible to movement, ellipsis, and so forth.[2] The radical proposal assumes that each spelled-out CU does not even merge with the rest of the structure, the final process of interphrasal association being accomplished in the performative components.[3] I will briefly detail each of these versions.

In the conservative version, the spelled-out phrase marker behaves like a word, so that it can associate with the rest of the structure; this means it must keep its label after Spell-Out. Technically, if a phrase marker $\{\alpha, \{L, K\}\}$ collapses through Spell-Out, the result is $\{\alpha, \langle L, K \rangle\}$, which is mathematically equivalent to $\{\alpha, \{\{L\}, \{L, K\}\}\}$.[4] Since this object is not a syntactic object, it clearly can behave like a "frozen" compound. As a consequence, we need not add any further stipulations: the collapsing procedure of Spell-Out itself results in something akin to a word.

To see how we reach this conclusion, we need to take seriously Chomsky's (1995) notion of *syntactic object*. Syntactic objects can take two forms.

(4) a. Base: A word is a syntactic object.
     b. Induction: $\{\alpha, \{L, K\}\}$ is a syntactic object, for L and K syntactic objects and α a label.

(4a) speaks for itself, although it is not innocent. The general instance is not too complicated: a word is an item from the lexicon. However, the Minimalist Program permits the formation of complex words, whose internal structure and structural properties are not determined by the syntax. (Indeed, the object resulting from Spell-Out also qualifies as a word, in the technical sense of having a label and a structure that is inaccessible to the syntax.) (4b) is obtained through Merge and involves a labeling function that Chomsky argues is necessarily *projection*. What is relevant here is how a label is structurally expressed.

(5)   Within a syntactic object, a label α is not a term.
(6)   K is a term if and only if (a) or (b):
    a.   Base: K is a phrase marker.
    b.   Induction: K is a member of a member of a term.

(6a) hides no secrets. (6b) is based on the sort of object that is obtained by merging K and L: one set containing K and L, and another containing $\{L, K\}$ and label α – namely, $\{\alpha, \{L, K\}\}$. This whole object (a phrase marker) is a term, by (6a). Members of members of this term (L and K) are also terms, by (6b). Label α is a member of the first term, hence not a term. All of these results are as desired.

Consider next the collapse of $\{\alpha, \{L, K\}\}$ as $\{a, \langle L, K\rangle\}$, equivalent to $\{\alpha, \{\{L\}, \{L, K\}\}\}$. By (6b), $\{L\}$ and $\{L, K\}$ are terms. However, $\{L, K\}$ is not a syntactic object, by either (4a) or (4b). Therefore, $\{\alpha, \{\{L\}, \{L, K\}\}\}$ cannot be a syntactic object by (4b); if it is to be merged higher up, it can be a syntactic object only by (4a) – as a word. This is good; we want the collapsed object to be like a compound, that is, essentially a word: it has a label, and it has terms, but they are not objects accessible to the syntax.

Note that set-theoretic notions have been taken very seriously here; for example, such notions as linearity have been expressed without any coding tricks (angled brackets, as opposed to particular sets). In essence, the discussion has revealed that generally merged structures (those that go beyond the head–complement relation) are fundamentally nonlinear, to the point that linearizing them literally destroys their phrasal base. This conclusion lends some credibility to Chomsky's conjectures that (a) Merge produces a completely basic and merely associative set-theoretic object, with no internal ordering, and (b) only if collapsed into a flat structure can this unordered object be interpreted at PF.

Though the current notation does the job, the appropriate results can be achieved regardless of the notation. Various positions can be taken, the most radical having been mentioned already. In the version that ships spelled-out phrase markers to performance, one must assume a procedure by which already processed (henceforth, "cashed out") phrase markers find their way "back" to their interpretation site. Plausibly, this is the role agreement plays in the grammar.

It is interesting to note that, according to present assumptions, MSO applies to noncomplements (which are not part of CUs). Similarly, agreement does not manifest itself in complements, which makes it reasonable to suppose that what agreement does is "glue together" separate derivational cascades that are split at Spell-Out, the way an address links two separate computers.

In either version of MSO, we have now deduced (1b), which stipulates that the elements dominated by γ in a CU precede whatever γ precedes. That γ should precede or be preceded by the other elements in its CU was shown in section 10.1. The fact that the elements dominated by γ act as γ does within its CU is a direct consequence of the fact that γ has been spelled out separately from the CU it is attached to, in a different derivational cascade. The elements dominated by γ cannot interact with those that γ interacts with, in the "mother" CU. Thus, their place in the structure is as frozen under γ's dominance as would be the place of the members of a compound γ, the syllables of a word γ, or worse still, elements that have already "gone to performance."[5]

I should point out one final, important assumption I am making. The situation we have been considering can be schematized as in (7). But what prevents a projection like the one in (8)?

(7)

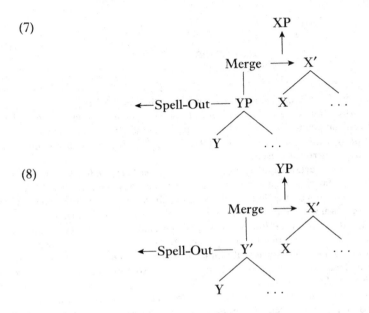

In (8), it is the spelled-out category Y′ that projects a YP. This results in forcing the linearization of X's projection prior to that of Y's, contrary to fact.

[. . .]

Within the conservative implementation of MSO, (8) can be prevented if *only lexical items project*. Again, MSO is designed to collapse a phrase marker into a compound of sorts. Yet this "word" cannot be seen as an item that projects any further; it can merge with something else, but it can never be the item that supports further lexical dependencies. This might relate to some of Chomsky's (to appear) conjectures regarding a fundamental asymmetry indirectly involved in the labeling of the Merge function; in particular, it may be that Merge (like Move) implies a form of Attract, where certain properties of one of the merging items are met by the other. It is conceivable that properties relevant to Attract are "active" only in lexical items within the lexical array, or numeration, that leads to a derivation, and not in words formed in the course of the derivation. This would include collapsed units of the sort discussed here, [. . .]. At any rate, the price to pay for unequivocal attachment of spelled-out noncomplements is to have two (perhaps not unreasonable) notions of terminals: lexicon-born ones and derived ones.

Under the radically performative interpretation of MSO, there is a trivial reason why a spelled-out chunk of structure should not project: it is gone from the syntax. The price to pay for equivocal attachment of spelled-out noncomplements is, as noted earlier, the agreement of these elements with corresponding heads.

[. . .]

I have essentially shown how the base step of the LCA may follow from economy, and how the induction step may follow from a minimalist architecture that makes central use of MSO, thus yielding dynamically bifurcated access to interpretive components.

Notes

1   For instance, in Bresnan (1971), Jackendoff (1972), or Lasnik (1972). Tree-adjoining grammars explored in, for example, Kroch (1989) also have the desired feature.

2   The reasons why compounds and spelled-out phrase markers are "frozen" are completely different (a real compound does not collapse), but the formal effect is the same.

3   This would be very much in the spirit of Hoffman's (1996) idea that syntactic unification is not given by the derivation itself.

4   I assume the standard definition of a sequence $\langle a, b \rangle$ as a set $\{\{a\}, \{a, b\}\}$ (see, for instance, Quine 1970: 65). Jim Higginbotham (personal communication) observes that the notation $\{a, \{a, b\}\}$ would also have the desired effects, although touching on a deep issue concerning whether one assumes the Foundation Axiom (or whether the individual a is allowed to be identified with the set $\{a\}$). For the most part, I would like to put these issues aside, although I cannot fail to mention two things. One, if one assumes Quine's notation, as we will see shortly, syntactic terminals will ultimately turn out to be defined as objects of the form $\{terminal\}$, rather than objects of the form *terminal*. Two, this might not be a bad result, given that in general we want to distinguish labels from terms, which could be done by way of the definition of term in (6), stating that labels are members of (set) phrase markers that are not terms. Then the problem is terminal items, which clearly are terms but need to be labeled as well. One possibility is to consider a given terminal term as labeled only after it has been linearized, hence having been turned by the system to a $\{terminal\}$ (the whole object is a term; thus, *terminal* is its label).

5   Note that the most natural interpretation of the radical version of MSO ships noncomplements to performance prior to the rest of the structure, thus proceeds top-down.

References

Bresnan, J. 1971. Sentence stress and syntactic transformations. *Language* 47: 257–81.

Chomsky, N. 1994. *Bare phrase structure. MIT Occasional Papers in Linguistics 5*. Cambridge, MA: MITWPL. [Published in P. Kempchinsky (ed.) (1994), *Evolution and revolution in linguistic theory: Essays in honor of Carlos Otero*, Washington, DC: Georgetown University Press, pp. 51–109. Also published in G. Webelhuth (ed.) (1994), *Government and binding theory and the minimalist program*, Cambridge. MA: MIT Press, pp. 383–439.]

Chomsky, N. 1995. *The Minimalist Program*. Cambridge, MA: MIT Press.

Chomsky, N. 1998. Minimalist inquiries: The framework. [Published in R. Martin, D. Michaels and J. Uriagereka (eds.) (2000), *Step by step: Essays on minimalism in honor of Howard Lasnik*, Cambridge, MA: MIT Press, pp. 89–155.]

Epstein, S. D. 1999. Un-principled syntax: The derivation of syntactic relations. In S. D. Epstein and N. Hornstein (eds.), *Working minimalism*, Cambridge, MA: MIT Press, pp. 317–45.

Higginbotham, J. 1983. A note on phrase markers. *Revue québécoise de linguistique* 13: 147–66.

Hoffman, J. 1996. *Syntactic and paratactic word-order effects.* Doctoral dissertation, University of Maryland, College Park.

Jackendoff, R. 1972. *Semantic interpretation in generative grammar.* Cambridge, MA: MIT Press.

Kayne, R. S. 1994. *The antisymmetry of syntax.* Cambridge, MA: MIT Press.

Kroch, A. 1989. Asymmetries in long-distance extraction in a Tree Adjoining Grammar. In M. Baltin and A. Kroch (eds.), *Alternative conceptions of phrase structure*, Chicago: University of Chicago Press, pp. 66–98.

Lasnik, H. 1972. *Analyses of negation in English.* Doctoral dissertation, MIT.

Martin, R. and J. Uriagereka. In progress. Collapsed waves in syntax. Ms., University of Tsukuba and University of Maryland, College Park.

Quine, W. V. O. 1970. *Philosophy of logic.* Englewood Cliffs, NJ: Prentice-Hall.

Uriagereka, J. 1998. *Rhyme and reason.* Cambridge, MA: MIT Press.

Weinbeng, A. 1999. A minimalist theory of human sentence processing. In S. D. Epstein and N. Hornstein (eds.), *Working minimalism*, Cambridge, MA: MIT Press, pp. 283–315.

CYCLICITY AND EXTRACTION DOMAINS

Jairo Nunes and Juan Uriagereka

1 Introduction

If something distinguishes the Minimalist Program of Chomsky (1995, 1998) from other models within the principles-and-parameters framework, that is the assumption that the language faculty is an optimal solution to legibility conditions imposed by external systems. From this perspective, a main desideratum of the program is to derive substantive principles from interface ("bare output") conditions, and formal principles from economy conditions. It is thus natural that part of the minimalist agenda is devoted to reevaluating the theoretical apparatus developed within the principles-and-parameters framework, with the goal of explaining on more solid conceptual grounds the wealth of empirical material uncovered in the past decades. This paper takes some steps towards this goal by deriving Condition on Extraction Domains (CED) effects (in the sense of Huang 1982) in consonance with these general minimalist guidelines.

Within the principles-and-parameters framework, the CED is generally assumed to be a government-based locality condition that restricts movement operations (see Huang 1982 and Chomsky 1986, for instance). But once the notion of government is abandoned in the Minimalist Program, as it involves nonlocal relations (see Chomsky 1995: ch. 3), the data that were accounted for in terms of the CED call for a more principled analysis.

Some of the relevant data regarding the CED are illustrated in example (1) [This] shows that regular extraction out of a subject or an adjunct yields unacceptable results. [. . .]

(1) a.   *[$_{CP}$ [which politician]$_i$ [$_{C'}$ did+Q [$_{IP}$ [pictures of t_i] upset the voters]]]
     b.   *[$_{CP}$ [which paper]$_i$ [$_{C'}$ did+Q [$_{IP}$ you read *Don Quixote* [$_{PP}$ before filing t_i]]]]

[. . .]

2 Basic CED Effects

Any account of the CED has to make a principled distinction between complements and noncomplements (see Cattell 1976 for early, very useful discussion).
Kayne's (1994) LCA [Linear Correspondence Axiom] has the desired effect: a given
head can be directly linearized with respect to the lexical items within its complement, but not with respect to the lexical items within its subject or adjunct.
The reason is trivial. Consider the phrase marker in (2), for instance (irrelevant
details omitted).

(2)

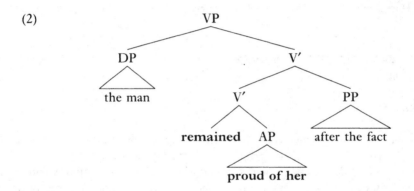

It is a simple fact about the Merge operation that only the terminal elements in
boldface in (2) can be assembled without ever abandoning a single derivational
workspace; by contrast, the terminal elements under DP and PP must first be assembled in a separate derivational space before being connected to the rest.

One can capitalize on this derivational fact in various ways. Let us recast Kayne's
(1994) LCA in terms of Chomsky's (1995) bare phrase structure and simplify its
definition by eliminating the recursive step, as formulated in (3).[1]

(3) *Linear Correspondence Axiom*
     A lexical item α precedes a lexical item β iff α asymmetrically c-commands β

Clearly, all the terminals in boldface in (2) stand in valid precedence relations, according to (3). The question is how they can establish precedence relations with the
terminals within DP and PP, if the LCA is as simple as (3).

Uriagereka (1999) suggests an answer, by taking the number of applications of
the rule of Spell-out to be determined by standard economy considerations and

not by the unmotivated stipulation that Spell-out must apply only once. Here we will focus our attention to cases where multiple applications of Spell-out are triggered by linearization considerations (see Uriagereka 1999 for other cases and further discussion). The reasoning goes as follows. Let us refer to the operation that maps a phrase structure into a linear order of terminals in accordance with the LCA in (3) as *Linearize*.[2] Under the standard assumption that phrasal syntactic objects are not legitimate objects at the PF level, Linearize can be viewed as an operation imposed on the phonological component by legibility requirements of the articulatory-perceptual interface, as essentially argued by Higginbotham (1983). If this is so and if the LCA is as simple as (3), the computational system should not ship complex structures such as (2) to the phonological component by means of the Spell-out operation, because Linearize would not be able to determine precedence relations among all the lexical items. Assuming that failure to yield a total ordering among lexical items leads to an illicit derivation, the system is forced to employ multiple applications of Spell-out, targeting chunks of structure that Linearize can operate with.

Under this view, the elements in subject and adjunct position in (2) can be linearized with respect to the rest of the structure in accordance with (3) in the following way: (i) the DP and the PP are spelled out separately and in the phonological component, their lexical items are linearized internal to them; and (ii) the DP and the PP are later "plugged in" where they belong in the whole structure. We assume that the label of a given structure provides the "address" for the appropriate plugging in, in both the phonological and the interpretive components.[3] That is, applied to the syntactic object K = {γ, {α, β}}, with label γ and constituents α and β (see Chomsky 1995: ch. 4), Spell-out ships {α, β} to the phonological and interpretative components, leaving K only with its label. Because the label encodes the relevant pieces of information that allow a category to undergo syntactic operations, K itself is still accessible to the computational system, despite the fact that its constituent parts are, in a sense, gone; thus, for instance, K can move and is visible to linearization when the whole structure is spelled-out. Another way to put it is to say that once the constituent parts of K are gone, the computational system treats it as a lexical item. In order to facilitate keeping track of the computations in the following discussion, we use the notation K = [γ ⟨α, β⟩] to represent K after it has been spelled out.

An interesting consequence of this proposal is that multiple Spell-out of separate derivational cascades derives Cattell's (1976) original observation that only complements are transparent to movement. When Spell-out applies to the subject DP in (2), for instance, the computational system no longer has access to its constituents and, therefore, no element can be extracted out of it. Let us consider a concrete case by examining the relevant details of the derivation of (4), after the stage where the structures K and L in (5) have been assembled by successive applications of Merge.

(4) *Which politician did pictures of upset the voters?

(5) a.   K = [$_{vP}$ upset the voters]

     b.   L = [pictures of which politician]

If the LCA is as simple as in (3), the complex syntactic object resulting from the merger of K and L in (5) would not be linearizable because the constituents of K would not enter into a c-command relation with the constituents of L. The computational system then applies Spell-out to L, allowing its constituents to be linearized in the phonological component, and merges the spelled-out structure L′ with K, as illustrated in (6).[4]

(6)

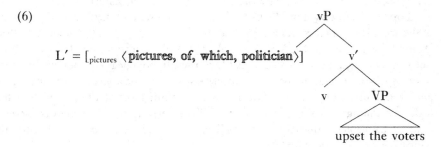

L′ = [$_{pictures}$ ⟨pictures, of, which, politician⟩]

Further computations involve the merger of *did* and movement of L′ to [Spec, TP]. Assuming Chomsky's (1995: ch. 3) copy theory of movement, this amounts to saying that the computational system copies L′ and merges it with the assembled structure, yielding the structure in (7).

(7)   [$_{TP}$ [$_{pictures}$ ⟨pictures, of, which, politician⟩] [$_{T′}$ did [$_{vP}$ [$_{pictures}$ ⟨pictures, of, which, politician⟩] [$_{v′}$ upset the voters]]]]

In the next steps, the interrogative complementizer Q merges with TP and *did* adjoins to it, yielding (8).

(8)   [$_{CP}$ did+Q [$_{TP}$ [$_{pictures}$ ⟨pictures, of, which, politician⟩] [$_{T′}$ did [$_{vP}$ [$_{pictures}$ ⟨pictures, of, which, politician⟩] [$_{v′}$ upset the voters]]]]]

In (8), there is no element that can check the strong *wh*-feature of Q. Crucially, the *wh*-element of either copy of L = [$_{pictures}$ ⟨pictures, of, which, politician⟩] became unavailable to the computational system after L was spelled out. The derivation therefore crashes. Under this view, there is no way for the computational system to yield the sentence in (4) if derivations unfold in a strictly cyclic fashion, as we are assuming. To put it in more general terms, extraction out of a subject is prohibited because, at the relevant derivational point, there is literally no syntactic object within the subject that could be copied.

Similar considerations apply to the sentence in (9), which illustrates the impossibility of "extraction" out of an adjunct clause.

(9)   *Which paper did you read *Don Quixote* before filing?

Assume, for concreteness, that the temporal adjunct clause of (9) is adjoined to vP. Once K and L in (10) have been assembled, Spell-out must apply to L, before

K and L merge; otherwise, the lexical items of K could not be linearized with respect to the lexical items of L. After L is spelled out as L', it merges with K, yielding (11). In the phonological component, Linearize applies to the lexical items of L' and the resulting sequence will be later plugged into the appropriate place, after the whole structure is spelled out. The linear order between the lexical items of L and the lexical items of K will then be (indirectly) determined by whatever fixes the order of adjuncts in the grammar.[5]

(10)   a.   K = [$_{vP}$ you read *Don Quixote*]
        b.   L = [$_{PP}$ before PRO filing which paper]

(11)   vP

[$_{vP}$ you read *Don Quicote*]   L' = [$_{before}$ ⟨ **Before, PRO, filing, which, paper** ⟩

What is relevant for the current discussion is that after the (simplified) structure in (12) is formed, there is no *wh*-element available to check the strong *wh*-feature of Q and the derivation crashes; in particular, *which paper* is no longer accessible to the computational system at the step where it should be copied to cheek the strong feature of Q. As before, the sentence in (9) is underivable through the cyclic derivation outlined in (10)–(12).

(12)   [$_{CP}$ did+Q [$_{TP}$ you [$_{vP}$ [$_{vP}$ read *Don Quixote*] [$_{before}$ ⟨before, PRO, filing, which, paper⟩]]]]

[. . .]

To summarize, CED effects arise when a given syntactic object K that would be needed for computations at a derivational stage D_n has been spelled out at a derivational stage D_i prior to D_n, thereby becoming inaccessible to the computational system after D_i.

Notes

1   For purposes of presentation, we ignore cases where two heads are in mutual c-command. For discussion, see Chomsky (1995: 337).
2   In Chomsky (1995: ch. 4), the term *LCA* is used to refer both to the Linear Correspondence Axiom and the mapping operation that makes representations satisfy this axiom, as becomes clear when it is suggested that the *LCA* may delete traces (see Chomsky 1995: 337). We will avoid this ambiguity and use the term *Linearize* for the operation.
3   See Uriagereka (1999) for a discussion of how agreement relations could also be used as addresses for spelled-out structures.
4   Following Uriagereka (1999), we assume that spelled-out structures do not project. Hence, if the computational system applies Spell-out to K instead of L in (5), the subsequent merger of L and the spelled-out K does not yield a configuration for the appropriate thematic relation to be established, violating the θ-Criterion. Similar considerations apply, *mutatis mutandis*, to spelling out the target of adjunction instead of the adjunct in example (10).

5   That is, regardless of whether adjuncts are linearized by the procedure that linearizes specifiers and complements or by a different procedure (see Kayne 1994 and Chomsky 1995 for different views), the important point to keep in mind is that, if the formulation of the LCA is to be as simple as (3), the lexical items within L' in (11) cannot be directly linearized with respect to the lexical items contained in the lower vP segment.

References

Cattell, R. 1976. Constraints on movement rules. *Language* 52: 18–50.

Chomsky, N. 1986. *Barriers*. Cambridge, MA: MIT Press.

Chomsky, N. 1995. *The Minimalist Program*. Cambridge, MA: MIT Press.

Chomsky, N. 1998. *Minimalist inquiries: The framework. MIT Occasional Papers in Linguistics 15*. Cambridge, MA: MITWPL. [Published in R. Martin, D. Michaels and J. Uriagereka (eds.) (2000), *Step by step: Essays on minimalism in honor of Howard Lasnik*, Cambridge, MA: MIT Press, pp. 89–155.]

Higginbotham, J. 1983. A note on phrase markers. *Revue Québécoise de Linguistique* 13: 147–66.

Huang, C.-T. J. 1982. *Logical relations in Chinese and the theory of grammar*. Doctoral dissertation, MIT.

Kayne, R. S. 1994. *The antisymmetry of syntax*. Cambridge, MA: MIT Press.

Uriagereka, J. 1999. Multiple spell-out. In S. D. Epstein and N. Hornstein (eds.), *Working Minimalism*, Cambridge, MA: MIT Press, pp. 251–82.

6

Copy Theory of Movement

From *LINEARIZATION OF CHAINS AND SIDEWARD MOVEMENT*
Jairo Nunes

1.2.4 Satisfaction of the Inclusiveness Condition

Still another conceptual advantage of assuming the copy theory from a minimalist perspective is that it satisfies the Inclusiveness Condition, which requires that an LF object be built from the features of the lexical items of the numeration (see Chomsky 1995: 228). The motivation underlying the Inclusiveness Condition is to restrict the reference set of derivations that can be compared for economy purposes. If the system could add material that is not present in the numeration in the course of syntactic computations, the role of the numeration in determining the class of comparable derivations would be completely undermined. Thus, given the minimalist assumption that economy matters in the computations from the numeration to LF, something like the Inclusiveness Condition must be enforced in the system.

This being so, the trace theory of movement violates the Inclusiveness Condition because traces are grammatical formatives that are not part of the initial array that feeds the computation. Under the copy theory, on the other hand, a trace is simply a copy of a lexical item of the numeration or a copy of an X-bar-theoretic object built from the items of the numeration. Put in different terms, the copy theory contributes to ensuring internal coherence in the framework.[1]

[. . .]

1.3 Traces and the Linear Correspondence Axiom

With Kayne's (1994) influential proposal that linear order is determined by hierarchical structure, as dictated by the Linear Correspondence Axiom (LCA) in (1) (see Kayne 1994: 33), an interesting question arises: are traces computed for purposes of linearization? The question is even more intriguing if one assumes that a trace is a copy of the moved element.

(1) *Linear Correspondence Axiom*
     Let X, Y be nonterminals and x, y terminals such that X dominates x and
     Y dominates y. Then if X asymmetrically c–commands Y, x precedes y.

Kayne (1994: 10) briefly mentions the question of linearization of traces under
the copy theory of movement when discussing the phrase markers in (2) and (3)
with respect to the LCA. According to Kayne, (2) is a well-formed phrase marker
because V asymmetrically c–commands N and therefore *see* is to precede *John*; in
(3), on the other hand, V and NP c–command each other and therefore no linear
order between *see* and *John* can be established.

(2)

(3)

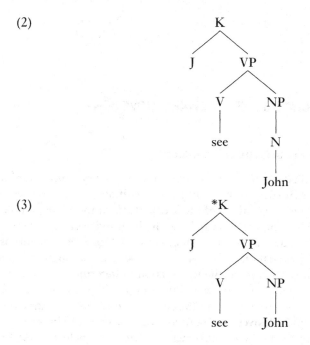

Assuming the distinction between phrase markers such as (2) and (3), Kayne considers two possibilities as to how structures containing traces may comply with the LCA:

> The question arises of what happens if *John* (or any phrase) is moved. If the result
> of movement is that DP (or NP) dominates just a trace, then *see* and that trace will
> not be ordered at all with respect to one another, since the internal structure of DP
> (or NP), which ensured antisymmetry, will have been lost. This might conceivably
> be a tolerable consequence, since traces are in any event not visible. It is notable,
> though, that this question does not arise if movement transformations leave a copy
> rather than a trace. (Kayne 1994: ch. 2, n. 3)

Given his claim that the LCA is the source of the major properties of standard
X–bar theory, Kayne (1994: 49) concludes that the LCA underlies the entire set
of syntactic representations. This entails, however, that S–Structure and LF should
not allow a structure containing a head and the trace of its complement for the

same reason a structure such as (3) should not be permitted: it violates the LCA. Kayne's suggestion that the "invisibility" of traces at PF exempts them from being subject to the LCA is therefore at odds with his conceptual argument that the LCA applies to all syntactic representations, including LF (see Kayne 1994: sec. 5.2).

On the other hand, as Kayne observes, there seems to be no problem in linearizing a given head and the trace of its complement under the copy theory of movement, provided that the trace has internal structure; in other words, traces do not differ from unmoved elements with respect to linearization considerations. We may thus draw the conclusion that the copy theory of movement is indeed a necessary component in Kayne's system in order to ensure consistency with respect to the well-formedness conditions that the LCA imposes on phrase markers.

Addressing the issue of whether or not traces should be subject to the LCA under the bare phrase structure approach, Chomsky (1995: 337) suggests that "there is no reason for the LCA to order an element that will disappear at PF, for example, a trace." I disagree with this suggestion. The null hypothesis under the copy theory of movement is that all copies should be subject to the same grammatical conditions; any proposed difference between heads of chains and traces should require strong motivation. Chomsky's suggestion could perhaps be better substantiated if reasons for deletion of traces were offered. Even so, it should be observed that the logic of the suggestion confers too much power on global computations. The linearization of a given element at a given derivational step is taken to be contingent on a deletion operation targeting that element later in the derivation. If this logic were to extend to morphological operations, for instance, one could ask why Morphology should not ignore traces, allowing contraction to proceed over them, given that they will be deleted later in the derivation. Clearly, this would yield wrong results with respect to *wanna*-contraction over *wh*-traces, for instance.

To my knowledge, there appears to be only one potential problem for the null hypothesis that heads of chains and traces are both subject to the LCA. If the links of a chain are in a sense the same element (under standard assumptions, a chain is a discontinuous object), any material intervening between two links of a given chain asymmetrically c-commands and is asymmetrically c-commanded by the same element. This state of affairs, however, is not compatible with the LCA and no linear order should obtain for structures containing chains.

In section 1.5, I turn this potential problem into a virtue by using the logic of its consequences to account for deletion of traces in the phonological component. Before we get to the discussion of how linearization considerations ultimately motivate deletion of traces, let us consider what are the main theoretical and empirical issues regarding deletion of traces and how successful some current analyses have been in addressing them.

1.4 Traces and phonetic realization

1.4.1 The issues

The most salient difference between heads of chains and traces is their phonetic realization: in the general case, only heads of chains are phonetically realized.

Thus, any analysis that adopts some version of the copy theory of movement
has to address the following questions: (i) why is it the case that (in general) a
nontrivial chain cannot have all of its links phonetically realized?, and (ii) why is
it the case that (in general) traces and not heads of chains are the links that are
deleted? That is, given the derivation sketched in (4), for instance, why is it
not possible for the structure in (4c) to yield the PF output associated with (5a)
or (5b)? [. . .]

(4)   a.   K = [$_{TP}$ T [$_{VP}$ was [$_{VP}$ kissed John]]]
       b.   *Copy*
             K = [$_{TP}$ T [$_{VP}$ was [$_{VP}$ kissed John^i]]]
             L = John^i
       c.   *Merge*
             [$_{TP}$ John^i [$_{T'}$ T [$_{VP}$ was [$_{VP}$ kissed John^i]]]]
(5)   a.   *John was kissed John.
       b.   *Was kissed John.
       c.   John was kissed.

      [. . .]

1.5   Linearization of chains and phonetic realization of chain links

1.5.1   Nondistinctiveness of copies

Once the copy theory of movement is assumed, one needs to determine whether
two terms with the same set of features are to be interpreted as distinct elements
or copies. Consider the structure in (6), for example. If the pair (*John, John*)
of (6) were to form a chain, it would satisfy both the Minimal Link Condition
and Last Resort; actual chain formation thus depends on whether or not the two
instances of *John* are nondistinct copies or elements distinctively specified in the
numeration.[2]

(6)   [$_{TP}$ John was [$_{vP}$ kissed John]]

I will follow Chomsky's (1995: 227) proposal that two lexical items *l* and *l'* selected
from a numeration should be marked as distinct for the computational system if
they are accessed by distinct applications of Select.[3] As for phrasal objects, I assume
that their labels encode the relevant piece of information regarding distinctiveness;
the DP [the man], for instance, is to be represented in bare phrase structure terms
as K = {the^i, {the^i, man^k}}. Given that Copy just replicates the targeted material
and does not alter distinctiveness markings, it is possible to determine, at any point
in a given derivation, whether two terms with identical sets of features are to be
interpreted as copies or distinct constituents.
      [. . .]
Let us explore the consequences of this conclusion for the linearization computations of the phonological component.

1.5.2 Linearization of nontrivial chains

If the notion of nondistinctiveness is available for early computations of the phonological component while syntactic structure is still present, it must certainly be available at the point where the system employs the operation *Linearize*, which I take to be the procedure that maps a given syntactic structure into a sequence of terminals, in compliance with the LCA. Assuming this to be so, let us consider the asymmetric c-command relations in (7), in order to determine how this structure should be linearized in accordance with the LCA.[4]

(7)   [John^i [was [kissed John^i]]]

Take the relation between the two copies of *John* and the copula *was*, for instance. Since the upper copy of *John* asymmetrically c-commands *was*, we should obtain the order ⟨*John^i was*⟩, according to the LCA; likewise, since the copula asymmetrically c-commands the lower copy of *John*, the order⟨*was, John^i*⟩ should be derived. Combining these two results, we should obtain the partial sequence σ = ⟨*John^i, was, John^i*⟩. Were the two instances of *John* distinct, σ would be a well-formed linear order, with the copula following an occurrence of *John* and preceding a different occurrence of *John*, as in *John said that John was kissed.* However, since the two instances of *John* in (7) are nondistinct, *was* is required to precede and be preceded by the same element, *John*. σ is therefore not a linear order because it lacks asymmetry (if α precedes β, then it must be the case that β does not precede α).

The structure in (7) also violates the irreflexivity condition on linear order (if α precedes β, then it must be the case that α ≠ β). Since the upper copy of *John* asymmetrically c-commands the lower one, the former should precede the latter in accordance with the LCA. Given that the two copies of *John* in (7) are nondistinct, that would amount to saying that *John* should precede itself.

Failure to yield a linear order thus provides a straightforward account of the fact that the structure in (7) cannot surface as the sentence in (8a); the attempted derivation of (8a) from (7) is canceled, because Linearize yields no output and no PF object is formed. To put it in general terms, if the links of a chain count as nondistinct for linearization purposes, we have an explanation for why a chain (in standard cases) cannot surface at PF with more than one link overtly realized: the syntactic object containing such a chain cannot be linearized.

(8)   a.   *John was kissed John.
       b.   John was kissed.

This is a welcome result. Recall that the derivations of (8a) and (8b) from (7) should be prevented from being compared for purposes of economy; if they were compared, the derivation of (8a) would incorrectly outrank the derivation of (8b) because it is more economical in not employing an application of deletion (see section 1.4.1). If the derivation of (8a) from (7) is canceled because it cannot be linearized, no questions of convergence or economy can be raised.[5]

I propose that deletion of chain links is thus required for a structure containing nontrivial chains to be linearized in accordance with the LCA. This proposal has the welcome conceptual advantage that it takes both heads of chains and traces to be subject to linearization. What is required at this point is an independent motivation for why deletion generally targets traces and not heads of chains and an account of how the presence of multiple copies may circumvent the LCA in some cases. These are the topics of the next sections.

1.5.3 Deletion of chain links and optimality considerations

1.5.3.1 *Full versus scattered deletion*

Consider the simplified structure in (9), in which the embedded object DP raises to the matrix subject position, leaving two copies behind.

(9)   [$_{TP}$[$_{DP}$ the [$_{NP}$ tall man]]^i appears [$_{TP}$[$_{DP}$ the [$_{NP}$ tall man]]^i to have been kissed [$_{DP}$ the [$_{NP}$ tall man]]^i]]

As discussed in section 1.5.2, such a structure cannot be linearized as is. The highest copy of *the tall man* asymmetrically c-commands the verb *appears*, for instance, which in turn asymmetrically c-commands the other two copies. Given that these three copies are nondistinct, no linear order between *the tall man* and *appears* can be established in accordance with the LCA. Thus, Linearize yields no output for further computations in the phonological component when applying to (9) and the derivation is canceled because no PF object is formed.

I proposed in section 1.5.2 that deletion may allow a structure containing nontrivial chains to be linearized by eliminating "repeated" material that induces lack of asymmetry and irreflexivity in the intended linear order. Nothing that has been said so far, however, prevents deletion from applying within the different links of a chain, in what may be called *scattered deletion*. For instance, deletion could in principle target different constituents in each of the links of the DP chain in (9), yielding a structure such as (10).

(10)   [$_{TP}$[$_{DP}$ the [$_{NP}$ ~~tall man~~]]^i appears [$_{TP}$[$_{DP}$ ~~the~~ [$_{NP}$ tall ~~man~~]]^i to have been kissed [$_{DP}$ ~~the~~ [$_{NP}$ ~~tall~~ man]]^i]]

Although the coindexed DPs in (9) are nondistinct, the constituents that survive deletion in (10) are distinct. (10) should then be linearized in accordance with the LCA, yielding the sentence in (11), which is, however, unacceptable.

(11)   *The appears tall to have been kissed man.

I propose that although the derivation of (11) converges at PF, it is not the most economical derivation starting from (9). To put it more broadly, scattered deletion does not yield an optimal derivation in the general case. Take (9), for example. Under the assumption that deletion for purposes of linearization only targets constituents (one constituent per application), the derivation of (10) from (9) requires that deletion apply (at least) five times, targeting the following constituents: the

NP of the chain link in the matrix subject position, the constituents *the* and *man* of the link in the intermediate subject position, and the constituents *the* and *tall* of the link in the object position. However, three other derivations starting from (9) that employ "full deletion" of chain links are more economical; if deletion targets the whole DP of two links of the chain in (9), the structures in (12) will be derived.

(12) a. $[_{TP}[_{DP}$ the $[_{NP}$ tall man$]]^i$ appears $[_{TP}[_{DP}$ ~~the~~ $[_{NP}$ ~~tall man~~$]]^i$ to have been kissed $[_{DP}$ ~~the~~ $[_{NP}$ ~~tall man~~$]]^i]]$

     b. $[_{TP}[_{DP}$ ~~the~~ $[_{NP}$ ~~tall man~~$]]^i$ appears $[_{TP}[_{DP}$ the $[_{NP}$ tall man$]]^i$ to have been kissed $[_{DP}$ ~~the~~ $[_{NP}$ ~~tall man~~$]]^i]]$

     c. $[_{TP}[_{DP}$ ~~the~~ $[_{NP}$ ~~tall man~~$]]^i$ appears $[_{TP}[_{DP}$ ~~the~~ $[_{NP}$ ~~tall man~~$]]^i]$ to have been kissed $[_{DP}$ the $[_{NP}$ tall man$]]^i]]$

Each structure of (12) can be linearized in accordance with the LCA, yielding the sentences in (13). Given that the derivation of any of the sentences in (13) employs only two applications of deletion, the derivation of (11), which requires (at least) five applications, is correctly blocked.

(13) a. The tall man appears to have been kissed.
     b. *Appears the tall man to have been kissed.
     c. *Appears to have been kissed the tall man.

Under the assumption that deletion targets one constituent per application, economy considerations concerning the number of applications of deletion thus block scattered deletion in the general case, favoring full deletion of chain links. I refer to the operation of the phonological component that converts (9), for instance, into structures such as (10) or (12) as *Chain Reduction* (see Nunes 1995: 279).

(14) *Chain Reduction*
Delete the minimal number of constituents of a nontrivial chain CH that suffices for CH to be mapped into a linear order in accordance with the LCA.

Although I will assume the formulation in (14) for expository purposes, it is actually unnecessary to specify that Chain Reduction delete the *minimal number* of constituents; that is, Chain Reduction need not count. Economy considerations regarding the length of a derivation may indirectly determine the number of elements to be deleted, by enforcing the minimal number of applications of deletion. All things being equal, a short derivation should block a longer derivation (see Chomsky 1995: 314, 357); hence, a derivation in which constituents are unnecessarily deleted is longer, therefore less economical, than a competing derivation where no such deletion occurs.

[. . .]

Note that the derivation of (11) . . . from the structure in (9) was ruled out on the basis of *economy*, rather than convergence considerations. The system proposed here actually allows instances of scattered deletion if full deletion of chain links does not yield a convergent derivation. For instance, if a derivation crashes because full deletion leads to violations of other constraints of the phonological component, it will not compete with corresponding derivations involving scattered deletion.

A rather persuasive example of this possibility is found in Bošković's (2001) analysis of the contrast between Macedonian and Bulgarian with respect to the location of clitics, as illustrated in (15) and (16).

(15) *Macedonian* (from Rudin et al. 1999)
    a.   Si mu (gi) dal li parite?
          are him-DAT them given Q the-money
    b.   *Dal li si mu (gi) parite?
          given Q are him-DAT them the-money
          'Have you given him the money?'
(16) *Bulgarian* (from Rudin et al. 1999)
    a.   *Si mu (gi) dal li parite?
          are him-DAT them given Q the-money
    b.   Dal li si mu (gi) parite?
          given Q are him-DAT them the-money
          'Have you given him the money?'

Bošković argues that in both languages the complex head [si+mu+gi+dal] left-adjoins to the interrogative particle *li*, leaving a copy behind, as represented in (17).

(17) $[si+mu+gi+dal]^i+li \ldots [si+mu+gi+dal]^i$

Deletion of the lower copy of [si+mu+gi+dal], as shown in (18), yields a well-formed result in Macedonian (see (15a)), because in this language pronominal clitics are proclitic and *li* is enclitic. The unacceptability of (15b) then follows from the general ban on scattered deletion imposed by economy considerations regarding the number of applications of deletion.

(18) $[si+mu+gi+dal]^i+li \ldots$ [s̶i̶+̶m̶u̶+̶g̶i̶+̶d̶a̶l̶]^i

In Bulgarian, on the other hand, both *li* and the pronominal clitics are enclitics; thus, deletion of the lower copy of the complex head does not lead to a convergent result (see (16a)). Bošković argues that the system then resorts to scattered deletion, as shown in (19), allowing the chain to be linearized yet at the same time satisfying the additional requirements of the phonological component.

(19) $[$s̶i̶+̶m̶u̶+̶g̶i̶+̶dal$]^i+li \ldots [si+mu+gi+$d̶a̶l̶$]^i$

[. . .]

To summarize, by taking the number of applications of deletion under Chain Reduction to be determined by economy considerations, we can account for (i) why scattered deletion within chains is in general not an optimal option (it employs more applications of deletion than necessary); (ii) why convergence requirements may override the preference for deletion of entire chain links (only convergent derivations count for economy computations) [. . .].

1.5.3.2 *Deletion of traces versus deletion of heads of chains*

We are still left with a problem from section 1.5.3.1: the derivations that convert a structure such as (20) into the PF output associated with any of the sentences in (21) were taken to be equally economical, for they employ the same number of applications of deletion under Chain Reduction; however the only derivation that yields an acceptable sentence is the one in which both traces are deleted.

(20) $[_{TP}[_{DP}$ the tall man$]^i$ appears $[_{TP}[_{DP}$ the tall man$]^i$ to have been kissed $[_{DP}$ the tall man$]^i]]$

(21) a. The tall man appears to have been kissed.
      b. *Appears the tall man to have been kissed.
      c. *Appears to have been kissed the tall man.

I show below that the choice among the links to be deleted is contingent on the elimination of formal features in the phonological component. But first, let us review Chomsky's (1995) proposal regarding the deletion of formal features in a derivation, starting with the computation from the numeration to LF.

Formal features may or may not be assigned an interpretation at the conceptual-intentional interface, depending on their type and on the category they are associated with. For instance, a Case-feature presumably does not receive an interpretation at the conceptual-intentional interface, whereas ϕ-features (gender, number, and person) receive an interpretation if they are part of a noun, but not if they are part of a verb. In case formal features are uninterpretable at the conceptual-intentional interface, they must be eliminated by LF, in order for the derivation to converge. Chomsky (1995) proposes that deletion of uninterpretable features takes place under feature checking, where *deletion* is taken to render a given feature "invisible at LF but accessible to the computation" (Chomsky 1995: 280).[6] Since interpretable features need not be deleted, they are always accessible to the computational system and may participate in more than one checking relation; uninterpretable features, on the other hand, cannot enter into a checking relation once checked.[7]

In addition to being relevant for LF computations, formal features are arguably relevant for morphological computations in the phonological component. Thus, Spell-Out must allow formal features to feed both the covert and the phonological component. The problem, however, is that formal features are not legible at the PF level (only phonological features are); if shipped to the phonological component, they should then lead the derivation to crash at PF. Dealing with this problem, Chomsky (1995: 230–1) proposes that there must be an operation of the phonological component applying after Morphology that eliminates formal features that are visible at PF. Let us call this operation *FF-Elimination* and take it to proceed along the lines of (22) (see Nunes 1995: 231), where deletion targets a single feature per application.[8]

(22)   *Formal Feature Elimination (FF-Elimination)*
Given the sequence of pairs $\sigma = \langle (F, P)_1, (F, P)_2, \ldots, (F, P)_n \rangle$ such that σ is the output of Linearize, F is a set of formal features, and P is a set of phonological features, delete the minimal number of features of each set of formal features in order for σ to satisfy Full Interpretation at PF.

The difference between the head of a chain and its traces regarding phonetic realization now follows from the number of checking relations a given copy is associated with. The discussion of the relation between interpretability of formal features and checking theory has so far been restricted to the mapping from the numeration to LF: checking operations render uninterpretable features invisible at LF, eventually allowing the derivation to meet Full Interpretation and converge at this level. A natural extension of this approach is to take checking operations to render uninterpretable features invisible at PF as well; after all, no formal feature is interpreted at the articulatory-perceptual interface.[9] Assuming this extension of Chomsky's (1995) checking theory, let us reconsider the derivation of (20), repeated in (23) with the relevant Case-features represented (unchecked features are in bold and checked/deleted features are subscripted).

(23) $[_{TP}[_{DP}$ the $[_{NP}$ tall man$]]^i$-$_{CASE}$ appears $[_{TP}[_{DP}$ the $[_{NP}$ tall man$]]^i$-**CASE** to have been kissed $[_{DP}$ the $[_{NP}$ tall man$]]^i$-**CASE**$]]$

After being assembled and merged with the verb *kissed*, the DP *the tall man* raises to the specifier of each T head in order to check their strong D-features; in addition, the Case-feature of the topmost copy of *the tall man* enters into a checking relation with the Case-feature of the matrix T. Since Case is an uninterpretable feature, this checking relation renders the Case-feature of the highest copy of *the tall man* invisible at LF and, according to the extension of the checking theory proposed above, invisible at PF as well. The Case-features of the lower copies of *the tall man*, on the other hand, are unaffected by the Case-checking relation involving the highest copy.

Let us then see how the DP chain of (23) is to be reduced. As discussed in section 1.5.3.1, the optimal reduction of this chain involves only two applications of deletion targeting any two of its links, as shown in (24).

(24)   a. $[_{TP} [_{DP}$ the $[_{NP}$ tall man$]]^i$-$_{CASE}$ appears $[_{TP} [_{\rm DP}$ the $[_{\rm NP}$ tall man$]]^i$-CASE to have been kissed $[_{\rm DP}$ the $[_{\rm NP}$ tall man$]]^i$-CASE$]]$

     b. $[_{TP} [_{\rm DP}$ the $[_{\rm NP}$ tall man$]]^i$-$_{CASE}$ appears $[_{TP} [_{DP}$ the $[_{NP}$ tall man$]]^i$-**CASE** to have been kissed $[_{\rm DP}$ the $[_{\rm NP}$ tall man$]]^i$-CASE$]]$

     c. $[_{TP} [_{\rm DP}$ the $[_{\rm NP}$ tall man$]]^i$-$_{CASE}$ appears $[_{TP} [_{\rm DP}$ the $[_{\rm NP}$ tall man$]]^i$-CASE to have been kissed $[_{DP}$ the $[_{NP}$ tall man$]]^i$-**CASE**$]]$

If the DP chain of (23) is reduced as in (24a), no further application of FF-Elimination is required to delete the Case-feature of *the tall man* in order for Full Interpretation to be satisfied; this feature has been deleted and is therefore invisible at PF. The PF output in (21a) is then derived after further applications of phonological rules. By contrast, if the DP chain is reduced as in (24b) or (24c), the convergent PF outputs in (21b) and (21c) are obtained only if FF-Elimination deletes the unchecked Case-feature of the copy that survives. Thus, the derivation in (24a), in which the head of the chain survives Chain Reduction, ends up being more economical than the derivations in (24b) and (24c), in which other links survive Chain Reduction, because it requires fewer applications of deletion by FF-Elimination – hence the pattern of acceptability in (21).[10,11]

Exploring the null hypothesis regarding the copy theory of movement, the above proposal thus takes the position that both heads of chains and traces should in principle be subject to phonetic realization. According to the logic of the proposal, there is nothing intrinsic to lower copies that prevents them from being pronounced. If Chain Reduction proceeds in such a way that only a trace survives, the derivation may eventually converge at PF. The fact that in most cases such a derivation yields unacceptable sentences is taken to follow from *economy* considerations, rather than convergence at PF. Since the highest chain link is engaged in more checking relations, it will require fewer application of FF-Elimination than lower chain links, thereby being the optimal candidate to survive Chain Reduction and be phonetically realized, all things being equal.

Things are not equal, however, if the phonetic realization of the head of the chain violates other well-formedness conditions of the phonological component. One such scenario is discussed by Franks (1998) in precisely these terms. Given the paradigm in (25), which shows that clitics in Serbo-Croatian generally appear in second position, Franks addresses the problem of exceptional placement triggered by prosodic considerations, as illustrated in (26) with an appositive clause [. . .].

(25) *Serbo-Croatian* (from Franks 1998)
    a.   Zoran *mi*   stalno   kupuje knjige.
         Zoran *me-DAT* constantly buys   books
    b.   *Zoran stalno   *mi*   kupuje knjige.
         Zoran constantly   *me-DAT* buys   books
         'Zoran is constantly buying me books.'

(26) *Serbo-Croatian* (from Franks 1998)
    Ja, tvoja mama, obećala   *sam*   *ti*   sladoded.
    I   your mother promised *AUX-1SG* you-DAT ice cream
    'I, your mother, promised you ice cream.'

[. . .]
Assuming that second position clitics move overtly to the highest functional head available and leave copies at all the intermediate sites, Franks (1998: sec. 2.6.2) proposes that "the puzzle of clitic placement reduces to the issue of which copy is the one pronounced." More specifically, he summarizes his proposal in the following way: (i) "Deletion of all but the highest copy does not occur if retention of the highest copy would result in a PF crash"; and (ii) "Economy considerations then dictate that the next highest copy is pronounced, unless again the result fails to converge." Under this view, the apparently exceptional sentence in (26) [is] derived

from the representation in (27) (Franks's (78) and (79a)), where "#" indicates an intonational phrase boundary.

(27)   [ja #tvoja mama# ~~[sam ti]~~ⁱ obećala [sam ti]ⁱ ~~obećala~~ sladoded]

Given that Serbo-Croatian clitics are enclitics, the intonational boundary induced by the appositive *tvja mama* in (27) blocks left-adjunction of the adjacent copy of the clitic cluster *sam ti*. If the lower copy of the clitic cluster were deleted, as in standard cases, then the higher copy would not be prosodically licensed, leading to a derivational crash at PF; the higher copy is then deleted and the lower copy phonologically attaches to the element to its left, yielding the sentence in (26).
[. . .]
Bošković (2000, 2002) extends Franks's (1998) analysis to apparent exceptions to obligatory *wh*-movement. Consider the Serbo-Croatian sentences in (28) and (29), for instance. (28) is representative of the general paradigm in Serbo-Croatian, with movement of all *wh*-phrases, whereas (29b) apparently shows an exceptional instance where a *wh*-phrase is prohibited from moving.[12]

(28)   *Serbo-Croatian* (from Bošković 2000, 2002)
       a.   Ko šta   kupuje?
            who what buys
       b.   *Ko kupuje šta?
            who buys   what
            'Who buys what?'
(29)   *Serbo-Croatian* (from Bošković 2000, 2002)
       a.   *Šta šta   uslovljava?
            what what conditions
       b.   Šta uslovljava šta?
            what conditions what
            'What conditions what?'
       c.   Šta neprestano šta   uslovljava?
            what constantly what conditions
       d.   *?Šta neprestano uslovljava šta?
            what constantly conditions what
            'What constantly conditions what?'

Given that the exceptional pattern in (29b) arises only when the sentence resulting from obligatory *wh*-movement involves adjacent occurrences of *šta*, as shown by the contrast between (29c) and (29d), and that the interpretation of (29b) does not differ from that of (29c) in the relevant respects, Bošković (2000, 2002) argues that the unexpectedly acceptable sentence in (29b) also involves overt movement of the object *wh*-phrase; however, a morphological restriction blocking adjacency of identical *wh*-words prevents the phonetic realization of the upper copy of the object chain, and the lower copy is realized instead, as represented in (30).[13]

(30)   [šta ~~šta~~ⁱ uslovljava štaⁱ]

Bošković (2002) presents compelling evidence for this approach by showing that comparable instances of "exceptional" *wh*-in-situ in Romanian, as illustrated in (31b), are able to license parasitic gaps, as shown in (32). Under the standard assumption that in-situ arguments do not license parasitic gaps, the acceptability of (32) can be accounted for if the *wh*-object actually moves overtly, licensing the parasitic gap, and the trace is phonetically realized instead of the head of the chain.

(31)   *Romanian* (from Bošković 2002)

    a.   *Ce   ce   precede?
          what what precedes

    b.   Ce   precede ce?
          what precedes what
          'What precedes what?'

(32)   *Romanian* (from Bošković 2002)

    Ce   precede ce   fara   sa   influenteze?
    what precedes what without SUBJ.PRT influence-3P.SG
    'What precedes what without influencing?'

[. . .]

By showing that both traces and heads of chains are in principle equally pronounceable, Franks's (1998) analysis of exceptional clitic placement and its extension by Bošković (2000, 2002) to exceptional lack of *wh*-movement provide compelling empirical evidence for the null hypothesis under the copy theory of movement.[14] The only piece missing in Franks's analysis is an independent explanation for why the best candidate for pronunciation is the *highest* chain link if possible, then the second *highest*, and so on.[15]

Under the approach developed in this section, however, this hierarchy is what we should expect. The ranking of best candidates for pronunciation from the highest to the lowest chain link follows from economy considerations regarding checking relations in overt syntax and applications of FF-Elimination in the phonological component. Since syntactic objects keep checking their features as they move, the higher a given chain link is, the fewer its unchecked features that FF-Elimination must delete. In other words, if a higher link survives Chain Reduction, the applications of FF-Elimination are minimized.

To sum up, lack of phonetic realization is not an intrinsic property that should characterize traces as grammatical primitives. Traces may indeed be phonetically realized if the pronunciation of the head of the chain causes the derivation to crash at PF. The fact that traces in the general case are not phonetically realized follows from the interaction of two independent factors: (i) since nontrivial chains induce violations of the LCA, they must undergo Chain Reduction; and (ii) the choice of the link to survive Chain Reduction and be phonetically realized is determined by economy considerations regarding the number of applications of FF-Elimination: given that the head of a chain participates in more checking relations than its trace(s), it will require fewer applications of FF-Elimination, becoming the optimal option for phonetic realization.

1.5.3.3 Phonetic realization of multiple copies
In this section, I examine some chains that have more than one full link phonetically realized and discuss why they do not cause problems for linearization.

1.5.3.3.1 Wh-elements   As mentioned in section 1.4.1, some languages may allow
wh-traces to be phonetically realized in addition to the head of the *wh*-chain. The
sentences in (33)–(34) exemplify this phenomenon.
    [. . .]

(33)   *German* (from McDaniel 1986)
        Wen   glaubt Hans *wen* Jakob gesehen hat?
        whom thinks Hans *wen* Jakob seen   has
        'Who does Hans think Jakob saw?'
(34)   *Romani* (from McDaniel 1986)
        Kas   misline   *kas*   o Demìri dikhlâ?
        whom you-think *whom* Demir   saw
        'Who do you think Demir saw?'

    [. . .]
    At first sight, these sentences constitute counterevidence to my proposal that
deletion of chain links is triggered by linearization considerations (see section 1.5.2):
if the *wh*-phrases of each of the sentences are nondistinct copies, they should prevent
their structures from being linearized and cause the derivation to be canceled.[16] I show
below that when closely inspected, these sentences actually provide additional evidence in favor of the proposal regarding linearization of chains pursued in this chapter.
Before getting into the analysis proper, let us consider two other kinds of data that
show that the phenomenon illustrated in (33)–(34) is very restricted in these languages.
    The first thing to note is that in languages that allow multiple *wh*-copies,
phonetic realization of traces is restricted to intermediate traces, as shown by the
contrast between (35) and (36), for instance. In both sentences, three *wh*-copies
are phonetically realized. The difference between them is arguably due to the fact
that in (35), only the intermediate *wh*-traces are realized, whereas in (36), the tail
of the *wh*-chain is realized as well.

(35)   *German* (from Fanselow and Mahajan 1995)
        Wen denkst Du *wen* sie meint   *wen* Harald liebt?
        who think you *who* she believes *who* Harald loves
        'Who do you think that she believes that Harald loves?'
(36)   *German*
        **Wen*   glaubt Hans *wen* Jakob *wen* gesehen hat?
         whom thinks Hans *whom* Jakob *whom* seen   has
         'Who does Hans think Jakob saw?'

    Second, as mentioned in section 1.4.1, the intermediate trace cannot contain a
full *wh*-phrase, as illustrated by the German and Romani sentences in (37) and (38),
which should be contrasted with (33) and (34).

(37)   *German* (from McDaniel 1986)
     Wessen Buch glaubst du *wessen Buch* Hans liest?
     whose book think you *whose book* Hans reads
     'Whose book do you think Hans is reading?'

(38)   *Romani* (from McDaniel 1986)
     Save chave mislinea *save chave* o Demìri dikhlâ?
     which boy you-think *which boy* Demir   saw
     'Which boy do you think Demir saw?'

In order to account for the whole paradigm described above, I will rely on a suggestion by Chomsky (1995: 337) regarding the linearization of two heads in a relation of mutual c-command, as illustrated in (39), under the bare phrase structure approach. Since the bare phrase structure system does not allow vacuous projections, neither m nor p in (39) asymmetrically c-commands the other and no linear order between them can be established in consonance with the LCA.

(39)

A derivation containing a structure such as L in (39) should therefore be canceled, unless, as Chomsky (1995: 337) suggests, "the structure $N = [_L \ m \ p]$ has changed by the time the LCA applies so that its internal structure is irrelevant; perhaps N is converted by Morphology to a 'phonological word' not subject internally to the LCA, assuming that the LCA is an operation that applies after Morphology."[17] The suggested morphological reanalysis may be implemented in terms of the operation *fusion* of Distributed Morphology (see Halle and Marantz 1993), which takes two terminal heads that are sisters under a single category node and fuses them into a single terminal node, reducing the number of independent morphemes in a structure.

Assuming Chomsky's (1995: 337) proposal that the LCA does not apply word-internally, the data in (33)–(38) can then be accounted for if (i) successive-cyclic *wh*-movement in these languages may proceed by adjunction to an intermediate C^0, as schematically represented in (40);[18] and (ii) Morphology in these languages may convert the adjunction structure $[_{C^0} \ WH \ [_{C^0} \ C^0]]$ in (40) into a single terminal element, along the lines suggested by Chomsky with respect to $[_L \ m \ p]$ in (39). That is, once the intermediate *wh*-copy and C^0 undergo morphological fusion, the *wh*-element becomes part of the single terminal element dominating C^0 and therefore invisible to the LCA. The order of the reanalyzed *wh*-element with respect to the other elements of (40) is then indirectly determined by the position of C^0, very much the way a morpheme or a consonant is indirectly ordered with respect to the other elements of the structure containing them, based on the position of the terminal element that contains them.

(40)

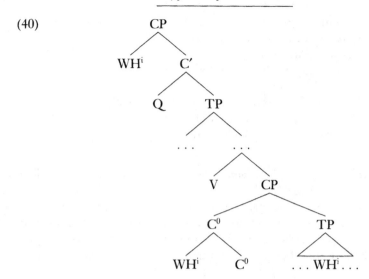

Bearing these considerations in mind, let us examine the possible outputs of (40) given in (41), after Morphology fuses the structure [$_{C^0}$ WH [$_{C^0}$ C^0]] into a single terminal element (as represented by "# . . . #").

(41) a. *[$_{CP}$ WH^i . . . [$_{CP}$ #[$_{C^0}$ WH^i [$_{C^0}$ C^0]#] [$_{TP}$ . . . WH^i . . .]]]
      b. *[$_{CP}$ WH^i . . . [$_{CP}$ #[$_{C^0}$ ~~WH^i~~ [$_{C^0}$ C^0]#] [$_{TP}$ . . . ~~WH^i~~ . . .]]]
      c. *[$_{CP}$ ~~WH^i~~ . . . [$_{CP}$ #[$_{C^0}$ WH^i [$_{C^0}$ C^0]#] [$_{TP}$ . . . WH^i . . .]]]
      d.   [$_{CP}$ WH^i . . . [$_{CP}$ #[$_{C^0}$ WH^i [$_{C^0}$ C^0]#] [$_{TP}$ . . . ~~WH^i~~ . . .]]]

According to the proposals made in section 1.5.2, a structure containing a non-trivial chain cannot be linearized in accordance with the LCA; since the chain links are nondistinct, they induce violations of the asymmetry and irreflexivity conditions on linear order. By deleting chain links, Chain Reduction circumvents this problem and allows structures containing chains to be properly linearized. Recall, however, that the number of applications of deletion of constituents by Chain Reduction is determined by general economy conditions regarding derivational length (see section 1.5.3.1); thus, all things being equal, Chain Reduction employs deletion as little as possible. In (41a), for instance, the intermediate link becomes invisible to the LCA after morphological fusion and need not be deleted. The other two links, however, remain visible for the LCA and prevent the whole structure from being linearized – hence the unacceptability of sentences such as (36), where all the links of the *wh*-chain are realized. In turn, (41b) is excluded by economy: since the intermediate link is invisible to the LCA, it need not – therefore, must not – be deleted by Chain Reduction; in other words, since Chain Reduction can allow the linearization of (40) with a single application of deletion, as shown in (41c) and (41d), further applications are blocked. Finally, the choice between (41c) and (41d) is the familiar one regarding deletion of heads of chains versus deletion of traces. Assuming that the head of the *wh*-chain participates in more checking relations, it requires fewer applications of FF-Elimination in the phonological component and becomes the optimal candidate for phonetic realization (see section 1.5.3.2) – hence the choice of (41d), empirically illustrated in (33)–(34).

In turn, contrasts such as the one between (33) and (34), on the one hand, and (37) and (38), on the other, are due to the fact that morphological fusion deals with heads, but not with maximal projections.[19] If Morphology is in general unable to deal with nonminimal maximal projections adjoined to heads (see Chomsky 1995: 319), *wh*-movement involving full phrases must then proceed through the intermediate Spec, CP rather than adjoining to C^0, as illustrated in (42).

(42) $[_{CP}[_{wh} \cdots]^i [_{C'} Q \cdots [_{CP}[_{wh} \cdots]^i [_{C'} C^0 [_{TP} \cdots [_{wh} \cdots]^i \cdots]]]]]$

Once all copies of the full *wh*-phrase in (42) are visible to the LCA, Chain Reduction must delete all but one link – hence the unacceptability of (37) and (38), for instance.[20]

Independent evidence for the proposed morphological restructuring of $[_{C^0}$ WH $[_{C^0} C^0]]$ as a single terminal element is provided by the dialect of German spoken in the Berlin-Brandenburg area, which, according to Fanselow and Mahajan (1995: 152–3), distinguishes multiple copies of regular PPs, as in (43a), from multiple copies of PPs that involve incorporation and independently function as simple morphological words, as in (43b).

(43)   *German* (from Fanselow and Mahajan 1995)
    a.   **An wen* glaubst Du *an wen* sie denkt?
        of whom believe you *of whom* she thinks
        'Who do you believe that she thinks of?'
    b.   *Wovon* glaubst Du *wovon* sie träumt?
        what-of believe you *what-of* she dreams
        'What do you believe that she dreams of?'

From the perspective explored here, dialectal and idiolectal variation in this regard (see note 19) is due not to syntactic computations proper, but to the degree of permissiveness of a given dialect or idiolect with respect to morphological reanalysis. As a rule, the more complex a constituent, the smaller the likelihood that it will undergo morphological reanalysis and become invisible to the LCA. The impossibility of a morphological reanalysis involving the higher complementizer in (40), for instance, is arguably due to its [+wh] feature, which makes it morphologically heavy in the relevant sense; in other words, only [–wh] C^0s are light enough to permit morphological reanalysis and render an adjoined *wh*-element invisible to the LCA.

    [. . .]

1.7   Conclusion

In this chapter, I have argued that the reason why traces usually are not phonetically realized follows from the interaction between the fact that traces are subject to the LCA and economy considerations concerning the number of applications of deletion to eliminate unchecked formal features in the phonological component (the FF-Elimination operation). A syntactic object containing a nontrivial chain CH in principle cannot be linearized in accordance with the LCA; since the links of CH are nondistinct, they induce violations of the asymmetry and irreflexivity conditions on linear order, canceling the derivation because no PF object is formed. In order to prevent this state of affairs, the phonological component can resort to the operation Chain Reduction, which in the general case deletes all but one link of a nontrivial chain.

Assuming that a given head only checks the relevant features of the chain link that is in its checking domain, the head of a chain CH will always have fewer unchecked formal features to be deleted by FF-Elimination than the lower links of CH. Thus, a derivation in which Chain Reduction deletes all the links except the head of the chain is in principle more economical than a derivation in which Chain Reduction deletes all of the links of the chain except for one trace. However, if the pronunciation of the head of the chain violates other well-formedness conditions of the phonological component, leading to a derivational crash at PF, the head of the chain is deleted and a trace is pronounced instead.

The analysis developed here also accounts for cases where more than one chain link is phonetically realized. The additional possibilities are tied to the possibility of morphological restructuring. Assuming that the LCA does not apply word-internally (see Chomsky 1995: 337), if a trace is reanalyzed by Morphology as part of a single terminal element, it becomes invisible to the LCA and need not – therefore, must not – be deleted by Chain Reduction. The economy considerations that prevent all chain links from being deleted (the issue of recoverability of deletion) are thus the same as the ones allowing multiple copies when morphological reanalysis takes places: deletion should be employed as little as possible.

[. . .]

Overall, then, compelling evidence of different kinds supports the null hypothesis concerning the copy theory of movement in the minimalist framework, namely, that traces do not have distinct intrinsic properties that would characterize them as grammatical primitives. In particular, I have shown that traces do not intrinsically differ from heads of chains with respect to linearization or phonetic realization.

Notes

1   Note that it is not the introduction of objects in the course of the derivation by itself that is problematic, for both traces and copies are introduced in this way. The difference is that while the copy theory creates an object by manipulating material that is available in the numeration that feeds the computation (the same applies to the structure-building operation Merge), the trace theory introduces a completely new element.

2   The motivation for treating terms related by the Copy operation as nondistinct rather than identical has to do with feature checking. If (6) has been formed by movement, for instance, the higher copy of *John* checks its Case-feature against T, whereas the Case-feature of the lower copy is still unchecked. In this scenario, the two instances of *John* in (6), although nondistinct in terms of the initial numeration, are not identical.

3 As Chomsky (1995: 227) observes, this proposal is at odds with the Inclusiveness Condition on the mapping from the numeration to LF, because the identification marks are not present in the numeration. It might be possible to determine whether or not a term is a copy of another term in compliance with the Inclusiveness Condition, if we keep track of the history of the derivation. If two contiguous derivational steps S_1 and S_2 differ in that a new term T is introduced into the computation, two possibilities arise: if from S_1 to S_2 the numeration has been reduced, T is to be interpreted as distinct from all the other syntactic objects available at S_2; if the numerations of S_1 and S_2 are the same, T must be a copy of some syntactic object available at S_1. In case there is more than one element at S_1 with the same set of features as T, independent conditions on chain formation could then determine which candidate is the only option that yields a convergent derivation. In a structure such as (i), for instance, only the pairs (*John⁴, John³*) and (*John², John¹*) could in principle form a chain; forming a chain with the pair (*John⁴, John¹*), for instance, would violate the Minimal Link Condition because the other two instances of *John* intervene, whereas forming a chain with the pair (*John³, John²*) would violate Last Resort because *John²* has its Case-feature checked and is inert for the computational system (see Lasnik 1995; Chomsky 2000, 2001).

(i) [$_{TP}$ John⁴ T [$_{vP}$ John³ [$_{v'}$ said [$_{CP}$ that [$_{TP}$ John² was [$_{vP}$ kissed John¹]]]]]]

Whether or not it is desirable that the recognition of copies by the computational system proceeds along these lines remains to be determined. For expository purposes, I will adopt Chomsky's (1995: 227) proposal mentioned in the text.

4 Here I put aside the question of how two heads in a mutual c-command relation can be linearized; I will return to it in section 1.5.3.3.

5 The unacceptability of the sentence in (ib) with two distinct instances of *John*, resulting from the structure in (ia), has nothing to do with linearization. The ill-formedness of (ia) is due to the fact that the lower instance of *John* cannot have its Case-feature checked.

(i) a. [$_{TP}$ John^i [$_{T'}$ was+T [$_{vP}$ kissed John^k]]]
   b. *John was kissed John.

6 Borrowing a metaphor suggested by Bob Frank (personal communication), it is as if deletion paints features blue and the interface is unable to see deleted features because it wears blue glasses.

7 Chomsky's (1995) proposal regarding feature deletion under checking is actually more complex in that it also resorts to an additional operation of erasure, which "is a 'stronger form' of deletion, eliminating the element entirely so that it is inaccessible to any operation, not just to interpretability at LF" (Chomsky 1995: 280). In this monograph, I will assume the gist of Chomsky's idea regarding the relation between interpretability at LF and accessibility to the computational system, but not its technical implementation in terms of erasure. All that is necessary for present purposes is to assume that a deleted feature cannot participate in a checking relation. For arguments against erasure, see Nunes (2000).

8 Similarly to the case of Chain Reduction, the specification of the number of features to be deleted by FF-Elimination may follow from economy considerations concerning derivational length: all things being equal, a derivation in which a given feature F is unnecessarily deleted by FF-Elimination will be longer than a derivation in which F is not deleted. As before, I will keep the description of FF-Elimination in (22) for expository purposes.

9 Notice that this extension does not prevent Morphology from accessing deleted features. According to Chomsky's (1995: 280) definition of deletion, which is adopted here, a feature that is deleted through a checking operation becomes invisible at LF but is accessible to the computation (see note 6). The proposal in the text only extends invisibility at LF to invisibility at PF, as well. For relevant discussion of these issues, see Nunes (2000).

10   As formulated in (22), FF-Elimination applies after a given syntactic object is linearized and, therefore, after Chain Reduction has applied. This is crucial in the reasoning; otherwise, if FF-Elimination could for instance apply to the DP chain in (23) before Chain Reduction, there would be no principled basis for distinguishing (24a) from (24b) and (24c). More generally, the account of why heads of chains are usually the optimal candidates for phonetic realization would be lost.

The required order of application between Chain Reduction and FF-Elimination may, however, be determined without stipulation (see Nunes 1999b for further discussion). According to the notion of derivational cost proposed by Chomsky (1995: 226), an operation is costless if it is required as a defining property of a derivation and costly if it is required to yield a convergent derivation. In the case at hand, if the DP chain in (23), for instance is not reduced, the structure containing it cannot be linearized and no PF object can be formed. Since a computation that does not yield the pair (PF, LF) does not count as a derivation (see Chomsky 1995: 225–6), Chain Reduction is required for a derivation to be obtained; as a defining property of a derivation, Chain Reduction is therefore costless. If FF-Elimination does not apply to (23), on the other hand, an illegitimate PF object may eventually be formed; hence, by being associated with PF convergence, FF-Elimination is derivationally costly. Thus, at the derivational step where a chain can in principle undergo either Chain Reduction or FF-Elimination, economy considerations will ensure its reduction.

I leave this discussion pending further research on the interactions of Chain Reduction and FF-Elimination with other operations of the phonological component. For relevant discussion, see Santos (2002). Santos suggests that prosodic parsing follows Chain Reduction and precedes FF-Elimination, citing the fact that in Brazilian Portuguese, traces do not block stress retraction, whereas pro does.

11   Consider the structure of the sentences in (i) within Chomsky's (1995) system, as represented in (ii).

(i)   a.   I believe John to be likely to be kissed.

      b.   What did John say that Mary bought?

(ii)   a.   [$_{TP}$ I believe [$_{TP}$ John^i-N to be likely [$_{TP}$ John^i-N to be kissed John^i-N]]]

      b.   [$_{CP}$ what^i-WH did+Q John say [$_{CP}$ what^i-WH that Mary bought what^i-WH]]

In each step of both instances of successive-cyclic movement, it is the categorial feature (an interpretable feature) of the moved element that enters into a checking relation with a feature of the target (an EPP-feature in (iia) and a strong *wh*-feature in (iib)). If interpretable features remain unaffected by checking operations, as Chomsky (1995: 280) proposes, the links of DP chains and *wh*-chains should be identical with respect to the only checking relation that takes place overtly, as represented in (ii), providing no principled basis for why deletion of traces should be the optimal solution in the analysis we are entertaining.

Notice that this potential problem does not arise if an exceptional Case-marking subject occupies a Case position (see Postal 1974; Lasnik and Saito 1992; Koizumi 1993; and Lasnik 1999, among others) or if *wh*-phrases have an uninterpretable feature to be checked against an interrogative complementizer (see Chomsky 2000, 2001). Under these assumptions, both the head of the DP chain associated with *John* in (ia) and the head of the *wh*-chain in (iib) would have checked more features, thus being the optimal links for phonetic realization, as desired.

Within the confines of the assumptions in Chomsky (1995), the technical problem posed by (i) can be circumvented if my proposal that uninterpretable features become invisible at PF after being checked is extended to interpretable features, as well. Chomsky's (1995: 280) proposal that an interpretable feature is able to participate in multiple checking relations can then be reinterpreted in the following way. When participating in an overt checking relation, an interpretable feature can optionally be deleted with respect to PF, becoming invisible at this level. If it is deleted with respect to PF, it patterns with deleted uninterpretable features in not being able to enter into any further checking relation; if it is not deleted, it is allowed to enter into another checking relation. Under this view, the sentences in (i) are derived after Chain Reduction deletes the lower copies of the structure in (iii), where the subscript convention is now generalized to mean 'invisible at the relevant interface' (PF for interpretable features, and LF and PF for uninterpretable features).

(iii)   a. $[_{TP}$ I believe $[_{TP}$ John^i-$_N$ to be likely $[_{TP}$ John^i-N to be kissed John^i-N]]]
        b. $[_{CP}$ what^i-$_{WH}$ did+Q John say $[_{CP}$ what^i-WH that Mary bought what^i-**WH**]]

12   Bošković (2000, 2002) attributes the observation regarding the contrast between (28a) and (28b) to Wayles Browne (personal communication).

13   Bošković (2000, 2002) shows that the same reasoning accounts for the contrast in (i) in Bulgarian, which was observed by Billings and Rudin (1996). As Bošković (1997) argues, only the highest *wh*-phrase in Bulgarian is subject to the Superiority Condition; the order between the other *wh*-phrases is free, as (ii) illustrates. The unacceptability of (ib) should thus be due to the occurrence of two adjacent identical *wh*-elements.

(i)   *Bulgarian* (from Billings and Rudin 1996)
      a.   Koj kogo na kogo e pokazal?
           who whom to whom is pointed–out
           'Who pointed out whom to whom?'
      b.   *Koj na kogo kogo e pokazal?
           who to whom whom is pointed–out
(ii) *Bulgarian* (from Bošković 2000, 2002)
      a.   Koj kogo kak e tselunal?
           who whom how is kissed
           'Who kissed whom how?'
      b.   Koj kak kogo e tselunal?
           who how whom is kissed

14   See also Bobaljik (1995, 1999), where it is proposed that a shifted object may be pronounced in the lower position if adjacency between I and the verb is disrupted, and Stjepanović (1999), where free word order in Serbo-Croatian is analyzed as resulting from the phonetic realization of different chain links, depending on stress assignment.

15   Franks (1998: 31) hints that "presumably, the fact that all but the highest copy usually deletes is an economy property of PF, trying to preserve as much as possible of what the overt syntax provides it with at Spell Out," but he does not elaborate further on the precise nature of such an economy property. This suggestion is similar to Brody's (1995: 107) conceptual justification for the principle of Transparency and, as such, it is not obviously applicable to cases where multiple copies are phonetically realized (see section 1.5.3.3).

16   This led me in Nunes (1995) to attempt (unsuccessfully) to analyze the identical elements in (33)–(34) as distinct elements. The current analysis builds on and expands the account offered in Nunes (1999a).

17   Evidence that the LCA may not determine the order of morphemes in words formed in the course of the derivation is provided by the European Portuguese sentence in (ia), which is arguably derived from (ib) after the preposition *de* adjoins to the auxiliary *hei* and the resulting X^0 adjoins to C^0. If the LCA applied word-internally, we would incorrectly predict that in (ia) *de* should precede rather than follow *hei*, given that the preposition asymmetrically c-commands the auxiliary in the final structure. Thanks to Ana Maria Martins for helpful discussion.

(i)　a.　O que hei-de　　　eu fazer?
　　　　　what　have.1SG-to I　do
　　　　　'What can I do?'

　　　b.　$[_{CP}\ C^0\ [_{TP}$ eu [hei [de [fazer [o que]]]]]]

18　Elements adjoined to a head H are in the checking domain of H (see Chomsky 1995: 268); hence, *wh*-movement via adjunction to C^0 in (40) is able to license whatever feature checking takes place in intermediate C positions. On the optimality of adjunction to heads versus movement to specifiers, see Nunes (1998).

19　Under this view, sentences such as (i) should involve fusion between the preposition and the *wh*-word, followed by fusion with the intermediate C^0.

(i)　*German* (from McDaniel 1986)
　　　Mit wem glaubst du *mit wem* Hans spricht?
　　　with whom thinks　you *with whom* Hans talks
　　　'With whom do you think Hans is talking?'

20　Fanselow and Mahajan (1995) propose that in German, intermediate traces may cliticize to C^0 in the phonological component, thereby becoming invisible to deletion. Although this proposal can explain why full *wh*-traces cannot be phonetically realized in intermediate trace positions, it does not have a principled explanation for why traces in general cannot be phonetically realized.

References

Billings, L. and C. Rudin. 1996. Optimality and superiority: A new approach to multiple wh-ordering. In J. Toman (ed.), *Formal approach to Slavic linguistics 3: The College Park Meeting*, Ann Arbor, MI: Michigan Slavic Publications, pp. 35–60.

Bobaljik, J. D. 1995. *Morphosyntax: The syntax of verbal inflection*. Doctoral dissertation, MIT.

Bobaljik, J. D. 1999. A-chains at the interfaces: Copies, agreement, and "covert" movement. Ms., McGill University. [Revised version published as A-chains at the PF-interface: Copies and "covert" movement. *Natural Language and Linguistic Theory* 20: 197–267, 2002.]

Bošković, Ž. 1997. Superiority effects with multiple wh-fronting in Serbo-Croatian. *Lingua* 102: 1–20.

Bošković, Ž. 2000. What is special about multiple wh-fronting? In M. Hirotani, A. Coetzee, N. Hall and J.-Y. Kim (eds.), *Proceedings of the 30th Annual Meeting of the North East Linguistic Society*, Amherst, MA: GLSA, pp. 83–107.

Bošković, Ž. 2001. *On the nature of the syntax–phonology interface: Cliticization and related phenomena*. Amsterdam: Elsevier.

Bošković, Ž. 2002. On multiple wh-fronting. *Linguistic Inquiry* 33: 351–83.

Brody, M. 1995. *Lexico-logical form: A radically minimalist theory*. Cambridge, MA: MIT Press.

Chomsky, N. 1995. *The Minimalist Program*. Cambridge, MA: MIT Press.

Chomsky, N. 2000. Minimalist inquiries: The framework. In R. Martin, D. Michaels and J. Uriagereka (eds.), *Step by step: Essays on minimalism in honor of Howard Lasnik*, Cambridge, MA: MIT Press, pp. 89–155.

Chomsky, N. 2001. Derivation by phase. In M. Kenstowicz (ed.), *Ken Hale: A life in Linguistics*, Cambridge, MA: MIT Press, pp. 1–52.

Fanselow, G. and A. Mahajan. 1995. Partial wh-movement constructions in Hindi and German. In U. Lutz and G. Muller (eds.), *Papers on wh-scope marking. Arbeitspapiere des*

Sonderforschungsbereichs 340, Stuttgart and Tübingen: University of Stuttgart and University of Tübingen, pp. 131–61. [Revised version published as Partial movement and successive cyclicity. In U. Lutz, G. Müller and A. von Stechow (eds.) (2000), *Wh-scope marking*, Amsterdam/Philadelphia: John Benjamins, pp. 195–230.]

Franks, S. 1998. Clitics in Slavic. Paper read at the Comparative Morphosyntax Workshop, Bloomington, Indiana.

Halle, M. and A. Marantz. 1993. Distributed morphology and the pieces of inflection. In K. Hale and S. J. Keyser (eds.), *The view from Building 20: Essays in linguistics in honor of Sylvain Bromberger*, Cambridge, MA: MIT Press, pp. 111–76.

Kayne, R. S. 1994. *The antisymmetry of syntax*. Cambridge, MA: MIT Press.

Koizumi, M. 1993. Object agreement phrases and the split VP hypothesis. In J. D. Bobaljik and C. Phillips (eds.), *Papers on Case and agreement I. MIT Working Papers in Linguistics 18*, Cambridge, MA: MITWPL, pp. 99–148.

Lasnik, H. 1995. Last resort and Attract F. In *Papers from the 6th Annual Meeting of the Formal Linguistics Society of Mid-America*, Bloomington: Indiana Linguistics Club, pp. 62–81.

Lasnik, H. 1999. *Minimalist analysis*. Malden, MA/Oxford: Blackwell.

Lasnik, H. and M. Saito. 1992. *Move α*. Cambridge, MA: MIT Press.

McDaniel, D. 1986. *Conditions on wh-chains*. Doctoral dissertation, University of New York.

Nunes, J. 1995. *The copy theory of movement and linearization of chains in the Minimalist Program*. Doctoral dissertation, University of Maryland, College Park.

Nunes, J. 1998. Bare X-bar theory and structures formed by movement. *Linguistic Inquiry* 29: 160–8.

Nunes, J. 1999a. Linearization of chains and phonetic realization of chain links. In S. D. Epstein and N. Hornstein (eds.), *Working minimalism*, Cambridge, MA: MIT Press, pp. 217–49.

Nunes, J. 1999b. Some notes on Procrastinate and other economy matters. *Revista de Documentação de Estudos em Lingüística Theórica e Aplicada (D.E.L.T.A.)* 15: 27–55.

Nunes, J. 2000. Erasing erasure. *Revista de Documentação de Estudos em Lingüística Theórica e Aplicada (D.E.L.T.A.)* 16: 415–29.

Postal, P. M. 1974. *On raising: One rule of English grammar and its implication*. Cambridge, MA: MIT Press.

Rudin, C., C. Kramer, L. Billings and M. Baerman. 1999. Macedonian and Bulgarian *li* questions: Beyond syntax. *Natural Language and Linguistic Theory* 17: 541–86.

Santos, R. 2002. Categorias sintáticas vazias e retração de acento em português brasileiro. *Revista de Documentação de Estudos em Lingüística Theórica e Aplicada (D.E.L.T.A.)* 18: 67–86.

Stjepanović, S. 1999. *What do second-position clitics, scrambling, and multiple wh-fronting have in common?* Doctoral dissertation, University of Connecticut, Storrs.

From "MORPHOSYNTAX: THE SYNTAX OF VERBAL INFLECTION"
Jonathan Bobaljik

2 Copy pronunciation: single output syntax

The more or less standard account of "covert" movement operations is that they are syntactic movement operations which occur after the split in the grammar which takes a single input and leads to separate phonological (PF) and semantic (LF) representations:

(1) *Model T Grammar*

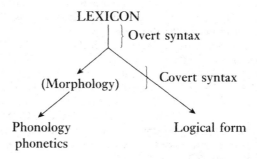

LEXICON

} Overt syntax

} Covert syntax

(Morphology)

Phonology
phonetics

Logical form

The considerations of Chapter II, I believe, lead in a slightly different direction. In particular, I will argue that the account I will provide leads us to a model of grammar where the syntax produces a single output representation from a given input, and that this output representation is then interpreted by semantic and morphophonological components. In Chomsky's terms, what I am proposing is that Spell Out is after LF movement operations (as noted, see Groat and O'Neil (1994) for an implementation of this idea within a framework of assumptions very close to Chomsky's; see also Pesetsky (in prep.) and Brody (1992) for related ideas in different frameworks).

(2) *Novel T: Single Output Syntax (SOS)*

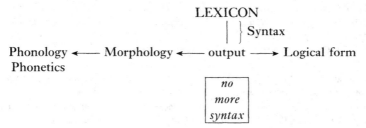

LEXICON

} Syntax

Phonology ⟵── Morphology ⟵── output ──⟶ Logical form
Phonetics

*no
more
syntax*

From "A-CHAINS AT THE PF-INTERFACE: COPIES AND 'COVERT' MOVEMENT"

On this view, then, 'covert' and 'overt' movement are distinguished not by sequential ordering in the derivation, but rather by which copy is pronounced and which copy is not. The theory of covert movement becomes thus a theory of mismatches between the interpretive (LF) and phonological (PF) interfaces regarding the privileging of copies. As schematized in (3), this theory yields a four-way typology of movement operations, where $copy_1$ c-commands $copy_2$.

(3) Privileged copies:

a. copy$_1$ ... copy$_2$ 'overt movement no reconstruction' PF LF	b. copy$_1$ ... copy$_2$ 'LF movement' LF PF
c. copy$_1$ ... copy$_2$ 'overt movement + reconstruction' PF LF	d. copy$_1$ ... copy$_2$ 'LF movement, + reconstruction' PF LF

If the LF and PF interfaces both choose to privilege the higher copy in a given chain, we derive the effect of simple overt movement: the moved element is interpreted in the position in which it is pronounced (3a). 'Reconstruction' (3c) involves the PF-privileging ('pronunciation') of the higher copy, but LF-privileging ('interpretation') of the lower copy, along the lines familiar from Chomsky (1993), Hornstein (1995), and others. The standard case of upwards (leftwards) 'LF-movement' is represented as in (3b): LF interpretation of a copy higher than that pronounced. Finally, the copy + delete theory of movement leads us to expect a fourth possibility (3d): the case in which something moves from the point of view of syntax, creating a sequence of two copies (i.e. a chain), but for which both LF and PF privilege the lower copy.

References

Brody, M. 1992. *Lexico-logical form*. Ms., University College London. [Published as *Lexico-logical form: A radically minimalist theory*. Cambridge, MA: MIT Press, 1995.]

Chomsky, N. 1993. A minimalist program for linguistic theory. In K. Hale and S. J. Keyser (eds.), *The view from Building 20: Essays in linguistics in honor of Sylvain Bromberger*, Cambridge, MA: MIT Press, pp. 1–52. [Reprinted in Chomsky (1995), *The Minimalist Program*, Cambridge, MA: MIT Press, pp. 167–217.]

Chomsky, N. 1995. *The Minimalist Program*. Cambridge, MA: MIT Press.

Groat, E. and J. O'Neil. 1994. Spell-out at the LF interface. Ms., Harvard University. [Published in W. Abraham, S. D. Epstein, H. Thráinsson and J.-W. Zwart (eds.) (1996), *Minimal ideas: Syntactic studies in the Minimalist framework*, Amsterdam: John Benjamins, pp. 113–39.]

Hornstein, N. 1995. *Logical form: From GB to minimalism*. Malden, MA: Blackwell.

Pesetsky, D. In prep. Optimality principles of sentence pronunciation. [Revised version published as Some optimality principles of sentence pronunciation, in P. Barbosa, D. Fox, P. Hagstrom, M. McGinnis and D. Pesetsky (eds.) (1998), *Is the best good enough? Optimality and competition in syntax*, Cambridge, MA: MIT Press. pp. 337–83.]

7

Existential Constructions

From "A MINIMALIST PROGRAM FOR LINGUISTIC THEORY"
Noam Chomsky

3.5 Extensions of the Minimalist Program

The question of economy of derivations is more subtle. We have already noted two cases: Procrastinate, which is straightforward, and the Last Resort principle, which is more intricate. According to that principle, a step in a derivation is legitimate only if it is necessary for convergence – had the step not been taken, the derivation would not have converged. NP-raising, for example, is driven by the Case Filter (now assumed to apply only at LF): if the Case feature of NP has already been checked, NP may not raise. For example, (1a) is fully interpretable, but (1b) is not.

(1)   a.   there is [$_\alpha$ a strange man] in the garden
       b.   there seems to [$_\alpha$ a strange man] [that it is raining outside]

In (1a) α is not in a proper position for Case checking; therefore, it must raise at LF, adjoining to the LF affix *there* and leaving the trace t. The phrase α is now in the checking domain of the matrix inflection. The matrix subject at LF is [α-*there*], an LF word with all features checked but interpretable only in the position of the trace t of the chain (α, t), its head being "invisible" word-internally. In contrast, in (1b) α has its Case properties satisfied internal to the PP, so it is not permitted to raise, and we are left with freestanding *there*. This is a legitimate object, a one-membered A-chain with all its morphological properties checked. Hence, the derivation converges. But there is no coherent interpretation, because freestanding *there* receives no semantic interpretation (and in fact is unable to receive a θ-role even in a θ-position). The derivation thus converges, as semigibberish.

     The notion of Last Resort operation is in part formulable in terms of economy: a shorter derivation is preferred to a longer one, and if the derivation D converges without application of some operation, then that application is disallowed. In (1b) adjunction of α to *there* would yield an intelligible interpretation (something like 'there is a strange man to whom it seems that it is raining outside'). But adjunction is not permitted: the derivation converges with an unintelligible interpretation. Derivations are driven by the narrow mechanical requirement of feature checking only, not by a "search for intelligibility" or the like.

Note that raising of α in (1b) is blocked by the fact that *its own requirements* are satisfied without raising, even though such raising would arguably overcome inadequacies of the LF affix *there*. More generally, Move α applies to an element α only if morphological properties of α itself are not otherwise satisfied. The operation cannot apply to α to enable some different element β to satisfy *its* properties. Last Resort, then, is always "self-serving": benefiting other elements is not allowed. Alongside Procrastinate, then, we have a principle of *Greed*: self-serving Last Resort.

Consider the expression (2), analogous to (1b) but without *there*-insertion from the lexicon.

(2)   seems to [α a strange man] [that it is raining outside]

Here the matrix T has an NP-feature (Case feature) to discharge, but α cannot raise (overtly or covertly) to overcome that defect. The derivation cannot converge, unlike (1b), which converges but without a proper interpretation. The self-serving property of Last Resort cannot be overridden even to ensure convergence.

From "CATEGORIES AND TRANSFORMATIONS"
Noam Chomsky

4.4.5   Covert raising

The shift of perspective just outlined has broader consequences. In the case of *wh*-movement, if the operator feature [wh-] is unchecked, it raises to an appropriate position, covertly if possible (by Procrastinate) and thus without pied-piping. If raising is overt, then pied-piping will be determined (we hope) by PF convergence and morphological properties of the language. Similarly, if the grammatical object Obj raises for checking of Case or some other formal feature, then the formal features FF[F] of its head raise derivatively, and the operation carries along a full category only if the movement is overt. If raising is overt, then Obj becomes [Spec, Agr_O]. If it is covert, then the features FF[F] raise alone, adjoining to Agr_O, which has V (or its relevant features) already adjoined to it.[1]

The same should hold for raising of subject Subj. Its unchecked features are eligible for raising. The operation is substitution with pied-piping if overt (say, to satisfy the EPP [Extended Projection Principle]), and it is adjunction to the appropriate head without pied-piping if covert (perhaps in VSO languages).

Subj and Obj should function in much the same way at LF whether they have raised overtly as full categories or covertly as features. In either case the raised element contains at least FF(LI), LI the head of Subj or Obj. FF(LI) includes the categorial feature of the nominal phrase and should have argument (A-position) properties, including the ability to serve as a controller or binder. In their reanalysis and extension of observations of Postal (1974), Lasnik and Saito (1991) argue that this is true for object raising: Obj raised covertly to [Spec, Agr$_O$] for Case checking has basically the same properties as an overt object in this regard, as illustrated for example in (1), with judgments somewhat idealized.

(1) a.   the DA [proved [the defendants to be guilty] during each other's trials]
     b.   *the DA [proved [that the defendants were guilty] during each other's trials]
     c.   the DA [accused the defendants during each other's trials]

For the conclusions to carry over to the Move F theory, it must be that the features adjoined to Agr$_O$ also have A-position properties, c-commanding and binding in the standard way. There is every reason to assume this to be true.

Consider such expletive constructions as (2a–b).[2]

(2) a.   there is a [book missing from the shelf]
     b.   there seem [*t* to be some books on the table]

Agreement is with the associate of the expletive (namely, *book-books*), which in our terms requires that the φ-features of the associate raise to the checking domain of matrix I. But the operation is covert. Therefore, it is not the associate that raises but its unchecked features, leaving the rest in situ. The natural assumption, once again, is that these features adjoin to I, not to its specifier *there*.[3]

Interpretations of (3) would therefore be roughly as in the paired cases (4) – though only roughly, because on this analysis, only formal features of the associate raise, leaving its semantic features behind.

(3) a.   there is considerable interest (in his work)
     b.   there aren't many pictures (on the wall)
     c.   there are pictures of many presidents (on the wall)
(4) a.   interest is considerable (in his work)
     b.   pictures aren't many (on the wall)
     c.   pictures are of many presidents (on the wall)

Similarly in other cases. The general conclusions about expletive constructions follow. Specifically, the associate must have unchecked features in order to be accessible for raising, so that we account for such standard examples as [*There seem that a lot of people are intelligent*]; we will return to some other locality effects. The HMC [Head Movement Constraint] is largely inoperative, however it is understood to apply to feature movement.[4]

It also follows that the expletive *there* cannot have checked all the features of I; if it had, I would not be a legitimate target for the associate. Plainly, *there* checks the strong feature of I (EPP); otherwise, expletive constructions such as (3) would not exist in the first place. But *there* must lack Case or ϕ-features, or both; otherwise, all features of I will be checked and the associate will not raise. There will be no way to express agreement of matrix verb and associate; (5a) will have the same status as (5b).

(5)   a.   *there seem to be a man in the room
      b.   there seems to be a man in the room

Covert raising to Agr_S places the features of the associate in a structural position with the essential formal properties of [Spec, Agr_S]. We therefore expect the associate to have the binding and control properties of the overt subject, analogously to the case of covert object raising to Agr_O (see (1)). The issues take a somewhat sharper form in a null subject language. Here we expect that the counterparts to such expressions as (6) should be admissible, contrasting with (7).

(6)   a.   there arrived three men (last night) without identifying themselves
      b.   there arrived with their own books three men from England
(7)   a.   *I met three men (last night) without identifying themselves
      b.   *I found with their own books three men from England

That appears to be correct. Thus, we find the following contrasts between Italian (8a–b) and French (8c–d):[5]

(8)   a.   sono entrati tre   uomini senza   identificarsi
           are   entered three men   without identifying themselves
           'three men entered without identifying themselves'
      b.   ne   sono entrati tre   *t* senza dire una parola
           of. them are   entered three   without saying anything
           'of-them three entered without saying anything'
      c.   *il   est entré   trois hommes sans   s'annoncer
           there is entered three men   without identifying themselves
      d.   *il   en   est entré   trois *t* sans   s'annoncer
           there of. them is   entered three   without identifying themselves

In Italian, with null subject expletive sharing the relevant properties of English *there*, LF raising to I of Subj (actually, its formal features) assigns A-position properties to Subj for binding and control, including the case of *ne*-extraction that makes it clear that Subj is overtly in the internal domain of the verb ("object position," basically). In French, with the full NP expletive *il* analogous to English *it*, the LF operation is barred, all features of the matrix I-phrase, the potential target, having already been checked by the expletive. Accordingly, there is no covert raising, hence no binding or control.

Consider the German analogue (9).

(9)   es   sind gestern   viele Leute angekommen, ohne
      there are   yesterday many people arrived   without

sich   zu identifizieren
themselves to identify
'many people arrived yesterday without identifying themselves'

Here agreement is with the associate, not the expletive, and the binding and control properties are as in (8), as predicted.[6]

Agreement with the associate, then, appears to correlate with matrix-subject binding and control properties for the associate, as expected on the minimalist assumption that Case and agreement are local Spec-head relations and that features raise under Last Resort, covertly if possible. We will return to a closer look at the factors involved.

Note that the entire discussion relies on the assumption that Case and ϕ-features of a noun N are part of its internal constitution, either intrinsic to it or added optionally as N is selected from the lexicon for the numeration. Therefore, these features form part of FF[N] and function within the "package" of formal features that drive computation, raising as a unit. We have seen that the conclusion is motivated on independent grounds; it is confirmed by the central role it plays within the computational system, which will be further confirmed as we proceed. Abandonment of the conclusion (say, by taking Case or ϕ-features of N to be separate lexical categories with their own positions in phrase markers) would cause no slight complication.

Though core predictions appear to be verified, many questions arise. One immediate problem is that the raised associate *cannot* be a binder in such expressions as (10), where t is the trace of *there* (see Lasnik and Saito 1991).

(10) *there seem to each other [t to have been many linguists given good job offers]

We know that this is an expletive-associate construction with associate agreement, as shown by replacing of *each other* with *us*. That leaves us with an apparent direct contradiction: the associate both can and cannot bind.

The solution to the paradox might lie within binding theory. Suppose that the LF anaphor movement approach proves correct. Then the head of the matrix clause of (10), at LF, would have the structure (11a) or (11b), depending on how covert operations are ordered, where An is the anaphor and α is the X^0 complex formed from I and the matrix V.

(11) a. [$_I$ An [FF(*linguists*) α]]
      b. [$_I$ FF(*linguists*) [An α]]

On reasonable assumptions, neither of these structures qualifies as a legitimate binding-theoretic configuration, with An taking FF(*linguists*) as its antecedent. No such problem would arise in the examples (6) and (8), or in such standard examples as (12).

(12) they seemed to each other [t to have been angry]

These phenomena provide further evidence that the features of the associate raise to I rather than adjoining to the expletive, over and above the fact that this operation is the normal one while adjunction from the associate position to the expletive would be without any analogue. If adjunction were in fact to the expletive, then there might be no relevant difference between (10) and (12). The phenomena also provide additional evidence for an LF movement analysis of anaphora.

[. . .]

4.5.3 Expletives

Suppose that a derivation has reached the stage [*I(nfl) seems [that John is intelligent]*] and the numeration contains an expletive, so that we can derive, for example, (13).[7]

(13)   *there seem [that [$_{Subj}$ a lot of people] are intelligent]

The expletive *there* checks the strong feature of I (EPP), but it fails to check some feature of H = [I, *seem*] that is −Interpretable and must be erased for convergence. The −Interpretable features of H are its Case and ϕ-features. Once again, we see that the expletive must lack Case or ϕ-features, or both (see discussion of (5)).

Suppose that *there* has Case, so that only the ϕ-features of H remain unchecked. But the ϕ-features of Subj are Interpretable, so Subj (actually, the formal features of its head) can raise covertly, checking the ϕ-features of H and allowing the derivation to converge − incorrectly, with an interpretation similar to 'it seems that a lot of people are intelligent'. It follows that *there* must lack Case.

Suppose that the expletive has ϕ-features. Suppose that these do not match the features of its associate, as in (5a), repeated here, with *there* plural and its associate *a man* singular, and the raising verb plural, matching *there*.

(14)   *there seem to be [a man] in the room

The ϕ-features of *seem* are erased in the Spec-head relation with *there*. The ϕ-features of *there*, being −Interpretable for an expletive, are also erased under this checking relation. The Case feature of *seem* is erased by raising of the associate *a man*. Since the ϕ-features of *a man* are Interpretable, they need not be checked. The derivation of (14) therefore converges, incorrectly.

We conclude, then, that the expletive has neither Case nor ϕ-features. FF(*there*) contains only D, which suffices to satisfy the EPP: the expletive has no formal features apart from its category.

Notice that agreement is overtly manifested on the verb that has *there* as subject. Earlier we considered the suggestion that overt manifestation of ϕ-features is a reflection of the [Spec, H] rather than [$_H$ F H] relation. The observation about agreement with expletives is consistent with this proposal, but it would conflict with the alternative idea that the distinction reflects overt rather than covert agreement. The two suggestions are empirically distinct in this case, perhaps only this case.

Suppose that *there* is a pure expletive lacking semantic features as well as formal features apart from its category D. We therefore expect it to be invisible at LF, to satisfy FI [Full Interpretation]. We know that *there* cannot be literally erased when checked; that would violate the fundamental condition [A term of Σ cannot erase.] forming an illegitimate syntactic object that would cancel the derivation. [. . .]

Since the expletive necessarily lacks Case, it must be the associate that provides the Case in ordinary expletive constructions such as (15a–c).

(15) a. there is a book on the shelf
      b. there arrived yesterday a visitor from England
      c. I expected [there to be a book on the shelf]

The associate must therefore have the Case that would be borne by DP in the constructions (16a–c), respectively.

(16) a. DP is . . .   (DP = nominative)
      b. DP arrived . . .   (DP = nominative)
      c. I expected [DP to be . . .]   (DP = accusative)

We therefore cannot accept the partitive Case theory of Belletti (1988).

There is a distinction between expletives that have Case and φ-features and the "pure expletives" that lack these features: in English, *it* and *there*, respectively. The distinction is neither clear nor sharp, but it is adequate for our limited purposes.[8] The former satisfy all properties of the I–V head they check, erasing the relevant features, and therefore bar associate raising. The latter do not erase the –Interpretable features of the I–V head. Therefore, raising is permitted, targeting this element; and it is required for convergence.

Two consequences follow. The direct prediction is that expletive constructions will manifest verbal agreement with the associate just in case the expletive lacks Case and φ-features: English *there*, German *es*, and Italian *pro* – but not English *it* and French *il*, which have a full complement of features. Note that the distinction is only partially related to overt manifestation.[9] A more interesting prediction, and one that will be more difficult to confirm if true, is that just in case the expletive lacks Case and φ-features, the associate will bind and control as if it were in the surface subject position. We have seen some reason to believe that this is true.

[. . .]

At LF, Exp is simply the categorial feature [D]. Any phonetic features would have been stripped away at Spell-Out, and we have seen that Exp has no other formal features. Lacking semantic features, Exp has to be eliminated at LF if the derivation is to converge: its D-feature is –Interpretable and must be deleted by some operation. Therefore, [D] must enter into a checking relation with some appropriate feature F. As we have just seen, T does not offer a checking domain to which Exp can raise,[10] so F must raise to the checking domain of Exp, which means that F must adjoin to it. What is F? Independently, there is good reason to believe that the categorial feature [N] adjoins to [D] regularly, namely, in the D–NP construction (Longobardi 1994). The optimal assumption, then, would be that it is adjunction of the feature [N] to Exp that eliminates its (sole remaining) feature. The feature [D] of Exp cannot be erased in this configuration: that would eliminate the category completely, leaving us with an illegitimate syntactic object. Therefore, checking of the categorial feature of Exp (its entire content) deletes it but does not go on to erase it, by the general principles already discussed.

The optimal assumption requires nothing new. Exp has no complement, but in the relevant formal respects, the head-complement relation that allows N-raising to D is the same as the [Spec-α] relation holding between Exp in Spec and the X′ projection of T. In a properly formed expletive construction, the formal features FF(A) of the associate A adjoin to matrix I (which we now take to be T^{0max}), checking Case and agreement and allowing matrix-type binding and control. The categorial feature [N] of A comes along as a free rider and is therefore in the right position to adjoin to Exp, forming [$_D$ N Exp]. The configuration so formed places [D] in a checking configuration with raised [N], as in the D-complement structure.[11] Like D that takes a complement, expletive D has a strong [nominal-] feature, which attracts [N] – a residue of the earlier adjunction-to-expletive analysis.

Notes

1   An ambiguity might arise if the features F that raise constitute the entire head (so that there is no generalized pied-piping) and the head happens also to be an X^{max}. In that case it would not be clear whether the movement is adjunction to a head or substitution in Spec. I will assume tentatively that this possibility cannot arise; the raised features FF(LI) do not constitute the entire head LI.

2   Note that we must distinguish *there be NP* constructions with strong existential import from the expletive constructions with small clauses, such as (2), which are much weaker in this respect, differing in other properties as well. For example, (2a) may be true even if there is no book, just a space on the shelf where a book should be, in contrast to *there is a book that is missing from the shelf*, which is true only if the book exists. Similarly, *John has a tooth missing* does not entail the existence of a tooth, now or ever. A fuller analysis of expletive constructions and related ones will also bring in focal stress and other relevant questions that have yet to be examined properly, to my knowledge.

3   As is well known, agreement with the associate is sometimes overridden, as for example in *there's three books on the table, there's a dog and cat in the room* (vs. *a dog and cat is in the room*). The phenomenon, however, seems superficial: thus, it does not carry over to *is there three books . . .*, *there isn't any books . . .*, and so on. The form *there's* simply seems to be a frozen option, not relevant here.

4   One might, however, explore its possible relevance for the definiteness effect, with D taken to be a target for N-features so that it cannot be skipped, and specificity (in the relevant sense) understood as a property of D. On D-N relations, see Longobardi (1994). A perhaps more exotic proposal is that overt N → D raising, as in Italian though not English under Longobardi's analysis, obviates the effect, as appears to be true for Italian. See Moro

(1994) for extensive discussion, from a different point of view. Note that the status of the definiteness effect is obscure for many reasons, including the fact that it distinguishes inter-pretations, not well-formedness strictly speaking, and interacts with other properties, such as focus. See note 2.

5   Thanks to Anna Cardinaletti and Michal Starke for the data. They observe that the con-trast seems independent of V-movement. Thus, the sentence is bad even if V moves to C in French.

(i)   *en   arrivera-t-il un sans casser la porte
      of.them will.arrive   one without breaking the door

They also point out that the French examples, though sharply distinguished from the Italian ones, have a more equivocal status than in the idealization here. On the general phenomenon, see Perlmutter (1983); Aissen (1990).

6   Anna Cardinaletti (personal communication). The same is reported for Icelandic (Dianne Jonas, personal communication) and Mainland Scandinavian (Cardinaletti 1994, citing Tarald Taraldsen).

7   On the infinitival analogue *there seem [a lot of people to be . . .], see [Chomsky (1995: 4.9)], an analysis that should carry over to it seems [John to be . . .] and should also exclude the counterparts even in languages that permit [*John [I (nfl) seems [that t is intelligent]]].

8   As the concepts are clarified, we should be able to distinguish the possible residual con-tent of such elements as expletive there and it from true semantic features.

9   See Cardinaletti (1994) for cross-linguistic confirmation and for closer analysis of the feature content of expletives.

10 It is also necessary to show that there is no other feature that could do so, a question that is not entirely trivial, but that I will ignore.

11 Some interesting questions arise about the category D: if it stands alone, as a pure head, does the derivation crash because the strong [nominal-] feature is not checked? If so, demon-stratives and pronouns either would have to involve complements or would have to raise, as in cliticization. [. . .]

References

Aissen, J. L. 1990. Towards a theory of agreement controllers. In P. M. Postal and B. Joseph (eds.), *Studies in relational grammar 3*, Chicago: University of Chicago Press, pp. 279–320.

Belletti, A. 1988. The case of unaccusatives. *Linguistic Inquiry* 19: 1–34.

Cardinaletti, A. 1994. Agreement and control in expletive structures. Ms., MIT. [Published in *Linguistic Inquiry* 28: 521–33, in 1997.]

Chomsky, N. 1995. *The Minimalist Program*. Cambridge, MA: MIT Press.

Lasnik, H. and M. Saito. 1991. On the subject of infinitives. In L. Dobrin, L. Nichols and R. Rodriguez (eds.), *Papers from the 27th Regional Meeting of the Chicago Linguistics Society*, Chicago: Chicago Linguistics Society, pp. 324–43. [Reprinted in Lasnik (1999), *Minimalist analysis*, Malden, MA Oxford: Blackwell, pp. 7–24.]

Longobardi, G. 1994. Reference and proper names: A theory of N-movement in syntax and logical form. *Linguistic Inquiry* 25: 609–65.

Moro, A. 1994. The raising of predicates. Ms., Centro "Fondazione San Raffaele," Milan; and Istituto Universitario Lingue Moderne, Milan. [Published as *The raising of predicates*. Cambridge: Cambridge University Press, 1997.]

Perlmutter, D. 1983. Personal vs. impersonal constructions. *Natural Language and Linguistic Theory* 1: 141–200.

From "LAST RESORT"
Howard Lasnik

3　Existential constructions

The precise nature of the Last Resort condition is of fundamental importance for the treatment of simple existential constructions. In a series of articles, beginning with Chomsky (1986), Chomsky has argued that the "associate" of *there* moves to *there* in LF in such a sentence as (1).

(1)　There is a man here

This provides the basis for an account of the familiar superficially bizarre agreement paradigms displayed by these constructions, with the verb agreeing with something that is not its formal subject:

(2)　a.　There is/*are a man here
　　　b.　There are/*is men here

Chomsky (1986) proposed that the LF movement of the subject is substitution, with the associate replacing *there*. There are, however, difficulties with substitution. For example, it would result in identical LFs for (3) and (4).

(3)　A man is likely to be here
(4)　There is likely to be a man here

But the interpretive possibilities diverge. In (3), *a man* can evidently have wide or narrow scope with respect to *likely*, while (4) allows only narrow scope for *a man*. Party for this reason, Chomsky (1991) modified his (1986) substitution analysis, proposing instead that the associate adjoins to *there*, the latter being a sort of LF clitic.[1] As for the driving force for the movement, Chomsky claims that this movement is A-movement and, as in many other instances of A-movement, it is motivated by the Case requirements of the moved item. Chomsky thus maintains that the Case of the argument in the constructions under consideration is not licensed without movement to subject position, but is licensed in that position. This would be in accord with Greed.

　　Note, though, that Case checking in this affixation configuration raises a conceptual question. Chomsky (1993) proposes that the "properties and relations [of the grammar] will be stated in the simple and elementary terms of X-bar Theory." In particular, he argues that such notions as government by a head, clearly not a core X-bar relation, must be dispensed with. All structural Case is thus recast in terms of the Spec–head relation. However, just as "government" was an extension of the core head–complement relation, Chomsky extends the Spec–head relation to "checking domain." This notion includes not just the Spec of a head, but also items adjoined to the Spec. It is this latter configuration that is relevant to

Case licensing in existential constructions, according to Chomsky. There is, thus, reason to suspect that Case does not in fact provide the driving force for the movement. Belletti (1988) and Lasnik (1992) provide further arguments for this conclusion, and propose that *be* (and unaccusatives) are Case licensers (licensing a Case that Belletti calls "partitive"), so that the Case of the associate is licensed without movement to the expletive. Further, if *there*, like other NPs in A-positions, must bear a Case of its own, "partitive" will be the only Case available for the associate of *there*.

Note that the familiar agreement paradigm with existentials and similar constructions, which provided the primary motivation for movement in the first place, potentially raises the same technical problem as Case licensing. If the movement of the associate to the position of *there* is not driven by Case, and if Case and agreement are but two sides of the same coin, one would not a priori expect agreement. Further, even if Case and agreement are divorced, relationship between a head and an adjunct of a specifier is problematic in that it goes beyond core X-bar relations, as noted just above. At this point, I suggest that the apparent Spec–head agreement in these constructions could actually be the result of a constraint on affixation. Suppose that *there* is freely generated with any φ-features, and, as usual, its associate must adjoin to it. The relevant constraint is that a category and an affix cannot disagree in φ-features.[2] Below I will consider an alternative.

Chomsky (1995a) in passing indicates acceptance of the conclusion that *be* licenses Case, but indicates that Greed can still be maintained, suggesting that it is the **agreement** features of the associate that need to be licensed by the movement. This seems unlikely, however. First, even if the φ-features of the associate have to be checked, they would already be checked against the Agr projection that Chomsky assumes constitutes the small clause in which the associate originates. In an existential construction such as (5),

(5)   There is someone available

this agreement would be manifested on the adjective (as it is overtly in languages with richer morphology than English). Further, there are reasons to doubt that NPs do have to be so checked. First, in a coordinate NP, it isn't clear how the individual conjuncts could be checked, particularly when they disagree in φ-features ("Mary and the boys"). Additionally, in a language like English with "natural" (as opposed to purely formal) agreement features on NPs, these features are semantically relevant so presumably must survive to the LF level, hence cannot be checked in Chomsky's sense, since that would entail deletion.[3]

4   Enlightened self interest

We have arrived at the conclusion that there are no features of the associate that need to be checked by the movement, thus, that Greed is too strong a constraint. Now if any version of Last Resort is correct, the movement must satisfy **some** formal requirement of some item. One candidate for that item is *there*, and there is one formal property of *there* that could be relevant. In contrast with the Chomsky (1986) treatment of *there*, in which *there* is replaced by its associate in LF, for Chomsky (1991, 1993), the movement is adjunction; *there* is an LF affix, as mentioned above. This could be a relevant formal "inadequacy." Lasnik (1981) proposed a general stranded affix constraint demanding that underlying freestanding affixes ultimately be attached to an appropriate host. The concern there was overt morphology, but the null hypothesis is that the same constraint should hold of covert LF morphology. That is, if *there* is an LF affix, the LF will crash unless the associate of *there* adjoins to it.[4] Plausibly, this would suffice to drive the LF movement at issue in much the same way that the strong NP feature of Tense drives overt subject raising in English. In the former instance, without movement, we would be left with an illegitimate LF object. In the latter instance, we would be left with an illegitimate PF object. Consider then a slightly weakened version of Greed, which I will call "Enlightened Self Interest." These two versions of Last Resort are stated in (6).[5]

(6) a. Greed: Movement of α to β must be for the satisfaction of formal requirements of α.

  b. "Enlightened Self Interest": Movement of α to β must be for the satisfaction of formal requirements of α or β.

Even apart from Case properties of existential constructions, there are reasons for favoring (6b) over (6a). Chomsky (1993) proposes that raising of a *wh*-operator to [Spec, CP] is driven by the need for a morphological Q-feature to be checked. In a simple interrogative clause, C has this feature, as does the operator that raises to it. Further, if the Q-feature of C is strong, the raising will be overt, as in English. Thus, it seems that the operator raises to check its own feature, and in so doing, it satisfies the feature of the head it raises to. So far so good. But what of multiple interrogation? Chomsky (1993) argues, exactly along the lines of Chomsky (1973), that the *wh*-phrases that are *in situ* overtly remain *in situ* at LF, and are interpreted in the appropriate Comp without movement to that Comp at any level of representation. As Martin (1996b) notes, for the one *wh* that actually does move, we must identify a driving force, in particular, (under Greed) a morphological feature of that *wh* that must be checked. Further, that feature must distinguish the *wh* that moves from the ones that do not, because if all had the feature, the unmoved ones would cause the derivation to crash. Or, just as bad as far as Chomsky is concerned, they should all move. Alternatively, if the feature is simply freely assigned to any *wh*-phrase, then there is no description of standard Superiority effects, as in (7).

(7) *What did who buy

This is so since we could have freely assigned Q to *What* and not to *who*, with the result that *What* would be the highest *wh* capable of moving. These problems disappear once Greed is relaxed to Enlightened Self Interest. All that needs to be said is that interrogative C has the Q-feature, that the feature is strong, and that it can be checked by any *wh*-operator, and that the Q-feature of the operator need **not** be checked (it can survive to the interface level).[6] None of this goes beyond what is explicitly or tacitly assumed in most discussions of the phenomenon. Enlightened Self Interest, but not Greed, allows the movement of an operator to [Spec, CP] to be entirely for the benefit of the target C.

ECM constructions such as (8) create a similar difficulty for Greed under standard assumptions (assumptions which I will, however, reconsider below).

(8)   I believe John to be clever

There must be some strong feature of non-finite tense driving the overt movement of *John* to subject position. But the relevant feature is not a Case feature, since Case in ECM [exceptional Case marking] constructions is checked in the Spec of the higher Agr_o, in association with *believe*. Further, as briefly discussed above, the raising of the NP cannot in general be driven by any agreement needs of the NP itself. There is, thus, no feature of the NP that needs to be satisfied. Yet Greed, unlike Enlightened Self Interest, demands that there be one. The same difficulty for Greed arises in even more extreme form in successive cyclic raising constructions:

(9)   John is believed [*t* to be likely [*t* to be arrested *t*]]

What features of *John* itself could possibly demand to be checked in *every* subject position it passes through? It is phenomena of this type that require the computationally complex global property of Greed mentioned earlier. Presumably *John* must move through the intermediate *t* positions in order for it to successfully arrive at its ultimate goal: the nominative Case checking position in the highest clause.[7] Given this, the possibility arises that Enlightened Self Interest is actually a **stronger** constraint than Greed in one regard. If an instance of movement of α to β can be driven by the needs of β (the feature instantiating the EPP (Extended Projection Principle], in the instances under discussion), the computation can be strictly local. *Every* step of movement will immediately satisfy a requirement; no look-ahead will be required or permitted.

The Enlightened Self Interest approach to Last Resort advocated here finds additional support in consideration of simple intransitives. Consider the point in the derivation of (10) where the VP has been projected, as in (11) (under the VP-internal subject hypothesis).

(10)   Someone laughed
(11)   [$_{VP}$ someone [$_{V'}$ laughed]]

The VP (11) is further embedded in a series of functional Tense and Agreement projections. Finally, in the derivation of (10), *someone* is raised to [Spec, Agr_s]. But just at that point in the derivation, an option existed, given the assumptions of Chomsky (1993): instead of *someone* raising, [$_{NP}$ there] could be inserted into that Spec position. Clearly, this latter option must exist, for both possibilities surface with unaccusatives, as in (12)–(13).

(12)   Someone arrived
(13)   There arrived someone (with *someone* in its initial position as complement
        of V)

But no such alternative exists for (10), as evidenced by the extreme ungrammaticality of (14).

(14)   *There someone laughed (with *someone* in its initial position as [Spec, VP])

For Chomsky, *someone* in (14) ought to be able to adjoin to *There* in LF, getting
its nominative Case checked. Thus, there would be no morphological violation.[8]
Further, the result would seem to be perfectly coherent semantically: "There was
someone who laughed." (14) is thus mysterious. Exactly the same difficulty arises
for Chomsky (1995a), the only difference being that (12), (13) and likewise (10),
(14) would have completely independent derivations, depending on whether the
initial numeration of lexical items includes *there*. (14), with an initial numeration
including *there*, is again mistakenly allowed. No such difficulty arises on the partitive Case view, however. In (14), there is no way that *someone* can have partitive
Case checked.[9] And if, as speculated above, *there* checks nominative Case when it
is subject of a finite clause, no Case at all is available for *someone*, so the latter is
presumably an ill-formed LF object. Thus, the ungrammaticality of (14) follows
immediately from the theory advocated here.

   So far, we have seen that several of the arguments for Greed can be overcome
in a principled fashion, and, in addition, that Greed (and the more general theory
including it) is problematic in a number of respects. However, there is one remaining
argument for Greed that cannot be so easily dismissed. Chomsky (1993) considers
the ungrammatical (15).

(15)   *There seems to [$_\alpha$ a strange man] [that it is raining outside]

In this instance "α has its Case properties satisfied internal to the PP, so it is not
permitted to raise, and we are left with a freestanding *there*." Chomsky takes this
freestanding *there* to be a legitimate LF object, satisfying all morphological
requirements. The derivation of the example is thus legitimate. Only the interpretation of the example, and not its structural form, is faulty. This illustrates
Chomsky's view of the "Last Resort" nature of movement: "Derivations are driven
by the narrow mechanical requirement of feature checking only, not by a 'search
for intelligibility' or the like." I follow Chomsky on this point.

   Chomsky argues that (15) displays another related property of the system at the
same time. This is that Last Resort is "self-serving," conforming to Greed: ". . .
raising of α in [(15)] is blocked by the fact that *its own requirements* are satisfied
without raising, even though such raising would arguably overcome inadequacies
of the LF affix *there*." Chomsky does not specify just what these inadequacies of
there are. In fact, on his account, there do not seem to be any relevant inadequacies, though I have suggested above that the affixed nature of *there* might constitute an inadequacy. Martin (1992) and Groat (1995) make the alternative proposal

that the deficiency of *there* is that it lacks ϕ-features. The raising of the associate in well-formed existential constructions is then driven by the need for Agr to discharge its ϕ-features. This analysis, like the one suggested above, favors Enlightened Self Interest over Greed, unless we assume, with Groat, that the ϕ-features of an NP also have to be checked, a possibility that Chomsky (1995a) also seems to favor (in accord with apparent acceptance of the partitive Case analysis). However, as already discussed, it is unlikely that NPs have to be so checked. Thus, even under the Martin/Groat proposal, it would still follow that Greed is too strong a constraint: the relevant movement is altruistic.[10]

Once Greed is weakened to Enlightened Self Interest, Chomsky's account of (15) is no longer available, assuming that *there* has formal inadequacies.[11] While it is still true that the morphological requirements of α and of Tense are satisfied without movement of α to *there*, the LF morphological requirement of *there* that follows from its affixal nature is not satisfied (or, on the Martin/Groat view, the ϕ-features of Agr are not checked). Hence, movement is motivated under Enlightened Self Interest. The derivation should converge, and, according to Chomsky, it should be semantically coherent. As noted, Greed would correctly exclude the derivation. However, we have now seen several reasons for rejecting Greed. Further, even Greed would not explain the impossibility of a version of (15) with *to* replaced by *TO*, where *TO*, analogous to Chomsky's *HIT* considered earlier, is like *to*, but lacking a Case feature. To address this new problem, and simultaneously to reconcile (15) with Enlightened Self Interest, I suggest, as perhaps the simplest possibility, that the semantic difficulty that Chomsky attributes to (15) with *a strange man in situ* might arise even if *a strange man* were to move. In the absence of any precise theory of what the semantic difficulty is, there is no obvious reason to reject this account.

As an alternative possibility, one might conjecture that *there* does indeed have a relevant LF morphological property, but one that is slightly more specific than I suggested above. Note that there are constraints on the associate of *there*. For example, it must be an NP, and not a clause:

(16)   *There is likely [that John is tall]

In fact, (15) can be seen, on one derivation (with the CP moving to *there*), as illustrating this same constraint. In the terms of the present discussion, *there* must be an LF affix on an NP. (15) suggests that the constraint is still tighter: that *there* must be an affix on an NP with partitive Case. Since *to* does not check partitive Case (as evidenced by the lack of definiteness effects in its complement, on Belletti's theory), the derivation of (15) in which *a strange man* adjoins to *there* in the LF component will yield a morphological violation. The same analysis carries over to (17).

(17)   *There strikes John/someone that Mary is intelligent

Again, *there* will be an illicit freestanding LF affix. And, again, while Chomsky's Greed account would carry over to this example, it would fail to explain the non-existence of *STRIKE*, a verb like *strike* but lacking a Case feature.[12] Beginning immediately below, I will reconsider the nature of the deficiency of *there* and the effects of that deficiency on syntactic derivation.

5   LF feature movement

Chomsky has recently suggested, in a series of lectures (and later in Chomsky 1995b), a somewhat different theory of the LF movement involved in expletive constructions, as part of a revised theory of LF movement more generally. Beginning with the standard Minimalist assumption that all movement is driven by the need for formal features to be checked, Chomsky argues that, all else equal, movement should then never be of an entire syntactic category, but only of its formal features.[13] PF requirements will normally force movement of a category containing the formal features, via a sort of pied-piping, under the reasonable assumption that a bare feature (or set of features) is an ill-formed PF object. For LF movement, on the other hand, pied-piping will normally not be necessary, hence, by economy, will not even be possible. Only the formal features will move, and they will move exactly to the heads that have matching features.[14] In a standard existential sentence like (18), then, the associate *someone* does not move to *there*.

(18)   There is someone here

Rather, only the formal features of *someone* move, and only to a corresponding functional head (or heads). The affixal account of *there* does not seem stable in such a theory. Rather, we are led to something much more like the Martin/Groat analysis. If *there* lacks agreement features, then the features of Agr will not be checked in overt syntax. The features of the associate will therefore have to move to Agr (in LF, because of Procrastinate). Note, in addition, that this overcomes the technical problem noted earlier for the Martin/Groat analysis, since the checking configuration is now allowed even under strict assumptions. In effect, it is a head–head configuration.

The problematic (15), repeated here as (19), which I dealt with (on one account) by appeal to specific requirements on the LF affixation of *there*, now once again has no formal account.

(19)   *There seems to [$_\alpha$ a strange man] [that it is raining outside]

Given that the deficiency of *there* is that it lacks agreement features, the features of *a strange man* should be available in the LF component for attraction to Agr$_s$.[15] All formal requirements would then be satisfied. (17), repeated as (20), raises the same difficulty.

(20)   *There strikes John/someone that Mary is intelligent

Chomsky claims, roughly along the lines of his earlier account, that *there* lacks not only agreement features, but also Case features. Thus, in examples like these, the

Case feature of Tense would not be checked by *there*. Further, it also could not be checked by *a strange man* (or *John/someone*), since that NP must check the Case feature of *to* (or *strike*). But we have already seen reason to reject the assumption that *there* does not check Case. The argument based on (14) above, repeated as (21), carries over unchanged in the feature movement theory.

(21)   *There someone laughed

If *there* does not check nominative Case, that Case should still be available for (the Case feature of) *someone*. Further, as John Frampton (personal communication) observes, (22), from Lasnik (1992), should also then be well-formed.

(22)   *There is likely [there to be a man here]

Given all of this, I will continue to assume that *there*, like other NPs, does have a Case feature. If a formal, as opposed to semantic, account for (15) and (17) is required, one might be constructed on the following lines: Assume with Chomsky that any visible feature of a head can "attract" a corresponding feature, resulting in the movement of a bundle of formal features (LF movement) or a syntactic constituent (overt movement). But in addition suppose that it is exactly a visible Case feature that makes the feature bundle or constituent available for "A-movement." Once Case is checked off, no further movement is possible.[16] In (15) and (17) the agreement features of Agr_s will not be checked either by *there* (it has no agreement features) or by the associate of *there* (it can move no further after it checks its Case feature against *strike* or *to*), resulting in an ill-formed LF. One additional example that is problematic even for Chomsky can also be easily accounted for in these terms. In (23) the movement of *a man* to satisfy the EPP requirement of the infinitive ought to be permitted, given Enlightened Self Interest, or its incorporation into Chomsky's feature attraction.

(23)   *The belief [a man to seem [t' is [t here]]]

Under the present proposal, once *a man* checks nominative in the lower clause, it is no longer available for further A-movement.[17] The same analysis extends to *BELIEVE*, a verb like *believe*, but with no Case feature. Consider (24).

(24)   *John BELIEVEs [a man to seem [t' is [t here]]]

Again, once *a man* has its Case checked, no further movement of it is possible. This proposal is in the nature of a compromise between Greed and Enlightened Self Interest. As with Greed, the NP that will move (or whose formal features will) must have a Case feature that has not been checked off. But as with Enlightened Self Interest, any particular instance of movement of that NP might be solely for the satisfaction of requirements of the target.

One major problem for Greed carries over, so must be dealt with now. If *be* and unaccusatives check Case (as argued by Belletti 1988 and Lasnik 1992), the agreement features of Agr_s in (25) will remain unchecked.

(25)   There is a man here

Note that this is precisely the type of sentence where *be* would necessarily participate in Case checking on the Belletti/Lasnik theory.[18] Hence (the formal feature bundle of) *a man* would not be available for further movement to Agr$_s$. However, even this problem disappears if we follow Belletti (1988) and Lasnik (1992) that the specific Case borne by the associate of *there* is one with semantic import. It would then not be checked off even if it participated in checking. Being not merely a formal feature, it would survive to the LF interface level, so would be visible throughout the syntactic derivation.[19]

Before turning to several advantages of the feature movement theory, I must acknowledge an apparent descriptive disadvantage of this theory *vis-à-vis* the LF affixation analysis of *there*. Recall the affixation account of (16), repeated as (26).

(26)   *There is likely [that John is tall]

The proposal was that *there* must be an LF affix on a particular sort of NP. (26) ran afoul of that requirement, since the only potential host for *there* is the complement clause. The converse situation, as in (27), could have been similarly handled.

(27)   *It is a man in the room

Descriptively, the associate of *it* must be a clause, arguably always a CP, as discussed (in slightly different terms) by Chomsky and Lasnik (1977). This too could have been captured by an affixation constraint: *it* must be an LF affix on a CP. Without such affixation, how can these association constraints be captured? The association requirement for *there* is relatively straightforward, if we assume that clauses do not have agreement features. Under that assumption, the agreement features of Agr$_s$ in (26) will never be checked. A possible bar to such an account is the apparent existence of sentential subjects, as in (28).

(28)   That John is tall is likely

For present purposes, I will simply assume that something along the lines of Koster (1978) is correct, and that apparent sentential subjects are actually in a presentential position, the true subject being a null pronominal (possessing, like other NPs, a set of φ-features). (27) is more difficult. By hypothesis, *a man* can bear a Case feature that will be checked by *be*. And the Case and agreement features of the Infl complex will be checked against those of *It*. I speculate that there is some feature of expletive *it* that must be checked against a feature of C. Since *it*, in addition to being a maximal projection, is simultaneously a head, the configuration needed for feature movement does obtain.

The feature movement theory has the potential to address several problems concerning existential constructions. For example, in connection with (3)–(4) above, I alluded to Chomsky's argument, based on scope facts, against a substitution analysis of expletive replacement. [. . .] [A]s he points out, in his example (29), it is not the case that there is no scope relation between *not* and *many students*.

(29)　There aren't many linguistics students here

Rather, *many linguistics students* necessarily has narrow scope.
　　[. . .]
The feature movement analysis of existential constructions has the potential to solve this scope problem. If in LF, only the formal features of *many linguistics students*, rather than the entire expression, move to a functional head or heads above negation, it is reasonable to conclude that the quantificational properties remain below negation. Then, if it is this structure that determines scope (that is, if QR either cannot alter these hierarchical relations or does not exist[20]) the desired results are obtained.

There are further phenomena that are suggestive of the same conclusion. For example, [Lasnik and Saito (ch. 2.1, this volume)] above shows that with respect to anaphora, the associate of *there* in an ECM configuration behaves as if it is unmoved. (30) contrasts with (31).

(30)　The DA proved [two men to have been at the scene] during each other's trials
(31)　*The DA proved [there to have been two men at the scene] during each other's trials

In (30) *two men* behaves as if it c-commands an item that is in the higher clause, an argument related to several presented by Postal (1974).[21] If the ECM subject raises into the higher clause, as conjectured in [Lasnik and Saito (ch. 2.1, this volume)] and by Chomsky and Lasnik (1993), this can be explained.[22] However, one would expect that *there* in (31) also raises into the higher clause. And if *two men* has adjoined to *there*, we would incorrectly expect (31) to have the status of (30) [. . .].

Negative polarity items display similar contrasts, as seen in (32) vs. (33).

(32)　The DA proved [no-one to be at the scene] during any of the trials
(33)　*The DA proved [there to be no-one at the scene] during any of the trials

Once again, the ECM subject (*no-one*) behaves as if it c-commands an item in the higher clause (*any*), while the associate of *there* does not display this behavior.

Not surprisingly, standard subject raising to subject position patterns with the "subject raising to object position" of ECM constructions. Thus, a raised subject can antecede an anaphor in the higher clause, but the associate of a raised expletive cannot:

(34)　Some linguists seem to each other [*t* to have been given good job offers]
(35)　*There seem to each other [*t* to have been some linguists given good job offers]

Similarly, a raised negative subject licenses a polarity item in the higher clause while the negative associate of a raised expletive does not:

(36)   No good linguistic theories seem to any philosophers [*t* to have been formulated]

(37)   *There seem to any philosophers [*t* to have been no good linguistic theories formulated]

All of the pairs involving overt raising to subject position are straightforward on the feature movement view. When the movement is overt (examples summarized in (38)), the **entire** NP moves.

(38)   a.   Some linguists seem to each other [*t* to have been given good job offers]
        b.   Many linguistics students aren't [*t* here]
        c.   No good linguistic theories seem to any philosophers [*t* to have been formulated]

As a result, the properties (referential, quantificational, etc.) relevant to licensing an anaphor or negative polarity item or determining scope will be in the required structural position. On the other hand, when the movement is covert (examples summarized in (39)), only the formal features raise.

(39)   a.   *There seem to each other [*t* to have been some linguists given good job offers]
        b.   There aren't many linguistics students here
        c.   *There seem to any philosophers [*t* to have been no good linguistic theories formulated]

The properties relevant to anaphora and scope remain below, failing to provide a higher licensing or scope position.

Further, the ungrammatical ECM examples involving an expletive and an associate (summarized in (40)) are easily accounted for in similar fashion.

(40)   a.   *The DA proved [there to have been two men at the scene] during each other's trials
        b.   *The DA proved [there to be no-one at the scene] during any of the trials

What is now mysterious, though, is the original phenomenon that [Lasnik and Saito (ch. 2.1, this volume)] set out to describe. Consider again the examples that were paired above with those in (40):

(41)   a.   The DA proved [two men to have been at the scene] during each other's trials
        b.   The DA proved [no-one to be at the scene] during any of the trials

What [Lasnik and Saito (ch. 2.1, this volume)] were concerned with, along lines similar to Postal (1974), was the apparent higher behavior of subjects of infinitives. That this behavior is related to ECM is seen in the contrast between the infinitival complements in (41) and the corresponding finite complements in (42).

(42) a. ?*The DA proved [that two men were at the scene] during each other's trails

  b. ?*The DA proved [that no-one was at the scene] during any of the trials

Similarly, for scope purposes, an ECM subject behaves as if it is in the higher clause while a nominative subject does not. Postal noted the contrast in (43): the scope of *few students* includes the higher clause in (43a).

(43) a. The FBI proved few students to be spies
  b. The FBI proved that few students were spies

All of these licensing and scope phenomena indicate that an ECM subject may behave as if it is in the higher clause. A further example discussed by Postal suggests that the ECM subject **must** behave that way:

(44) a. *Joan believes [him$_i$ to be a genius] even more fervently than Bob$_i$ does
  b. Joan believes [he$_i$ is a genius] even more fervently than Bob$_i$ does

If *him* is raised to the higher clause in (44a), while (uncontroversially) *he* remains in the lower clause in (44b), the contrast can be explained by whatever derives Condition C effects.

6   Raising to [Spec, Agr$_o$]: covert or overt?

We have now arrived at a virtual contradiction.[23] The phenomena in (39) argue that when raising is in LF, only the formal features of an NP raise, leaving behind those properties involved in anaphora, scope, etc. But (41), (43), and (44), which involve the same class of phenomena, argue that referential and scopal properties in ECM constructions do raise, along with the formal features. At this point, I will consider two possible ways out of this dilemma.[24]

[. . .]

A second approach would rely, instead, on the already postulated distinction between overt and covert movement. Recall Chomsky's conjecture that for PF reasons, overt movement is always of a category, not just formal features, while covert movement is merely of formal features, since the entire category need not (hence, must not) move. The relevant movement in the *there* constructions considered above is covert, so the account of those constructions is exactly as in the first approach. Only the features move, so for all other purposes, it is as if no movement took place. For ECM constructions, also, the standard Minimalist assumption is that the movement is covert. This was the source of the paradox. But Koizumi (1993),[25] revising and extending ideas of Johnson (1991), argues that accusative Case is checked overtly in English, just like nominative Case. The accusative NP overtly raises to [Spec, Agr_o] (with V raising to a still higher head position). If this is correct, the seemingly paradoxical asymmetry is immediately reduced to the independent pied-piping asymmetry. In the *there* construction, the only movement is the covert movement of the formal features of the associate to the Agr head. For an ECM subject (or, for that matter, the object of a simple transitive) the movement is overt, hence, of the entire NP.

Both of these approaches correctly entail that, among the NPs considered so far, only the associate of *there* shows lower behavior. All the others show higher behavior. It is also worthy of note that on both of the approaches, the Case of the associate of *there* is apparently licensed independently of *there*, as in the approach of Belletti (1988).

A further distinctive property of the movement hypothesized to be involved in *there* constructions is noted by Hornstein (1994). Hornstein argues that the apparent infinite regress in antecedent contained deletion (ACD) constructions is resolved not by QR, as on the classic account of May (1985), but by raising to [Spec, Agr_o]. Lasnik (1999: ch. 3) and Takahashi (1996) present similar arguments. As Hornstein observes, this provides a derivation for (45).

(45)   John expected [[no-one that I did [$_{VP}$ *e*]] to be electable]

In the structure given in (45), the null VP seems to be contained within its antecedent, the larger VP headed by *expected*. But if [no-one that I did [$_{VP}$ *e*]] raises to [Spec, Agr_o] above *expected*, the regress can be avoided. Hornstein notes that (45) contrasts sharply with (46).

(46)   *John expected [there to be no-one that I did electable]

Hornstein concludes that "there is no expletive replacement . . . If expletive replacement obtains, then at LF [(45)] and [(46)] should have analogous structures with *there* and *no-one that I did* forming a complex and raising to the matrix [Spec, Agr_o] for Case checking." Hornstein doesn't indicate how he proposes to deal with the standard arguments, going back to Chomsky (1986b), **for** expletive replacement, namely, the agreement facts mentioned above and the A-chain like locality between expletive and associated argument. Again, there is a seeming paradox. There is a strong argument that movement is not involved, and an equally strong argument that it is. But the resolution of the paradox is already at hand. [. . .] Only the formal features of the associate of *there* move. Consequently, *no-one that I did* in (46) remains *in situ*, leaving the null VP internal to its antecedent. Further, on both of the approaches, in (45) that NP necessarily raises out of the VP, freeing the null VP from its antecedent.[26]

   [. . .]

7 Conclusion

In conclusion, I have argued for a version of the Last Resort condition that incorporates the basic property of Enlightened Self Interest: an instance of movement must be for the satisfaction of some feature, where that feature might be of the moved item or of the target. The condition still embodies one residual element of Greed: that an NP (or its set of formal features) is no longer available for "A-movement" when its Case has been checked off. Finally, in terms of the feature movement theory of (LF) movement, I have suggested, based on binding and ellipsis phenomena, that the movement involved in accusative Case checking in English is overt, as argued by Koizumi (1993), roughly following Johnson (1991). While the general direction seems quite promising, more comprehensive Minimalist theories of Case licensing, and, indeed, of anaphora and of ellipsis, await further investigation.

Notes

1   This does not entirely resolve the scope issue, as I will discuss below. A related matter is that, as noted in [Lasnik and Saito (ch. 2.1, this volume)], substitution creates binding theoretic difficulties as well. I will return to this issue also.

2   A parallel account for the *Case* of the associate would not be available since the Case feature of an NP must literally be checked while, as I will discuss immediately below, agreement features of an NP need not. See Lee (1994) on these two types of features.

3   Since the agreement in sentences like (5) is also manifested on the verb, we have yet more evidence that agreement features of an NP are not checked off, even when the NP participates in a checking relation.

4   Željko Bošković reminds me that this line of reasoning is inconsistent with my analysis of verbal morphology in [Lasnik (ch. 4.1, this volume)], where it is argued, contra recent strictly lexicalist proposals, that Infl morphology in English is an independently generated affix (as in Chomsky 1957). It is crucial to the analysis I present that the affixal property of Infl **not** suffice to drive raising of the verb, so that only a PF coalescence process will be available. Below, I will examine an alternative account of *there* that does not demand that it be an affix, but that is still inconsistent with Greed.

5   Given the considerations of note 4, we will see that "formal" must be strengthened to "featural" (where I take the property of being an affix not to be featural in the relevant sense).

6   Again, this is as expected if the feature has semantic content.

7   For present purposes, I will continue to follow Chomsky on this point, but it is not obviously correct. Chomsky (1991) argues that in overt syntax, VP-internal subject moves directly to [Spec, IP]. This move seems to violate shortest move by skipping [Spec, Agr$_o$]. However, Chomsky claims that [Spec, Agr$_o$] need not exist until LF, so it is not actually skipped. This leaves open the possibility that [Spec, IP] similarly need not exist overtly. Granted, if it did not, the EPP would be violated. But under Greed, that should be of no concern to the NP that is moving. See Takahashi (1994) for important discussion of the shortest move condition.

8   Note that the seemingly parallel (i) will be unproblematic.

(i)   *There someone arrived

In this instance, nothing would drive the overt movement of *someone* to [Spec, VP], so (at the very least) Procrastinate would be violated.

9   This assumes with Lasnik (1992), and contra Belletti (1988), that partitive Case licensing
     ability is not a property of all verbs, but rather is limited to *be* and unaccusatives.

10   Note that this account again raises the technical problem of checking in a configuration
     that is not precisely a Spec–head configuration.

11   If we were to follow Chomsky in assuming that *there* has no formal inadequacies, then the
     example would be blocked even by Enlightened Self Interest. Neither α nor β would benefit
     formally from the move.

12   Roger Martin observes that neither account explains the non-existence of *STRIKE* in a
     sentence like (i).

     (i)   *John STRIKES *t* that Mary is intelligent

     Pending an account of this fact, the discussion in the text remains tentative, though, as
     Željko Bošković points out, the crucial question is not whether *STRIKE* exists, but whether
     there are any verbs at all with the relevant properties. Bošković suggests that middles and
     passives are plausible candidates.

13   And, further, that an unchecked feature of the target drives movement, much in the spirit
     of Enlightened Self Interest.

14   Note that this provides hope of making Procrastinate a true economy condition: waiting
     until LF to move entails moving less material.

15   This is so even if there is an Agreement head above the PP that needs to be checked, since,
     as discussed above, the agreement features of an NP are not "checked off" even if they
     participate in a checking relation.

16   That this reinstates much of the redundancy that I earlier indicated was problematic
     for Greed suggests that there is more to be said on this matter. See Bošković (1995) for
     discussion.

17   As an alternative, Ormazabal (1995) argues that complements of ECM verbs are CPs (while
     control complements are IPs), the reverse of the widely accepted proposal of Chomsky (1981).
     The impossibility of nominalizations of such constructions then follows, on Ormazabal's
     account, from general constraints on the incorporation of the zero complementizer.

18   One additional problem in Belletti's original proposal, and carried over in the successive
     revisions in Lasnik (1992) and Lasnik (1999: ch. 4) persist: the apparent optionality of "par-
     titive" Case. In (i), and even more strikingly in (ii), it evidently must be true that *be* need
     not discharge its Case.

     (i)   A man is here
     (ii) John is here

     I know of no fully satisfactory solution to this problem, so for present purposes I will give
     a merely technological answer: *be* and unaccusative verbs come in doublet pairs with and
     without the Case feature. So-called middle constructions might involve similar doublets,
     thereby permitting the object of a normally transitive verb to move to a Case checking
     subject position.

19   Something like Ormazabal's proposal of note 17 might be necessary for (i).

     (i)   *The belief [a man to be [*t* here]] . . .

     Suppose *a man* bears partitive Case, and *be* checks that Case. By hypothesis, *a man* is still
     available for further movement, so it should be able to move to [Spec, IP] in (i) thus sat-
     isfying the EPP. All formal requirements are then met. Only one other possibility occurs
     to me. If, as argued in Lasnik (1999: ch. 4), the configuration for partitive Case checking
     is not created until LF (*here* raising to the "light" verb *be*, and the complex raising to Agr_o;

a man in [Spec, Agr$_o$] then *a man* would not have its Case checked overtly. To have its Case checked, *a man* would have to lower covertly. If (contra Lasnik and Saito 1984, 1992) there is a general prohibition of such lowering, then *a man* could not get its Case checked at all.

20 Among recent work on this, see Lasnik and Saito (1992) for the former possibility and Kitahara (1992) for the latter.

21 I put aside consideration of the precise nature of the constraint on anaphor–antecedent relations, and of other similar relations to be discussed immediately below.

22 Further, as also discussed in [Lasnik and Saito (ch. 2.1, this volume)] given that objects of simple transitives also behave as if they c-command adverbial adjuncts, even objects must raise to a higher position (on standard, but not completely uncontroversial, assumptions about phrase structure and c-command).

23 The conclusion of [Lasnik and Saito (ch. 2.1, this volume)] was similar, and, as will be seen, for similar reasons.

24 Bošković (1994), operating under a slightly different set of assumptions, suggests an additional way out. He proposes, following Chomsky (1991) and Lasnik (1999: ch. 4), that *there* is an affix. Further, following Lasnik (1999) he takes that affixal nature to be a formal inadequacy driving movement. However, departing from Lasnik (1999) he proposes that rather than the associate raising and adjoining to *there*, *there* lowers and adjoins to the associate (a sort of Affix Hopping). This immediately gives the result that for LF purposes, the behavior of the associate is in accord with its S-structure position.

25 See Ura (1993) for a related proposal.

26 The theory of Bošković (1994) also correctly handles the ACD paradigms, as Bošković observes.

References

Belletti, A. 1988. The case of unaccusatives. *Linguistic Inquiry* 19: 1–34.

Bošković, Ž. 1994. *Wager*-class verbs and existential constructions. Ms., University of Connecticut, Storrs.

Bošković, Ž. 1995. *Principles of economy in nonfinite complementation*. Doctoral dissertation, University of Connecticut, Storrs. [Revised version published as *The syntax of nonfinite complementation: An economy approach*. Cambridge, MA: MIT Press, 1997.]

Chomsky, N. 1957. *Syntactic structures*. The Hague: Mouton.

Chomsky, N. 1973. Conditions on transformations. In S. Anderson and P. Kiparsky (eds.), *A Festschrift for Morris Halle*, New York: Holt, Rinehart, and Winston, pp. 232–86.

Chomsky, N. 1981. *Lectures on government and binding*. Dordrecht: Foris.

Chomsky, N. 1986. *Knowledge of language: Its nature, origin, and use*. New York: Praeger.

Chomsky, N. 1991. Some notes on economy of derivation and representation. In R. Freidin (ed.), *Principles and parameters in comparative grammar*, Cambridge, MA: MIT Press, pp. 417–54. [Reprinted in Chomsky (1995), *The Minimalist Program*, Cambridge, MA: MIT Press, pp. 128–66.]

Chomsky, N. 1993. A minimalist program for linguistic theory. In K. Hale and S. J. Keyser (eds.), *The view from Building 20: Essays in linguistics in honor of Sylvain Bromberger*, Cambridge, MA: MIT Press, pp. 1–52. [Reprinted in Chomsky (1995), *The Minimalist Program*, Cambridge, MA: MIT Press, pp. 167–217.]

Chomsky, N. 1994. *Bare phrase structure. MIT Occasional Papers in Linguistics 5*. Cambridge, MA: MITWPL. [Published in P. Kempchinsky (ed.) (1994), *Evolution and revolution in linguistic theory: Essays in honor of Carlos Otero*, Washington, DC: Georgetown University Press, pp. 51–109. Also published in G. Webelhuth (ed.) (1994), *Government and binding theory and the minimalist program*, Cambridge, MA: MIT Press, pp. 383–439.]

Chomsky, N. 1995a. Bare phrase structure. In G. Webelhuth (ed.), *Government and binding theory and the minimalist program*, Cambridge, MA: MIT Press, pp. 383–439. [Also published in P. Kempchinsky (ed.) (1995), *Evolution and revolution in linguistic theory: Essays in honor of Carlos Otero*, Washington, DC: Georgetown University Press, pp. 51–109.]

Chomsky, N. 1995b. Categories and transformations. In Chomsky (1995), *The Minimalist Program*, Cambridge, MA: MIT Press, pp. 219–394.

Chomsky, N. and H. Lasnik. 1977. Filters and control. *Linguistic Inquiry* 8: 425–504.

Chomsky, N. and H. Lasnik. 1993. The theory of principles and parameters. In J. Jacobs, A. von Stechow, W. Sternefeld and T. Vennemann (eds.), *An international handbook of contemporary research*, Berlin/New York: Walter de Gruyter, pp. 506–69. [Reprinted in Chomsky (1995), *The Minimalist Program*, Cambridge, MA: MIT Press, pp. 13–127.]

Groat, E. 1995. English expletives: A minimalist approach. *Linguistic Inquiry* 26: 354–65, 1993.

Hornstein, N. 1994. An argument for minimalism: The case of antecedent-constrained deletion. *Linguistic Inquiry* 25: 455–80.

Johnson, K. 1991. Object positions. *Natural Language and Linguistic Theory* 9: 577–636.

Kitahara, H. 1992. Checking theory and scope interpretation without quantifier raising. In S. Kuno and H. Thráinsson (eds.), *Harvard University Working Papers 1*. Cambridge, MA: Department of Linguistics, Harvard University, pp. 51–71. [Revised version published as Raising quantifiers without quantifier raising, in W. Abraham, S. D. Epstein, H. Thráinsson and C. J.-W. Zwart (eds.) (1996), *Minimal ideas: Syntactic studies in the Minimalist framework*, Amsterdam: John Benjamins, pp. 189–98.]

Koizumi, M. 1993. Object agreement phrases and the split VP hypothesis. In J. D. Bobaljik and C. Phillips (eds.), *Papers on Case and agreement I. MIT Working Papers in Linguistics 18*, Cambridge, MA: MITWPL, pp. 99–148.

Koster, J. 1978. Why subject sentences don't exist? In S. J. Keyser (ed.), *Recent transformational studies in European languages*, Cambridge, MA: MIT Press, pp. 53–64.

Lasnik, H. 1981. Restricting the theory of transformations: A case study. In N. Hornstein and D. Lightfoot (eds.), *Explanation in linguistics*, Harlow: Longman, pp. 152–73.

Lasnik, H. 1992. Case and expletives: Notes toward a parametric account. *Linguistic Inquiry* 23: 381–405.

Lasnik, H. 1993. *Lectures on minimalist syntax. University of Connecticut Occasional Papers in Linguistics 1*. Cambridge, MA: MITWPL. [Reprinted in H. Lasnik (1999), *Minimalist analysis*, Malden, MA: Blackwell, pp. 25–73.]

Lasnik, H. 1994. Verbal morphology: *Syntactic structures* meets the Minimalist Program. Ms., University of Connecticut, Storrs. [Published in H. Campos and P. Kempchinsky (eds.) (1995), *Evolution and revolution in linguistic theory*, Washington, DC: Georgetown University Press, pp. 251–75, and reprinted in Lasnik (1999), *Minimalist analysis*, Malden, MA: Blackwell, pp. 97–119.]

Lasnik, H. 1999. *Minimalist analysis*. Malden, MA/Oxford: Blackwell.

Lasnik, H. In press. Case and expletives revisited: On Greed and other human failings. [Published in *Linguistic Inquiry* 26: 615–33 (1995), and reprinted in H. Lasnik (1999), *Minimalist analysis*, Malden, MA: Blackwell, pp. 74–96.]

Lasnik, H. and M. Saito. 1984. On the nature of proper government. *Linguistic Inquiry* 15: 235–55.

Lasnik, H. and M. Saito. 1991. On the subject of infinitives. In L. Dobrin, L. Nichols and R. Rodriguez (eds.), *Papers from the 27th Regional Meeting of the Chicago Linguistics Society*, Chicago: Chicago Linguistics Society, pp. 324–43. [Reprinted in Lasnik (1999), *Minimalist analysis*, Malden, MA: Blackwell, pp. 7–24.]

Lasnik, H. and M. Saito. 1992. *Move α*. Cambridge, MA: MIT Press.

Lee, R. K. 1994. *Economy of representation*. Doctoral dissertation, University of Connecticut, Storrs.

Martin, R. 1992. Case theory, A-chains, and expletive replacement. Ms., University of Connecticut, Storrs.

Martin, R. 1996. On LF wh-movement and wh-islands. In E. Laurençot, R. Lee and M.-K. Park (eds.), *University of Connecticut Working Papers in Linguistics 5*, Cambridge, MA: MITWPL, pp. 25–44.

May, R. 1985. *Logical form*. Cambridge, MA: MIT Press.

Ormazabal, J. 1995. *The syntax of complementation: On the connection between syntactic structures and selection*. Doctoral dissertation, University of Connecticut, Storrs.

Postal, P. M. 1974. *On raising: One rule of English grammar and its implication*. Cambridge, MA: MIT Press.

Takahashi, D. 1993. On antecedent-contained deletion. Ms., University of Connecticut, Storrs.

Takahashi, D. 1994. *Minimality of movement*. Doctoral dissertation, University of Connecticut, Storrs.

Takahashi, D. 1996. On antecedent-contained deletion. In E. Laurençot, R. Lee and M.-K. Park (eds.), *University of Connecticut Working Papers in Linguistics 5*, Cambridge, MA: MITWPL, pp. 65–80.

Ura, H. 1993. On feature-checking for wh-traces. In J. D. Bobaljik and C. Phillips (eds.), *Papers on Case and agreement I. MIT Working Papers in Linguistics 18*, Cambridge, MA: MITWPL, pp. 215–42.

7.1   Recent Developments

From "DERIVATION BY PHASE"
Noam Chomsky

Consider raising constructions with unaccusatives, abstracting for the moment from English-specific idiosyncrasies so that (1a) converges as (1b).

(1)   a.   [C [T be likely [Expl to-arrive a man]]]
      b.   there is likely to arrive a man

The expletive Expl has the uninterpretable feature *person*. Under local Match, Expl agrees with T and raises to [Spec, T]. The operation deletes the EPP-feature of T and the person feature of Expl, but the φ-set of T remains intact because Expl is incomplete [. . .]. Therefore, Agree holds between the probe T and the more remote goal *man*, deleting the φ-set of T and the structural Case feature of *man* (assuming, as throughout, George and Kornfilt's (1981) thesis that structural Case is a reflex of agreement). The values assigned under Agree are trans-mitted to the phonological component: the values of *man* for the φ-set of T, nom-inative for structural Case. Uninterpretable features delete, and the derivation converges as (1b).

Suppose the smallest strong phase is v^*P, not CP.

(2)   a.   [C [we [$_{v^*P}$ v^*-expect [Expl to-arrive a man]]]]
      b.   we expect there to arrive a man

If the derivation is parallel to (1), then Agree holds of (v^*, Expl), deleting the person feature of Expl but leaving v^* intact so that Agree holds of (v^*, *man*). The

Existential Constructions

φ-set of v^* deletes; structural Case of *man* is assigned the value accusative and deletes. If v^* lacks an EPP-feature here, then (1) and (2) differ in that there is no raising to [Spec, v^*].[1]

In (1) and (2), no intervention effect is induced by Expl. That follows for (1) under the principle (3), conceptually plausible and empirically supported. (See [Chomsky 2000]).

(3)   Only the head of an A-chain (equivalently, the whole chain) blocks matching under the Minimal Link Condition (MLC).

For (2), the same principle would suffice if raising takes place in ECM [extended Case marking] constructions.[2]

Notes

1   A separate question is whether Expl raises to a position within the v^* complement. [. . .]
2   The observation is irrelevant if Case is assumed to be assigned to the object in situ.

References

Chomsky, N. 2000. Minimalist inquiries: The framework. In Roger Martin, David Michaels, and Juan Uriagereka (eds.), *Step by step: Essays on minimalist syntax in honor of Howard Lasnik*, Cambridge, MA: MIT Press, pp. 89–155.
George, L. and J. Kornfilt. 1981. Finiteness and boundedness in Turkish. In F. Heny (ed.), *Binding and filtering*, Cambridge, MA: MIT Press, pp. 105–27.

From "MINIMALIST INQUIRIES: THE FRAMEWORK"
Noam Chomsky

The general conclusions are these:

(1)   a.   Long-distance agreement is a T-associate (probe-goal) relation.
       b.   The EPP can be satisfied by
             i.   Merge of expletive
             ii.   Merge of associate
             iii. Merge of α closer to T than the associate

Case (1bi) is illustrated by T-associate agreement, with the definiteness effect. Case (1bii) exhibits agreement of [Spec, T] and T, but that is ancillary to the T-associate relation. In case (1biii) there is no definiteness effect and long-distance T-associate agreement holds with embedded accessible nominative; or, if such an associate is lacking, T is default.

More generally, we should not expect Spec-head relations to have any special status. Within bare phrase structure, we cannot, for example, take the result of first Merge to α to be sometimes a specifier and sometimes a complement, as in an X-bar-theoretic analysis that takes the object of α to be its complement (*see John, proud* [*of John*]) but the subject of objectless α to be its specifier (base forms of *John eat, John proud*). The restriction to a single specifier is also questionable: rather, we would expect first Merge, second Merge, and so on, with no stipulated limit.

From "BEYOND EXPLANATORY ADEQUACY"
Noam Chomsky

We therefore conclude that in addition to Merge, there is a relation Agree holding between probe P and goal G, which deletes uninterpretable features if P and G are appropriately related. It remains to determine its properties.

There considerations lend further support to the conclusion that the Spec-head relation does not exist. [. . .]

(1)   Apparent Spec-H relations are in reality head-head relations involving minimal search (local c-command).

If there is no Spec-head relation, then the EPP-feature OCC cannot be satisfied by Merge alone.[1] It follows that internal Merge requires Agree. Therefore, Move = Agree + Pied-piping + Merge. Note the weakness of the hypothesis. It would be refuted only by a configuration H-XP in which any arbitrary term of XP could raise to Spec-H. But it seems that the raising of α from XP is always restricted to some category of constituents of XP, hence some feature F of α (or complex of features) that matches OCC. The (nontrivial) question then reduces to what F is.[2]

It also follows that external Merge does not suffice to check OCC. The only relevant case is expletive EXPL. EXPL externally merged in Spec-T must delete the OCC-feature of T and lose its own uninterpretable features (if T is complete). The interesting case is a *there*-type EXPL lacking theta role. EXPL must have some feature [uF], or it could not be raised.[3] ·Suppose EXPL is a simple head, not formed by Merge. In a label-free system, EXPL is accessible without search as a probe and can match and agree with the goal T. If T is selected by C (hence complete), then [uF] is valued and disappears, and the derivation can converge. If T is defective, EXPL will await a higher complete probe (either C-T or *v*). Whatever probe values and deletes, [uF] must still seek a complete goal, to eliminate its own uninterpretable features: the normal case of *there* constructions with long-distance agreement. Suppose that EXPL has all φ-features, like French *il*. When merged in Spec-T, T complete, it can no longer raise: therefore, T must value and eliminate the φ-features of EXPL. But that can happen only if T finds a goal to value its own features – which, however, are overridden by the EXPL-T relation (possibly a reflection of the property of richness of morphological realization already mentioned). We conclude that such expletives must be simple heads and that there is an additional empirical argument in favor of Collins-style label-free phrase structure – noting that some problems remain unresolved, at least in any clean way.

Notes

1 The feature OCC means "I must be an occurrence of some β", taking an occurrence of β to be its sister.

2 One might seek to appeal to universal conditions C: α is allowed to raise only if it satisfies C. Even if this is possible, to show that Merge alone checks OCC, it would be necessary to show that C does not invoke head–head relations (as in standard formulations of MLC [Minimal Link Condition]). A technical question is how checking of the EPP-feature by internal Merge (Move) is effected by a head–head relation alone. Neither Agree nor (by assumption) Merge can check the feature, so it must be a property of Pied-piping, still in many ways a mysterious operation.

3 Perhaps, for example, structural Case, as proposed by Lasnik (1999: ch. 4).

Reference

Lasnik, H. 1999. *Minimalist analysis*. Malden, MA/Oxford: Blackwell.

8

Syntax/Semantics Interface

From "ECONOMY AND SCOPE"
Danny Fox

1 Introduction

In this paper I will provide evidence that the syntactic scope of quantifiers is affected by economy considerations. In particular, I will argue that altering this scope at LF incurs a cost which economy considerations seek to minimize.

There are basically two operations which have the determination (and the altering) of scope as their sole purpose. One is Quantifier Raising (QR); the other is Quantifier Lowering (QL). I will claim that these Scope Shifting Operations (SSOs) are restricted by economy considerations. What could be the content of such a claim? In general, economy considerations are believed to choose the most optimal derivation from a set of competitors (a "reference set"). It is also believed that optimality is achieved by reducing instances of moving or by minimizing their length. The content of the claim is, therefore, that minimizing SSOs, both in quantity and length, enters among the considerations that choose the optimal derivation from the reference set.

Here a highly controversial issue arises. How is the reference set constructed, and what are its members? This issue shows up in almost every approach to economy and, in fact, is central to the question of optimality in general (cf. Chomsky 1994; Grimshaw 1993; Pesetsky (in prep.), among others). This paper will argue that the reference set (at least the one relevant for SSOs) includes *only derivations that end up with the same semantic interpretation*. In this respect I follow Golan (1993) and Reinhart (1994), who have also argued for a semantic determination of the reference set.[1]

I will show that Economy seeks to reduce the cost associated with SSOs. More specifically, I will show that an instance of an SSO is blocked if there is a competing derivation in the reference set (i.e. a derivation that ends up with the same semantic interpretation) which involves a shorter SSO, or avoids it altogether. Put simply, an SSO can apply only if it yields a semantic interpretation which would be impossible without its application. In other words, SSOs are allowed only when necessary (as a last resort) for achieving a designated interpretation.

Following Chomsky (1994, 1995), I will assume that the reference set is constructed on the basis of an initial choice of lexical items to be used throughout the derivation (a Numeration). All the derivations in the reference set must be constructed with the use of all and only those lexical items in the Numeration. The paper will extend Chomsky's suggestion by assuming that the designated Numeration is accompanied by a designated interpretation as well.[2] In other words, under the assumptions made in this paper, all derivations in the reference set are going to use the same lexical items and end up with the same interpretation.[3]

To understand the nature of the claims that are going to be made in this paper, consider QR and its relevance for sentences such as those in (1) and in (2). These sentences differ in that in (1) the interpretations are different when the subject has scope over the object and when the scopal relation is reversed, whereas in (2) the interpretations under the two scopal relations are identical. I will try to show that sentences such as those in (2) differ from their counterparts in (1) in not allowing their objects to move by QR over the subject.

(1) a.   A boy loves every girl.
     b.   Many boys love every girl.
(2) a.   John loves every girl.
     b.   Every boy loves every girl.

To see how this follows from the version of Economy that is herein suggested, let us compare the effects of Economy on (1a) and (1a). Consider first (1a). As mentioned, this sentence will have different interpretations when the subject has scope over the object and when the scopal relation is reversed. Call these two interpretations M_S and M_O respectively. If the reference set is constructed with M_S as the designated interpretation, the optimal derivation will be the one ending with the LF in (1'a).[4,5] If the reference set is constructed with M_O as the designated interpretation, there will be no way of avoiding QR over the subject and the optimal derivation will be the one ending with the LF in (1'b). Because the results are not logically equivalent, the derivation without QR over the subject is not compared to the one involving this movement; both LFs in (1') are possible.

(1') a. $[_{IP}$ a boy$_1$ . . . $[_{VP}$ every girl$_2$ $[_{VP}$ t$_1$ loves t$_2]]]$
      b. $[_{IP}$ every girl$_2$ $[_{IP}$ a boy$_1$ . . . $[_{VP}$ t$_1$ loves t$_2]]]$

Consider now (2a). Contrary to (1a), this sentence will have the same interpretation under its two possible scopal relations. Call this interpretation M. Because every interpretable LF that might result from (2a) will have M as its interpretation, we need to consider only one reference set (the one constructed with M as the designated interpretation). This reference set includes (among others) the derivations resulting in the LFs in (2'). Economy considerations prefer (2'a) over (2'b), and the latter is blocked.

(2') a. $[_{IP}$ John$_1$ . . . $[_{VP}$ every girl$_2$ $[_{VP}$ t$_1$ loves t$_2$]]]
      b. *$[_{IP}$ every girl$_2$ $[_{IP}$ John$_1$ . . . $[_{VP}$ t$_1$ loves t$_2$]]]

The same claim is going to be made with respect to QL. In other words, it will be claimed that QL distinguishes between (3) and (4) in the same way that QR distinguishes between (1) and (2). In (3), QL will yield an interpretation which would be impossible without its application. The two derivations do not compete; they result in the two admissible LFs in (3'). In (4), by contrast, the derivations with and without QL result in logically equivalent LFs; they compete, and Economy blocks the LF in (4'b).[6]

(3) An American runner seems to Bill to have won a gold medal.

(4) John seems to Bill to have won a gold medal.

(3') a. An American runner$_1$ seems o Bill $[_{IP}$ t$_1$ to have won a gold medal]
      b. __ seems to Bill $[_{IP}$[an American runner] to have won a gold medal][7]

(4') a. John$_1$ seems to Bill $[_{IP}$ t$_1$ to have won a gold medal]
      b. *__ seems to Bill [[John] to have won a gold medal]

The nature of the claim being made ensures that simple evidence will not be found. The claim is that SSOs are blocked when their application doesn't have semantic effects. Evidence for the claim could, therefore, be found only if we had ways for deciding on the LF position of a quantifier in the cases in which semantics could not distinguish between the different possibilities. We need to utilize our knowledge about other mechanisms (besides the mechanisms that interpret LFs) that might be sensitive to the syntactic position of quantifiers. What could such mechanisms be? I can think of two possibilities.

The first possibility is that there are grammatical constraints which are sensitive to the LF position of syntactic elements. If such constraints exist, they could perhaps tell the location of a quantifier even when semantics fails to differentiate among the possibilities. In this paper I will utilize two constraints of this form. One constraint will be the widely discussed constraint on parallelism in ellipsis constructions, and the other will be the Coordinate Structure Constraint.

The second possibility is more complicated. Before going into it, I think it is important to understand that the ideas presented in this paper go against a prevailing assumption regarding the architecture of the grammar. According to this assumption, the workings of the computational system are not affected by the workings of later performance systems which interpret its outputs. In particular, the workings of the syntax are not affected by semantics – syntax is autonomous.[8] Here the claim is that syntax is *not* completely autonomous. The computational system that constructs the reference set sees certain aspects of interpretation. The question is, obviously, *to what extent* syntax is non-autonomous. That is, how much of interpretation is syntax capable of seeing?[9] [. . .]

It seems to me that the prevailing assumption regarding the autonomy of syntax is correct as a null hypothesis. Further, it seems to me that counterevidence of the type present does not motivate total abandonment of this null hypothesis. Rather, it will motivate a very local amendment. I will demonstrate that syntax must see the semantic effects of the relative scope of two quantifiers (the difference between (1) and (3), on the one hand, and (2) and (4), on the other). However, this will not motivate the claim that syntax can see everything having to do with the workings of later interpretative mechanisms.[10] In the absence of further evidence, the amendment of the autonomy hypothesis would be that syntax can see the semantic effects of quantifier scope (and perhaps other aspects of compositional semantics which form a natural class with the interpretation of scope) but nothing else.

[. . .]

2   VP ellipsis

It is widely known that ellipsis sometimes disambiguates constructions involving multiple quantification. More specifically, a construction involving multiple quantification, which would normally show scopal ambiguity, sometimes loses this ambiguity when it serves as an antecedent for ellipsis.

Consider the fact exemplified in (5, 6). The standard scopal ambiguity in a sentence like (5) disappears when the sentence is the first conjunct of a VP ellipsis construction like (6). For (6) to be true, there must be a single boy who admires all of the teachers, whereas in (5) the boys can vary with the teachers.

(5)   Some boy admires every teacher.   (ambiguous)
(6)   Some boy admires every teacher and Mary does too.[11]   (unambiguous)

This phenomenon has already been noted by Sag (1976) and Williams (1977). However, as we will see, it has not yet received a satisfactory explanation.

Williams wanted the contrast in (5–6) to follow from a general constraint which bars the existence of free variables in syntax. His idea was that in order for the object to get wide scope in (5), it must QR over the subject, as represented in (7a). Such QR would be followed in (6) by LF reconstruction of the elided VP. This reconstruction, presented in (7b), would result in an unbound variable in the second conjunct, t', and would thus be ruled out. The only way to reconstruct the elided VP in (6) without violating the ban on free variables is by adjoining the quantifier to VP, as demonstrated in (7c). The resulting structure allows only narrow scope interpretation for the object of the first conjunct in (6), and the contrast is thus explained.

(7)   a.   [$_{IP}$ every teacher [$_{IP}$ some boy [$_{VP}$ admires t]]]
       b.   *[$_{IP}$ every teacher [$_{IP}$ some boy [$_{VP}$ admires t]]] and Mary [$_{VP}$ admires t']
       c.   [$_{IP}$ some boy [$_{VP}$ every teacher [$_{VP}$ admires t]]] and Mary [$_{VP}$ every teacher [$_{VP}$ admires t]]

[. . .]

There are strong empirical reasons for abandoning this explanation. The crucial feature of this explanation is that it is based on a theory of ellipsis whereby moving the object over the subject in (6) yields a VP that cannot be reconstructed. If this account is right, scopal ambiguities should always disappear in VP ellipsis constructions. Hirschbühler (1982) showed that this consequence is false. Despite ellipsis, the sentences in (8) allow the object to have wide scope with respect to the subject.

(8) a. A Canadian flag is in front of every building and an American flag is too.
     b. One guard is standing in front of every building and one policeman is too.
     c. Some boy admires every teacher and some girl does too.

As noted by Hirschbühler, the sentences in (8) cannot be analyzed as involving across-the-board scope, an analysis that, under a certain set of assumptions, could perhaps salvage the original approach to (5).[12] In other words, it is impossible to claim that the object quantifier in the first conjunct has scope over both the conjuncts, with an interpretation paraphrasable (in the case of (8a)) as *For every building, it is the case that there is a Canadian flag in front of it and an American flag in front of it too*. This is demonstrated by the sentences in (9). (9a) can be true when there is no building which has both an American and a Canadian flag on it, as long as there are two sufficiently large subsets of buildings (one with a Canadian flag on each of its members and one with an American flag). For this truth to hold, the LF of (9a) must be something like $(9'a_1)$ and not like $(9'a_2)$. The same can be shown for (9b), though it requires considering a more complicated situation (see Hirschbühler 1982).

(9) a. A Canadian flag is in front of many buildings and an American flag is too.
     b. A Canadian flag is in front of most buildings and an American flag is too.

$(9')$ a_1. many buildings$_1$ [a Canadian flag is [$_{VP}$ in front of t_1]] and many buildings$_2$ [an American flag is [$_{VP}$ in front of t_2]]

        a_2. *many buildings$_1$ [a Canadian flag is [$_{VP}$ in front of t_1]] and [an American flag is [$_{VP}$ in front of t_1]]

We therefore confront a puzzle: what is the difference between (6) and (8)? Why can't (6) have wide scope for the object quantifier while (8) can? In other words, why is (6′) an impossible LF for (6), and (8′) a possible LF for (8)?

(6′) *every teacher$_1$ [some boy admires t_1] and
      every teacher$_2$ [Mary admires t_2]

(8′) every teacher$_1$ [some boy admires t_1] and
      every teacher$_2$ [some girl admires t_2]

Previous attempts to deal with this puzzle (e.g. Cormack 1984 and Diesing 1992) assumed that the relevant difference between (6) and (8) has to do with the grammatical properties of the subject of the second conjunct. In (6) the subject of the second conjunct is a referring expression. In (8), by contrast, the subject is a quantifier.

However, this assumption is wrong. Although the relevant difference does concern properties of the second conjunct, it is not determined by the properties of the subject alone. Rather, as we shall see, it relates to a semantic property of the conjunct as a whole. I will argue that the crucial difference concerns the fact that in (6) the second conjunct, *Mary admires every teacher*, does not display any semantically relevant scope ambiguity, whereas its counterpart in (8c), *some girl admires every teacher*, does. In other words, the truth conditions of *Mary admires every teacher* are the same whether *Mary* has wide scope with respect to *every teacher* or vice versa. In contrast, the two possible scopal relations yield different truth conditions for *some girl admires every teacher*.

2.1 The Ellipsis Scope Generalization

Here we will see that the relevant difference between (6) and (8) has to do with whether or not the second conjunct is semantically ambiguous. In other words, we will see that the correct generalization is the following:

(10) *Ellipsis Scope Generalization (ESG)*: The relative scope of two quantifiers, one of which is in an antecedent VP of an ellipsis construction, may differ from the surface c-command relation only if the parallel difference will have semantic effects in the elided VP.

The ESG states that a second conjunct disambiguates the first conjunct (in constructions such as (6) and (8) above) if and only if it is itself semantically unambiguous. To see that this is the correct generalization, we will go over the paradigm in (11–18) below. This paradigm is constructed by minimally varying the semantic properties of the second conjunct. Scopal ambiguity is once more possible in the first conjunct only when a similar ambiguity is possible in the second conjunct.

In the (a) sentences of (11–12) the first conjuncts are unambiguous, because the second conjuncts – *the organizer of the film festival admires every movie* in (11a) and *the principal knows the capital of every country* in (12a) – have the same meaning under both scopal relations.

(11) a. One of the film reviewers admires every movie, and the organizer of the film festival does too.   (unambiguous)

   b. One of the film reviewers admires every movie, and the director/the audience does too.   (ambiguous)

(12) a. One student (in the school) knows the capital of every country, and the principal (of the school) does too.   (unambiguous)

   b. One student knows the capital of every country, and the prime minister (of that country) does too.   (ambiguous)

The second conjuncts of the (b) sentences, by contrast, have different truth conditions under the two scopal relations. To see this, consider the second conjunct of (11b). Under one scopal relation (subject wide scope) the sentence can be true only if there is a single director who admires all of the movies. Under the other scopal relation (object wide scope) the directors can vary with respect to the movie.[13] Because of the ambiguity of the second conjunct, the first conjunct can be ambiguous as well.[14]

It is important to point out that there is probably a syntactic difference between the subjects of the second conjuncts in the (a) and the (b) sentences in (11–12). The difference is that in the (b) sentences the subjects of the second conjuncts can contain an implicit variable, which can get bound by a quantifier. One might suggest that this difference be utilized for an account in the spirit of Diesing and Cormack. However, that would be the wrong way to go. First, consider (13) below. In this sentence there is an implicit variable within the subject of the second conjunct. Nevertheless, the second conjunct still disambiguates the first conjunct. The reason is that the variable in the subject of the second conjunct cannot be bound by the object quantifier. For this reason, there is no ambiguity in the second conjunct, and the first conjunct is unambiguous as well.[15]

(13)   At each festival, one of the film reviewers praised every movie and the organizer did too.

Consider now (14) below. In this sentence the subject of the second conjunct is a bona fide quantifier. Nonetheless, contrary to Diesing and to Cormack, the first conjunct is unambiguous. The reason for the lack of ambiguity is that the second conjunct, *every girl admires every teacher*, doesn't show a parallel ambiguity. (The relative scope of two universal quantifiers doesn't affect truth conditions.)[16]

(14)   Some boy admires every teacher, and every girl does too.   (unambiguous)

Now consider (15–16).

(15)   a.   One of the film critics admired every movie, and everyone at the film festival did too.   (unambiguous)
        b.   One of the film critics admired every movie, and everyone in the audience did too.   (ambiguous)
(16)   a.   One student (in the school) knows the capital of every country, and every teacher (in the school) does too.   (unambiguous)
        b.   One student knows the capital of every country, and every minister (in that country) does too.   (ambiguous)

The (a) sentences in (15–16) are just like (14) in that the second conjuncts involve two universal quantifiers and are thus not semantically ambiguous. The second conjuncts of the (b) sentences involve two universal quantifiers as well. However, in these cases wide scope for the object allows the domain of quantification of the subject universal quantifier to be determined by the elements that the object quantifies over. In other words, in (15b) wide scope for the object allows the audiences to vary with respect to the movies. Similarly, in (16b) wide scope for the object allows the ministers to vary with respect to the countries.[17] In both (15b) and (16b), there are semantic consequences to object wide scope in the second conjunct, and, thus, object wide scope is possible in the first conjunct as well.

The sentences in (17–18) differ minimally from (12) and from the (a) sentences in (15–16). The difference is that the semantic properties of the subject quantifier in the second conjuncts in (17–18) make the truth conditions different under the two different scopal relations.

(17) a. One of the film critics admired every movie, and almost everyone at the film festival did too. (ambiguous)
      b. One of the film critics admired every movie, and most visitors to the film festival did too. (ambiguous)
(18) a. One student (in the school) knows the capital of every country, and almost every teacher (in the school) does too. (ambiguous)
      b. One student knows the capital of every country, and most/many teachers do too. (ambiguous)

In the (a) sentences, the fact that we inserted the modifier *almost* into the second conjunct's subject allows for scopal ambiguity within this conjunct. When the subject in (17a), for example, has wide scope, the sentence can be true only if there is a set of people in the film festival that is sufficient in cardinality to be considered 'almost everyone', and if each member of this set admires all of the movies. However, when the object of (17a) has wide scope, the sentence can be true also when the set of admiring people varies with respect to the movies. In other words, the sentence can be true even when there is no single sufficiently large set of people that admires all of the movies. All that is required is that for each movie there be a sufficiently large set of admirers. The second conjunct is thus semantically ambiguous, and therefore allows for the first conjunct to be ambiguous as well. The other sentences in (17–18) are parallel to (17a), and again the first conjunct can be ambiguous.

To summarize, (11–18) demonstrate that the first conjunct of a VP ellipsis construction can show a scopal ambiguity only if the second conjunct can show a parallel ambiguity. To make this point clear, below I list the second conjuncts that disambiguate the first conjunct in (A) and those that do not in (B). The difference is that in (A) wide scope for the object does not affect truth conditions, while in (B) it does.

(A) a. Mary likes every teacher. (unambiguous)
     b. The organizer of the film festival praised every movie. (unambiguous)
     c. Everyone in the film festival enjoyed every movie. (unambiguous)
(B) a. Some girl likes every teacher. (ambiguous)
     b. The audience/the director admires every movie. (ambiguous)
     c. Everyone in the audience admires every movie. (ambiguous)

    d.   Almost everyone at the film festival admires every movie. (ambiguous)

    e.   Most visitors to the film festival admire every movie. (ambiguous)

    f.   An American flag is in front of many buildings. (ambiguous)

2.2 Explaining the ESG

The paradigm in (11–18) demonstrated the correctness of the ESG, which is repeated in (19).

(19)   *Ellipsis Scope Generalization (ESG)*: The relative scope of two quantifiers, one of which is in an antecedent VP of an ellipsis construction, may differ from the surface c-command relation only if the parallel difference will have semantic effects in the elided VP.

What are the principles from which the ESG follows? I would like to argue that this generalization has two parts. One part follows from a well-known constraint which requires parallelism between elided/reconstructed material and its antecedent (see, among many others, Tancredi 1992; Rooth 1992; Fiengo and May 1994). The other part follows from the principle of Economy outlined at the start of this paper. The two principles interact in the following way to yield the ESG. From Economy it follows that the object can move by QR over the subject only if the movement yields an interpretation which would be unavailable otherwise. From parallelism it follows that the object moves by QR over the subject in one of the conjuncts if and only if a parallel instance of QR applies in the other conjunct.[18] The ESG is derived from these two principles in the following way. If the second conjunct is ambiguous, Economy is not at stake, and the first conjunct can have both scopal interpretations as long as parallelism is maintained. If, on the other hand, the second conjunct is not ambiguous, then (*a*) Economy doesn't allow long QR in the second conjunct; therefore (*b*) parallelism doesn't allow long QR in the first conjunct; and consequently (*c*) the first conjunct cannot be ambiguous.[19]

Let us illustrate how Economy and parallelism interact to explain the ESG by a look at the way they affect (6) and (8). Consider first (8c) and its four conceivable LFs in (20). Since the two conjuncts are ambiguous, Economy allows QR in both. Parallelism rules out non-parallel QR; thus (c) and (d) are ill-formed.

(20) a.   some boy$_1$ [every teacher$_2$ [t$_1$ admires t$_2$]] and
           some girl$_1$ [every teacher$_2$ [t$_1$ admires t$_2$]]

      b.   every teacher$_2$ [some boy$_1$ [t$_1$ admires t$_2$]] and
           every teacher$_2$ [some girl$_1$ [t$_1$ admires t$_2$]]

      c.   *some boy$_1$ [every teacher$_2$ [t$_1$ admires t$_2$]] and
           every teacher$_2$ [some girl$_1$ [t$_1$ admires t$_2$]]

      d.   *every teacher$_2$ [some boy$_1$ [t$_1$ admires t$_2$]] and
           some girl$_1$ [every teacher$_2$ [t$_1$ admires t$_2$]]

Consider now (6) and its four potential LFs in (21). Parallelism rules out the non-parallel scopal relations (c, d) just as it did in (20). At the same time, Economy disallows QR of the object over the subject in the second (unambiguous) conjunct, thus ruling out (21b).

(21)   a.   some boy$_1$ [every teacher$_2$ [t$_1$ admires t$_2$]] and
            Mary$_1$ [every teacher$_2$ [t$_1$ admires t$_2$]]
       b.   *every teacher$_2$ [some boy$_1$ [t$_1$ admires t$_2$]] and
            every teacher$_2$ [Mary$_1$ [t$_1$ admires t$_2$]]
       c.   *some boy$_1$ [every teacher$_2$ [t$_1$ admires t$_2$]] and
            every teacher$_2$ [Mary$_1$ [t$_1$ admires t$_2$]]
       d.   *every teacher$_2$ [some boy$_1$ [t$_1$ admires t$_2$]] and
            Mary$_1$ [every teacher$_2$ [t$_1$ admires t$_2$]]

The ESG provides strong evidence that QR is restricted by the particular consideration of Economy outlined in the beginning of this paper. The evidence is strong because parallelism is needed independently of the ESG, and because Economy is exactly what is needed to fill in the gap between the effects of parallelism and an account of the ESG (i.e. to rule out LFs such as (21b)).

Let me conclude this subsection with a short discussion of pseudo-gapping and the way it further supports the explanation I provide for the ESG.[20] Pseudo-gapping is a construction similar to VP ellipsis in its compliance with parallelism. In that respect pseudo-gapping can serve the same role that ellipsis did in the argument that QR is allowed only when it yields a semantically significant scopal relation. However, pseudo-gapping is also different from VP ellipsis (and superficially similar to gapping) in that part of the VP is not elided.[21] This property of pseudo-gapping is important for our purposes because it allows us to vary the semantic properties of a sentence (which must comply with parallelism) while keeping its subject constant.[22] Such an experiment can give the final blow to the possibility that the difference between the ambiguous and unambiguous sentences in ellipsis is solely related to properties of the subject in the second conjunct.

Consider the instance of pseudo-gapping in (22a) below. In this sentence there is ambiguity in both the first and the second conjunct. The sentence thus conforms to the ESG. It also exemplifies the fact that pseudo-gapping obeys parallelism. In this sentence there must be parallelism between the two conjuncts with respect to the relative scope of the two quantifiers. If the sentence allows the boys to vary with respect to the professors, it must also allow the girls to vary with respect to the parents. Similarly, if variance is disallowed for the boys, it is also disallowed for the girls.

(22)   a.   A boy was introduced to every professor and a girl was to every parent.
            (ambiguous)
       b.   A boy was introduced to every professor and a girl was to Jane.
            (unambiguous)
       c.   A boy was introduced to every professor and a girl was to some parent.
            (unambiguous)

Consider now (22b) and (22c). In both cases the subject must have wide scope over the object. The reason should by now be clear. In both sentences the second

conjunct is unambiguous (*a girl was introduced to Jane* in (22b) and *a girl was introduced to some parent* in (22c)). Thus, according to the ESG, the first conjunct
cannot be ambiguous either. These examples are important because they show
decisively that the relevant difference between (6) and (8) cannot be traced to properties of the subject of the second conjunct. All of the sentences in (22) have the
same subject, and yet some group with (6) and some with (8).
    [. . .]

2.4   Quantifier Lowering

In the previous section we have seen evidence from VP ellipsis that Quantifier
Raising is restricted by economy considerations and is allowed only when it yields
an interpretation which would be unavailable otherwise. In this section we will see
that the same holds for Quantifier Lowering.[23]

Consider the sentence in (23). This sentence is ambiguous with respect to the
relative scope of the subject quantifier and of the attitude verb *seems*. If the subject quantifier has wide scope, the sentence can be true only if Bill has some American
runner in mind, and only if it seems to Bill that that particular American runner
won a gold medal. If the attitude verb has wide scope, the sentence merely requires
that Bill have the belief that some American runner or other won a gold medal.
Bill need not have any particular American runner in mind. The sentence would
be true in a situation in which Bill sits in the Olympic cafeteria, hears the American
anthem and concludes that an American runner won the medal.

(23)   An American runner seems to Bill to have won a gold medal.

The two readings of (23) are the result of the two positions in which the subject
can be interpreted. If the subject is interpreted in its S-structure position, it
has wide scope with respect to the attitude verb. However, if it is lowered to the
embedded IP at LF, the attitude verb has wide scope. (See, among others, May
1985 and Diesing 1992; see also notes 6 and 7.) The two LFs for (23) are thus
represented in (24).

(24)   a.   An American runner$_1$ seems to Bill [t$_1$ to have won a gold medal].
       b.   __ seems to Bill [[an American runner] to have won a gold medal].

Consider now what happens if we embed (23) in a VP ellipsis construction such
as (25). (25) is ambiguous, just as (23) is. However, since parallelism must be maintained, the relative scope of the subject and the attitude verb must be the same in
the two conjuncts. Bill could know the identity of the Russian and the American
runner, or alternatively he could be sitting in the cafeteria hearing the consecut-
ive playing of the two anthems. What is important, however, is that if Bill is required
to know the identity of the American runner, he must also know the identity of
his Russian colleague and vice versa. (26a, b) are possible LFs for (25), while (26c,
d) are not.

(25) An American runner seems to Bill to have won a gold medal and a Russian athlete does too.   (ambiguous, with parallelism)

(26) a.   An American runner₁   seems to Bill
                       [t₁ to have won a gold medal] and
             a Russian athlete₁   seems to Bill
                       [t₁ to have won a gold medal]

      b.   __ seems to Bill [[an American runner] to have won a gold medal] and
           __ seems to Bill [[a Russian athlete] to have won a gold medal]

      c.   *An American runner₁ seems to Bill [t₁ to have won a gold medal] and
           __ seems to Bill [[a Russian athlete] to have won a gold medal]

      d.   * __ seems to Bill [[an American runner] to have won a gold medal] and
           a Russian athlete₁ seems to Bill [t₁ to have won a gold medal]

Consider now (27). This sentence, contrary to (25), is not ambiguous. For it to be true, Bill must know the identity of the American runner.

(27) a.   An American runner seems to Bill to have won a gold medal and Sergey does too.   (unambiguous)

This follows naturally from the assumption that QL is restricted by Economy considerations. If QL, just like QR, is a costly operation, it can apply in a structure only if it has semantic consequences. Since in a sentence such as (28) the meaning remains the same whether or not QL takes place, QL is impossible. For the same reason QL cannot apply to the second conjunct in (27), and because of parallelism it cannot apply to the first conjunct. (29c, d) are ruled out by parallelism, and (29b) is ruled out by Economy.

(28) Sergey seems to Bill to have won a gold medal.

(29) a.   An American runner₁   seems to Bill
                       [t₁ to have won a gold medal] and
             Sergey₁   seems to Bill
                       [t₁ to have won a gold medal]

      b.   __ seems to Bill [[an American runner] to have won a gold medal] and
           __ seems to Bill [[Sergey] to have won a gold medal]

      c.   *An American runner₁ seems to Bill [t₁ to have won a gold medal] and
           __ seems to Bill [[a Russian athlete] to have won a gold medal]

      d.   * __ seems to Bill [[an American runner] to have won a gold medal] and
           Sergey₁ seems to Bill [t₁ to have won a gold medal]

Notes

1   To the best of my knowledge, the idea that Economy should compare only derivations that end up semantically equivalent was first presented in Golan (1993). Golan shows that a semantically sensitive economy principle has the potential of solving a certain puzzle for superiority noted by Lasnik and Saito (1992). Space limitations don't permit me to go over

the analysis. Reinhart (1994, 1995a, 1995b) embeds Golan's idea within a global view of the architecture of the grammar and suggests extensions in a variety of domains. Independently, she has suggested an extension of Golan's idea to QR along the lines presented here (drawing on certain observations about Weak Crossover (WCO) which she attributes to Eddy Ruys). For further extensions to the ideas presented here, see Fox (forthcoming) and Fox and Percus (in prep.). For a somewhat different idea about the way QR might interact with Economy, see Cresti (1995).

2   There has been a long and difficult debate in both the linguistic and the philosophical literature regarding the ontological status of the interpretations that are assigned to sentences. I will not take a position on this matter. For the purposes of this paper, it is enough to assume what is accepted by almost all participants in the debate, namely that sentences are interpreted, and that the interpretations consist, somehow, of instructions for the performance systems that interact with the language faculty. When I say that two LF structures have the same interpretation, I mean that they provide identical instructions to the performance systems that (immediately) interact with the computational system. Because we don't know in advance what these performance systems are like, we can't be certain when two LF structures have the same interpretation. For now I will assume that interpretations are identical when they are logically equivalent. Later on, this view will be modified (see notes 8 and 9). For expository purposes, I will sometimes adopt the terminology of a truth-theoretic semantics and use 'interpretation' and 'truth conditions' interchangeably.

3   The reference set cannot be defined only by reference to an interpretation, for reasons that have been stressed by Chomsky on many occasions. A sentence such as *A knife was used by John to slice the salami* should not be blocked by a sentence such as *John sliced the salami with a knife*. The reference set for Economy must be limited in some way so as to include only derivations with a similar choice of lexical items. The claim made in this paper is that the reference set should be further restricted so as to include, from the set of derivations with a similar choice of lexical items, only the subset of those which end up having the same semantic interpretation.

4   In the LFs I suggest, I assume that a quantifier must be above VP at LF. Assuming the VP-internal subject hypothesis and a semantic theory whereby a quantifier is a second order predicate (type $\langle\langle e, t\rangle, t\rangle$), this is the lowest position where a quantifier can be interpreted (see Heim and Kratzer 1994). However, as pointed out to me by Tanya Reinhart, the claims made in this paper are consistent with the assumption that quantifiers can remain in situ and move only when they have wide scope with respect to a S-structure c-commanding quantifier. For some discussion, see Reinhart (1995a).

5   If one adopts an Agr theory of case, then the object would be interpretable in Spec of Agr-O, and there would be no motivation for QR when M_s is the designated interpretation. Adopting such a theory would result in something similar to the proposal made by Reinhart (see note 4) in that a scope shifting operation would be needed only when the LF scopal relation is the reverse of the S-structure c-command relation (but see note 23).

6   Given a copy theory of movement, there is a possibility that the narrow scope for the subject in (3) is not the result of QL. It is possible that this narrow scope reading is achieved by interpreting the subject in the position of the trace (cf. Hornstein 1994 and Pica and Snyder 1994, among others). However, it is still possible that QL is involved. In fact, arguments against reconstruction and in favor of a lowering operation adjoining the quantifier to IP are presented in Chomsky (1995: ch. 4, sec. 7.4). In this paper, I will assume QL. One might claim that my arguments that the narrow scope reading is preferred by Economy support QL. That Economy should disprefer movement seems obvious. That it should have preferences with respect to the possible positions for the interpretation of a moved constituent seems less obvious. Of course, it is not impossible. In Chomsky (1993) it was stipulated that in A'-chains there is a preference to minimize restrictors. For A-movement it is possible to make the opposition stipulation.

7   The graphics I use might suggest that QL is an operation that restores a quantifier to its trace position. However, this is just an artifact of notation. The claims I make about QL are independent of its specific landing site. As far as I am concerned, QL could restore a quantifier to its trace position. However, it could also involve adjunction to a position that c-commands the trace (see Chomsky 1995: ch. 4, sec. 7.4).

8   The term "autonomy of syntax" has been used over the years in two different (and in fact unrelated) ways. Under one usage, the autonomy thesis is a methodological claim about the way one should go about constructing a theory of the computational system. According to this thesis, one should only consult evidence that relates to the acceptability of sentences, not to their interpretation. As far as I can tell, no one has ever argued in favor of this thesis, only against it. (For some discussion, see Chomsky 1979.) Under the other usage, the autonomy thesis is a working hypothesis about the organization of the grammar. According to this hypothesis, the computational system is modular in a sense somewhat akin to that of Fodor (1983). In particular, it is assumed that information which is the result of the workings of different interpretive systems is unavailable to the computational system. The discussion of autonomy in the text is related to the organization of the grammar and is completely unrelated to the methodological question.

9   Work in semantics sometimes assumes a predetermined division of labor among interpretive systems. Thus, for example, many assume a distinction between semantics and pragmatics (which relates, though is not completely identical, to the distinction made in the philosophical literature, e.g. by Pierce and Carnap). Under this distinction, semantics is the study of formal features of interpretation, which can be captured (among many other ways) by a truth theory. Pragmatics is (more or less) everything else. It seems to me that this assumption is a reasonable working hypothesis. But, like any working hypothesis, it should not be treated as a given reality. It seems to me that a discovery of certain aspects of "truth-conditional" semantics which are visible to the computational system should be viewed as an opportunity to replace the working hypothesis with more intricate claims about the internal structure of interpretive mechanisms. This approach is perhaps controversial. Thus Hintikka (1977), who suggested that certain aspects of interpretation might be relevant for the working of the computational system (the licensing of negative polarity items), concluded that all aspects of interpretation are relevant, and that, therefore, certain problems of undecidability arise. (See Chomsky 1979 for some discussion.)

10 For some methodological discussion, see Fox and Percus (1994).

11 Almost all of the points about ellipsis which are made in this paper could be carried over to constructions involving phonological deaccenting. See note 22.

12 This observation also argues against the analysis proposed by Hirschbühler, who acknowledged it as an unsolved problem.

13 I will not go into the syntax and semantics of the definite description in (11b) and (12b) that allows for this reading. It is probably the case that the nominal predicates *director* and *prime minister* contain a variable that can be determined by context. For some discussion, see Partee (1989). As pointed out by Kai von Fintel (pers. comm.), the contrast between the (a) and the (b) sentences of (11) and (12) probably indicates that if the implicit variable obeys Weak Crossover [WCO], violations of WCO must be weaker than violations of both Parallelism and Economy (see the explanation in subsection 2.2). See Partee (1989) for a discussion of the fact that violations of WCO are weaker with implicit variables than with overt ones.

14 The status of (11b) and (12b) raises some interesting questions regarding the interaction of grammar and world knowledge. As pointed out to me by Noam Chomsky, the knowledge that the director or the audience, contrary to the organizer of the film festival, can be different for each choice of a movie is part of our knowledge of the world; it cannot be part of semantics. Here a problem might arise for the explanation I will provide in subsection 2.2. The potential problem is that for the semantic module, if there is one, there is no

difference between the case of *every movie* having wide scope over *the director* and the case of it having wide scope over *the organizer of the film festival*. As far as semantics is concerned, in both cases the wide scope is different from the narrow scope. In both cases, two different sets of instructions are given to the conceptual intentional system. Semantics cannot care about the fact that in the case of *the organizer of the film festival* the conceptual intentional system happens to treat the two sets in the same way.

I think that Chomsky's remark is very interesting. However, I think it doesn't really expose a problem for my proposal. Rather, it forces a more careful rephrasing. What I would like to suggest is that definite descriptions are ambiguous. They can include an empty variable that can be syntactically bound (in the sense of Partee 1989). However, such a variable is not obligatory. As is normal, by the time the definite description is interpreted by performance systems that access world knowledge, one of the options could be ruled out. If *the organizer of the film festival* in (11a) includes a variable which is to be syntactically bound, it is uninterpretable in the context that comes to mind. The reason is that there is no natural pairing between movies and organizers of film festivals. By contrast, a pairing between movies and directors is trivial. That is why *the director* in (11b) is interpretable with a syntactically bound variable. (This difference is probably the explanation for the contrast between *Every movie was admired by its director* and #*Every movie was admired by its film festival organizer*.) If *the organizer of the film festival* is inserted with a variable, QR is allowed. However, the DP is uninterpretable. If it is inserted without a variable, QR is not allowed. For *the director* both options exist. [. . .] I thank Noam Chomsky, Irene Heim, David Pesetsky, and Tanya Reinhart for discussion of this matter.

15　I thank an anonymous *NALS* reviewer for providing me with this fact.

16　I thank Kyle Johnson for suggesting this line of research.

17　In the (b) sentences of (15–16), just like in the (b) sentences of (11–12), there is probably a variable within the nominal predicate. (See note 13.)

18　For now I expect the reader to take a leap of faith and believe that this kind of parallelism is needed independently of the ESG. [. . .] Notice that all of the ambiguous cases we have seen are ambiguous with parallelism; the scopal relations between the different operators are always identical in the two conjuncts.

19　This analysis crucially assumes that QR in one conjunct can never be licensed in order to allow an interpretation of the other conjunct which would otherwise be impossible. [. . .]

20　I thank Martha McGinness for suggesting pseudo-gapping as a further test for the validity of the ESG.

21　It seems reasonable to claim that pseudo-gapping involves movement of material out of the VP, followed by VP ellipsis. For analyses along these lines, see Jayaseelan (1990) and Lasnik (1993).

22　Phonological down-stressing has the potential of serving the same role that pseudo-gapping does. If conjunctions involving phonological down-stressing in one of the conjuncts must obey parallelism (see Lasnik 1972; Chomsky and Lasnik 1993; Tancredi 1992), then the absence of full ellipsis could allow us to vary the lexical choices within the VP. However, I found that judgments with these constructions were difficult to obtain. Speakers couldn't provide judgments about scope while still insuring that they were down-stressing the VP.

23　Recent attempts to eliminate QR assume that all scopal ambiguities are achieved by quantifier reconstruction. Given a checking theory of case, objects move out of the VP independently of scope. Thus narrow scope for the subject can be achieved by reconstruction (cf. Hornstein 1994; Pica and Snyder 1994; Kitahara 1994). As they stand I see many problems with these approaches. One obvious problem is that they have to stipulate that all PPs move to a case position. Further, it is not clear how they would account for cases of ambiguity other than those involving two arguments of a verb. For example, it is not clear how they would deal with the scopal ambiguity of object quantifiers and heads such as modals, negation, and attitude verbs [. . .], or with cases of inverse linking. Yet another problem is that they cannot deal with certain cases in which scope is not clause-bound (see Kennedy 1995).

References

Chomsky, N. 1979. *Rules and representations*. New York: Columbia University Press.

Chomsky, N. 1993. A minimalist program for linguistic theory. In K. Hale and S. J. Keyser (eds.), *The view from Building 20: Essays in linguistics in honor of Sylvain Bromberger*, Cambridge, MA: MIT Press, pp. 1–52. [Reprinted in Chomsky (1995), *The Minimalist Program*, Cambridge, MA: MIT Press, pp. 167–217.]

Chomsky, N. 1994. *Bare phrase structure. MIT Occasional Papers in Linguistics 5*. Cambridge, MA: MITWPL. [Published in P. Kempchinsky (ed.) (1994), *Evolution and revolution in linguistic theory: Essays in honor of Carlos Otero*, Washington, DC: Georgetown University Press, pp. 51–109. Also published in G. Webelhuth (ed.) (1994), *Government and binding theory and the minimalist program*, Cambridge, MA: MIT Press, pp. 383–439.]

Chomsky, N. 1995. *The Minimalist Program*. Cambridge, MA: MIT Press.

Chomsky, N. and H. Lasnik. 1993. The theory of principles and parameters. In J. Jacobs, A. von Stechow, W. Sternefeld and T. Vennemann (eds.), *An international handbook of contemporary research*, Berlin/New York: Walter de Gruyter, pp. 506–69. [Reprinted in Chomsky (1995), *The Minimalist Program*, Cambridge, MA: MIT Press, pp. 13–127.]

Cormack, A. 1984. VP anaphora: Variables and scope. In F. Landman and F. Veltman (eds.), *Varieties of formal semantics*, Dordrecht: Foris, pp. 81–102.

Cresti, D. 1995. *Indefinite topics*. Doctoral dissertation, MIT.

Diesing, M. 1992. *Indefinites*. Cambridge, MA: MIT Press.

Fiengo, R. and R. May. 1994. *Indices and identity*. Cambridge, MA: MIT Press.

Fodor, J. A. 1983. *Modularity of mind*. Cambridge, MA: MIT Press.

Fox, D. Forthcoming. Condition C effects in ACD. [Published in R. Pensalfini and H. Ura (eds.) (1995), *Papers on minimalist syntax. MIT Working Papers in Linguistics 27*, Cambridge, MA: MITWPL, pp. 105–19.]

Fox, D. and O. Percus. 1994. On the autonomy of the computational system. Ms., MIT.

Fox, D. and O. Percus. In preparation. A note on existential constructions.

Golan, Y. 1993. Node crossing economy, superiority, and D-linking. Ms., Tel Aviv University.

Grimshaw, J. 1993. Minimal projections, heads, and optimality. [Revised version published as Projections, heads, and optimality, *Linguistic Inquiry* 28: 373–422, 1997.]

Heim, I. and A. Kratzer. 1994. Class notes.

Hintikka, J. 1977. Quantifiers in natural languages: Some logical problems. *Linguistics and Philosophy* 1: 153–72.

Hirschbühler, P. 1982. VP deletion and across-the-board quantifier scope. In J. Pustejovsky and P. Sells (eds.), *Proceedings of the 12th Annual Meeting of the North East Linguistic Society*, Amherst, MA: GSLA, pp. 132–39.

Hornstein, N. 1994. An argument for minimalism: The case of antecedent-constrained deletion. *Linguistic Inquiry* 25: 455–80.

Jayaseelan, K. A. 1990. Incomplete VP deletion and gapping. *Linguistic Analysis* 20: 64–81.

Kennedy, C. 1995. Antecedent-contained deletion and the syntax of quantification. Ms., University of California, Santa Cruz. [Published in *Linguistic Inquiry* 28: 662–88, 1997.]

Kitahara, H. 1994. Raising quantifiers without raising quantifier raising. Ms., Harvard University. [Published in W. Abraham, S. D. Epstein, H. Thráinsson and C. J.-W. Zwart (eds.) (1996), *Minimal ideas: Syntactic studies in the Minimalist framework*, Amsterdam: John Benjamins, pp. 189–98.]

Lasnik, H. 1972. *Analyses of negation in English*. Doctoral dissertation, MIT.

Lasnik, H. 1993. Lectures on minimalist syntax. *University of Connecticut Occasional Papers in Linguistics 1*. Cambridge, MA: MITWPL. [Reprinted in Lasnik (1999), *Minimalist analysis*, Malden, MA: Blackwell, pp. 25–73.]

Lasnik, H. and M. Saito. 1992. *Move α*. Cambridge, MA: MIT Press.

May, R. 1985. *Logical form*. Cambridge, MA: MIT Press.

Partee, B. H. 1989. Binding implicit variables in quantified contexts. In C. Wiltshire, B. Music and R. Graczyk (eds.), *Papers from Chicago Linguistic Society 25*, Chicago: Chicago Linguistic Society, pp. 342–65.

Pesetsky, D. In preparation. *Syntax at the edge: Optimality effects in sentence grammar*.

Pica, P. and W. Snyder. 1994. Weak crossover, scope, and agreement in a minimalist framework. [Published in R. Aranovich, W. Byrne, S. Preuss and M. Senturia (eds.) (1995), *Proceedings of the 13th West Coast Conference on Formal Linguistics*, Stanford: CSLI, pp. 334–49.]

Reinhart, T. 1994. Wh-in-situ in the framework of the Minimalist Program. *OTS Working Papers*. Utrecht University. [Published in *Natural Language Semantics* 6: 29–56, 1998.]

Reinhart, T. 1995a. Quantifier scope – How labor is divided between QR and choice functions. [Revised version published in *Linguistics and Philosophy* 20: 335–97, 1997.]

Reinhart, T. 1995b. Scrambling and focus. Ms., Utrecht University.

Rooth, M. 1992. Ellipsis redundancy and reduction redundancy. In S. Berman and A. Hestvik (eds.), *Proceedings of the Stuttgart Ellipsis Workshop. Arbeitspapiere des Sonderforschungsbereichs 340 Nr. 29*, Heidelberg: IBM Germany.

Sag, I. 1976. *Deletion and logical form*. Doctoral dissertation, MIT.

Tancredi, C. 1992. *Deletion, deaccenting and presupposition*. Doctoral dissertation, MIT.

Williams, E. 1977. Discourse and logical form. *Linguistic Inquiry* 8: 101–39.

From "RECONSTRUCTION, BINDING THEORY, AND THE INTERPRETATION OF CHAINS"
Danny Fox

5 Where Does Binding Theory Apply

[. . .]

What I would like to claim now is that binding theory, or at least Condition C, applies *only* at LF. My argument will have two steps familiar from Chomsky (1993). The first step – which was actually already taken by Chomsky and in which I will basically, follow his assumptions (though perhaps not the mode of his implementation) – argues that, contrary to initial appearances, there is a coherent story to be told in which binding theory applies only at LF. The second step argues that the alternative, in which binding theory (and specifically Condition C) also applies at other levels of representation, is empirically inferior. This second step is based on Fox (1995a).[1]

5.1 The first step of the argument (Chomsky 1993)

Let us begin by reviewing the evidence that is taken to show that Condition C applies at S-Structure. Consider the contrast between (1) and (2). Under certain assumptions about the nature of covert QR [Quantifier Raising] (Chomsky 1977;

May 1977, 1985), the LF structures of the sentences in (1) are those in (3). With respect to Condition C, these structures are identical to the S-Structure representations in (2). If Condition C applied only at LF, there would be no obvious way of accounting for the contrast. If it applied at S-Structure as well, the contrast would follow straightforwardly.[2]

(1)   a.   */??You bought him$_1$ every picture that John$_1$ liked.
      b.   *He$_1$ bought you every picture that John$_1$ liked.
(2)   a.   [[Which picture that John$_1$ liked] [did you buy him$_1$ t]]?
      b.   [[Which picture that John$_1$ liked] [did he$_1$ buy you t]]?
(3)   a.   [[Every picture that John$_1$ liked] [I bought him$_1$ t]].
      b.   [[Every picture that John$_1$ liked] [he$_1$ bought you t]].

5.1.1 Chomsky's proposal

Chomsky (1993), however, provides a way of accounting for the contrast without the assumption that Condition C applies at S-Structure. In particular, he suggests that Ā-movement always leaves a copy and that this copy (under certain circumstances) yields a Condition C effect, even if Condition C applies only to the output of movement. In (1) the true output of QR is quite different from (3). Specifically, it still has a copy of the moved constituent at the position of the trace, and it is the r-expression within this copy that yields the violation of Condition C. In (2), Chomsky claims (following Lebeaux 1988), Ā-movement applies prior to the insertion of the relative clause that contains the r-expression. Therefore, in (2) the copy of the moved constituent does not yield a Condition C effect. The difference between overt and covert movement under this proposal is related not to their respective ordering relative to binding theory but to their respective ordering relative to lexical insertion.[3] Covert movement is never followed by lexical insertion and therefore never appears to circumvent a Condition C violation.

As it turns out, certain cases of overt movement are similar to the case of covert movement in that they are unable to circumvent a Condition C violation. These cases are demonstrated by Lebeaux's (1988) contrast between (4a) and (4b).

(4)   a.   [Which argument *that John made*]
                 did he believe t?
      b.   ??/*[Which argument *that John is a genius*]
                 did he believe t?

Chomsky accounts for this contrast on the basis of a distinction between the timing of adjunct insertion and the timing of complement insertion, which he also borrows from Lebeaux. According to this distinction, complements, in contrast to adjuncts, must be inserted prior to movement (in accordance with the extension/projection principle). From this it follows that complements, such as the italicized phrase in (4b), in contrast to adjuncts, such as the relative clause in (4a), cannot obviate Condition C via overt Ā-movement.[4]

It turns out that overt Ā-movement of certain phrases (phrases that contain complements and no adjuncts) is identical to covert movement with respect to Condition C. This weakens the argument from (1) and (2) that Condition C makes an overt/covert distinction. Nevertheless, this provides only the first stage of the argument that Condition C applies only at LF. It is still *possible* to account for all the data under the assumption that Condition C applies both at S-Structure and at LF (see Lebeaux 1988, 1994). In the remainder of this section, I would like to present the argument from Fox (1995a) that Condition C must apply only at LF. The argument is based on an observation by Fiengo and May (1994) that certain cases of covert movement do in fact obviate Condition C. This observation cannot be accounted for under the assumption that Condition C applies at S-Structure.

5.1.2   The interpretation of Ā-chains: a slight modification

The discussion thus far has not spelled out the nature of the structures that are interpreted. As noted by Chomsky (1993), interpreting an operator-variable construction probably requires some alterations of the copies created by movement. In particular, Chomsky suggests that the output of movement in structures such as (5), which is fully represented in (6), undergoes a later process that forms one of the structures in (7).

(5)   Which book did Mary read t?
(6)   which book did Mary read which book
(7)   a.   which book$_x$ did Mary read x
      b.   which$_x$ did Mary read book x[5]

Further, he stipulates that the structure in (7b) is preferred to the structure in (7a), thus accounting for the Condition C violation in (4b). I will basically follow this assumption, but will modify the implementation slightly. This modification will make the interpretation of the QRed structures more straightforward and will perhaps allow the stipulation to follow from general principles of economy. Under the modification, the two structures are those in (8).

(8)   a.   which book$_x$ did Mary read x *(ruled out by economy)*
      b.   which book$_x$ did Mary read book x

(8a) is interpreted standardly. For (8b), something novel needs to be proposed. Various possibilities come to mind. For concreteness, I follow a suggestion made by Sauerland (in progress). (See also Rullmann and Beck 1998.) According to this possibility, *book x* is interpreted as a definite description, *the book identical to x*, yielding an interpretation paraphrasable as *which is the book, x, such that Mary read the book identical to x*.[6] The specifics of this proposal are not crucial for present purposes. What is crucial is that there is a not implausible semantic method for interpreting (8b). Assuming this method is secure, we can conclude that general principles of economy prefer (8b) to (8a) since the former is closer to (6). In other words, (8b) involves fewer operations (of deletion) on (6) and is thus preferred.[7]

For QR, similar issues arise. A sentence such as (9) has (10) as the output of QR, which can in turn be converted to one of the structures in (11).[8] Economy principles determine that the interpreted structure is (11b).[9]

(9) John$_1$ [$_{VP}$ t$_1$ likes every boy].
(10) John$_1$ [every boy [$_{VP}$ t$_1$ likes every boy]]
(11) a. *John$_1$ [every boy$_x$ [$_{VP}$ t$_1$ likes x]] *(ruled out by economy)*
     b.   John$_1$ [every boy$_x$ [$_{VP}$ t$_1$ likes boy x]]

The inability of QR to obviate Condition C is explained in the same way as the inability of overt *wh*-movement to do so. The explanation is based on an economy principle that prefers structures in which the restrictor of the quantifier is not eliminated from the base position.

5.2   The second step of the argument (Fox 1995a)

With this much in hand, we can proceed to the argument that Condition C must apply only at LF. The logic of the argument is based on the nature of economy principles. These principles choose an object from a set of competitors (a reference set). If, under certain circumstances, the reference set is restricted so as not to include the most optimal object, it is predicted that an otherwise unacceptable object will be licensed. In the present case it is predicted that (11a) will be licensed under circumstances in which (11b) is not a member of the reference set. Under such circumstances, QR should obviate Condition C effects. The question is whether such circumstances exist.

In Fox (1995a) I suggest that they do. In particular, I suggest that in cases involving antecedent-contained deletion (ACD), the counterpart of (11b) is not licensed and the counterpart of (11a) is the only element in the reference set and hence is acceptable. As is well known, QR is needed in ACD constructions in order for VP-deletion to be licensed (e.g. Sag 1976; May 1985; Kennedy 1997). However, the problem of ACD is solved only if the restrictor is eliminated from the base position. For illustration, take (12) and suppose a theory of VP-ellipsis that involves PF deletion (of the material in angle brackets) licensed by LF Parallelism. If (14a) were the interpreted structure, all would be well; the antecedent VP (in square brackets) would be identical (up to alphabetical variance) to the elided VP. If, however, (14b) were the chosen structure, Parallelism would not be obeyed; the antecedent VP would still contain a copy of the elided VP.[10] For this reason, it is plausible to assume that (14a) is the only element in the reference set and is therefore licensed.[11]

(12) John$_1$
         [$_{VP}$ t$_1$ likes every boy Mary does ⟨likes t⟩]
(13) John$_1$
         [every boy Mary does ⟨likes t⟩ [$_{VP}$ t$_1$ likes every boy Mary does ⟨likes t⟩]]

(14) a.   John₁ [every boy Mary does ⟨likes *x*⟩]ₓ
            [_vp t₁ likes *x*]

      b.   *John₁ [every boy Mary does ⟨likes *x*⟩]ₓ
            [_vp t₁ likes *x* boy Mary ⟨likes *x*⟩]
            (does not obey Parallelism)

Given these considerations, we predict that QR in ACD constructions will obviate Condition C. In fact, this seems to be the case, as noted by Fiengo and May (1994).[12] Consider the contrast between (15) and (16). The sentences in (15) end up with the logical forms in (17), which violate Condition C. The sentences in (16), however, involve ACD and thus end up with the logical forms in (18), which do not violate Condition C.

(15) a.   ??/*You sent him₁ the letter that John₁ expected you would write.
      b.   ??/*You introduced him₁ to everyone John₁ wanted you to meet.
      c.   ??/*You reported him₁ to every cop that John₁ was afraid of.
(16) a.   You sent him₁ the letter that John₁ expected you would.
      b.   You introduced him₁ to everyone John₁ wanted you to.[13]
      c.   You reported him₁ to every cop that John₁ was afraid you would.
(17) a.   you [the letter that John₁ expected you would write]ₓ
            [sent him₁ *x* letter that John₁ expected you would write]
      b.   you [everyone that John₁ wanted you to meet]ₓ
            [introduced him₁ to *x* one that John₁ wanted you to meet]
      c.   you [every cop that John₁ was afraid of]ₓ
            [reported him₁ to *x* cop that John₁ was afraid of]
(18) a.   you [the letter that John₁ expected you would ⟨send him *x*⟩]ₓ
            [sent him₁ *x*]
      b.   you [everyone that John₁ wanted you to ⟨introduce him to *x*⟩]ₓ
            [introduced him₁ to *x*]
      c.   you [everyone that John₁ was afraid you would ⟨report him to *x*⟩]ₓ
            [reported him₁ to *x*]

This line of reasoning makes many additional predictions. To see the nature of these predictions, we must examine the analysis of ambiguous ACD constructions such as (19). This construction is ambiguous with respect to the size of the VP that has been elided (with the two options specified in (19a) and (19b)).

(19) I expected John₁ to buy everything that he₁ thought I did.
      a.   ⟨bought⟩
      b.   ⟨expected him to buy⟩

In addition, there is a potential ambiguity with respect to the relative scope of the universal quantifier and the intensional verb *expect*. Putting aside Parallelism, (19) is potentially four-ways ambiguous: the universal quantifier may take scope either below or above the intensional verb *expect*, and VP-ellipsis may target either the embedded or the matrix VP. Under the copy theory of movement and the

assumption that Ā-movement has an intermediate VP-adjunction step, (19) has
the four potential LF structures in (20).

(20) a.   I expected John₁ to
           [_QP everything that he₁ thought I did ⟨buy t⟩]
              buy [_QP everything that he₁ thought I did ⟨buy t⟩]
                                              (embedded scope; embedded ellipsis)

      b.   I expected John₁ to
           [_QP everything that he₁ thought I did ⟨expected him₁ to buy t⟩]
              buy [_QP everything that he₁ thought I did ⟨expected him₁ to buy t⟩]
                                              (embedded scope; matrix ellipsis)

      c.   I
           [_QP everything that he₁ thought I did ⟨buy t⟩]
              expected John₁ to
                 [_QP everything that he₁ thought I did ⟨buy t⟩]
                    buy [_QP everything that he₁ thought I did ⟨buy t⟩]
                                              (matrix scope; embedded ellipsis)

      d.   I
           [_QP everything that he₁ thought I did ⟨expected him₁ to buy t⟩]
              expected John₁ to
                 [_QP everything that he₁ thought I did ⟨expected him₁ to buy t⟩]
                    buy [_QP everything that he₁ thought I did ⟨expected him₁ to
                    buy t⟩]
                                              (matrix scope; matrix ellipsis)

However, as pointed out by Larson and May (1990), (20b) has no way of achieving Parallelism. We are thus left with (20a), (20c), and (20d). Each of these must
be converted into an operator-variable construction under the economy principle that minimizes deletion of copies. This economy principle chooses the most
optimal operator-variable construction that obeys Parallelism. We thus end up with
the three structures in (21).

(21) a.   I expected John₁ to
           [_QP everything that he₁ thought I did ⟨buy t⟩]
              buy t
                                              (embedded scope; embedded ellipsis)

      b.   I
           [_QP everything that he₁ thought I did ⟨buy t⟩]_x
              expected John₁ to
                 [_QP x thing that he₁ thought I did ⟨buy t⟩]
                    buy t
                                              (matrix scope; embedded ellipsis)

      c.   I
           [_QP everything that he₁ thought I did ⟨expected him₁ to buy t⟩]
              expected John₁ to buy t
                                              (matrix scope; matrix ellipsis)

In (21) there is a single instance of QR, hence a single chain; in (21b) and (21c) there are two chains. In all three constructions Parallelism forces a simple trace at the θ-position. (21b) and (21c) differ in that Parallelism requires the elimination of the intermediate trace in the former but not in the latter.

Now consider (22). This sentence differs from (19) in that it allows only matrix VP-ellipsis. This is exactly what is predicted; structures (23a) and (23b), which involve embedded VP-deletion, violate Condition C, whereas structure (23c) does not.

(22)   I expected him$_1$ to buy everything that John$_1$ thought I did.
    a.   *⟨bought t⟩
    b.   ⟨expected him$_1$ to buy t⟩
(23)   a.   I expected him$_1$ to
          [$_{QP}$ everything that John$_1$ thought I did ⟨buy t⟩]
             buy t

                                      (embedded scope; embedded ellipsis)
    b. I
          [$_{QP}$ everything that John$_1$ thought I did ⟨buy t⟩]$_x$
            expected him$_1$ to
               [$_{QP}$ x thing that John$_1$ thought I did ⟨buy t⟩]
                 buy t

                                        (matrix scope; embedded ellipsis)
    c. I
          [$_{QP}$ everything that John$_1$ thought I did ⟨expected him$_1$ to buy t⟩]
            expected him$_1$ to buy t

                                        (matrix scope; matrix ellipsis)

The proposal predicts that QR would bleed Condition C only if the QR is long enough to get out of the c-command domain of the "dangerous" pronoun, and only if the QR is needed for ACD resolution and thus requires elimination of the offending material at the tail of the chain.

   [. . .]

In this section I have shown that (a) it is possible to maintain that Condition C applies only at LF despite what appears to be evidence to the contrary (Chomsky 1993) and (b) this stance is virtually necessary on empirical grounds (Fox 1995a).

Notes

1 Chomsky (1993) also presents the second step of the argument. However, his argument is based on Condition A and is unrelated to scope.

2 Given the proposal made in Fox (1995b), the structures in (1) involve very short QR, or perhaps no QR at all. Under this proposal, the LF structures of (1) are very different from (3), and it is thus far from obvious that they pose a problem for the assumption that Condition C applies only at LF. However, it turns out that the argument based on (1) carries over to structures for which this objection does not hold.

   (i) a.   */??A different girl bought him$_1$ every picture that John$_1$ liked.
       b.   *A different girl wanted him$_1$ to buy every picture that John$_1$ liked.

(ii) a. A different girl bought John₁ every picture that he₁ liked.
      b. A different girl wanted John₁ to buy every picture that he₁ liked.

3   Note that the claim that overt and covert movement differ in their ordering relative to lexical insertion is strongly motivated on independent grounds. There is strong independent motivation for the claim that lexical insertion cannot follow covert operations (at least not without severe constraints). If this claim were false, it is hard to imagine how any correspondence between meaning and sound could be accounted for.

4   One might wonder whether the possibility of inserting adjuncts at various points in the derivation is consistent with the observation in section 2 that Ā-reconstruction feeds Condition C. In section 6 I will show that it is consistent. The basic idea is that scope reconstruction is the result of interpreting a large part of the copy at the base position. I will show that such an interpretation is available only if the adjunct is inserted at the base position; the option of late insertion necessarily yields the nonreconstructed interpretation.

5   It is conceivable that these structures should be interpreted via quantification over choice functions (Reinhart 1995; Kratzer 1998; Winter 1995; Engdahl 1980: 131–41). However, as pointed out by Irene Heim, Uli Sauerland, and Yoad Winter (personal communications), it is not clear how such an analysis would extend to proportional quantifiers (e.g. *most, almost, every*). This is one of the motivations for the modification that follows.

6   Rullmann and Beck consider this possibility as a method for interpreting *wh*-in-situ (and provide a variety of interesting arguments in its favor). Sauerland, who has independently suggested a similar semantic approach, shows that it can also provide an interpretation for the tail of moved *wh*-phrases/QPs in structures such as (8b) and (11b). In previous versions of this article, I assumed that the restrictor at the tail of the chain is interpreted as a predicate that is interpreted via coordination. For reasons of space, I cannot discuss the differences between this proposal and the proposal by Sauerland that I assume here.

7   For similar though not identical ideas, see Cresti (1996).

8   I assume, on the basis of Fox (1995b), that in sentences such as (9) QR is limited to the VP level.

9   Note that the assumption that economy principles prefer (11b) to (11a) is very similar to the assumption that economy principles prefer feature movement to category movement. On the basis of this similarity, I suggest in Fox (1995a) a restatement of the ideas reported here in terms of feature movement.

10   I believe there is good evidence for a theory of ellipsis involving PF deletion. (See Lasnik 1972; Tancredi 1992; Chomsky and Lasnik 1993; Fox 1995b; Wold 1995.) However, the ideas developed here do not depend on such a theory. They could just as easily be stated in a theory involving LF copying such as that suggested by Williams (1977). Under such a theory, (12b) would be eliminated from the reference set because it would not allow LF copying without an infinite regress problem (May 1985).

11   A plausible conclusion from Fox (1995b) is that Parallelism is not accessible to economy considerations (see Fox 2000). If we put Fox (1995a) together with Fox (1995b), the forced conclusion is that Parallelism is not accessible to the economy conditions that determine whether or not QR is to apply. However, it is accessible to the considerations that determine how the output of QR is to be converted to an operator-variable construction.

12   Fiengo and May account for this under the assumption that there is an algorithm that determines at what levels of representation Condition C applies. In standard cases the algorithm determines that Condition C applies at all levels of representation, and in ACD constructions it determines that Condition C applies only at LF. In Fox (1995a) I present various arguments against Fiengo and May's proposal. The most direct argument is the observation that the proposed algorithm, which is based on a notion of an index token, predicts that Condition C would apply only at LF in the sentences in (i). In order to account for the ungrammaticality of these sentences, one would need to appeal to the copy theory of

movement. Once such an appeal is made, the algorithm is no longer needed, and the conclusion that Condition C applies only at LF is virtually forced. (For an additional argument
against Fiengo and May's proposal, see note 13.)

(i)   a.   *He$_1$ introduced his$_1$ mother to [$_{QP}$ everyone that John$_1$ liked].
      b.   I expected him$_1$ to introduce his$_1$ mother to [$_{QP}$ everyone that John$_1$ thought I
           did] *⟨introduce his mother to t⟩

13   Fiengo and May (1994) claim that the sentences in (16) contrast with the sentences in (i),
     which do not include deletion but are identical in all other respects. All the speakers I have
     consulted disagree with this judgment.

(i)   a.   You sent him$_1$ the letter that John$_1$ expected you would [send him$_1$].
      b.   You introduced him$_1$ to everyone John$_1$ wanted you to [introduce him$_1$ to].

As long as the bracketed VPs in (i) are downstressed, the sentences are acceptable. Since
downstressing, just like ellipsis, must obey Parallelism (Tancredi 1992; Rooth 1992), this
result is expected under the proposal presented here. However, it is highly problematic for
Fiengo and May's proposal. (Thanks to an *LI* reviewer for stressing the importance of this
point.)

Kennedy (1997) discusses the fact that there is no detectable contrast between the examples in (ii).

(ii) a.   Polly introduced him$_1$ to everyone Erik$_1$ wanted her to.
      b.   Polly introduced him$_1$ to everyone Erik$_1$ wanted to meet.

In Fox (1995a: 116–18) I provide an account of this fact based on the theory of Parallelism
for phonological deaccenting. The basic idea is that in (iib), in contrast to the sentences
in (15), the embedded VPs can be downstressed (given what Rooth calls "implicational
bridging"). When they are downstressed, Parallelism forces the otherwise uneconomical
deletion at the tail of the chain.

References

Chomsky, N. 1977. On WH-Movement. In P. Culicover, T. Wasow and A. Akmajian (eds.),
    Formal Syntax, New York: Academic Press, pp. 71–132.
Chomsky, N. 1993. A minimalist program for linguistic theory. In K. Hale and S. J. Keyser
    (eds.), *The view from Building 20: Essays in linguistics in honor of Sylvain Bromberger*,
    Cambridge, MA: MIT Press, pp. 1–52. [Reprinted in Chomsky (1995), *The Minimalist Program*,
    Cambridge, MA: MIT Press, pp. 167–217.]
Chomsky, N. and H. Lasnik. 1993. The theory of principles and parameters. In J. Jacobs,
    A. von Stechow, W. Sternefeld and T. Vennemann (eds.), *An international handbook of
    contemporary research*, Berlin/New York: Walter de Gruyter, pp. 506–69. [Reprinted in Chomsky
    (1995), *The Minimalist Program*, Cambridge, MA: MIT Press, pp. 13–127.]
Cresti, D. 1996. Economy and the scope of amount phrases. In J. Camacho, L. Choueiri and
    M. Watanabe (eds.), *Proceedings of the 14th West Coast Conference on Formal Linguistics*, Stanford,
    CA: CSLI, pp. 79–94.
Engdahl, E. 1980. *The syntax and semantics of questions in Swedish*. Doctoral dissertation,
    University of Massachusetts, Amherst.
Fiengo, R. and R. May. 1994. *Indices and identity*. Cambridge, MA: MIT Press.

Fox, D. 1995a. Condition C effects in ACD. In R. Pensalfini and H. Ura (eds.), *Papers on minimalist syntax. MIT Working Papers in Linguistics 27*, Cambridge, MA: MITWPL, pp. 105–19.

Fox, D. 1995b. Economy and scope. *Natural Language Semantics* 3: 283–341.

Fox, D. 2000. Economy and semantic interpretation. Cambridge, MA: MIT Press and MITWPL.

Kennedy, C. 1997. Antecedent-contained deletion and the syntax of quantification. *Linguistic Inquiry* 28: 662–88.

Kratzer, A. 1998. Scope or pseudoscope? Are there wide scope indefinites? In S. Rothstein (ed.), *Events in grammar*, Dordrecht: Kluwer, pp. 163–96.

Larson, R. and R. May. 1990. Antecedent containment or vacuous movement: Reply to Baltin. *Linguistic Inquiry* 21: 103–22.

Lasnik, H. 1972. *Analyses of negation in English*. Doctoral dissertation, MIT.

Lebeaux, D. 1988. *Language acquisition and the form of the grammar*. Doctoral dissertation, University of Massachusetts, Amherst.

Lebeaux, D. 1994. Where does the binding theory apply? Ms., University of Maryland, College Park. [Published in R. Echepare and V. Miglio (eds.) (1995), *University of Maryland Working Papers in Linguistics 3*, College Park, Maryland: Department of Linguistics, University of Maryland, pp. 63–88.]

May, R. 1977. *The grammar of quantification*. Doctoral dissertation, MIT.

May, R. 1985. *Logical form*. Cambridge, MA: MIT Press.

Reinhart, T. 1995. *Interface strategies. OTS Working Papers*. Research Institute for Language and Speech, Utrecht University.

Rooth, M. 1992. Ellipsis redundancy and reduction redundancy. In S. Berman and A. Hestvik (eds.), *Proceedings of the Stuttgart Ellipsis Workshop. Arbeitspapiere des Sonderforschungsbereichs 340 Nr. 29*, Heidelberg: IBM Germany.

Rullmann, H. and S. Beck. 1998. Presupposition projection and the interpretation of which-question. In *Reconstruction: Proceedings of the 1997 Tübingen Workshop (Arbeitspapiere des Sonderforschungsbereichs 340, Bericht Nr. 127)*. Universität Stuttgart and Universität Tübingen, pp. 223–56.

Sag, I. 1976. *Deletion and logical form*. Doctoral dissertation, MIT.

Sauerland, U. In progress. The making and meaning of chains. Doctoral dissertation, MIT. [Defended as *The meaning of chains*, 1998.]

Tancredi, C. 1992. *Deletion, deaccenting and presupposition*. Doctoral dissertation, MIT.

Williams, E. 1977. Discourse and logical form. *Linguistic Inquiry* 8: 101–39.

Winter, Y. 1995. On the formalization of choice functions as representing the scope of indefinites. In G. V. Morrill and R. T. Oehrle (eds.), *Formal grammar. Proceedings of the Conference of the European Summer School in Logic, Language, and Information*, Barcelona: Universitat Politécnica de Catalunya, pp. 275–90.

Wold, D. 1995. Identity in ellipsis: Focal structure and phonetic deletion. Ms., MIT.

From "MINIMALISM AND QUANTIFIER RAISING"

Norbert Hornstein

My aim in this chapter is to eliminate Quantifier Raising (QR) as a rule of Universal Grammar. In Government-Binding (GB) style theories, QR is the operation that targets quantified NPs (QNPs) in A-positions and moves them to Ā-positions. QNPs contrast with nonquantified expressions (e.g. names) in being uninterpretable unless moved to Ā-positions from which their relative scopes and binding domains are determined (see, e.g. May 1985; Chierchia and McConnell-Ginet 1990). To deny that QR exists is to claim that no rule targeting QNPs as such obtains. Rather, the relative scope and binding properties that QNPs manifest is parasitic on the movements that all NPs undergo to satisfy grammatical demands such as Case requirements and other species of feature checking. This attitude toward QR reflects a more general sentiment concerning interpretation: semantic structure is a by-product of grammatical operations driven by formal concerns. Grammars seek morphological rectitude, not meaning. What meaning there is, is the unintended consequence of this mundane quest.[1]

This global vision motivates the desire to eliminate rules like QR that syntactically target expressions for essentially semantic reasons. This is buttressed by additional theory-internal reasons for dispensing with QR in the Minimalist Program. These largely boil down to the fact that QR and minimalism fit together awkwardly. Consider some illustrations.

First, the Minimalist Program presumes that movement serves to check morphological features. Thus, if QR obtains, its end must be the checking of Q-features. However, in contrast to *wh*-features or focus features or topic features, each of which has overt morphological realization in some language, Q-features are virtually unattested overtly. This suggests that Q-features do not exist and that no movement exists whose concern is to check them.

Second, like wh-, topic, and focus movement, QR yields an Ā-structure. However, QR seems able to append a quantified NP (QNP) to virtually any maximal projection.[2] Thus, it appears that Q-features, if they exist, have no particular position of their own. Rather, they can be sprinkled on any XP to yield the desired abstract movement at LF. Once again, this contrasts with the more familiar features (such as *wh*-features and topic features) that induce Ā-movement to rather specific IP-peripheral positions. One cannot move a *wh*-feature to the front of just any XP or focus an expression by adjoining it to any arbitrary projection.

Third, eliminating QR is a step toward eliminating the antecedent government part of the Empty Category Principle (ECP) from the grammar. Antecedent government does not fit well into minimalism. Its key notions – blocking category, barrier, γ-marking, and so forth – are not easily defined in minimalist terms. Nonetheless, the ECP is critical to theories that employ LF Ā-movement operations. It prevents them from overgenerating. However, if LF Ā-operations like QR (and *wh*-raising) are dispensed with, then the need for antecedent government likewise recedes.[3]

Fourth, if quantifier-scope interactions (QSI) piggyback on the structure of A-chains (i.e. the chains that result from operations that check L-related features), then the clause-boundedness of QSIs in natural languages can be directly accounted for.[4] The general clause-boundedness of quantifier interaction effects reduces to the very local nature of A-movement. In other words, if A-chains define the limits of quantifier scope, then the observed restricted scopal reach of natural language quantifiers follows trivially.

Fifth, the elimination of QR (and other Ā-movements) from LF allows apparent S-Structure conditions like Subjacency and parasitic gap licensing to reposition to LF.[5] For the Minimalist Program, this is a very desirable result. A core tenet is that there are only two grammatical levels – LF and PF – and that only the former has significant phrasal structure. A consequence of this is that all grammatical conditions that GB distributes among D-Structure, S-Structure, LF, and PF must now be largely relocated to LF. LF Ā-movement operations like QR greatly complicate this task. As an illustration, consider parasitic gap (PG) licensing.

Since Chomsky (1982), it has been standardly assumed that PGs must be licensed at S-Structure. This is required in a GB theory to distinguish the acceptable (1a) from the unacceptable (1b).

(1) a.   which book did John read t without reviewing pg
     b.   *John read every book without reviewing pg

The problem (1) poses can be directly traced to the presence of QR, for its application renders the two sentences in (1) structurally analogous at LF.

(2) a.   [which book$_i$ [John read t_i [without reviewing pg_i]]]
     b.   [every book$_i$ [John read t_i [without reviewing pg_i]]]

Thus, if LF Ā-operations exist, then PG licensing cannot be stated neatly at LF. This is a problem for minimalism given the absence of any other suitable level at which to state the condition. However, if QR is eliminated, then there is no difficulty relocating the PG licensing condition to LF. The reason is that there is no more Ā-structure at LF than the overt syntax provides; hence, (1a,b) are no more structurally similar at LF than they are prior to Spell-Out. So, if PG licensing is sensitive to Ā-dependencies (as standardly assumed), then eliminating QR allows one to state this condition at LF without empirical loss – and this is what the Minimalist Program, a theory that eschews S-Structure, requires.

The above points provide part of the motive for what follows: a reanalysis of QSI effects without the benefit of QR. There is one further methodological reason with a minimalist resonance. For the standard instances of QSIs, QR is not required. But if not required, it is not desirable either. The argument below rests on the observation that given the minimalist theory of Case, it is easy to construct an empirically adequate account of quantifier scope exploiting technical machinery already in general use. As I will suggest, the opportunity for exploiting Case chain structure to serve as the basis of QSIs exists in the Minimalist Program for one main reason: the structural configurations for the realization of Case and θ requirements are very different. In GB theories, government unifies all core grammatical relations. Moreover, the domains of Case and θ-assignment are essentially identical in GB. For example, an object is assigned its θ-role in roughly the same position in which it meets its Case requirements.[6] Though the Minimalist Program still retains (more or less) the GB approach to θ-assignment, it construes morphological feature checking in a very different way. It is this difference that the proposal below exploits.

The rest of the chapter is organized as follows. In section 3.1, I outline a way of representing QSIs via the structure of Case chains. In section 3.2, I argue that the theory sketched in section 3.1 has empirical payoffs. In section 3.3, I consider some crosslinguistic QSI data from Japanese, Hungarian, and the Romance languages. [. . .]

3.1 The basic proposal

Assume as background the version of the Minimalist Program set out in Chomsky (1993). The key elements are listed in (3).

(3) a. The VP-internal subject hypothesis: NPs in English begin in VP-internal positions.
     b. NPs in VP-internal positions move to [Spec, Agr] positions to check Case features. In particular, subjects move to [Spec, Agr_S] in overt syntax, and objects move to [Spec, Agr_O] at LF.
     c. Movement is copying and deletion.
     d. LF is the sole structured grammatical level, and all grammatical conditions hold here.

(3a) has been amply motivated and is no longer controversial (see Kuroda 1988; Koopman and Sportiche 1991). In the Minimalist Program, it reflects the conviction that all θ-roles are assigned within lexical projections.[7] If one further assumes, as Chomsky (1995) does, that all θ-roles are assigned to trivial chains, and that the θ-Criterion is a convergence condition, then all NPs must begin inside lexical shells for derivations to converge. [. . .] For now, I assume the theory of Case presented in Chomsky (1993). Its distinctive feature is that a D/NP marked with accusative Case is checked in a configuration analogous to one in which a D/NP marked with nominative Case is checked – namely, in a specifier-head configuration with the Case-checking head outside the VP shell. This specifier-head configuration is realized for accusatives in English at LF with the object raising from the VP shell to [Spec, Agr_O]. (3c,d) are both standard assumptions. Both are used in accounting for the data in section 3.2.[8]

I make two additional assumptions.

(4) A QNP Q_1 takes scope over a QNP Q_2 iff Q_1 c-commands Q_2.
(5) At the conceptual-intentional (C-I) interface, an A-chain has at most one and at least one member.

(4) is innocuous. It is the commonly assumed algorithm for translating syntactic c-command relations into semantic scope dependencies.[9] (5) is *not* trivial. It generalizes the assumptions concerning deletion in Ā-chains (Chomsky 1993) to all chains.[10] It forces deletion of all copies in an A-chain save one. (5) does not specify which chain members delete. The optimal assumption is that the process is free. It is not important here whether one takes this deletion process to be a fact about the interface interpretation procedure or one about the structure of LF phrase markers themselves. For present purposes, it is immaterial whether all but one member of the LF chain actually delete or whether the members of the chain remain intact until some post-LF interpretive module where only one member of the chain is "chosen" to be interpreted. If the latter is correct, then "deletion" simply amounts to being uninterpreted. If the former is correct, then deletion is an actual grammatical operation and (5) is a convergence requirement. Nothing below chooses

between these two interpretations of the deletion process. What is crucial is that some form of deletion exist in A-chains. This is controversial. In section 3.4, I rebut arguments that reconstruction in A-chains is illicit.

(3)–(5) suffice to provide an analysis of QSIs in English. Consider a typical instance. (6) is ambiguous; either the universally quantified object or the indefinite subject is interpreted as taking wide scope.

(6)   someone attended every seminar[11]

The LF structure of (6) prior to deletion of copies is (7).[12]

(7) $[_{Agr_S}$ someone $[_{TP}$ T $[_{Agr_O}$ every seminar $[_{VP}$ someone attended every seminar]]]]]

Someone raises to [Spec, Agr$_S$] to check its nominative Case in the overt syntax. At LF, *every seminar* moves to [Spec, Agr$_O$] to check accusative Case. Each move leaves a copy of the moved expression behind. Conforming to (5) requires deleting one member of each of the two A-chains. Four possible structures result (deleted expressions are in parentheses).

(8)   a. $[_{Agr_S}$ someone $[_{TP}$ T $[_{Agr_O}$ every seminar $[_{VP}$ (someone) [attended (every seminar)]]]]]
      b. $[_{Agr_S}$ someone $[_{TP}$ T $[_{Agr_O}$ (every seminar) $[_{VP}$ (someone) [attended every seminar]]]]]
      c. $[_{Agr_S}$ (someone) $[_{TP}$ T $[_{Agr_O}$ (every seminar) $[_{VP}$ someone [attended every seminar]]]]]
      d. $[_{Agr_S}$ (someone) $[_{TP}$ T $[_{Agr_O}$ every seminar $[_{VP}$ someone [attended (every seminar)]]]]]

Using the interpretive principle (4), we can represent the ambiguity of (6). (8a–c) are LF structures in which *someone* takes scope over *everyone*. In (8d), this QSI is reversed.[13]

The above discussion shows that QSIs in transitive sentences in English can be represented without QR by exploiting the structure of A-chains in a minimalist theory. The assumptions in (3)–(5) are crucial. For example, in the absence of copying and deletion, determinate scope relations among QNPs would not be represented and quantifier-scope dependencies would be grammatically underdetermined.[14]

More interestingly, VP-internal subjects are instrumental in allowing objects to take scope over subjects. So too is the assumption that objects check accusative Case outside the VP shell in [Spec, Agr$_O$]. In fact, the VP-internal subject hypothesis and the assumption that accusative Case is checked outside the VP shell in [Spec, Agr$_O$] are actually flip sides of the same minimalist intuition, namely, that the grammar segregates morphological Case and agreement properties from θ-properties. The domain of θ-assignment is the VP shell. Case, in contrast, is checked in a specifier-head relation outside this lexical shell. This separation of functions is a constant refrain within minimalism. It is interesting to observe, therefore, that representing QSIs without QR requires exploiting both halves of this central minimalist dichotomy.[15] The converse is also true. One can interpret QR as the technical price a theory that grammatically represent QSIs must pay if it identifies the domains and relations of Case theory and θ-theory.

3.2   Some empirical benefits

Having shown how to represent QSIs without the benefit of QR, in this section I provide evidence in favor of this approach. Two features of the analysis are crucial. First, quantifier scope is parasitic on the structure of A-chains. Second, what scope an expression has is a function of which member of its A-chain survives the deletion process.[16]

Consider first different scope interactions manifest in raising and control structures.

(9)   a.   someone seemed to attend every seminar
      b.   someone hoped to attend every seminar

Every seminar can be interpreted as having scope over *someone* in (9a) but not in (9b). This follows from the different structures of the two sentences. At LF, prior to deletion, (9a) has the structure in (10a) typical of a raising construction, whereas (9b) has the structure in (10b) characteristic of control.[17]

(10)   a.   [someone [T [seem [someone [to [every seminar [someone [attend every
             seminar]]]]]]]]
       b.   [someone [T [someone [hope [PRO [to [every seminar [PRO [attend
             every seminar]]]]]]]]]

Observe that through judicious deletions it is possible to get a copy of *someone* c-commanded by a copy of *every seminar* in (10a), as in (11).

(11)   [(someone) [T [seem [(someone) [to [every seminar [someone [attend
       (every seminar)]]]]]]]]

At no point do the chains headed by *someone* and *every seminar* interleave in (10b). Hence, for this structure, no amount of deletion can duplicate the effect found in (11).

In sum, if relative scope piggybacks on A-chain structure and reflects relative c-command after deletion, we expect matrix subjects to be able to take scope under embedded–clause objects in raising constructions but not in control structures. This accounts for the contrast in (9).

Consider a second pair of sentences. (12) illustrates that QSIs are sensitive to the Tensed-S Condition. It is possible to interpret *someone* in (12a) as within the scope of *every Republican*. This reading is absent in (12b).

(12)   a.   someone expected every Republican to win
       b.   someone expected that every Republican would win

This contrast follows from previous assumptions. (12a) is an exceptional-Case-marking (ECM) construction. The embedded subject raises to the matrix [Spec, Agr_O] to check its accusative features at LF. The embedded subject in (12b) is marked nominative; its Case is checked in the embedded [Spec, Agr_S]. Prior to deletion at LF, the two sentences have the structures in (13).

(13) a. $[_{Agr_S}$ someone $[_{Agr_O}$ every Republican $[_{VP}$ someone [expected $[_{Agr_S}$ every Republican $[_{VP}$ every Republican to win]]]]]]]

    b. $[_{Agr_S}$ someone $[_{VP}$ someone [expected $[_{Agr_S}$ every Republican would $[_{VP}$ every Republican win]]]]]

Note that the chains headed by *someone* and *every Republican* interleave in (13a) but do not in (13b). Consequently, *every Republican* can c-command (and hence take scope over) *someone* after the relevant deletions, as shown in (14).

(14) $[_{Agr_S}$ (someone) $[_{Agr_O}$ every Republican $[_{VP}$ someone [expected $[_{Agr_S}$ (every Republican) $[_{VP}$ (every Republican) to win]]]]]]]

No combination of deletions will allow *every Republican* to c-command *someone* in (13b) and so the analogous interpretation is unavailable for this structure.

The above accounts both rely on Case chains undergirding quantifier scope. For these data, the structure of Case chains alone accounts for the indicated scope contrasts.[18] In GB-style theories, both sorts of data are accounted for in terms of the ECP (see, e.g. Aoun and Hornstein 1985). As the ECP is an unwelcome condition in the Minimalist Program, a side benefit of this approach is that it can handle these contrasts without invoking it.

Let us turn next to a different set of interactions, ones that highlight the effect of assumption (5). The Minimalist Program assumes (see (3d)) that there is only a single level at which grammatical conditions can apply: LF. I now review some data that rely on the combination of (3d) and (5). Consider the interaction of relative quantifier scope and binding.

Higginbotham (1980) observes that (15a) is ambiguous, with either the subject or the object taking widest scope. (15b) is similarly ambiguous so long as the pronoun is not interpreted as bound by *someone*. However, on the bound reading, the sentence can only be interpreted with the indefinite subject outside the scope of the *every* phrase.

(15) a.   someone played every piece of music you knew
    b.   someone$_i$ played every piece of music he$_i$ knew

The requirement that *someone* take wide scope in (15b) follows from the assumptions made above. The LF structure of the sentence prior to deletion is (16a). To be interpreted as bound, the pronoun must be c-commanded by its antecedent at LF (for the standard discussion of this, see Higginbotham 1980). However, this forces *someone* to c-command the *every* phrase. Given (4), this in turn leads to an LF structure in which *someone* takes scope over the *every* phrase, as in (16b,c).

(16) a. [$_{Agr_S}$ someone [$_T$[$_{Agr_O}$[every piece of music he knew] [$_{VP}$ someone [$_{VP}$ played
          every piece of music he knew]]]]]

      b. [$_{Agr_S}$ someone$_i$ [$_T$[$_{Agr_O}$[every piece of music he$_i$ knew] [$_{VP}$ (someone) [$_{VP}$
          played (every piece of music he knew)]]]]]]

      c. [$_{Agr_S}$ (someone$_i$) [$_T$[$_{Agr_O}$[(every piece of music he$_i$ knew)] [$_{VP}$ someone [$_{VP}$
          played every piece of music he knew]]]]]]

Given the minimalist assumptions in Chomsky (1995), these data cannot be similarly handled in a theory that represents QSIs via QR. The problem is as follows.
Chomsky argues that Ā-chains minimize the restrictor in Ā-position at LF. In effect,
this forces QR to move bare Qs. But if just bare Qs move, then (17) is a legitimate LF structure where the pronoun can be bound by the variable t_j while *some* is
c-commanded by *every*.[19]

(17) [$_{IP}$ every$_i$ [$_{IP}$ some$_j$ [$_{IP}$ t_j [$_{VP}$[t_j one] played [t_i piece of music he knew]]]]]]

There are further cases of interactions between quantifier scope and binding.
A classic one is discussed by Aoun (1982). He observes that in a raising structure
– (18a) – *someone* can be interpreted as within the scope of the embedded *every*
phrase. However, if the raised subject binds a matrix pronoun or anaphor, this
reading disappears and *someone* must be interpreted as having wider scope than
the *every* phrase – (18b,c).

(18) a. someone seemed (to Bill) to be reviewing every report
      b. someone$_i$ seemed to his$_i$ boss to be reviewing every report
      c. someone$_i$ seemed to himself$_i$ to be reviewing every report

The LF structures of (18b,c) are shown in (19).

(19) a. [someone$_i$ seemed to his$_i$ boss [(someone) to be [every report [(someone)
          reviewing (every report)]]]]]
      b. [someone$_i$ seemed to himself$_i$ [(someone) to be [every report [(someone)
          reviewing (every report)]]]]]

If *someone* is to bind the matrix pronoun/anaphor in (19), the embedded copy
must delete. This makes it impossible for the *every* phrase to c-command *someone*. Consequently, *someone* must be interpreted as outside the scope of the *every*
phrase.

Similar effects occur in simple clauses with adjuncts. (20a,b) are ambiguous, with
either the *every* phrase or *someone* taking wide scope. (20c,d), with *someone* binding into the adjunct, are no longer ambiguous. *Someone* must take wide scope.

(20) a. someone serenaded every woman
      b. someone reviewed every brief

c. someone$_i$ serenaded every woman before he$_i$ left the party

d. I got someone to review every brief without leaving the office

We can account for these interactions between scope and binding just as we did above if we assume that adjuncts are adjoined to VP or higher.[20] if *someone* is to bind into the adjunct, the copy inside the VP shell must delete, as this copy does not c-command the adjunct. The copy in [Spec, Agr$_S$] thus determines the scope of *someone*. However, the *every* phrase cannot take scope over this position, as no *every* copy c-commands it. (21a,b) are the relevant LF structures.

(21) a. [$_{Agr_S}$ someone$_i$ [$_T$ every woman [$_{VP}$[$_{VP}$ (someone) serenaded (every woman)] [before he$_i$ left the party]]]]

b. [$_{Agr_S}$ someone$_i$ [$_T$ to [$_{Agr_O}$ every brief [$_{VP}$[$_{VP}$ (someone) review (every brief)] [without PRO$_i$ leaving the office]]]]]

This reasoning further implies that if the object (rather than the subject) binds into the adjunct, then scope ambiguities will persist. This seems to be correct, as (22a) can be read with *someone* either in the scope of the *every* phrase or outside it. This is because (22a) has two well-formed LF structures. In (22b), the extant *every* phrase c-commands the undeleted *someone*. In (22c), the opposite c-command relations obtain.

(22) a. someone questioned every suspect$_i$ before he$_i$ was released

b. [$_{Agr_S}$ (someone) [$_{Agr_O}$ every suspect$_i$ [$_{VP}$[$_{VP}$ someone questioned (every suspect$_i$) [before he$_i$ left]]]]]

c. [$_{Agr_S}$ someone [$_{Agr_O}$ every suspect$_i$ [$_{VP}$[$_{VP}$ (someone) questioned (every suspect$_i$) [before he$_i$ left]]]]]

This theory has another consequence. I have argued that subjects that bind into adjuncts must take wide scope because VP-internal subjects fail to c-command adjuncts. This implies that if a subject binds into a complement rather than an adjunct, it should be able to take scope inside the object since the VP-internal subject position c-commands the complement position. Hence, the copy in [Spec, Agr$_S$] can delete and binding will remain licit. This is illustrated in (23). Here, *someone* can be interpreted within the scope of the *every* phrase with the indicated binding. The relevant LF structures are provided in (24).

(23) a. someone$_i$ asked every attendant if he$_i$ could park near the gate

b. John got someone/at least one patron$_i$ to tell every critic that he$_i$ hated the play

(24) a. [$_{Agr_S}$ (someone) [$_{Agr_O}$ every attendant [$_{VP}$ someone$_i$ asked (every attendant) if he$_i$ could park near the gate]]]

b. John got [$_{Agr_S}$ (someone/at least one patron) to [$_{Agr_O}$ every critic [$_{VP}$ someone/at least one patron$_i$ tell (every critic) that he$_i$ hated the play]]]

The interaction between scope and binding illustrated here cannot be easily duplicated in a grammar that delivers quantifier scope via QR yet retains the standard binding theory. The problem arises because in such a theory, relative quantifier scope is sensitive to the Ā-positions of Ā-chains whereas binding is sensitive to the A-positions of these chains. For example, a quantified object can take scope over a subject by QRing over it while the subject remains outside the VP shell in some [Spec, IP] from which it can bind into the adjunct. So, for example, with QR in the LF arsenal, (25) is a perfectly fine LF representation of (20c). Here, the object takes scope over the subject, and the subject binds into the adjunct.

(25)   [every woman$_i$ [someone$_j$ [$_{Agr_S}$ t_j [$_{Agr_O}$ t_i [$_{VP}$[t_j [$_{VP}$ t_j serenaded t_i] before he$_i$ left the party]]]]]]

In sum, a QR-based theory fails to capture dependencies between relative quantifier scope and binding. The reason is that the grammatical expression of quantifier scope – the QRed expression – is different from the object relevant for Case and binding effects in such a theory. The former is a matter of Ā-chain structure whereas the latter is the province of A-chain configuration. The present proposal identifies scope markers and anaphoric anchors. The c-command domain of the same grammatical element determines both its binding properties and relative scope. We thus expect one to potentially restrict the other.[21]

3.3   Some crosslinguistic considerations

Thus far, I have argued that English QSIs can be accounted for without LF Ā-movement. The structure of A-chains suffices. The Ā-operation I have considered has been QR, and the A-chains at issue are those driven by Case theory. However, the logic of the proposal is more general than this. Japanese scrambling constructions manifest a version of the same logic.[22]

Saito (1992) demonstrates that clause-internal scrambling (CIS) and long-distance scrambling (LDS) are quite different operations. CIS is an instance of A-movement, LDS an instance of Ā-movement. A-movement is distinguished from Ā-movement in two ways. A-movement rescinds weak crossover (WCO) effects and licenses anaphoric binding. English raising constructions illustrate this.

(26)   a.   no one$_i$ seems to his$_i$ mother [t_i to be ugly]
       b.   the men$_i$ seem to each other$_i$ [t_i to be ugly]

The matrix subjects in (26) are able to licitly bind the indicated pronoun/reciprocal. The fact that this is possible indicates that the trace in the embedded clause is the residue of A-movement. When the trace is the residue of Ā-movement, neither binding is permitted.

(27)   a.   *who$_i$ does it seem to his$_i$ mother [t_i is ugly]
       b.   *which men$_i$ does it seem to each other$_i$ [t_i are ugly]

In Japanese, CIS functions like raising whereas LDS resembles *wh*-movement. (28) indicates that CIS obviates WCO effects. (29) shows that it licenses reciprocal binding.

(28) a. ?*[Masao-wa [Hanako-ga   pro$_i$ yomu mae-ni] dono   hon$_i$-o
          Masao-TOP Hanako-NOM   read   before   which book-ACC
          yondal] no
          read   Q
          'Masao read which book before Hanako read'

    b. dono hon$_i$-o   [Masao-wa [Hanako-ga   e$_i$ yomu mae-ni]
          which book-ACC Masao-TOP Hanako-NOM   read   before
          [t$_i$ yonda]] no
            read   Q
          'which book did Masao read before Hanako read it'

(29) a. ?*[Masao-ga   [[otagai$_i$-no   sensei]-ni [karera$_i$-o
          Masao-NOM   each other-GEN teacher to   they-ACC
          syookaisita]]] (koto)
          introduced   (fact)
          'Masao introduced them to each other's teachers'

    b. [karera$_i$-o [Masao-ga   [[otagai$_i$-no   sensei]-ni [t$_i$
          they-ACC Masao-NOM   each other-GEN teacher to
          syookaisita]]]] (koto)
          introduced   (fact)
          'them, Masao introduced to each other's teachers'

In contrast, LDS induces WCO effects and fails to license reciprocal binding, as in (30a) and (30b), respectively.

(30) a. *dono ronbun$_i$-ni-mo [sore$_i$-no tyosya]-ga [John-ga   t$_i$
          every paper-DAT   it-GEN   author-NOM John-NOM
          manzokusita to]   omotteiru (koto)
          was satisfied COMP thinks   (fact)
          '*every paper$_i$, its$_i$ author thinks that John was satisfied with'

    b. *[karera$_i$-o [Masao-ga [otagai$_i$-no   sensei]-ni [$_{CP}$[$_{IP}$
          them-ACC Masao-NOM each other-GEN teacher to
          Hanako-ga   t$_i$ hihansita] to]   itaa]] (koto)
          Hanako-NOM   criticized COMP said (fact)
          '*them$_i$, Masao said to each other's teachers that Hanako criticized t$_i$'

What happens with respect to relative quantifier scope? As is well known, without scrambling, relative quantifier scope in Japanese reflects S-Structure c-command relations.[23] Interestingly, CIS induces ambiguities. LDS, in contrast, does not. (31a) is unambiguous. The nominative subject *dareka-ga* must be interpreted as having wide scope. In (31b), however, the accusative *dareka-o* has been clause-internally scrambled, and now either the subject can take scope over the object or conversely. In other words, CIS, a species of A-movement by the standard diagnostic tests, fosters novel QSIs.

(31) a. dareka-ga   daremo-o   semeta
          someone-NOM everyone-ACC blamed
          'someone blamed everyone'
      b. [dareka-o [daremo-ga [t_i semeta]]]

What of LDS? It is inert. Overt LDS to an Ā-position does not permit the scrambled expression to take wide scope. In (32), *daremo-ni* cannot take scope over the
matrix *dareka-ga* despite having been overtly moved there. ((32) is from Bošković
and Takahashi 1998.)

(32) daremo$_i$-ni   dareka-ga   [Mary-ga t_i atta to] omotteiru (koto)
      everyone-DAT someone-NOM Mary-NOM   met that thinks   (fact)
      'everyone, someone thinks that Mary met'
      = for some person x, x thinks that Mary met every y
      ≠ for every person y, some person thinks that Mary met y

Saito (1992) provides independent evidence from the scrambling of *wh*-morphemes
that LDS in Japanese is semantically inert. He observes that *wh*-elements scrambled
outside the domain of their related Q-morphemes are nonetheless licensed at LF,
as in (33).

(33) dono hon$_i$-o   [Masao-ga   [$_{CP}$[$_{IP}$ Hanako-ga t_i tosoyokan-kara
      which book-ACC Masao-NOM   Hanako-NOM   library-from
      karidasita]   ka] siritagatteiru]   (koto)
      checked out Q   wants-to-know (fact)
      '*which book, Masao wants to know Hanako checked out from the library'

Saito assumes that lowering is both possible and required at LF. That this is
possible follows if indeed the position to which LDS moves a scrambled expression is semantically inert. Were it not, lowering the *wh*-morpheme at LF would
violate Full Interpretation.
     For our purposes, the interesting fact is that this form of overt Ā-movement
seems incapable of altering quantifier-scope patterns whereas A-movement can.
This supports the view that QSIs are sensitive to A-movement rather than LF Ā-
movement.
     This said, things cannot be quite so simple. There are well-known cases of
languages in which *overt* Ā-movement does appear to determine the relative scope
of quantified expressions. One of the best-studied cases is Hungarian. In Hungarian, D/NPs, whether quantificational or not, are typically moved from IP to
various presentential positions. This movement fixes the relative scopes of the
QNPs (see É. Kiss 1991 and Szabolcsi 1995; examples are from the latter). (34)
illustrates this.

(34) a. sok   ember mindenkit felhívott
          many men   everyone   phoned
          = many men > everyone

b.   mindenkit sok ember felhívott
     = everyone > many men

It appears, however, that in the absence of this movement, Hungarian overt structure does *not* disambiguate quantifier scope. Szabolcsi (1995) provides examples
of postverbal QNPs that have not been Ā-moved. She indicates that these QNPs
enjoy the same scope ambiguities attested in English. In short, for these cases,
S-Structure fails to determine relative scope.

(35)   egy keddi   napon harapott meg   hatnál több kutya minden fiút
       a   Tuesday day-on bit-PFX more than six   dogs bit   every   boy
       'it was on Tuesday that more than six dogs bit every boy'
       = more than six dogs > every boy
       = every boy > more than six dogs

How are we to interpret these Hungarian facts? First, it seems that relative
quantifier scope can piggyback on Ā-chains. This is consistent with the larger picture outlined in the introductory paragraphs, the central idea being that there are
no rules *specifically* for fixing quantifier scope. There is no rule of grammar whose
concern it is to ensure that quantified expressions reside in scope positions. This,
however, does not prohibit quantifier scope from piggybacking on the structure
of Ā-operations required for other reasons, as in Hungarian.
   Szabolcsi (1995) makes a very interesting proposal in this regard. She argues
that pre-IP positions in Hungarian make rather specific informational demands on
the expressions that inhabit them. In contrast to positions occupied by expressions
in Japanese LDSs, these positions are semantically active. As evidence for this,
Szabolcsi argues that the QNPs in presentential position in Hungarian are not actually interpreted as (generalized) quantifiers, in contrast to the interpretation of such
expressions in postverbal positions in Hungarian or quite generally in English.
Rather, the pre-IP positions in Hungarian have more specific interpretive requirements associated with them. The structure of the clause, she proposes, is (36).[24]

(36)   [Topic* [Quantifier* [Focus [Negation [Verb [NP*]]]]]]

Nominal elements in the first three positions, Szabolcsi insists, are not interpreted
simply as quantifiers. This is not surprising for elements in Topic and Focus
positions, whose informational contributions to interpretation have been well studied.
However, Szabolcsi argues that even QNPs in the "Quantifier" slot are not interpreted as generalized quantifiers but rather "provide subjects of predication" in
more or less complex ways. Only some kinds of D/NPs can do as much. Those
that cannot are barred from this position just as certain D/NPs are barred from
being Foci or Topics because they cannot fulfill the informational requirements
these positions demand.
   If Szabolcsi is correct, then it is possible to combine the English and Japanese facts with the Hungarian ones as follows. Deletion of copies is free, but the

resulting LF structure must be interpretable. If pre-IP positions make interpretive demands, then the deletion process must leave a copy in these positions. But because only one copy can survive to the C-I interface, this will freeze the relative scopes of expressions that move there. This is what happens in Hungarian, if Szabolcsi is correct. If, however, the landing sites of movement are not associated with any specific informational tasks, as for example in Case positions or LDS positions, then the general properties of the grammar have free play and we end up with the English and Japanese data reviewed above.

One further point is worth mentioning in the context of the Minimalist Program. The considerations in the introductory paragraphs strongly suggest that if Ā-movement obtains in a grammar, it should be overt. What is minimalistically awkward is covert Ā-movement. This is consistent with the data above.

The overall picture that emerges concerning QSIs is the following. Relative quantifier scope is computed from structures required for independent grammatical reasons. There are no quantifier scope rules per se in the grammar. Rather, quantifier scope is determined by deleting copies that movement induces, leaving but one at the C-I interface. Which copy survives determines what sort of binding can occur, what the relative scopes of the expressions can be, and what informational structure the sentence can bear. The interaction of all of these factors should be the norm.

Notes

1   For a contrasting vision of how grammars integrate quantifiers, see Beghelli (1993).
2   This assumption holds in most of the theories of QR in the GB literature. See, for example, May (1985) and Aoun and Li (1993). These two influential works allow (and empirically require) QPs to adjoin to any XP.
3   It is also necessary to eliminate the other Ā-movement operations at LF, such as *wh*-raising. See Hornstein (1995) for some suggestions. For alternatives, see Reinhart (1995), Tsai (1994).
4   The clause-boundedness of QR has been widely observed (see Aoun and Hornstein 1985; Chomsky 1975; Chierchia 1995; Cooper 1983; May 1977).
5   This point was brought to my attention by Alan Munn.
6   I emphasize "roughly," for not all Case positions are thematic.
7   Chomsky, adverting to Hale and Keyser (1993), suggests that this in turn follows from an interpretation of θ-roles as essentially relational.
8   Uriagereka [ch. 5, this volume] argues that the Minimalist Program does not require that LF and PF be levels. The analysis presented below survives using his alternative assumptions.
9   (4) is not a principle of grammar. Rather, it is a correspondence rule relating grammatical structure to semantic interpretation. It observes that there is a correlation between semantic scope and syntactic c-command and states what the relation is. Why this relation obtains is an interesting question. A natural answer is that semantic interpretation rules exploit syntactic structure (e.g. interpretation is bottom up using LF trees). Why c-command is the relevant notion is addressed by Epstein [ch. 5, this volume] and Uriagereka [ch. 5, this volume].
10 This means that it rejects the view that "reconstruction" can be reduced to some yet-to-be-specified property of operator-variable structures as Chomsky suggests.

11 There have been persistent claims that the reading in which the object takes scope over the subject is in some ways marked (see Chomsky 1995; Pica and Snyder 1995; Reinhart 1995). Even if this is so, which I believe is unclear at best, it is quite easy to force the "marked" readings. Thus, on the favored reading of (i), each poem is recited by a different girl; that is, the object takes scope over the subject.

(i)   a different girl recited every poem

The substantive points argued for in this section can be made using *a different N* in place of the simple indefinite.

12 I abstract away from possible V-movement at LF. [. . .]

13 Juan Uriagereka has pointed out to me that the fact that the subject is interpreted as taking scope over the object in three out of four of the grammatical LF structures could be the source of the reported preference for interpreting the subject as having wide scope.

14 Several theories of QSI have this character (see, e.g. May 1985; Aoun and Li 1993). This said, a grammatical theory is more empirically exposed, and thus more interesting, to the degree that it structurally disambiguates interpretation. Of course, this demand might have other untoward consequences. However, methodologically, it is the one to start with.

15 QNPs inside PPs also enter into QSIs in English. The approach outlined above can be extended to accommodate these cases as well. For details, see Hornstein (1995: 175–7).

16 It is not chains that have scope but members of chains. This contrasts with approaches in terms of "chain" scope (see Aoun and Li 1993; Barss 1986).

17 This assumes that control is not reduced to movement as proposed in Hornstein (1998). If control is reduced in this way, further assumptions are required to cover these facts (for details, see Hornstein 1999). Interestingly, it appears that not all control structures block QR. In effect, many seem to pattern like raising structures, though others do not. For the nonce, I assume that the standard description (due to Burzio 1986) is correct: control contrasts with raising in blocking QR.

18 This is an important point. The structure of Case (A-) chains is motivated quite independently of the theory of quantifier scope. The fact that it suffices to handle an interesting range of QSIs as well puts a considerable methodological burden on those who wish to augment the theory of grammar by including QR, a rule whose sole purpose is to integrate quantificational data into linguistic theory.

19 We can interpret this LF structure as follows. Assume propositions are interpreted post-LF in tripartite fashion (in the style of Heim 1982); that is, the proposition is divided into quantifiers, restrictors, and nuclei. This puts the quantifiers out on the left, followed by the restrictors and then the nuclear scope. This gives an LF structure like (17) the interpretation (i).

(i)   every x, some y [[(musician y) & (x piece of music y knew)] $\rightarrow y$ played x]

20 This is contra Larson (1988). It is consistent with the assumptions in Chomsky (1995).

21 GB theories that determine scope at S-Structure similarly predict interactions between scope and binding. The problem with these theories is that they are incapable of accommodating the basic quantifier scope facts unaided. In effect, QR-like rules are introduced. See Williams (1986); Hornstein and Weinberg (1990) for discussion. More recent proposals in Reinhart (1995) suffer from similar failings.

22 I assume in what follows that scrambling is indeed movement to the scrambled position. See Saito (1992) for discussion. However, there is another option (explored in Bošković and Takahashi 1998), in which the "scrambled" expression is lowered at LF. Bošković

and Takahashi's analysis is compatible with the proposal in section 3.1, so I consider the implications of the more standard treatment here.

23 See Aoun and Li (1993) for the most elaborate discussion of this. For a reanalysis of their results in a framework similar to the one outlined in section 3.2, see Hornstein (1995: ch. 8).

24 The "*" indicates that several of these expressions can occur here. Szabolcsi notes that (36) is inspired by work by Beghelli (1993).

References

Aoun, J. 1982. On the logical nature of the binding principles: Quantifier Lowering, double raisings of "there" and the notion empty element. In J. Pustejovsky and P. Sells (eds.), *Proceedings of the 12th Annual Meeting of the North East Linguistics Society*, Amherst, MA: GLSA, pp. 16–35.

Aoun, J. and N. Hornstein. 1985. Quantifier types. *Linguistic Inquiry* 16: 623–36.

Aoun, J. and Y.-H. A. Li. 1993. *Syntax of scope*. Cambridge, MA: MIT Press.

Barss, A. 1986. *Chains and anaphoric dependence*. Doctoral dissertation, MIT.

Beghelli, F. 1993. A minimalist approach to quantifier scope. In A. Schafer (ed.), *Proceedings of the 23rd Annual Meeting of the North East Linguistic Society*, Amherst, MA: GSLA, pp. 65–80.

Bošković, Ž. and D. Takahashi. 1998. Scrambling and last resort. *Linguistic Inquiry* 29: 347–66.

Burzio, L. 1986. *Italian syntax: A government and binding approach*. Dordrecht: Reidel.

Chierchia, G. 1995. *Dynamics of meaning: Anaphora, presupposition, and the theory of grammar*. Chicago: University of Chicago Press.

Chierchia, G. and S. McConnnell-Ginet. 1990. *Meaning and grammar: An introduction to semantics*. Cambridge, MA: MIT Press.

Chomsky, N. 1975. Questions of form and interpretation. *Linguistic Analysis* 1: 75–109. [Reprinted in Chomsky (1977), *Essays on form and interpretation*, Amsterdam: North-Holland, pp. 25–59.]

Chomsky, N. 1982. *Concepts and consequences of the theory of government and binding*. Cambridge, MA: MIT Press.

Chomsky, N. 1993. A minimalist program for linguistic theory. In K. Hale and S. J. Keyser (eds.), *The view from Building 20: Essays in linguistics in honor of Sylvain Bromberger*, Cambridge, MA: MIT Press, pp. 1–52. [Reprinted in Chomsky (1995), *The Minimalist Program*, Cambridge, MA: MIT Press, pp. 167–217.]

Chomsky, N. 1995. Categories and transformations. In Chomsky (1995), *The Minimalist Program*, Cambridge, MA: MIT Press, pp. 219–394.

Cooper, R. 1983. *Quantification and syntactic theory*. Dordrecht: Reidel.

Epstein, S. D. 1999. Un-principled syntax: The derivation of syntactic relations. In S. D. Epstein and N. Hornstein (eds.), *Working minimalism*, Cambridge, MA: MIT Press, pp. 317–45.

Hale, K. and S. J. Keyser. 1993. On argument structure and the lexical expression of grammatical relations. In K. Hale and S. J. Keyser (eds.), *The view from Building 20: Essays in linguistics in honor of Sylvain Bromberger*, Cambridge, MA: MIT Press, pp. 53–109.

Heim, I. 1982. *The semantics of definite and indefinite noun phrases*. Doctoral dissertation, University of Massachusetts, Amherst.

Higginbotham, J. 1980. Pronouns and bound variables. *Linguistic Inquiry* 11: 679–708.

Hornstein, N. 1995. *Logical form: From GB to minimalism*. Malden, MA: Blackwell.

Hornstein, N. 1998. Movement and chains. *Syntax* 1: 99–127.

Hornstein, N. 1999. Movement and control. *Linguistic Inquiry* 30: 69–96.

Hornstein, N. and A. Weinberg. 1990. The necessity of LF. *The Linguistic Review* 7: 129–67.

É. Kiss, K. 1991. Logical structure in linguistic structure. In C.-T. J. Huang and R. May (eds.), *Logical structure in linguistic structure*, Dordrecht: Kluwer, pp. 111–48.

Koopman, H. and D. Sportiche. 1991. The position of subjects. *Lingua* 85: 211–58.

Kuroda, S.-Y. 1988. Whether we agree or not: A comparative syntax of English and Japanese. *Lingvisticae Investigationes* 12.

Larson, R. 1988. On the double object construction. *Linguistic Inquiry* 19: 335–91.

May, R. 1977. *The grammar of quantification*. Doctoral dissertation, MIT.

May, R. 1985. *Logical form*. Cambridge, MA: MIT Press.

Pica, R. and W. Snyder. 1995. Weak crossover, scope, and agreement in a minimalist framework. In R. Aranovich, W. Byrne, S. Preuss and M. Senturia (eds.), *Proceedings of the 13th West Coast Conference on Formal Linguistics*, Stanford: CSLI. pp. 334–49.

Reinhart, T. 1995. *Interface strategies. OTS Working Papers*. Research Institute for Language and Speech, Utrecht University.

Saito, M. 1992. Long-distance scrambling in Japanese. *Journal of East Asian Linguistics* 1: 69–118.

Szabolcsi, A. 1995. Strategies for scope taking. In *Working papers in the theory of grammar 2.1*, Research Institute for Linguistics, Hungarian Academy of Sciences, Budapest. [Reprinted in A. Szabolcsi (ed.) (1997), Ways of scope taking, Dordrecht: Kluwer, pp. 109–54.]

Tsai, D. W.-T. 1994. *On economizing the theory of A-bar dependencies*. Doctoral dissertation, MIT.

Uriagereka, J. 1999. Multiple spell-out. In S. D. Epstein and N. Hornstein (eds.), *Working minimalism*, Cambridge, MA: MIT Press, pp. 251–82.

Williams, E. 1986. A reassessment of the functions of LF. *Linguistic Inquiry* 17: 265–99.

Index

CPSIA information can be obtained
at www.ICGtesting.com
Printed in the USA
FSOW03n1409111217
42004FS